The Visionary Realism of German Economics

ANTHEM OTHER CANON ECONOMICS

The **Anthem Other Canon Economics** series is a collaboration between Anthem Press and The Other Canon Foundation. The Other Canon – also described as 'reality economics' – studies the economy as a real object rather than as the behaviour of a model economy based on core axioms, assumptions and techniques. The series includes both classical and contemporary works in this tradition, spanning evolutionary, institutional and Post-Keynesian economics, the history of economic thought and economic policy, economic sociology and technology governance, and works on the theory of uneven development and in the tradition of the German historical school.

The Visionary Realism of German Economics: From the Thirty Years' War to the Cold War

Erik S. Reinert

Edited by Rainer Kattel

ANTHEM PRESS

Anthem Press
An imprint of Wimbledon Publishing Company
www.anthempress.com

This edition first published in UK and USA 2019
by ANTHEM PRESS
75–76 Blackfriars Road, London SE1 8HA, UK
or PO Box 9779, London SW19 7ZG, UK
and
244 Madison Ave #116, New York, NY 10016, USA

British Library Cataloguing-in-Publication Data
A catalogue record for this book is available from the British Library.

ISBN-13: 978-1-78308-903-1 (Hbk)
ISBN-10: 1-78308-903-2 (Hbk)

This title is also available as an e-book.

CONTENTS

INTRODUCTION

Erik S. Reinert

This volume attempts to present a period of around three hundred years of the German-language tradition in economic theory. The German tradition originated as part of a larger Continental tradition in economics, the origin of which can be seen as the massive impact of Italian economist Giovanni Botero's 1588 bestselling *On the Greatnesse of Cities*[1]—soon incorporated into a larger work on the *Reason of State*—which appeared in about 45 editions in Italian, Latin, Spanish, French and German between 1588 and 1666. Reflecting the cosmopolitical nature of Jesuit activism, Botero's connection to Germany and *Mitteleuropa* was strong. His first four publications appeared, respectively, in Krakow, Würzburg, Nürnberg and Frankfurt.[2] Before the Thirty Years' War—which marks the starting point for the present volume—there were already four Latin editions of Botero's *Greatnesse of Cities* published in Germany.[3]

The broad and cross-disciplinary social science tradition started by Botero came to dominate economics in Germany more and longer than in other nations. We can find partial explanations for this in the fact that Germany—compared to countries like Holland, England or France—was a relative latecomer: *eine verspätete Nation*. Until the end of the nineteenth century, Germany also consisted of many states—several hundred states after the Thirty Years' War (1648) and still around 30 three centuries later. We can speculate if the diversity and large number of small competing states with small populations may have encouraged researchers to be cross-disciplinary. To paraphrase Adam Smith, the small size of the partly regional markets for social sciences may have limited the division

---

I would like to thank Rainer Kattel for all his assistance in the publication of this volume. A note of deep gratitude goes to Fernanda Aars Reinert, my wife, librarian, muse, and proofreader for the last almost 50 years. The Heilbronn Symposia, organized by Jürgen and Ursula Backhaus, provided a demand which led to the production of several chapters in this volume. Theirs has been a most important work.

1 For a discussion of Botero and his influence on economics, see Reinert, Erik, and Kenneth Carpenter, "German Language Economic Bestsellers before 1850, with Two Chapters on a Common Reference Point of Cameralism and Mercantilism", *The Other Canon Foundation and Tallinn University of Technology Working Papers in Technology Governance and Economic Dynamics*, No. 58, 2014, technologygovernance.eu/eng/the_core_faculty/working_papers/.

2 See Firpo, Luigi, *Gli scritti giovanili di Giovanni Botero*, Florence: Sansoni, 1960, pp. 12–22.

3 The first edition in German followed in Frankfurt only in 1657.

of labor. This may also have reinforced a cultural tendency to attempt to understand large and complex structures in a holistic way: the desire for a *Ganzheitslehre*.[4]

German philosopher Johann Gottlieb Fichte (1762–1814) certainly thought German political diversity, rather than unity, would cause increased learning and emulation:[5]

> How fortunate we are in this regard that there are still so many distinct and separate German states! What is so often said to be to our disadvantage can perhaps work to our advantage in this important national matter. Perhaps imitation on the part of the majority, and the desire to get ahead of the others, will bring about something that the tranquil self-satisfaction of the individual states would not; for it is plain that the one state among all German states that makes a start with this will gain a definite lead in the respect, love, and gratitude of all; it will be the supreme benefactor and true founder of the nation. It will give the others courage, provide an instructive example, and become their model.[6]

Until its swan song as a result of World War II, German economics followed Botero's approach of blending economics, in its narrow sense, not only with what is now called sociology but also with anthropology, political science, demography, and facts and figures from any other field that seemed to be relevant for the questions at hand. Relevance, as opposed to available tools, was the starting point for any analysis in this tradition. Botero's second major work, *Relazioni Universali*,[7] is organized more by geography and ethnicity than by nation-states proper. As one observer says, Botero "brought together an immense mass of geographical and anthropological information, which he tried to organize according to broad methodological categories (like 'resources', 'government', and 'religion')."[8] During the 200 years following the first 1591 Italian edition, Botero's *Relazioni Universali* was published in an incredible 84 editions[9]—in Italian, German, Latin, English, Spanish and Polish.[10]

The first six chapters of this book trace the German tradition as it was methodologically part of mainstream Continental European economics. Already early on, in the seventeenth century, English economics, so-called mercantilism, started to be dominated by commercial interest and traders, men like Thomas Mun, Josiah Child and John Cary.

---

4 Austrian economist Othmar Spann (1878–1950) represents both an extreme example of this holistic approach and how it could degenerate into totalitarianism.

5 For the role of emulation in the growth and development of Europe, see Reinert, Sophus, *Translating Empire: Emulation and the Origins of Political Economy*, Cambridge, MA: Harvard University Press, 2011.

6 Fichte, Johann Gottlob, *Addresses to the German Nation*, trans. with introduction and notes by Isaac Nakhimovsky, Béla Kapossy and Keith Tribe, Indianapolis, IN: Hackett, 2013, p. 141. Originally published in 1808.

7 The first three parts of which were published in Rome in 1591 (presso Giorgio Ferrari).

8 Rubies, Joan-Pau, *Travel and Ethnology in the Renaissance*, Cambridge: Cambridge University Press, 2000, p. 294.

9 The main bibliographical source on Botero is Assandra, Giuseppe, "Giovanni Botero. Note biografiche e bibliografiche di Giuseppe Assandra suo concittadino" (edited by Gino Borghezio), in *Bollettino storico-bibliografico subalpino*, vol. XXVIII, Turin, 1926, pp. 407–42, and vol. XXX, 1928, pp. 29–63, 307–51.

10 There were three early Polish translations: 1609, 1613 and 1659. Botero's biographer Assandra indicates that the lack of a French translation was the result of this work being banned there.

German economists, the so-called Cameralists, were largely recruited from the ranks of public employees of the many small states. While English economists tended to see the world through the lenses of long-distance traders, German economists often saw the world through the lenses of tax collectors of small states. The English emphasis on trade and barter, rather than on production, still today continues to be a key characteristic of mainstream economics. However, maximizing trading profits and maximizing public revenue gave very different perspectives. The third branch of early economics, French Colbertism, had perspectives not dissimilar from the German ones, but it was decidedly marked by the fact that France had been a unified monarchy centuries before Germany. While the end of the Hundred Years' War in 1453 unified France, the end of the Thirty Years' War in 1648 split Germany into hundreds of small states.

David Ricardo's 1817 *Principles of Economics*—with an even more extreme focus on barter rather than production as the determining factor in the international economy—moved economics to a much higher level of abstraction. As opposed to the German-language tradition right, left and center—Joseph Schumpeter, Karl Marx and Rudolf Hilferding, respectively—Ricardo did not separate the financial sector from the real economy. This came to limit today's understanding of financial crises.

Ricardo's foundation of international trade theory as represented by the barter of qualitatively identical labor hours, void of any qualities, is in my opinion perhaps the largest barrier to our present understanding of two main problems in the world economy today: poverty and large-scale migration. To the nineteenth-century latecomers—like Germany, United States, Japan and Russia—Ricardo's trade tended to be seen almost like an insult to common sense, an attempt to reduce the rest of the world to suppliers of raw materials to English industrial and de facto colonial might. The less abstract German tradition was to therefore become the dominating nineteenth-century economic tradition in the other main latecomer nations, not only in Continental Europe but also in the United States,[11] Japan[12] and Russia.[13]

The liberalist school labelled the adherents of the German Historical School of economics as *Kathedersozialisten*—or socialists of (academic) chairs. In our focus on German authoritarianism, we tend to forget that the Iron Chancellor Otto von Bismarck said to Gustav Schmoller that he was really also a *Kathedersozialist* but did not have time for such activities. It can be discussed if Bismarck's remark originated in a paternalistic view toward labor, if it originated in an understanding that it was politically necessary to improve the well-being of the working masses to prevent revolution, if it originated in a

---

11 German economics was also influenced from the United States and the periphery of the British Isles. See Reinert, Erik S., "Daniel Raymond (1820): A US Economist Who Inspired Friedrich List, with Notes on Other Forerunners of List from the English-Speaking Periphery," in Peukert, Helge (ed.), *Taking Up the Challenge! Festschrift für Jürgen Backhaus*, Marburg: Metropolis, 2015.

12 For a discussion, see Sugiyama, Chuhei, and Hiroshi Mizuta, *Enlightenment and Beyond: Political Economy Comes to Japan*, Tokyo: University of Tokyo Press, 1988.

13 The foremost German influence on Russian economics was Count Sergei Witte, Friedrich List's Russian translator. Witte held several influential ministerial posts in Russia from 1892 onward and was an initiator of Russian industrialization and of the Trans-Siberian Railroad. See Narcave, Sidney, *The Memoirs of Count Witte*, Armonk, NY: Sharpe, 1990; and von Laue, Theodore, *Sergei Witte and the Industrialization of Russia*, New York, NY: Columbia University Press, 1963.

love for mankind, or in all of the above. The important thing is that the movement originating in the *Verein für Sozialpolitik* (1882–1932)—the genetic material of which is contained in 188 volumes of economic deliberations on my shelves—created the European welfare state and gave important impetus to similar movements abroad.

Richard Ely, one of the founders of the American Economic Association in 1885, described the German influence on the founders thus:

> The young men who gathered at Saratoga in 1885 to form the American Economic Association had very generally returned from Germany about 1880.[14] Ideals of freedom were strongly cherished and very precious to us all. So as not to commit others I will describe my own feelings as a student of economics in Germany, but I believe I speak for many others. I had the feeling when I went there that I had entered into a new heritage of freedom, and a certain joyous expansion was one of the most pronounced feelings which I experienced. There was a free and large spirit on the part of professors of economics in the Fatherland, as well as other professors in the German university, to which I had not been accustomed. I felt that in the atmosphere of the German universities there was room for growth and encouragement of the development of individuality, which was something new to me.[15]

Unfortunately, to many these are not the values Germany came to represent during the twentieth century, but there is all the more reason to try to understand why German economics in its golden age inspired so many and could still serve as a major inspirational source to poor and rich nations alike. That is, if we manage to eliminate the negative leftovers from a relatively brief period (from the 400 years' perspective of this volume) in the twentieth century.

Apart from Francis Walker, already the president of MIT by then, the first elected officials of the American Economic Association were the following: Henry C. Adams, who from 1887 until his death in 1921 was a professor of political economy and finance at the University of Michigan; Edmund J. James, at the time at the University of Pennsylvania where he became the director of the Wharton School of Finance and Economy and later president of the University of Illinois; John Bates Clark, later a professor at Columbia University; Richard T. Ely, at the time a professor and the head of the Department of Political Economy at Johns Hopkins University; and Edwin Seligman, who spent his whole career at Columbia University as a professor of political economy.[16]

---

14 The exception, who had no educational background from Germany, was Francis Amasa Walker, the first president, who at the time was the president of the Massachusetts Institute of Technology (MIT). Walker was a law graduate from Harvard.

15 Ely, Richard T., "The American Economic Association 1885–1909," *American Economic Association Quarterly*, 3rd series, vol. 11, no. 1, Papers and Discussions of the Twenty-Second Annual Meeting: Being the Twenty-Fifth Anniversary of the Founding of the Association. New York City, December 27–31, 1909 (April 1910), pp. 67–68.

16 Adams had studied in Heidelberg and Berlin, James in Halle under Johannes Conrad (Conrad's students had strong influence on Harvard's economics department), Clark in Zürich and Heidelberg (under Karl Knies), Ely in Heidelberg under Knies, and Seligman in Berlin, Heidelberg, Geneva and Paris.

One reason I relate the distinguished careers of the founding officers of the American Economic Association in such detail is that the association's Wikipedia entry reads as follows: "The AEA was established in 1885 in Saratoga, New York by younger economists trained in the German historical school; *since 1900 it has been under the control of academics*."[17] This curious phrasing clearly indicates that the distinguished group of economists and university presidents related here were not "academics" by Wikipedia standards. Unfortunately such slants are not uncommon in Wikipedia articles on economics.

Richard Ely's autobiography *Ground under Our Feet*[18] details a young American scholar's meeting with German economic thought and method, and how rugged individualism was mellowed by an understanding for a state. Indeed, the German school of economics at the time distanced itself equally from both political extremes, from communism and from what was then referred to as Manchester Liberalism—from what Gustav Schmoller, dean of German economics at the time, in his inaugural speech at the University of Berlin called "the ahistorical twins":

> The simplistic optimism of "laissez-faire" and the childish and frivolous appeal to revolution, the naive hope that the tyranny of the proletariat would lead to world happiness, increasingly showed their real nature, that they were twins of an ahistorical rationalism. [...] The old doctrines of individualistic natural law were transformed from the humanistic idealism of an Adam Smith to the hard mammonism of the Manchester School and (were useless for the present situation). [...] The period 1870–1890 led to the theoretical and practical bankruptcy of both the old schools.[19]

This type of economics—which I have called the Other Canon[20] of economics—can be distinguished from today's mainstream economics in several ways. One is that it is based on the study of historical events rather than on abstract axioms. Another is that there is an emphasis on qualitative understanding—on *verstehen*, as one would profoundly understand, for example, a person. This is in contrast to the approach of the natural sciences, which is more explaining (*erklären*).[21] In this sense, Other Canon economics represents the opposite of the *physics-envy* of today's economic mainstream.

---

17 https://en.wikipedia.org/wiki/American_Economic_Association, accessed July 30, 2015. Italics added.

18 Ely, Richard, *Ground under Our Feet*, New York, NY: Macmillan, 1938.

19 Schmoller, Gustav, *Wechslende Theorien und faststehende Wahrheiten im Gebiete der Staats- und Socialwissenschaften und die heutige deutsche Volkswirtschaftslehre*, Berlin: W. Büxenstein, 1897, p. 22. My translation. Downloadable on www.othercanon.org.

20 See Reinert, Erik S., and Arno Daastøl, "The Other Canon: The History of Renaissance Economics. Its Role as an Immaterial and Production-Based Canon in the History of Economic Thought and in the History of Economic Policy," in Reinert, Erik S. (ed.), *Globalization, Economic Development and Inequality: An Alternative Perspective*, Cheltenham: Edward Elgar, 2004, pp. 21–70.

21 See Drechsler, Wolfgang, "Natural versus Social Sciences: On Understanding in Economics," in Reinert, Erik S. (ed.), *Globalization, Economic Development and Inequality: An Alternative Perspective*, Cheltenham: Edward Elgar, 2004, pp. 71–87.

Employing *verstehen* as a scientific method involves a particular form of objectivity. Real objectivity is not achieved by observing and quantifying a phenomenon with great accuracy; objectivity in the Other Canon tradition is of the type described by Nietzsche:

> The only seeing which exists is a seeing in perspective, a seeing with perception; and the more feelings we allow to get involved about an issue, the more eyes—different eyes—that we mobilise to observe one thing, the more complete will our concept of this thing, our objectivity, be. Would not eliminating the will [...] be the same as to castrate the intellect?[22]

Quantification does not imply understanding; in fact, quantification may produce a false sense of understanding. As Jerome Ravetz put it in a recent conference in Brussels, "We may be ignorant of our ignorance but at least we can measure it to two significant digits."

Yet another angle from which to explain the difference to today's mainstream economics is to focus on the level of abstraction: German economics and the Other Canon tradition, facing a question or a policy problem, consistently attempt to place themselves at a level of abstraction where they are likely to find an answer to the question or problem at hand. Whereas abstraction often has been seen as synonymous of science itself, in the German tradition pragmatism and *Praxisnähe*—relevance and closeness to reality—have always been highly regarded. The opposite is represented by what one of the economists represented in this volume calls *verschimmelte Schulweisheiten*[23]—"mouldy school truths"—or what a rector of the University of Berlin[24] scorned as *Stubengelehrten*—drawing-room academics—persons who lack experience and have acquired his or her knowledge only from books and never tried them out in real life.

The insistence on adjusting the analysis to a level of abstraction where a relevant reply is likely to be found automatically opens up both for a very large toolbox and for cross-disciplinarity. It also opens up for understanding that some factors, perhaps extremely important ones, have had to be sacrificed due to the restrictive assumptions needed in order to use the tools economists have chosen to use. As Schumpeter puts it, "The general reader will have to make up his mind, whether he wants simple answers to his questions or useful ones—in this as in other economic matters he cannot have both."[25]

---

22 "Es gibt nur ein perspektivisches Sehen, nur ein perspektivisches 'Erkennen'; und je mehr Affekte wir über eine Sache zu Worte kommen lassen, je mehr Augen, verschiedene Augen wir uns für dieselbe Sache einzusetzen wissen, um so vollständiger wird unser 'Begriff' dieser Sache, unsre 'Objektivität' sein. Den Willen aber überhaupt eliminieren, die Affekte samt und sonders aushängen, gesetzt, daß wir dies vermöchten: wie? Hieße das nicht den Intellekt kastrieren?," Nietzsche, Friedrich, *Werke*, Digitale Bibliothek Band 31, Berlin, Directmedia (CD-ROM), 2000. 7394–95. My translation.

23 Bücher, Karl, *Lebenserinnerungen*, Tübingen: Laupp, 1919, p. 197.

24 Wagner, Adolph, *Die akademische Nationalökonomie und der Socialismus*, Rede zum Antritt des Rectorats der Königlichen Friedrich-Wilhelms-Universität in Berlin am 15, October 1895, Berlin: Julius Becker, 1895, p. 7.

25 Schumpeter in Zeuthen, Fredrik, *Problems of Monopoly and Economic Welfare*, London: Routledge, 1930.

One important criticism of today's mainstream economics would be precisely this: a level of abstraction that has led to irrelevance.

The influential Columbia University economist Edwin Seligman—already mentioned as one of the founders of the American Economic Association—described the program of German economics as follows:

- It discards the exclusive use of the deductive method, and stresses the necessity of historical and statistical treatment.
- It denies the existence of immutable natural laws in economics, calling attention to the interdependence of theories and institutions, and showing that different epochs or countries require different systems.
- It disclaims belief in the beneficence of the absolute laissez-faire system.
- It maintains the close interrelations of law, ethics and economics.
- It refuses to acknowledge the adequacy of the presumption of self-interest as the sole regulator of economic action.[26]

The chapters in this volume—attempting to resurrect and show the relevance of a now virtually distinct type of economic theory—were written over a period of twenty years. Their publication is spread over a variety of books and journals, and—since they all relate to the overarching subject of the now decidedly unfashionable German-language approach to economics—it seems useful to unite them in a single volume. In this volume they are primarily organized in chronological order from the earliest German economist to the last representative of the German historical school.[27]

Chapter 1 gives an overview of German-language economics as it relates to economic development. Chapter 2 discusses the role of the state in the process of economic growth, where a key feature of German economics is that both the individual *and* society are seen as relevant units of analysis. Chapter 3 introduces the life and work of Veit Ludwig von Seckendorff (1626–1692) and the birth of German-language economics after the Thirty Years' War. Chapter 4 introduces Christian Wolff (1679–1754) and the role of innovation and new knowledge in economics. Chapter 5 discusses Johann Heinrich Gottlob von Justi (1717–1771) and his generation of economists. Chapter 6 introduces Jacob Bielfeld (1717–1770) and his theory of the decline of nations. Chapter 7 focuses on Friedrich List (1789–1846) and his perspectives on free trade. Chapter 8 presents a discussion of the mechanisms that have historically compensated for technological unemployment, an issue that was discussed by Karl Marx (1818–1883). Chapter 9 looks at Karl Bücher (1847–1930) and his view of the geographical dimensions of techno-economic change. Chapter 10 discusses Austrian economics—part of which is presently decidedly

26 Seligman, Edwin, *Essays in Economics*, New York, NY: Macmillan, 1925, p. 15–16.

27 The most important German economist not specifically treated in this volume is Gustav Schmoller (1838–1917). For introductions to Schmoller, see Backhaus, Jürgen (ed.), *Gustav von Schmoller and the Problems of Today*, Oxford: Berg, 1989; and Balabkins, Nicholas W., *Not by Theory Alone: The Economics of Gustav von Schmoller and Its Legacy to America*, Berlin: Duncker & Humblot, 1988.

fashionable—from the point of view of Other Canon economics. Chapter 11, written with my youngest son Sophus Reinert, looks at Friedrich Nietzsche (1844–1900) and his relationship to the German historical school of economics. Chapter 12, written with my eldest son Hugo, discusses the origins and use of the term *creative destruction*—generally associated with Joseph Schumpeter (1883–1950)—back to Werner Sombart (1863–1941) and to Nietzsche.

Chapters 13 and 14 look at the work of Joseph Schumpeter more in detail: Chapter 13 discusses him in the context of the history of economic thought, focusing on his ambivalent relationships as torn between historical analysis and highly abstract theory. Chapter 14 looks at poverty and underdevelopment in a Schumpeterian context. Chapter 15 is a plea for establishing a synthesis of German and Austrian economics in order to fight world poverty. Chapter 16, written with Rainer Kattel, was a warning issued in 2004—at the time of the large European Union enlargement eastward—that this integration worked contrary to previous EU integration schemes, done in the spirit of Friedrich List, and predicting a Latinamericanization of the European Union: that the differences between the rich and the poor would become much more marked. Chapter 17 looks at the present crisis in the European Union from the point of view of three German economists, Heinrich von Thünen (1783–1850), Friedrich List and Joseph Schumpeter. Chapter 18 looks at financial crises as seen by Joseph Schumpeter, US economist Hyman Minsky and Venezuelan social scientist Carlota Perez. Chapter 19 takes us back to an overview of the history of economic thought based on a prize essay by German mathematician and economist Johann Jacob Meyen (1731–1797). The final Chapter 20 discusses Werner Sombart (1863–1941) and the swan song of a German economic tradition that had lasted about three hundred years, an economic tradition that had created the welfare state and provided inspiration to virtually all countries that emulated England's road to industrialization.

In an interview, Paul Krugman essentially admitted the helplessness of an economics profession that has been defined by its employing certain tools:

> I think there's a pretty good case to be made that the stuff that I stressed in the models is a less important story than the things that I left out because I couldn't model them.[28]

Faced with such a degree of helplessness—being locked into a partly irrelevant toolshed of economics and having lost the key to get out—one would expect a cry of common sense to return to an economics profession that, because it is less formal, goes beyond the present tools in order to solve the many pressing problems of mankind. Indeed, Krugman seems to find himself in the situation described by Nietzsche above: the intellect has been disabled—castrated, in Nietzsche's words—by a self-imposed inability to work outside the models. This is a situation that would seem to appeal to normal and healthy common sense, in German philosophy called *der gesunde Menschenverstand*.

---

[28] Paul Krugman in the *New Yorker*, March 1, 2010.

Someone trained in the German historical school of economics would have understood that the deindustrialization of the Southern European periphery over the past years would cause precisely the "transfer union" that German politicians fear. Someone trained in the German historical school would have understood why people flee Northern Africa, with 40 inhabitants per square kilometer, for lack of jobs but find jobs when they come to the Netherlands, with 400 inhabitants per square kilometer. This lack of understanding—which is now the elephant in the room in European (and North American) politics—was well understood in economics all the way back to Giovanni Botero's *On the Greatnesse of Cities* until fairly recently.

After World War II, Germany itself was saved by a German-type economic analysis with roots back to Botero: the sustainable population level of a nation is determined by its economic structure. A deindustrialized nation will not be able to retain its former population. The organs of the Marshall Plan that turned the formerly approved Morgenthau Plan—a 1943 plan to deindustrialize Germany—into a reindustrializing Marshall Plan was largely the product of a fact-finding mission of former president Herbert Hoover, who, in January 1947, had been asked by President Truman "to go to Germany and Austria to address the food and economic problems in the British and American occupation zones."[29] By January 1947, the huge unforeseen consequences of the Morgenthau Plan had become evident.

In March 1947, Herbert Hoover reported back to President Truman what was the strongest statement in development economics ever:

> There is the illusion that the New Germany left after the annexations can be reduced to a "pastoral state." It cannot be done unless we exterminate or move 25,000,000 out of it.[30]

There is virtually no trace of this understanding to be found in Germany and in the EU today. The Euro straitjacket relentlessly deindustrializes growing parts of the EU periphery. As we have noted, Germany's nineteenth-century Iron Chancellor Bismarck professed to be a *Kathedersozialist*, someone with a pronounced social consciousness. Today's Iron Chancellor Angela Merkel is, according to one biographer, better known for her "Werteabstinenz," her absence of values.[31]

After World War II, Germany was saved from a deindustrializing Morgenthau Plan by the Marshall Plan. I therefore see it as a very strong moral obligation on Germany not to continue applying de facto Morgenthau Plans on the EU periphery and Africa. Most educated Germans know that a key element in Hitler's coming to power was that after World War I the Allies attempted to collect a debt from Germany that was unpayable. I therefore see it as a very strong moral obligation on Germany not to attempt to collect an equally unpayable debt from Greece. If Friedrich List had been here today, he would most likely have scorned his fellow Germans in the same way he scorned England in the

---

29 http://www.trumanlibrary.org/hoover/documents.php?page=3.

30 For a German view on this issue, see Baade, Fritz, "Gruß und Dank an Herbert Hoover," in *Weltwirtschaftliches Archiv*, vol. 74, no. 1, 1955, pp. 1–6.

31 Höhler, Gertrud, *Die Patin: Wie Angela Merkel Deutschland umbaut*, Zürich: Orell Füssli, 2012.

1840s. After having climbed to wealth employing a certain type of economic wisdom, Germany now prohibits other nations from following the same road to wealth, throwing away the very ladder it has used in the past.[32]

It is my hope that this volume, presenting a less formal approach to economics—which can solve the issues Krugman sees as important but cannot model—will contribute to raising interest in the now defunct German tradition in economics. At present, the European Union seems to get the worst of all worlds: German authoritarianism based on neoclassical economics instead of the economics understanding of Bismarck and his contemporaries.

List of (Mostly) Forgotten German-Language Economists[33]

Veit Ludwig von Seckendorff (1626–1692)
Philipp Wilhelm von Hörnigk (1640–1714)
Gottfried Wilhelm Leibniz (1646–1716)
Simon Peter Gasser (1676–1745)
Christian Wolff (1679–1754)
Georg Heinrich Zincke (1692–1769)
Jacob Bielfeld (1717–1770)
Johann Heinrich Gottlob von Justi (1717–1771)
Johann Friedrich von Pfeiffer (1718–1787)
Johann Jacob Meyen (1731–1797)
Johann Beckmann (1739–1811)
Johann Gottfried Herder (1744–1803)
Johann Gottfried Hoffmann (1765–1847)
Johann Heinrich von Thünen (1783–1850)
Friedrich List (1789–1846)
Bruno Hildebrand (1812–1878)
Wilhelm Roscher (1817–1894)
Karl Marx (1818–1883)
Heinrich Bernhard Oppenheim (1819–1880)
Karl Knies (1821–1898)
Eugen Dühring (1833–1921)
Adolph Wagner (1835–1917)
Gustav Schmoller (1838–1917)

---

32 "Es ist eine gemeine Klugheitsregel, daß man, auf den Gipfel der Größe gelangt, die Leiter vermittelst welcher man ihn erklommen, hinter sich werfe, um andern die Mittel zu benehmen uns nachzuklimmen" (from List's *Das nationale System der politischen Oekonomie: Der internationale Handel, die Handelspolitik und der deutsche Zollverein*, Stuttgart & Tübingen: Gottascher Verlag, 1841, p. 501).

33 Source: Reinert, Erik S., *Warum manche Länder reich und andere arm sind. Wie der Westen seine Geschichte ignoriert und deshalb seine Wirtschaftsmacht verliert*, Stuttgart: Schäffer-Poeschel, 2014, p. 233. These economists are all cited in the book.

Carl Menger (1840–1921)
Lujo Brentano (1844–1931)
Karl Bücher (1847–1930)
Werner Sombart (1863–1941)
Franz Oppenheimer (1864–1943)
Max Weber (1864–1920)
Rudolf Hilferding (1877–1941)
Joseph Alois Schumpeter (1883–1950)
Fritz Redlich (1892–1987)
Friedrich von Hayek (1899–1992)
Hans Singer (1910–2006)

The original publication data for the articles in this book is as follows:

Chapter 1. German Economics as Development Economics: From the Thirty Years War to World War II. In Jomo, K.S. and Reinert, Erik (eds.), *The Origins of Development Economics: How Schools of Economic Thought Have Addressed Development*, London, Zed, 2005, pp. 48–68.

Chapter 2. The Role of the State in Economic Growth, *Journal of Economic Studies*, vol. 26, no. 4/5, 1999, pp. 268–326.

Chapter 3. A Brief Introduction to Veit Ludwig von Seckendorff (1626–1692), *European Journal of Law and Economics*, 19, 2005, pp. 221–230.

Chapter 4. Exploring the Genesis of Economic Innovations: The religious gestalt-switch and the duty to invent as preconditions for economic growth (with Arno Daastøl), *European Journal of Law and Economics*, vol. 4, no. 2/3, 1997, pp. 233–283.

Chapter 5. Johann Heinrich Gottlob von Justi (1717–1771): The Life and Times of an Economist Adventurer. In Backhaus, Jürgen (ed.), *Johann Friedrich Gottlob von Justi: The Beginnings of Political Economy: Johann Friedrich Gottlob von Justi, series The European Heritage in Economics and the Social Sciences*, New York, Springer, 2009, pp. 33–74.

Chapter 6. Jacob Bielfeld's On the Decline of States (1760) and its Relevance for Today, *The Other Canon Foundation and Tallinn University of Technology Working Papers in Technology Governance and Economic Dynamics*, No. 47, 2013.

Chapter 7. Raw Materials in the History of Economic Policy; or, Why List (the Protectionist) and Cobden (the Free Trader) Both Agreed on Free Trade in Corn. In Parry, G. (ed.), *Freedom and Trade*: 1846–1996, London, Routledge, 1998, pp. 275–300.

Chapter 8. Compensation Mechanisms and Targeted Economic Growth – Lessons from the History of Economic Policy. In Vivarelli, Marco and Mario Pianta (eds.), *The Employment Impact of Innovation*, London, Routledge, 2000, pp. 182–206.

Chapter 9. Karl Bücher and the Geographical Dimensions of Techno-Economic Change. Backhaus, Jürgen, (editor) *Karl Bücher: Theory – History – Anthropology – Non-Market Economies*, Marburg, Metropolis Verlag, 2000, pp. 177–222.

Chapter 10. Austrian Economics and the Other Canon: The Austrians between the Activistic-Idealistic and the Passivistic-Materialistic Traditions of Economics. In Backhaus, Jürgen (ed.), *Evolutionary Economic Thought. European Contributions and Concepts*, Chelthenham, Elgar, 2003, pp. 160–207.

Chapter 11. Nietzsche and the German Historical School (with Sophus Reinert). In Backhaus, Jürgen and Wolfgang Drechsler (eds.), *Friedrich Nietzsche 1844–2000: Economy and Society, series The European Heritage in Economics and the Social Sciences*, Boston, Springer, 2006, pp. 111–135.

Chapter 12. Creative Destruction in Economics: Nietzsche, Sombart, Schumpeter' (with Hugo Reinert). In Backhaus, Jürgen and Wolfgang Drechsler (eds.), *Friedrich Nietzsche 1844–2000: Economy and Society, series The European Heritage in Economics and the Social Sciences*, Boston, Springer, 2006, pp. 55–85.

Chapter 13. Schumpeter in the Context of two Canons of Economic Thought. *Industry and Innovation*, vol. 6, no. 1, 2002, pp. 23–39.

Chapter 14. The role of technology in the creation of rich and poor nations: Underdevelopment in a Schumpeterian system. In Aldcroft, Derek H. and Ross Catterall (eds.), *Rich Nations – Poor Nations. The long run perspective*, Aldershot, Edward Elgar, 1996, pp. 161–188.

Chapter 15. Towards an Austro-German Theory of Uneven Economic Development? A Plea for Theorizing by Inclusion. *Review of Austrian Economics*, vol. 20, nos. 2/3, June 2007.

Chapter 16. The qualitative shift in European integration: towards permanent wage pressures and a 'Latin-Americanization' of Europe? (with Rainer Kattel). *PRAXIS Working Papers* No. 17, 2004.

Chapter 17. Primitivization of the EU Periphery: How the European Union hollowed out Heinrich von Thünen's model and put both Friedrich List and Joseph Schumpeter into Reverse Gear. *Informationen zur Raumentwicklung / Informations on Spatial Development*, Bonn, Germany, No. 1, 2013.

Chapter 18. Mechanisms of Financial Crises in Growth and Collapse: Hammurabi, Schumpeter, Perez, and Minsky. *Jornal Ekonomi Malaysia*, vol. 46, no. 1, 2012, pp. 85–100.

Chapter 19. Full Circle: Economics from Scholasticism through Innovation and back into Mathematical Scholasticism. Reflections around a 1769 price essay: 'Why is it that Economics so Far has Gained so Few Advantages from Physics and Mathematics? *Journal of Economic Studies*, vol. 27, no. 4/5, 2000, pp. 364–376.

Chapter 20 is modified from Reinert, Erik S., *Warum manche Länder reich und andere arm sind. Wie der Westen seine Geschichte ignoriert und deshalb seine Wirtschaftsmacht verliert*, Stuttgart: Schäffer-Poeschel, 2014.

In Chapters 7 and 9 the page numbers from the original publication are found in brackets, indicating the start of a new page in the original publication.

Chapter One

GERMAN ECONOMICS AS DEVELOPMENT ECONOMICS: FROM THE THIRTY YEARS' WAR TO WORLD WAR II

Erik S. Reinert

Three main elements make a study of the German economic tradition) particularly rewarding for development economists. First of all, German economics was born late and at a time when the nation was particularly backward, poor and ravaged by the Thirty Years' War (1618–48), which had cost the lives of up to 70 per cent of the civilian population in some areas. Therefore, from its very inception, German economics was that of a backward nation attempting to catch up with its wealthier neighbours. As opposed to English and American economics, whose philosophical base changed radically when the nations attained world economic power, the analytical base of German economics was not modified as the nation grew wealthier. Second, German economics has consistently, through the centuries, seen the economy from a different vantage point with different metaphors: essentially from the point of view of production rather than trade, and operating at a much lower level of abstraction than today's mainstream economics and its predecessors. Third, the scope of economics in the German tradition has been much wider than in the Anglo-Saxon mainstream. Factors such as geography and history, technology and technical change, government and governance, and social problems and their remedies, have all been central to the approach since its very inception.[1]

A frequent theme in German historical writing is the idea of the country as a *verspätete* nation, a laggard nation, as compared to the rest of Europe. In such a situation, the state plays a very different role than in the more developed nations.[2] As Keynes said, 'the worse the situation, the less laissez-faire works.' It was therefore only natural that other latecomers — in particular, the United States and Japan — built their economic theories and policies on the German model.[3] During the nineteenth century, united in a common position against English economics, economics in Germany and the United States strongly influenced and fertilized each other. These catching-up nations formed

---

1 In this chapter, the term 'German economics' will be used to cover all economics originally written in the German language.

2 For a discussion of the role of the state in the German economic tradition, see Reinert (1999).

3 For a discussion of the choice of the German model in Japan, both after the Meiji Restoration and after 1945, and in the United States, see Reinert (1995).

a common theoretical front against England, a nation that not only made it politically clear that she saw it as a primary goal to prevent other nations from following the path of industrialization, but also — for the first time in the history of economics — possessed an economic theory that made this goal a legitimate one. From a policy perspective, the novelty of the economics of Smith and Ricardo was that they made colonialism morally defensible.[4]

The nineteenth century produced important German–American economic exchanges and alliances against English classical economics. Friedrich List, a German political refugee in the United States, was inspired by the vision and arguments of US economists: publications by Daniel Raymond and Mathew Carey in 1820 and 1821 provided List with new ammunition and inspiration. Later in the century, another German–American pair of economists, Henry Carey and Eugen Diihring, supported and defended each other. During the nineteenth century, both US and Japanese economists were trained in German economics: US economists through their graduate studies at German universities, and Japanese economists through their training under not only German economics professors in Japan but also a large number of German-trained US professors teaching in Japan (see Sugiyama and Mizuta 1988). There were no graduate schools in economics in the United States at that time, and most US economists received their Ph.D.s at German universities, as did all the founders of the American Economic Association. Reading knowledge of German was mandatory for a Ph.D. in economics in the United States until World War II.

We should not, however, exaggerate the differences between the German economic tradition and that of the rest of continental Europe. In the long term, the most important dividing line was between the English economic tradition and the continental European traditions seen as a whole. The works available in English on the German economic tradition tend to be seen from an Anglo-Saxon viewpoint, where German economics is seen in contrast to the English tradition without recognizing its similarities to the rest of the continental tradition. To most historians of economic thought, cameralism — the particular German form of economics — is solely a German phenomenon. Many are not aware that both the term 'cameralism' itself and the works of the cameralist authors spread from Sweden and Russia to Spain and Italy.[5] The textbook written by the first professor of economics outside Germany, Anders Berch in Uppsala (Berch 1747), used the term 'cameralism' in its title. The first professor of economics in northern Italy in the 1760s, Cesare Beccaria, was one of 'cameral sciences'.

The only two German-language economists broadly studied in the rest of the world — Karl Marx and Joseph Alois Schumpeter — are, in fact, much less original in the context of the German tradition than they appear in the standard historiography of economic thought. Marx and Schumpeter indeed shared a typical 'German' view of productive forces bringing about change in society. In his Foreword to the Japanese edition of *The Theory of Economic Development* (reproduced in Clemence 1951: 158–63),

[4] This is documented in Reinert, ed. (2004c).
[5] This is also the case of Tribe (1988, 1995).

Schumpeter stressed the similarities between Marx' approach and his own, contrasting their approach with Walrasian and Marshallian economics. In the German production-based tradition, capital per *se* has no value, and this is reflected both in Schumpeter and in Marx. As a result, the interest rate under perfect equilibrium in Schumpeter's system would be zero. This finds its parallel in Marx's proposition that constant capital does not produce any surplus value. However, these similarities, according to Schumpeter, are 'obliterated by a very wide difference in general outlook' (in Clemence 1951: 161).

Seen from the perspective of German economics, the part of Marx's work alien to this tradition was his use of Ricardo's labour theory of value. Marx's contemporaries among German economists, starting with Eugen Diihring who was the first to comment on his work, therefore tended to be sympathetic towards Marx's economic analysis but not to his turning the social pyramid upside down as the solution to society's ills. Still, Marx's influence on the German economists who followed him is clear. In fact, in his book review of Werner Sombart's main work, *Der moderne Kapitalismus,* Gustav Schmoller, the oldest of the giants of the New Historical School, chided his younger colleague for being too greatly influenced by Marx.

Permanent Characteristics of the German Economic Tradition

It is possible to distinguish an economic tradition in Germany from after the end of the Thirty Years' War in 1648. Prior to this date, in the tradition of Xenophon, a literary tradition generally labeled *Hausvaterliteratur* gave advice on how to run estates, small and large. *Fürstenspiegel* (Wings' Mirror'), of which the best known is *Sachsenspiegel* from the twelfth century, were books that collected the laws and customs of the German states. During the three hundred years from 1648 until the German economics tradition dissolved after World War II in 1945, a continuity of principles and approaches can be observed that clearly distinguished this type of economics, both from English economics after 1776 and from today's mainstream economics. In the chapter on 'Mercantilism and Economic Development' in this volume, we point to the similarities between English economics before 1776 and the German tradition.

Different types of economics tend to be influenced by the professions from which the economists are recruited. English economists were, to a large extent, merchants and traders who brought their professional perspective with them. Adam Smith spent many years as a customs inspector, adding to the commercial bias of English economic theory. Indeed, a common German criticism of English classical economics has been that it reduced the science of economics to *catalectics,* to a science limited to the study of barter, trade and exchange. German economists, by contrast, were involved in the management of the many small German states. The term cameralism itself originates in the *camera principis* or *Kammer,* that is, treasury. The perspective of the cameralists was that of public management, of taxes and institutions, laws and regulations. Their view of economic development was, therefore, very practical, and led them to a consideration of production — rather than trade alone — and the balance between different economic activities. For example, the need for creating a healthy base for taxation led them to favour the promotion of mechanized manufacturing, whose employees would gain a taxable income and whose owners were much better tax subjects than farmers or small artisans. German economists were, almost to a man,[6] in ardent opposition to the French Physiocrats, who established agriculture as the only producer of 'net wealth' (see also the chapter on 'The Italian Tradition of Political Economy' in this volume).

The German economic tradition focuses on the state as an important economic facilitator and occasionally also as an entrepreneur of last resort in difficult situations (Reinert 1999). Probably also as a legacy of the chaos of the Thirty Years' War, a chaos similar to that of any 'failing state' today, pragmatism called for an orderly environment, with the state as a necessary facilitator in order to create individual opportunity and happiness. The state is seen as something through which, rather than against which, individual liberty and progress are gained within the framework of a *common weal?* Through this tradition, German economics provides key insights for contemporary economies where the 'natural order' is non-productive rent-seeking involving raw materials and/or cheap labour, and where the 'natural order', at times, is utter chaos.[7]

German economics is above all an *Erfahrungswissenschaft* — a science based on experience. There is little metaphysical speculation and high abstractions; many considered the economic theories of David Ricardo to be an example of 'metaphysical speculation'.[8] *Strukturzusammenhänge* — structural coherence and connections — among economic factors, and between the economy and the rest of society, are not only obvious, understanding such connections is also most important for both economic theory and policy. Synergies would be one example of this. Compared to Anglo-Saxon economics, the German approach has therefore always been holistic. Economics was to become an umbrella science of the social sciences. There was only one criterion for what was to be included under the heading of 'economics': relevance. To the degree that nutrition might be important to the economy at one point in time, it would be a part of economics.

Praxisnähe — closeness to reality — and relevance have been key criteria for academic quality in this tradition. There is also a fundamental understanding that important economic factors are irreducible to mere figures and symbols. A frequent criticism is that standard economics often produces *qualitätslose Grössen,* quantities that are devoid of any qualitative understanding. Even the most accurate and comprehensive description of a human being by all his or her quantifiable aspects — height, weight, percentage of water and trace minerals — would leave out the key factor in economic development, what Friedrich Nietzsche called *Geist and Willenskapital:* the wit and will of mankind.

As it developed, German economics came to be solidly based on the philosophical foundation of Gottfried Wilhelm von Leibniz (1646–1716) and Christian Wolff (1679–1754),[9] arising from the legal tradition of *Naturrecht* or natural law.

---

6 The exceptions are August Schlettwein (1731–1802) and Theodor Schmalz (1760–1831), both marginal figures in the history of German economic thought.

7 I am indebted to Wolfgang Drechsler for assistance in formulating this paragraph.

8 A very useful discussion of different ways of understanding economic phenomena in German versus mainstream economics is found in Drechsler (2004).

9 For a discussion, see Reinert and Daastol (1997).

The devastation of the Thirty Years' War created a need for a common basis of law regardless of creed. In the natural 'uncivilized state', the natural law tradition maintains that man still has moral obligations, the origins of which are to be found in nature. Modern state theory also emerged in the same period. At the core of the system of Christian Wolff, who came to be the basis of German economics starting around 1750, rests the presupposition that man is essentially a social, peaceful and rational being. Related to this is a fundamental belief in man's common sense: *der gesunden Menschenverstand.*

Schumpeterian elements are deeply embedded in the German economics tradition. A focus on learning and progress, very clear in Leibniz and Wolff, is based on the *Gottesähnlichkeit* of man: man's near-God-like quality of being able to create new things. Being born in the image of God meant that it was man's pleasurable duty to invent. At its most fundamental level, the contrast between English and German economics lies in the view of the human mind. To John Locke, man's mind is a blank slate — a *tabula rasa* — with which he is born, and which passively receives impressions throughout life. To Leibniz, man has an active mind that constantly compares experiences with established schemata, a mind both noble and creative.

Of Adam Smith's ideas, the one most repudiated by German economists was that man is essentially an animal that has learned to barter. In the tradition that followed Smith, ideas and inventions have been produced outside the economic system. Karl Menger, the founder of the Austrian School of Economics, dedicated a whole chapter in his *Grundrisse* to refute Smith's view on this point. In the German tradition, including Marx and Schumpeter, the view is that man is an animal who has learned to invent. Nietzsche later added the point that man is the only animal that can keep promises, and therefore creates laws and institutions. Putting these elements together, we have an impressionistic picture of what differentiates English from German economics — barter and 'metaphysical speculation', on the one hand, and production and institutions, on the other.

To sum up, the following are the main characteristics that distinguish the German economic tradition — from Gottfried Leibniz and Christian Wolff, via Johann Gottlob von Justi and Friedrich List, to the *Verein fur Sozialpolitik* and the Historical Schools:

- Centre of theory: man and his needs: *Der Mensch and seine Bedürfnisse.*
- A non-mechanical understanding of the world: qualitative *(verstehen,* as opposed to purely quantifiable '*begreifen*' (Drechsler 2004).
- An *activist–idealist* approach to economic policy based on morality and ethics, as opposed to *a passive–materialistic* attitude to economic policy (these are Werner Sombart's terms).
- 'History matters': theory and policy must be based on the context and should understand the cumulative mechanisms in economics.
- Technology and new knowledge are the driving forces of the economy.
- Focus on production, rather than trade.
- Economic activities are seen as qualitatively different as carriers of economic growth.

- Economic harmony is man-made, not natural. Passivity is more likely to create 'spontaneous disorder' than 'spontaneous order'.

Cameralist Economic Policy: From Veit von Seckendorff (1626–1692) to Wilhelm von Hörnigk (1640–1714)

Veit Ludwig von Seckendorff (1626–1692) has been called the 'Adam Smith of Cameralism' (Small 1909), and justifiably so. His times were violent and extremely difficult for Germany. The Thirty Years' War (1618–48) was a religious war, initially intra-German, which gradually came to involve several European powers at the time, including Spain, France, Denmark and Sweden. The war had no winner, but it became obvious to a number of German intellectuals of the next generation that the real loser was civilized society as such. When Seckendorff was 16 years old, his father, a German in the service of the Swedish army, was executed as an alleged spy. By the time Seckendorff died at the age of 66, the armies of Louis the XIV of France had recently utterly destroyed one German state, the Palatinate *(Pfalz)*. In between, there were wars with the Turks and two more wars with France that led to the loss of Strasbourg, where Seckendorff had studied. Cameralism, in our view, cannot be properly understood outside this context of a simultaneous reconstruction of a civilized society and of what would today be called 'failed states': states where economic life and basic institutions had to be built, virtually, from scratch. The 'natural order' of the day was barbarism.

Seckendorff entered the service of a former official in the Swedish army, Duke Ernst of Sachsen–Gotha, called Ernst *der Fromme* or Ernst the Pious. Seckendorff loyally identified himself with the *common weal* of the state he served, but was also patriotic about greater Germany. He is referred to as one of the most learned men of his times; he corresponded with Leibniz, among others, and his high ethical standards made him a prototype for later German bureaucrats.

In 1656, at the age of 30, Seckendorff finished his most important work and the first book in the cameralist literature, *Der Teutsche Fürstenstaat (The German Principality)*. The book became the standard handbook for economic policy in Germany and went through a number of editions over the next 98 years. The *Fürstenstaat* is a kind of 'owner's manual' for a small state. There are accurate descriptions of history, population, economic conditions, administration, school system, law and justice. The principles followed in the very successful reconstruction of the state of Sachsen–Gotha and its institutions after the Thirty Years' War are described. Seckendorff's approach was clearly a holistic and organic one, where the state is an organism and its *common weal* can only be understood in its totality *(Ganzheit)*. His views were similar to those of the Italian economists of the Renaissance. The emphasis on the totality, on *Ganzheit*, was to be a hallmark of German economics and German philosophy for the next 300 years.[10]

---

[10] Othmar Spann (1878–1950) represented an extreme case of 'holistic economics'.

Seckendorff travelled to the Netherlands, accompanying Count Ernst. The wealth and religious tolerance he observed there made a huge impression on him (Stolleis 1995:158). Early economic policy in Europe was frequently based on benchmarking against the successful states — the Netherlands (Reinert, ed. 2004c) and Venice being the obvious cases — and against Spain, with its inflow of gold accompanied by deindustrialization and increasing poverty, as the case to avoid. To Seckendorff, the Dutch appeared as 'examples of the wisest and in production and trade *(in Gewerb)* the most experienced people' (Seckendorff 1665). From the Netherlands, Seckendorff understood the crucial need for manufactures and also the need to cluster economic activities, both arguments that Antonio Serra had already raised at a theoretical level in 1613. Seckendorff's economic measures included promotion of manufactures and resettlement of artisans from the countryside in the cities, where they were likely to make a much better living. He promoted the extension of agriculture and of activities adding value to the produce of the land. He also eased the mobility of labour by eliminating fees required for settlement and resettlement. With him, we find the origins of the welfare state, of care for the poor and of government responsibility for the elderly. In his wish to limit the powers of the guilds, he showed liberal tendencies well ahead of his times.

Seckendorff's policies were, to a large extent, reflected in von Hörnigk's principles published eighteen years later, which we shall discuss in detail below. Seckendorff established in the eighteenth century what Albert Hirschman calls 'a multi-level conspiracy for development'. He was an early proponent of a school of economists and political writers that was to dominate Europe in the next century: writers who convinced the kings and rulers that their *right to rule* a state or country also entailed a *duty to develop* that state. The thirteenth-century idea of a common good, originating in Italian humanism, was slowly being transformed into an idea of public happiness, and the ruler was put in charge of the project. Wilhelm Roscher coined the descriptive term 'enlightened despotism' for this kind of rule (Roscher 1868: 77).

The enlightened ruler — the 'philosopher–king' in Christian Wolff's terms — was in charge of this 'developmental dictatorship', and the job taken up by the cameralists following Seckendorff was to advise, assist, guide, correct, flatter and cajole the ruler into doing his job properly. The logic that emerged was, the better the ruler, the wealthier the people. Instead of judging his success by his own wealth, the ruler's success would be based on the wealth and happiness of his people.[11]

Of the cameralists, the first true economist was Johann Joachim Becher (1635–1682), whose varied career matched that of the 'economist adventurers' of the next century. Here, however, we concentrate on Becher's university companion and brother-in-law, Philipp Wilhelm von Hörnigk (1640–1714), who delivered economic policy measures in the most succinct way. Like Johann Heinrich Gottlob von Justi in the next century, Hörnigk was a German-born economist in the service of Austria. His book *Österreich über alles, wann es nur will (Austria Supreme (if it so wishes))* was published anonymously in

[11] An example of an English translation of a German book on this subject is Wolff (1750).

1684, and was the most successful German-language economics book of the period. Like Seckendorff, Hörnigk corresponded with Leibniz, the famous and practically inclined philosopher of the time. Hörnigk's economics was 'reality economics', based on intensive studies of the actual situation in the country. His 1684 book reached at least sixteen editions and remained in print for a full hundred years (Carpenter 1977: 10). The centenary edition was published in 1784 under the title *Bemerkungen über die österreichische Staatsökonomie (Remarks on the Economy of the State of Austria)*. In this edition, it was claimed that Austria could thank Hörnigk's book for most of her wealth.

As in the case of Seckendorff, understanding Hörnigk requires an understanding of the setting. Civilization, as it was known then, was under threat. Just two years before Hörnigk's book was published, the Turks had ended one of several unsuccessful sieges of Vienna. Austria suffered great famines during 1648–50,1692–94,1698–1702 and 1712–13, and devastating epidemics in the 1630s, 1650s and 1680s. To the north, the once powerful Hanseatic League had long been in decline, and to the south, neighbouring Venice and Italy had started on a similar downward path. These were challenging times for Austria.

Hörnigk distrusted merchants and complained that wealthy people who had the funds to invest did not do so. He recommended a different kind of shock therapy from that of today's economists and the Washington Consensus: complete prohibition of luxury goods from abroad that would prompt the rich to invest in national manufacturing. Like William Petty in England at that time, Hörnigk was an early proponent of 'political arithmetic'. Among other things, he calculated the income from artisans in a successful Dutch city.

We shall summarize below Hörnigk's 'Nine Points of Economic Policy' from his 1684 book, and briefly comment on the circumstances in which such policies, most unusual today, would be appropriate and efficient. Hörnigk's recommendations were representative not only of German economic policy, both then and later, but also of principles that, to varying degrees, were typical of Europe's way out of underdevelopment.[12]

Hörnigk's *first* point was 'to inspect the country's soil with the greatest care, and not to leave the agricultural possibilities of a single corner or clod of earth unconsidered. Every useful form of *plant* under the sun should be experimented with, to see whether it is adapted to the country.' In this type of economic theory that was famous for its bias towards manufacturing, it is most interesting that the first reference should be to agriculture. Agricultural productivity advanced extremely slowly for centuries; so, typically, the economists of the day saw that the only way to raise production was by extending the arable area through the draining of marshes, etc. Most interesting was the 'Schumpeterian' element of introducing new crops.

Second, 'all commodities found in a country, which cannot be used in their natural state, should be worked up within the country, since the payment for *manufacturing* generally exceeds the value of the raw material by two, three, ten, twenty, and even a hundred fold'. Unemployment and underemployment represented huge problems at the time,

---

[12] This part of Hörnigk's book was translated by Arthur Monroe (1930).

and this 'multiplier effect' of manufacturing was commonly found, both in terms of value added and employment. The first instance was probably Fernando Ortiz's memorandum to the king of Spain in 1558 (see the chapter titled 'Mercantilism and Economic Development' in this volume for a further discussion).

Third: For carrying out the above two rules, there will be need of people, both for producing and cultivating the raw materials and for working them up. Therefore, attention should be given to the population, that it may be as large as the country can support, this being a well-ordered state's most important concern, but, unfortunately, one that is often neglected. And the people should be turned by all possible means from idleness to remunerative *professions;* instructed and encouraged in all kinds of *inventions,* arts, and trades; and, if necessary, instructors should be brought in from foreign countries for this.

Fourth, once in the country, gold and silver, whether from its own mines or obtained by *industry* from foreign countries, are, under no circumstances to be taken out for any purpose, so far as possible, or be allowed to be buried in chests or coffers, but must always remain in *circulation;* nor should much be permitted in uses where they are at once *destroyed* and cannot be utilized again. For under these conditions, it will be impossible for a country that has once acquired a considerable supply of cash, especially one that possesses gold and silver mines, ever to sink into poverty; indeed, it is impossible that it should not continually increase in wealthy and property.

The emphasis on gold and silver was what the mainstream history of thought told us to expect, an emphasis supposedly exposing the 'primitiveness' of these theories. However, see Perrotta (1991) for an alternative view.

Therefore, *fifth,* 'the inhabitants of the country should make every effort to get along with their domestic products, to confine their luxury to these alone, and to do without foreign products as far as possible.' As Perrotta (1993) argues, import substitution was a key aspect of mercantilism. The first, and hugely successful, such import substitution strategy was the English 'Tudor plan' from 1485–1603 (see Reinert 1995; and the chapter on 'The Italian Tradition of Political Economy' in this volume).

Sixth: 'In case the said purchases were indispensable because of necessity or *irremediable* abuse, they should be obtained from these foreigners at first hand, so far as possible, and not for gold or silver, but in exchange for other domestic wares.' This was the clearing system that was operating also in Europe in the years after World War II, in order to avoid balance of payments deficits.

Seventh: 'Such foreign commodities should in this case be imported in unfinished form, and worked up within the country, thus earning the wages of *manufacturing there.'* The multiplier mechanism of manufacturing applied both to the value added effect and the employment effect, and, additionally, solved the balance of payments problem.

Eighth: 'Opportunities should be sought night and day for selling the country's superfluous goods to these foreigners in manufactured form, so far as this is necessary, and for gold and silver; and to this end, *consumption,* so to speak, must be sought in the farthest ends of the earth, and developed in every possible way.' The 'cult of export' was not invented by the Washington Consensus. This was another way of improving balance of payments deficits endemic to poor countries, where Keynesian measures alone may only suck in imports.

Ninth: Except for important considerations, no importation should be allowed under any circumstances of commodities of which there is a sufficient supply of suitable quality at home; and in this matter neither sympathy nor compassion should be shown to foreigners, be they friends, kinsfolk, *allies,* or enemies. For all friendship ceases, when it involves my own weakness and ruin. And this holds good, even if the domestic commodities are of poorer quality, or even higher priced. For it would be better to pay for an article two dollars which remain in the country than only one which goes out, however strange this may seem to the ill-informed.

This sums up the value added, employment and balance of payments arguments, arguments that may also be presented in a neoclassical production possibility frontier-type analysis.

The Eighteenth Century: The Birth of Academic Economics and of Specialization in the Field

The eighteenth century, the Age of Enlightenment, was characterized by a very considerable literary production, including of the cameralist sciences. *Bibliografie der Kameralwissenschaften,* the main bibliographical source, lists 14,040 items — with some duplication — over 1,184 pages (Humpert 1937), the majority of the publications. Johann Heinrich Gottlob von Justi (1717–1771), the most influential German economist of the century, was also the most prolific writer among the economists, with a total of 67 published books (Reinert 2004a). Thirteen different contemporary translations were made of eight of Justi's books, into five different languages.

This was also the century of the first economics journals, mixing practical advice, theory and news on the whereabouts of economists, in typical cameralist style. The best known German economists of the time — Justi, Georg Heinrich Zincke (1692–1769) and Johann Beckmann (1739–1811) — published their own journals. Practical works on agriculture, arts, inventions and manufacturing also abounded all across Europe at the time. In addition to being an age of discoveries, the eighteenth century was an age of science and scientific academies, with the founding of large museums in Europe.

The world's first two professorships in economics (and cameralism) were established in Germany in 1727, about a century before the first such professorship in England. The first professorship in economics outside Germany was in Uppsala in Sweden, starting some time in the 1830s. The countries to follow suit were Finland (then part of Sweden), at the Åbo (Turku) Academy; then Austria, with Justi being named professor in the cameral sciences in 1752 in Vienna; and Italy, where Antonio Genovesi was appointed professor of political economy, University of Naples, in 1754.

Since the early 1970s, Kenneth Carpenter, a librarian at Harvard University, has collected large amounts of material documenting the translations of economics books in

Europe before 1850. He describes a pattern of frequent translations between continental European languages but less frequent translations to and from English.[13] The material is not yet fully systematized, but the section on Sweden, which is finished but remains unpublished, shows that out of 207 economics publications translated into Swedish before 1850, 84 were from German, 55 from French and 51 from English. The rest were from Danish and multilingual sources. The widespread myth, of English origin, that German economics has been the 'odd man out' in the history of economic thought, seems to be thoroughly unfounded.[14]

Johann Heinrich Gottlob von Justi was probably the most representative German economist of the period. He was both a synthesizer and a modernizer of the German tradition, absorbing the important novelties of the 1700s into the consensus of the late 1600s. One example of a new institution was fire insurance. Perhaps the most important novelty of the century was the discovery of important synergies between manufacturing and agriculture: by promoting manufacturing, one would not be punishing agriculture, but quite the contrary. The segmentation of the field of cameralism into subfields, with their own publications and textbooks, was a sign of a maturing science. Justi himself wrote a book on the theory of finance, and his 1754 inaugural lecture as professor of the cameral sciences in Vienna was about the relationship between science and economic welfare, a theme that was to be the subject of a book by Johann Gottfried von Herder (1744–1803) some twenty years later.

Geography had been an important element in continental European economics since the books by Giovanni Botero (1588) and Antonio Serra (1619). From the eighteenth century, it became fashionable to describe economics in stages: from hunting and gathering, to herding, agriculture and, finally, agriculture and manufacturing (Reinert 2000). Justi placed these historical stages on a geographical plane using concentric circles, placing the urban increasing returns sector at the centre. This is the tool normally attributed to Johan Heinrich von Thünen (1783–1850). Both Justi and von Thünen thoroughly understood the importance of nurturing and protecting the manufacturing area, both geographically and economically the core of any nation-state (Reinert 2004a). When a German economist stated, 'It is known that a primitive people do not improve their customs and institutions later to find useful industries, but the other way around' (Meyen 1770: 11), he was expressing something that could be considered the common sense of the time.

Also, technology had always been an integral part of cameralism; in the 1770s, from the economics professor Johann Beckmann at the University of Gottingen, the world got its first economics textbook focusing on technology. Beckmann built on Justi's foundations, publishing a third edition of Justi's two-volume book, *Factories and Manufacturers.*

Johann Friedrich von Pfeiffer (1718–1787) wrote a successful cameralist textbook (Pfeiffer 1764–65, 1777–78), as well as a very early history of economic thought covering

---

13 The preliminary results are published in Carpenter (1977).

14 This point is also forcefully made by the Spanish historian of economic thought, Ernest Lluch (1996: 163–75).

about thirty authors — German, French, English and Italian — in six volumes (Pfeiffer 1781–84). As previously mentioned, virtually all the German economists were opposed to Physiocracy, and Pfeiffer provided a systematic theoretical refusal of Physiocratic doctrines in a book entitled *The Anti-Physiocrat* (Pfeiffer 1780).

Joseph Schumpeter compared German mercantilism with English classical economics succinctly:

> He (Justi) saw the practical argument for laissez-faire not less clearly than did A. Smith, and his bureaucracy, while guiding and helping when necessary, was always ready to efface itself when no guidance or help seemed needed. (Schumpeter's footnote here: 'This was not merely a dream. It will be pointed out below that the bureaucracy in the typical German principality actually tried to behave like this.') Only he saw much more clearly than did the latter all the obstacles that stood in the way of its working according to design. Also, he was much more concerned than A. Smith with the practical problems of government action in the short-run vicissitudes of his time and country, and with particular difficulties in which private initiative fails or would have failed under the conditions of German industry of his time. His laissez-faire was a laissez-faire plus watchfulness, his private-enterprise economy a machine that was logically automated but exposed to breakdowns and hitches which his government was ready to mend. For instance, he accepted as a matter of course that the introduction of labour-saving machinery would cause unemployment: but this was no argument against the mechanization of production because, also as a matter of course, *his* government would find equally good employment for the unemployed. This, however, is not inconsistency, but sense. And to us who are apt to agree with him much more than we do with A. Smith, his (Justi's) vision of economic policy might look like laissez-faire with the nonsense left out. (Schumpeter 1954: 172)

The 'Historical Schools' of the Nineteenth and Twentieth Centuries

After an initial period of resistance to the ideas of David Ricardo and English economics, the 1830s and, particularly, the 1840s saw the growth of a very strong belief in the merits of laissez-faire capitalism. This period has a lot in common with the triumphalist period following the fall of the Berlin wall that came to mark the 1990s. This first period culminated in the repeal of the corn laws in England in 1846, when the English, for a while, extremely skilfully managed to convince the rest of the world to no longer protect its manufacturing industry by no longer protecting their own agriculture. There are many parallels between the 1840s and the period in which we now live: never since, until now, has such blind faith in the virtues of free markets dominated academia and policy-making to such an extent. The route from the overwhelming social problems of the mid-nineteenth century to the national welfare states that were to follow decades later, therefore, contains clues on how contemporary problems, this time on a global rather than a national scale, can be handled.

Perhaps the most essential feature of mercantilist economic policy was to diversify the economy away from agricultural monoculture into diversified manufacturing.

Protecting agriculture would mean protecting the old feudal order that one wished to get rid of. The English bluff — withdrawing the protection of agriculture to convince the rest of the world to stop protecting manufacturing industry — would easily have been called by the great continental economists of the eighteenth century — by a Montesquieu in France, by a Galiani or a Genovesi in Italy, by a Justi in Germany. The same would have been true for the economists of the preceding seventeenth century, to whom the proposal would have appeared even more ridiculous. From 1820 onwards, however, resistance to Ricardian economics was to come not from Europe but from the United States, with important policy-focused publications by Daniel Raymond and Mathew Carey in that year, and important theoretical work against Smithian economics by John Rae in 1834. In Europe, during this period, there was mainly one lonely voice speaking out against the economic policy of liberalism and peripheral deindustrialization: Friedrich List (1789–1846). Once an American citizen, List was clearly inspired by the arguments forwarded by Daniel Raymond, a Baltimore lawyer.

List himself was converted from a free trader to one who saw the need to protect agriculture after he saw the devastating results of deindustrialization in France following the fall of Napoleon. Most of what Friedrich List wrote has never been translated from German into other languages, so the very strong opinion many mainstream economists have of List is narrowly based. List tells us the way things work, but does not generally tell us why. He convincingly argues that the cultivation and protection of agriculture will not yield the same results as the protection of manufacturing (Reinert 1998). He tells us that the producers of olive oil will be poor in the absence of manufacturing, but not really why. With some justification, therefore, he may be criticized as a theorist. List's policy recommendations were fine, and his feel for the right historical sequencing of policy measures was probably unique, but, as compared to Antonio Serra, he failed to explain their underlying mechanisms. List's theoretical concepts were vague, or, as Werner Sombart said about him: 'His concepts levitate like undelivered souls on the banks of Hades' (Sombart 1928: 929). However, his holistic vision of the synergies of economic development and national wealth creation, products of increasing return activities and of heavy investments in infrastructure, as the driving forces behind national wealth, was almost unprecedented.

From the perspective of German economics, Friedrich List was the great free trader who forged the German customs union, the *Zollverein*. The rest of the world sees him as the great protectionist. List was also the first to have a vision of a European common market. Most economists today fail to understand how one can be protectionist in one context and a free trader in a different context. In List's vision, global free trade was desirable only after every nation had achieved a comparative advantage in increasing return activities. Only when the asymmetries of colonial and neocolonial trade had been eliminated would all parties benefit from free trade. List's vision was fully compatible with the European mercantilist mainstream of the preceding 300 years, and with Serra's theoretical explanation.

Historically based and context-specific economic theories were to dominate German economic theory from around 1850 to the hundred years that followed. This period is normally divided in three — into the 'older', 'younger' and 'youngest' historical schools. As has also been suggested by others, it is convenient to treat List as representing a 'proto-historical school'. He raised the Italian arguments — from Botero and Serra to Galiani — that the cities and their manufacturing activities are the keys to personal freedom, to the arts, to the division of labour and, indeed, to civilization itself. A point made by German economists as early as Leibniz, and so masterfully restated by Galiani, was repeated by List, who insisted that manufacturing was also the key to creating wealth in agriculture, 'the only way to liberate agriculture from its chains'.

The first shot in the long fight between the German historical schools and English classical economics was fired in the year 1848, by a book by Bruno Hildebrand (1812–1878). A few years later, Karl Knies (1821–1898), perhaps the most under-rated of these economists, presented his theoretical work on the historical method in economics. Knies inspired the most prominent and influential economist in the United States at the turn of the nineteenth century, Richard Ely (1854–1943), founder and then president of the American Economic Association from 1899 to 1902, at that time classified as a 'Christian socialist'.

In 1886, another influential US economist inspired by German economics, Edwin Seligman (1861–1939), outlined the programme of the German Historical School as follows. For Seligman, the School:

1. Discards the exclusive use of the deductive method, and stresses the necessity of historical and statistical treatment.
2. Denies the existence of immutable natural laws in economics, calling attention to the interdependence of theories and institutions, and showing that different epochs or countries require different systems.
3. Disclaims belief in the beneficence of the absolute laissez-faire system.
4. Maintains the close inter-relations of law, ethics and economics, and refuses to acknowledge the adequacy of the presumption of self-interest as the sole regulator of economic action.

Key members of the 'older' Historical School were Hildebrand, Knies and Wilhelm Roscher (1817–1894). Key members of the 'younger' Historical School were Gustav von Schmoller (1838–1917), Adolph Wagner (1835–1917) and Lujo Brentano (1844–1931). The 'youngest' Historical School was represented by Werner Sombart (1863–1941) and Max Weber (1864–1920). In the next section, we discuss the policies emanating from this school of economics.[15]

The foundations of Schumpeterian economics were also laid by the Historical School. Schumpeter's best known concept in economics, 'creative destruction', was first used by Werner Sombart, who was heavily influenced by Friedrich Nietzsche (see Reinert and Reinert (2004).

[15] For a discussion of the Historical School, see Shionoya, ed. (2001).

The Social Problem and the *Verein für Sozialpolitik*

> Ricardo, and still more those who popularized him, may stand as an example for all time of the extreme danger which may arise from the unscientific use of hypothesis in social speculations, from the failure to appreciate the limited applications to actual affairs of a highly artificial and arbitrary analysis. His ingenious, though perhaps over-elaborated reasonings became positively mischievous and misleading when they were unhesitatingly applied to determine grave practical issues without the smallest sense of the thoroughly abstract and unreal character of the assumptions on which they were founded. (H.S. Foxwell, professor of economics, Cambridge University, 1899)

1848, also the year of publication of *The Communist Manifesto,* saw a 'backlash' against Ricardian and laissez-faire economics. In all the European languages, 'the social problem', which had lingered under the surface ever since the end of the Napoleonic Wars, suddenly surfaced with incredible vigour, and produced both revolutions across Europe and a lot of literature on the subject. But, as Galiani had so eloquently pointed out 70 years before, mankind is a great connoisseur of effects but a poor judge of causes. In our view, Professor Foxwell's comments about Ricardo anticipate what Schumpeter was later to call the Ricardian vice of economics.

The reaction of German economists to this challenge is slightly confused by frequent mention of three overlapping categories or groups of economists: the German Historical School; the *Kathedersozialisten* ('Socialists of the Professorial Chair'); and the Association for Social Policy, *Verein fur Sozialpolitik*. This requires some clarification.

The German Historical School is a term later introduced to refer to these generations of German mainstream economists. *Kathedersozialist* is a somewhat unfortunate term imposed on a group of economists by a contemporary journalist; in the same year the majority of them founded the *Verein fur Sozialpolitik.* The first term used by the journalist was 'freshwater sailors', a derogatory reference made by European sailors to colleagues who thought they were sailors but had never experienced 'the real thing', that is, the reality and perils of the ocean (Oppenheim 1872). The intent was the same: to accuse these economists of trying to improve the real world without having much experience of it themselves. Unlike Ricardian economics, however, these economists were much closer to analysing 'the real thing', the context and reality of economics. Compared to English classical economics, Ricardo was the 'freshwater sailor' in a sea of arbitrary assumptions, while the *Kathedersozialisten* were attempting — successfully, in the long term — to tackle the world as it really was.

Probably a quotation from Gustav Schmoller's opening speech at the founding meeting of the *Verein für Sozialpolitik,* in a private home in Eisenach on Sunday, 6 October 1872, best explains the background for its creation:

> The deep cleavage in our society separating entrepreneurs and workers, owning and not owning classes, represents a threat of a social revolution. This threat has drawn closer. In wide circles there have been serious doubts whether the economic doctrines which dominate on today's market — and which were expressed at the Economic Congress — forever will keep

their dominance. Will the introduction of the free right to carry on business *(Gewerbefreiheit)* and the elimination of all mediaeval legislation on guilds really create the perfect economic conditions that the hotheads *(Heißsporne)* of that tradition predict?

It was the original *Verein fur Sozialpolitik,* active from 1872 to 1932, that built the theoretical and practical foundations of twentieth-century European welfare states. The Scandinavian welfare states, which were to become the most prominent, took over not only many German institutions, but often also their names in literal translation. Significantly, the *Verein* ceased to exist the year Hitler came to power, but its work had largely been completed by then.

The creators of the welfare state then were economists whose common trait was that they were anti-Ricardian, people who disliked communism just as much as they disliked liberalism. However, when these economists, their theories and political opinions are carefully studied, they come across as a very diverse group. The question that arises is, how a group with these differences managed to be so productive, and to create so many new institutions and social reforms. The *Verein* continued a tradition that started with Seckendorff and Leibniz, producing what to modern economists would look like microscopic analyses of economies and economic history. From the accumulation of such micro-data, context-dependent policy conclusions were drawn at a high level of abstraction. The method of the Historical School can be compared with the case-study method of the Harvard Business School at a national, rather than a company, level. The case-study method was established by the Harvard School's first dean, an enthusiastic student of Schmoller, Edwin Gay (1867–1946), whose own studies of economics and economic history in German-speaking Europe lasted more than twelve years.

An important element that kept the *Verein* together was a common research agenda, around which facts were gathered from all regions of German-speaking Europe, with papers written and presented at annual meetings. One year they would discuss problems caused by the lack of health insurance, another year how to create a system protecting workers from unemployment, and the next year the consequences of 'Fordist' mass production. A fascinating issue of the time was how to address the poverty of areas that specialized in economic activities that had not been mechanized and/or remained highly intensive in unskilled labour. The 'home workers', *Heimarbeiter,* were mostly paid by piece.

Such specialization in 'unmechanizable' production bereft of scale effects and untouched by the ruling techno-economic paradigm clearly parallels today's *maquilas* (low-tech assembly plants). However, unlike the Mexican *maquila* workers of today, these workers were theoretically free to move to other, more industrialized areas of Germany at the time.

It has been argued that the *Verein fur Sozialpolitik* rarely disagreed with the imperial economic policy of Bismarck, implying that they were uninfluential or 'puppets' of the regime. In our view, causality runs the other way: Bismarck's economic policy rarely disagreed fundamentally with the views of the *Verein.* Bismarck understood social reality and problems, and also that the liberals had no cure; he therefore relied heavily on the recommendations of the *Verein,* which, as noted earlier, covered an unusually wide political spectrum.

As we saw, the scholarly output of cameralism was enormous, as was the scholarly production of the next century of German economics, particularly following 1848. The papers and reports of the *Verein fur Sozialpolitik* conferences fill 188 volumes and occupy five metres of shelf space. The first century of *Schmoller's Jahrbuch* (1871–1971), the most influential journal of the same group of economists, fills almost seven metres of shelf space. In addition, there are literally dozens of other journals and an enormous number of books and monographs. We do not have to accept the neoliberal claim that 'there is no alternative'; here lie the bases for a full-fledged alternative to neoclassical economics, unfortunately locked in a language that was once the lingua franca of economics but which today is relatively inaccessible.[16]

The famous *Methodenstreit* between German and Austrian economists, a kind of civil war inside German-language economics, started in the 1880s between Gustav Schmoller and Carl Menger (see Reinert 2003a). Viewed from today's vantage point, this occasionally vitriolic academic discussion was essentially a quibble over details. Carl Menger, the academic who supposedly argued against the use of history in economics, stated: 'A highly developed theory of economic phenomena is inconceivable without the study of economic history'; 'No reasonable person conceals the importance of historical studies for research in the field of political economy'; and 'History is indispensable for theoretical economics.' Schmoller and Menger, both agreed that both induction and deduction were needed, and the *Methodenstreit* was apparently about who was to be in the driver's seat — over which of the two was going to be the 'main science' and which would be the 'auxiliary science'.

In spite of the *Methodenstreit* civil war, German economics probably reached its highest point of influence around 1900. Both in the United States and in Japan, economic theory and policy were heavily influenced by German economics. Much to the satisfaction of German economists, John Stuart Mill had recanted on two key features of English classical economics relating to economic development: the wage funds doctrine (which limited the resources available for wages and salaries) and the free trade doctrine (Mill admitted the usefulness of industrial tariffs). It was generally agreed that Ricardo's abstract system had produced social disasters. A symptom of the loss of influence was Cambridge economist W. Cunningham's book, *The Rise and Decline of the Free Trade Movement* (London: Clay/Cambridge University Press), 1904. It was, therefore, with a certain justification that Gustav Schmoller, in his inaugural lecture as *Rektor* of the University of Berlin in 1897 (Schmoller 1897), celebrated the victory of empirically oriented economics over dogmatic economics, both left and right.

---

[16] Prof. Jürgen Backhaus, now of Erfurt University, has, for almost two decades, organized the Heilbronn Symposia, the main purpose of which is to render important German economic analyses accessible in the English language.

1945–47: The Morgenthau Plan Validates the German Economics Tradition

German economics, with an unbroken tradition from about 1650 to 1950, is uniquely valuable as a full-fledged alternative to today's mainstream economics. This tradition represents the most consistent bulwark against mechanistic and simplistic economic solutions of all political shades. We have attempted to build on this theoretical tradition in constructing the Other Canon of economics (www.othercanon.org). Creating, motivating, directing and controlling market forces in order to enhance human welfare has been the *leitmotiv* of German economic theory since its inception after the Thirty Years' War. After World War II, German-type economics continued to dominate German economic policy in its 'social market economy'.

The economic integration of Europe, at least until the 2004 extension, followed Friedrich List's prescriptions of symmetrical integration. In Europe, German pragmatism ruled at home, recently with a huge emphasis on innovation, while neoclassical economics became an export article ruling Europe's relationship with the rest of the world. As a theoretical tradition, the German tradition of economics was essentially thrown out — in our view, totally unjustifiably — with the bath water of Nazism. Policies based on this theoretical tradition developed not only Europe, but also the United States and Japan; indeed, such policies have been a mandatory passage point for all successful national transitions out of poverty.

After World War II, the core idea of cameralism as development economics — the idea that national development needs an increasing returns manufacturing sector — was vindicated through a large-scale experiment, the Morgenthau Plan. The purpose of this plan, named after Henry Morgenthau, the US Secretary of the Treasury during 1934–45, was to prevent Germany from ever starting a war again (Morgenthau 1945). This was to be achieved by deindustrializing Germany, making it a pastoral economy by closing factories, taking the industrial machinery out of the country, and filling the mines with water. The plan was approved in an Allied meeting in 1943, and carried out after the German capitulation in May 1945.

The Morgenthau Plan was abruptly stopped in 1947 when ex-President Herbert Hoover of the United States, on a fact-finding mission, reported back from Germany: 'There is the illusion that the New Germany left after the annexations can be reduced to a "pastoral state". It cannot be done unless we exterminate or move 25,000,000 out of it.' Hoover had rediscovered the wisdom of the cameralist and mercantilist population theorists: an industrialized nation has a much larger carrying capacity in terms of population than an agricultural state. The deindustrialization process had also led to a sharp fall in agricultural yields and to institutional collapse, providing evidence of the importance of the linkages between the industrial and agricultural sectors that were a hallmark of cameralist economics. Less than four months after Hoover's alarming report from Germany, the US government announced the Marshall Plan, which aimed to achieve exactly the opposite of the Morgenthau Plan: Germany's industrial capacity was to be brought back to its 1938 level at all costs. It cannot be emphasized enough that the Marshall Plan was not just a financial plan but, principally, a *reindustrialization plan*.

After years of neglect, the Morgenthau Plan was resurrected *de facto* by the Washington Consensus, starting in the 1980s and, even more strongly, after the end of the Cold War in 1991. This new *de facto* plan came with the label of 'structural adjustment', which often had the effect of deindustrializing third world nations (Reinert 2004c). These two ideal types of economic policy — the Marshall Plan and the Morgenthau Plan — embodied the 'virtuous' and 'vicious' circles that were fashionable, but not well explained, in the heyday of development economics during the 1950s and 1960s (Reinert 2003b).

In 1947, the United States understood the destructive forces that had been put in motion with the Morgenthau Plan. In his Harvard speech in June 1947, announcing what came to be called the Marshall Plan, US Secretary of State George Marshall stressed that 'the farmer has always produced the foodstuffs to exchange with the city-dweller for the other necessities of life'. This division of labour, that is, between increasing return activities in the cities and the countryside, was 'at the present time … threatened with breakdown'. George Marshall then made a remarkable recognition of cameralist and mercantilist economic policy: 'This division of labor is the basis of modern civilization.' Civilization requires increasing return areas, something that people from Antonio Serra to Abraham Lincoln and Friedrich List had been saying for a long time. However, this core of five centuries of economic theory has always eluded the trade-based English economics and its successor, today's mainstream economics. Its conceptual and instrumental tools fail to grasp this factor — a blind spot in mainstream economics that causes untold human suffering today. Herein lies the key to understanding the growing number of 'failed states' that have followed in the wake of the Washington Consensus. In 1953, George Marshall was awarded the Nobel Peace Prize.

I am indebted to Wolfgang Drechsler, Rainer Kattel and the editor for helpful comments on this chapter. The usual disclaimer applies.

References

Berch, Anders (1747), *Inledning til allmänna Hushalningen, innefattande Grunden til Politie, Oekonomie och Cameralwetenskaperna* (Stockholm: Lars Salvius).

Carpenter, Kenneth (1977), *Dialogue in Political Economy: Translations from and into German in the 18th Century,* Kress Library Publications No. 23 (Boston: Harvard Business School).

Clemence, Richard V. (1951), *Essays of J.A. Schumpeter* (Cambridge, Massachusetts: Addison-Wesley).

Drechsler, Wolfgang (2004), 'Natural versus Social Sciences: On Understanding in Economics', in Erik S. Reinert, ed. (2004c).

Humpert, Magdalene (1937), *Bibliografie der Kameralwissenschaften* (Cologne: Schroeder).

Lluch, Ernest (1996), 'El Cameralismo mas alla del mundo germanico', in *Revista de Economia Aplicada,* 4 (10): 163–75.

Meyen, Johan Jacob (1770), *Wie kommt es, dass die Oekonomie bisher so wenig Vortheile von der Physik und Mathematik gewonnen hat; und wie kann man diese Wissenschaften zum gemeinen Nutzen in die Oekonomie einführen, und von dieser Verbindung auf Grundsätze kommen, die in die Ausübung brauchbar sind?* (Berlin: Haude & Spener).

Monroe, Arthur (1930), *Early Economic Thought: Selections from Economic Literature prior to Adam Smith* (Cambridge, Massachusetts: Harvard University Press).

Morgenthau, Henry, Jr. (1945), *Germany is Our Problem: A Plan for Germany* (New York: Harper).

Oppenheim, H.B. (1872), *Der Katheder-Sozialismus* (Berlin: Oppenheim).

Perrotta, Cosimo (1991), 'Is Mercantilist Theory of the Favourable Balance of Trade Really Erroneous?' *History of Political Economy,* 23 (2): 301–36.

——— (1993), 'Early Spanish Mercantilism: The First Analysis of Underdevelopment', in Lars Magnusson, *Mercantilist Economics* (Boston: Kluwer): 17–58.

Pfeiffer, Johann Friedrich von (1764–65; 1777–78), *Lehrbegriff sämtlicher oeconomischer und Cameralwissenschaften,* 6 volumes (Stuttgart und Mannheim: Johann Christoph Erhard und C.F. Schwan).

——— (1780), *Der Antiphysiocrat, oder umstandliche Untersuchung des sogenannten Physiocratischen Systems* (Frankfurt: Esslingersche Buchhandlung).

——— (1781–84), *Berichtigungen berühmter Staats- Finanz- Policei- Cameral- Commerz- und okonomischer Schriften dieses Jahrehunderts, von dem Verfasser des Lehrbegriffs sämtlicher Öconomischen und Cameralwissenschaften,* 6 volumes (Frankfurt: Esslingersche Buchhandlung).

Reinert, Erik S. (1995), 'Competitiveness and Its Predecessors: A 500-year Cross-National Perspective', *Structural Change and Economic Dynamics,* 6: 23–42.

——— (1998), 'Raw Materials in the History of Economic Policy; or, Why List (the Protectionist) and Cobden (the Free Trader) Both Agreed on Free Trade in Corn', in G. Parry, ed., *Freedom and Trade: 1846–1996* (London: Routledge).

——— (1999), The Role of the State in Economic Growth', *Journal of Economic Studies,* 26 (4/5).

——— (2000), 'Karl Bücher and the Geographical Dimensions of Techno-Economic Change', in Jürgen Backhaus, ed., *Karl Bücher: Theory, History, Anthropology, Non-Market Economies* (Marburg: Metropolis Verlag).

——— (2003a), 'The Austrians and the Other Canon', in Jürgen Backhaus, ed., *Evolutionary Economic Thought: European Contributions and Concepts* (Cheltenham: Edward Elgar).

——— (2003b), 'Increasing Poverty in a Globalized World: Marshall Plans and Morgenthau Plans as Mechanisms of Polarization of World Incomes', in Ha-Joon Chang, ed., *Rethinking Economic Development (London:* Anthem Press).

——— (2004a), 'Johann Heinrich Gottlob von Justi (1717–1771): The Life and Times of an Economist Adventurer', in Jürgen Backhaus, ed., *Johann Heinrich Gottlob von Justi: The Beginning of Political Economy* (Boston: Kluwer).

——— (2004b), 'The Dutch Republic 1500–1750: Economic Strategy and Economic Performance in the Views of Contemporary European Economists', in Oscar Gelderblom, ed., *The Political Economy of the Dutch Republic.*

———, ed. (2004c), *Globalization, Economic Development and Inequality: An Alternative Perspective* (Cheltenham: Edward Elgar).

Reinert, Erik S. and Arno Daastol (1997), 'Exploring the Genesis of Economic Innovations: The Religious Gestalt-Switch and the *Duty to Invent* as Preconditions for Economic Growth', *European Journal of Law and Economics,* 4 (2/3): 233–83.

Reinert, Erik S. and Hugo Reinert (2004), 'Creative Destruction in Economics: Nietzsche, Sombart, Schumpeter', in Jürgen Backhaus and Wolfgang Drechsler, eds, *Friedrich Nietzsche 1844–2000: Economy and Society* (Boston: Kluwer).

Roscher, Wilhelm (1868), 'Der Sächsische Nationalokonom Johann Heinrich Gottlob von Justi', in *Archiv fur die Sächsische Geschichte:* 76–106.

Schmoller, Gustav (1897), *Wechselnde Theorien und Feststehende Wahrheiten im Gebiete der Staats- und Socialwissenschaftlichen und die Heutige Deutsche Volkstwirtschaftslehre, Rede bei Antritt des Rectorats* (Berlin: W. Büxenstein).

Schumpeter, Joseph (1954), *History of Economic Analysis* (New York: Oxford University Press).

Seckendorff, Veit Ludwig von (1665), *Additiones oder Zugaben und Erleuterungen zu dem Tractat des Teutschen Fürstenstaat* (Frankfurt: Götzen).

Shionoya, Yuichi, ed. (2001), *The German Historical School: The Historical and Ethical Approach to Economics* (London: Routledge).

Small, Albion W. (1909), *The Cameralists: The Pioneers of German Social Polity* (New York: Burt Franklin).

Sombart, Werner (1928), *Der Moderne Kapitalismus,* Vol. 2: *Das Europäische Wirtschaftsleben im Zeitalter des Frühkapitalismus* (Munich and Leipzig: Duncker & Humblot); 2-volume edition 1902, 4-volume edition 1919, 6-volume edition 1928.

Stolleis, Michael, ed. (1995), *Staatsdenker in der frühen Neuzeit* (Munich: Beck).

Sugiyama, Chuhei and Hiroshi Mizuta (1988), *Enlightenment and Beyond: Political Economy Comes to Japan* (Tokyo: University of Tokyo Press).

Tribe, Keith (1988), *Governing Economy: The Reformation of German Economic Discourse 1750–1840* (Cambridge: Cambridge University Press).

——— (1995), *Strategies of Economic Order. German Economic Discourse (1750–1950)* (Cambridge: Cambridge University Press).

Wolff, Christian (1750), *The Real Happiness of a People under a Philosophical King Demonstrated; Not only from the Nature of Things, but from the Undoubted Experience of the Chinese under their first Founder Fohi, and his Illustrious Successors, Hoam Ti, and Xin Num* (London: M. Cooper).

Chapter Two

THE ROLE OF THE STATE IN ECONOMIC GROWTH[1]

Erik S. Reinert

Abstract

This paper attempts to trace and describe the role played by the government sector – the state – in promoting economic growth in Western societies since the Renaissance. One important conclusion is that the antagonism between state and market, which has characterised the twentieth century, is a relatively new phenomenon. Since the Renaissance one very important task of the state has been to create well-functioning markets by providing a legal framework, standards, credit, physical infrastructure and – if necessary – to function temporarily as an entrepreneur of last resort. Early economists were acutely aware that national markets did not occur spontaneously, and they used "modern" ideas like synergies, increasing returns, and innovation theory when arguing for the right kind of government policy. In fact, mercantilist economics saw it as a main task to extend the synergetic economic effects observed within cities to the territory of a nation-state. The paper argues that the classical Anglo-Saxon tradition in economics – fundamentally focused on barter and distribution, rather than on production and knowledge – systematically fails to grasp these wider issues in economic development, and it brings in and discusses the role played by the state in alternative traditions of non-equilibrium economics.

Keywords: *Economic growth, Central government, Economic systems*

Without the Utopians of other times, men would still live in caves, miserable and naked. It was the Utopians who traced the lines of the first city … Out of generous dreams

[1] SUM – Centre for Development and the Environment, University of Oslo, Working Paper No. 5, 1997. The author thanks Moses Abramowitz for extensive comments on this paper. The author also gratefully acknowledges the creative suggestions and criticisms of Arno Daastøl contributing to this paper. The usual disclaimer applies. A much shortened version of the paper is forthcoming in Toninelli, Pier Angelo (Editor), *The Rise and Fall of State Owned Enterprise in the Western World*, Cambridge University Press.

come beneficial realities. Utopia is the principle of all progress, and the essay into a better future (Anatole France (cited in Fuz, 1952)).

1. Introduction: "The Renaissance State" vs "Natural Harmony"

In 1338 Ambrogio Lorenzetti finished his frescoes *Allegory of Good and Bad Government* in the Town Hall of Siena. The fresco symbolising good government shows thriving shops, fine buildings and dancing citizens enjoying their leisure. Bad government is shown as ruin, rape, robbery and murder. The *Allegory of Good and Bad Government* represents the optimistic Renaissance view of Man's untapped potential to improve his own situation. Theirs was a view of history being a continuous optimisation process where "Man's wit and will", applied to harnessing the forces of Nature, held enormous potential for improving his lot: "the never ending frontier of knowledge."

The starting point for Renaissance economics, and the birth of the modern State, was an acute awareness of the suboptimality of the present situation of Mankind – steeped in the ignorance and poverty of the Middle Ages. This situation could clearly be improved, and this optimisation was chased as an ever-moving target in the distance. The propellant of this process was learning – the acquisition of new knowledge. This process resembles today's evolutionary economics at its best (see, for example, Lundvall, 1994; dynamic optimisation is discussed in Nelson, 1995).

The usefulness of a State in this process arises out of the Renaissance concept of the common weal[2] – or the "common good" – a systemic dimension which is lost in the atomistic and static structure of today's mainstream economics. In this paper we use the term "Renaissance State" for a type of activistic and idealistic State which, we shall attempt to show, has been an "obligatory passage point" for all presently industrialised nations, bringing the nation into economic activities creating a common weal through increasing returns and self-enforcing feedback mechanisms. At a very simple level, a common weal arises out of the synergies stemming from the sharing of fixed costs – resulting either from specialised tools or from specialised knowledge, like the old story of the blind man and the deaf man whose weal was improved by acting together. We shall argue that the growth of complex economies has important similarities to the growth of complex technological systems – and that, in both cases, increasing returns are at the core of positive feedback mechanisms which increase welfare. Such systemic synergies are further based upon diversity – just as both the very existence and the common weal of a household fundamentally rest on synergies arising from Man and Woman being different. A common weal, then, is systemic and synergy-based – it is a dynamic concept in a process which increases the size of the economic pie – much as the process described by Adam Smith, who prior to his meetings with the French physiocrats in *The Theory of*

[2] It is interesting to note that people promoting the "common weal" were seen as being the enemies of the tyrants, as in this phrase from 1579: "Ridding good Commonwealmen out of the way, that he may maintaeine himself stil in his tyranny" (Golding, De Mornay, quoted in *The Oxford English Dictionary*, Oxford, The Clarendon Press, 1933, Vol. 3, p. 696).

Moral Sentiments (Smith [1759], 1812) recommends government intervention to promote a certain industry (which operated under increasing returns), to help neither the consumer nor the producer, but because it benefited the system as a whole – the "common weal". At this point it is important to point out that the actions emanating from an understanding of a "systemic common weal" are very different from the idea of distributive collective action – in a setting of static rent-seeking and zero-sum games – in modern Anglo-Saxon economics[3].

The economics of State involvement in the Renaissance was both immensely activistic and idealistic. Albert Hirschman (1991), discusses the arguments which, since the late eighteenth century, have been used against this type of activistic and idealistic interference with the "natural harmony" created by the market mechanism. Hirschman in his book gives us the history of ideas listing the arguments why Ambrogio Lorenzetti's optimistic frescoes expressing Man's ability to improve his own destiny were, at best, naïve and futile. Hirschman has collected the arguments in favour of passivity as a strategy[4] – a natural corollary to Ricardo's "dismal science". In this paper we shall discuss the role of the State in economic growth and in the history of economic thought as being torn between two fundamentally different economic outlooks: a production-centered and activistic-idealistic Renaissance tradition and a barter-centered and passivistic-materialistic tradition of Adam Smith, David Ricardo and neo-classical economics.

Hirschman divides the arguments against any active strategy on the part of the State in three categories, and finds to his surprise that both the traditional "right" and the traditional "left" gradually started to make the same kind of arguments:

(1) *Perversity*. Any attempt at improving the economic or social order will have the opposite effect of that intended. This argument is clearly present already in Adam Smith's late works.
(2) *Futility*. Any attempt at changing the social or economic order is doomed to fail.
(3) *Jeopardy*. Any attempt at changing the social or economic order will carry with it costs that are so high as to jeopardise what has previously been achieved.

The *zeitgeist* of the late 1990s is clearly closer to that described by Hirschman than to the optimism of Lorenzetti and his times. But the fall of the Berlin wall now gives us an opportunity to re-examine the role of the State in economic development under less ideological pressure than, not only since the start of the Cold War, but since the Ghost of Communism entered the stage 150 years ago. However, we are seriously hampered by the fact that at the core of present-day mainstream economics – as a result of the standard assumptions of neo-classical theory – there still lies a "natural harmony", in a

3 Our analysis is based on the role of positive and dynamic systemic effects influencing the size of the economic pie. This is a very different argument from that which shows that distributional conflicts over the sharing of the pie – both statically and over time – may very well reduce its size, as in the anti-social collective actions described, for example, in the works of Mancur Olson.

4 I owe this term to Arno Daastøl.

world void of any systemic effects, of Samuelson's factor price equalisation: the natural harmony which will make all wage earners of the planet equally rich – if we can only "get the prices right" and "provide a level playing field".

Out of these philosophies of "natural harmony" rises the rejection of the State as such, as in the "Civil disobedience" of Henry David Thoreau (1849) and its present-day manifestations, as in the 1995 bombing of the US Federal Building in Oklahoma City. We live in a society caught between, on the one hand, the wish for the simple individualistic life of Thoreau, with its roots in the late eighteenth century, whose ideal is living outside any society ("Why are people so worried", says Thoreau. "The one who does not eat, does not have to work.") On the other hand, we are addicted to a standard of living which can only be kept up in the network of a fine grained specialization, the synergies and scale of which are essential to the production of systemic effects, to the common good of Renaissance economists. These economists observed the wealth of populous and economically diversified cities – like Venice – in stark contrast to the poverty of the undiversified economic base in the countryside and in agricultural/administrative cities like Naples. Even the pessimistic Machiavelli, who "wants to present us with Mankind in its most negative and depressing aspects" (Canina, 1937), says it this way: "Il bene commune è quello che fa grandi le città" – "The common good is what makes the cities great".

However, today considerable tension is created by the fact that any systemic effects in the economy – and consequently any role of the State – are external to the core of the ruling economic theory. This fact is all the more harmful because, as we shall attempt to show in this paper, the experiences of the presently industrialised countries indicate that the need for State interventions is stronger, the poorer the country. Those who produce economic theory all live in nations where a strong State is taken for granted – where the "obligatory passage point" of a Renaissance-type state is long history.

The assumptions of neo-classical theory correspond to a world which fits Henry Thoreau's ideal: no human institutions and no systemic effects. Reading Thoreau is the key to understanding the dissatisfaction of the average American with Governments of any kind. Thoreau shares with Adam Smith a strong aversion to any type of human institutions and collective action, a view – clearly inspired by Rousseau – that the institutions of civilised society have corrupted Mankind. To Adam Smith all human institutions – private and public – "so invariably produce 'absurd' results that they have no presumptive legitimacy" (McCraw, 1992).

Neo-classical economics has kept Thoreau's and Adam Smith's myth alive by failing to internalise the systemic synergies of societies, among multitudes of professions, each with a minimum efficient size of operation, which, in turn, also cause societies themselves to have a minimum efficient size. This minimum efficient size of societies grows as more knowledge is added and more professions are formed – increasing the standards of living – and forming the fundamental connection between geography and economics (Bücher, 1918–19; Polanyi, 1957). These same factors led to the creation – in succession – first of the medieval city economies, then of national economies, and finally of "globalisation". The needs for a State essentially arise from the same synergies and interdependencies, and from the differing abilities of economic activities to provide the increasing returns which are at the core of this system.

One of the problems of today's mainstream is, then, that – through its assumptions of a complete absence of increasing returns to scale and of perfect information – it has produced a theory which is as individualistic as Henry David Thoreau's visions: there are no systemic external effects present at the core of the theory. Economic theory today fails to tell us why we cannot have our cake (atomistic individualism) and eat it too (a high standard of material living). This is essentially the reason why theories of the State, of the Firm, or of any other human institutions are external to the core of economic theory. Renaissance economists tell us that the State exists because of the systemic effects in an economy, effects which also the early Adam Smith glorifies (see the cover of this paper). Today's practice of labeling – in a rather *ad hoc* manner – all unexpected economic effects either as "externalities" or "market failures" contributes little to the understanding of economic systems. *Ad hoc* exceptions are more easily seen, and acted upon, close to home, in the industrialised countries, rather than far away in the Third World. For this reason, the fundamental argument for the single market in the European Union is the existence of increasing returns observed in practice (The Cecchini Report), but without any ties to trade theory. On the other hand, the theoretical foundation for the EU policy against the Third World is that such increasing returns do not exist (conventional trade theory which does not allow for asymmetrical trade between increasing and diminishing return activities). This frequent and inconsistent "assumption-juggling" in economic theory was denounced already by Joan Robinson. From the point of view of the Third World this may be seen as an alternative version of "The Golden Rule" – the one who has the gold makes the rules. We see it as an important task ahead for economic theory to internalise the externalities which produce welfare: the systemic synergies of scale and scope which have their origin in the creation and implementation of new knowledge in those production processes which are subject to increasing returns.

The World Bank 1997 World Development Report – to be entitled "The State in a Changing World" – will focus on the role of state in economic development. Predictably it will continue the discussion on the role of the State which was started with the publication of *The East Asian Miracle* (1993). This paper discusses the historical role of the State in a different framework of assumptions from that of the World Bank. These assumptions are spelled out in section 2. In our view, the successful East Asian nations essentially follow very similar strategies to those followed first by England (starting in the 1480s) and later by all other presently industrial nations in the early stages of development. World Bank studies do not go back more than 50 years, so these similarities are unlikely to be uncovered in their normal process. Likewise, the history of economic thought having today largely been reduced to a genealogy of neo-classical economics, the record of the past economic policies of the presently industrialised countries has to a large extent been "unlearned". There is no such thing as an academic sub-discipline called "History of Economic Policy", and the industrial powers of Europe and North America seem to be unified in a common misconception about their own past, about the role of the State in bringing them out of poverty.

In this paper we attempt to lift the field of vision beyond the post-World War II era, in order to show that in this 500-year perspective, the active role of the State in the East Asian "miracle" – as described by authors like Amsden (1989) and Wade (1990) – is essentially business as usual: "an obligatory passage point" in the transition from underdevelopment to development. In section 2 we provide a different set of assumptions from that of mainstream economics as to how economic welfare is created and distributed. In section 3 we attempt to produce an inventory of the roles historically played by the State to promote the common weal. Section 4 takes a closer look at the systemic theories behind these policy measures. In section 5 we attempt to show that – while making little sense in a limited neo-classical framework – these policies of Schumpeterian mercantilism are fully compatible with a variety of recent new approaches to economic theory. Section 6 looks at this in the perspective of two parallel economic canons. Section 7 relates the demise of "Renaissance economics", and section 8 briefly comments on the role of State-owned enterprises in this system. Section 9 looks at the role of Adam Smith in making new knowledge into a zero-sum game in economic theory, and section 10 provides the conclusions.

2. Mechanisms causing and diffusing economic growth and welfare: the view of the production-based and activistic-idealistic renaissance tradition

A paper purporting to trace the influence of the State on economic growth must – implicitly or explicitly – be based on a model of the mechanisms which cause economic growth. Below we shall attempt to clarify how our assumptions differ from those of Adam Smith and of the neo-classical system. Partly using the terminology of Werner Sombart, we base our analysis on a production-centered, activistic-idealistic set of assumptions, in contrast with today's mainstream, which in this context can be labeled barter-centered and passivistic-materialistic.

Our set of assumptions differs from that of today's mainstream economic theory, and therefore also concludes with a different view of the role of the state in economic growth. To clarify: if the conditions of "real world" did correspond to the assumptions of neo-classical theory, we would have shared the view that any attempt to influence income growth and distribution would be futile. However, as we shall argue, the factors causing uneven economic development – where State intervention may play a role – are the very factors which neo-classical theory assumes away. When neo-classical theory is "right", it is, on key points, "right for the wrong reason". We would for example argue that the benefits from international trade are mainly caused by what Schumpeter called historical increasing returns – a blend of increasing returns and technical change – rather than on the static gains in the Ricardian theory. The need for "governing the market" arises from such factors which are left out of mainstream theory.

There seem to be three important aspects to this question:

(1) how economic growth is created;
(2) the alternative mechanisms through which growth and welfare are diffused between and within the nation-states, and to the individual; and
(3) how this alternative understanding is based on a different philosophical basis.

These three aspects are briefly discussed in the next three sub-sections.

2.1. Assumptions about the causes of economic growth

One important starting point is that, in our view, today's mainstream economics – as a cluster of variants around the neo-classical paradigm –fundamentally lacks a theory of economic development beyond seeing it as a process of adding capital to labour. In 1956 Stanford economist Moses Abramowitz showed that capital accumulation only accounted for 10–20 per cent of US economic growth – which he then referred to as "a measure of our ignorance about the causes of economic growth".

What are the forces creating welfare? It seems that search process for "the approximate causes of growth", as Abramowitz calls them, follows the path of Ibsen's Peer Gynt, to whom the onion – and his inner self – only revealed layer after layer, but no core. We would argue that the factors listed below should be seen as "reactants", factors which, when they are all present – and only then – produce economic welfare. These "reactants" have been uncovered layer after layer in modern economics, starting at the top of the following list. The causes of increased economic welfare are:

- Markets.
- Capital.
- Technology (the *techno-* part: new hardware/tools).
- Technology (the *-logy* part: new human skills and new knowledge).
- The attitude to new knowledge (men's and nations').
- Systemic aspects giving rise to positive feedback mechanisms (increasing returns, "scale and scope").
- Man's rational will ("wit and will").

Today's mainstream economic theory basically limits itself to the first two factors only. Markets and capital are clearly necessary, but far from sufficient building blocks for a theory of economic growth. New research under the heading of "evolutionary economics", as sponsored by the OECD under the title TEP (Technology and Economy Programme), also includes factor 3, and increasingly also factor 4. Another striking feature of the economics of Adam Smith – in addition to his distaste for human institutions already mentioned – is his long and deliberate proofs that the production of knowledge, from the point of view of the individual as well as for society, is a zero-sum game. This is probably where Adam Smith most clearly breaks with the Renaissance tradition, and a key point which we shall discuss in more detail in section 9 of this paper. Today – partly as an effect of the TEP programme – the opposite message of Adam Smith's is slowly sinking in: the driving forces of the economic system are innovations created by new knowledge. Nations which stop innovating do not keep their standard of living, they lose their standard of living even though they keep the same efficiency.

2.2. Assumptions about the mechanisms which diffuse growth and welfare

Another, and most important, dimension to the phenomenon of economic growth is that it seems to be a product of a number of systemic effects which are not captured by theories atomistically studying only the single actors in the system. These aspects – synergies, economies of scope, or systemic economies of scale – are the starting points of positive feedback mechanisms – virtuous circles – in the economy, and they only appear in view when the system as such is the object of analysis. The presence or absence of such factors determines how economic growth spreads in the economy – essentially in one of two forms: either as higher wages to man-the-producer or as lowered prices to man-the-consumer. In a closed system, the two modes of collecting the benefits from technical change make no practical difference. In international trade between two different labour markets with an asymmetrical trade pattern (trading increasing return products for diminishing return products) which of the two models operates makes all the difference.

In a previous paper we have referred to these two alternative mechanisms as the collusive and the classical modes of distributing the benefits of technological change (Reinert, 1994). The collusive mode of income distribution took place system-wide and in parallel in all industrialised countries behind the barriers to entry created by Fordist mass production. Demands for higher monetary wages to labour were met, while at the same time money supply was increased at least at the pace of the increase in national physical productivity. In the perfectly competitive classical model of income distribution, people should have got richer by having their purchasing power increased through falling prices – just as Adam Smith and Ricardo predicted – not through the raising of monetary wages. We have also argued that the term "competitiveness" and its historical equivalents have been used to describe the existence of such systemic results of dynamic imperfect competition and of a collusive spread of the benefits from technological change (Reinert, 1995).

The practical consequences in world income distribution, created by the two different modes of distributing the benefits of technical change, can best be seen in the traditional service sector. In this huge sector in any economy there is normally very little difference in productivity between First World and Third World workers. A bus driver, a barber, or a chambermaid are about as productive in Bolivia or Haiti as they are in Norway or Italy. Why then do the barbers or bus drivers in Bolivia or Haiti have real wages which are only a fraction – 10–20 per cent – of the real wages of a barber or a bus driver in Norway or Italy? Why does the invisible hand reward people with the same productivity so widely differently in different economies? We would argue that this is the result of *Strukturzusammenhänge* – of systemic effects – created by the fact that a large part of the benefits resulting from technological change in increasing return activities are spread in the collusive mode, i.e. as higher monetary wages in the local labour market rather than as lowered prices internationally. In the perspective from a poor sub-Saharan nation, what we see as "economic development" basically appears as a system based on "industry rent" from increasing return activities which spreads throughout the national labour markets. The existence of increasing return activities – and their accompanying barriers to entry – creates a national common weal which gives the Norwegian bus driver real wages which are five times higher than his equally productive Bolivian counterpart.

We would argue that the origin of such systemic effects is found in the fixed costs which accompany Man's tools: the increasing sophistication of tools (and accompanying fixed costs) and of specialised human skills to work the tools, leads to increasing minimum efficient sizes of operations in an ever-increasing number of professional specialisations and in an ever-increasing diversity of products and services. This causes cumulative causations and path dependency. As an example: the village which had enough volume to support its own blacksmith (fixed cost of energy in hearth), had a clear advantage over a smaller village with no blacksmith in the next cumulative step up the ladder of technological sophistication. This is the reason why "the division of labour is determined by the size of the market", Adam Smith's deep insight which later disappeared from neo-classical economics. This is also the explanation for the great importance of a large population which is held unanimously by pre-Smithian economists.

2.3. The different philosophical underpinnings of the activistic-idealistic tradition

Promoting new knowledge was a fundamental driving force for the economic policies of the Renaissance – and later of all *realökonomisch* mercantilism, cameralism and Colbertism. If one puts together a list of economic interventions in Renaissance economics, such as later in Figure 2.1, it becomes clear that the element uniting these seemingly most diverse economic policies is the promotion and protection of new knowledge. These policies further rested on the assumption, implicit or explicit, that some knowledge was more valuable than other. Consequently, it was in the interest of the State to create and protect such knowledge. On a philosophical level, this valuable knowledge emanates from the mind of Man. Therefore, any theory not taking Man's mind and Man's soul into consideration will not understand the increase in Man's material condition, i.e. economic growth.

In the activist-idealistic tradition, economics and the social sciences require a different kind of understanding from the natural sciences. The social sciences, concerned with the ends and values instead of laws, should aim to understand (*verstehen*). The natural sciences, on the other hand, aim mainly to describe and conceptualise (*begreifen*). Qualitative relationships are at the core of the *Geisteswissenschaften* – the humanities, or literally, the sciences of the mind. A crucial aspect of these sciences is therefore their irreducibility to natural science. Although economics is also about numbers, there is also a basic incommensurability between numbers (quantities) and some fundamental aspects of economic science, like Man's wit and will. The German economic tradition continued the Renaissance tradition. Here the inner unity (*Strukturzusammenhang*) of

The Establishment of Scientific Academies.
- Bacon's 'New Atlantis': Salomon's House.
- Leibniz: Inspires the establishment of the academies of Berlin, Vienna and St. Petersburg.

Encouragement and Assistance to Inventors.
- Bacon: 'Upon every invention of value we erect a statue to the inventor, and give him a liberal and honorable reward'.
- Wolff: 'We should forbid mockery of inventors.'

Diffusion of new Knowledge/Education.
- Bacon: 'We have circuits of visits, of divers principal cities of the kingdom; whereas it cometh to pass we do publish* such new profitable inventions as we think good.'
- Wolff as the 'educator of the German Nation'

Establishing an Apprentice System.
- In England under Elizabeth I (1558-1603)
- In Germany as a result of the teachings of Leibniz and Wolff.

Patent Protection for new Inventions (Venice, 15th Century).
- Showing a sophisticated understanding of the *appropriability problem* of new knowledge.

State-owned Manufactures as 'Places of Learning'.
- Emphasized by Werner Sombart.

Subsidies to Firms in Industries new to the Nation or Region.
- Serra: the number of different professions as a key factor in explaining the wealth of a city.

Tax Breaks and Bounties to Firms bringing in new Technology.
- Systematically applied in England starting under Henry VII in 1485.
- Import of skilled labour

Travel Restrictions for skilled Labour.
- Under penalty of death for certain skills in Venice.

Prohibition against the Export of Machinery.
- In force in England until the 1830s.

Prohibition against the use of Machinery in the Colonies.
- The heritage of this economic policy is still felt in many Third World counties, which, like Haiti, specialise in the economic activities which have not yet been mechanised.

Export Duties on Raw Materials
- Ensuring that local manufacturing industries have lower prices on raw materials than foreign competitors.

Import Duties on manufactured Goods, while national Competition insured.
- Machines seen as a proxy for new knowledge; this measure maximises the flow of capital and labour to activities producing with machines, not manual power.

Strengthening the Navy.
- Taking advantage of 'the economies of scale in the use of force'.

Source: Bacon (n.d. (1930s)), p. 272

Note: *"Publish" here in its meaning of "to make generally accessible, to disseminate, offer to the public", (see *The Oxford English Dictionary*, Vol. VIII, pp. 1561-2)

Figure 2.1 Schumpeterian mercantilism: promoting and protecting new knowledge in the economic policy of the Renaissance (starting in the sixteenth century).

the *Geisteswissenschaften* – e.g. the refusal to isolate "economic man" from the rest of the human being – shines through from Leibniz to Werner Sombart. The common weal in Renaissance economics is also the result of such a synergetic *Strukturzusammenhang*. The fact that our two equally efficient bus drivers – one in Bolivia and the other in Norway – have such widely different real wages, is a product of economic *Strukturzusammenhänge*, of which today's atomistic economic theory and economic policy are totally ignorant.

The economic policies resulting from theories of this kind were carried out with varying degrees of understanding of the underlying principles. These policies were, in our meaning of the word, not based on what we would normally call scientific analysis. These theories were based on "clues", on a mode of inference called abduction – or phronesis, Aristotle's third form of knowledge. (For a more general discussion of these issues, see Reinert and Daastøl, 1995.) This tradition is continued by the Italian philosopher Giambattista Vico (1668–1744), by the US philosophical tradition of C.S. Pierce, and in economics in Kaldor's "stylised facts". (For a discussion of Kaldor's use of stylized facts see Lawson, 1989.) According to Pierce, "(Induction) can never originate any idea whatever. No more can deduction. All the ideas of science come to it by the way of Abduction. Abduction consists of studying facts and devising a theory to explain them. Its only justification is that if we are ever to understand things at all, it must be in that way" (1867). Pierce here describes the role played by the formulation of hypotheses as the fundamental element in the creation of new knowledge, in the German eighteenth century philosophers Leibniz and Wolff.

We shall explain how policy is generated through abductive reasoning with a parallel from the history of medicine: starting in the twelfth century sailors in the Mediterranean used lemons to prevent scurvy (Villner, 1986). This was a very effective policy. However, the explanation as to why this policy worked only appeared in 1929, with the discovery of Vitamin C (Mervin, 1981). Likewise, we would claim that it is entirely possible to establish good economic policies for a time, without fully understanding the factors involved. For example, identifying "progress", or ability to pay more taxes, with the use of machinery in an increasing number of industries would result in a beneficial public policy, even if the causal relationship between the use of machinery and wealth were not clearly established, or had been "unlearned". The intuitive abduction often precedes what we would think of as a more "scientific" type of knowledge. This view that abduction anticipates "science" was expressed by the English economist Edward Misselden in 1623: "Wee felt it before in sense, but now wee know it by science" (Misselden, 1623).

We would argue that business decisions are made – mostly under high degrees of uncertainty – based on such intuitive abduction about what is good for the firm, on what at business schools is called "management by gut feeling". Early statesmanship seems to have worked in a similar way. Going through the voluminous letters and instructions of Colbert (Clément, 1861–1872), one is struck by his role as being that of a businessman in charge of a huge empire: as an entrepreneurial input-coordinator for France Inc., in a venture to get into knowledge-based activities, he was faced with what historians of technology call "reverse salients" (for a discussion of this concept, see Wiebe et al., 1989) – of dynamic bottlenecks – retarding the system and demanding managerial attention.

By differentiating intuitive abduction from "science", the position of writers like Friedrich List comes in a new and different light. List is full of interesting ideas and has an intuitive understanding of the mechanisms at work (he sees that lemons will do the job against scurvy, and argues for their use), but he fails to develop concepts which explain to us clearly what's going on (he fails to point clearly to Vitamin C). As Werner Sombart says about List: "His concepts levitate like undelivered souls on the banks of Hades"[5]. However, just as lemons helped against scurvy 800 years before the exact mechanisms through which they work were established, economic growth was successfully promoted using "new knowledge" and "use of machinery" as proxies for the underlying factors causing systemic economic growth.

3. The three roles of the State

For the purpose of the paper we find it useful to divide the roles of the State into three broad categories:

(1) The State as a *provider of institutions* – in the widest sense ("establishing the rules of the game"/"providing an even playing field").
(2) The State as a *provider of income distribution* and as an "insurance company" (preventing evil/"sharing the pie").
(3) The State as a *promoter of economic growth* (promoting happiness/ "increasing the size of the pie").

There are, of course, other alternative classifications of the roles of the State. Wilhelm von Humbolt says: "A State then, has one of two ends in view; it designs either to promote happiness, or simply to prevent evil" (Humbolt, 1996, p. 19). Another German economist, Adolph Wagner, divides the role of the State into two different categories of objectives: Law and Power (*Rechts- und Machtzweck*) and Culture and Welfare (*Kultur- und Wohlfahrtszweck*)[6]. However, for our purpose it is important to divide the welfare aspect expressed in the other classification into two very different categories: the creation vs the distribution of income.

This paper essentially deals with point 3 – the role of the State in the creation – rather than the distribution – of income, but a few remarks on points 1 and 2 are necessary to draw lines of delimitation, and to clarify where and how the categories overlap.

To point 1 – "The State as a provider of institutions". These institutions may, on the one hand, be seen as preconditions required by the invisible hand in order to get on with its job of creating economic growth. On the other hand, they may be seen as part of a wider and more active strategy as that under point 3, the State as actively "increasing the

---

5 "... seine Begriffe 'schweben' umher wie die unerlösten Seelen an den Ufern des Hades", Sombart, 1928, p. 929.

6 Wagner in *Handwörterbuch der Staatswissenschaften*, Vol. 7, 4th edition, Gustav Fischer, Jena, 1926, p. 773.

size of the pie". However, we choose to put these fundamental institutions – which hardly come under the attack of the thesis of futility, jeopardy and perversity – in this separate category. These basic institutions include private property and the well-worn German concept of a *Rechtsstaat* (Civil- or Legal-State). As standards of living grow, secondary demands are created and the State is extended into a *Kulturstaat* (a Culture State), providing institutions for education, science, charity, sanitation, etc. (Cohn, 1895). Summing up, one German author says: "Food, drink, clothing, shelter, amusement, social intercourse – these are the primary wants with the covering of which private economy is mainly occupied; peace, order, security, culture, relief – these are the higher needs which are mainly served by the public economy" (Cohn, 1895, p. 73; also quoted in Baumol, 1952).

To point 2 – "Sharing of the pie and distributing risk": The thought of distributing the inevitable risks of life is a very old one – the participants of the camel caravans of the Near East 2200 BC had a risk sharing system. Modern insurance traces its root to the middle of the fourteenth century. The same ideas of risk sharing are present during the beginnings of the welfare state, already in the Byzantine Empire, where the idea of sharing the risks of life gradually develops into a role of income distribution. Thoughts around welfare are found very clearly in the writings of German philosophers Gottfried Wilhelm Leibniz (1646–1716) and Christian von Wolff (1679–1754). Leibniz suggested that a national health system should be established[7]. The health system should be the basis for a welfare guaranteed by the State (Müller *et al.*, 1973). Wolff specifies clearly that he wants a State which secures welfare for the individual, but not one which automatically provides for him ("Ein Wohlfahrtsstaat, aber kein Versorgungsstaat" (Namslau, 1932)) – a most difficult balance to this very day.

Clearly "sharing the pie" is not a wholly independent exercise from that of "increasing the size of the pie". Economic arguments for income redistribution include the argument that a certain income distribution is required to create and maintain a mass market. This argument seems to be one used to defend the enormous transfer payments within the European Community; i.e. "Poverty is bad for business". One can further argue that an unequal income distribution threatens the social fabric of society, and therefore the nation itself and its economy. A most important argument – similar to that used by nineteenth century US economists – is that a continuous increase in the price of labour relative to the price of capital is a key factor in the virtuous circle created by State intervention: the increasing relative price of labour is a strong incentive for further mechanisation, which again allows for even higher wages and higher profits, and so on. By making labour more skilled, it is made more valuable. This was also an important argument of nineteenth century US economists against the dismal pauperisation theories in English classical economics, and formed the basis for the dual policy of "the high wage strategy" and "the American system of manufactures" giving protection to increasing return activities. We would see this argument for income distribution as part of the virtuous circles which are created by State intervention under the next point.

---

[7] In his *Directiones ad Rem Medicam Pertinentes*, 1672.

To point 3 – "The role of the State in increasing national wealth (increasing the size of the pie)". Clearly the institutions in points 1 and 2 are necessary, but in our view not sufficient, conditions for economic growth. The objective of this paper is to look at the more active role of the state in economic development – "the developmental State". We most look behind the State as a provider for institutions for which there is a "natural demand" into another role of creating demand for things which are necessary, but for which there is no articulated demand. If people do not want to educate their children – because they are themselves not educated, and because they need their daily labour – the State plays a new role: the State uses "its power of coercion in order to create a general demand for the institutions which it has established", says Cohn (1895). Here enters a more visible hand – the role of "the State as a factor of production" to use Luigi Einaudi's (1942) term, originally from Adam Müller (1809). It is the role of this visible hand which forms the core of this paper. The role played by the State is contained in the felicitous term coined by Robert Wade (1990): "governing the market". It is clearly particularly to this role of the state that the message of futility, perversity, and jeopardy is directed.

Historically the roles of the State as a promoter of economic growth can be listed under the following headings:

- *Getting the nation into "the right business"*, i.e. recognising, as a historical starting point, the activity-specific nature of economic growth. We intuitively understand that Japan could not have reached her present position by making inexpensive shirts, rather than inexpensive cars or electronics, and that Pavarotti could not have made the same fortune washing dishes as singing, but this intuitive knowledge is not compatible with today's barter-centered economic theory. Historically all presently industrialised nations (see Reinert, 1980; 1994; 1995) – for the right or for the wrong reasons – have passed through an initial stage with a policy based on the understanding that not all economic activities are equally feasible as starting points for the self-enforcing positive feedback system which we call development.
- *Creating a comparative advantage in "the right business"*. A common element of all successful strategies for catching up with richer nations is the conviction that free trade is not wanted until the nation has created a comparative advantage in the "right" economic activities (which, among other things, means skill-based, not resource-based). There is an important underlying perception in this that in a world economic system, if there is world demand both for skilled (well paid) and for unskilled (poorly paid) labour, a nation may end up locked into a permanent comparative advantage in being poor and unskilled.
- A very strong emphasis on the role of the State as *a supplier of infrastructure*. This is a unifying element of most "enemies" of classical and neo-classical economists, from Colbert (canals, turnpikes, ports, merchant marine, navy) to Friedrich List (known in Germany as "the father of the German railway system") and to Al Gore/Robert Reich (the electronic super-highway). Infrastructure is, as all other systemic elements of the economy, conspicuously absent from today's economic theory (e.g. not to be found in *The New Palgrave*). Infrastructures are key factors in extending markets and are

"highways" which the positive feed-back mechanisms need in order to displace themselves geographically.

- *Setting standards* has been a very important task of the state, from the neo-classical point of view to lower transaction costs, from the evolutionary point of view to form a basis for standardised mass production. A visitor to the Renaissance towns of Italy can to this very day observe the iron bars fastened to the church wall on the main square, establishing the standard units of measurement valid in the city. Each city had different measurements, which made information and conversion tables on these issues an important task for early economic books[8]. Today the setting of standards is important to hi-tech products like mobile telephony. Clearly the state also has an important role in setting legal standards and providing a social virtue which is crucial to prosperity[9]. This was a point much emphasized by Renaissance philosophers, and is rediscovered today in Fukuyama's (1995) book *Trust.*
- A responsibility of the State *to provide skilled labour and entrepreneurship* if in short supply. Early policy measures – often helped by religious wars – were aimed at bringing in skilled labour and entrepreneurs from abroad by granting exclusive rights (patents) for a limited time, or through bounties, tax relief, etc. The State is also an entrepreneur of last resort.
- Unless one firmly believes in Say's Law – that supply creates its own demand – the State clearly has an important role in *creating demand* in general. Out of the Victorian slums with only subsistence demand, a better income distribution of a growing economic pie paved the way for the mass markets. This development made industrial production and "Fordism" possible, e.g. through the establishment of minimum wages. Nineteenth century US economists saw particularly well the role of raising labour skills to increase their market value – the policy which was called "The High Wage Strategy". There is reason to believe that the sharp fall in economic welfare experienced by weakly industrialized nations in the wake of "structural adjustment" in part was due to the elimination of demand created by the State. In this context it is important to keep in mind that what we call "economic development" is little more than a collective "industry rent", the national distribution of which – in spite of our *laissez-faire* mythology – is the result of decades of "artificial" redistribution, partly due to the activities of labour unions. Our understanding today of the connection between the key variables: growth of demand, income redistribution and higher wages pushing mechanisation, is very limited. In several nations today – as, for example, in Peru – there is evidently a break in the positive circuit created by these factors.
- The State has played a very strong role pushing the technological frontier by being *a supplier of high-quality demand* for national production, of demand for goods at the borderline of what, at any time, was technically feasible. Key mechanisms here have been

---

8 An example of such a book comprising 218 pages, first published in 1503 and going through five editions, is (di Pasi, B.), *Tariffa di pesi e mesure* (sic) *correspondenti dal Levante al Ponente; da una terra al laltra* (sic)*: e a tutte le parte del mondo*, Bindoni, Venice, 9 October 1521.

9 I am indebted to Arne Disch for this point.

infrastructure projects and warfare. Werner Sombart, in 1913, describes the destruction of war as being the starting point both for the creative spirit of Man (Sombart, 1913a) – for searches for synthetic substitutes for raw materials in short supply – and also for the organizational capabilities of the State[10]. This is a most important argument in the spirit of Chandler and Lazonick. Not only was State demand crucial for purposes of war and infrastructure, but also the personification of the State – royalty and nobility – served as Porterian demanding customers for luxuries, and provided the basis for future technological expansion into lower-cost mass production. Historically the demand for luxury has played a role similar to that played by people who, ten years ago, paid $4,000 for a cellular phone, enabling later mass production to deliver better phones for $80 today. Again, the function of State demand for luxury is brilliantly described by Werner Sombart (1913b).

- An emphasis on the value of knowledge and education *per se*. See the list of policy measures collected as *Schumpeterian Mercantilism* in Figure 2.1. (Scientific academies, education, patent laws and copyright protection, tariffs protecting the few activities where the production of new knowledge was focused, etc.).
- A long-term goal similar to what in the nineteenth century USA was called *The High Wage Strategy* – i.e. seeing high wages *per se* as a goal. At the core of this economic thinking was Man and his Needs ("Der Mensch und seine Bedürfnisse"), rather than a "dead equilibrium" which reduces Man to one of several factors of production, the high or low reward of which has no place in the system. The importance of the wage level in explaining GNP is illustrated by the fact that today wages are typically 70 per cent of GNP: i.e. maximising wealth essentially means maximising national wages.
- An understanding of the importance of a *legal system* built to strengthen the above structures. To Christian Wolff – the eighteenth century German economist and philosopher of law – a system of property rights assisting the dynamic symbiosis between "persons who collected knowledge and people who collected money"[11] was seen as the core of a system creating – like Francis Bacon's system before him – a never-ending frontier of development.
- The State as an *entrepreneur and capitalist of last resort*. There is no reason to assume a "sufficient" supply of entrepreneurship at any point in time and in any culture – the poorer the nation, the less so. As we shall discuss in the short chapter on State-owned enterprises, moving the State into a role of capitalist or entrepreneur resulted from "reverse salients" in the system, rather than from any ideological preference.

We would argue that – as economic agents – States exist for fundamentally the same reasons that firms exist, both of them for reasons not well captured by today's economic theory, which focuses on barter and atomism. We suggest that the absence of a theory

[10] Sombart's argument is one of creative destruction: "Wiederum steigt aus der Zerstörung neuer schöpferischer Geist empor …" (Sombart, 1913, p. 207). Schumpeter's German term for creative destruction is *schöpferischer Zerstörung*.

[11] See Reinert and Daastøl (1995).

of the firm in modern economic theory is caused by the same reasons which cause the absence of the theory of the State in the same body of theory. Both firms and states are institutions which are brought to life by the kind of systemic synergies which are excluded in neo-classical theory through the assumptions of full divisibility of resources, of perfect information, perfect competition, and of the absence of increasing returns.

To continue this analogy between the State and the Firm, we would argue that the size and strength of a firm to a large extent are determined by the sum of the countervailing forces of economies of scale and diseconomies of scale. Large chemical firms are the product of huge economies of scale in production, advertising and finance; coupled with the opposite effect – the diseconomies of bureaucratisation – in administration and coordination. Similarly the strength and size of the State are also torn between two opposite effects, well captured by Humbolt (1996, p. 22): "The highest good" which arises from associations, like the State, "is the very variety arising from the union of numbers of individuals". This variety is a core part of the synergies creating the common weal, and in my view also the underlying principle why, as in Adam Smith's argument, "the division of labour" is so important (see also Serra (1613), discussed later in this paper, on this point). However, "this variety is undoubtedly merged into uniformity in proportion to the measure of State interference". Thus, the existence of a State tends to produce "uniformity and inertness", which is the very reverse of what caused State intervention in the economy in the first place, which was the need for "variety and activity" – i.e. the establishment of a large number of professions ("division of labour") through entrepreneurship.

The extent and size of a firm are a result of competitive powers – which are industry- and product-specific – on the underlying trade-off of increasing and decreasing returns to scale. Similarly, the extent and activity of the State (what we could call "The Optimal State") should, at any point in time, reflect the paradox that, having united in order to exploit the synergies and economies of scope which result from the variety and activity of Mankind, the potentially perverse effect[12] of producing uniformity and inertness is likely to occur. This uniformity and inertness threaten the variety and activity, the synergies of which the State was established to foment and exploit in the first place. In the case of both the firm and the State, one important answer to the diseconomies of scale produced by size and growing complexities lies in the concept of organizational capabilities. The Managerial Revolution was, in the world of business, the reply to these challenges (see Chandler, 1977; 1990).

The role of the state in industrialised countries is often seen as one of protecting "civil liberties", or the form of freedom which we would call "freedoms to". However, the role of the State in the early stages of economic development is one of jump-starting the systemic effects which were to secure the "freedoms from" – freedom from hunger, freedom from injustices, freedom from ignorance. With time, however, another aspect of the dynamic balancing creating an "optimal state" appears when the actions of the State to provide "freedoms from" are gradually seen as encroaching upon Man's "freedoms to".

---

[12] See the reference to Hirschman's "perversity thesis" in the introduction to this paper.

The Smithian revolt against Renaissance economic policy can be seen as such a conflict, as seen in Turgot's arguing against the excesses of Colbertism. In England at the time, the policies of the "development state" had entered into an area of diminishing returns of static and individual rent-seeking rather than the synergetic collective rent-seeking. Clearly a big dose of "markets" was needed. However, as German, US, and Japanese economists in the nineteenth century were so eager to point out, this did not mean that nations which had not reached the level of England could use the same policies there and then. The role of the State – like the particular balance of emphasis on freedoms *to* and freedoms *from* – is highly context-specific.

4. New knowledge, systemic effects and positive feedback-loops in Renaissance economics: the consequent role of the State

Renaissance was brought into reality by philosopher-statesmen like Francis Bacon (1561–1626), who consciously used his Utopian tract *The New Atlantis* as an essay in forecasting the future in order to inspire and influence it, a process he himself called "feigned history" (Crother, 1960). Bacon's *New Atlantis* (published 1627) and his *Essay of Innovations* (about 1605), describe the development of society as being propelled by new inventions and innovations, and should, in my view, be considered as the earliest tracts of what we today would call "Schumpeterian economics". In this paper we shall attempt to show that the economic policies carried out by the European nation-states starting with the Renaissance, although making little sense from the perspective of neo-classical economics, make eminent sense when seen in the perspective not only of Schumpeterian economics, but also of other recent developments in economic theory.

Not only in Bacon's "feigned history", but also in real history, these early inventions and innovations came about as the result of what, using a Chandlerian vocabulary, ought to be called the organizational capabilities of the State (see Chandler, 1990; Lazonick, 1991). During this century's conflict between planned economies and market economies, the relationship between the State and private entrepreneurs is still frequently seen as one of natural animosity. Historically, however, the roles of the State and of private entrepreneurs have been more in the spirit of complementarity and partnership, where the State facilitated and coerced private entrepreneurs into business, and – this failing – also moved in as an entrepreneur of last resort. The motivating force behind the European Commission's 1995 "Green Paper on Innovation" – 30,000 copies of which have been distributed – was precisely again to promote the organizational capabilities of the modern European states in maintaining the "competitiveness" of Europe by strengthening its National Innovation Systems (see Lundvall, 1992; and Nelson, 1993).

The foreword to the most recent advanced textbook in economic growth states that "economic growth comes largely from the accumulation of knowledge" (Barro and Sala-i-Martin, 1995). We shall attempt here to show that a principal historical role of the State from the Renaissance onwards has been precisely one of promoting and protecting new knowledge and innovations. In Figure 2.1 we have assembled what we consider the most important government interventions in economic policy starting in the Renaissance. We would argue that the common theme of these economic policies – the thread which unites them – is just this concern for the creation and protection of new knowledge. Looking at history from a simple perspective of barter, not production, and under diminishing returns/single equilibrium/perfect information, the importance of these policies is lost. In the diminishing return/equilibrium perspective, any and all factors causing unequal economic growth are lost, creating the world of artificial harmony and world-wide factor-price equalisation. As we shall attempt to show later, a most important historical role of Adam Smith's was precisely that of laying the ground for "perfect markets" and "natural harmony" by making the quest for knowledge into a zero-sum game – using the metaphor of a lottery – from the point of view of both the individual and the State. In this way Adam Smith effectively removed the quest for imperfect competition through new knowledge which was so important to Renaissance thinking. This is the root of why new knowledge and new technology hits today's mainstream economics as "manna from heaven".

Pre-Smithian economic thinking takes a holistic starting point – the People, the State. A fundamental underlying idea exists that the situation of each individual can be improved by measures which take into consideration the collectivity of individuals. In other words, there are systemic effects which cannot be found if one limits the horizon atomistically to study individuals alone. We shall argue that the existence of such systemic effects is the fundamental reason why the State has a role to play in economic growth. We still find the strong belief in this systemic approach in the early Adam Smith – before his conversion by the physiocrats. This is shown in the quote from *The Theory of Moral Sentiments* on the title page of this paper. In the later Adam Smith the atomism of John Locke takes over, but Smith's fundamental insight that "the division of labour is limited by the size of the market" is the description of one such systemic effect. We argue that the division of labour is only important if systemic economies of scale are at work. "The division of labour" is, of course, lost in neoclassical theory. In this section we shall discuss the theories of the time as they relate to economic growth, and also try to see these theories in the perspective of modern evolutionary economics.

As we have said, the goal of the economic policy of the State was to increase the common weal, i.e. the prosperity of the community. This is the starting point of virtually all economic writing of the period. To the Renaissance economists systemic effects seem first to have arisen from the observation that widespread wealth seemed to accumulate in the cities – not in the countryside. This was the fundamental observation of one of the earliest best-selling books in economics, *Delle Cause della Grandezza delle Città* written by Giovanni Botero (1543–1617) (Botero, 1590). The English translation, published in London in 1606, is entitled *The Cause of the Greatnesse of Cities*. But there were also huge differences between cities, between the opulence of Venice and the poverty of Naples, and this issue would be thoroughly discussed by Antonio Serra in 1613. In the best theoretical works of the time, this difference between the wealth and poverty of cities and countryside, and between cities, is explained in terms of the following main factors:

- The size and density of population.
- The different "qualities" of economic activities.

- The presence or absence of diversity of economic occupations, and the different capacities of economic activities to initiate "virtuous circles" or positive feed-back mechanisms.

4.1. The size and density of the population

One key aspect of this set of theories is the importance of having a large population. "The power of a State is not the result of its territorial extension, but of its number of people, and its good government." This phrase is found with little variation in the writings of virtually all economists and philosophers of the time, by Mun, Child, Petty, and Davenant in England, by Montchrétien, Forbonnais and Necker in France, and by Leibniz, Wolff, Becher, and Justi in Germany. One of the reasons for the great seventeenth century interest in China was its large population density which was seen as proportionate to the degree of knowledge and wisdom. This way of thinking is very far from today's *zeitgeist*, which has completely internalised the dismal science of Ricardo and Malthus in this respect. Because we have excluded knowledge and technology from today's economics, we fear overpopulation in Bolivia (with a population of five persons per square km) and in Peru (with 15 persons per square km), but we are not worried about Holland with 400 persons per square km.

The population argument makes sense if, as Adam Smith claims, "the division of labour is limited by the extent of the market". If there are fixed costs and minimum efficient scale (Chandler, 1990) involved in establishing new professions, which is certainly the case, then the argument makes sense that a larger population contributes to a larger division of labour. We shall see that Antonio Serra's 1613 work clearly stresses the importance of the division of labour, thus anticipating Petty by about 70 years and Adam Smith by about 160 years. One observation which can be made here is that Adam Smith's key contribution of the division of labour is not really compatible with the assumptions of neo-classical trade theory: If there are no economies of scale – i.e. no fixed cost – and perfect information, there is little reason for any division of labour at all. Samuelson's theory which proves factor price equalisation seems to be based on assumptions which take away the very incentives which cause the division of labour.

4.2. The different "qualities" of economic activities

"Renaissance economics" presented several levels of arguments for policy intervention, which may roughly be classified in three categories as follows: from observations of isolated and activity-specific differences in welfare, through the description of systemic synergies emanating from these activities, to the description – particularly perfected in one case – of fully-fledged positive feedback systems:

- Observations of higher welfare in some economic activities rather than in others, a static and non-systemic observation of welfare being activity specific. (As if today lawyers make more money than people picking lettuce; therefore a nation of lettuce pickers will be poorer than a nation of lawyers.)

- Some economic activities as core of systemic synergies which produce and spread welfare locally or nationwide ("where there are many people working with machines, also the shopkeepers are wealthier than in other places where machines are not used").
- There are degrees of understanding how these systemic synergies develop into positive feedback systems, but the top performance is that of Antonio Serra in 1613, who has a description of Venice as a true autocatalytic system where increasing returns and diversity – the latter expressed as the number of different professions in a nation (i.e. degree of division of labour) – are identified as being at the core of virtuous circles which generate wealth. Naples is the example of the opposite effect in Serra's system, because the production of raw materials is not subject to increasing returns. (We also find Adam Smith in *The Wealth of Nations* asking himself: Why is there so little division of labour in agriculture? On the other hand, agriculture is to him the only "natural" activity. Smith fails, however, to make the connection that the "unnatural" imperfect competition is a product of a sophisticated division of labour.)

Just as we today would see a career of washing dishes in a restaurant as having a limited potential for creating income compared with a career as a lawyer, the Renaissance economists extended this argument to apply to the common weal as well. In other words, they believed that the factors which created differences in welfare within an economy were the same factors which created differences in income between nations. As a result of the process of pre-Ricardian common sense, no factor-price equalisation would be achieved by putting all the people washing dishes in one nation and all the lawyers in another and open up for free trade between the two nations. In these theories economic growth is "activity-specific"; it is only available in some economic activities subject to dynamic imperfect competition, and not in others. As we shall see later in this paper, Adam Smith, in his late work, goes out of his way to prove that differences in income between professions do not exist. We are here talking about differences in wages – which constitutes more than 70 per cent of GNP in an industrialised economy – and not in profits.

What, Giovanni Botero asked in 1590, is more important for making a nation wealthy, the fertility of its soil or industry? No doubt, industry, says Botero. First of all "because the things produced by the able hands of man are many more, and have a much higher price, than the things produced by nature[13]. Nature gives the material, but the object … is the work of Man. Wool is a simple, coarse material of nature. How many beautiful objects, varied in form and shape, the Arts can produce from this…"

We find the same line of reasoning among the German cameralist economists. The German writers of economics were – as opposed to their English counterparts – mostly employed by the rulers of the small German states. One of their main tasks was to increase the income from taxes to the regent. Their observations coincided with those of the Italian economists: the subjects who worked with machinery were able to pay much higher taxes than those working without machines. In this way the use of machinery

[13] Botero (1590), p. 362, my translation.

became a proxy for a type of profession desired in a nation. The beginning of the industrial revolution in England – Henry VII's establishment of textile industries – was based on this same line of reasoning[14].

Understanding economic development as being activity-specific leads to two different policy measures by the State. One is a set of positive measures, taken in order to bring domestic economic activities into the "right" industries, those where the particular time period allowed for the build-up of new knowledge, the use of machinery, etc. The same understanding of the activity-specific nature of economic growth opens up for a set of negative measures, taken in order to prevent other nations from getting into that "right" type of activities. Prohibiting the use of machinery in the Colonies was one such measure. Other measures aiming at the destruction of already established high-quality activities include the British policies in Ireland starting 1699, when the prosperous exports of high-skilled woollen manufactures were prohibited, and the more labour intensive and less mechanizable linen manufacture was brought in (Hely-Hutchinson, 1779). In the beginning of the nineteenth century similar policies were in force against Indian textile manufacture. At the same time contemporary US sources describe English commercial policy at the time as being aimed at preventing the USA's industrialisation. As late as in 1904, the official history of the US Republican Party, which carries a laudatory foreword by President Theodore Roosevelt, comments: "We had suffered quite enough before the Revolution from the policy of Great Britain in checking our industrial and mechanical aspirations, and keeping us a buying instead of a making people …" (Curtis, 1904, p. 42). The English debates made no secret of the fact that their strategy was one of keeping other nations from industrialising. In 1816 Brougham explained the English strategy in the House of Commons:

> It is well worth while to incur a loss upon the first exportation, in order, by the glut, to stifle in the cradle those infant manufactures in the United States which the (Napoleonic) war has forced into existence (Curtis, 1904, p. 40).

We would argue that this is a fairly typical nineteenth century comment. Also Richard Cobden – the champion of free trade – saw the elimination of the Corn Laws as means to weaken other nations' manufactures. Cobden saw the high price of corn as the basic reason why England had not been able to hold on to her near-monopoly of world manufacturing. To Cobden free trade in corn was above all a means to prevent other nations from threatening the British near-monopoly of manufacturing exports:

> The factory system would, in all probability, not have taken place in America and Germany; it most certainly could not have flourished, as it has done, both in these states, and in France, Belgium, and Switzerland, through the fostering bounties which the high-priced food of the British artisan has offered to the cheaper fed manufacturer of those countries (this point is discussed in Reinert, 1996).

---

14 See Reinert (1994) for a discussion of this.

Historically the economic policies recommended in production-based economics follow two alternative lines of argument:

(1) The risks and perils of a resource-based economy – being specialised in economic activities not requiring high labour skills and subject to diminishing returns. These two effects may combine into a lock-in effect trapping a nation in poverty (the "Bolivia Syndrome"), which technical change will not solve. Exporting natural resources constituted "bad trade" in the orthodoxy of English economic policy until long after Adam Smith and David Ricardo. The most clear statement of this orthodoxy is contained in three volumes published by Charles King in 1721 (King, 1721). In King's Taxonomy exporting raw materials was "bad trade". We later find this same line of argument in nineteenth century USA, Germany, and Japan, and in twentieth century Australia and Canada.

(2) The benefits of concentrating a nation's economic activities in mechanisable, skill-absorbing activities, subject to increasing returns – a cluster of characteristics which for a long time could be efficiently shorthanded as manufacturing. Exporting goods from these activities qualified as "good trade" in King's Taxonomy – the English orthodoxy which built her national strength. The Canadian and Australian arguments later added to this by showing that the presence of a national manufacturing base upgraded skills in the resource-based activity and prevented these activities from going into Diminishing Returns – making raw material exports from a manufacturing country a viable strategy.

What, then, are the characteristics of growth inducing – "good" – economic activities? We have, in several publications, provided a "quality index" of economic activities, listing the characteristics which, in a system of dynamic imperfect competition, ranks economic activities according to their ability to provide increasing economic welfare to a nation. This "quality index" is reproduced in Figure 2.2.

Differences in wage levels, both nationally and between nations, seem to result from varying degrees of imperfect competition – caused by both static and dynamic factors. The factors at work have long been identified both by businessmen and in industrial economics, and they are correlated. Figure 2.2 attempts to create an area from light to dark grey where "the quality" of economic activities at any time can be roughly plotted on a scale from white: "perfect competition" – to black: "monopoly". The latter is only a temporary state, as new technologies fall towards a lower score as they mature.

4.3. Diversity, synergies and positive feed-back mechanisms in Renaissance economics

The static observation of higher welfare in some economic activities than in others is very frequent. Daniel Defoe gives us a systemic extension of this argument as the line of reasoning which persuaded Henry VII to start an English textile industry when he came to power in 1485: while living with his aunt in France, the future King of England had observed not only that the French textile producers (who got all their raw materials – wool

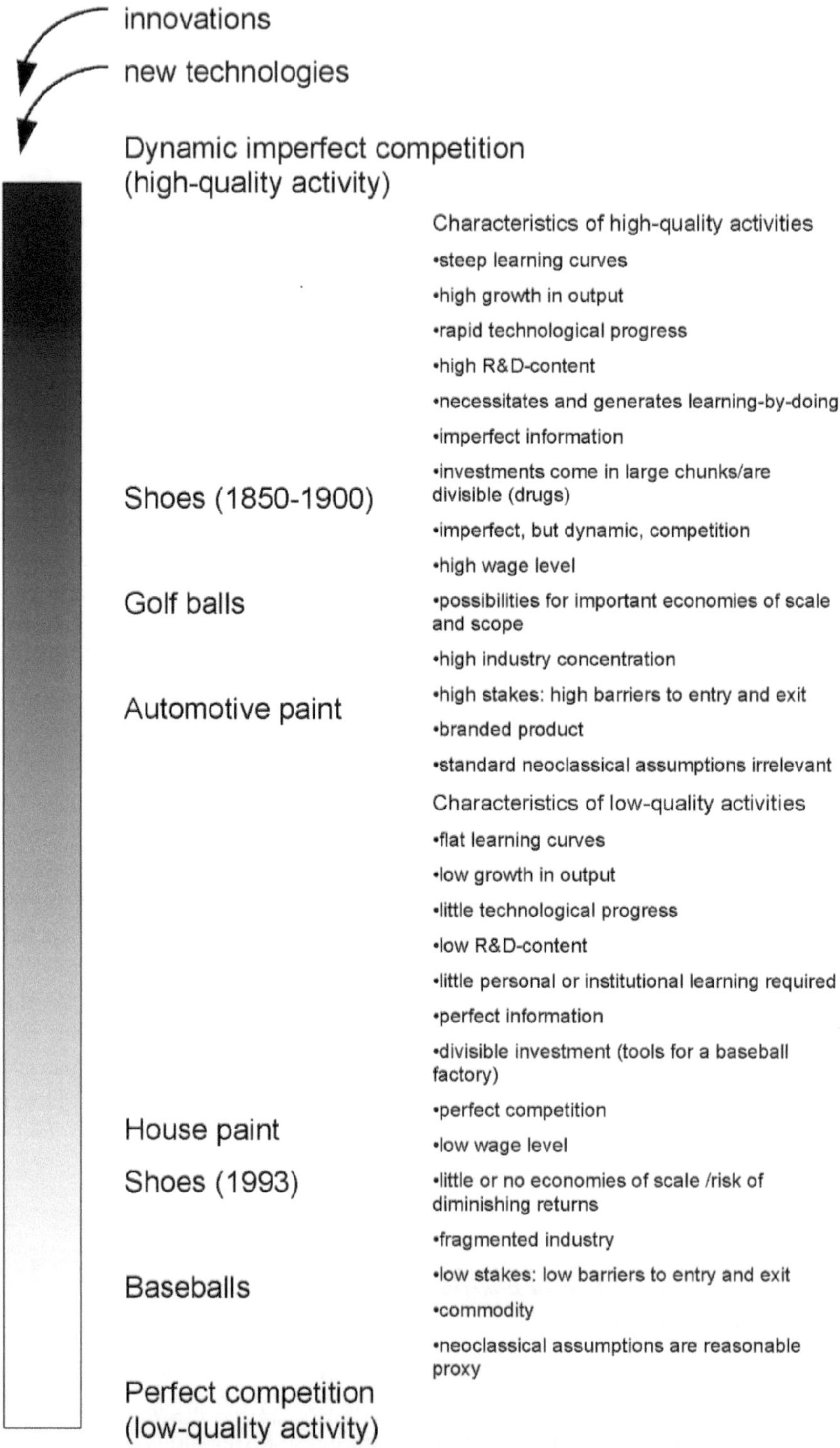

Figure 2.2 The quality index of economic activities.

and Fuller's Earth – from England) were much richer than their English providers of raw materials, but also that wealth spread to the whole community: where there was manufacturing, also the shopkeepers were richer. There were synergetic effects between manufacturing industry and the common weal of people outside the manufacturing sector.

There are several arguments founded on this kind of systemic synergy caused by manufacturing. Adam Smith's *The Theory of Moral Sentiments* – from before his meeting with the French physiocrats – shows him as a relatively traditional mercantilist in this aspect. The reasons given by German philosophers and statesmen Leibniz and Wolff for why a State is needed include an emphasis on learning which triggers positive systemic effects. The reason why there is so little conflict between the interest of the individual and the common weal in their system is precisely that increased knowledge produces more of both individual and collective profits, something like: "The incoming tide (of knowledge) raises all boats". Wolff observes that "Some people collect knowledge like other people collect money", and indicates the benefits to society of putting these two types of people together.

The most remarkable of all economic treatises before Adam Smith is, in this author's opinion, no doubt the 1613 book by Antonio Serra, *A Brief Treatise on the Causes which can make Gold and Silver Plentiful in Kingdoms where there are no Mines* (Serra, 1613). The title corresponds to our stereotypes of mercantilist tracts, that they are only about gold and silver (Coquelin and Guillaumin, 1854). In fact Serra produces a most sophisticated model, producing, on the one hand, systemic economic development and, on the other, underdevelopment.

Serra's starting point is knowledge. On the dedicatory page he denounces "ignorance as the cause and starting point of all evil". He further comments on "everybody's innate desire for knowledge". He outlines the plan of his work as: 1. Understanding why some nations, even though they have no mines, are very rich, and 2. Based on this understanding, to explain the apparent paradox that his own nation, the Kingdom of Naples, although abounding in natural resources has reached such an abysmal level of poverty that "it does not leave us to breathe nor to enjoy what nature has given us". Serra is the first economist to describe increasing returns (Roscher, 1882; Schumpeter, 1951) and with the increasing returns as his starting point, he describes positive feedback mechanisms which lead to virtuous circles of development in a national system.

Serra has two types of factors which cause the wealth of nations:

(1) Particular (or specific) factors (*accidenti propri*), which can occur only in one nation and not in others; and
(2) Common (or general) factors (*accidenti communi*), which may occur in any nation.

Particular factors

The first particular factor in Serra's system is a surplus of products for export. His phrase "The surplus (*soprabbondanza*) of goods which are produced in a kingdom in excess of its own needs and conveniences" reminds us of an Adam Smith type of "vent for surplus" theory of international trade, but this is only the beginning of Serra's long and sophisticated reasoning. Serra explains that he lists this as a particular factor – rather than as a general or common one, by pointing out that a surplus – or a positive balance of trade – cannot apply to all nations. His second particular factor is the geographical position (*il sito*) of the nation "relative to other kingdoms and parts of the world ... being a potent occasion, and almost a cause, of extensive trading of a kingdom". Rating nations according to their geographical position, "Venice holds the first place".

General factors

Serra lists four common or general factors which bring wealth, and, most importantly, how these factors interact with each other and with the particular factor of the geographical position of a nation listed above:

(1) *The number and variety of industrial professions* (*La quantità degli artifici ... diversi*). I see the "number of professions" as fundamentally the same concept as "the division of labour", in which case Serra anticipates this concept in William Petty's watch factory by 64 years and in Adam Smith's pin factory by 173 years. Clearly the number of industrial professions in a nation is a symptom of – and a proxy for – a variety of economic factors: technological sophistication, a sophisticated pattern of demand, a large diversity of skills, and – due to a minimum efficient scale of production in each profession – a large market. Serra rates this factor higher than the "vent for surplus" factor which he has listed under particular factors. This is because to Serra industrial professions, most importantly, behave differently from agricultural.

(2) *The quality of the population* (*la qualità delle genti*). The quality of a population is good "when the inhabitants thereof are by nature industrious, or diligent and ingenious in building up trade not only in their own industry, but outside, and on the watch for opportunities to apply their industry." On this factor Genoa gets the highest score, followed by Florence and, only third, Venice, which "though it has more commerce than all the cities of Italy together, will nevertheless hold third place with respect to this factor." Serra clearly relates the barrenness of the Genoese republic (*il loro paese sterilissimo*) to their industriousness and their wealth.

(3) *The presence of a great commerce* (*il traffico grande*). Here we find Serra's description of how the various factors creating wealth interact with and mutually reinforce each other in creating virtuous circles of development. In the case of Venice, "she is aided by her extensive manufactures; a factor which brings a great many people there, not only because of the trades themselves, in which case the effect would be attributed to them, but also as a result of the concurrence of these two factors together, because one gives strength to the other, the great concourse due to commerce and due to the geographical situation being increased by the manufactures, and the manufactures being increased by the great concourse due to commerce, while commerce is made

greater by the same concourse of people"[15]. It cannot be emphasized enough that the starting point for the virtuous circles described by Serra are to be found in the increasing returns of manufacturing.

(4) *The regulations of the State* (*la provvisione di colui che governa*). Here Serra emphasizes the role of government policy in order to create national wealth. This is a most difficult task, he says, because one policy measure can have very different effects in different industries: "like the sun which makes clay hard, but makes wax soft, like a low whistle which irritates the dog, but quietens the horse." (One could here, for example, think of an economic policy assisting innovation by subsidising research, which would greatly benefit the pharmaceutical industry, but not at all help the printing industry, whereas a policy of subsidising the purchasing of advanced machinery would help the printing industry, but hardly affect the pharmaceutical industry.) In spite of these difficulties, Serra makes it clear that economic policy is the most important factor causing the wealth of nations.

5. The role of the Renaissance State in the light of recent economic theory

We argue that the pre-twentieth century involvement of the State in economic growth, starting in the Renaissance – while making virtually no sense in the "fatally simple structure" of neo-classical economics[16] – is eminently compatible with new approaches in the evolutionary economics of complex systems of, for example, W. Brian Arthur (1990) and Paul David. It is also compatible with the key elements of the new trade theory, with the theories of Paul Krugman (1986) from the 1980s (rather than those of the 1990s) and of Grossman (1992) and Helpmann and Krugman (1985), and to the debate on strategic trade policy (Krugman, 1986). This is precisely because Renaissance economists did not see the economy as being deterministic, predictable, and mechanistic.

As we have attempted to show, synergetic and systemic economic effects, which modern economists see as being typical of activities subject to increasing returns, were typically recognised – with varying degrees of sophistication – by a vast number of pre-Smithian economists, and used to argue for specific State intervention. The mechanisms creating these cumulative causations were much more clearly described by Antonio Serra in 1613 than by Friedrich List in the 1840s or by Gunnar Myrdal in the 1950s. Today the most surprising aspect of the new theories emphasising increasing returns is that they are applied either to technological systems – where income distribution is not an issue – or to what we would call symmetrical trade, to trade between groups of nations all involved in

---

15 "..ma ancora giova la quantità dei artifici che in essa si ritrovano, il di cui accidente causa concorso grandissimo di gente, non solo per gli artefici, mentre in tal caso a quelli si attribuirebbe la causa, ma per il concorso di questi due accidenti insieme, poiche´ l'uno somministra forza all'altro, e il concorso grande che vi e´ al rispetto del traffico e della ragione del sito cresce per la quantità degli artefici, e la quantità degli artifici cresce per il concorso grande del traffico, il quale per il concorso predetto diventa maggiore."

16 A term used by English philosopher of science Jacob Brunowski.

activities subject to cumulative causations. In such cases the logic of State intervention is infinitely less than in the cases of asymmetrical trade, in the cases of Third World countries which are historically locked into exporting products produced under conditions of diminishing returns, and importing goods produced under conditions of increasing returns (this argument is developed in Reinert, 1980). The existence of symmetrical trade between nations at the same level of development, mutually in increasing return activities, is an argument for free trade and no intervention. Charles King had argued already in 1721 (King, 1721) that trading manufactured goods for other manufactured goods was "good trade", beneficial to both trading nations, whereas exporting raw materials and importing manufactured goods was "bad trade".

These new theories, based on increasing rather than diminishing returns, open up for a process-dependent, organic world, where historical cumulative causations, positive feedbacks, and lock-in effects give multiple solutions – also clearly suboptimal ones. The external economies of Alfred Marshall, the growth pools of Perroux, the linkages identified by Albert Hirschman (1958) and the observation of Michael Porter that innovations thrive in clusters (Porter, 1990) are also recognitions of important systemic effects of economic development – in all these theories past history reinforces into positive feedback systems and creates path-dependence. Other recent works on technological change – of authors like Christopher Freeman and Giovanni Dosi – also describe the path dependent nature of technological change. Surprisingly many early economic writers also recognise such systemic effects, and describe them.

An important insight from these modern theories is that small differences early in the history of an industry may have huge effects further on – like the "butterfly effect" in chaos theory – whether the nation is going to be specialised in increasing or diminishing return industries. This clearly opens up a huge area for State intervention, and we argue that this is exactly the kind of intervention that what we have labeled Schumpeterian mercantilism has provided from England in the 1480s to Korea in the 1980s. Joshua Gee, in his 1738 treatise, presents a similar argument to the modern one:

> The Trade of a Nation is a mighty Consequence (*sic*), and a Thing that ought to be seriously weighed, because the Happiness or Misfortune of so many Millions depend upon it. A little Mistake in the Beginning of an Undertaking may swell to a very great one. A Nation may gain vast Riches by Trade and Commerce, or for want of due Regard and Attention, may be drained of them.

We argue that this dynamic view of the world finally opens up for a much larger role of "human wit and will" – private and collective – in influencing the wealth of nations, rather than this wealth being a product of the invisible hand of Providence. Since increasing returns are most typical in manufacturing, these new theories inadvertently create theoretical support for the century-long mercantilist preference for manufacturing over the production of raw materials. In these early theories the use of machinery was often a proxy for "good trade". Again, this theory is being vindicated by recent theoretical development on the important role of machinery in economic growth (see De Long and Summers, 1991).

The fundamental problem of neo-classical theory, and of the thinking behind the policies of the World Bank today, is that they are based on the implicit assumption that all economic activities are "alike". These theories fail to open up for the presence and absence of increasing returns and consequently of asymmetrical trade – trade between nations exporting products from increasing return activities (which create "autocatalysing systems") and nations exporting diminishing return activities. "New Growth Theory" explicitly combines increasing returns with perfect competition, which, in my view, is based on a fundamental misrepresentation of how new knowledge is produced and spread. In this way, although opening up for the benefits of increasing returns, most of these economists perpetuate factor-price equalisation. Some few articles in new growth theory open up for the world view on which this paper is based – i.e. for inherent differences between economic activities as being the starting point for explaining the present wealth and poverty of nations. The most notable exception is Robert Lucas Jr – last year's winner of the Nobel Prize in economics – whose 1988 and 1993 papers explicitly open up for this possibility (Lucas, 1988; 1993).

Borrowing our terminology from the study of complex technological systems, we argue that these differences between economic activities made a strong (rather than a large) state into an "obligatory passage point" (for a discussion of this concept see Bijker, 1995) for economic development. Seeing a nation as a complex system – like a firm or a technological system – the need for input coordination arises. In the development of a technological system – just as in the development of nations – obligatory passage points "represent instances of power, because they discipline the interactions of actors" (Bijker, 1995, p. 266).

As nations evolve – just as when large technological systems evolve – there are "components" in the system which may fall behind others, limiting its potential efficiency. In the study of large technological systems, these are called "reverse salients" (Bijker et al., 1989) ± a dynamic conception of what in a static system would be called a bottle-neck, and where, at certain stages, innovative energy has to be focused (Bijker et al., 1989, p. 4). We would argue that, in all presently industrialised countries, an active State has historically been an "obligatory passage point" providing the necessary function of removing "reverse salients", and of coordinating and coercing the various "reactants" which together produce economic wealth.

We would argue that the role played by the State of Henry VII of England starting in 1485, of coercing entrepreneurship in order to establish a textile industry in England, is essentially an expression of an understanding of the same obligatory passage point to development as could be observed when the Korean government coerced Samsung from trading activities into the manufacturing of semiconductors in the early 1980s. Also the other policy measures – some types of bounties, cheap credit, temporary protection of local market, etc. – are strikingly similar in both instances. The same reasoning underlies the two State actions 500 years apart: a fundamentally Renaissance notion that new learning is the basis for economic development, and that this new learning is able to create development – through what we would call virtuous feed-back systems – in some economic activities rather than in others. In both cases, resource-based activities – in the absence of a manufacturing base – were not seen as being able to do the job of lifting the nation out of poverty. This is what we refer to as the activity-specific element of economic growth; the fact that only nations which include a large enough percentage of activities subject to dynamic increasing returns have been able to develop, and that, in this light, the phenomenon that we call "development" is essentially a "dynamic rent" which labour, capital and governments collect from such a dynamic feed-back system.

Based on the abundance of evidence of similar production- and learning-based, activity-specific strategies for early economic development since the late 1400s – they were clearly at the core of the now forgotten nineteenth century development strategies of the USA, Germany and Meiji Japan – we argue for the existence of an alternative 500-year canon of economic theory. In the perspective of this alternative knowledge-based canon, the period of dominance of classical and neo-classical barter-based canon stands out as a 200-year old parenthesis.

In this system where growth is activity-specific, the State has played the necessary role of active midwife for all developed nation-states, much in the same way as entrepreneurs have played the initial role of strong input-coordination and midwifery in all big corporations. However, both companies and States grow up, and the role of the autocratic leader and champion is reduced in both cases. Once positive feed-back systems (autocatalytic systems) have put a nation on the path of dynamic increasing returns – having started what in the study of complex technological systems sometimes is called "historical snowballing" – the role of the State is reduced to a more indirect one of maintaining the national innovation system, and of generating demand for new skills. In other words, the closer a nation finds itself to the virtuous circles of knowledge generation operating near the world "frontier of knowledge", the more the nation-state has to depend on indirect measures of influencing the economy. The biggest "latecomer advantages" of being able to catch up to a known technological frontier have been lost. For this reason the mythical MITI plays a very different role in the Japanese economy today from that after World War II.

Once the vested interests of the ruling classes have been moved from resource-based activities (which, in the absence of a manufacturing sector, do not produce positive feed-back systems)[17] and into manufacturing, the positive feedback system also embraces the political system: private rent-seeking has been brought into the activities which also brings with it collective rent-seeking, and "what's good for General Motors is good for the United States." With this, we explicitly suggest that in some economic activities, much more than in others, there is a community of interest between the vested interests of the entrepreneur and the vested interests of the nation as a whole. This point was very clearly made by nineteenth century US economists, particularly by Henry Carey (1851), who also made it clear that such effects could not be produced in the absence of manufacturing industry.

Because of this, perhaps the most important historical role of the State has been to bring the economic activities of the nation into such positive feedback activities. This factor is the fundamental common element between England in 1485 and Korea in the

17 Reinert (1996) elaborates on this point.

1980s. This was also the core argument of the "American System of Manufactures" and of the "High Wage Strategy" which completely dominated the economic policy of nineteenth century USA. The US Civil War was a war between the free traders of the South and the politicians of the North which argued that no national wealth could be created without the protection of domestic manufactures. Reading of the contemporary US sources leaves little doubt that "Free Trade, Slavery, and Secession were … sworn allies" (Logan, 1886; Curtis, 1904). In this context, Latin America is best seen as a group of nations where the "South" – the groups with vested interests in resource-based activities – won the civil wars (Gootenberg, 1989; McEvoy, 1994).

This kind of argument – and the strategies of Henry VII and Korea 500 years apart – are essentially only dynamic versions of an industrial policy which Alfred Marshall recommends in the first edition of his *Principles*: "A tax … on the production of goods which obey the Law of Diminishing Return, and devoting the tax to a bounty on the production of those goods with regard to which the Law of Increasing Returns acts sharply" (Marshall, 1890). We would argue that Marshall here describes the most typical economic policy of what we today despise as "mercantilism". We find the same kind of reasoning again as the fundamental mechanism causing uneven economic development in Frank Graham's 1923 theory of international trade (Graham, 1923, pp. 199–227). Most unfortunately, with the mathematisation of general equilibrium theory all such elements were gradually thrown out of economic theory as being "not compatible with equilibrium" or "as inconsistent with free competition, and therefore as outside the scope of the present discussion" (Viner, 1937). In this way economics moved increasingly further into the realm of pure ideology, the ideology being hidden in the assumptions, as Joan Robinson and others have claimed. The nations producing behind the barriers to entry created by the largest effects of increasing returns and with the most exclusive new information were the very nations forcing upon the world a model assuming no increasing returns and perfect information. In our view, the seriousness of the long-term practical consequences of this on the poor world will only dawn upon us over the next decade. The further removed an economy operates from the assumptions of neo-classical economics, the greater its vested interests in making other nations operate as if this theory were a true reflection of reality[18].

We would argue that, since the end of the Second World War, "Cold War Economics" has contributed to strengthen this development even further: The political need for an economic theory providing an ideological defence line against communism, and the further mathematisation of general equilibrium economics mutually reinforced each other. The historical coincidence is that both these forces demanded that the elements which created anything but a harmonious and even economic growth be eliminated. Economic theory developed, as Paul Krugman put it, along "the perceived line of least

---

[18] This is certainly true in the short term – and according to nineteenth century US economists and politicians this was a main feature of English classical economy – but in the very long term it is in nobody's interest that whole regions of the world remain poor and outside the world market.

mathematical resistance" (Krugman, 1990). At the height of the Berlin Blockade Paul Samuelson proved the universal harmony of "factor-price equalization" based on the standard assumptions of neo-classical theory. At the height of McCarthyism, Milton Friedman defended the use of these seemingly counterfactual assumptions as the basis of economic theory. The crossfire of mathematisation of a static neo-classical theory and of political demands – both needing perfect markets – cleaned out of economic theory all the factors which cause uneven economic growth, and consequently also most of the factors which bring about a need for a State intervention.

The following is an example of the poverty-equilibrium which the historical absence of a development state is likely to create: the world's most efficient producers of baseballs for the American sport are located in Haiti: their wages are 30 US cents per hour. Their technology is the same as the US producers' – all baseballs are sewn by hand. All the skills and capital of the USA have not managed to mechanise this production – it is a relic left over from a techno-economic paradigm long past. Just as in Keynes' unemployment equilibrium, such poverty-equilibria may lock nations into a comparative advantage of being poor and ignorant, in industries requiring low skills. This in spite of their being the most efficient producers in the world with the best available technology. Historically the "development state" has taken a nation into economic activities which require higher skills, and thus established a platform from which successive growth becomes more self-sustaining with much less intervention.

We consequently argue that the presence of a "development state" – taking the nation-state into increasing return activities – as an obligatory passage point is determinant for economic welfare. The most interesting aspect of such poverty traps is how the systemic aspects of development create widely differing wages in professions where productivity of labour and capital are essentially the same the world over. The cumulative effects, which today generally have their roots in the export sector, spread through the labour market also to activities which, by themselves, are not subject to increasing returns: the vast majority of workers in any nation are employed in the traditional service sector. Productivity in these activities vary very little from nation to nation, as in our example with the bus drivers in Norway and in Bolivia. The systemic effects accompanying economic growth – which are created by increasing returns – produce what we in the next section shall call a collusive distribution of the gains from technological change: in the Fordist mass production paradigm – centred on the nation-state – the gains from technological change spread to a large extent as higher domestic monetary wages – rather than as lowered prices internationally.

6. The two canons of economic theory

Next year's European Conference on the History of Economics – in Athens – is based on the "role of the canon in the history of economics." The call for papers notes that in most sciences the authority of the "classics" has been challenged – not so in economics, "where the canonical sequence of Smith, Ricardo, Marx, etc. still constitutes the skeleton for most teaching and scholarly discussion". The question of whether alternative "canons" exist is also raised.

In this paper we argue that a parallel tradition – an alternative canon – exists. The theoretical conflict between the forefathers of today's mainstream economics and the forefathers of the alternative canon has existed since the 1622–23 debate between Gerard De Malynes (Malynes, 1622, 1623) and Edward Misselden (Misselden, 1622, 1623), where Malynes represented a static theory rooted in barter and Misselden represented a theory centred on learning and production. In the history of economic thought, their debate is interpreted as being about exchange controls and the balance of trade[19]. However, by going back to the sources, one finds that the main line of attack by Misselden against Malynes is his "mechanical" view of man – Malynes has left out Man's "art" and "soul". Misselden quotes at length a paragraph from Malynes, where Malynes reduces trade to three elements, "namely, Commodities, Money, and Exchange" (Misselden, 1623, p. 8). Objecting to this definition, Misselden says: "It is against Art to dispute with a man that denyeth the Principles of Art". Misselden scorns Malynes for not seeing the difference between a heap of stones and logs and a house – because Man's productive powers produce the house but his soul has been left out. A similar criticism can be made of neo-classical economics.

Misselden represents the acute Renaissance awareness of the enormous territory to be covered between Mankind's present poverty and ignorance, and the enormous potentials. This released enthusiasm and energy. The situation recalls Keynes' frustration with the suboptimal situation of the world under the Great Depression. We shall attempt to show that both to the Renaissance philosophers/economists as well as to Keynes, the formula needed to "free" society from its suboptimal position was what Keynes called "salvation through knowledge" (Misselden, 1623, p. 102).

In the late eighteenth century a new type of economic theory came into being, focusing on the "natural harmony" of Nature. This was truly a paradigm shift in Kuhn's sense. The incentives of Renaissance economics to produce knowledge through a process which we have labeled dynamic and knowledge-producing rent-seeking – or Schumpeterian Mercantilism – had in many cases degenerated into static rent-seeking. Whereas the optimistic theory of the Renaissance focused on the limitless potential of "Man the producer", the new economic theory came to focus on "Man the trader and consumer". The two theories were steeped in very different realities – the old one in Man's ability to create and produce, and the new one in a world of barter, based on the mechanics of an *ordre naturel* – the "Natural order". The old theory was dynamic and organic and centred on "thought" (Logos) and "*werden*" (becoming), the new theory was mechanical and static, centred on "matter", and "*sein*" (being). In the old theory the market was present in the role of a servant of active human beings who knew where they were going, in the new theory the market acquired many of the characteristics of "Providence" (on this point, see

[19] Schumpeter discusses the controversy between the two men in his *History of Economic Analysis*, Oxford University Press, New York, 1954, pp. 344–5. See also their respective entries in "The New Palgrave". In all cases these references are purely to the mechanics of money and exchange.

Viner, 1972), as the manifestation of the *ordre naturel.* Werner Sombart fittingly calls the Renaissance economics activistic-idealistic, and the economics from Adam Smith onwards passivistic-materialistic (Sombart, 1928, p. 919).

Just as Renaissance economics sees no limits to progress – they truly see "a never ending frontier of human knowledge" – in Adam Smith's system nations reach a stationary state where they can "advance no further", when that "full complement of riches which the nature of its soil and climate … allowed it to require" had been reached (Smith, 1976, p. 106). It is only here that we see the practical consequences of Adam Smith and the "deep ecology" movement sharing the same assumptions – no new knowledge entering the system. The only logical consequences of a theory which does not allow for the production of new knowledge is either a stationary state (Adam Smith) or an "ecological disaster." This disaster can be predicted by simple extrapolations. However, each level of knowledge carries with it its own level of "sustainability." As we shall discuss later, "knowledge" and "institutions" are the conspicuously and "actively absent" factors in Adam Smith's system, i.e. these factors are not only ignored, but it is actively argued that they have no relevance.

Just as the focus of Renaissance economics was on production, the focus of neoclassical economics is on barter and exchange. Leibniz, in 1671, sees the origin of barter as being in production, and quotes Aristotle: "Nam Mercator transfert tantum, Manufactura gignit" – Trade can carry only as much as the factories produce. To Leibniz, the poverty of the producing artisans was an important argument for the establishment of an active State. "After all, is not the entire purpose of Society to release the artisan from his misery? The farmer is not in need, since he is sure of his bread, and the merchant has more than enough" (Leibniz, 1992).

The fundamental characteristic of the new "classical' economic theory was its conscious de-emphasis on the role of human knowledge which comes across very clearly in Adam Smith's late work, i.e. *The Wealth of Nations.* The new economics of the late eighteenth century was to produce the "dismal science" of Malthus and Ricardo, and fundamentally to change Man's view of the role of the State. The old theory emphasized systematic effects emanating from *das Ganze* – from the whole as a system. The new theory, starting with Adam Smith and reaching its apex with Paul Samuelson's factor-price equalisation in 1950, had the individual as its sole unit of analysis. However, not even the whole individual became the unit of analysis, only a part of the individual labeled *Homo Oeconomicus* who engaged in barter. Excluded was not only the state, but also *Homo Faber* – man the innovator and producer.

In economics, the mechanical world view is centred on barter, accumulation, physical metaphors, equilibrium, and optimality. In this mechanical view, a fundamental characteristic of Man is his propensity to barter. The organic view in economics is centred on inventions, production, evolution, biological metaphors, and disequilibrium. In an evolutionary system, almost by definition, no optimality exists, except as an ever-moving target in the distance (this point is discussed in Nelson, 1995). In this organic view a fundamental characteristic of Man is his propensity to explore, to invent, and cumulatively and continuously to create new knowledge. In this perspective, today's evolutionary economics still may be seen as being too "mechanistic" – substituting biology-envy for "physics envy" in a process where the role of conscious human effort – individual and collective – as the main engine propelling evolutionary change is still missing.

One fundamental difference between the two world views appears when authors from the two schools describe how Man differs from animals. The most famous representative of the barter-centred theory of development says it this way:

> The division of labour arises from a propensity in human nature to ... truck, barter and exchange one thing for another ... It is common to all men, and to be found in no other race of animals, which seem to know neither this nor any other species of contracts ... Nobody ever saw a dog make a fair and deliberate exchange of one bone for another with another dog (Adam Smith, *The Wealth of Nations* (1976), Chicago edition, p. 17).

The reply from the production-centred theory of development:

> ... Beavers build houses; but they build them nowise differently, or better, now than they did five thousand years ago ... Man is not the only animal who labours; but he is the only one who improves his workmanship. These improvements he effects by Discoveries and Inventions ... (Abraham Lincoln, Speech of the 1860 Presidential Campaign).

The roots of the problems of today's mainstream economics can be traced back to these conflicting views on Man. We would argue that it is time for economic theory to find again the knowledge-based and production-based alternative to today's economic tradition. This tradition is traced over the last 500 years in Figure 2.3.

Adam Smith's nineteenth century enemies in the USA would ask how Adam Smith's theory explains economic growth. How do you get more bones into the economy by teaching dogs to barter and to make contracts? And, how do you explain with Adam Smith's theory why dogs today eat canned dog food and not bones? Although Adam Smith has a "general tendency of things to improve" in the background, these improvements descend on mankind as "manna from heaven" – not as a result of organised conscious effort – and hit everybody at the same time.

The term *laissez-faire* is today used as a slogan for no government intervention. However, from the context of how and when the remark was made, a different interpretation is possible. The term is known through the French physiocrats, but the term was not invented by them. Quesnay perpetuated the term as a slogan for the non-intervention of government. However, the physiocrats picked up an expression which long before had been used by a merchant called Legendre[20], who was consulted, around 1680, by Colbert, as to what could be done to promote trade and welfare. This merchant then dropped the words which became famous: "laissez-nous faire", to which later Quesnay added: "Ne pas trop gouverner" – "Do not govern too much" (Garnier in Cognelin and Guillaumin, 1854, Vol. 2, p. 19). However, it seems important to keep in mind that Legendre at this point had the whole arsenal of Schumpeterian mercantilism at his disposal – he may very well have expressed the feeling that this was all the government

[20] This account is given in Roscher, 1882, Section X (10), p. 36.

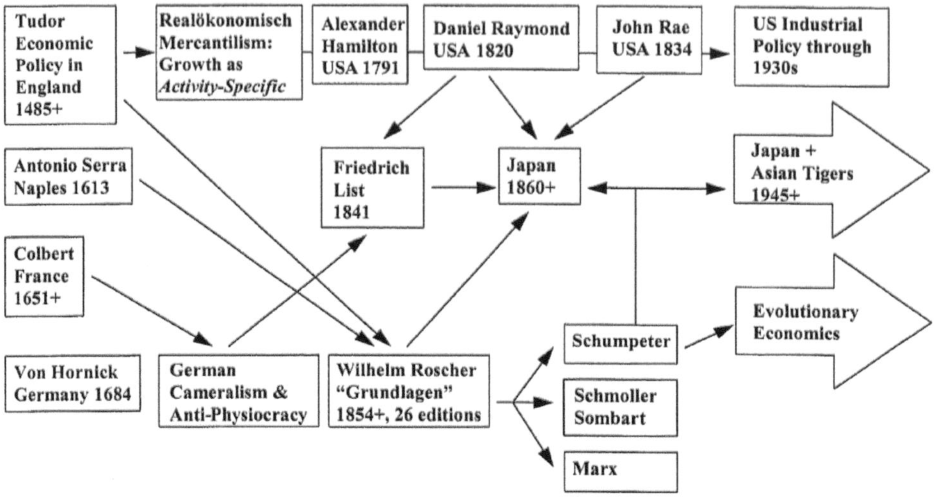

Figure 2.3 The knowledge- and production-based canon of economic theory.
Source: Roscher, *Principles of Political Economy*, Callaghan, Chicago, 1882.

could be expected to do – that the maximum point of government intervention had been reached, that the rest was up the entrepreneurs.

7. "United by a common misconception about our past" – the decline and fall of Renaissance economics

> Es evidente que hay muchas maneras de hacer historia, casi tantas como de deshacerla (José Ortega y Gasset, *La Rebelión de las Masas*, 1937)[21].

"A nation", said Harvard political scientist Karl Deutsch, "is a group of persons united by a common error about their ancestry and a common dislike of their neighbours" (Deutsch, 1969). This saying is presumably valid for all tribes – including academic tribes. The same maxim seems most appropriate when applied to our understanding of the role of the state in bringing Mankind out of poverty and ignorance. The history of Renaissance economics in today's textbooks is not unlike a history of Rome written by the Huns.

Just as the Black Legend – *la leyenda negra* – has disfigured Spanish history, our view of mercantilism has been deformed by the "Midas legend" – the legend that the mercantilists were only interested in gold. Modern civilized society was formed during the Renaissance; all artists and scientists of the Renaissance – from Galileo to Michelangelo – are our

[21] "There are many ways to make history. Almost as many as to unmake it," Espasa-Calpe, Madrid, 1964, p. 163.

heroes. Renaissance Man is still a term denoting profound knowledge in many fields. Yet, we are told by virtually all modern histories of economics that the economic theory behind all this was only about collecting gold.

In the field of Cold War Economics, just as in the cold war politics of a Latin American banana republic, those not siding clearly with either of the two superpowers were the ones most at risk; they would – literally – be shot at from both sides (or not get a university appointment). Cold War Economics was in many ways a battle of Utopias, where, as Colin Clark once put it, "theory" was mistaken for "science". This was a relatively unsophisticated scientific war between "good guys" and "bad guys", as in the Western movies of the time, where the market was seen as either "good" or "bad". This led to a polarisation of economic theory – the combined effect of the Cold War and the process of mathematisation of a static system crowded out other and most relevant aspects. Focusing on the quantifiable factors in their barter-based models, the economics profession came to be prisoners of their own limited toolbox. As the history of economic thought also slowly came to be filtered through neo-classical lenses, the debates of the past were reinterpreted to fit the Cold War mold. Historical authors were given labels as free traders (good guys) or protectionists (bad guys), while both the historical context and the other often very sophisticated aspects of these older theories were lost. This is the history of economic thought with which we still live.

Another feature of this is that some nations come to be curiously at odds with their own past. Nowhere is this more clear than in the USA. US banknotes provide a portrait gallery of people whose economic policy today would be ridiculed both by the World Bank and in American university textbooks in economics – from the views of Benjamin Franklin[22] that "protection and competition" was the only way to make manufactures cheap in the USA (Whatley, 1774), to George Washington who, for the same reasons, insisted on a necessarily primitive American-made suit at the first presidential inauguration, via the protectionists Hamilton and Jackson, to Thomas Jefferson's attempt to prohibit the works of Ricardo in the US, to the view of Abraham Lincoln (quoted earlier) that at the origin of wealth there are inventions and innovations. The uncomfortable fact that the US Civil War – to a large extent a war between the free traders of the Southern Confederacy against the protectionist North – was won by the "bad guys", who represented despicable mercantilist theories of economic development, is today seriously played down. With this development the real treasure of US economic theory, which even today is very relevant – a century of thought from Daniel Raymond to John Rae, E. Peshine Smith and Simon Patten – is all but deleted from the national collective memory, and from the history of economic thought. Most nineteenth century

22 Benjamin Franklin is the author of the laudatory footnotes to this effect in the second edition of Whatley, 1774. This book title succinctly puts together two important points: that effective protectionism leading to dynamic national rent-seeking must lean on freedom to establish new business, on competition (as opposed to the static rent-seeking resulting from protectionism in India or post-war Latin-America), and that, from the point of view of the real wages paid in non-industrialised nations, manufactured imports appear very expensive. The solution was to establish a competitive economy based on manufacturing in the USA.

US economists made it very clear that their economic policy was specific to the situation of the US economy then; they would not have recommended protectionism as a solution for the problems of the USA today. One of several studies puncturing the myth that US economic policy during its first 100 years was one of a weak State and of *laissez-faire* was written by a Harvard historian: *Economic Policy and Democratic Thought*[23].

We seem to be still suffering from the illusion in nineteenth century economic theory of an automatic development – a view also largely shared by Marx. However, this view had its strong opponents also in the nineteenth century, particularly in Germany and the USA. German economist Eugen Dühring, the great defender of US economist Henry Carey in Europe, scorns *die Karrikierer des Merkantilismus* – the caricature makers of mercantilism – who "only too often spoke as if the businesspeople and the statesmen of the day almost believed that precious metal could be used as food for the human body"[24]. The important systemic aspects of this theory – the promotion of the common weal – are mostly left out of today's accounts.

Welfare is clearly a product of conscious human will, not of any invisible hand of Providence. Johann Gottfried Hoffman in his *Theory of Taxation* (1840) puts it this way: "The delusion that security of life and property, the productivity of labor, and the consequent possibility of acquisition and enjoyment, and even the elevation of the spiritual and the ennobling of the moral nature – that these goods came to Man in the gift of gratuities, is itself a proof of the advanced stage of culture which the greater part of Europe at present occupies. As the grown man has long since forgotten the pains it cost him to learn to speak, so have the peoples, in the days of their mature growth of the State, forgotten what was required in order to free them from their primitive brutal savagery" (Hoffman, J.G., introduction to *Lehre von den Steuern*, Cohn, 1895, p. 60). Another German economist, Gustav Cohn, who was born in the year Hoffman's Theory appeared, picks up the argument and continues: "In point of fact, how significant was the involuntary testimony which the eighteenth century, with its repudiation of the historic State and its yearning after the primordial state of nature, bore to the blessings of the inherited culture which it ungratefully enjoyed" (Cohn, 1895, pp. 60–61). This description – written more than 100 years ago – also fits the *zeitgeist* of today. Again today "repudiation of the State" and "the end of the nation-state" – based on English classical and neo-classical economics – are mixed with the "yearning after the primordial state of nature" from the "deep ecology" movement. In fact such anti-modernist movements seem to occur towards the end of techno-economic paradigms. Rousseau and Adam Smith represented the eighteenth century version of this movement. The nineteenth century *fin de siècle* movement comprised nihilism, and towards the end of the twentieth century we see a postmodernism bordering on nihilism. Out of the late nineteenth century *fin de siècle* mood grew both the *Blut und Boden* movement and the conservative revolution of the 1920s and 1930s, paving the way for irrational Nazism.

---

23 Harvard University Press, Cambridge, MA, 1948. Prepared under the direction of The Committee on Research in Economic History, Social Science Research Council.

24 Dühring, Eugen, *Kritische Geschichte der Nationalökonomie*, 1879, quoted in Sombart, 1928, p. 913.

The new type of economic theory brought with it a very different view of the role of government. There were good objective reasons for this. The old mercantile system had degenerated, and Adam Smith's basic idea that the English and French economies now needed a heavy dose of market was no doubt correct. However, Adam Smith was so successful in ridiculing all economists before the Physiocrats that the whole production-based tradition in economics was slowly lost.

Reconstructing a new economic theory which exogenised both knowledge and State was clearly much less risky to advanced nations than to the more backward ones. Adam Smith's only mention of the invisible hand in *The Wealth of Nations* can easily be read as the description of a virtuous circle which takes on the character of a *perpetuum mobile* – of "historical snowballing" – once it has properly been put into motion. The closer a nation is to the frontier of human knowledge, the less the State has to contribute in direct interventions. Or, as Keynes said in 1923: "The more troublous the times, the worse does a *laissez-faire* system work." The issue was therefore not, said Keynes, one between collectivism and *laissez-faire,* but between targeted state action and a socialism which was out of date and contrary to human nature[25]. This requires a strong State, but not a big State.

The Midas Legend is more deeply entrenched than ever. Anyone who dares to comment positively on any aspect of economic theory before Adam Smith can make Werner Sombart's words his own: "Ich sage das auf die Gefahr hin, als Neo-Merkantilist abgestempelt und in das Raritätenkabinett unseres Faches übergeführt zu werden" (Sombart, 1928, p. 925).

8. The role of public enterprises in this system

Although other papers of this conference will cover this subject more fully, I shall add a few comments in an attempt to reconstruct the role of public enterprises within the now unlearned logic of pre-Ricardian economics. In this section, I shall largely follow the subject as treated by Werner Sombart (Sombart, 1928, pp. 847–57). Unfortunately Sombart's profound understanding of the growth of the capitalist system is mainly accessible in German[26]. This problem of inaccessibility is strengthened by the most unfortunate neglect of pre-war German economic theory, a neglect today apparently promoted by the Germans themselves. This nation has all reason to be proud of their heritage in economic theory, but Germany seemingly attempts to unlearn this tradition collectively together with less fortunate aspects of the past. This sad state of affairs, coupled with the US misconceptions – bordering on denial – of their own nineteenth century economic theory and economic policy, in my view bereaves the world of the only existing fully-fledged and viable alternative to the neo-classical tradition.

25 Quoted in Skidelsky and Keynes (1995, p. 152).

26 A small group under the leadership of Prof. Jürgen Backhaus of the University of Limburg in Maastricht in The Netherlands – the "Heilbronn Group" – is attempting to resurrect German economic theory and make it accessible in English, based on a conviction of its relevance today. A result of one of their annual conferences in Heilbronn, Germany, three volumes have just been published in English on the economics of Werner Sombart (Backhaus, 1996).

Sombart makes the point that the reasons given for the establishment of State-owned industries in the historical record do not give justice to their importance:

> The importance of (State-owned enterprises) for the creation of modern industry cannot be overestimated. These served to set, not only a protoype example of industry, but also the pace and pattern for the new form of organisation. It was the State-owned enterprises which, due to the demands they created, often served as catalysts for the development of capitalist industries. These enterprises are so essential that they cannot be left out of an account of the development of capitalism, which – although their conceptual roots lay elsewhere – they furthered in thousands of ways[27].

In the quote at the cover of this paper, the early Adam Smith explains how government intervention is made to help neither the consumers nor the producers, but for the interest of the system, the State, the common weal. Similarly, state-owned enterprises were primarily established in the interest of the State. The following were the main motivations:

- *Administrative reasons.* On occasion the State administration found that, in certain industries, the only practical way of carrying out the necessary controls was by State ownership. This was most often done for reasons of financial policy, particularly in the case of mining of precious metals.
- *To meet the needs of the ruler and the court.* Many state-owned manufactures were set up seemingly with the sole objective of providing luxury goods to the King. Rulers and ruled took pride in showing off the skill level and production capacity of their nation – be it in producing china, silk or tapestries – seemingly much in the same way nations are proud of their athletes today. As already mentioned when discussing the role of the State in providing demand for skills – of the State as a Porterian demanding customer – the effect of the mass production of luxuries clearly had an effect of making such goods more accessible further down the social ladder, and, more importantly, of building up technical and managerial skills which spread to other activities.
- *For reasons of statesmanship/to further the common weal.* As already frequently mentioned, the State intervention was often made under this heading. Reasons given were those of creating employment, increasing exports, reducing dependence on foreign nations, etc. Often State ownership appears as "entrepreneurship of last resort". Also tariffs were used to promote industries out of the same logic, the State trying to establish industries with the minimal tariff which would attract investors. Certain industries were seen as

[27] "Für die Entstehung der modernen Industrie kann man die Bedeutung dieser Gründungen nicht hoch genug einschätzen. Denn sie sind es, die vielfach als Muster, noch öfter als Schrittmacher neuer Organisationen dienen. Sie sind es, die durch ihre Nachfrage oft genug als den Kristallisationspunkt für die Entwicklung auch der kapitalistischen Industrie bilden. Ihre Erwähnung … darf … in einer Darstellung des Werdegangs des modernen Kapitalismus nicht fehlen, den sie aus den angegebenen Gründen in tausendfaltiger Weise gefördet haben, trotzdem sie ihrem Geiste nach aus anderer Wurzel erwachsen sind" (Sombart, 1928, p. 847).

being mandatory for the common weal, and this results in the obvious pattern that the most backward nations tended to have the highest tariffs.

- *For reasons of national defence.* The importance of national defence for technological development has been enormous – from the earliest history to the contribution of Reagan's Star War program to cellular telephone communication. A main challenge to statesmen of today is to devise mechanisms of financing technological developments other than as unintended by-products of warfare. To this point we refer to Sombart's "Krieg und Kapitalismus", which we have cited in section 3. Obvious State industries in this respect are gunpowder and armaments, but also industries closer to the core of industrial and commercial development, like iron foundries and shipbuilding. However, the technologies and logistics needed to supply the huge armies also contributed to develop skills, scale, and scope in the State-owned production and distribution of goods like bread and clothing. The shortage of natural raw materials for the purposes of war is clearly a most important reason for research and inventions in the field of synthetic materials.

State-owned industries seems to have been part of the role of the "obligatory passage point" played by a strong and active State. These companies were – as Sombart emphasises – "places of learning", not only for technical skills, but also for organizational and social capabilities. These are deep and elusive, but nevertheless indispensable skills for the process of economic development. Military demand seems to have had the same positive effect in the USA as in Europe. Ely Whitney financed the development of the revolutionary "cotton gin" from the profits from selling rifles to the Revolutionary Army, and the whole concept of production with interchangeable parts – paving the way for industrial mass production – originated in the production of rifles in the USA. However, in the USA a much larger role was played by private entrepreneurs than in Europe. Although in their trade policy and in terms of "getting the nation into the right business" the USA was clearly in line with Europe, we here face a difference in historical development. We can only speculate if this was because of a considerably better supply of entrepreneurship in the USA – a crucial factor in economic development – if it was a result of a later industrialisation when a historical prototype of industrialisation was evident in Europe, of ideological preference, of having a more developed industrial structure before really threatening foreign wars appeared in US history (WWI), or all of the above.

Clearly the staring point of many technological trajectories was statal or para-statal demand, not only from war but also from the construction of infrastructure, power generation, a national telephone system, etc. Examples abound: that the automotive industry in Japan has its origins in the demand for trucks for the Imperial Army (see Odigari and Gota, 1993) is a typical one. Import substitution based on reasons of national security seems to have played an extraordinarily important role through the centuries. Over time this led to a convergence of industrial structure, establishing a common platform of technological knowledge in all advanced countries. With this relatively similar industrial structure as a starting point – from this common platform – the process of specialisation and globalisation today mutuallybenefits the advanced countries.

The need for national security supplies forced nations into increasing return activities, even though their natural comparative advantage may originally have been elsewhere. National security considerations helped create a new comparative advantage in the production of skill-intensive increasing return goods. Our problem today is, however, that having unlearned this historical insight, we pretend that the nations which have not been through this process of cumulative knowledge-building – the nations which have not reached this platform of knowledge – will equally benefit from the globalisation process. In terms of skills and scale, this common platform of knowledge creates the basis for a symmetrical pattern of international trade among the advanced countries, of a pattern of specialised trade between people with similar levels of skill, like that of lawyers trading with physicians. The asymmetrical trading relationships between the North and the South are more like a nation of skilled lawyers trading with a nation of unskilled lettuce pickers – there are no logical reasons why any factor-price equalisation should take place between the two, unless some technological development opens up for lettuce-picking profitably to absorb as much human capital as the study of law. In the existence or not of a common "platform of technological knowledge and organisational skills" seems to lie the main historical difference separating the two convergence groups in the world economy – the rich "North" and the poor "South".

9. Exogenizing the engines of growth: Adam Smith and the loss of knowledge, institutions and systemic effects in economic theory

At the time of the publication of Adam Smith's *The Wealth of Nations* in 1776, no doubt the mercantilist system had developed from its Renaissance origins of a dynamic and wealth-producing quest for dynamic rents from new knowledge, to a system often characterised by static rent-seeking. Adam Smith's prescription of a heavy dose of market was no doubt a correct one. However, Adam Smith did much more than prescribing more market and less intervention. He produced a system which removed the very engines of growth from the previous world view:

- He efficiently argued that knowledge was of no value either to society or to the individual (see below). This counterintuitive reasoning is retained in today's economic theory when it predicts equalisation of wages between nations exchanging goods produced at extremely different skill levels.
- His theory removed human institutions. (Adam Smith) exhibits a powerful aesthetic aversion to any type of collective action, a visceral distaste bordering on revulsion. For him "human institutions" so invariably produce "absurd" results that they have no presumptive legitimacy (McCraw, 1992, p. 364).
- His atomistic view removed all systemic effects and constructs a theory of individuals void of any uniqueness, all governed by their "human nature" which is the same in all human beings.

The paradox of Adam Smith is that he saw an important Renaissance-type systemic effect – the division of labour – as being the source of wealth, an idea which was there both in Serra (1613) and very explicitly in Petty (1691). Yet, Smith's other assumptions – atomism, no increasing returns, no institutions, no new knowledge – ousted this key systemic insight forever from classical and neo-classical theory. Says US economist George Stigler: "Almost no one used or now uses the theory of division of labour, for the excellent reason that there is scarcely such a theory … There is no standard, operable theory to describe what Smith argued to be the mainspring of economic progress"[28].

The loss of human knowledge, of institutions, and of any notion of systemic common weal in economic theory is, in this writer's opinion, a fundamental reason for our failure to capture why the world polarises into two convergence groups of nations – one wealthy and one poor. We argue for the importance of recognizing that what got Mankind from the cold and draughty caves into economic welfare was more than the discovery of barter and of "getting the prices right" – that it required immense addition of knowledge and skills. A basic assumption running through pre-Smithian economics was that different economic activities contributed differently to the common weal – that the uneven advances of human knowledge were intimately tied to the process creating uneven growth. The professions which absorbed more knowledge – embodied or disembodied – were seen as the carriers of the common welfare of a nation. On this background it is interesting to go through Adam Smith's works with one particular question in mind: What is the role of knowledge in Adam Smith's system?

In Chapter X of Book I, Adam Smith explains what causes differences in wages between professions – i.e. in a national economy. Wages constituting more than 70 per cent of GNP in a modern industrial nation; differences in national income between nations are principally a result of differences in wages, rather than differences in profits. We would further argue that, with an international economy with increasing factor mobility, the distinction between a theory of international trade as opposed to a theory of national trade is losing its importance. The only aspect which divides a theory of international from a theory of national trade is the question of factor immobility. Therefore Adam Smith's answer to the question as to which circumstances, "either really, or at least in the imagination of men, make up for a small pecuniary gain in some (employments), and counter-balance a great one in others", is of great interest.

Smith lists five reasons why some people are paid better than others. The list is remarkable in that in each and every point raised, Adam Smith goes out of his way to explain why human knowledge and human skills do not produce a higher standard of living than ignorance – neither to society nor to the individual. If people with more knowledge and more skills have higher incomes – which was also observable at the time of Adam Smith – it is never due to the fact that skills and knowledge produce value, but due to one of the following five reasons:

(1) *Wages vary with the agreeableness of the employment.* For this reason, "the most detestable of all employments, that of the public executioner, is, in proportion to the quantity of work done, better paid than any common trade whatever" (Smith, 1776, p. 113).

[28] Stigler quoted in McCraw (1992, p. 362).

Under this point Adam Smith also discusses why human skills and talent are often very well rewarded – attempting to explain what he sees as the "exorbitant rewards" of artists, "opera-singers &c.". The rewards to these talents are to Smith a direct result of "the discredit which attends the employment of them as the means of subsistence." To Smith the fact that society rewards extraordinary talent is a direct result of the fact that "we despise their persons". "While we do the one (i.e. despise them), we must of necessity do the other (i.e. pay exorbitant rewards)." "Should the public opinion or prejudice ever alter with regard to such occupations, their pecuniary recompense would quickly diminish" (Smith, 1776, p. 120). Smith argues that if we would just stop despising our actors, artists and sportsmen, their incomes would fall to the level of an agricultural laborer. His system does not allow for a pecuniary reward which is coupled with admiration – his natural system has to pair "high reward" with "despise".

(2) *Wages vary with the cost of learning the business.* Smith makes it very clear, however, that "the cost of apprenticeship accounts for the wages of manufacturers being higher than those of country labour" (Smith, 1776, p. 114). There are therefore no advantages to manufacturing over agriculture; although the earnings in manufacturing "may be somewhat greater, it seems, however, to be no greater than what is sufficient to compensate the superior expense of their education". In other words, the mercantilist tradition that nations who export the products from professions of higher skills will be wealthier than nations exporting products with low skills is here strongly denied. From the point of view of both society and the individual, adding knowledge to labour is, in Smith's system, clearly a zero-sum game.

(3) *Wages vary with constancy of employment.* For this reason, professionals like masons and bricklayers who "can neither work in hard frost and foul weather", and who are not secured constant demand for their services, will have a higher wage than people who are permanently employed. "The high wages of these workmen, therefore, are not so much the recompense of their skill, as the compensation for the inconsistency of their employment" (Smith, 1776, p. 116). Again, any role of skill and knowledge is denied.

(4) *Wages vary with the trust to be reposed.* Some professions – Smith mentions goldsmiths, physicians, lawyers, and attorneys – are higher paid because of the "great trust which must be reposed in the workmen" (Smith, 1776, p. 117). We have to have confidence in these people, says Smith, and the reason we pay them more is that we do not have confidence in people who are not well paid. "Such confidence could not safely be reposed in people of a very mean or low condition. Their reward must be such, therefore, as may give them that rank in society which so important trust requires" (Smith, 1776, p. 118). To Adam Smith, in other words, we do not pay lawyers and doctors better than people who wash dishes because their skills are more valuable, but because we have to trust these people, and could not dream of having confidence in people from the lower classes of society.

(5) *Wages vary with the probability of success.* "Put your son apprentice to a shoemaker, there is little doubt of his learning to make a pair of shoes: But send him to study law, it is at least twenty to one if ever he makes such proficiency as will enable him to live

> by his business." For this reason, Adam Smith looks at the skilled professions like a lottery: "those who draw the prizes ought to gain all that is lost by those who draw the blanks". Since, according to Smith, only one in 20 lawyers makes something out of their profession, this one lawyer "ought to receive the retribution of his own so tedious and expensive education, but that of more than twenty others who are never likely to make anything by it" (Smith, 1776, p. 118–119). Again, to society, knowledge is a zero-sum game.

As opposed to today's economists, Adam Smith is consistent in carrying his anti-mercantilist theory down to the family level. Few economists today recommend their children to get a job washing dishes rather than to go to university, using the argument that "factor-price equalization is just around the corner anyway". Privately – but not at the national level – today's economists not only see the value of human capital, but they also accept US economist Daniel Raymond's most important point from 1820 (Raymond, 1820): Different professions have different capacities profitably to absorb capital (human or other) – different professions have different "windows of opportunity" for creating welfare. One cannot profitably add as much human capital to the job of washing dishes as to the job of being a lawyer. For this reason economists would recommend to their children professions which require a university education – although by doing this they express what they – at the level of a nation – would describe as "a mercantilist preference for one profession to another." Adam Smith, however, is very consistent on this point: all risks consider it is safer to let your son become a shoemaker's apprentice than to become a lawyer (Adam Smith had no children).

Today's economic theory addresses the problem of differing absorption capacities of knowledge by assuming that all activities have the same production function – that the necessary extension of skills is automatically brought to life by the addition of capital to labour. This describes a process of creating economic growth which is similar to the process of adding water to instant coffee: one assumes that the knowledge necessary in order to increase productivity is already there in equal measure in all human activities.

Adam Smith further argues that the choice of profession is of no importance, and he dispenses with skill and knowledge as economic factors based on two assumptions:

(1) He assumes that labour comes from the same pool of people: "If, in the same neighbourhood, there was any employment either more or less advantageous than the rest, so many people would crowd into it in the one case, and so many would desert it in the other, that its advantages would soon return to the other employments."
(2) He assumes that skills can be learned extremely fast. Investing in machines and instruments may take a long time, says Smith, "but when both have been fairly invented and are well understood, to explain to any young man, in the completest manner, how to apply the instruments and how to construct the machines, cannot well require more than the lessons of a few weeks: perhaps those of a few days might be sufficient. In the common mechanical trades, those of a few days might certainly be sufficient."

Adam Smith's discussion on what causes a difference in retribution between professions leads up to a severe criticism of the English statutes of apprenticeship. These dated from Elizabeth I – from the time of the cultivation of knowledge *per se*, which provided apprenticeships of up to seven years. Adam Smith saw apprenticeships as an extreme waste, since he is of the opinion that everything could be learned "in a few days". Unlike some later economists, like Alfred Marshall, Adam Smith was not a practical man – he "seemed the unlikeliest of guides to the practical world" in the words of Harvard Business School professor Thomas McCraw (McCraw, 1992).

In both Adam Smith and in neo-classical theory there is in some fundamental way a contradiction between the notion of perfect markets and the way the economy adds knowledge. This problem spills over to how economic theory today explains profits (Naples and Aslanbeigui, 1996). There is no incentive to produce new knowledge in perfect markets – the possibility of appropriating the fruits of new knowledge is absent. By letting new knowledge enter the system like "manna from heaven", the very engine of growth – the search for new knowledge which creates imperfect competition – is excluded from mainstream theory. For this reason, an understanding of how different degrees of imperfect competition is caused by conditions of production is at the very core of any understanding of economic growth. Economic theory, however, does not have a relevant theory of production, and of the role of human knowledge in this process. Thorstein Veblen in his "The preconceptions of economic science" says it this way: "To sum up: classical economics, having primarily to do with the pecuniary side of life, is a theory of the process of valuation" (Veblen, 1919). Production is left out. In the words of Werner Sombart: "There is like a tacit agreement in (the profession) that one has reached the conviction that the science of economic life, in so far as this is studied by the economics profession, is a science of the circulation and distribution of goods" (Sombart, 1928).

Did Adam Smith believe that the invisible hand would produce factor-price equalization? Hardly. In *The Theory of Moral Sentiments* Smith explains how the invisible hand promotes income distribution. However, to a modern ear, his arguments are hardly convincing. Smith bases his argument on the principle that the rich have a limited capacity to consume, and therefore are forced to share with the poor: "It is to no purpose, that the proud and unfeeling landlord views his extensive fields, and without a thought for the wants of his brethren, in imagination consumes himself the whole harvest that grows upon them. The homely and vulgar proverb, that the eye is larger than the belly, was never more fully verified than with regard to him. The capacity of his stomach bears no proportion to the immensity of his desires … The rest he is obliged to distribute … The rich … consume only little more than the poor. They are led by an invisible hand to make nearly the same distribution of the necessaries of life, which would have been made, had the earth been divided into equal portions among its inhabitants …" (Smith, 1812).

10. The loss of the state and the revenge of the centaur

One of the most moving paintings of the Renaissance is Sandro Botticelli's *Pallas and the Centaur*, painted in the late 1480s. This work shows Pallas – the ancient goddess of wisdom – mildly and somewhat condescendingly caressing the head of a centaur, symbolising Man's past of ignorance and violence. The expression of embarrassment on the centaur's face is precious – he is so obviously ashamed of his wild and ignorant past. The symbolism – the victory of reason, wisdom and peace – comes across in an atmosphere densely filled with harmony, a feature which makes Botticelli's works so unique.

The economists of that time – and pre-Smithian economists in general – seem to have been aware of this ongoing battle between the wisdom and peace of Pallas and the violent ignorance of the centaur. Channeling the passions and energies of the centaur into productive – rather than destructive – activities was a main challenge of the Renaissance (Hirschman, 1977). This was a matter which could not be left to any self-organising invisible hand. The prominent and influential German economist J.F. von Pfeiffer (1715–1787) – an ardent anti-physiocrat – puts it this way: "You can make of human beings what you want. The way he is governed commends Man to good, or to evil. The advantage of the nation must be the advantage of its members. He who separates these advantages is an ignorant who damages the public body (*Staatskörper*)" (von Pfeiffer, 1777).

This paragraph in Pfeiffer summarises two important aspects of the pre-Smithian development state. The quality of the "system" makes Man good or evil, and as in Chandler's works on managerial capitalism, there is a conscious and visible hand – Man's wit and will – which holds this system together. The second point, which Pfeiffer saw as being connected, belies the present Anglo-Saxon notion that pre-Smithian economics – and especially German cameralism – collectivistically subdued the interest of the individual to the interest of the State. Just as in the quote from the early Adam Smith on the cover of this paper, the overall growth of the system prevented the need for any static concerns for Pareto optimality: "The incoming tide lifts all boats".

The invisible hand starts working when conditions have been created bringing the vested interests looking for private rate of return in line with the interests of the public rate of return – when, like Pfeiffer says, what is in the interest of the individual also is in the interest of the collectivity. This happens when a critical mass of labour in a nation is employed in activities subject to increasing returns, and when the fruits of these increasing returns are allowed to filter out, to a large extent, as higher monetary wages inside the producing nation, rather than as lowered prices for foreign customers. In this way the core of society escapes from the static economics of zero-sum games: where the gain of one individual is the loss of another. Such activities – which "raise all boats" – are the starting point of what the historians of technology call the process of "historical snowballing" – of the virtuous circles of development. Under such conditions – in increasing return activities and when appropriate mechanisms for the distribution of dynamic rents have been established – the saying attributed to Alfred P. Sloan is true to a surprising extent: "What is good for General Motors is good for the United States." In Appendices 1 and 2 we have outlined (Reinert, 1980) the self-reinforcing virtuous and vicious circles of development and underdevelopment – of "historical snowballing" and the lack of it – as described in this paper.

The metaphor of "the invisible hand" was frequently used by Adam Smith in his works on astronomy and in *The Theory of Moral Sentiments*. It is only once mentioned in

The Wealth of Nations – and in a context which, if read in the perspective of the preceding chapters of this paper, can be taken to indicate an awareness of just such a process of historical snowballing. The chapter in question (Chapter II of Book IV) starts with a description of how protective duties have created a number of industries in Great Britain. Smith thereafter describes a centripetal system whereby merchants – because they prefer to trade closer to home – bring their capital there. This argument is really the description of the start of a virtuous circle. It is this tendency, for reasons of risk/distance, of capitalists to support domestic rather than foreign industry – implicitly assuming that such an industry exists – which is the starting point of the beneficial work of the invisible hand in Smith's system. If one reads the whole chapter, it can be argued that Smith uses the "invisible hand" in the context of historical snowballing. But it is most important to keep in mind that the starting point of this system is – in Smith's narrative – the fact that all industries of Great Britain were created by mercantilist protectionism.

The negative counterpart of historical snowballing – rendered in Appendix 2 – produces poverty, violence and ignorance. In the 1490s, Botticelli – who was also a novelist – experienced the Renaissance backlash of Savonarola's violent revolution against the Medicis in Florence, when the books authored by him were burned. In the late twentieth century we are also experiencing the comeback of the centaur – of Man's ignorant and violent past: in Somalia and Liberia the State as a civilizing agent, for all practical purposes, has ceased to exist. In Rwanda and Burundi tribal wars commit mutual genocide. A similar "system of unreason" bothered Keynes during the First World War: "When reason dies, monsters are born." No doubt these processes are partly produced by diminishing returns in agriculture in a situation of population pressure, when there is no employment outside the diminishing return sector. In this case, the failure of neo-classical economics to distinguish between increasing and diminishing return activities seems to be closely linked to the failure of the international community to improve the situation.

This retrogression of civilisation suggests the fragility of the veneer of what we would call a civilized society which holds the primitive centaur at bay. Today seemingly more and more countries are threatened by the process of "Somalisation" – the return to power of what the international press describingly labels as "war lords." The same development threatens part of the former communist nations. In Russia we can only be baffled by the fact that a notoriously inefficient planned economy managed to produce a GNP per capita which was clearly considerable higher than what the "free" market is able to produce today. We probably cannot continue to explain this through the new science of "transitology" for much longer. This proves the point of nineteenth century mainstream US and German economics: having a relatively inefficient industrial sector – in the process of being educated to graduate into participation in a bigger market – is infinitely better than not having an industrial sector at all.

There is no doubt that Renaissance economists would have put together a very different strategy for the transition of the former communist nations from that which has been done in the 1990s: above all they would have established an appropriate legal system and adopted long-term mechanisms to save and upgrade the manufacturing industries. Deindustrialising nations is equal to removing most of the increasing return activities which increase the common weal system-wide – the activities which not only create isolated pockets of welfare. Reducing nations to resource-based activities (subject to diminishing returns) and to a traditional service sector only is tantamount to "bombing them back to the Stone Age." Today economic policy too often lets the ideological criterion of a nation's "openness" to foreign imports overrule the concern for keeping increasing return activities in business. This not only reduces local GNP and world welfare; such a policy also creates the kind of nature-based poverty which is the main threat to global sustainability. People and nations who are not in the position to make a living from their knowledge may easily end up with no other alternatives for survival than making a living raping the environment.

And these retrogressing countries are "market economies." It is difficult to blame the state of affairs on excessive government intervention or on their "having got the prices wrong". Cohn's nineteenth century explanation, essentially that we have unlearned that societies have to go through a process of Renaissance-type State building, is still fundamentally correct. We argue that a strong State – leading a nation into increasing return activities – historically has been an obligatory passage point in the development of any nation. If this is the case, to what extent does a world economic order based on an ahistorical and atomistic neo-classical economic theory – with its thesis of futility, perversity and jeopardy – contribute to the "barbarisation" which we are witnessing? In our view, quite a lot. We see the present *zeitgeist* as being a product of a few very fundamental influences – of a "handful of metaphors", to use McCloskey's term. We are still victims of the excesses of Adam Smith's (at the time justified) criticism of a mercantilism which had lost much of its original content and had degenerated into protecting monopolies rather than creating and protecting knowledge. Our ideas are still locked into a pattern shaped by a 100-year fight with communism, when the Utopia of communism fought the Utopia of factor price equalisation – a fight which led to the demise of all alternative economic theories after the Second World War.

The glorification of Adam Smith's primitive faith in the invisible hand of Providence – rather than in the rational will of Man – is in our view the product of a most unfortunate combination of events: the assumptions needed in order to turn Adam Smith into an unassailable theoretical bastion against communism coincided fully with the assumptions which were needed in order to convert economics into mathematics. In a world where the increasing disparities between rich and poor are clearly attributable to imperfect knowledge, imperfect competition and increasing returns, the assumption of perfect competition is powerfully cemented. The welfare of the rich nations is clearly a product of a dynamic "industry rent" which, in the short term, is not hurt by neo-classical adjustment policies. However, the same adjustment policies in a relatively backward economy will kill off what little there is of advanced economic activities in these nations – through what we have elsewhere called the Vanek effect – and destroy welfare.

The World Bank and the IMF tend to use the criterion of "openness of the economy" as the main criterion for success. Clearly an advanced nation with high skills is better off in an open economy than in a closed one. A favorite example is the success of Chile as an open economy – after a century of natural and State-sponsored protection (including under Pinochet). To this Friedrich List and the nineteenth century US economists would have unanimously responded: of course, Chile's advanced economy – especially when seen in relation to those of her neighbours – was mature to graduate into the world economy. But "Openness" as a criterion for success is meaningless without a reference to the degree of skills contained in a nation's exports.

"If the rod be bent too much one way, says the proverb, in order to make it straight you must bend it as much the other", says Adam Smith (when discussing the French physiocrats). This proverbial maxim seems to apply to the general attitude towards the State after the fall of the planning paradigm: since the market economy was clearly "wrong" and is dead, we can continue to assume that markets must be perfect and atomistic. In such a framework it is difficult to find a place for the State in the promotion of economic development. It is not clear today how a reasonable balance can be restored. It is a very long way from the appearance of theoretical "toy models" showing the importance of increasing returns – as we see today – to a World Bank interference with the market through a systematic nourishing and protection of such activities in the Third World. The ideological barriers seem difficult to overcome. When science is wrong, the burden is unequally distributed. During the centuries, when bleeding the patient was a cure-all in the medical science, the weakest were the ones whose situation deteriorated the most. Similarly, in a world economic order based on an atomistic economic theory void of human institutions, on perfect competition and the absence of increasing returns, where "deregulation" and "openness" to imports are seen as a cure-all, the poorest nations are again the ones who suffer.

We are now again facing a battle which will prove to be at least as long and unrelenting as Keynes' battle against the monetary orthodoxy. Many nations of the world are trapped in an "underdevelopment equilibrium" which is not unlike the "unemployment equilibrium" of the interwar period. To get the world out of "the unemployment equilibrium", Keynes had to slay the dragon defending the gold standard. Belatedly, economists came to recognize, with Keynes, that national welfare can be positively influenced by monetary stimuli: the thesis of futility, perversity and jeopardy had been proved wrong.

What is the formula to get a large part of the world population out of this "poverty equilibrium"? E.A.G. Robinson recalls the "burning sense of the world's stupidities" which animated Keynes as a lecturer on the economic situation of his day[29]. According to Keynes, slayer of the foregoing dragon, the recipe for gaining long-term influence in the face of massive theoretical disagreement is "violent and relentless truth-telling", which will work "even if slowly"[30]. This time the battle is carried inside the "black box" of economics, in order to show that the contents of the black box – the "quality" and diversity of the activities in which a nation is engaged – are perhaps the main determinant of the standard of living of nations. In addition to this, a relatively equitable income distribution is an indispensable factor, but income distribution without the nation being in the right activities is a futile exercise. As previously mentioned, economic development should be seen as the product of a set of "reactants", all of which have to be present in order to set off the desired reaction leading into "autocatalytic" – self-reinforcing – systems. The

[29] Quoted in Skidelsky and Keynes, 1995, p. 652.
[30] Quoted in Skidelsky and Keynes, 1995, p. 21.

dragon which has to be slain is the dragon defending the assumptions of perfect information, perfect competition and constant returns to scale – a set of assumptions which must be got rid of *en bloc* – not cautiously investigated one by one and then put back into the theory as is done in new growth theory.

The result will, in my view, confirm the common sense of Daniel Raymond's 1820 thesis on the US economy updated to the global economy: the factors which determine the differences in standard of living between nations are essentially the same factors which determine the differences in standard of living within nations: levels of knowledge and skill which create successions of temporary oligopoly power based on dynamic imperfect competition. However, the spread effects of the leading sectors are such that the standards of living of the vast majority of wage earners of a nation, in the traditional service sector (barbers, bus drivers etc.) – whose efficiency is virtually the same in rich and poor nations – are determined by the skill level of the export sector. A Bolivian barber and bus driver are just as efficient as their Norwegian or German counterparts, but the systemic effects of the world economy is such that their real wages are just a fraction of that of their First World counterparts. This is a result of what we have called the collusive spread of the benefits from technological change – the fact that these benefits in large part are taken out as higher real wages in the producing countries rather than being distributed in the classical way, as lowered prices to the world markets.

For this reason, a more equitable distribution of world income cannot be achieved by distributing income as such – which inevitably will result in putting whole nations on the dole. A better world income distribution can only be achieved by distributing production of skill-intensive "high quality" activities – those which produce systemic feedback systems in the local labour market – to poor countries. This is also the activity-specific lesson from The Asian Tigers. This is a dynamic consideration beyond any concern of static "Pareto optimality" – by increasing the skills of the "laggard" countries by distributing production, they will buy more, not less, from the First World. This was the point made by the defenders of the nineteenth century "American System of Manufacturing" in their discussions with English economists: the US demand for imports would increase as a result of more industrialisation, and above all, this demand would be upgraded to more skill-intensive articles. They proved to be right, and proved their point that mutually optimal solutions – what Henry Carey called the harmony of interests – in the case of asymmetrical economic development, can only be found with the help of a visible hand of the State, which makes a conscious economic policy based on theories which have internalised the causes of uneven economic growth.

Successful State interventions have created dynamic imperfect competition – a process of dynamic and collective national rent-seeking – which increases enormously the size of the pie. The State has given temporary help, and with clear strings attached. Unsuccessful State interventions may at a first glance look similar to the successful ones, e.g. because also they protect national manufacturing industries. However, the less successful State interventions – as in India and many Latin American nations – have created static rent-seeking through relatively permanent protection with no strings attached, leading to a "shallow" industrialisation, to inefficient monopolies with a limited potential to increase the pie. In spite of their inefficiencies, however, it is important to keep in mind that a relatively inefficient industrial sector produces a much higher GNP than having no industrial sector at all – this is one of the lessons of the "transitology" of former communist states. Deindustrialising inefficient nations is not a viable option if one has a minimum concern for human welfare. This dilemma is very similar to that facing Germany in the 1830s; a situation with more than 30 small states, each with an extremely protective tariff. The solution in Germany was a first stage which removed the tariff between the 30 German states, and created an enormous competition among nations of fairly similar skill levels. Within this symmetrical trade pattern the nation continued to build skills, finally to "graduate" to compete openly in the world markets. In this way the State completes its most important historical function – to establish the nation solidly in economic activities subject to increasing returns, and to set up a dynamic national system where innovations are an essential by-product of the way its national industry competes.

Appendix 1

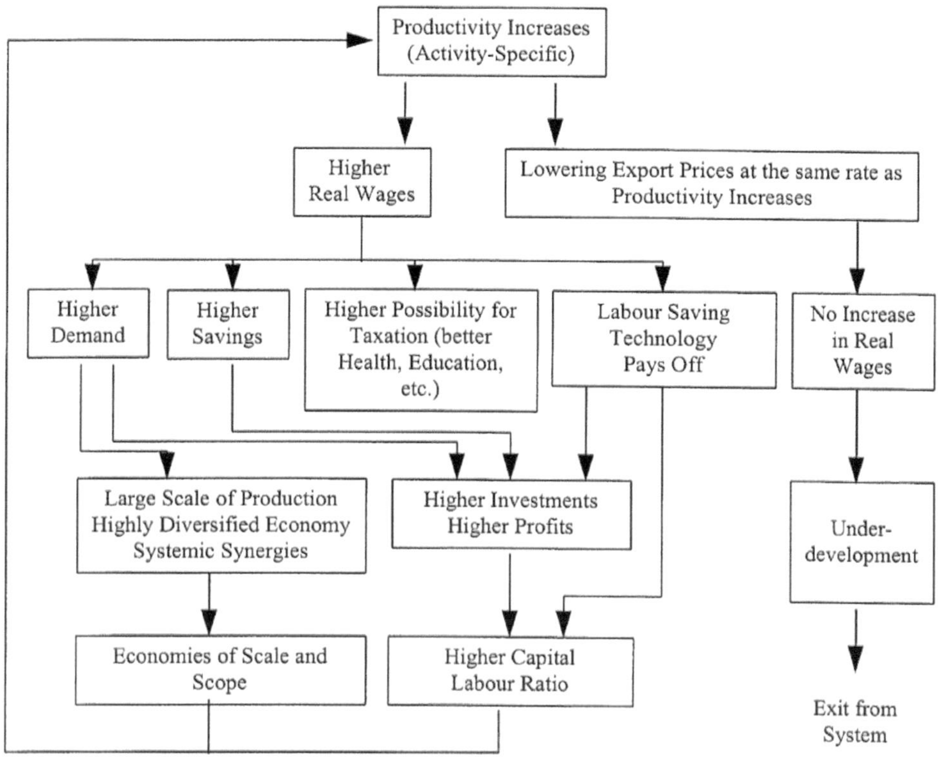

Note: In a closed system, with constant employment rate, the only way GNP per capita can grow is through the "Virtuous Circle." However, the system can be cut-off at any one point, e.g., if higher demand goes to foreign goods alone, the circle will break.

Source: Reinert (1980, p. 39).

Figure A1 The "virtuous" circle of economic development.

Appendix 2

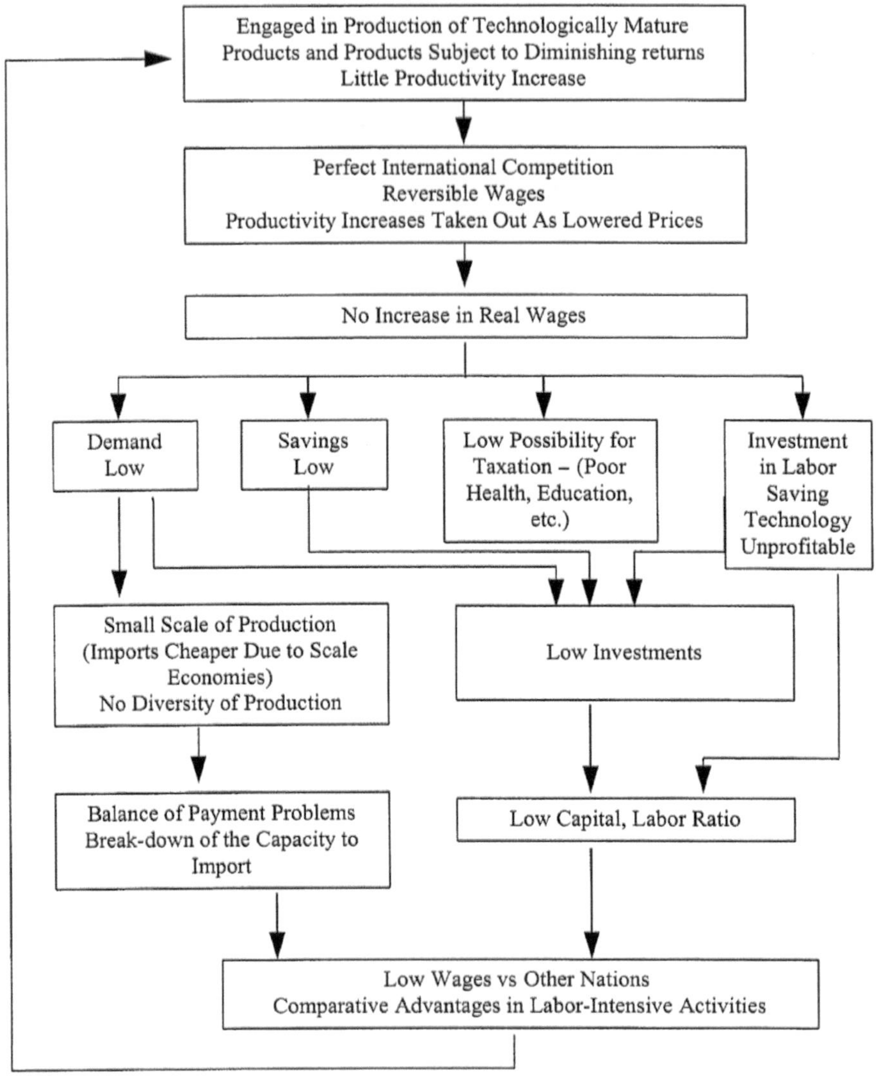

Note: It is futile to attack the system at any one point, e.g. increasing investment when wages are still low and demand is absent. An instance of this is poor capital utilisation and excess capacity in Latin American LDCs.

Source: Reinert (1980, p. 41).

Figure A2 The "vicious" circle of economic underdevelopment.

References and further reading

Amsden, A. (1989), *Asia's Next Giant: South Korea and Late Industrialization*, Oxford University Press, New York, NY.

Arthur, W.B. (1990), "Positive feedbacks in the economy", *Scientific American*, February, pp. 80–5.

Backhaus, J. (Ed.) (1996), *Werner Sombart – Social Scientist*, Metropolis Verlag, Marburg.

Bacon, F. (n.d. (1930s?)), "New Atlantis", in Andrews, C.M. (Ed.), *Famous Utopias*, Tudor Publishing, New York, NY, p. 272.

Barro, R.J. and Sala-i-Martin, X. (1995), *Economic Growth*, McGraw-Hill, New York, NY, p. xvi.

Baumol, W. (1952), *Welfare Economics and the Theory of the State*, Longmans, Green, London, pp. 153–4.

Bijker, W. (1995), *Of Bicycles, Bakelites, and Bulbs. Towards a Theory of Sociotechnical Change*, MIT Press, Cambridge, MA.

Bijker, W., Hughes, T.P. and Pinch, T. (Eds) (1989), *The Social Construction of Technological Systems*, MIT Press, Cambridge, MA.

Botero, G. (1590), *Delle Cause della Grandezza delle Città*, Vicenzio Pellagalo, Rome.

Bücher, K. (1918–19), *Die Entstehung der Volkswirtschaft* (i.e. "The Emergence of National Economies"), Laupp, Tübingen, 2 Vols.

Canina, A. (1937), *Il Pensiero Finanziario di Niccolò Machiavelli*, Zanichelli, Bologna, p. 168.

Carey, H. (1851), *Harmony of Interests*, Skinner, Philadelphia.

Chandler, A. (1977), *The Visible Hand: The Managerial Revolution in American Business*, Harvard University Press, Cambridge, MA.

Chandler, A. (1990), *Scale and Scope: The Dynamics of Industrial Capitalism*, Harvard University Press, Cambridge, MA.

Clément, P. (Ed.) (1861–1872), *Lettres, Instructions et Mémoires de Colbert*, Paris, Imprimerie Impériale/Imprimerie Nationale, 7 Vols. in 10 + 1 Volume "Errata Général et Table Analytique."

Cohn, G. (1895), *The Science of Finance*, translated by Thorstein Veblen, Economic Studies of the University of Chicago, No. 1, University of Chicago Press, Chicago, IL.

Coquelin and Guillaumin (1854), *Dictionnaire de l'Économie Politique*, Guillaumin & Hachette, Paris, p. 610.

Crother, J.G. (1960), *Francis Bacon, The First Statesman of Science*, Cresset Press, London, p. 17.

Curtis, F. (1904), *The Republican Party. A History of its Fifty Years' Existence and a Record of its Measures and Leaders 1854–1904*, Vol. 1, 2 Vols, Putnam, New York, NY.

De Long, B. and Summers, L. (1991), "Equipment investment and economic growth", in *Quarterly Journal of Economics*, Vol. 106, May, pp. 445–502.

Deutsch, K. (1969), *Nationalism and its Alternatives*, Knopf, New York, NY, p. 3.

Einaudi, L. (1942), "Del concetto dello 'stato fattore di produzione', e delle sue relazioni col teorema del risparmio dall'imposta", Estratto dal *Giornale degli Economisti e Annali di Economia*, CEDAM, Padova.

Fukuyama, F. (1995), *Trust*, Free Press, New York, NY.

Fuz, J.K. (1952), *Welfare Economics in English Utopias from Francis Bacon to Adam Smith*, Martinius Nijhoff, The Hague, p. 1.

Gootenberg, P. (1989), *Between Silver and Guano, Commercial Policy and the State in Post-independence Peru*, Princeton University Press, Princeton.

Graham, F. (1923), "Some aspects of protection further considered", *Quarterly Journal of Economics*, Vol. 37, pp. 199–227.

Grossman, G.M. (Ed.) (1992), *Imperfect Competition and International Trade*, MIT Press, Cambridge, MA.

Helpmann, E. and Krugman, P. (1985), *Market Structure and Foreign Trade*, MIT Press, Cambridge, MA.

Hely-Hutchinson, J. (1779), *The Commercial Restraints of Ireland Considered*, William Hallhead, Dublin.

Hirschman, A.O. (1958), *The Strategy of Economic Development*, Yale University Press, New Haven.

Hirschman, A.O. (1977), *The Passions and the Interests*, Princeton University Press, Princeton.

Hirschman, A.O. (1991), *The Rhetoric of Reaction. Perversity, Futility, Jeopardy*, Harvard University Press, Cambridge, MA.

King, C. (1721), *The British Merchant or Commerce Preserv'd*, John Darby, London, 3 Vols, Vol. 1, p. 3.
Krugman, P. (Ed.) (1986), *Strategic Trade Policy and the New International Economics*, MIT Press, Cambridge, MA.
Krugman, P. (1990), *Rethinking International Trade*, MIT Press, Cambridge, MA, p. 4.
Lawson, T. (1989), "Abstraction, tendencies and stylised facts: a realist approach to economic analysis", in Lawson, T., Gabriel Palma, J. and Sender, J. (Eds), *Kaldor's Political Economy*, Academic Press, London.
Lazonick, W. (1991), *Business Organization and the Myth of the Market*, Cambridge University Press, Cambridge.
Leibniz, G.W. (1992), "Society and economy" (1617), reprinted in *Fidelio*, Vol. 1 No. 3, Fall, p. 54.
Logan, J.A. (1886), *The Great Conspiracy, its Origin and History*, Hart, New York, NY, p. 30.
Lucas, R. Jr (1988), "On the mechanics of economic development", *Journal of Monetary Economics*, Vol. 22, pp. 3–42.
Lucas, R. Jr (1993), "Making a miracle", *Econometrica*, Vol. 61, pp. 251–72.
Lundvall, B.-Å. (Ed.) (1992), *National Systems of Innovation*, Pinter, London.
Lundvall, B.-Å. (1994), *The Learning Economy – Challenges to Economic Theory and Policy*, paper presented at the EAEPE-Conference, Copenhagen, October.
McCraw, T. (1992), "The trouble with Adam Smith", *The American Scholar*, Vol. 61 No. 3, Summer, p. 364.
McEvoy, C. (1994), *Un proyecto nacional en el siglo XIX, Manuel Prado y su visión del Perú*, Universidad Católica, Lima.
Malynes, G. (1622), *The Maintenance of Free Trade, According to the Three Essentiall (sic) Parts . . . Commodities, Moneys and Exchange of Moneys*, William Sheffard, London.
Malynes, G. (1623), *The Center of the Circle of Commerce, or A Refutation of a Treatise, lately published by E.M.*, Nicholas Bourne, London.
Marshall, A. (1890), *Principles of Economics*, Macmillan, London, p. 452.
Mervin, L. (1981), *Vitamin C*, Thorsons Publishers, Willingborough, pp. 14–15.
Misselden, E. (1622), *Free Trade and the Meanes (sic) to Make Trade Flourish*, Simon Waterson, London.
Misselden, E. (1623), *The Circle of Commerce or the Ballance (sic) of Trade*, Nicholas Bourne, London.
Müller, A. (1809), *Elemente der Staatskunst*, Vol. 5, Sander, Berlin.
Müller, K., Schepers, H. and Totok, W. (Eds) (1973), *Studia Leibniziana Supplementa*, Vol XII, Band 1, Franz Steiner Verlag, Wiesbaden, p. 234.
Namslau, G. (1932), "Rechtfertigung des Staates bei Christian Wolff", in Kraus, H. (Ed.), *Internationale Rechtliche Abhandlungen*, Dr. W. Rothschild, Berlin, p. 96.
Naples, M. and Aslanbeigui, N. (1996), "What does determine the profit rate? The neo-classical theories presented in introductory textbooks", in *Cambridge Journal of Economics*, Vol. 20, pp. 53–71.
Nelson, R. (Ed.) (1993), *National Innovation Systems*, Oxford University Press, New York, NY.
Nelson, R. (1995), "Recent evolutionary theorizing about economic change", *The Journal of Economic Literature*, Vol. XXXIII No. 1, March, pp. 58–9.
Odigari, H. and Gota, A. (1993), "The Japanese innovation system: past, present and future", in Nelson, R.R. (Ed.), *National Innovation Systems. A Comparative Analyisis*, Oxford University Press, New York, NY.
Pierce, C.S. (1867), Hartshorne, C. and Weiss, P. (Eds) *Collected Papers of Charles Sanders Pierce,* Harvard University Press, Cambridge, MA.
Polanyi, K. (1957), *The Great Transformation, the Political and Economic Origins of our Time* (1944), Beacon Press, Boston, MA.
Porter, M. (1990), *The Competitive Advantage of Nations*, Macmillan, London.
Raymond, D. (1820), *Principles of Political Economy*, Fielding Lucas, Baltimore, MD.
Reinert, E. (1980), *International Trade and the Economic Mechanisms of Underdevelopment*, University Microfilm, Ann Arbor, MI.

Reinert, E.S. (1994), "Catching-up from way behind, a Third World view perspective on First World history", in Fagerberg, J. *et al.*, *The Dynamics of Technology, Trade, and Growth,* Edward Elgar, London.

Reinert, E.S. (1995), "Competitiveness and its predecessors – a 500-year cross-national perspective", *Structural Change and Economic Dynamics,* Vol. 6, pp. 23–42.

Reinert, E. (1996), "Raw materials in the history of economic policy; or, why List (the Protectionist) and Cobden (the Free Trader) both agreed on free trade in corn", paper presented at the conference on the Repeal of the Corn Laws, Manchester, March.

Reinert, E. and Daastøl, A. (1995), "Exploring the Genesis of economic innovations: the religious gestalt-switch and the duty to invent as preconditions for economic growth", Norwegian Institute of Foreign Affairs (NUPI), Working Paper No. 540, December.

Roscher, W. (1882), *Principles of Political Economy,* Callaghan, Chicago, IL.

Schumpeter (1951), *History of Economic Analysis,* Oxford University Press, New York, pp. 258–9.

Serra, A. (1613), *Breve trattato delle cause che possono far abbondare li regni d'oro e argento dove non sono miniere,* Lazzaro Scoriggio, Naples.

Skildelsky, R. and Keynes, J.M. (1995), *The Economist as Saviour 1920–1937,* Vol. 2, Penguin, Harmondsworth.

Smith, A. (1976), *The Wealth of Nations* (1776), University of Chicago Press, Chicago, IL.

Smith, A. (1812), *The Theory of Moral Sentiments,* in *The Collected Works of Adam Smith,* Cadell and Davies, London, Vol. 1, p. 317–18.

Sombart, W. (1913a), "Krieg und Kapitalismus", *Studien der Entwicklungsgeschichte des modernen Kapitalismus,* Duncker und Humblot, München and Leipzig.

Sombart, W. (1913b), "Luxus und Kapitalismus", *Studien der Entwicklungsgeschichte des modernen Kapitalismus,* Duncker und Humblot, München and Leipzig.

Sombart, W. (1928), *Der moderne Kapitalismus, Vol. 2: Das europäische Wirtschaftsleben im Zeitalter des Frühkapitalismus,* Duncker & Humblot, München and Leipzig, p. 917.

Veblen, T. (1919), "The preconceptions of economic science", in *The Place of Science in Modern Civilisation and other Essays,* Huebsch, New York, NY, p. 144.

Villner, K. (1986), *Blod, Kryddor och Sott,* Carlsson Bokförlag, Stockholm, pp. 110–13.

Viner, J. (1937), *Studies in the Theory of International Trade,* Harper, New York, NY, p. 473.

Viner, J. (1972), *The Role of Providence in the Social Order. An Essay in Intellectual History,* American Philosophical Society, Philadelphia.

von Humbolt, W. (1996), *The Sphere and Duties of Government* (1854, German original in 1852), Thoemmes Press, Bristol, pp. 19, 22.

von Pfeiffer, J.F. (1777), *Lehrbegriff sämtlicher öconomischer und Cameralwissenschaften,* Schwan, Mannheim, Vol. 3 Tome 1 (Des dritten Bandes erster Teil), p. 2.

Wade, R. (1990), *Governing the Market. Economic Theory and the Role of Government in East Asian Industrialization,* Princeton University Press, Princeton, NJ.

Whatley, G. (1774), *Principles of Trade. Fredom (sic) and Protection are its best Suport(sic): Industry, the only Means to render Manufactures cheap,* Brotherton and Sewill, London.

Wiebe, B., Hughes, T.P. and Pinch, T. (Eds) (1989), *The Social Construction of Technological Systems,* MIT Press, Cambridge, MA.

World Bank (1993), *The East Asian Miracle, Economic Growth and Public Policy,* Oxford University Press, New York, NY.

Chapter Three

A BRIEF INTRODUCTION TO VEIT LUDWIG VON SECKENDORFF (1626–1692)

Erik S. Reinert

Abstract

Veit Ludwig von Seckendorff is widely regarded as the 'founder' of early economics in Germany, of Cameralism. Having survived the horrors of the Thirty Years' War and the resulting economic, political, and moral break-down of society, Seckendorff conceived of a holistic science of public administration fit to reconstruct the more than 300 independent German principalities recognized by the Peace of Westphalia. The science he envisioned was both theoretical and practical, covering all the needs of a small principality. The same union of active and contemplative characterizes Seckendorff's own life, as he devoted himself both to administrating the Court of Gotha and the University of Halle, both to write an "owner's handbook" to small principalities and one of the most celebrated defenses of Lutheranism. This introduction will explore how these many facets came together in the figure of Seckendorff, what his main influences were, and how the historical context helped shape his writings.

Keywords: Seckendorff, Veit Ludwig von (1626–1692), Germany, history of economic thought

JEL Classification: B11, N00

1. Introduction

Germany has often been referred to as 'eine verspätete Nation'—a delayed nation—in the historiography of the country. This 'lateness', usually thought of in social and political terms, is also reflected in the development of economics and the neighbouring social sciences. The first uniquely German economic tradition, known as cameralism after the *Kammer* or provincial treasury of German principalities, only emerged after the 1648 Peace of Westphalia with the writings of Veit Ludwig von Seckendorff. Economic and related social sciences developed early in Italy with Giovanni Botero (1588) and Antonio Serra (1613), in France with Barthélemy Laffemas (1598) and Antoine de Montchretien

(1615) and in England with writers such as John Hales (1549) and particularly Francis Bacon (1561–1626). Bacon was the first scientist to create a strong focus on learning and innovation (e.g. his 'Essay on Innovation' and 'Essay on Human Learning'). A similar emphasis on innovation and learning also appears later in the German context, principally in the works of Gottfried Wilhelm Leibniz (1646–1716) and Christian Wolff (1679–1754) (Reinert and Daastøl, 1997).

It has been argued that economics did not develop in the rich states and nations as a way to get richer, but rather as a science of imitating the productive structure of the successful nations in laggard areas. Venice and the Dutch Republic offered the ideal models to emulate, while Spain, whose deindustrialization and gradual decline was increasingly evident from the 1550s onwards, remained the one to avoid throughout the early modern period (Laspeyres, 1863/1961; Perrotta, 1993; Reinert and Reinert, 2003; Reinert, 2004; Reinert and Reinert, 2005). In this picture, Veit Ludwig von Seckendorff—the 'Adam Smith of Cameralism' (Small, 1909)—follows the typical pattern. Giovanni Botero had attempted to explain what caused wealth by studying the economic structures of wealthy cities in his seminal 1588 *Delle cause della grandezza delle città* and his subsequent 1589 *Della ragion di stato*, and Antonio Serra's 1613 *Breve trattato* was an attempt to make Naples wealthy by imitating the economic structure of Venice, and Seckendorff also looks abroad for inspiration. Seckendorff's writings on economics and economic policy appear mainly in the 1665 *Additiones* to his main work *Der Teutsche Fürstenstaat*, written, tellingly, after a visit to the Dutch Republic.

2. The Thirty Years' War and the context of Seckendorff's writings

Seckendorff's life and work mainly unfold in Thuringia, in the geographical centre of present Germany, in what sometimes is referred to as 'the central cultural province of Germany' ("Die mitteldeutsche Kulturprovinz"). Thuringia has historically been a melting pot of the German tribes, both culturally and in terms of language development, and thus constitutes an area with a large cultural diversity. The Thuringian city of Weimar was a cultural center long before Goethe, Schiller, and the later Bauhaus movement made it famous. In Seckendorff's times, the province was also at the crossroads of international influences. At the court in Dresden and in other smaller Thuringian courts, Italian influences were particularly strong— in music, theatre, and opera, for example, the interplay of German and Italian traditions produced great results. In nearby Mannheim and Kassel, English influences were more prevalent, in art, in music, and in alchemy (Yates, 1999). All in all, 17th century Thuringia exemplified the crossroads of diversity which no doubt have been a key factor in Europe's cultural, intellectual and economic development. It contained a large number of cities and city-states with a diverse topography, and the bourgeoisie of the cities were hard-working. Thus, the local peasants enjoyed an unusual degree of freedom and absence of serfdom from relatively early on.

Seckendorff's times were, however, violent and extremely difficult for Germany. The Thirty Years' War (1618–1648) was a religious war, initially intra-German, which gradually came to involve several European powers at the time, including Spain, France,

Denmark and Sweden. The war had no winner, but it became obvious to a number of German intellectuals of the next generation that the real loser was civilized society as such. When Seckendorff died at the age of 66, the armies of Louis the XIV of France had recently utterly destroyed one German state, the Palatinate (*Pfalz*). In between, there were wars with the Turks, and two more wars with France that had led to the loss of Strasbourg, where Seckendorff had studied. Seckendorff's conception of Cameralism can, in our view, not be properly understood outside this context of a simultaneous reconstruction of a civilized society and of what would today be called 'failed states', states where economic life and basic institutions had to be built, virtually from scratch. The 'natural order' of the day was barbarism.

The Thirty Years' War had indeed left Germany 'an economic wasteland' (Inama-Sternegg, 1864). The long war and the presence of foreign troops had created massive destruction throughout the German principalities, cities had been destroyed and thousands of villages burnt. On top of this, wide-scale deforestation in order to export wood made the countryside reflect the conditions of the cities. The agricultural base of the region had been largely destroyed, causing several famines that added to the mounting death-toll. It has been estimated that between half and two thirds of the German population died during the war and in its immediate aftermath, or an incredible 12–13 million dead.[1] Lawlessness disrupted trade between city and country, forced recruitments led to a scarcity of workers, and lack of capital, falling prices of agricultural products and agricultural land, heavy taxation, frequent payments of customs duties in internal trade, debasement of coinage, loss of law and security, and rampant vagrancy were just some of the many factors that came together to dismantle German economy and society. Contemporary sources indicate that this resulted in increasing apathy, in a general reduction in the number of educated people, and in the end a growth of superstition—in other words, the Thirty Years' War caused widespread 'primitivization' and 'retrogression' in the German territories. These losses meant Germany was unable to compete with even the most rudimentary foreign imports from England and Holland, causing further deindustrialization, unemployment, and poverty. To enumerate one such example, the decline of textile production in Osnabrück in the period following the war elucidates a larger trend:

1656 189 masters produce 3.156 pieces of cloth
1672 130 masters produce 2.270 pieces of cloth
1679 104 masters produce 1.280 pieces of cloth
1686 60 masters produce 886 pieces of cloth
1693 50 masters produce 544 pieces of cloth

Berthold Brecht powerfully dramatized the losses incurred by this war in his *Mother Courage*.

---

1 Inama-Sternegg adds up local accounts and finds these estimates plausible.

Even in the larger cities spared from most of the violence of the war, such as Hamburg, Bremen and Lübeck, the nearby fighting had devastating consequences. The war, for example, sealed the fate of the once proud Hansa traders, their name kept only 'as a precious relic' (Inama-Sternegg). The Danes had begun dominating the Hansa already in the 1620s, but their power was broken completely by the end of the Thirty Years' War. It was at this time that the Dutch Republic rose to become the center of Northern European economic hegemony, contested only by the English.

The Thuringian city of Erfurt, however, located as it was in the middle of the German theatre of war, was among those hardest hit. The surrounding counties suffered immense destruction as well; the former county of Henneberg saw 19 of its villages destroyed, and it would take almost 200 years before the population and wealth of the region had been brought back to the 1634, pre-war, level.

YEAR	1634	1649	1849
Families	1773	316	1916
Houses	1717	627	1558
Cows	1402	244	1994
Horses	485	73	107
Sheep	4616	–	4596
Goats	158	26	286

Source: 'Denkwürdigkeiten aus Frankens und Thüringens Geschichte und Statistik', quoted by Inama-Sternegg.

By war's end, the Holy Roman Empire was left in political shambles, divided into *more than 300 independent German states*: 'large and small; partly secular, partly ecclesiastical; partly monarchies, partly republics; partly aristocratic, partly democratic; which all of them had full sovereignty, and—when they felt strong enough—could take foreign trade in their own hands, make alliances and wage war' (Inama-Sternegg). This economic fragmentation was still to be cursed by Friedrich List in the 1840s, he referred to the German *Kleinstaaterei* although the number of states by then were down to less than 40.

3. Secckendorff's life

Veit Ludwig von Seckendorff[2] descended from a family of Franconian knights, and was proud of his heritage. Particularly, he held his great-grandfather Schertel von Burtenbach, a Protestant army commander in the *Schmalkaldischen Krieg* (1546–1547) between catholic and protestant rulers, in high regard. Seckendorff spent the first twenty-two years of his life entirely in the shadow of war. At the age of eight he lost his family home in Franconia, and at sixteen he lost his father, an officer in the Swedish Army, who was executed as a supposed spy in the market square of Salzwedel (Between Hannover and Berlin in today's Sachsen-Anhalt). The war forced his mother on the road with her children, living in the Thuringian towns of Coburg, Mühlhausen and Erfurt. The family was supported economically by former colleagues of Seckendorff's father in the Swedish army. Fürst

2 Biographical information is mainly from Lüdtke (1939).

Ernst *der Fromme* of Gotha had fought on the side of the Swedish King Gustav Adolf at the Battle of Lützen (1632), and Joachim Ludwig von Seckendorff—Veit's father—had been of one of Fürst Ernst's eight company commanders. Veit first came into contact with Duke Ernst the Pious, then holding court in Coburg, at the age of thirteen, and later moved with him to Gotha in 1640.

Seckendorff's education was noteworthy for his times. Under Fürst Ernst's protection, he attended the famous *Gymnasium* in Gotha from 1641 to 1642, and continued his studies at the University of Strasbourg the same year. The town, an important center of trade and stronghold of Lutheranism, was saved from destruction during the Thirty Years' War, and the university was thus allowed to function uninterrupted throughout the period. It was generally considered to be Germany's most distinguished university at the time, and, like Thuringia, it was a nexus of cultural influences close to the French sphere of influence. Seckendorff tells us he rather would have focused his studies in the field of theology, but obeys the wishes of his father's comrade in arms in the Swedish army, Colonel Montaigne, and thus mainly studies law, with some philosophy, history and theology on the side.

His teachers in Strasbourg gave Seckendorff the intellectual foundations on which he was later to build. He studied classics, German history starting with *Tacitus*, German national humanism, and constitutional law. Prof. Johann Heinrich Böcler in Strasbourg was central in forming Seckendorff's views. Böcler came from antiquity, bible, and philosophy and ended in contemporary history and politics. Here in Strasbourg we find the roots of Seckendorff's view of the need to build the state on *Sittlichkeit*—morality and morals—in a system where the welfare of the state was the main goal. Subsequently Seckendorff also studied for a period in Marburg.

After finishing his studies, Seckendorff considered both a military and a scientific career. However, the economic conditions of his family forced him to go into government service. In 1646 he entered the service of *Ernst der Fromme* in Gotha as *Hofjunker*. Since 1640 Fürst Ernst had been working hard at reconstructing and unifying his state based on strong *Geist* und *Willen* (spirit and will), a strength given him by the Lutheran sense of duty blended with military traits. Seckendorff soon established strong personal relations with the Fürst. As responsible for the library,[3] Seckendorff continued his studies, read to Fürst Ernst, made book résumés and had to give written replies to his questions.

A long sequence of new positions attests to his lightening career in Gotha: in 1648 we find him as *Kammerjunker*, in 1651 as *Hof- und Justizrat und Mitglied der Ratsstube*, in 1655, as *Geheimer Hof- und Kammerrat*, Seckendorff brings the finances of the state in impeccable order. In 1664, at the age of 38, Seckendorff reached the highest possible position in Gotha: *Direktor des Geheimen Rates*. In the same year, for reasons that are not clear, he left the service of Fürst Ernst.

From 1665 to 1682 Seckendorff was in the service of Duke Moritz of Sachsen-Naumburg-Zeitz, holding various administrative posts. In 1669 he worked in Dresden,

---

3 For the turbulent history of libraries, including the Gotha library, during the The Thirty Years' War, see Walde (1930).

experiencing the luxurious life at the court there, a sharp contrast to the pious Gotha court. Seckendorff left the service of the duchy shortly after the death of Duke Moritz in 1682.

In 1682 Seckendorff retired as an 'independent scholar' to the estate Meuselwitz, near Altenburg, which he had purchased in 1676. At this point he reverted to his early desire at the University of Strasbourg to dedicate himself to the study of theology. He carried out an extensive correspondence with Leibniz and Philipp Jacob Spener (1635–1705), the founder of Lutheran pietism. In 1692 he accepted the position of Chancellor at the University of Halle where the world's first professorship in economics would be established 35 years later—but passed away just after arriving in Halle. Seckendorff's life was indeed well balanced between the two old ideals of a *vita activa* and a *vita contemplativa*.

4. Seckendorff's writings

For posterity, Seckendorff's fame rests on three main works, of which the latter two are on religion. At the age of 30, in 1656, Seckendorff published his main work in the social and administrative sciences, the *Teutsche Fürstenstaat.* This work was to remain in print, continuously in new editions, for the next 100 years. In 1664 he completed the *Additiones* to the *Fürstenstaat*, which were published with a reprint of the original work in 1665.

In 1685, Seckendorff's second important work, the *Christenstaat*, was published, and his third important work, the *Commentarius historicus et apologeticus de Lutheranismo*, was published complete in 1692. This work is a response to an anti-protestant tract, *Histoire du, Luthéranisme* (Paris 1680), by the French Jesuit Luis Maimbourg (1610–1686). A first part of this work was published in 1688.

The *Fürstenstaat* is a kind of 'owner's manual' for a small state. The work brings together two overlapping older traditions: (1) the *Fürstenspiegel* or Princes' Primer on how to rule, and (2) the tradition of accurate country surveys and descriptions dating back to *De magnalibus urbis mediolani* of Bonvesin de la Riva (1288) and later works on the Florentine state. Such descriptive surveys were, 100 years before the publication of the *Teutsche Fürstenstaat*, the purpose of costly and extensive *visitas* in the Spanish provinces of the New World, the result of which were published. Duke Ernst's *Generalvisitation* (1641–1645) and the *grosse Gerichtsvisitation* (1652, 1662) must be seen in this tradition. Phillipp von Hörnigk's survey of Austria was the basis for his own influential 1684 work, an important follower of Seckendorff in the German cameralist tradition (Hörnigk, 1684). Like Seckendorff's *Fürstenstaat*, Hörnigk's work was to remain in print, in a large number of editions, for a century after its first publication.

The *Fürstenstaat* contains accurate descriptions of history, population, economic conditions, administration, school system, law and justice. The principles followed in the very successful reconstruction of the state of Sachsen-Gotha and its institutions after the Thirty Years' War are described. Seckendorff's approach is clearly a holistic and organic one, where the state is an organism and its *common weal* can only be understood in its totality (*Ganzheit*). Seckendorff's views are similar to those of the Italian economists of the

Renaissance. The emphasis on the totality, on *Ganzheit*, was to be a hallmark of German economics, and German philosophy for the next 300 years.

We know that Seckendorff travelled to the Netherlands, accompanying Duke Ernst. The wealth and religious tolerance he observed there made a huge impression upon him (Stolleis, 1995, p. 158). Early economic policy in Europe is frequently based on benchmarking against the successful states—the Netherlands and Venice being the obvious cases—and against Spain, with its inflow of gold accompanied by deindustrialisation and increasing poverty, as the case to avoid (Reinert, 2004). To Seckendorff, the Dutch appear as 'examples of the wisest and in production and trade (*in Gewerb*) the most experienced people' (Seckendorff, 1665).

The inspiration Seckendorff found in Holland is well reflected also in the writings of his English contemporaries. Josuah Child, the famous mercantilist, opens his 1668 book (published 12 years after Seckendorff's *Fürstenstaat*), with a comment on 'the prodigious increase of the Netherlanders' which is 'the envy of the present and may be the wonder of all future generations. And yet, the means whereby they have thus advanced themselves, are sufficiently obvious, and in a great measure imitable by most other nations…, which I shall endeavour to demonstrate in the following discourse'. In a later work Child elaborates further: 'If we intend to have the Trade of the World, we must imitate the Dutch, who make the worst as well as the best of all manufactures, that we may be in a capacity of serving all Markets, and all Humors' (Child, 1693, p. 90).

From the Netherlands, Seckendorff understood the crucial need for manufactures (already in the early 1500s more than 30 per cent of all employment in the Dutch Republic was in manufacturing), and also the need to cluster economic activities. Seckendorff's economic measures included the promotion of manufactures and the resettlement of artisans from the countryside in the cities, where they were likely to make much better livings. He promoted the extension of agriculture and activities adding value to the produce of the land. Seckendorff also eased the mobility of labour by eliminating fees required for settlement and resettlement. With him, we also find the origins of the welfare state, of care for the poor, and of government responsibility for the care of the elderly. In his wish to limit the powers of the guilds, he showed liberal tendencies well ahead of his times.

Seckendorff was to establish what could be called 'a multi-level conspiracy for development'. The 13th century idea of a common good—originating in Italian humanism—is slowly being transformed into an idea of public happiness, and the ruler is put in charge of the project. Wilhelm Roscher coined the descriptive term 'enlightened despotism' for this kind of rule (Roscher, 1868, p. 77). The enlightened ruler—the 'Philosopher-King' in Christian Wolff's terms (Wolff, 1750)—was in charge of this 'developmental dictatorship'. The logic that emerged was: the better the ruler, the wealthier the people. Instead of judging his success by his own wealth, the ruler's success will be based on the wealth and happiness of his people. These elements of economic theory are mainly contained in the *Additiones*, written after Seckendorff's visit to the Dutch Republic (see Sophus Reinert in this volume).

5. Seckendorff as a mercantilist/cameralist

Seckendorff's *Fürstenstaat* —especially the *Additiones*—contains a number of key policy prescriptions that are to be found in the work of later cameralists. Seckendorff represents mercantilism in Gustav Schmoller's sense of *statebuilding:* a wise policy of simultaneously building state and economy (*Staatsklugheit*) is at the core of his work. Seckendorff also represents mercantilism in Cosimo Perrotta's sense of *import substitution*, and in core sense of adopting policies *creating employment.*

In Seckendorff we can recognize many elements of later cameralist thought. Indeed many of the elements that distinguish the German economic tradition as it was to develop until World War II are already there in Seckendorff (Reinert, 2005):

- The emphasis on *Staatsweisheit, Staatsklugheit* and *Staatswissenschaft,* an integration of administration, policy and economic theory. This develops not into a state theory but into a science of administration (*Verwaltungslehre*).
- The need to shape 'the quality of the people', a frequent concern with early economists. The skills and knowledge of the inhabitants are to be upgraded ('Staatsbildung bedeutet Menschenformung')
- The emphasis on education. Mandatory school attendance was established in Weimar in 1619 and in Gotha in 1642.
- The interest in 'learned societies', foreshadowing founding of scientific academies by Leibniz and Christian Wolff. In 1660 Seckendorff published a pamphlet as member of the *Fruchtbringende Gesellschaft.* In 1633 the *Aufrichtige Gesellschaft der Tannen* had been founded at the University of Strasbourg, and Seckendorff is likely to have been a member.
- A view of the state as the *corpus politicum—der Staat als Organismus*—continues the mediaeval 'body metaphor' of economics. This is typical for later German economic thinking, in sharp contrast to Anglo-Saxon economics which produces statements like Margaret Thatcher's 'there is no such thing as society'.
- A 'duty based system' where *Pflicht* (duty) and market both rule.

The following eleven economic principles can be distilled from Seckendorff's *Additiones*:

1. Industrialization of domestic raw materials.
2. Stop export of raw materials and re-import of finished product. Local industrialization.
3. *Gewerbefreiheit* and the elimination of guilds.
4. Introduction of new economic activities, i.e. increasing the division of labour.
5. Careful tax and tariff policy.
6. Protection of local production.
7. Loosening the binding of the artisans to the towns.
8. Renting out government land with increasing population pressure.
9. Putting the school system in line with the economic policy.
10. Building out a welfare policy.
11. A very 'modern' policy of adult education.

6. Conclusion: The *right to rule* becomes the *duty to develop* the nation

The first professor of economics anywhere, Simon Peter Gasser in Halle, starts his textbook in economics (Gasser, 1729) with a long poem from Seckendorff's *Additiones* (reproduced below), fittingly illustrating Seckendorff's position as the founding father of the science in Germany. This poem describes the old ideal of a king, an able hunter, horseman, and fencer, and the modern king whose success is measured in the justice and welfare found in his state. Thomasius—who delivers Seckendorff's funeral oration—also uses the *Teutsche Fürstenstaat* as textbook in Halle. Seckendorff feeds directly—and prominently featured— into the cameralist mainstream.

Seckendorff represents an early case of the principle where a sovereign's *right to rule* is consciously converted into a *duty to develop* the state he heads. The king under whom he served, Ernst the Pious of Sachsen-Gotha, also became the early prototype of this type of ruler. Seckendorff may be seen as an early theorist of the developmental state, a type of rule which bases its ideology and legitimacy on an ability to promote sustained economic development. The ability to improve the economic conditions of its inhabitants becomes both the goal of the ruling elite and a means to keep power.

The poor countries of Europe could not aspire to the more democratic type of rule found in Florence, Venice or the Dutch Republic. The necessary urban elites were just not there in sufficient numbers. So the poor periphery had to make do with what they had: a King or *Fürst*. Seckendorff and the cameralists following him transformed the ruler and his *Weltanschauung*, attempting to copy the economic structures—rather than the economic policies—found in the successful and wealthy states of Europe. The result was *the enlightened ruler*—the *philosopher-king* or the *enlightened despot*—who was put in charge of a 'developmental dictatorship'. The job of men like Seckendorff and his successors was to advice, assist, guide, correct, flatter and cajole the rulers to do their job properly. Here Seckendorff was to set a pattern that was followed by the German economists succeeding him all through the 18th Century.

Teutsches Fürsten-Blut, lass Künste Künste seyn
Und ob ein andrer gleich mit Reiten, Jagen, Hetzen
Im Fechten und im Spiel, und in dem eiteln Schein
Des tollen Kleider-Drachts, Wohlreden, Reimen setzen
Dir überlegen ist, hat er gleich mehr studirt
Und kann in fremder Sprach auch ganze Bücher schreiben,
Versteht die Mahlerey, schnitzt, drechselt und poßirt,
Begreifft des Himmels-Lauf, kann Alchimie treiben,
So sey du eingedenck, was dein Beruf und Stand,
Dein Thun und Hauptwerck sey; *O lerne wohl regieren*
Dein anvertrautes Volck, im Friede laß dein Land,
Durch gute Policey, Nahrung und Recht floriren

Dem der sich unterwirft; dem mache seine Last
So leicht du immer kanst, verschone des Elenden
Hingegen wisse wohl die Kräfte die du hast,
Zum Zwang des stolzen Feinds sieghaftig anzuwenden.

References

Child, J. (1668). *Brief Observations Concerning Trade and Interest of Money*, London: Calvert and Mortlock.

Child, J. (1681). *A Treatise Concerning the East-India Trade*, London: Printed for the Honorable East India Company.

Gasser, S. P. (1729). *Einleitung zu den Oeconomischen Politischen und Cameral-Wissenschaften*, Halle: Verlegung des Waysenhauses.

Hörnigk, P. W. von (1684). *Österreich über alles wenn es nur will*, no place, no publisher.

Inama-Sternegg, K. T. von. (1864). "Die volkswirtschaftlichen Folgen des Dreißigjährigen Krieges für Deutsch-land." *Historisches Taschenbuch*. 4.F. 5

Jacobsen, R. (2002). "Die Brüder Seckendorff und ihre Beziehungen zu Sachsen-Gotha." Jacobsen & Ruge (2002:95–120).

Jacobsen, R. & Ruge H.-J. (eds.). 2002. *Ernst der Fromme (1601–1675). Staatsman und Reformer. Wissenschaftliche Beiträge und Katalog zur Ausstellung*, Bucha bei Jena: Quartus.

Klinger, A. (2002). *Der Gothaer Fürstenstaat- Herrschaft, Konfession und Dynastie unter Herzog Ernst dem Frommen*, Husum: Matthiesen Verlag.

Laspeyeres, E. (1863/1961). *Geschichte der volkswirtschaftlichen Anschauungen der Niederländer und Ihrer Literatur zur Zeit der Republik*, Niewkoop, de Graaf (reprint).

Lüdtke, W. (1939). "Vitus von Säckendorff als deutscher Staatsmann und Volkserzieher des 17. Jahrhunderts." *Jahrbuch der Akademie zu Erfurt*, Erfurt: Villaret.

Müller, V. (1967). *Karl Theodor von Inama-Sternegg- Ein Leben für Staat und Wissenschaft*, Dissertation zur Erlangung des Doktorgrades an der philosophischen Fakultät der Universität Wien.

Perrotta, C. (1993). "Early Spanish Mercantilism: The First Analysis of Underdevelopment." In L. Magnusson (ed.), *Mercantilist Economics*, Boston: Kluwer.

Reinert, E. S. (2004). "Benchmarking Success: The Dutch Republic (1500–1750). as seen by contemporary European Economists." In E. Reinert (ed.), *How Rich Nations got Rich. Essays in the History of Economic Policy*, SUM Working Paper 2004.01, University of Oslo, Centre for Development and the Environment.

Reinert, E. S. (2005). "German Economics as Development Economics: From the 'Thirty Years' War' to World War II." In K. S. Jomo and E. S. Reinert (ed.), *Origins of Development Economics*, London: Zed Books.

Reinert, E. S. & Daastøl, A. (1997). "Exploring the Genesis of Economic Innovations. The Religious Gestalt-switch and the Duty to Invent as Preconditions for Economic Growth." *European Journal of Law and Economics*, 233–283.

Reinert, E. S. & Reinert, S. A. (2003). "An Early National Innovation System: The Case of Antonio Serra's 1613 *Breve Trattato*." *Institutions and Economic Development/Istituzioni e Sviluppo Economico*, 1(3).

Reinert, E. S. & Reinert, S. A. (2005). "Mercantilism and Economic Development: Schumpeterian Dynamics, Institution Building and International Benchmarking." In K. S. Jomo and E. S. Reinert (ed.), *Origins of Development Economics*, London: Zed Books.

Roscher, W. (1868). "Der sächsische Nationalökonom Johann Heinrich Gottlob von Justi." *Archiv für Sächsische Geschichte*. 76–106.

Small, A. (1909). *The Cameralists: The Pioneers of German Social Polity*, New York: Burt Franklin.

Stolleis, Michael (ed.) (1995). *Staatsdenker der frühen Neuzeit*, Munich: Beck.

Strauch, S. (2002). "Ernst der Fromme und Veit Ludwig von Seckendorff- zwei Kämpfer für das Luthertum." *Jacobsen & Ruge* pp. 127–135.
Walde, O. (1930). *Storhetstidens Litterära Krigsbyten. En Kulturhistorisk Bibliografisk Studie*, Uppsala: Almqvist & Wicksell.
Wandel, U. J. (2002). "Herzog Ernsts Schiffahrts- und Kanalpläne." *Jacobsen & Ruge* pp. 227–248.
Wolff, C. (1750). *The Real Happiness of a People under a Philosopher King*, London: M. Cooper.
Yates (1999). *The Rosicrucian Enlightenment*, London: Routledge.

Chapter Four

EXPLORING THE GENESIS OF ECONOMIC INNOVATIONS: THE RELIGIOUS GESTALT-SWITCH AND THE DUTY TO INVENT AS PRECONDITIONS FOR ECONOMIC GROWTH

Erik S. Reinert & Arno Mong Daastøl

Abstract

This paper discusses changes in the level of knowledge—i.e. learning—as a key source of economic growth, and argues that historically a radical change in attitude towards new knowledge has been a necessary precondition for economic growth. The Renaissance created this radically new attitude in Europe, and this paper discusses contributions to economic theory and economic policy of some of the most influential scientists involved in this process: Francis Bacon (1561–1626) in England, and Leibniz (1646–1716) and Christian Wolff (1679–1754) in Germany. It is argued that these polyhistors viewed economic change as a dynamic knowledge-based process—a view that has important similarities with modern evolutionary or Schumpeterian economics. These similarities have so far not been recognized, and the paper suggests that modern economic theory would benefit from studying the theoretical and practical economics of these philosophers who laid the foundations for the industrial revolution.

Keywords: duty, knowledge, economic growth, technological change

Introduction

This is a paper about economic growth, and implicitly also about the lack of it. We postulate a religious/philosophical *gestalt-switch*—a fundamental change of Man's world view—as a necessary pre-condition for economic growth. Our contention is that the *attitude to creation of new knowledge*—which is changed by this gestalt-switch—is a basic but neglected explanatory variable for economic growth and its absence.

In order to explain the nature of this gestalt-switch we construct two categories—two ideal types—of *Weltanschauungen*, or 'world views': One mechanical and static, centered around 'matter', and 'sein' (being), and one dynamic and organic, centered around 'thought' (Logos) and 'werden' (becoming). These categories also find their counterparts in the sphere of economics. In economics, the mechanical world view is centered around barter, accumulation, physical metaphors, equilibrium, and optimality. In this mechanical view, a fundamental characteristic of Man is his propensity to barter. The organic view in economics is centered around inventions, production, evolution, biological metaphors, and disequilibrium. This paper endeavours to show that this non-mechanical and organic model of economics—evolutionary economics—has its historic origins not in Darwinist or Lamarckian biology, but in the philosophy and economics of the Renaissance. The scarce historiography of evolutionary economics[1] has so far neglected these authors, who were no doubt extremely influential at the time.

In any evolutionary system, almost by definition, no optimality exists, except as an ever-moving target in the distance[2]. In this organic view a fundamental characteristic of Man is his propensity to explore, to invent, and cumulatively and continuously to create new knowledge. We argue that in this perspective today's evolutionary economics may be seen as being too 'mechanistic'. Evolutionary dynamics has been added to economic theory, but this brand of evolutionary economics seems to underestimate the role of *conscious human effort*—individual and collective—as the main engine propelling evolutionary change. If evolutionary economics only means substituting 'biology-envy' for the previous 'physics-envy', economics will still suffer from *Entgeistung*—from being devoid of *Geist* or Mind—a term used by 19th Century German theory in criticising English classical economics. We shall also argue this alternative non-mechanical economic theory—which was at the core of the Renaissance—contrasts with the 'natural selection' analogy which e.g. Hodgson claims as the basis for the new wave of evolutionary modellers.[3] The alternative non-mechanical tradition—from the Renaissance through the economics of Nicholas

---

1 The most comprehensive work on the history of evolutionary economics is contained in Hodgson, Geoffrey M., *Economics and Evolution, Bringing Life Back into Economics*, Cambridge, Polity Press, 1993. Early reference points to evolutionary economics are normally the quote that 'the Mecca of the economist lies in economic biology' appearing in the 7th edition of Alfred Marshall's *Principles of Economics*, (London, Macmillan, 1907) and the 1898 article by Thorstein Veblen 'Why is Economics not an Evolutionary Science' (*The Quarterly Journal of Economics*, vol. xii, July 1898, reprinted in Veblen, *The Place of Science in Modern Civilisation and other Essays*, New York, Huebsch, 1919.)

2 This point is discussed in Nelson, Richard, 'Recent Evolutionary Theorizing About Economic Change', in *The Journal of Economic Literature*, Vol. XXXIII, No. 1, March 1995, pp. 58–59.

3 Hodgson, *op. cit.*, p. 149.

Kaldor—tended to be based on an untraditional mode of inference: on *abduction*[4] rather than on induction or deduction.

We shall argue that the conflict between a mechanical world view and a dynamic one, based on Man's rational being and soul, also was at the core of an important early debate in English economics. This fundamental philosophical debate between Misselden and Malynes in 1622–23 now appears in the history of economics—filtered through the lenses of neo-classical economics—merely as debate on exchange control and the balance of trade.

The two ideal types—the organic and the mechanical—are probably both always present in every human being and in every society. However, in every human being, as well as in every historical period, the balance between them differs. Some individuals, just like some historical periods, are more creative than others. The dynamic and organic world view creates a changing world of imbalances and insecurity. The mechanical world view restores the picture of a stable, balanced, and apparently organized world.

Sequentially, it would appear that initially a dynamic and inventive world view creates wealth, whereas a mechanical world view moves in later in order to explain and to create order, an order which to some extent probably is only a mental illusion. The cycle of ascent and decline and nations somehow seems to relate to changes in relative importance of the two contrasting *Weltanschauungen*.

It would also appear that, seen in time, a *techno-economic paradigm*[5] essentially consists of one such sequence of a creative burst, followed by a period of increasingly mechanistic and uncreative human activity, until the next creative burst explodes. A new paradigm is created by a radical innovation, e.g. steam power or electricity, which affects most activities, setting fundamentally new technical standards and 'rules of the game'. Inside one techno-economic paradigm, less dramatic and incremental changes take society down a new learning curve. This learning curve, initially steep, gradually flattens out as the potentials of the paradigm are exhausted. Simultaneously the more mechanical *Weltanschauung* gains predominance, until a burst of human creativity again 'creatively destroys' the old stagnant order, forming a new techno-economic paradigm. Since different nations or regions, at any point in time, will be in different stages of this process, they appear to us as slowly ascending or declining in economic importance.

We would argue that we today collectively suffer from problems attributable to an overdose of 'order', of mechanical economics. This falsely creates a 'Harmonielehre'[6]—a passive system of automatic harmony both in income creation and in income

---

4 For a discussion of this, see chapter 5 below.

5 See Perez, Carlota, 'Structural Change and the Assimilation of New Technologies in the Economic and Social System', in *Futures*, Vol. 15, 1983, No. 4, pp. 357–375, Freeman, 'The Nature of Innovation and the Evolution of the Productive System', in *Technology and Productivity. The Challenge for Economic Policy*, Paris, OECD, 1991.

6 Lionel Robbins in *The Theory of Economic Policy in English Classical Economy*, London, Macmillan, 1952, claims that the excessive formalisation of the classical economists in neo-classical economics create an artificial 'Harmonielehre'.

distribution. This focus on order and formality in economic theory carries with it costs to society in terms of

a) neglecting the importance of invention and new knowledge as one of the preconditions for economic growth, thereby curtailing wealth creation, and
b) leaving an unnecessarily large part of mankind in poverty. Through its basic assumptions, today's standard theory has created a 'blind spot' for anything but an even distribution of wealth.[7] Our limited understanding of wealth creation is intimately tied to our limited understanding of how wealth is distributed.

It would also seem that a paradigm shift affects sciences in a sequence which may vary according to the nature of the particular paradigm-shift. One scientific discipline will be the leader, another the laggard. In our opinion, economic science is presently a laggard, being a prisoner of its own toolbox. Like many others, we would argue the need for a careful but 'creative destruction' of the axioms of economic science, creating a new and more dynamic *gestalt.* In our view, however, economics should venture well beyond the constrains of natural sciences—be they physics or biology—to place itself in a framework of the *Geisteswissenschaften*—the 'sciences of the mind', the Humanities.

We would suggest that the new and coming gestalt will have to carry with it important insights from the previous gestalt-switch which took place in the Europe of the Renaissance. An important philosopher and economist, who was pivotal in laying the theoretical foundation for Germany's economic ascent, is **Christian Wolff** (1697–1754). Wolff was the junior collaborator of Europe's leading philosopher and scientist at the turn of the eighteenth Century, Gottfried Wilhelm Leibniz (1646–1716). Wolff is mainly known for his work of structuring Leibniz' ideas and making them more accessible to the general public, just as Leibniz himself had wished. In fact, Leibniz' main philosophical work, *New Essays* (1695)—an attack on the epistemology of John Locke—was only published, posthumously, in 1765. But, as often is the case in such instances, Wolff added to and subtracted from Leibniz' ideas. Wolff's more systematic approach was also more formal, but less metaphysical, than Leibniz' own. 'Wolff says that Leibniz' system begins at a point where his own stops'.[8] In addition, it seems that Wolff's attitude was less 'romantic socialist' and more 'realistic' than Leibniz' own.

Wolff, like Leibniz, was a true polyhistor, laying the foundations for all later German philosophy, and contributing in a fundamental way to such diverse sciences as mathematics, physics, meteorology, linguistics and international law. A modern Swedish historian of law describes Wolff as the most important contributor to European philosophy of

[7] Paul Samuelson (1949 and 1950) proved that, under the standard assumptions of neo-classical theory, perfect information and no increasing returns to scale, the world would achieve *factor-price equalisation*— i.e. everybody would be equally rich—if the world was only opened to free trade.

[8] Corr, Charles A., 'Christian Wolff and Leibniz', *Journal of Historical Ideas*, Vol. 36, 1975, pp. 241–262, p. 256

law since Emperor Justitian's *Corpus Juris Civilis* from 529–534 A.D.[9] Wolff and Leibniz represent a legal tradition which consciously tried to construct the basis for a modern welfare state.[10] By bringing together those 'who collect money' and those 'who collect knowledge' in a suitable framework of property rights, Leibniz and Wolff attempted to develop a basis for a 'civilized society'. In their opinion this could only take place if Mankind sought new knowledge, new crafts, and new technologies, i.e. through the development of a manufacturing industry. With hindsight, Erik Anners, the legal philosopher, today agrees that, in the absence of such a legal structure, an industrial revolution would have been impossible.[11] and holds the relatively advanced and systematic West-European legal practice to be a prime reason why Europe advanced economically relative to the Greek- and Russian-Orthodox nations and to the Arab cultures.[12] The obstacles created for economic development by the lack of a suitable legal structure, is brought to evidence today as we observe the economic transformation in Russia.

Wolff's collected works comprise tens of thousands of pages, and his role in the transformation of Germany was a crucial one. 'The centre of scientific life in Germany during the eighteenth century was formed by the teaching and school of Christian Wolff', according to a classic work in the history of philosophy[13]. Before Wolff, several philosophers, including Leibniz, had tried to overthrow the Aristotelian system of Melanchton which had dominated Germany. But, 'The Man who finally overthrew Melanchton's system was Christian Wolff'.[14] Without Wolff, Kant, as well as Hegel and German eighteenth-century idealism in philosophy, is unthinkable.

In economics Wolff represents a 'vital' and organic school, in strong opposition to a static, mechanical and deterministic world view. We shall examine his basic teachings as they relate to economic change, and argue that his insights are very useful to the process of vitalisation needed in economics today.

---

9 'From the rationalist school of natural rights, Christian Wolff is the writer who has exerted the most influence on the development of European Law, with an influence which reaches into our present time', Anners, Erik, *Den europeiske rettens historie*, Oslo, Universitetsforlaget, 1983, p. 197. (our translation).

10 'Leibniz had derived the conceptions of right (or law) from the most general principles of practical philosophy, following the examples of the ancients. Wolff followed him in this respect also, but made it on this account the end of the political compact to secure the mutual furtherance of individuals in behalf of their mutual perfecting, enlightening, and happiness; according to him, therefore, the state has to care, not merely for external safety, but also for the general welfare in the broadest extent. The consequence of this is that Wolff assigns to the state the right and duty of a thorough tutelage of the great mass of unenlightened men who are controlled by error and passion, and of intermeddling even in their private relations in the way of education.' Windelband, Wilhelm, *A History of Philosophy*, (1893), Westport, Conn., Greenwood Press, 1979, p. 518

11 Anners, *op.cit.*, pp. 177, 183

12 Anners, *op.cit.*, p. 173

13 Windelband, Wilhelm, *A History of Philosophy*, (1893), Westport, Conn., Greenwood Press, 1979, p. 444.

14 I.e. the so-called peripatetic system of Melanchton, see: Ronald S. Callinger, 'The Newtonian-Wolffian Controversy', *Journal of Historical Ideas*, Vol. 30, 1969, pp. 319–330.

A few remarks are needed on the importance of the legal system, and on Wolff's position within the philosophy of law, since it is impossible to separate his impact both on philosophy and on economics from this:

The reformation removed the scholastic foundations of late Medieval natural law, aimed at creating Christian subjects. At that time around half of the German population—in some areas two thirds—had been killed in the Thirty Years' War. To Leibniz and Wolff it was therefore of utmost importance to create a common basis of law regardless of creed. The new philosophy of law reintroduced some Hellenistic ideas, but it still cannot be characterized as secular. The philosophy of natural law maintains that law has a solid moral foundation, and this was elaborated into a coherent and consistent system. Morality is supposed to rest upon nature, the interpretation of which is central to all systems. This is fundamentally where the various philosophers of the tradition diverge from each other. In the natural 'uncivilised' state, Aquinas still holds that man has certain obligations, whereas Hobbes holds that there would only be one: staying alive. At the core of the axioms in Wolff's system rests the presupposition that man essentially is a social, peaceful and rational being.

Leibniz and Wolff completed the synthetic method within philosophy of law by placing any problem into a system of superior and subordinated rules in a strict geometrical system. As in geometry these rules were built on exact definitions of concepts. This rationalistic philosophy of natural law gained importance in the 18th century. Wolff's students developed the method further, and created the foundation of jurisprudence of concepts and codifications of the 19th Century. This system was used as a political weapon in the hands of the Enlightenment in order to change the institutions of society. Acceptable axioms were chosen and the conclusions drawn with mathematical certainty and this had an enormous impact as the conclusions appeared to be unimpeachable. However, many will argue that the axioms were subjective, just as many would argue today that science itself is essentially subjective.[15]

The first part of this paper briefly discusses a fundamental problem in economics: The tension between creativity and formalism. Part two gives a description of the search for the 'proximate causes' of economic growth in the post-war era as a continuous uncovering of new factors, or 'reactants'. Part three discusses the contrasts between neo-classical and evolutionary economics in this context. Part four traces the evolution of the *religious gestalt-switch* which fundamentally changed our attitude to knowledge, and in which Wolff played an important part. Part five briefly discusses the English version of the *gestalt-switch*, which happened before the German one. Part six discusses the holistic, organic and dynamic system of economics created by Leibniz and Wolff. Part seven discusses the role of Man's will, invention, and creativity in Wolff's 'System of Duties'. The concluding part constitutes part eight. An appendix brings a partial translation of Wolff's main work as regards economic change and innovation.

---

[15] See Corr, Charles A, 'Christian Wolff's Treatment of Scientific Discovery', *Journal of the History of Philosophy*, Vol. 10, No. 3, pp. 323–334.

1. The tension between creativity and formalism in economics

Central figures in the history of economic thought come across as being in two minds—one could almost say schizophrenic—in their attempt to reconcile the creative and dynamic world view with the formal and static one. We shall give two examples of this. An important and creative economist living in the eternal tension between mechanical stability and creative growth was Joseph Schumpeter. On the one hand the equilibrium-centered formalist Walras was his favourite economist, on the other hand he himself is known to posterity for his theory for putting *disequilibrium*, and factors which are very difficult to formalise, like 'creative destruction', at the center of economic theory. Schumpeter admired the exactness of the mathematical language of equilibrium analysis, but his own contribution to economics was centered around an evolution of knowledge not captured by formal deductive mathematics.

Alfred Marshall on one hand states that 'the Mecca of economics is in biology'[16]. At the same time, in the appendix of the very same book, Marshall lays the foundations for an economic science which brings to an end all biological metaphors in economics, opening up for a science based exclusively on physical metaphors ('physics-envy'). Still, in order to create equilibrium, Marshall paradoxically had to restore to a *biological* metaphor. Increasing returns had been an important argument for industrial policy ever since Antonio Serra in 1613[17] all through the 19th Century. In order to reconcile the existence of increasing returns with equilibrium, Marshall uses a lengthy metaphor of firms growing and dying like trees in the forests.[18] This evolutionary growth process supposedly counteracts the tendency towards uneven accumulation caused by increasing returns to scale.[19] The argument which killed all future biological analogies in neo-classical economics, was a biological analogy. This biological analogy was important in making economics into what it is today, a profession where a physics-inspired equilibrium is the central gestalt.

Once the biological metaphors were gone, economic inquiry embarked upon 'the path of least mathematical resistance', to quote Paul Krugman.[20] In this process the economics profession gained much in terms of analytical rigor. However, for the understanding of **economic growth**, this rigor proved to be a *rigor mortis*. When the process of mathematization had been perfected, that subject was gone.

The choice of language is important to whether ideas can be transmitted. For a discussion of the different properties of snow, Swahili would be a poor choice. Communicating on this subject in an Eskimo or Lapp language would certainly lead

---

16 Marshall, Alfred, *Principles of Economics*, London, Macmillan, 1890, p. iv.

17 Serra, Antonio, *Breve trattato delle cause che possono far abbondare li regni d'oro e argento dove non sono miniere*, Napoli, Lazzaro Scoriggio, 1613.

18 Marshall, op. cit., pp. 315–316.

19 This problem is discussed in Hart, Neil, 'Increasing returns and economic theory: Marshall's reconciliation problem', University of Western Sydney, *Discussion Paper Series*, No. E9004, 1990.

20 Krugman, Paul, *Rethinking International Trade*, Cambridge, Mass., MIT Press, 1990, p. 4. It is interesting to note Krugman's view of economics as path-dependent, a concept which is otherwise foreign to the theoretical tradition he represents.

to a much better understanding. Similarly, linear mathematics based on 19th Century physics has proved unsatisfactory for understanding the creative processes underlying economic change.

2. Exploring the sources of growth and forever finding new ones

Thomas Kuhn[21] describes a process where contradictions between the realities observed and the ruling theoretical paradigm build up towards a paradigm shift. In the 1990's there is a growing awareness among economists of the inadequacy of our understanding of economic growth. As a result, there is a renewed interest in the sources of growth. During the exceptional growth period after the 2nd World War, what French economists refer to as the 40 years of *gloire*, only the Third World gave us a continuous reminder that there were still things to be understood. During the long post-war boom, anyone with a vision limited to Europe and the United States, could, under the circumstances, be forgiven for reasoning that by solving the cyclical problems of the economy we had simultaneously solved the problems of long-run growth. For many years, economic growth was largely seen as a mechanical result of the accumulation of capital.[22] This was already pointed out by Friedrich List in his criticism of Adam Smith's theory.[23]

A change in attitude has slowly built up and gathered momentum in the 1990's—perhaps due to a new and different demand on US economists to explain the lack of growth and the lack of 'competitiveness'. A collective complacency has slowly given way to uneasiness. 'The Economist', normally a staunch defender of the profession, declared in 1992 that 'True enough: economists are interested in growth. The trouble is that, even by their standards, they have been terribly ignorant about it. The depth of that ignorance has long been their best-kept secret.'[24]

Signs of an inadequate understanding of growth had been around long for those who wished to see them. In the Third World it became increasingly clear that we were addressing the symptoms rather than the causes of economic welfare. In 1956 Moses

---

[21] Kuhn, Thomas, *The Structure of Scientific Revolutions*, 2nd Edition, Chicago, University of Chicago Press, 1970.

[22] We would tend to attribute this lack of interest to a basic complacency with the situation in the industrialized world at the time. This led to a lack of demand for alternative explanations. Clearly, the theoretical development was also influence by the cold war. In this period, theories showing the perfection of the market system were most welcome. The theoretical development proceeded down a path created by the choice of methodology and tools made by economists in the late 19th Century. Thereby one symptom and necessary companion of growth—capital accumulation—was mistaken for its true cause. Searching for the sources of growth was not in the natural 'path' of this theory, which was essentially centered around barter, exchange, and equilibrium.

[23] According to List, the fundamental problem here was that Smith's system was a theory of *exchange*, and not of *production*. See e.g. List, Friedrich, *The National System of Political Economy*, London, Longman's Green & Co., 1885, p. 137.

[24] 'Explaining the mystery', January 4th, 1992, p. 17.

Abramowitz of Stanford University showed that capital accumulation only accounted for 10–15% of US economic growth. The remainder—the 'residual' of 85–90%—he referred to as 'a measure of our ignorance'. In the first instance this led to a relatively fruitless search, essentially for the factor capital hidden in other factors, generally referred to as 'growth accounting'. Many years later, in 1993, noting the lack of progress in explaining the 'residual', Abramowitz teases us by questioning whether it can get much worse. Can we be more than 100% ignorant? Yes, he says, we can be more than 100% ignorant. 'What worries me is not what we don't know, it is the things we think we know that ain't so'.[25]

Starting from a capital-centered view of growth, the economics profession has moved through various layers of explanations—unknowingly approaching the understanding of economic growth much in the same way one would peel an onion, ever finding a new issue once the previous issue had been brought into view. Very early theories of development tended to focus on geography and climate. In the neo-classical tradition *capital*, of course, is the main factor which virtually alone was supposed to account for the growth process. Schumpeter once referred to this as 'the pedestrian view that it is the accumulation of capital *per se* that propels the capitalist engine'[26]. Outside the mainstream human creativity, in the form of *entrepreneurship*, was studied. Also here, in the atomistic tradition of modern economics, focus was mostly on individuals, not on society or its institutions.

In the late 1960's focus shifted to *technology*. An early and important book in this tradition was David Landes' *The Unbound Prometheus*[27]. Technology is normally seen as consisting of two parts, a 'hard' part—the tool or machine—and a 'soft' part—human knowledge. For a long time, the study of technology concentrated on the 'hardware', the machine. Implicitly, knowledge was seen in the light of neo-classical 'perfect information', and therefore not important to technological change. Consequently 'technology transfer' came to be seen as a transfer of hardware, of machinery, while little attention was paid to human knowledge. Knowledge was seen to be 'codified'—as in instruction booklets—and easily transferred. This is the formal and static interpretation of knowledge, as opposed to an alternative view which is more tacit, intuitive, and creative.

As a next step the entrepreneur and the machine came to be seen as part of a *system* which continuously created innovations—a 'National Innovation System'[28]. This brand of evolutionary or Schumpeterian approach got its 'seal-of-approval' by the establishment through a large OECD programme, 'Technology and Economy', which was finished in

---

25 Abramowitz, Moses 'Sources of ignorance, old and new', *Journal of Economic History*, March 1993.

26 Schumpeter, Joseph A., *History of Economic Analysis*, New York, Oxford University Press, 1954, p. 468.

27 Cambridge, Cambridge University Press, 1969.

28 Lundvall, Bengt-Åke (ed.), *National Systems of Innovation*, London, Pinter, 1992, and Nelson, Richard (ed.), *National Innovation Systems*, New York, Oxford University Press, 1993.

1992.[29] The layer which required understanding after 'the machine'—the hardware of technology—was 'knowledge'. Slowly the concept of *knowledge* itself was brought into focus—and the importance of 'tacit' or uncodified knowledge was acknowledged.

Just as 'werden'—becoming, is a dynamic version of 'sein'—being, learning is the dynamic version of knowledge. All forms of *learning* have lately come into focus[30] in evolutionary economics: Institutional learning, learning-by-doing, learning by interaction, etc. A sign of the times is that the last OECD economic conference, in Copenhagen in November 1994, was held under the title: 'Conference on Employment and Growth in the Knowledge-based Economy.' The inadequacy of the neo-classical theoretical framework, with perfect information at its core, is becoming increasingly clear, as *human knowledge* more and more is seen as the basis for wealth creation. Even in the latest mainstream textbook in economic growth, the foreword states that 'Economic growth comes largely from the accumulation of knowledge'[31]. Economic thinking is entering this new and, economists presume, unchartered territory.

The present zeitgeist points out *knowledge* as the key factor in explaining growth. This honour had previously been bestowed on *capital* and on *technology*. But, as our understanding of these factors increased, their inadequacy in explaining economic welfare also became apparent. Economic growth must be seen as a product of several '*reactants*', each one a necessary but in itself insufficient factor. These reactants include geographical circumstances like climate, natural infrastructure (e.g. waterways), capital, entrepreneurship, institutions—like a systematic framework of law—, a technological 'window of opportunity', technological hardware and *changes in the stock* of human knowledge, i.e. learning. But, this is clearly not the end of the search for the 'proximate causes'[32] of economic growth. We are—like Ibsen's *Peer Gynt*—peeling an onion and always seeing new layers. Which one will appear beneath the factor 'knowledge'?

As when technology was put into focus, it seems that David Landes—professor of history emeritus at Harvard University—is again at the frontier of finding the proximate causes—or new reactants—for creating economic welfare. Landes now states that picking up *The Unbound Prometheus*, with its emphasis on technological hardware, is 'like walking into a kitchen built in the 1960's'.[33] Pushing the frontier of knowledge beyond factor technology, the next question in Landes' own *onion*—after light has been shed on the previous layer—regards the distributive aspects of technological change. In particular he looks at why the center of economic gravity at a certain point in history moved from the South of Europe to the North. Why did the Mediterranean lose its scientific

29 OECD, *Technology and Productivity. The Challenge for Economic Policy*, Paris, OECD, 1991, and *Technology and the Economy. The Key Relationships*, Paris, OECD, 1992.

30 See e.g. Lundvall, Bengt-Åke, 'The Learning Economy—Challenges to Economic Theory and Policy', paper presented at the EAEPE Conference in Copenhagen, October 1994.

31 Barro, Robert J. and Xavier Sala-i-Martin, *Economic Growth*, New York, McGraw-Hill, 1995. p. xvi. What in the static neo-classical framework is referred to as 'Accumulation of knowledge', is what we would call 'learning'.

32 This is Moses Abramowitz' term.

33 Stated at a seminar at the University of Oslo, May 16, 1995.

and economic leadership to Holland and England? In Landes' book—*The Wealth and Poverty of Nations*—the factor explaining the relative decline of the South and the rise of the North is ***attitude to knowledge***. To Landes 'mark 1996', the center of economic gravity from Southern to Northern Europe came as a result of *differences in attitude towards new knowledge*.

In order to explain historical attitudes to knowledge, religion will automatically enter the picture as an explanatory variable. Religion as a factor in explaining economic growth has centered around the debate following Max Weber's 1929 book *Protestant Ethics and the Spirit of Capitalism*. This factor had earlier been pointed out by authors like Adam Müller, Wilhelm Roscher, and Ernst Troeltsch. Landes quotes Kurt Samuelson's discussion of the Weber controversy.[34] Max Weber and Werner Sombart[35] each saw different religious systems of belief as promoting the values of growth and capitalism. The English historian Tawney, on the other hand, saw the *decline* of religion as the cause of capitalism.[36] In this paper we shall argue that the relationship between religion and economic welfare is not directly a question of a Protestant vs. a Catholic view, nor of an ascent or decline of religion as such. An important factor in the rise and shifts of gravity in capitalism seems to have been fundamentally different attitudes towards new knowledge. This phenomenon is not unrelated to the Reformation, but, as Weber's critics have pointed out, the question is much broader and older than that.

Variations in religious interpretation of Man's position in relation to Nature and God seem to have determined the scope and energy of the searching process for new knowledge—whether this process is wide and energetic and breaks with old routines, or weak, 'bounded', constrained by taboo, and myopic. If, e.g., the Church does not allow autopsies, little progress will be made in the medical sciences. Ultimately the difference in attitudes towards new knowledge reflects two fundamentally different views of the nature and image of Man. In this system, the decline of the Mediterranean and the ascent of Northern-Central Europe is a result on one hand of a growing hostile attitude towards new knowledge in the South, exemplified by the trials of the likes of Galileo and Giordano Bruno. On the other hand, Northern Europe took up the new view of Man and his 'duty to explore and invent'—exemplified in the writings of Christian Wolff which we shall discuss later in the paper.

The processes of accumulation of knowledge in the North were evidently helped by the emigration of refugee scholars from the South, especially from Italy,[37] just as Italy earlier had been blessed with refugees from Constantinople, both before and after its conquest by the Turks.[38] These refugee scholars transferred knowledge much in the same

---

34 *Ekonomi och Religion*, KF:s Bokförlag, Stockholm, 1957.

35 *Die Juden und das Wirtschaftsleben*, Leipzig, Duncker & Humblot, 1911.

36 Tawney, Richard, *Religion and the Rise of Capitalism; A Historical Study*, London, J. Murray, 1926.

37 This is discussed in Cassirer, Ernst, *The Platonic Renaissance in England* (1932), New York, Gordian Press, 1970, and in Venturi, Franco, *Italy and the Enlightenment. Studies in a Cosmopolitan Century*, New York, New York University Press, 1972.

38 This refers to the influx of neo-Platonists to the Florentine Academy, see Windelband, Wilhelm, *A History of Philosophy*, (1893), Westport, Conn., Greenwood Press, 1979, p. 359

way that entrepreneurs and industrialists, subject to religious prosecution, were instrumental in the spreading of industrial skills across Europe.

In the search process for the approximate causes of growth, the question arises whether we are bound to follow the path of Ibsen's Peer Gynt, to whom the onion—and his inner self—only revealed layer after layer, but no core. The important French philosopher Descartes banished final causes, on the grounds that we cannot know God's purposes. The alternative tradition presented in this paper would argue that there is a core. The core of Man is rational, Leibniz and Wolff would claim, and he therefore has the potential to understand God's purposes. In this tradition it is important that Man was made in God's own image. God is active, rational, creative and perfect. It is therefore Man's **duty** to strive for this same kind of perfection through learning, explorations and inventions. This will lead him to happiness. In this tradition, starting with the Egyptians and Plato, the *soul of Man* becomes the core, not only of the layers of explanations which lead us to understand economic growth and welfare, but of science in general.

We shall argue that this territory has been well charted before, but 'unlearned', particularly in economics. In our opinion this loss is due to emergence of empiricism as the dominating philosophical paradigm. An understanding of the crucial change in the attitude towards knowledge which creates growth, and changed the center of economic gravity from Southern to Northern Europe, can best be understood through the study of a religious *gestalt-switch* which started evolving through the late Middle Ages. The new attitude to knowledge was a precondition for sustained economic growth. The existence of a market clearly was another precondition. But, without the new attitude towards learning and creativity, the goods exchanged in the marketplace today would essentially have continued to be the same as during the Centuries before the Renaissance.

The new attitude towards knowledge can best be understood in the context of the 'system of duties' created, among others, by German philosopher Christian Wolff. In such a system, the industrial revolution and economic progress was 'willed', it was a product of a conscious collective decision to improve Man's material conditions, and through that, his happiness. We would argue that beyond this, the next, and probably last, layer of causes of economic welfare will be found in the study of the 'image of Man'—in the Platonic tradition rather than in the Aristotelian tradition of philosophy. In this tradition 'true essential reality … could be grasped only by thought, in contrast with perception.… the Platonic system thus becomes immaterialism.'[39] The **idea** is the core, not sensual perceptions of reality.[40] The essential moving force behind the physical and monetary flows of an economy is Man's ideas.

---

39 Windelband, Wilhelm, *op. cit.*, p. 108–109.

40 See Plato, *Phaedo*, Translated with an Introduction and Commentary by R Hackforth, Cambridge, Cambridge University Press, 1972, especially 97c to 108c in the Greek pagination, and his *Parmenides*, Translated into English and with an Introduction by A.E. Taylor, Oxford, Clarendon Press, 1934, 132b to 136e, and 'Epistle VII', in *Plato, with an English Translation*, Vol VII, (edited by R.G. Bury), Loeb Classical Library, London, Heinemann 1929, 342b to 344d. See also Cornford, F.M., *Plato's Theory of Knowledge*, London, Routledge, 1935.

What other economists have identified as the moving force of the economy, are all dependent on Man's ideas: The term 'capitalism' indicates that capital is the moving force of the economy, but others suggest that the accumulation is the result of imperfect competition resulting e.g. from technical change[41]. Adam Smith sees Man's propensity to barter as the moving force. Marx sees Man's use of tools as the key feature. US economist E. Peshine Smith[42] claimed that Man's domination of the forces of Nature is the most important feature. Schumpeter sees innovations at the moving force. These are all necessary conditions, but they one and all rest on Man's **rational will** and **ideas**. The ultimate moving force of the economy is thus ideas. The other moving forces—barter, tools, innovations, domination of Nature—all originate from Man's ideas, and are as such mere symptoms of progress, not causes. In a sense, the name capitalism is therefore somewhat of a misnomer. Unfortunately the word **idealism** is already in use with different connotations.

3. Evolutionary vs. neoclassical economics—the historical roots of the conflict

As a result of the growing uneasiness with the shortcomings of neoclassical theory, this theory is being challenged by an alternative evolutionary world view. Nelson and Winter's 1982 book *An Evolutionary Theory of Economic Change*[43] is considered as the starting point for today's renewed interest in evolutionary economics, although its origins are well-rooted in the teachings of Schumpeter. Prof. Erich Streissler has traced the influence of 19th Century German and Austrian economics on Schumpeter[44]. It is however, possible to trace the origins of today's conflict between neo-classical and evolutionary economics much further back: Here Christian Wolff, not surprisingly to those who know the roots of German economics, comes across as one of the spiritual forerunners of evolutionary economics. The counterpoint of the conflict is—in shorthand—the *static equilibrium* of neo-classical economics vs. a *dynamic evolution*.

Today a group of philosophers and historians of economics discusses neo-classical economics as being modelled on late 19th Century physics, and how the concept of equilibrium, Marshall's scissors of supply and demand, came to be its central *gestalt*. In his book *More Heat than Light. Economics as Social Physics, Physics as Nature's Economics*[45], Philip Mirowski attacks the 'physics-envy' of present-day economics. Mirowski quotes

---

[41] The first clear statement of this is found in John Rae's *Statement of some New Principles on the Subject of Political Economy*, Boston, Hilliard Gray, 1834.

[42] Smith, E. Peshine, *A Manual of Political Economy*, New York, Putnam, 1853.

[43] Cambridge, Mass., Harvard University Press, 1982.

[44] 'The Influence of German and Austrian Economics on Joseph A. Schumpeter', in Shinoya, Yuichi and Mark Perlman, *Schumpeter in the History of Ideas*, Ann Arbor, University of Michigan Press, 1994.

[45] Cambridge, Cambridge University Press, 1989, see also De Marchi, Neil (editor), *Non-natural Social Science: Reflecting on the Enterprise of 'More Heat than Light'*, Durham, Duke University Press, 1993.

Argentine author Borges' assertion that 'universal history is the history of a handful of metaphors'. Mirowski's counterpoint becomes neo-classical economics with its metaphors from physics vs. an alternative theory based on 'natural images' or biological metaphors.[46]

The two focal points, mentioned above, in the economics profession today are essentially based on similar critical attitudes towards static theory and its physical metaphors. The two groups have a lot of common ground, but do not seem to communicate. Their origins go back to Leibniz and Wolff, among others. With these 18th Century Germans, the modern approach shares a dynamic world view, which emphasises the 'never-ending frontier' of science and innovation. However, Leibniz, 'his faithful henchman Christian Wolff'[47], and their followers differ from Schumpeter, Nelson, Mirowski and today's evolutionists on a crucial point. Leibniz and Wolff emphasise the role of *conscious human will* as a moving force in economics. This human will acts both on an individual and on a collective level. Compared to Leibniz and Wolff, today's evolutionists are in some sense too 'mechanical'.

The science of Leibniz and Wolff is not the dismal science of the English classical economists, but, as we shall see, a science of duties leading to joy and harmony. The pessimism of the young Malthus as regards population is an example in point. This contrasts sharply with the typical German cameralist view—later followed by List and Schmoller—that the greatness of population was a main determinant of wealth: A successful country was one where the creativity of the human mind would *more than compensate* any diminishing returns from land. These effects were to be accomplished through new knowledge and new technology. Leibniz argues that 'the true power of a kingdom consists in the number of men, (and) manufacturing especially is to be considered the most useful occupation in accomplishing this result.'[48] Manufacturing could absorb and utilize more inventions than agriculture, and it was seen to contribute more to the systemic effects which improved society, to what Renaissance economists called *the common weal*. Recent economic research on *positive feedback systems*[49] confirms the 'mercantilist' idea that manufacturing—which is subject to increasing returns—is able to create positive feedback mechanism which supplies a system-wide common good, whereas resource-based activities—subject to diminishing returns—do not have this ability.

---

46 Mirowski, Philip, *Natural Images in Economic Thought*, Cambridge, Cambridge University Press, 1994.

47 '... the great name of Leibniz and that of his faithful henchman, Christian Wolff'. Quoted from Schumpeter, Joseph Alois, *History of Economic Analysis*, New York, Oxford University Press, 1954, p. 117.

48 *Gottfried Wilhelm Leibniz*, Guhrauer's edition, vol. II, p.312, quoted in Stangeland, Charles Emil, *Pre-Malthusian Doctrines of Population*, Chicago, University of Chicago Press 1904, p. 207. See also: *Essai de quelque Raissonnements noveaux sur la Vie humaine et sur le Nombre des Hommes*, in *Works*, (Klopp edition) first series, Vol. V, pp. 326–337, referred to in Stangeland, p. 207.

49 For an overview, see Arthur, W. Brian, 'Positive Feedbacks in the Economy', in *Scientific American*, February 1990, pp 80–85.

Building on his own experience as a mining engineer and administrator in Harz, south of Hannover, between 1680 and 1686, Leibniz imagined that new knowledge could unleash Man's creativity both in the process of shaping technology and by creating spare time, as the heavy burden of daily life would be lifted. In these ways technology potentially was not only the necessary means to the liberation of Man but also the highest expression of true love and spirituality.[50] In particular Leibniz expressed great hope in the development of steam power as a controllable and reliable source of energy.

Leibniz and Wolff, as Cusa before them and Schmoller after them, opposed the compartmentalisation of different aspects of life and science which followed as a result of the materialistically oriented Enlightenment. They stressed the necessity of multi-disciplinary knowledge, and of the normative basis of all science. This ethical and inter-disciplinary attitude contrasts sharply with the simplistic concept of *Economic Man* in the atomistic classical and neo-classical tradition. The question of interdisciplinarity formed the core of the important *Methodenstreit* in economics of the 1870s, between Carl Menger and Gustav Schmoller.

The point of divergence between neo-classical economics and evolutionary economics can be traced back to pre-19th Century philosophy. The Plato-Cusanus-Bruno-Leibniz-Wolff tradition has a dynamic world view emphasizing *new knowledge* and *production*— cast in the mode of 'werden', or becoming. The modern Anglo-American tradition is cast around the concept of 'sein'—being. It emphasises a mechanical division of labour, and at its core we find the process of *barter and exchange* rather than production. To Adam Smith Man is different from other animals above all because of his *propensity to barter*. Adam Smith illustrates this by contrasting Man with a dog, because dogs never consciously barter.[51] To Adam Smith the division of labour is the cause of progress. In the spirit of Wolff one would argue that there would be no division of labour, except as a result of the creativity and inventiveness of Man. Consequently what distinguishes a human being from a dog is not the propensity to barter, but, in Adam Smith's terms, the *propensity to invent new ways in which to divide labour*. To Wolff, the fact that these products later have to be bartered in a market, would have been a secondary, and much less important consideration.

In the Plato-to-Wolff tradition, Man is different from animals because of his ability to think rationally according to principles, e.g. abstraction. Economics in this tradition

---

[50] As laid out in his 'On the Establishment of a Society in Germany for the Promotion of the Arts and Sciences', 1671, translated from the German by John Chambless, reproduced in *Fidelio*, Vol. 1, no. 2, 1992, pp. 63–69, see in particular pp. 66–68

[51] Adam Smith sees the division of labour to be caused by the propensity to barter: '(The propensity to barter) is common to all men, and to be found in no other race of animals, which seem to know neither this nor any species of contracts .... Nobody ever saw a dog make a fair and deliberate exchange of one bone for another with another dog.' Wealth of Nations, *op. cit.*, p. 17. In evolutionary terms, however, the division of labour is caused by inventions and specialised knowledge. The division of labour can only depend on the size of the market if there are fixed costs and consequent economies of scale in the system. Therefore, in some fundamental sense, the division of labour is incompatible with equilibrium.

becomes an optimistic science, because of Man's seemingly unlimited capacity to invent. Economics in the English barter-centered tradition becomes a dismal science because, following up in Adam Smith's metaphor, it is not clear why and how more dog bones, not to speak of canned dog food, would suddenly appear among a society of bartering dogs. The failure of neo-classical economics to incorporate technical change is deeply rooted in this tradition of seeing Man essentially as a bartering animal, and not as a creative and inventing one. Smith's crucial insight on the 'division of labour', which in the end could not be attributable to barter alone, has not been incorporated into present mainstream economics. Mainstream economics focuses on 'Man the Consumer', whereas in the Wolff tradition focus is on 'Man the Producer'.

Another sign of Smith's failure to see the importance of new ideas, is his view that the rate of profit will have to fall. It is not well known that this idea, which was later to gain much prominence with Marx, actually originates with Adam Smith. In the absence of new ideas and inventions, the rate of profit will fall for three reasons, and it is not clear which of the three, or all, Smith refers to[52]. First, the rate of profit will fall because of a tendency towards a more perfect competition. Secondly, the rate of return on capital will fall because there will be more capital around, and more capital chasing the same number of investment opportunities will lead to a falling rate of profit. Thirdly, continuing progress would depend on a further division of labour. This Smith saw as tied to geographically expanding markets, which eventually will be saturated. Both Smith and Ricardo fail to understand that all these tendencies will be counteracted by a flow of new ideas and inventions which will both a) Increase the demand for capital in a growing economy, and b) Add new products which initially will be traded under conditions of temporary monopolies. This mechanism, whereby capitalists continuously have to seek new ideas and innovations in order to keep up the profit rate, is at the core of the Schumpeterian system. In this system, the fall of nations is accompanied by capital flight which starts when the national system fails to produce innovations.[53] This phenomenon could be observed from Venice and Holland to England as England ascended, and from England to the US as England descended. The mechanism is a fairly straightforward one: Inward capital flows are determined by a nation's propensity to invent and innovate; in other words by *investment opportunities*. These investment opportunities are provided by inventions and new products, in a process which is greatly facilitated by government initiatives, e.g. in education, infrastructure, and warfare.

In the English-based mainstream economics, under the assumption of perfect information, new learning is absent—or must be seen as 'manna from heaven'. It is not clear that human will—in the form of inventions, business strategies, or economic policies—in any way can affect the size of the flow of manna. The connection between learning and welfare is here, at best, indirect through mechanical forces which are not

---

52 This is discussed in Verdera, Francisco, 'Adam Smith and the Falling Rate of Profit: A Reappraisal', in *Scottish Journal of Political Economy*, Vol. 39, No. 1, February 1992.

53 Both Smith and Ricardo discuss the problem of capital outflows, but it in a static framework with no possibility for new inventions at home to counteract the problem.

consciously created. In neo-classical economics all economic activities, for all practical purposes, tend to become 'alike'. The world is populated by cloned 'representative firms', and government policy is supposed not to differentiate between firms or industries. In the Leibniz-Wolff cameralist tradition, as well as today's evolutionary economics, the variety and uniqueness of human economic activities are central to the system. Canadian economist John Rae (1834) was the first to point out the connection between a society's propensity to save and its propensity to *invent*: Savings were to Rae basically not a result of thrift, but of retained earnings from imperfect competition created by inventions and technical change.[54]

Leibniz' 'vitalist' view contrasts sharply with the static mechanisms of modern economic theory. To Leibniz the world is not to be understood in terms of *geometrical* principles, as it is with Descartes and Newton, but according to *dynamic* principles. Compared to Descartes and Newton, Leibniz inverts the order of explanation of how the world is to be understood: Descartes and Newton explain the organic world based on the understanding of *inorganic* phenomena—understanding 'the living from the dead'. This leads to the 'physics-envy' of today's economic theory. Leibniz, and later Goethe, on the contrary, explain 'the dead from the living', i.e. from energy, eventually from mental energy: thinking. They therefore basically explained everything from philosophical and idealistic points of view as opposed to philosophical materialism.[55] To them, lower level forms are to be explained by higher level forms. God's power of creation being the highest form, creativity looms high as an explanatory variable in Leibniz' world view. In the static Newtonian tradition of classical and neo-classical economics, Man is just another material factor of production, and the equilibrium of supply and demand is at the core. In the Leibniz-Wolff tradition Man's free will and creativity become the moving force of the economy. Economics becomes a dynamic, evolutionary and anthropocentric science, i.e. Man's creativity is at the very core.

In the 'physics envy' of neo-classical economics, economics and the social sciences are 'soft' disciplines, which are in some way inferior to the 'hard' natural sciences. The Leibniz-Wolff tradition, continued in the works of philosophers like Wilhelm Dilthey and Hans Georg Gadamer, refuses any such subordination. In Dilthey's view, the social sciences, concerned with the ends and values instead of laws, should aim to **understand** (verstehen). The natural sciences, on the other hand, aim mainly to **describe and conceptualise** (begreifen). Qualitative relationships are at the core of the *Geisteswissenschaften*—the Humanities, or literally, sciences of the mind. A crucial aspect of these sciences is therefore their *irreducibility to natural science*. Paradoxically, although economics is about numbers, there is also a basic incommensurability between numbers (quantities) and some fundamental aspects of economic science. In the German economic

[54] Rae, John, *Statement of Some New Principles on the Subject of Political Economy*, Boston, Hilliard, Grey & Co., 1834.

[55] For an account of Wolff's fight with the Newtonians at the Berlin Academy of Science, in particular Maupertuis, Euler and Frederick II's protégé Voltaire, see Ronald S.Callinger, 'The Newtonian-Wolffian Controversy', *Journal of Historical Ideas*, Vol. 30, 1969, pp. 319–330.

tradition, the inner unity (*Strukturzusammenhang*) of the *Geisteswissenschaften*—its refusal to isolate 'economic man' from the rest of the human being—shines through from Leibniz to Max Weber.

Near the core of this problem, we find the struggle between *nominalist* and *realist* conceptions of the status of the *common terms*—universalia—at the end of the Middle Ages. The former—nominalism—as a *quantitative* relationship, outward and accidental, and the latter—realism—as a necessary inner *qualitative* relationship concerned with structure and meaning. The former is typically represented by the British empiricism of Hobbes, and the latter by the Platonic tradition. This controversy continues today in the theory of science as a discussion of the role of theory: *instrumentalism* vs. *realism*. Discussing Mediaeval scholastic economics, Schumpeter mentions that 'in our own time, the Realism and Nominalism of the scholastic doctors have been linked with two other concepts, Universalism and Individualism ... the conflict between which runs through the whole history of sociological and economic analysis, and is indeed the essential fact behind all the other clashes of opinion that occurred throughout the ages.'[56] We would argue that this conflict is more profoundly is a question of materialism vs. idealism. In the last account, idealism and realism are the true defenders of individualism since all kinds of materialism, nominalism, biologism and other types of reductionism in the end deny the potential independence of the individual and his soul.[57]

4. The religious gestalt-switch: From religion as a deterrent, to religion as a promoter of economic growth

After Kuhn's *Structure of Scientific Revolution*[58] fundamental changes in the sciences have come to be called paradigm shifts. A paradigm shift is a fundamental change in the conception of reality. It involves a gestalt-switch—the gestalt in question is seen as being a totally different one, the world is no longer flat but round. We shall argue that the basis for the economic growth and welfare of the Western world was a religious gestalt-switch.

---

[56] The methodological conflict between universalism and individualism (methodological collectivism vs. methodological individualism) is usually fought within a materialist agenda. Liberalism, marxism as well as game theory and functionalism are usually all only seemingly contradictory parts of this same materialist tradition as opposed to idealist individualism. Such idealist individualism is really not opposed to collectivist explanations; they merge in historical research.

[57] This is profoundly argued in Hjalmar Hegge's thesis in philosophy—epistemologically and historically. Hegge argues in particular against superficial individualism, against the 'decisionistic' existentialism of Kierkegaard, Heidegger and Sartre and against the liberalists J. Locke, Adam Smith, John Stuart Mill, W. Humboldt, F.Hayek, J.Rawls, J.Habermas, as well against Marx. He claims they all represent various kinds of irrationalism. See Hjalmar Hegge, *Frihet, individualitet og samfunn*, Oslo, Universitetsforlaget 1988, see chapter 1; *Freedom and Individuality*, and chapter 17; *The Interior and Exterior Existence of Individuality*. Translated into the German as *Freiheit, Individualität und Gesellschaft*, Stuttgart, Verlag Freies Geistesle-ben, 1992.

[58] Kuhn, Thomas, *The Structure of Scientific Revolutions*, 2nd Edition, Chicago, University of Chicago Press, 1970.

This switch has long historical roots, building up within the Catholic Church through the late Middle Ages. At the same time, the switch is caused by a change in emphasis from one Greek philosopher to another. The driving force of the gestalt-switch was an increasing dissatisfaction with the fruitlessness of the static interpretation of Aristotle in the scholastic tradition, occupied with static relations of categories and syllogisms. The new gestalt was based on a dynamic interpretation of the newly introduced writings of Plato, which gave impetus to the Renaissance and totally dominated this period. Our interpretation of the changing philosophical emphasis, is based on the neo-Kantian tradition of Wilhelm Windelband and Ernst Cassirer.

The roots of the dynamic, holistic, and idealistic world view which came to be the characteristic feature of German economic thought, can be traced even further back than Plato, to Heraclitus (536–470 b.C.). He added a dynamic dimension, 'werden'—becoming—to the static material world of 'sein'—being. 'Being' was at the core of the world gestalt of his predecessors, in his lifetime represented by the Eleatic School of Xenophanes and Parmenides. The holistic world of Heraclitus and Plato was based on *Logos*, thought. In contrast, atomism was based on *matter*. The atomism which later was to characterise John Locke and English economic liberalism, was first made explicit by Leucippus (5th Century b.C.) and his pupil Democritus (460–370 b.C.). Epicureus (341–270 b.C.) developed atomism in the social sphere.[59]

Through the Middle Ages the Aristotelian-scholastic tradition caused religion to be a strong deterrent in the search for new empirical knowledge. The Holy Scriptures—supplemented especially by Aristotle—were seen to hold, 'at least implicitly, the sum of knowledge useful or indeed possible for men'.[60] In the mediaeval philosophical tradition, religion is at the core of the argument against searching for new knowledge outside the Scriptures and Aristotle. A search for knowledge outside these sources almost automatically became a heresy. Using such knowledge would 'disturb the equilibrium of nature'.

A necessary foundation for later economic growth was that *this religious argument was turned upside down*. The gestalt-switch was based in a new and dynamic interpretation of the same Scriptures. The Scriptures which previously served as a straightjacket preventing Man from seeking knowledge outside his immediate boundaries, could now be used to argue for the exact opposite case. The Holy Scriptures + a static interpretation of Aristotle deterred the supply of new knowledge. The same Scriptures, adding the long-forgotten views of Plato, provided for a world where explorations and inventions were not only tolerated—with Leibniz-Wolff they even became one of the main duties of Man. This was very much the spirit of the Renaissance. First in Roger Bacon (1214–1292), later in Nicolas of Cusa (1401–1464), Leibniz (1646–1716), and Wolff (1697–1754), the perfection of God was turned into an argument for searching new knowledge so that Man could strive towards Godly perfection.

---

59 This is discussed in Windelband, op. cit., Chapter 1, and in Cassirer, Ernst. *An Essay on Man*, New Haven, Yale University Press, 1944, and Cassirer, Ernst, *Das Erkenntnisproblem in der Philosophie und Wissenschaft der neuerer Zeit*, Vol. 1, Berlin, Verlag Cassirer, Berlin, 1906.

60 Taylor, Henry Osborn, *The Mediaeval Mind*, London, Macmillan, 1914, Vol. II, p. 521.

The remarkable central idea of Cusa that 'the Universe is the *explicatio* of God, that His work of creation consists in that He is all (*Creare Dei est esse Omnia*) and that, in thinking, the mind, as it were, *imitates this creative act*.'[61] Noting Cusa as a forerunner of Copernicus, Dijksterhuis notes that 'a scientific revolution might have taken place in the fifteenth Century if only the intellectual power that called these thoughts into existence had succeeded in inspiring kindred spirits among the students of the different sciences.[62] Thomas Kuhn mentions Cusa as the only forerunner Copernicus probably knew.[63]

This turnaround in the use of religious argumentation made it a duty, not a heresy, to discover, experiment, and invent. This transformation was based both on Platonic and Aristotelian traditions. According to Windelband, this transformation also involved in-fighting between the Aristotelians—empirically oriented Aristotelians in opposition to scholastic Aristoteleanism. However, the new spirit of the Renaissance was to be identified with the Platonic opposition which was new and therefore more interesting according to Windelband, and perhaps also more consistent.

Windelband, however, omits the crucial role played by the conscious emphasis on the use of *hypotheses*—or conjectures—in the philosophy of the Renaissance, which was the contribution of the neo-Platonists continued by Wolff. Cusa even named one of his works *De coniecturis* (1440–1444).[64] According to Wolff, philosophy is a study of the possible ('werden' = becoming) as opposed to the present reality ('sein' = being)[65]. He thereby relates back to the Greek pre-Socratic struggle of Heraclitus and Democritus referred to above. In fact, Wolff intended his life of work to culminate with a work on the art of the

61 E. J. Dijksterhuis: *The Mechanization of the World Picture*, 1950, Princeton University Press, Princeton 1986, p. 228.

62 Dijksterhuis, *op.cit.*, p. 231.

63 Thomas Kuhn, *The Copernican Revolution. Planetary Astronomy in the Development of Western Thought*, Cambridge, Harvard University Press 1957, renewed 1985., pp. 144, 197 and 233–235.

64 See the discussion in: Ronald Levao, *Renaissance Minds and Their Fictions. Cusanus, Sidney, Shakespeare*, Berkeley, University of California Press 1985, part I: *Nicholas of Cusa and the Poetics of Conjecture*. Levao points out the aesthetic 'perspective' dimension in Cusa's work which was to be elaborated by Kepler, Leibniz and Schiller in the areas of for example astronomy, painting, music and politics. Perspective can correct local errors in comprehension. Levao notes that Cusa anticipates several of Vico's convertibility of *verum* and *factum*; Man knows best what he has made.

65 Cassirer point out that this distinction—between present reality and the possible—is 'a universal problem of paramount importance for the whole character and development of human culture. Empiricists and positivists have always maintained that the highest task of human knowledge is to give us the facts and nothing but the facts. A theory not based on facts would indeed be a castle in the air, but this is no answer to the problem of a true scientific method; it is, on the contrary, the problem itself. For what is the meaning of a 'scientific fact'? Obviously no such fact is given in any haphazard observation or in a mere accumulation of sense data. The facts of science always imply a theoretical, which means a symbolic, element. Many, if not most, of those scientific facts which have changed the whole course of the history of science have been hypothetical facts before they become observable facts', Cassirer, An Essay on Man, op. cit., p. 58. This touches on Mirowski's and McCloskey's observations today, concerning metaphors, symbols and rhetoric in economic theory.

possible—i. e. invention—but this work never materialised. Hypotheses are the form in which new ideas appear; the essence of creativity. Hypotheses therefore characterise the difference between narrow fact-related empiricism and dynamic rationalism. They also mark the difference between formal logic (axiomatic deductivism/Euclidean geometry) and non-Euclidean geometry. Hypotheses characterize the essence and foundation of scientific progress and cannot be explained, nor furthered, through linear logic, but only through intuitively based analogies, metaphors and paradoxes. Linear logic cannot give anything more than what you already know; that which is inherent and implicit in the axioms. It can, however, structure what we do know.

Aristotle follows Plato in so far as they both see experience awakening the slumbering ideas within us. However, he does not follow Plato in recognizing that man potentially creates, through his self-moving spirit, new thoughts appearing in the form of lower and higher *hypotheses*. Based on sets of lower hypotheses on causal relations—what Kepler calls 'explanatory hypotheses'—Man is able to abstract higher hypotheses or *principles*—what Kepler calls 'true hypotheses'. It's man's duty to discover these principles, through experience, hypothesising, and experimenting—and to utilise and implement them through inventions. In a sense, the struggle between 'werden' and 'sein', today underlies the contrast between a relatively optimistic evolutionary economic science in a setting of 'werden', and a 'dismal' static neo-classical theory in a setting of 'sein'.

Newton strongly rejected the use of hypothesis, which he saw as being opposed to the idea of experience and experiments. Leibniz, on the other hand, insisted that hypotheses were needed to complement experience.[66] In spite of his opposition to using hypotheses, Newton naturally made many hypotheses himself.[67] By ignoring the role of hypotheses,

66 The is very clear in Leibniz' *On the Establishment of a Society in Germany for the Promotion of the Arts and Sciences* (1671), translated from the German by John Chambless, reproduced in *Fidelio*, Vol. 1, No. 2, 1992, pp. 63–69, section 19.

67 This is noted by Burtt, Edwin Arthur, *The Metaphysical Foundations of Modern Physical Science*, Garden City, N.Y., Anchor, 1954, pp. 215–220. In fact, book three of the first edition of Principia in 1687 started off with a list of hypotheses (page 1, book 3, 1.ed.). The following edition in 1713, however, not only opened with a foreword with a frontal attack on Leibniz, which is discussed in the next section, but he also quite consequently substituted *rules* for *hypotheses*. This is hardly known today, as only the third edition of 1727 was translated from Latin into English. Newton refused his collaborator Clarke to change back to the original use of the term *hypothesis*—for reasons which are open to speculations: Newton was a Christian heretic of the Arian sect (Arius, 250–336 A.D.). Clarke in 1741 had to disavow this belief after a new set of beliefs came to dominate the Royal Society. Newton's intention with scientific experiments was to look for signs showing that God had changed the rules of the world. If the rules had changed, this was seen as the surest sign that Christ was soon to return. Thus there was no place for hypotheses. Newton read the Bible as a collection of secret formulas in this regard. Leibniz criticized Newton's theory saying that both physics and theology would be absurd if God were to change the rules, and had reason to do so. To Leibniz this would have established God as a pathological ruler who interferes in the world with violence—a whimsical terrorist—as opposed to Leibniz' conception of a rational creator. Newton did not accept hypotheses—i.e. new interpretations of the world—only new observations (Rule IV, 2.ed., 1713). Newton's theory on the calculus was fairly similar to the earlier published theories of Leibniz and *Optics* was fairly similar to the earlier theories of Huygens, and his mechanical ideas fairly similar to

Newton established a model for the neo-classical school of economics which similarly was to insist on the permanent correctness of their axiomatic-deductive system—both concerning axioms and method.

Many pathbreakers for the religious *gestalt-switch* suffered persecutions as heretics. Bacon was arrested in 1277 because of his teachings, which contained 'suspitious innouations'(sic)[68]—*aliquas novitates suspectas*. He probably remained in jail until 1292. Nicolas of Cusa (from Kues near Trier in Germany) was Cardinal and Bishop of Brixen, present-day Bressanone in Italian South Tyrol. Also Cusa (or Cusanus) suffered from local prosecution. Giordano Bruno, his spiritual follower, was tried as a heretic and burned at the stake in Rome in the year 1600. Bruno laid the foundations for the works of Kepler, but also of the tradition of Galileo and Newton.

The emerging neo-Platonic world view saw in all creations the spirit of God—it was pantheistic. They thereby pointed out the need to explore and better understand Nature as a necessary way to know God. This conveyed an image of God as active, rational and creative. Since Man was created in the image of God, men also had the potential for these same qualities, both as individuals and collectively as the 'State'. As we shall see in Wolff, Man not only had permission to learn, explore, invent, and educate, but indeed a religious duty to do so. Creation was not ended on the 7th day, it was God's will that Man should be creative in order to improve the Creation—and thereby improve both his own condition and that of his fellow Man, both materially and spiritually. This contrasts sharply with the passive role given to Man in the Creation in the works of Adam Smith[69]. In the Leibniz-Wolff tradition, like in evolutionary theory today, there is no reason to think that the present situation is in any way optimal. As the foremost evolutionary economist says today, '… the equilibrium is strongly path dependent, and today's "optimum" may be very local and likely poor stuff compared to what might have been'[70].

This *obvious suboptimality of the present situation*, compared to the potential—the Unbound Prometheus—which lies in the creative forces of Man, caused Pufendorf, Leibniz, Wolff and other German philosophers to argue for coordinated intervention in the productive life. This need for coordination led to the need for the State. The core of German economic discourse became 'Der Mensch und seine Bedürfnisse'—Man and his Needs[71]. Somewhat surprisingly today, these needs also included an fundamental 'need to create'. A system created around a producing and inventing Man 'and his needs', obviously would develop very different values compared to a system where the self-interest of a

that of Galileo. Therefore, some scholars consider Newton's distinctive contribution to be that of methodology: substituting symbols for metaphors and substituting symbolism for theory.

68 For this term, see *The Oxford English Dictionary*, Vol. 5, p. 314.

69 This is especially clear in Adam Smith's *Theory of Moral Sentiments* (1759), Indianapolis, Liberty Classics, 1982, pp. 236–237.

70 Nelson, Richard, 'Recent Evolutionary Thinking About Economic Change', in *Journal of Economic Literature*, Vol. XXXIII (March 1995), p. 58.

71 An excellent discussion of this is found in Tribe, Keith, *Governing Economy. The Reformation of German Economic Discourse 1750–1840*, Cambridge, Cambridge University Press, 1988.

bartering and passively consuming 'Homo Oeconomicus' rules alone, as in the neoclassical economic system.

After 100 years of fighting totalitarianism, we have a tendency to classify any system not based on individual atomism as 'collectivist'. Interpreting the German economic system in this way is decidedly incorrect. 'The ultimate goal of the ordering of rights became the interest of the individual',[72] to quote Windelband, Schumpeter's favourite historian of philosophy.[73] The objective of the system was to maximize individual happiness, but, as opposed to the English liberalist tradition, there was no reason to believe that individual self-interest *alone* would lead to an optimal outcome.

In the English liberalist political economy, collective entities like people, society and nations tend to be considered as mere nominal abstractions. However, by Plato, his followers, and also in the German Cameralist tradition, these entities were considered real. This corresponds to the nominalist and realist points of view in the struggle over the universals, discussed here at the end of the above chapter, and indicates the practical implications of this metaphysical debate. In the static English liberalist tradition there is no need for governmental intervention. There is no evolution in the theory, and any intervention will just upset the 'natural' static equilibrium. In contrast, in the mercantilist tradition, the nation-state should intervene in the ongoing evolution in order to maximize the happiness and welfare of the individual citizen. Here lies the beginning of the welfare state as conceived by Christian Wolff. Leibniz anticipated him by suggesting that a national health system should be established.[74] The health system should be the basis for a welfare guaranteed by the State.[75] Wolff later specifies clearly that he wanted a state which secured welfare for the individual, but not one which automatically provided for him ('Ein Wohlfahrtsstaat, aber kein Versorgungsstaat'[76])

This rational pantheistic view opened for a new tolerance of other religions. In this world view morality was seen as having a totally rational base, which therefore could be understood by everybody. The principle of rationality forms the common basis for 'Natural Religion' which opens up for a reconciliation both with the diverse factions of Christianity and with Islam and Chinese Confucianism. Both Roger Bacon, inspired by Averroës[77],

---

[72] Windelband, *op. cit.*, p. 432.

[73] '... I shall name but one name, that of the man whose work seems to me to have been the peak achievement of the 'historical philosophy' of that or any other age: Wilhelm Windelband.', Schumpeter, Joseph Alois, *History of Economic Analysis*, op. cit., p. 775.

[74] In his *Directiones ad rem medicam pertinentes*, 1672.

[75] 'Leibniz verfolgt das Ziel einer Heilkunde im Zeichen der Aufklärung, das heißt für ihn, die Grundlage für einen ***staatlich zu garantierenden Wohlstand*** zu schaffen (Italics in original), Krüger, Mathias, 'Leibniz' Vorstellungen zur Organisation eines öffentlichen Gesundheitswesens', in Müller, Kurt, Heinrich Schepers and Wilhelm Totok (eds.), *Studia Leibniziana Supplementa*, Vol XII, Band 1, Wiesbaden, Franz Steiner Verlag, 1973, p. 234.

[76] Namslau, Günter, 'Rechtfertigung des Staates bei Christian Wolff', in Kraus, Herbert (ed.), *Internationale Abhandlungen*, Berlin, Dr. W. Rothschild, 1932. p. 96.

[77] See Windelband, Wilhelm, *A History of Philosophy*, (1893), Westport, Conn., Greenwood Press, 1979. p. 319.

and Cusanus, held positive views of Islam. Both Gottfried Wilhelm Leibniz and Christian Wolff held very positive views of Chinese society and Confucianism. China showed both a large population and economic welfare, and therefore, these authors argued, Chinese society[78] had to have found 'the philosophers' stone.', e.g. the rationally correct principles of life and society. It is interesting to observe the virility of Chinese entrepreneurship throughout South-East Asia today, and the strong emphasis of minority Chinese on high levels of education, in this light. The ethnic Chinese today show the qualities that Leibniz and Wolff underlined in their day. It is interesting to contrast this with Adam Smith's use of China—50 years later—as an example of a country where a dreadful state of affairs prevailed.[79]

Another source of inspiration to Leibniz, and therefore to Wolff, was the expansionist economic policy of Richelieu and Colbert in France. Young Leibniz was invited to Paris by Colbert's trusted leader of the Academy of Science, Christian Huygens. Leibniz spent long periods in Paris (1672–1676 and later 1690–1694), where he could observe Colbertism, a system which systematically promoted and protected the new knowledge which was continually being created in the manufacturing sector.[80] Seeing Colbertism in action clearly inspired Leibniz' thoughts. Richelieu originally moulded the core from which Colbert established the Academy of Science in Paris 1666, Leibniz was later instrumental in founding the Academies of Berlin and St. Petersburg. It is interesting to contemplate that it was observing the devastating consequences of the collapse of this French mercantilist system—after the Napoleonic wars—which caused another German, Friedrich List, to convert from being a free trader to favouring the protection of national manufactures in the German Zollverein.

5. The gestalt-switch and the industrialization of England

Although this paper is centered around the gestalt-switch based on German economist-philosophers, we feel it is important also rapidly to draw a picture of England to show the earlier, but parallel, development here.

The basic idea of *real-ökonomisch* mercantilism, cameralism and Colbertism, rested on the assumption, implicit or explicit, that *some knowledge was more valuable than other*. Consequently, it was in the interest of the State to create and protect such knowledge. On a philosophical level, this valuable knowledge emanates from the mind of Man. Therefore, any theory not taking Man's mind and Man's soul into consideration, will consequently not understand the increase in Man's material condition, i.e. economic growth.

---

78 Although we have no indication that this is true, it is interesting to note that a historical novel by Thomas Costain also portraits Roger Bacon as having a keen interest in China. *The Black Rose*, New York, Avon, 1973.

79 Smith, Adam, *Wealth of Nations* (1776), Chicago, University of Chicago Press, 1976. pp. 80–81.

80 For a description of this, see Joubleau, Félix, *Études sur Colbert*, 2. Vols., Paris, Guillaumin, 1856, and Gouraud, Charles, *Histoire de la Politique Commerciale de la France et son Influence sur le Progrès de la Richesse Publique*, 2 Vols., Paris, Durand, 1854.

The economic policies resulting from theories of this kind were carried out with varying degrees of understanding of the underlying principles. These policies were, in our meaning of the word, not based on what we today would normally call scientific analysis. These theories were based on 'clues', on a mode of inference called *abduction*—or *phronesis*, Aristotle's third form of knowledge[81]. This tradition is continued by the Italian philosopher Giambattista Vico (1668–1744), by the US philosophical tradition of C.S. Pierce, and in economics in Kaldor's 'stylised facts'.[82] According to Pierce, '(Induction) can never originate any idea whatever. No more can deduction. All the ideas of science come to it by the way of Abduction. Abduction consists of studying facts and devising a theory to explain them. Its only justification is that if we are ever to understand things at all, it must be in that way.'[83] Pierce here describes the role played by the formulation of hypotheses in the neo-platonic tradition of Leibniz and Wolff.[84]

We shall explain how policy is generated through abductive reasoning with a parallel from the history of medicine: Starting in the 12th Century sailors in the Mediterranean used lemons to prevent scurvy.[85] This was a very effective policy. However, the explanation as to why this policy worked only appeared in 1929, with the discovery of Vitamin C[86]. Likewise, we would claim that it is entirely possible to establish good economic policies for a time, without fully understanding the factors involved. For example, identifying 'progress' or ability to pay more taxes with the use of machinery in an increasing number of industries, would result in a beneficial public policy, even if the causal relationship between the use of machinery and wealth were not clearly established, or had been 'unlearned'. The intuitive abduction often precedes what we would think of as a more 'scientific' type of knowledge. The view that abduction anticipates 'science' was expressed by the English economist Edward Misselden in 1623: 'Wee felt it before in sense, but now wee know it by science'[87]. The important debate between Misselden and Malynes is referred to below.

When England started growing in the late 15th Century, the Republic of Venice was already based on such policies. Mercantilist policies aimed at the creation and protection of valuable knowledge included prohibition of emigration of skilled labour—under

---

81 The authors are indebted to Åke Uhlin for pointing out the relevance of abduction to this analyis.

82 For a discussion of Kaldor's use of stylised facts, see Lawson, Tony, 'Abstraction, tendencies and stylised facts: a realist approach to economic analysis', in Lawson, Tony, J. Gabriel Palma and John Sender (eds.), *Kaldor's Political Economy*, London, Academic Press, 1989.

83 Pierce, Charles S., in Hartshorne, C. and Weiss, P. (eds.), *Collected Papers of Charles Sanders Pierce*, Cambridge, Mass., Harvard University Press, 1867. Vol. V, p. 146. Quoted in Lawson, *op. cit.*, p. 68.

84 Pierce is often interpreted as belonging to a biological and instrumentalistic tradition opposed to the neo-platonic tradition. For an alternative interpretation which puts Pierce in the 'realist' and neo-Platonic tradition, see Schneider, *A History of American Philosophy*, New York, Colombia University Press, 1946, pp. 334 ff.

85 Villner, Katarina, *Blod, Kryddor och Sott*, Stockholm, Carlsson Bokförlag, 1986, pp. 110–113.

86 Mervin, Leonard, *Vitamin C*, Willingborough, Thorsons Publishers, 1981, pp. 14–15.

87 Misselden, Edward, *The Circle of Commerce*, London, Nicholas Bourne, 1623.

the penalty of death, and the protection of the home market. In Venice the use of protective tariffs as an instrument of industrial policy—as opposed to a measure to collect revenue—started around 1421[88], although it had been practised also in Byzantium (see below). Frequently the argument used for introducing tariffs, was to defend the high wages of the Venetian workers. Starting with Henry VII of England in 1485, and perfected by Elizabeth I, this type of economic policy slowly established itself as English mercantilism. A similar system had been implemented in France under Louis XI starting around 1462. An important mercantilist tool to encourage and protect the creation of knowledge, was the patent system.[89] Also this system was first created in Venice, where already in 1474 'patents of ten-year validity were available to all who registered a new device'.[90] A further logical policy to protect valuable knowledge embodied in machinery, was the prohibition of the export of machinery from England, which lasted until the 1830's.[91]

The encouragement and protection of knowledge which seemed particularly valuable was at the core of this system. The mercantilist logic was based on what we would call 'pre-Ricardian common sense'. This logic was most clearly stated by William Petty (1623–1687)[92]: If the average industrial workers have annual incomes which are four times those of a farmer, a nation of industrial workers will be much richer than a nation of farmers. This insight was killed off by Adam Smith's preference for agriculture as the most 'natural' activity, and by Ricardian trade theory. The static trade theory does not account for the phenomenon described by Petty, essentially because the factors causing these phenomena could not be grasped and formalised within the framework of the theory. Even today, international trade theory effectively removes as non-existent all factors which distinguish one economic activity from another, in some sense 'all economic activities become qualitatively alike'.

In a sense these policies correspond to Marshall's policy recommendations in the early editions of his *Principles of Economics*[93] that favourable results will arise from taxing

---

88 Sapori, Armando, 'I grandi problemi della storia economica di Venezia dal Secolo XI al XVI', in *Studi de Storia Economica*, Florence, Sansoni, 1967, Vol. III, p. 204.

89 For an excellent discussion of this, see MacLeod, Christine, *Inventing the Industrial Revolution. The English Patent System*, 1660–1800, Cambridge, Cambridge University Press, 1988.

90 Lane, Frederic C., *Venice. A Maritime Republic*, Baltimore, Johns Hopkins University Press, 1973. s. 320.

91 See Berg, Maxine, *The Machinery Question and the Making of Political Economy*, Cambridge, Cambridge University Press, 1980.

92 Petty, William, *Political Arithmetick, or a Discourse concerning the Extent and Value of Lands, People, Buildings; Husbandry, Manufacture, Commerce, Fishery, Artizans, Seamen, Soldiers; Publick Revenues, Interests, Taxes, Superlucration, Registries, Banks; Valuation of Men, Increasing of Seamen, of Militia's, Harbours, Situation, Shipping, Power at Sea &c. As the same relates to every Country in general, but more particularly to the Territories of His Majesty of Great Britain, and his neighbours of Holland, Zealand, and France*. London, Robert Clavel, 1691.

93 Marshall, Alfred, *Principles of Economics*, 1st edition, London, Macmillan, 1890, p. 452. This insight, contradicting the concept of equilibrium, disappeared from the later 2nd. to 8th. editions.

activities subject to diminishing returns in order to subsidising activities subject to economies of scale—especially if one visualises the term as Schumpeter's *historical increasing returns*.[94]

Later economic writers have no doubt that the economic ascent of England starts with the Tudors, particularly Henry VII and Elizabeth I. Daniel Defoe describes the transformation of the English economy, starting during the reign of Henry VII[95], from being a poor producer of raw wool in the periphery of Europe, to being a nation which based its increasing wealth on the processing of wool and the manufacture of woollen textiles. Friedrich List, many years later, was to comment that during centuries one simple maxim had been the substitute for all other economic theories in England: 'Export manufactured goods, import raw materials[96].

Did England experience a religious-philosophical gestalt-switch before Germany? We would claim it did. We have already mentioned the role of Roger Bacon. After Bacon, the Cambridge school of neo-Platonic philosophy did to England, what earlier the Academy of Florence had done to Italy. The original impetus of the Renaissance Revolution came to Florence—and to the Academy founded by Cosimo de' Medici (1389–1464)—from Byzantium, the East Roman Empire. Cusa visited Constantinople in 1435, but the key figure in injecting neo-Platonism in Florence and Europe was Byzantine philosopher and emigrant George Gemistos Plethon (ca. 1360–1452), who charged the teachings of the new Aristotelians with having an unchristian and materialistic character. From the point of view of economics, it is interesting to note that Plethon praised a protectionist policy in order to stimulate Byzantine industry and economy faced with Italian competition.[97] Giordano Bruno—a Neo-Platonic follower of Cusa—visited Paris several times, and had a long and influential stay in England from 1583, where he also acted as a counsellor to Elisabeth I. He was expelled from England after his satiric attacks on the Aristotelean 'pedantic grammarians' within the English establishment, and in particular at Oxford.[98] A trap was set for Bruno by the Venetian Inquisition in 1591, and he was later burned at the stake in Rome.[99]

Later Leibniz and Wolff were to be the philosophers of the gestalt-switch in Germany. According to Ernst Cassirer, the Cambridge School of philosophy 'is one of the piers of

---

[94] A term covering both the shift in the production function resulting from technical change *and* pure scale effects.

[95] Defoe, Daniel, *A Plan of English Commerce*, 2nd Edition, London, Charles Rivington, 1730, pp. 126–133

[96] This is discussed in Reinert, Erik, 'Catching-up from Way Behind: A Third World Perspective on First World History, in Fagerberg, Jan et. al. *The Dynamics of Technology, Trade and Growth*, Aldershot, Edward Elgar, 1994.

[97] See *The Oxford Dictionary of Byzantium*, New York, Oxford University Press, 1991. Vol. 1, p. 673.

[98] See Hall, Hall, A. Rupert, *The Revolution in Science 1500–1750*, London, Longman, Second Edition, 1983, and Frances D. Yates' critical *Giordano Bruno and the Hermetic Tradition*, Chicago, The University of Chicago Press 1964, reprint 1991. Chapters XII and XIII are both called *Giordano Bruno in England: The Hermetic Tradition.*

[99] See Rucker, Rudy, *Infinity and the Mind. The Science and Philosophy of the Infinite*, Princeton, Princeton University Press, 1995, p. 19.

that bridge linking the Italian Renaissance with German humanism in the eighteenth Century'[100]. Cassirer documents the Italian and English roots of what was to become the German gestalt-switch; 'how a certain group of ideas, which had taken root in Italy through Nicolas of Cusa and acquired a stable form in the Florentine Academy, retains its force in English Humanism and in English philosophy of the Seventeenth and Eighteenth Centuries, in order to finally undergo a rebirth, a sort of metamorphosis and metempsychosis, in the history of German thought.'[101] The Neo-Platonic heritage was taken to the New World by the Puritans—followers of the Cambridge School.[102] The impact of the new attitude to science is also discussed in a recent book on 'The Scientific Revolution in National Context'.[103]

A forerunner of the Cambridge school was St. Anselm of Canterbury (1033–1109), originally from Aosta in Italy. The philosophy of the Cambridge school strongly influenced economic policy starting with Francis Bacon (1526–1561), Lord High Chancellor and Reformer of England. Bacon, educated at Cambridge, was the man who turned neo-Platonic interest in Nature into a policy of changing Nature in order to benefit Man. Bacon was 'the impresario, propagandist, and publicist for the scientific revolution that has, in the last three hundred years, shaped our world'.[104] Reading Bacon's essay **'Of Innovations'**[105]—written about 450 years ago—brings to mind that there are clear parallels between static Mediaeval scholasticism, which is what Bacon fought against[106], and the closed-circuited and mechanical system of today's economic theory. Bacon's adversaries labelled his essays 'Good Advice for Satan's Kingdom'—anybody attempting to disturb the natural state of affairs in Nature's equilibrium were seen to promote Satan's Kingdom. Passively adopting—do nothing—was the only acceptable strategy to Bacon's adversaries in a debate which was not unlike the industrial policy debate in our times.

In common with his 13th Century predecessor, Roger Bacon, Francis Bacon held the view that the sciences are organically connected.[107] Man's power over nature was, in his view, an act of imitating the omnipotence of God—to strive for perfection. The parallel to Leibniz and Wolff is clear. To Bacon, experimental science was in itself a religious task. He saw science as 'an exalted co-operative enterprise'[108]. Bacon also writes a book

100 Cassirer, Ernst, *Platonic Renaissance in England* (1932), New York, Gordian Press, 1970, p. 201.

101 Ibid., p. 201.

102 Schneider, Herbert W, *A History of American Philosophy*, New York, Columbia University Press, 1946, Chapter 1–3. The first section of this book is entitled 'Platonism and Empiricism in Colonial America.'

103 Porter, Roy, and Mikulas Teich (Eds.), Cambridge, Cambridge University Press, 1992.

104 Bailey, Philip H., in 'Introduction' to *Complete Essays of Francis Bacon*, New York, Belmont Books, 1962, p. vii.

105 In *Complete Essays*, op. cit., pp. 78–79.

106 '... Bacon believed that he could set out new paths for science, and in this spirit he set up his New Organon as over against the Aristotelian', Windelband, *op. cit.*, p. 383.

107 *Encyclopaedia Brittanica*, 14th Edition, London, 1929, Vol 2, p. 886.

108 Burtt, Edwin Arthur, *The Metaphysical Foundations of Modern Physical Science*, Garden City, N.Y., Anchor, 1954, p. 125.

about the Reign of Henry VII[109], whom we consider an important point of departure for England's later ascent. Characteristically, Bacon's biography is entitled *Francis Bacon. The First Statesman of Science.*[110]

Bacon wrote a treatise which is interesting to economics: *New Atlantis*—a reminiscent of Plato's *Critias*. About the *New Atlantis* Windelband writes, in a phrase which does not belie its German origin: '... a happy island-people in carefully guarded seclusion is brought before us, which by skilful regulations receives information of the progress in civilisation made by all other peoples, and at the same time, by the systematic prosecution of research, discovery, and invention, raises to the highest point the control over Nature for the practical interests of human life. All kinds of possible and impossible inventions are related in fantastic prophecy, and the whole activity of the "House of Salomon" is directed towards the material state of society,...'[111] The inventions include the telescope, microphone, telephone, explosive material, flying machines, engines with air and water power, chemical discoveries, better culture of plants and animals, etc. The 'House of Salomon', in Bacon's utopian tract, played the role which was later to be played by Academies of Science and Universities. The utopias were at once a way indirectly to criticise the present order, and to present visions for alternative social orders.

In England, the influence of the Neo-Platonists and the Cambridge School yielded to the Empiricist philosophical counter-reformation led by Hobbes and John Locke (1632–1704). This conflict is also reflected in the main economic debate in early 17th Century England, in 1622–23 between Gerard De Malynes[112] and Edward Misselden.[113] In the history of economic thought, this debate is interpreted as being about exchange controls and the balance of trade.[114] However, by going back to the sources, one finds that the main line of attack by Misselden against Malynes is his 'mechanical' view of man—Malynes has left out Man's 'art' and 'soul'. Misselden quotes at length a paragraph from Malynes, where Malynes reduces trade to three elements, 'namely, Commodities, Money, and Exchange'[115]. Objecting to this definition, Misselden says: 'It is against Art to dispute with a man that denyeth the *Principles* of Art. This sentence (just quoted from Malynes)

---

109 Bacon, Francis, (Franc. Baconi), *De Verulamio Historia Regni Henrici Septimi, Anglia Regis. Opus Vere Politicum*, Lugd. Batavor, Franc. Hackium, 1647.

110 Crowther, J.G., *Francis Bacon. The First Statesman of Science*, London, Cresset Press, 1960.

111 Windelband, *op.cit*, p. 430.

112 Malynes, Gerhard, *The Maintenance of Free Trade, According to the three essentiall (sic) Parts ... Commodities, Moneys and Exchange of Moneys*, London William Sheffard, 1622, and *The Center of the Circle of Commerce, or, A Refutation of a Treatise,..., lately published by E.M.*, London, Nicholas Bourne, 1623.

113 Misselden, Edward, *Free Trade and the Meanes (sic) to Make Trade Flourish*, London, Simon Waterson, 1622, and, *The Circle of Commerce or the Ballance (sic) of Trade*, London, Nicholas Bourne, 1623,

114 Schumpeter discusses the controversy between the two men in his *History of Economic Analysis*, New York, Oxford University Press, 1954, pp. 344–345. See also their respective entries in 'The New Palgrave'. In all cases these references are purely to the mechanics of money and exchange.

115 Misselden, *op. cit.*, (1623), p. 8.

sheweth Malynes grosse ignorance, not to haue lern't to distinguish the *Principles* of naturall things from their Essence.... Homo constat anima & copore (sic): A man consists of soule and bodie. Now the *Matter* of a *Man* is a corporeall substance, common to other creatures: but the *Forme* of *Man* is his rationall soule: whereby he differeth from them all'.[116, 117] On the next page Misselden says: 'For a *Man* is not said to bee a *Man* in respect to his matter or corporeall substance: for then a beast should be a man: but in respect of his rational soule, whereby hee excelleth all other creatures.' According to Misselden, Malynes—by reducing commerce and economics only to its *matter*, i.e. merchandise and money—had left out Man's art and soul. Without Man's art and soul, 'there would be no traffique amongst men, not withstanding the materials of trade'.[118]

The conflict between the two economists Malynes and Misselden thus anticipates by some 250 years the German critique of the *Entgeistung* of economic theory and by some 350 years the present debate on 'physics-envy'. Misselden's equivalent of *Entgeistung* and 'physics envy' was—he quotes Aristotle on this—*privation*: 'Privation is not Ens or Beeing, because it is not in the subiect which is made by it.' To Misselden, economics is not in the 'Commodities, Money and Exchange', which are merely 'matters thereof'. In the same way 'An House is not an house in respect of the matter whereof it is made; for then all other stone & timber should be a house: but in respect to the *Forme* of it, whereby it is known to be a house.' In other words, the relationship between money and exchange on the one hand and economics on the other, is like the relationship between stone and timber on the one hand, and a house on the other.

The Malynes/Misselden debate emphasises the point that the debate on its own philosophical underpinnings has haunted economic theory from its very inception. It also goes to show that by generally lumping all mercantilists together in the history of economic thought, and by reading them almost exclusively second hand—almost invariably filtered through the lenses of a neo-classical *Weltanschauung*—we have lost sight of a vast number of valuable insights into our own profession.

After the debate of the 1620's in England, the 'mechanical' views of Malynes, Locke and Newton were soon to win the day. In his *Principia Mathematica* Isaac Newton launched his attack on Leibniz in 1687. The main attack of his best friend, John Locke, followed in 1690, and it was directed against Leibniz' neo-Platonist collaborators in Cambridge[119], the most important of whom was Henry More (1614–1687). Perhaps the easiest way to understand this conflict is by seeing Leibniz and Wolff as defending the idealist tradition of the neo-Platonic Renaissance against the attacks of the materialistic and mechanistic theories of the English and French Enlightenment. The severity of this conflict is

116 *ibid*, p. 9.

117 This contrast between *matter and form* or between *matter and ideas* is an old Platonic theme which has been thourougly discussed by Ernst Cassirer in his *Substanzbegriff und Funktionsbegriff*, Berlin 1910, English translation: *Structure and Function*, Chicago and London, 1923, and in *Freiheit und Form. Studien zur deutschen Geistesgeschichte*, Berlin 1916 and in *Philosophie der symbolischen Formen* 1–4, Berlin 1923–29.

118 *ibid*, p. 11.

119 Windelband, *op. cit.*, p. 450.

reflected in a quote by Rupert Hall's standard work on the scientific revolution: '... no man of genius has ever mounted so unscrupulous campaign against an opponent as Newton organised against Leibniz.'[120]

Hall sums up the situation like this: 'After the death of Huygens in 1695, all Europe except the English recognised Leibniz as its leading intellectual light: mathematician, philosopher, inventor, historian, friend and counsellor of monarchs, unlike Descartes always eminently respectable. That an English mathematician should set up his pretensions against such a figure was remarkable: That these pretensions should be upheld, widened and justified by an ample printed justification with, it seemed, the unanimous confidence of the Royal Society behind them was almost incredible.'[121] Newton was, himself, the chairman of the Royal Society in London, which makes the story less incredible. The humanist Jonathan Swift wrote a satiric attack on the practices of the Royal Society in *The Flying Island.*

In the political sphere, this intellectual development had its counterpart in the 'glorious revolution of 1688', which brought William III of the Dutch House of Orange to the English throne. With him came John Locke, who in his refuge in Holland had studied Cusa. On the practical side, we once more find the same parties engaged in a controversy. Locke defended the central elements of this 'glorious revolution' against Leibniz' criticisms—a revolution which cut the powers of the King, and in particular his right to levy taxes,[122] thereby also cutting his power to guide the social and economic development. This seems to be yet another case of the long standing European conflict between, on the one hand, the landed aristocracy and the plutocracy and, on the other hand, the King and the upcoming bourgeoisie. John Kells Ingram, the Irish historian of economics, comments on the development of the science of economics resulting from this: 'In England, after the transaction of 1688, by which the government was consolidated on the double basis of aristocratic power and official orthodoxy, the state policy became not so much retrograde as stationary,... there was for some time a noticeable check in the intellectual development, and Roscher and others have observed that, in economic studies particularly, the first three decades of the eighteenth century were a period of general stagnation, eclecticism for the most part taking the place of originality.'[123]

Italy experienced a similar development as England. In Windelband's view, 'Italy was made dumb by the counter-reformation.[124]'There, one consequence of this was the failure to establish a nation-state. In Italy, town-mercantilism did not develop into national mercantilism for yet another 200 years. The connection between the absence of

---

120 Hall, A. Rupert, *The Revolution in Science* 1500–1750, London, Longman, Second Edition, 1983, p. 310.

121 Hall, *op.cit.*, p.350

122 Anners, *op.cit.*, p. 191. See also, R.W.Meyer, *Leibnitz and the Seventeenth Century Revolution*, New York, Garland Publishing Inc., 1952 and 1985. A translation of the German original, *Leibniz und die europäische Ordnungskrise*, Hamburg, Hansischer Gildenverlage, 1948.

123 Ingram, John Kells, *History of Political Economy*, London, Black 1919, p. 54.

124 Windelband, *op. cit.*, p. 379.

a nation-state and the absence of economic development in Italy is clearly pointed out by Friedrich List and later by Immanuel Wallerstein.[125]

The Empiricist School reintroduced atomism and a mechanical world view, where the creative powers of Man lost their central part in the picture. Locke's empiricist tradition took over in the sphere of theoretical knowledge. In spite of this, in the long run English economic policy continued to be influenced by practical consideration, by vested interests, and by a practical view of steady progress materialising in machinery and science. Adam Smith's thesis of free trade did not have much practical influence during the first 100 years, and even then only when British vested interests suffered too much damage.[126] Practical policy was heavily influenced by practical men, who, like Andrew Ure[127] and Charles Babbage, saw the importance of technical change[128] and science[129].

The system developed into one where people like Babbage were listened to for domestic policies, and Smith and Ricardo were used for export. By this eclectic use of theory—by varying assumptions and theories according to the needs of England—both Babbage and Ricardo served England well. England shows that a mechanical and static economic theory will not do much harm a) as long as there is a steady supply of innovations, and b) as long as domestic policy-makers do not actually start believing in the static theory. England today, on the other hand, seems to be a country suffering simultaneously from a lack of innovations and from a political class which has come to embrace the static economic theory—where new ideas are irrelevant—as a 'natural law'.

6. Leibniz' and Wolff's system: Monads, duties and the holistic attitude to economics

It is in the works of Cusa, Kepler, Bruno, and Leibniz that one finds the origins of holistic German economic and social thought[130]. This contrasts with the atomism of the English Enlightenment, and with both classical and neo-classical economic theory. The views of Cusa[131], Bruno, Kepler, and Leibniz are Platonic rather than Aristotelian in their origin. They represent a world view of universal harmony, optimism and world joy. There was,

---

125 Immanuel Wallerstein, *Det Moderne Verdenssystem*, Oslo, Gyldendal, 1979, Vol. II, p. 93 (translation of *The Modern World System*, New York, Academic Press, 1974)

126 It has been calculated that the duty on cheap wine in 'free-trade England' during the 19th Century, in order to protect the interest of the brewers, reached 55.000%.

127 Ure, Andrew, *The Philosophy of Manufactures: or, an Exposition of The Scientific, Moral, and Commercial Economy of the Factory System of Great Britain*, London, Charles Knight, 1835.

128 Babbage, Charles, *On the Economy of Machinery and Manufactures*, London, Charles Knight, 1832.

129 Babbage, Charles, *Reflections on the Decline of Science in England* (1830), London, William Pickering, 1989. The publishing of this book led to renewed interest and investment in science. Note the timing of these works after Ricardo's *Principles* in 1817.

130 In continuation of the ancient Greek roots.

131 The close relationship between Plato and Cusanus is emphasized in Wyller, Egil A., *Enhet og Annethet*, Oslo, Dreyer, 1981, particularly pages 46–72. Wyller sees Cusanus as a great dialectician and theoretician of principles in the Platonic and Christian tradition.

as we shall see with Wolff, no conflict between a rigid system of duties and *Lebensfreude*—the joy of living. In the spirit of the Renaissance, the search for knowledge now took place in the nature created by God in his image, rather than confined in the libraries. The objective of the school created by Leibniz and Wolff was to improve the standard of living and to create employment—'to promote the happiness of Man'. This same objective, typical of the period, is contained in the title of one of Wolff's books: *Rational Thoughts on the Doings to be carried out by Men to promote their Happiness. Conveyed to Lovers of Truth by Christian Wolff.*[132]

To Cusa 'all substances are present in everything, that each thing therefore presents a microcosm, and yet that each has also its special principle of life and activity.'[133] From this, Giordano Bruno developed a system where the world consisted of units, called monads. This system was further developed by Leibniz. To him each monad was essentially different, but they also reflect the wholeness, *die Ganzheit*. Monads were the immaterial substances which made up the world, and their main characteristic was energy or force. Monads are individual, indivisible, and spiritual power centres. They are closed and cannot communicate, except through God.[134] Their force is constant, imperishable, immortal and bound to emanate in the direction of perfection. To Leibniz, and also to Wolff, there is a hierarchy of monads from passive and 'material' ones, to active and spiritual ones—the highest being God. They are compelled to act out their individual characteristics in a synchronised manner. Their actions correspond to each other in a harmony pre-established by God.[135] This harmony also exists between the world of the monads and the world of the phenomena experienced by Man. This harmony of ruling principles constitutes the world order. The duty of man is to explore and gain understanding of these principles: A joyful duty to learn and educate.

---

132 Our literal translation of the German original title: *Vernünftige Gedanken von der Menschen Thun und Lassen, Zur Beförderung ihrer Glückseeligkeit, den Liebhabern der Wahrheit mitgetheilt von Christian Wolffen, 1713*. The English edition carried the title *Logic, or Rational Thoughts on the Powers of the Human Understanding*, London, 1790.

133 Windelband, *op. cit.*, p. 371. Similar ideas were found in Baghdad in the 9th Century and later with the founder of Neo-Platonism, Plotinus. These same ideas find their counterparts in the Greek philosopher Anaxagoras, in the Egyptian Hermes and the Indian Vedanta philosophy of Brahman (God). This monism is opposed to the dualistic formal logic of Aristotle and Francis Bacon: *A* and *not-A*. This is what Ouspensky calls a higher intuitive logic. P.D. Ouspensky, *Tertium Organum*, London, Routledge, 1923, revised translation from the Russian 1981, chapters 8 and 21. Ouspensky claims that Aristotelain logic 'is quite sufficient *for observation*. But *for experiment* it is insufficient, for experiment takes place *in time*, whereas Aristotle's formulae do not take time into account.' Ouspensky claims that both Roger Bacon and later Francis Bacon observed this, but did not overcome the former insufficiency. *op.cit.*, pp. 73 ff. To this, note the loss of the time dimension in neo-classical economics.

134 i.e. through the rational principles constituted by God.

135 See, Gottfried Wilhelm Leibniz, *Monadology and Other Philosophical Essays*, London, Macmillan, 1965. See also, Ernst Cassirer, *Leibniz' System in seinen wissenschaftlichen Grundlagen*, Hildesheim, Georg Olms Verlagsbuchhandlung, 1962

This contrasts with the new English liberalist system of John Locke, in opposition to the earlier Cambridge School.[136] In Locke's view the mind of Man at birth was a *tabula rasa*, a blank slate upon which experience imprinted 'bits' of knowledge. Locke did not believe in self-moving intuition or conceptions, principles of thought which Man carried with him from birth as innate ideas. Human thought occurs when the different experiences are combined into more complex ideas. This makes the thought process of Locke's followers, among them Adam Smith and the English classical economists, into a process of associative psychology only.[137]

Bluntly put, *passive sensations* are at the core of Locke's system. As Leibniz and Wolff see it, Locke misunderstands the fundamental phenomenon of the mind, by attempting to find the basis of the mind in these passive impressions. To Leibniz and Wolff, the essence of the mind consists in *activity*, not in mere passivity.[138] The nature of the mind lies in its active energy and in its fertility—in its capacity to produce an unending series of ideas. The ego, then, is not merely the scene of ideas, but rather the source and origin of ideas: 'The fountain and source of a prescribed law of things about to be created.'[139] Leibniz sees the real perfection of Man's ego in this creative process: 'It is more perfect the more freely this production takes place.' The monadology also explains the existence of intuition, semiconscious monads, and opens up for what we today would call 'tacit knowledge'. The greater the force of the monad, the more fertile the mind and the more prolific the production of ideas. The creative production of a multitude of ideas originates in the freedom and unity of a monad/mind, and therefore in harmony. This harmony creates order and beauty, which in their turn awakens love and joy. Out of this comes Man's inclination to do good, his virtue. Will and reason interact to create happiness, 'an ever-enduring progress in wisdom and virtue …'.

As we shall see more clearly when discussing Wolff, in the Plato-Leibniz-Wolff- tradition public wealth is created by a system of 'private virtues'. This, of course, contrasts fundamentally with the classical and neo-classical tradition, based on Mandeville-Smith, that the essential wealth-producing mechanism of our economic system is a process by which *private vices* are converted into *public benefits*, i.e. 'we owe our daily bread to the greed of the baker, not to his kindness'.[140] In the Mandeville-Smith tradition, society, to the

---

136 See Gottfried Wilhelm Leibniz, *New Essays on Human Understanding*, Cambridge, Cambridge University Press, 1996, and also Nicolas Jolley, *Leibniz and Locke. A Study of the New Essays on Human Understanding*, Oxford, Clarendon Press, 1984.

137 'As a philosophy, Empirisism or Sensualism or Sensationalism, although brillliantly defended by Hume and by Mill … did not wear well. Leibniz raised the obvious but not decisive question—what is it?—… Associationist Psychology fared much better and in fact commanded the explicit or implicit allegiance of English economists and their continental allies until about 1900 and beyond', Schumpeter, *History of Economic Analysis*, op.cit, p. 121.

138 Cassirer, Ernst, *The Philosophy of the Enlightenment* (1951), Princeton, Princeton University Press, 1979, s. 121.

139 Leibniz' letter to de Volder, March 24, 1699, quoted in Cassirer (1951), 1979, *op. cit.*

140 Mandeville's private vices-public benefits was a parody on Leibniz' pre-established harmony. The main popularizer of Newton on the European Continent and main adversary of Wolff—Voltaire—ridiculed Leibniz for the same idea in his novel *Candide* with Leibniz in the figure of Dr. Pangloss.

extent that this exists, is balanced through a system of 'countervailing self-interests' (or greediness). In the Leibniz-Wolff tradition, society is in balance due to an innate human consensus—*consensus gentium*—and through legislation and governmental intervention. This *consensus gentium* was based on principles and patterns of thought which originated with Plato's dialogue 'Meno'.[141] In Europe the *consensus gentium* was important to the 15th Century Nicholas of Cusa and to Italy's Florentine Renaissance. This system continued with the late 17th Century Platonist School in Cambridge. It is first of all the adherents of this *consensus gentium* who come under the attack of John Locke in 1690. In the *consensus gentium* tradition, the difference between men and animals rests in Man's innate ability to think and communicate, based on abstract principles, which are shared by all men.

These abstract ideas form the basis of morality according to the neo-Platonic tradition; the skilful ability to distinguish between right and wrong[142]. In present-day economics, of course, '*right*' and '*wrong*' are phenomena which are totally external to the system. The Platonic tradition, however, was from the very start normative, and set out to change and better the conditions of Mankind in theory and practice; as a duty imposed on man by God, but also as a duty imposed by Man himself, as a spiritual being. Plato wrote the utopian *The Republic, The Statesman* and *Laws* and even engaged in a reform program with the King of Sicily. St. Augustin wrote the *De civitate Dei* and his followers became the closest advisors to Charlemagne. According to Schumpeter, Cusa, among all his other activities, set out to reform the tax system of the Holy Roman (German) Empire in 1440 proposing a system of income tax—an idea which was carried out in 1920. Jonathan Swift and Thomas More are later rational utopians in the same tradition, having similar ideas to those of Leibniz and Wolff as regards the creation of a welfare state.[143]

As a result of their monistic world-view, the monadology, Cusa[144] and Leibniz both advocated universal development since no human being can be happy and free when other fellow Men are not. Leibniz was explicit on what should be done to aid the development of other nations; 'by no means' should we lend money to the poorer nations. Leibniz suggested instead that giving *knowledge* to other nations in order to make them self-reliant would be the best means.[145] Wolff emphasised the need to institutionalize

---

141 Lamb, W.R.M. (Editor), *Plato, with an English Translation*, The Loeb Classical Library, Vol. IV, London, Heinemann, 1924. Greek standard pagination: 85 C.

142 In this tradition, human conscience serves as an *inner* force which balances society. This contrasts with the English philosophical tradition, where balance is created by *external* forces; by the despot in Hobbes, and by the competitive market in Locke.

143 See the third last section of chapter 4 on the conceptian of a Preussian welfare state.

144 In *De Docta Ignoratia*, 1439

145 In his *Society and Economy* (1671), translated from the German by John Chambless, reproduced in Fidelio, vol. 1, No. 3, 1992, pp. 54–55. Leibniz argues that Society should foster a harmony of interest between merchants and artisans through the establishment of a national industry: 'Monopoly is avoided, since this Society always desires to give commodities at their fair price, or even more cheaply in many cases, by causing manufactured goods to be produced locally rather than having them imported. It will especially preclude the formation of any monopoly of merchants or a cartel of artisans, along with any excessive accumulation of wealth by the merchants or excessive poverty of the artisans—which is particularly

national social relief in a manner which gives people the incentives to take care of themselves to the largest possible extent.

Although our emphasis is on new knowledge as it relates to technical inventions and economic growth, other, equally important, aspects should also be noticed. The religious-philosophical gestalt-switch liberated all human endeavour: The sciences, explorations, poetry, drama, and all the visual arts. The liberation came in a sequence where, from its Italian origins, the center of gravity of the Renaissance moved from Florence, to Cambridge and Paris, and then to Halle in Germany. Dante, Columbus, Leonardo da Vinci, Michelangelo, Drake, Shakespeare, Goethe, and Schiller were all products of the same liberating force of the new philosophy and theology.

7. Man's will, invention, and creativity in Wolff's 'System of Duties'

Wolff laid the foundations on which the German Historical school of economics was to build. Unfortunately, Wolff's system comes in a packaging which, at first glance, is neither easily accessible nor immediately attractive to a modern person.

- 'None of these (Wolff's) books is small or particularly delightful to read. In reading them, one cannot forget Wolff's definition of the 'German Logic': '*When a book is prolix.* If more of already known things is presented than is required by the purpose of the book, then the book contains superfluous things in it. Then it is prolix.' He illustrates what needs no illustration. He proves (often by proofs so invalid that the fastidious reader may squirm) what needs no proof and what admits no proof. He defines what needs no definition. He cites, by elaborate cross-references, his other works, which all too often are found not to elucidate the passages in question but to be almost equivalent to it. He moves with glacial celerity. He ruthlessly bores.'[146]

---

the case in Holland, where the majority of merchants are riding high, whereas the artisans are kept in continual poverty and toil. This is harmful to the republic, since even Aristotle maintains that artisanship ought to be one of the worthiest occupations. *Nam Mercaturs transfert tantum, Manufactura gignit.* ('For trade can only carry only as much as the factories produce.') And why, indeed, should so many people be poor and miserable for the benefit of such a small handful? After all, is it not the entire purpose of Society to release the artisan from his misery? ' Should money be invested in other countries? 'By no means. Each country shall, on the contrary, supply itself with those necessary commodities and manufactured goods which previously came from abroad, so that it will not have to procure from others what it can have for itself; each country shall be shown how properly to use its own domestic resources.... And thus no country among those which permit Society the proper degree of freedom, will be favored over the other; rather, each shall be made to flourish in those areas which God and Nature have allowed to excel. Manufacturing, therefore, shall always take place at the commodities' point of origin; whereas commerce, in accordance with its nature, shall be located at the rivers and oceans—an arrangement which only becomes disrupted (manufacturing being placed near commercial centers, far from its raw materials) when the necessary Society and cohesiveness is lacking in many locations, especially where there are no republics.'

146 Beck, L. W., *Early German Philosophy. Kant and his Predecessors*, Cambridge, Mass., Harvard University Press, 1969, p. 258.

This is a rather harsh judgement of Wolff. No doubt he is repetitive, but in our view his seemingly unnecessary definitions and proofs do contain some real gems. The narrative is carried forward by these definitions, rather than by analysis. Wolff's books are among the first best-selling non-religious texts. They were written as teaching texts, and were also used for spoken delivery. As a consequence, there is an emphasis on repetition. We would certainly agree with Keith Tribe, who, when discussing the Wolffian system, states that the style 'presents both a limitation and an opportunity. In the past it has been the limitation that has usually prevailed; perhaps it is now time to explore the opportunity.'[147]

Below we shall discuss the role of innovation and creativity as essential duties of Man, as these are outlined by Wolff in his *Rational Thoughts on the Doings to be carried out by Men to promote their Happiness. Conveyed to Lovers of Truth by Christian Wolff*, based on the 6th edition published in 1739.[148] References will be made according to the system of paragraphs employed by Wolff. The book contains more than 1.000 such paragraphs. We have tried to translate paragraphs which are representative for Wolff's view of economic evolution, innovation, science, and invention. Without sacrificing his style completely, we have tried to render Wolff's ideas in a readable English.

Reading Wolff continuously brings to mind flashbacks from the huge reservoir of German *Sprichwörter*, or aphorisms. It is as if these aphorisms, the foundations of our stereotype of the German character, were a product of a distillation process carried out in order to present the essence of Wolff's work.[149] Here we find the roots of *Gründligkeit* and tenacity. We also find an elucidation of the importance of learning-by-observing and learning-by-doing, i.e. of the philosophy which underlies the German apprentice system. Wolff was not only a highly respected scientist internationally, he was the *educator of the German people*. Wolff's is a science which carries the German high distinction of being *Praxisnah*, or near to practical life and reality. When business people today criticise

---

147 Tribe, *op. cit.*, p 17.

148 Wolff, Christian, *Vernünftige Gedanken von der Menschen Thun und Lassen*, Danish translation, *Fornuftige Tanker om det som Menneskene have at Giøre og Lade til Deres Lyksaligheds Befordring. Sandhedselskere meddelte af Christian Wolffen.* Første Gang trykket paa Dansk, paa Forleggerens egen Bekostning, efter det 6te Oplag som er trykket til Frankfurt og Leipzig, 1739. Kjøbenhavn, 1744. Trykket udi Hans Kongel. Majestæts af Universitæts Bogtrykkerie, af Johan Jørgen Hopffner, og findes sammesteds tilkiøbs. We have been working with the first Danish edition of this work, from 1744, based on the 6th edition, published in Frankfurt and Leipzig in 1739, but have checked the translations with the original German. German was more or less the official language—*Amtssprache*—in Denmark until about 1780. The Danish language was essentially a sophisticated *Plattdeutsch* dialect. In Danish new concepts which are difficult to translate to English or any language not close to German—like *Zeitgeist, Wissenschaft* (science, or literally 'knowledge creation'), *Erkenntnisdrang* (thirst for knowledge), *Gegenstand*—effortlessly find their direct equivalents in *Tidsånd, Videnskab, Erkjendelsestrang, Genstand.* In this particular case, we therefore have few qualms by not using the original. We are grateful to Hugo Reinert of Oxford University for valuable assistance in translating Wolff from Danish to English.

149 'Aller Anfang ist schwer', 'Übung macht der Meister', etc.

mainstream economic theory, what they in effect do, is to point out that this theory is not sufficiently *Praxisnah* to be useful.

Wolff's world view, as we shall see, strongly indicates the presence of cumulativeness and path dependency. Here we also find the rationale behind the refusal of the German Historical School of economics to separate 'economic man' from the wholeness of Man. We learn in Wolff that accumulating wealth is only one part of Man's desires, accumulating knowledge is another desire which to many individuals is more enjoyable that accumulating wealth.

Although Christian Wolff's world view is clearly evolutionary, his system of duties as the basis for social organization clearly also puts him in Sombart's category of *richtende Nationalökonomie*, economics as a normative science based on what 'ought to be'. It is therefore useful to compare Wolff's system briefly with other 'duty-based'—*richtende*—economic systems. In Wolff's system, one recognises the three parts which, in Sombart's view, characterise *richtende* (normative) economic systems:[150]

1) Insight into the final values (in Wolff's case: perfection of Man's knowledge)
2) Knowledge of the right means to achieve this (Wolff: a system of duties)
3) Appealing to the will to take the 'right' actions (Wolff: act to maximize learning)

As result of the discoveries, there seems to have been a great interest in alternative economic systems in Wolff's times. We have already commented on the interest in China, and on the role of utopias. It could be noted that probably the largest economy ever to be built exclusively on a *system of duties*—with the complete absence both of money and markets—was Tahuantinsuyo, or the Inca Empire. The important German cameralist economist Johann Gottlob von Justi published, in 1762, a book containing a long chapter on the organisation of the Inca Empire.[151] We should also mention Wolff's apparent similarity to a modern duty-based system, which consciously tried to abolish all traces of a market system. In his *Rational Thoughts*, Wolff draws a picture of Man which brings into memory the 'New Man' from Marx through to Ernesto 'Che' Guevara's 'Hombre Nuevo'. The New Man is—similarly with Wolff's Man as he is depicted in this book—moved by moral force. But there is a big difference, Wolff's Man also lives in a society with market-based checks and bounds in addition to the purely moral ones, i.e. in a market economy with private property and a sophisticated legal and institutional system. Wolff specifically attempts to create a system of property rights for new ideas, that is addressing the *appropriability problem* of new knowledge.

In our translations, we have emphasized the role of learning, education and innovation. However, in the same book Wolff explains the necessity of the institutions of a market-based society—private property, money, credit, rent, interest, etc.—and the

---

150 Sombart, Werner, *Die drei Nationalökonomien*, München und Leipzig, Duncker & Humblot, 1930, p. 77.

151 *Verglechung der Europäischen mit den Asiatischen und anderen vermeintlich Barbarischen Regierungen, in drei Büchern verfasst*, Berlin etc., Rüdigers, 1762, pp. 493–549.

normative relations between them. Chapter 3 of the book—On Man's duties in Relationship to Property, he starts out by explaining the need for private property, why a community of goods is impracticable. (Paragraph 887, see below).

In the first two paragraphs of these *Rational Thoughts* (there are other books by him with similar titles) Wolff portrays a world where Man's free will is faced with 'the decision of choosing the things which please us'. This freedom rests in Man's will or choice. Decisions are necessary, and they are the essential cause of change. The decisions will either improve or worsen Man's internal or external perfection. These paragraphs convey a picture of life as being a product of decisions—of both human life and human history as being the outcome of gigantic 'decision trees'.

'When deciding whether a decision or an act is good or bad, it is necessary to study its consequences'(No. 4). 'The basic rule to follow when making the decisions which are in our power to make, is: Do what makes your own condition, or that of others, more perfect. Refrain from doing what makes these conditions less perfect.'

'A rule, after which we are obliged to subjugate the decisions of our free will, is called a Law' (16). 'A rule is called a Law of Nature when nature obliges us to adjust our actions according to this law ...'(17).

'Nature requires us to do what makes us and our conditions more perfect' (19). In other words, it is our ***duty*** *to Nature* to make the best possible decisions. We have a responsibility towards 'das Ganze'—this is not a matter of personal decision. If we do not make the best decisions, the consequences are not ours alone. Like a monad, we are unique, but also a reflection of the totality.

In the next paragraph, Wolff specifies that our duties originate in Nature. Somewhat surprisingly for his time, he continues to state that these duties would exist 'even if there were no God.'(20) Being part of the whole, whether we believe in God or not, gives us duties towards ourselves and towards Mankind.

Paragraph 29 contains a very clear statement that 'Man and his conditions, either of perfection or imperfection, depend on their free acts'. Man basically holds the key to his own destiny, and his situation is a result of his own past decisions.

The judge as to whether our deeds are good or bad is called Conscience ... (73). 'For this (judgement, Man needs) an insight into the connections between the truths'.... 'Man has a conscience because he is able to reason' (90)

'Nature demands that Man do what makes his situation more perfect, and refrains from doing what does him and said situation less perfect.' Wolff goes on to explain three acts of duty: to perfect our soul, to perfect our body, and to perfect our outward condition (224). Man is taught to learn to understand his potential, and to 'find' his body, his soul and his condition (228).

To achieve this knowledge, Man has to study his fellow Man (229). It is Man's duty to find himself, but the way to achieve this *is to care about his fellow Man.* This concern is also a duty (230).

'Not everyone has the ability to invent. Man shall **not** only take care of himself, but also of others. Therefore, those whom GOD has given powers and possibilities to invent, have the duty to perform this work in the interest of others, and to inform others in writing,... (233) and through education' (235).

Gaining the necessary knowledge requires great diligence and thoroughness. Wolff makes it clear that sitting back, thinking that we have reached perfection, is not accepted. He warns against complacency (237). Here, as in many other paragraphs below, we get to know the Wolff who is considered the father of German thoroughness—'Gründligkeit'.

'As children, and others with similar intellectual capacity, will take after what they see in others,..., it is recommendable immediately to teach the children to notice what other people make and do, and to repeat the good, but refrain from the evil, which they may notice with others .... To this belongs that once a child has been decided (to a profession), immediately to set up as an example for him, a person who has done very well in this (same) profession'.(238). Here is the reasoning behind the German apprentice system, which is generally so much admired.

'To the three kinds of duties (see 224) correspond three kinds of good things: The good things of the mind, the good things of the body, and the good things of pleasure.' (242) We have the duty to strive for these good things. In other words, it is a *duty* to seek pleasure (243). As a foundation for German social sciences, Wolff presents us with a world view which is the opposite of the 'dismal science'. Life is not a zero-sum game. At the core of the mechanisms which increase the size of the pie, we find **creativity and inventiveness—not barter**.

In the appendix, we let Wolff elaborate on his own system of Man's duties to create and invent. The excerpts have been chosen with a view to illustrate Wolff as a precursor of evolutionary economics, with particular emphasis on his view of learning. In Wolff we find a view of history being propelled by the creation of new knowledge—in other words by **innovation**. Learning—changes in the level of knowledge—takes place through hypothesising and observing, but one finds other forms of learning, what we today would call learning-by-doing, learning-by-interaction, and learning-by-observing. To Wolff, the creation of knowledge is cumulative, and his world is also path-dependent. However, in contrast to modern evolutionary economics inspired by biological evolution, **human will** and **morality** play the crucial role in Wolff's system. In a Wolffian perspective, modern evolutionary economics in this sense carries with it much of the mechanistic world view of neo-classical economics. Both neo-classical, and much of evolutionary economics, are examples of what 19th Century German economists criticised as *die Entgeistung der Volkswirtschaft*—that the **human mind** had been left out of economic science.

8. Conclusion. Understanding Growth: Wolff and the duty to venture beyond a barter-centered economic theory

In this paper we have attempted to draw long parallel lines of two alternative theoretical traditions in the history of economic thought. The two lines are based on fundamentally different *Weltanschauungen*. The lines can be traced back to the period when the term economics was first used, to ancient Greece. One of these traditions is mechanistic and barter-centered, the other dynamic and production-centered. The first tradition belongs to what Werner Sombart calls *ordnende Nationalökonomie*, which is concerned about *organising* the economic sphere. The second tradition is what Sombart calls *verstehende*

Nationalökonomie[152]—what Nelson and Winter refers to as *appreciative economics*.[153] The first explains Man's economic activities in terms of physics (dead matter), the second in terms of biology (living matter). The two complement each other, one emphasizing *barter* and exchange of goods and services, the other their *creation* and production.

We have tried to show that a switch from a static, passive, and mechanical world view to an organic, active, and creative one, is a necessary precondition for economic growth. We would also argue that an understanding of the causes of uneven distribution of wealth—locally or on a world scale—can only come from studying the differing conditions and levels of knowledge present in the dynamic *production* of goods and services, not in the sphere of barter and exchange. It is argued that our present failure to understand economic growth—and particularly the uneven spread of this growth—is a consequence of a world economic system almost exclusively based on a static *theory of barter and consumption*.

As we quoted initially—to Adam Smith the basic difference between Man and beast was Man's propensity to barter. Smith illustrates the difference between Man and beast by pointing out that no one has ever seen two dogs deliberately exchange bones. In our opinion, the fundamental failure of neo-classical economic theory in capturing the essence of economic growth, rests precisely in this barter-centered world view. Today's economic theory carries with it this deadweight from Adam Smith and his intellectual predecessors, the French physiocrats. Theory essentially fails to understand the mechanisms which bring new 'bones'—very unevenly—into the system.

This is not to say that barter and markets are unimportant, to the contrary. But understanding economic growth requires a conception of the economy that goes well beyond the understanding of the more and less visible hands which operate in the marketplace. To follow up on Adam Smith's own example: What if we managed to teach dogs how to barter and enter into contracts? Would this in any way change economic growth among dogs by increasing world production of bones? Of course not, nor are we indicating that Adam Smith thought it would. In Adam Smith and the classical economists in general there is an underlying assumption of 'the tendency of things to improve' which, to Smith, was driven by 'the division of labour'. But, little curiosity is shown in investigating the causes of this tendency to improve. It is taken for granted, much as a steady supply of innovations was taken for granted after WW II. We have argued that Smith's 'division of labour' is a result of human ideas, a by-product of the fixed costs and specialisation associated with technological change. Economics has failed to formalise this most central of Smith's ideas—the division of labour is not part of today's economic theory[154].

---

152 Sombart, Werner, *Die Drei Nationalökonomien*, München und Leipzig, Duncker & Humblot, 1930.

153 Nelson and Winter, *op. cit.*

154 We would argue this is because the division of labour essentially is a result of fixed costs, and therefore must be accompanied by increasing returns to scale. These are the same fixed costs and consequent scale effects which cause firms to exist. It is the existence of these scale effects which causes the division of labour to be 'limited by the extent of the market'. The division of labour is therefore not compatible with perfect competition and equilibrium. Adam Smith himself speculates as to why there is less division of labour in agriculture, where the 'natural'

Income differentials between nations—just like inside nations—seem largely to be a result of different types of knowledge commanding different market prices. Efficiency *per se* seems to be relatively unimportant in explaining differentials in income. The difference in income between a medical doctor and a person washing dishes, is explained by the different value the market puts on their knowledge. The most efficient dishwasher earns only a fraction of the income earned by a mediocre doctor. Consequently a nation exporting dishwashing services will be much poorer that a nation exporting medical services.

We have argued that this kind of intuitive understanding was an important basis for pre-Ricardian economic policy. Herein lies the fundamental difference in the industrial policies emerging from the mechanical—*organising*—and the organic—*understanding*—school of economics. The organic and learning-based tradition will see economic development essentially as a shift into activities where learning is 'focused'[155] at any particular time. This was the basis for the industrial policy of the Republic of Venice, of England starting under Henry VII in 1485, of France under Louis XI and later Colbert, of Germany and the United States, and later of Japan and Korea. A mechanical and barter-centered theory, as in the neo-classical tradition, will only measure the *effects* of new ideas and of learning as they are translated into 'capital accumulation'—thereby *fundamentally inverting causes and effects* of the process of growth.

By seeing the learning process only as a process of accumulation of 'human capital', mainstream theory loses an important point: Human capital is only of measurable value where a technological 'window-of-opportunity'—a new idea—creates a demand for this knowledge. Where human capital is accumulated without the demand for knowledge, which is essentially created by new ideas, the result is unemployment and/or a 'brain drain'. Since new ideas and learning at any time will be focused in relatively few activities, economic development is an *activity-specific* process[156]. The supply of knowledge must be met by a demand for such knowledge, in the same way that the supply of capital has to be matched with a demand for capital generated by new ideas. This will be discussed in the next paragraph.

The tension between the mechanical and the creative view of the economic system can be expressed in various ways. The creative view can be labelled 'industrialism', the mechanical one 'financial capitalism'. 'Productive capitalism' will, by the weight of its own success, slowly be transformed into 'financial capitalism'. The decline of nations can be attributed to an excess of 'financial capitalism'(capital) in relationship to the flow new ideas (innovations) which is the propellant of 'industrialism'. As societies mature, more direct government effort is needed to channel investments back into production. This is made difficult, as the political power will have passed slowly to those protecting the vested

state of competition is found, than in manufacturing, but he fails to see the implications of this.

155 See Rosenberg, Nathan, 'The direction of technological change: inducement mechanisms and focus devices', Chapter 6 in *Perspectives on Technology*, Cambridge, Cambridge University Press, 1976.

156 This point is elaborated in Reinert (1994), *op.cit.*

interests of the financial institutions. Thus, the financial market which was needed to serve production, becomes itself the center of the economy; 'the tail wagging the dog'. Slowly, the lack of investment opportunities resulting from disregarding innovations in the non-financial sector, will erode the basis also for the financial capitalism, leading to massive capital flight.

William Lazonick ties the decline of the economic performance of the United States to an excess of 'Value Extraction' ('financial capitalism') compared to 'Value Creation' ('industrialism').[157] Michael Porter, in a little-quoted part of his latest book, expresses similar thoughts: Economic decline starts when a society moves from an 'innovation-driven' stage—we could have said 'idea-driven' ('industrialism')—to a 'wealth-driven' stage ('financial capitalism')[158]. The ill-defined concept of 'competitiveness' also conceals industrialism's search for the dynamic imperfect competition which accompanies innovations[159]. Since the creative process—new ideas as the moving force—is absent in standard economic theory, these concepts unfortunately make little sense in the framework of economic theory today.

The creation-centered economics of Christian Wolff seems to move the economics profession into metaphysics. We are presented with a world where economic progress is achieved through a process where Mankind climbs a hierarchy of 'monads' towards ever higher levels of understanding and of knowledge. However, we would like to point out that there is something decidedly metaphysical also about the Mandeville-Smith-neoclassical tradition, where the process of knowledge creation and growth essentially is one where 'private vices' ('greed') are automatically converted into 'public virtues' ('economic growth'). In Wolff's system, 'private virtues' are transformed into 'public virtues', in a process which, on that level, is clearly more rational and straightforward and less metaphysical than the neo-classical alternative.

Christian Wolff represents an economic tradition which, compared to neo-classical economics, is situated at the other extreme of an imaginary axis going from 'creativity only' to 'barter only' as the moving forces of the economic processes. To Wolff creativity are at the center; barter and commerce are a necessary consequence of creativity and production. In today's mainstream theory, barter is at the center, and creativity is totally absent. The human mind is nowhere present—economic theory suffers from *Entgeistung*.

The English classical economists focused on the incentives of the market place as an external driving force for man. Wolff, although acutely aware of the role of markets and contracts, emphasises Man's inner drive for learning, creating, and innovating. To Wolff, Man is not just an 'economic man'—as in the neo-classical tradition—but he is *also* an 'economic man'. We would argue that—in order to understand the *knowledge-based society*—time has come to focus again on the Wolffian tradition.

---

157 Lazonick, William, 'Creating and extracting value: corporate investment behaviour and American economic performance', in Bernstein, Michael and David Adler, *Understanding American Economic Decline*, Cambridge, Cambridge University Press, 1994.

158 Porter, Michael, *The Competitive Advantage of Nations*, London, Macmillan, 1990, pp. 550–551.

159 This is discussed in Reinert, Erik, 'Competitiveness and its Predecessors—a 500-year cross-national Perspective', in *Economic Dynamics and Structural Change*, March 1995.

Appendix 1: Excerpts from Wolff's *Rational Thoughts on the Doings to be carried out by Men to promote their Happiness*

References are, in the customary tradition, to paragraphs.

247—'As neither Nature nor GOD can oblige us to something impossible, we are not obliged to accomplish the Good Things which are not in our power …'

248—'But we must not say that something is not in our power, until we can prove it. Confusion in this area is very dangerous. He who holds, that something is not in his power, he does not make sufficient effort, and thus his progress towards higher perfection will be hindered, and he will not come to possess the Highest Good, which could have been within his reach on Earth. For example, it was believed that it was not in our power to develop the sciences and the arts beyond the point to which the ancient Greeks had brought them, but (only to continue to reinterpret them), and not to add any new knowledge. Therefore the rise of the sciences has been hindered, which otherwise could have been furthered the many brilliant heads, who have been limited by these preconceived judgements.'

249—'Thus, as long as we are not completely convinced that something lies not within our power, we must employ our full powers in order to achieve it … But if it is possible, it will cause us even more joy, that we were not discouraged by the difficulties we encountered. We must not doubt our own abilities, until tried and tried again and not succeeded.'

250—'And this practice will strengthen us from day to day, so that we do not immediately lose courage in the face of failure but persevere.… And from experience comes the saying of the ancients: nothing is too difficult for he who attempts it.'

251—'He who tries to gain what is good, and flee what is evil … Therefore one is freed from regret and shame, two contradictory afflictions,… and one can assure oneself that God, who has created the Heavens and the Earth for his intentions, has also allowed the contradictions afflicting him, to exist as a means to good.'

252—'On the other hand, when one immediately doubts one's own powers and dares nothing, but thus distorts good or contracts some disadvantage, one must blame oneself, when one later realises that it lay within one's grasp to gain what is good and avoid disadvantages. When one is now convinced by experience that it has been within our powers to sustain good and avoid disadvantage, one realises that one has done wrong, and conscience accuses us. Consequently, as the accusations of conscience bring discomfort, so one experiences discomfort. But how difficult this discomfort is to cure, and how difficult it is to calm the contradictory afflictions, has already been ascertained above (113).'

253—'We come now to the strange duties of Man, and consider first the duties to the soul, the obligations Man has in regards to his **soul**. We find, in the soul, both reason and will. Therefore we must examine that which Man is obliged to both in regards to his **reason** and his **will**. We begin with reason, for will is derived from it.'

254—'**Reason** is a force in the soul whereby the possible is clearly envisioned. As reason is more perfect, the more clearly it can envision things, so are we, in regards to our reason, obliged to do all that which increases the number and clarity of envisioned things, and to ignore that which can hinder them.'

255—'As we are obliged to yearn that our **reason** be able to envision more and more things, we must never ignore the opportunity to understand or learn something, and thus pursue as much knowledge as our circumstances permit.'

256—'When the chance arises to learn many different things, but lack of time or resources makes it impossible for us to acquire all this knowledge, it is obvious that one must prefer one for the other. As every human being chooses a certain way of life … he must prefer the knowledge which benefits those transactions he will undertake according to his way of life, and thus he errs when he prefers the other, from which he can not expect such benefit.'

257—'This does in no way excuse those who ignore or reject knowledge only because they believe it is of no gain to them in the profession they themselves have chosen or are skilled in: for this excuse is valid only in the circumstances where one, to learn the important, must set aside other concerns, but in no way in those circumstances where resources are sufficient.'

258—'He who in such a manner excuses himself in those circumstances where resources do not preclude it, one must show by example how unexpected situations could arise in his life, where knowledge of something could not only be of benefit, but even crucial,…'

259—'It even happens, that Man deludes himself in the matter of whether a knowledge is useful to his profession or not. He could, in his delusion, take for useless that which to him is most important. For he who believes it important not to ignore any knowledge that could be of use to him, will, as long as he is in doubt, rather take the safe path,…, since it is not harmful for him to have learned something useless without ignoring the necessary, whereas it most certainly is harmful for him to refrain from learning something that could be of benefit to him.'

269—'In truth, Man is not obliged to any knowledge beyond that which is made possible by his capacities; but one must take great care, when in unusual cases one is to judge whether our powers are sufficient for a knowledge or not. One must first try, and, as a skill comes with training, and training consists of the repetition of an action, keep trying … But as it is easiest to move Man by example, it is often beneficial to show him how lesser people have come to the same knowledge.'

261—'It is also true that Man is not obliged to acquire a knowledge which is not required by his circumstances, that is, if time or resources do not permit its acquisition …'

284—'The thoroughness of knowledge is based on the clarity of conclusions. Clarity of conclusions is a perfection of reason, and thus thorough knowledge is one of the perfections of reason. As Man is obliged to seek the perfection of reason it is also his duty to acquire thorough knowledge.'

293—'The ability to prove what one claims is called science. Seeing as Man is obliged to seek thorough knowledge, he is also *under an obligation to science.*'

294—'.... This ability to draw unknown truths from those already known, is called the art of invention.'[160]

295—'There is another way to show why one has the obligation to seek the art of invention ... As no human being should doubt that more knowledge is produced where the art of invention is present than where it is not, everyone must admit that the art of invention should be sought with the greatest intensity. One sees how much more progress has been made in the sciences today, practising the art of invention, than in the past, when one only learned what others had invented ...'

296—'.... It is possible to uncover hidden truths in two ways, either by experience or by reason; for in these two ways all knowledge of truth is acquired. He who seeks to invent only by experience, must observe what happens in the world and attempt much in many different ways, until finally something is brought to light. He who seeks to uncover by reason must, from correct deduction of accepted truths, extract others that are connected to these. For reason is an insight into the relations between truths, and conclusions bare these relations for the eye to see.'

297—'He who seeks to uncover truths through experience is served by his mental acumen. He must also be articulate as well as able to concentrate his thoughts.... The difference between experience and experimentation I have explained elsewhere. By experience, nature brings things and events to light, without our conscious effort, whereas in experimentation we must help nature, or it would not uncover anything ...'

298—'One trains oneself in the art of experience when one imagines the diligence others have shown in this area, for thus we acquire a conception of the art they have mastered and the methods they have employed to extract truths from the observation of nature. By imitating these methods, day by day we become skilled in the comprehension others have shown in observing the course of natural events, and the application of this in similar cases ... If we find that the other has shown an acumen we lack, we must investigate why the other noticed what we did not. This shall give us a rule we will be able to apply in other situations....'

299—'Nowhere has the art of experience been brought further than in the field of Astronomy.'

303—'... One can reach this goal when one practises invention: something which is done by investigating the inventions of others and the techniques they have used, and following them in similar cases ...'

306—'However, as new truth can not be invented except where it comes from familiar, known truths, so he who seeks to acquire the art of invention must familiarise himself with as many previous inventions as possible. The more truths are known, the more can be invented, when one possesses the skills which are necessary to invent. The truths one knows are comparable to the materials that are necessary for a work ...'

---

[160] This brings to mind both Arthur Koestler's idea of *bisociation*, 'creating new knowledge by combining previously unconnected facts', in *The Art of Creation*, London, Macmillan, 1964, and Edward De Bono's 'lateral thinking', see e.g. *Lateral Thinking for Management. A Handbook*, Harmondsworth, Penguin, 1982.

307—'It is also known that the strange rules of the art of invention are based on the experience of things, and could not be understood before many truths were uncovered and invented. So must he who for a class of truths seeks to gain the art of invention familiarise himself with all that which has been invented, but also consider how these truths have been derived according to the common rules, and how later on strange rules have been derived from the invented truths, how Man has been, and still is, able to continue …'

309—'Wit is an ease in finding similarities. Thus, that which enables us to see the similarity more easily brings us to greater wit …'

310—'… And he who in this manner seeks wit, will by his wit also prove reason …'

311—'But it also often happens that things share a similarity, but that it is lost among other, more obvious similarities.'

313—'We can also still in a normal manner prove that Man is obliged to acumen, skill at conclusions and thoroughness, the art of invention, wit, the art of experience, linguistics and all that which belongs to these perfections.'

314—'And thus science is a means to wisdom. Therefore we are obliged to wisdom, and in a new manner it is thus proved that we are obliged to science.'

317—'It is true that the greater part of humanity always, and all humans very often in such cases make use of expectations rather than science, (and) must also make use of this for lack of knowledge …'

345—'If one knows love of truth, and specifically also hungers after a science, it is plainly visible in the great joy he exhibits when it is spoken of: for he who loves a class of truths takes pleasure thereof …'

349—'Happiness and joy over truths as yet unknown are proof of a great devotion to the growth of science. For this is proof of a great love of truth, but the devotion stems from love. He who loves truths seeks to accumulate them, like the one who loves money seeks to hoard it.'

351—'That which at one time challenged divine intellect, may at another time, when progress has been made in the knowledge of truth and more techniques are known, be childishly simple.'

352—'As one can now judge the art of invention by the method by which the invention is arrived at, so one must here make a distinction between what is arrived at by experimentation, and what is arrived at by wit and reason …'

355—'If one had an accurate history of the sciences,[161] and of the men whose merit it is that they flourished, from all periods of history, it would serve not only to show the usefulness of the art of invention, but it would prove to be of much greater value. It would serve to firmly improve the reputation of the art of invention, through the truths thereby revealed, through the rules of the art of invention which one also would reveal,.... (In this way) one would know how much truth so far had been invented, and what was still missing, and thereby avoid wasting time and effort in seeking what was already known. This history would have to show how much light, and knowledge of truth, has been

[161] i.e. an encyclopaedia.

present in the world at any time.... One easily sees that such a history is not the work of one man, but many people must work with common efforts for a long time to create, and therefore I have referred them to the Academies of Science.'

664—'One can know the perfection of God by observing nature in two ways, either by only noticing what happens in nature, i.e. through **Natural History**, or by scrutinising the causes of what happens, i.e. through **Natural Science** ...'

665—'As no one promotes the glory of God but for he who knows his perfections, so is ignorance of God and his qualities a hindrance to the obligations to God ...'

767—'Man is obliged to perfect not only himself and his own condition, but also other humans and their conditions. And thus is he obliged to all those things whereby his and others' conditions may be perfected'

768—'... The obligations to others are the same as the obligations to oneself ...'

880—'The condition of Man where no one offends the other is called peace.'

887—'People with a community of property, would all have to be reasonable and love themselves as they love each other, sincerely. But, since it is not possible, that all men be of this predisposition, but experience unfortunately! (sic) tells us, how many are prone to vices, in such a way that some would only waste and not produce, others would see themselves superior to others and want to be more than the others are, others again would only seek make damage, and so forth. Therefore it is not possible to have the property that one uses for the necessities and conveniences of life in communal property. The communal property is more difficult the larger the population is, which lives in the same place, and the more affluent their way of life. The community of goods can only exist among those who love each other sincerely, and are of one mind. In other cases, not only will it produce utter disorder, but also give occasion to insults.'

936—'As we are obliged to help anyone to what he cannot reach without our help, so are we also obliged to share of our surplus with anyone in need. However, as no one can demand of us what he can reach on his own, we can demand it back when he is able to return it....'

Appendix 2. Excerpts from Leibniz' *On Wisdom*

Wisdom is nothing other than the science of happiness, that is to say it teaches us to attain happiness. Happiness is the state of a constant joy. Joy is a pleasure, which the soul feels in itself. The pleasure is the feeling of a perfection or an excellence, be it in us or in something other; for the perfection of another thing is also pleasant, as understanding, bravery, and especially, the beauty of other persons; also, as well, of an animal; yes, even of a lifeless creature, a painting, or a work of art....

One says in general: There is something, I know not what, that pleases me in the thing, which one calls sympathy. But those who search for the causes of things, more often find the foundation for this, and understand, that something lies under it which, although unperceived by us, yet truly proves useful....

Music gives a beautiful example of this....

I call all elevation of being perfection, for as sickness, as it were, is a degradation and a decline from health, thus is perfection something which soars above health; but even health itself lies in the middle and on the scales, and lays the ground for perfection.

Now just as sickness originates from a damaged action, such as the intelligent medical mind well observes, thus perfection shows itself on the contrary to work with power, since all being consists in a certain power; and the greater the power, the higher and freer is the being.

Moreover, in respect to all power, the greater it is, the more the many is found thereby to be from one, and in one, in that the One governs many outside of itself, and represents them in itself. Now, the Oneness in the Many is nothing other than harmony, and because one agrees more closely with this one than with that one, thus the order, from which all beauty comes, flows from it, and beauty awakens love.

Hence one sees now, how happiness, pleasure, love, perfection, being, power, freedom, harmony, order, and beauty are connected to each other, which is seen correctly by few....

Now when the soul feels in itself a great harmony, order, freedom, power or perfection, and hence feels pleasure therefrom, such produces a joy, so as is evident from all these and the above explanations.

Such joy is constant and cannot deceive, nor cause a future sadness, if it arises from knowledge and is accompanied by a light, out of which arises in the Will an inclination toward the Good, which is Virtue.

If, however, pleasure and joy are directed such that they indeed bring pleasure to the senses, but not to the mind, so can they just as easily lead to unhappiness as to happiness, just as a good-tasting meal can be unhealthy.

And thus must the sensuous desires be employed according to the rules of reason, like a meal, medicine, or invigoration. But the pleasure, such as the soul experiences in itself, in conformity with reason, is such a present joy, that it can even preserve our joy for the future.

From this it follows, that nothing serves happiness more than the illumination of the mind and the exercise of the Will to act at all times according to Reason, and to seek such illumination especially in the knowledge of things, which can bring our Mind always further to a higher light, while from this springs a perpetual progress in Wisdom and Virtue, also, consequently in Perfection and Joy, the profit of which also remains with the soul after this life....

Now when a high ranking person attains this, such that even in the midst of all wealth and honor, he still finds his great pleasure in the workings of his Understanding and his Virtue, I hold him doubly noble. On his own account, because of this his happiness and true joy, but for others, because it is completely certain, that this person can and will share his light and virtue with many others because of his power and reputation, since such sharing will reflect back upon himself and can give new light to those who have the same common purpose of helping each other in the search for Truth, the Knowledge of Nature, the augmentation of human powers and the promotion of the common good. Thus the noble happiness of high-ranking and thereby illuminated persons is apparent, because they can do as much for their happiness, as if they had a thousand hands and a thousand lives; yes, as if they lived a thousand times as long as they do. For so much is our life to be valued as a true life, as one does good in it. Who now does much good in a short time is equal to him who lives a thousand times longer; this occurs with those who can cause thousands and thousands of hands to work with them, through which in few years more Good can happen to their highest glory and enjoyment, than many hundreds of years could otherwise bring.

The beauty of nature is so great, and the contemplation of it has such a sweetness, also the light and good impulse, which arise therefrom, have such glorious benefits already in this life, that whoever has tasted them, holds a low opinion of all other delights by comparison. But if we add that the soul does not pass away, but that each perfection in it endures and must bear fruit, so one sees for the first time rightly, how true happiness, which arises thus out of wisdom and virtue, is totally effusive and unmeasurable beyond everything, that one could possibly imagine about it.

On Wisdom (1690), translated by Anita Gallagher,
Reproduced in *Fidelio*, Vol. 3, No. 2, 1994, pp. 78–80

Appendix 3. Excerpts from Leibniz' *OUTLINE OF A MEMORANDUM On the Establishment of a Society In Germany for the Promotion of The Arts and Sciences (1671)*

~1~

The topics of this memorandum are (1) whether and (2) how to set it up. Although, what we have to say about how to set it up, will serve to show that it is to be set up. To the extent that we think about its nature and characteristics, to that extent we must give an account of examples of its operation and usefulness.

~2~

If it is asked, whether it is to be set up, the answer is, yes, and, indeed, as much for the sake of the founders themselves as for the common good. Those who found it I take to be so constituted that, because of their distinguished position, power, and reputation, they have no need of anything other than a good conscience and immortal glory with those judges who cannot be deceived: God and posterity. Both will, of course, only render their judgement in the future; yet even in this life, for persons of high standing and especially for generous men—who are not pressed by necessity and who pay no heed, out of regard of their conscience and their health, to the pleasures of the body beyond necessity—there is nothing sweeter and nothing which promotes health more than that contentment, that joy, that peace of mind and, in a word, that heaven on earth, which gives a truthful foretaste of the future blessedness now, which is otherwise to be believed and hoped for from God and posterity, and which portrays to the mind in a glimpse, as it were, concentrated in a moment, the fruits of eternity. Thus it may be concluded that such a society is to be founded for the sake of (1) the good conscience and (2) the immortal glory of the founders, and also (3) for the common good. Although the common benefit of such a praiseworthy work, agreeable to both God and men, establishes the merit of the founders, their good conscience as well as their immortal name, is the true and infallible reason. Which is now to be shown, point by point.

~I7~

And therefore, I am of the opinion, that even the great moralists and politicians, who are not, however, naturalists, and who are neither conversant with nor pay attent**ion to the** wonders of nature, are missing a great part of the proper awe, the true knowledge and the devout **love of God**, and thus the perfection of their souls, to the **point that their art** of knowing and **ruling men is not** made good through excellent science and good practices. Therefore, **no one can** praise God with more zeal and greater energy than he who, with his eloquence and poetry, and also in true philosophy, goes beyond the boundaries of common knowledge.

~18~

Especially are those among men to be esteemed, however, who doubtless stand in the grace of God, who with the good intention of praising the Creator and of being of service to their neighbour, discover a glorious wonder of nature or art- it may only be an experiment, or a well-established harmony, and, as it were, just through that, honor God with perorating and poeticizing; just as empirical scientists are to be esteemed higher than orators or historians, and theorists higher than real poets, because the former conceive certain experiments which agree with nature—the latter only fictions—and conceive of rhyming hypotheses on the basis of experiments, and with that harmony praise the wisdom of God.

~19~

As often as a new structure is discovered by means of experiment by the now industrious anatomists, or a hitherto unknown function of a long known structure is conceived by means of hypotheses, just so often will the omnipotence and wisdom of God, as it were, be illuminated with living colours, and a rational man will be moved to an awe of the wisdom, a fear of the power, and to a love of the harmony of both, which is the beauty and goodness of his Creator, far more than he is through a thousand speeches, songs, and, indeed, even sometimes lectures and homilies. Correspondingly, one such discovery can be the material and source of more than a thousand beautiful songs of praise.

~20~

Therefore, any truth, any experiment or theorem, which is admirable and worthy of consideration, even if no problem could be made of it (which is seldom), even if it were not lucrative but only luciferous, is, as such, to be considered as a new-found mirror of the beauty of God, and to be esteemed as invaluable and more noble than the costliest diamond, and therefore also, what is used among honorable, God-fearing and rational people to the perfection of nature and the real arts, must be considered for the most holy cause and to the benefaction of the inexhaustible true glory of God.

~20~

Which is not even to mention, that most would have a benefit for human life, if our evil institutions, carelessnesses, and distractions did not make all our real and useful discoveries, of which there have been not a few in our century, worthless to us. As thus medicine is hardly improved at all by the newly discovered lacteal and lymphatic vessels, of circulation, and so many other ducts, nor by the light which was kindled by chemistry and thrown onto nature, and the methods of medicine remain in the same bad condition with practitioners, who are only greedy for money, as it has always been in the past.

~21~

For that reason, the third way to seek the glory of God, namely those who serve Him as moralists, as politicians, as those who guide public affairs, is the most perfect, since those not only endeavour to find the radiance of God's glory in nature, but also seek to emulate Him through imitation; and thus seek to honor Him not only through praise and devotion, or with words and thoughts, but also with good works, not only to consider the good He has done, but to sacrifice themselves to Him and offer themselves as an instrument and through that to do more good for society and in particular for the human race, as the best of all visible creatures, in those things which we have the power to effect, and for which we are ordered and created.

~22~

These are the ones who apply the discovered wonders of nature and art to medicine, to mechanics, to the comfort of life, to materials for work and sustenance of the poor, to keeping people from idleness and vice, to the operation of justice, and to reward and punishment, to preservation of the common peace, to the increase and welfare of the fatherland, to the elimination of times of shortage, disease, and war (insofar as it is in our power and is our responsibility), to the propagation of true religion and fear of God, indeed, to the happiness of the human race; and who endeavour to imitate in their domain what God has done in the world.

~23~

Such happiness of the human race were possible if a general agreement and understanding were not to be counted as chimeras, and placed along with More's *Utopia*, Campanella's *Civitate Solis*, and Bacon's *Atlantis*, and in general were not commonly too distant from the most powerful Lord Councillors of the common welfare. Nevertheless, it follows from reason, justice, and conscience that each does in his sphere of activity that by which he may be justified before God and the tribunal of his own conscience. If we are not able to do what we want, then we want what we can do. Perhaps through finding means, which though apparently of no great importance and involving no great costs, yet are for the common good, for the stimulus of the nation, for the support and maintenance of many men, for the glory of God and the discovery of His wonders, great results could be accomplished.

~24~

Among such means, one of the easiest and most important will be the establishment of a society or academy, well grounded although small at the start. Through that, the natural genius of the Germans will be inspired, according to the examples of all their neighbours, which it is hoped they will excel:

- an increased agreement and closer correspondence of skilled people will be aroused, creating opportunity and arrangements for many excellent and useful thoughts, inventions, and experiments, which are often lost, because now those having them will have the confidence to communicate and then to receive them back again;
- to supply and make useful resources and funds, and other things lacking, on a large scale;
- joining theory and experiment in a happy marriage, the one supplying the deficiencies of the other;
- establish a school of inventors and, as it which each could readily work out his tests and concepts; discover the kinds and advantages of experiences which increase of themselves not in the least by chance (even if in the beginning there is only a small number);
- indeed, means will be supplied to maintain the nourishment of the people, to establish manufacturing and consequently draw in commerce, and in time to establish workhouses and houses of discipline for the idle and criminal in which to work;
- erect warehouses filled with necessities for emergencies, and even in the future form a safe bank for rentiers who wish to invest their money;
- to enter into companies, enter into negotiations with those formed;
- to encourage the Germans to commerce on the sea, joining up with the Hanseatic cities;
- to improve the schools, furnishing the youth with exercises, languages, and the reality of the sciences before they unfortunately travel, and establish Gentlemen's Schools as well;
- to facilitate the crafts through improvements and tools, through always inexpensive fire and motion;
- to test and be able to work out everything in chemistry and mechanics, to work with glass, to create telescopes, machines, water devices, clocks, lathes, painting studios, presses, paint companies, weaving factories, steel and iron works, and even some quite useful things which, when done in a small way without organization are unfruitful;
- to support private laws in land before all else except for new inventions;
- to get support from high places, to support foundations and organizations for curiosities, to form a theatre of nature and the arts or chamber of arts, rarities and anatomy for easy learning of all things not in the now established herbal and other gardens and libraries;
- to summarize books and manuscripts and posthumous works, to bring together scattered reports, experiments, and letters of correspondence, to have everything in order and indexed;
- to support poor students and at the same time create institutions for their work which will be useful both to them and to society;
- to support impoverished eccentrics who have ruined themselves through extravagance, and merchants, ruined through misfortune as well, helping both for their own benefit and that of society;
- to support useful people on the land (who only wish to have provisions and materials for their nourishment, who for the most part, when they sense something is wrong in the world, leave the land and go over to foreign rule, much to the harm of themselves and the ruined fatherland, some falling into a life of dissipation, running off to war and

destroying themselves or being cut off or removed in their first bloom, when they and others like them could people bloom, when they and others like them could people the land with families and thus be useful); to put them to work; to preserve them from beggary, to nourish them with their wife and family; to guard them and theirs from sin, disgrace, and ruination of the soul.

On that basis, but without determining a definite time and place, rather everything being undertaken in a leisurely manner, this strategem must be brought into motion with a small fund and some small advantages.

~25~

This is the constant, indeed continuous charity, which will grow endlessly and increase of itself and be of benefit to many thousands of men, which is circumscribed by no limit in advance; which will not be like other foundations, with which the continuance, support, and even the goal are not always closely connected with the interests of the members and directors, and thus are subject to abuses; and which will not be easily ruined through war or death or other plagues of the country once it gets started; which is directed to the absolutely real things, to the highest glory of God and to universal approval and eternal benediction and gratitude of posterity, which will come after and will perhaps be able to enjoy it over a long period of time; for that purpose God has given many beautiful circumstances, on which to allow delay would be irresponsible; which God hopefully will bless, indeed, in order to carry out what begins so piously, will reward us with health and long life and, finally, which all rational men most highly wish for, with eternal blessedness for our immortal souls and the prayers and blessings and witnesses of so many souls, who have been taken thereby from misery and ruination and at last can receive a decent wage. And in conclusion, this point: that whoever has the power to do something on this work, should not, for the glory of God and the sake of his own conscience, fail to reflect upon it.

translated by John Chambless, Reproduced in *Fidelio*,
Vol. 2, No. 1, 1992, pp. 63–69

Chapter Five

JOHANN HEINRICH GOTTLOB VON JUSTI (1717–1771): THE LIFE AND TIMES OF AN ECONOMIST ADVENTURER

Erik S. Reinert

Table of Contents:

Introduction: 'State Adventurers' in English and German Economic History

The term *merchant adventurer* was applied to the earliest medieval English merchants who made their wealth and fame in new and hazardous markets (Carus-Wilson, 1967). A similar spirit of hazardous economic adventure *cum* economic career characterized the life of economist and social scientist Johann Heinrich Gottlob von Justi (1717–1771) as well as several of his cameralist contemporaries in Germany and Austria. Justi epitomizes the heyday of the German brand of mercantilist writing, cameralism. These traditions represent the reasoning on economics and state sciences that laid the necessary groundwork for the creation of all European nation-states and for the Industrial Revolution, but was later excluded from the more narrow and barter-based economics of the English tradition. Justi was both a synthesizer and a modernizer of this tradition, absorbing the important novelties of the 1700's into the already existing consensus of the late 1600's. Justi was, as far as we can judge, probably also the most prolific writer of all economists in any language, publishing a total of 67 books of which 8 works were translated into five languages (See Reinert & Reinert: 'A Bibliography of J.H.G. von Justi' in this volume).

As a profession, these early German-speaking economists stand out as being of a very different class and type than their English contemporaries. This is emphasized by Keith Tribe, the English-speaking author who in a very thorough work has devoted more time and space to Justi than anyone else in the English language (Tribe 1988). However, when comparing Justi's writings with the economics traditions in the rest of the European continent – from Spain to Sweden and Finland – rather than with England, it is in fact the English tradition that stands out as being 'different'. Whereas most early English economists were themselves merchants, the professional career of the typical German economist at the time tended to be tied to the administration of the many small German states. The activities of these German-speaking economists tended to cover a very broad spectrum. Their careers include both theory and *Praxis* – teaching, administration and entrepreneurship – and also activities on very different levels of abstraction: from theoretical philosophy to government administration and practical matters of production and starting new enterprises.

Justi and his contemporary economist adventurers Georg Heinrich Zincke (1692–1769, from Saxony) and Johann Friedrich Pfeiffer (1718–1787, from Berlin) all suffered similar tragic fates towards the end of an active life of teaching, writing, public administration and public entrepreneurship. They had all been soldiers as a preface to their eventful lives as economist adventurers or *gelehrte Abenteurer* ('scholarly adventurers'). Both Justi, Zincke and Pfeiffer rose to fame as accomplished writers of economics and *Staatswissenschaften* (political science) and trusted administrators; but all of them ended their careers in varying degrees of disgrace, all accused of embezzlement. Some of the important works of Zincke and Pfeiffer are listed in the bibliography of this paper, for the works of Justi see our separate bibliography in this volume. Johann Joachim Becher (1635–1682), arguably the first German mercantilist (see Becher 1668), also suffered a similar fate. Forced into exile in Holland and England by his creditors in Vienna, Becher dies in London in deepest poverty. These economist adventurers – Justi himself calls them 'State Adventurers' *(Staatsabenteuerer)* – were active in fields far beyond the work of their English contemporaries. Their *Praxisnähe* led them to alternate between the need for a better theoretical understanding of the world and the need for carrying their theories into practice.

From the point of view of today's society, Justi's career covered the functions of a university professor of economics and political science, an economic advisor to governments, a publisher and organizer of translations (*Übersetzungsunternehmer*), a personal national research council in several fields, a manager of government investments, a prospector of mines, and an entrepreneur of last resort on behalf of the State. As we shall see, his many books covered an unusually wide range of subjects, although not all with the same skill. In addition, for most part of his nomadic life, he edited his own journals.

Like the founders of German economics – Gottfried Wilhelm von Leibniz (1646–1716) and Christian Wolff (1697–1754) – the cameralists tended to be men both of theory and of action, of *Praxis*. Theory was there only as a basis for human action, an action in which they themselves wished to take part. Typically Johann Joachim Becher complains that 'he could have used his time better through inventions, practicing and traveling' (quoted in Klaus & Starbatty 1990: 14). No doubt, their inclination for practical action rather than theory alone, their shared enthusiasm for new inventions and their aspiration and efforts aimed at converting these inventions into practical innovations, led so many German cameralists into high-risk ventures and eventually into precarious financial situations, dependent as they were on the changing favours of rulers and noblemen.

The uneventful life of Adam Smith as a theoretical university professor and customs inspector – as far as possible removed from any practical problems of production and inventions – provides a stark contrast to the Cameralist drive to combine theory with *Praxis*, philosophy with entrepreneurship, and invention with practical innovations. Their respective theories of economic development reflect their respective lives: Adam Smith built an economic theory based on barter and trade, where the conditions of production, knowledge, technology and inventions were exogenised. To the Cameralists nothing was exogenous, their criterion was whether a factor was relevant or not. Their theories represented a *Praxisnahe* and Faustian-holistic attempt to capture all relevant factors: *zuerst war die Ganzheit*. From Adam Smith's system, based on trade, economics developed as a *Harmonielehre*[1] where 'passivity as a national strategy' would create automatic harmony, and where structural change and novelty was exogenised. The cameralist system was one of production and of nations in competition, where economic development meant radical structural change, and where learning, new knowledge, new technology, and new institutions to handle them, had to be continuously created. In this setting the nation-state – like any big corporation today – needed a well-established strategic vision of where it was headed in order to maximise the welfare of its citizens. As Tribe (1988) perceptively points out, at the core of German economic theory was 'Man and his needs', *der Mensch und seine Bedürfnisse*.

Werner Sombart divided the science of economics into two categories, the Renaissance economics tradition which he calls **activistic-idealistic,** and the economics from Adam Smith onwards which he calls **passivistic-materialistic** (Sombart 1928: 919). This article focuses on Johann Heinrich Gottlob von Justi and his contemporaries in the period of 30–40 years before the publication of Adam Smith's *Wealth of Nations* (1776). We shall argue that Justi and his contemporaries, while still working in the activistic-idealistic Renaissance tradition that we call The Other Canon of economics[2], had already absorbed the most important contribution from the passivistic-materialist tradition started by Dutchman Bernhard Mandeville (Mandeville 1714/1724): the role of self-interest as an important propellant of economic growth. We claim that this was a type of economics that represented, quoting Schumpeter's characterization of Justi's economics, 'laissez-faire with the nonsense left out' (Schumpeter 1954: 172).

1 Se Robbins (1952) for a discussion of economics as *Harmonielehre*.
2 See www.othercanon.org

1. Justi's Life

Three accounts of Justi's life and work have been published, one in French (by D.M., an anonymous female admirer, in 1771, reprinted in 1777) and two in German (Roscher 1868 and Frensdorff 1903/1970). Additional biographical information, mainly attempting to correct the misleading information first published in the French journal, is found in Beckmann's economic periodical (Beckmann 1770–1806, Vol. 10, 1779, pp. 458–460) and in Höck (1794).

In addition, during Justi's own lifetime, his colleague Georg Heinrich Zincke (see above) also frequently reports on Justi's whereabouts, his new discoveries and publications in his periodical *Leipziger Sammlungen von Wirthschafftlichen Policey- Cammer- und Finanz-Sachen* (Zincke 1746–1767). The *Generalregister* – general index – to the first twelve volumes of Zincke's *Leipziger Sammlungen* (1761: 609–610) lists the 41 journal entries dealing with Justi's life and work. It should be noted that his contemporary Zincke seems to be the only person who reports on Justi in a generally favourable tone. Zincke frequently refers to Justi's humility, a term otherwise not normally connected with his character. Notes in English on Justi's life are found in Small (1909) and Tribe (1988), as well as in Tribe's article in the New Palgrave (Tribe 1987).

Johann Beckmann – an important successor in Justi's economic tradition and the editor of the third edition of Justi's book on manufacturing and factories (Beckmann 1789) – was extremely upset by the poor quality of the first account of Justi's life, full of factual errors (Beckmann 1770–1806, 1779: 459–460)[3]. These misleading and exaggerated accounts were later spread to other publications, adding to the confusion about a life that was adventurous enough in real life. 'Justi would have deserved that the story of his strange fate be collected and published', says Beckmann in his *Physikalisch-ökonomische Bibliothek* (Vol. 10, 1779: 459). Our account here is based on the accounts found in Zincke (1746–1767), in Roscher (1868 & 1874), in Beckmann (above) and, above all, in Frensdorff (1903/1970) which gives by far the most detailed account of Justi's life. Recently Rieter et. al. (1993) provides bibliographical and also some biographical information on Justi.

As is to be expected in the biography of a personality sometimes surrounded with an air of almost mythical qualities, the first disagreements around the life of Johann Heinrich Gottlob von Justi start with his date of birth. On Beckmann's authority the most likely date was considered December 25, 1720, in Brücken an der Helme, Sangerhausen (near Halle) in Thüringen. Other candidates are 1705 and 1717. Roscher (1868:78) assumes that the difficulty of tracing Justi's birth may be due to his being born out of wedlock. However, Frensdorff's later research makes it likely that Justi was born on Christmas Night 1717, and baptised in the local Lutheran church on December 28.

---

3 'Der ganze Aufsatz ist aus so vielen Unwahrheiten und falschen Urtheilen zusammengesetzt, dass es eine weitläufige Arbeit seyn würde, ihn durchaus zu verbessern'. ...'Mit einer unbegreiflichen Unverschämtheit hat diese Dame, die durch Verschweigung ihres Namens ihre Ehre gedeckt hat, Unwahrheiten von Sachen hingeschrieben, die im geringsten nicht bekannt gewesen sind'.

Justi's father, George Heinrich Justi, a court official, died already on November 20, 1720. Justi had two elder sisters, about whom we know nothing. His mother remarried, and from this marriage Justi had a half-brother, Christoph Traugott Delius, born in 1728, and later author of a work on mining. Initially the two brothers enjoyed good relations, and Christoph contributed to Justi's first publication, the 'Deutsche Memoires', which was published in 1741. (Justi 1). Much later Christoph published a work on mining (Vienna 1773), and – like his brother – found employment in Austria. Later, the relationship between the two brothers deteriorated into 'sharp polemics' around Justi's publications on mining and geology. It must be noted already here that while Justi's publications in economics and political science represented the state of the art – it is probably fair to say that he was the man who first systematised the science of economic policy and public administration – his more journalistic writings seem to be of varying quality.

We do not have complete knowledge of Justi's education. In his writings, he informs his readers that he attended the Gymnasium in Quedlinburg (Justi J2, 1754: 457). This school was at the time under the leadership of Tobias Eckhart, a well-known educator. The information about his university years is contradictory, Höck claims he studied cameralism in Jena under Zincke, but Frensdorff's research concludes that neither did Zincke ever teach in Jena nor did Justi ever study there (Frensdorff. 1903/1970: 7). Frensdorff found, however, Justi's matriculation at the University of Wittenberg, dated October 19, 1842. Already here, Justi published his first collection of essays, written by himself and others (Justi 1). His first written work, *Der Dichterinsel* ('Poets' Island'), was probably written in 1737, but only published in 1745 (Justi 3, reprinted in Justi 38).

Before going to university, according to the author himself, Justi had already started his career as a soldier in 1741, during the Austrian War of Succession (1741–42). In the army he finds a mentor in Lieutenant Colonel Wigand Gottlob von Gersdorff, who awakens Justi's interest in the sciences. The meeting with von Gersdorff is a turning point in Justi's life. Gersdorff makes him his private secretary and, at the end of the war, supplies him with the necessary means to pursue his law studies in Wittenberg. Here Justi studies under Prof. Augustin Layser, and on July 18, 1744 he defends his thesis *De Fuga Militiae*, on the punishment for military dissertations (Justi 2).

After finishing his thesis, Justi goes back to the army, but his mentor von Gersdorff falls in the Battle of Hohenfriedberg on June 4th, 1745. At this point Justi leaves the army, but keeps his residence in Dresden and publishes his first journal *Ergetzungen der vernünftigen Seele aus der Sittenlehre und der Gelehrsamkeit überhaupt* (Justi J1). Here, in 1746, Justi marries Gertrud Feliciana Johanna Pietsch, daughter of a priest. The marriage is not a happy one, the itinerant Justi seems not always to be accompanied by his wife. After the marriage ends in a dramatic divorce, Justi writes a two-volume work on marriage law (Justi 23).

During 1747 Justi leaves Dresden and moves back to the county of his birth, Sangerhausen in present Sachsen-Anhalt, where he enters the service of the widowed Duchess of Sachsen-Eisenach. Here, in the forth volume of his monthly journal (Justi J1), the author declares that the journal from now on will also contain material on metaphysics and philosophy. He writes a price essay on monadology for the Academy of Sciences in Berlin (Justi 5), and receives a price of 50 ducats. However, he comes down on the side of Newton and against the German tradition in this debate, and arouses the rage of several authors (Anonymous 1747 & 1748). His most severe critic, however, is Christian Wolff, who writes about 'an arrogant and audacious, and at the same time impertinent quibbler called Justi' (*einen hochmüthigen und verwegenen, dabei unverschämten Rabulisten, namens Justi*) (quoted in Frensdoff 1903/1970: 21).

After this stint at metaphysics and philosophy, his last, in the summer of 1750 Justi leaves both Germany and his previous career behind and moves to Austria. His stay in Vienna will set the path that he will follow for the rest of his life. Until now he has covered a whole range of subjects with his journalistic abilities, but his 'speculative' period is over. From now on he starts studying economics as it was defined at the time. Justi starts experimenting with producing a colorant from local plants to serve as a substitute for the expensive indigo. His first publication in Vienna (Justi 11) is on this subject.

Justi probably did not have a job when he left for Vienna. He was there because of the plant experiments, and while there he made himself known through a publication on international law which was relevant in Austria at the time (Justi 12). This caused him to be called to a chair in *eloquentia Germanica,* German language, rhetoric and writing (see Justi 10 & 17). This was a job where lawyers were seen as the best qualified. Justi arrives in Vienna as Empress Maria Theresia reorganises the Austrian administration, and his professorship is at the Theresanium, which she founded in 1746. The scope of this academy is to 're-educate' the impoverished Austrian nobility. When Justi later translates and edits a French book on the conversion of the old fashioned nobility to a merchant nobility (Justi 19), this is a reflection of the same challenges that led to the foundation of the Theresianum as a *Ritterakademie.*

Justi's appointment is confirmed on August 31st, 1750, and his inaugural lecture on December 16 is on 'The Connection Between the Flowering of the Sciences and the Means which Make a State Powerful and Happy' (Justi 13). This work is published, with continuous pagination, following Justi's complete and succinct plan, syllabus, and student exercises for the teaching of the cameral sciences at the Theresianum, a most impressive work. The latter publication is dated in Vienna on October 15, 1752, and both works are published, together, in 1754, in Leipzig. This is, in our view, perhaps the most interesting of all Justi's works, laying the foundations for his work on cameralism, which is all subsequent to this work.

This basic work is, surprisingly, an exceedingly rare publication. An extensive search has only found seven copies in public libraries worldwide, four in Germany, one in Austria (*Österreichische Nationalbibliothek)* and two in the Unites States. It was probably never made ready for publication before Justi left Vienna in 1753, and was only published in Leipzig in 1754 – without indication of a publisher – by an admirer who is known by his initials D.E.v.K., and who also wrote an introduction. Frensdorff (1903/1970: 27, footnote 4) also comments on the rarity of this book which is found neither in Göttingen nor in Berlin, he says. He only knows about its existence from the Berlin catalogue.

It seems then, that Justi spends his first two years in Vienna organising the field of cameral sciences as an academic subject. In 1752, he gets the Professorship for *Praxis im Cameral-, Commercial- und Bergwesen* (i.e. mining). On the subject of minerals and fossils Justi publishes his first books in 1756 and 1757 (Justi 18 & 21).

Justi leaves Austria about the middle of the year 1753. The details surrounding his departure are even less clear than those of his arrival. The theories of why he left are many. It could be either a) because he created large expectations around new silver mines in Niederösterreich, which never really materialised, or b) had never converted to Catholicism and came in conflict with the Jesuits, or c) as the loyal colleague Zincke reports in the *Leipziger Nachrichten* (Vol. XI (1755): 260) 'because of poor health caused by the Viennese air', which was probably just an excuse, or d) all of the above. But, regardless of the reasons for his departure, Justi's legacy in economics and public administration continues in the official economic textbooks in Austria well into the 1840's, through the books of Sonnenfels that were based on Justi's system and teachings (See Tribe 1988)

At the end of 1753 we find Justi in Mansfeld, near Halle, in his native Saxony. Here he founds a new periodical *Neue Wahrheiten zum Vorteil der Naturkunde und des Gesellschaftlichen Lebens der Menschen* (Justi J2). As Frensdorff puts it, 'Justi cannot live without such a medium in which to communicate with the public'.

In 1755 Justi moves to Leipzig, at the time the most important German town of authors and publishers. His first large works on the cameral sciences are published here in the same year as his arrival (Justi 14 & 15). Here he also publishes, anonymously, a tract on monetary policy: *Entdeckte Ursachen des verderbten Münzwesen Deutschlands* (Justi 16, reprinted in Justi 50, 'Gesammelte Politische und Finanzschriften'). But in the same year Justi moves on again, this time to Göttingen, where he is the first person to teach economics at the local university. As in Vienna, his teaching is combined with a practical job in the local administration.

During the Seven Years' War (1756–1763), Prussia, allied with England, fights Austria (Maria Theresa) allied with France, Russia, and Saxony-Poland. Here Justi gets himself involved in international politics, plotting against the catholics and particularly against the Jesuits as 'dangerous enemies'. This was Justi active as a political *Projectmacher*, in order to get paid for his intelligence work and political writings. The most fantastic element in this story is the supposed existence of a Jesuit treasure to be used to convert Protestants. The whole story is *Romanhaft* – like a work of fiction – writes Frensdorff. The political intrigues spun around and by Justi are well covered in Frensdorff (pp. 38–58).

Instead of delving into the details of political intrigue during the Seven Years' War, we shall devote a paragraph here to Justi's position towards the Jesuits and his place in the history of anthropology. When Justi in 1762 writes his remarkable work admiring Chinese and Peruvian institutions and culture *Vergleichchungen der Europäischen mit den Asiatischen und andern vermeintlich barbarischen Regierungen* (Justi 64), he adopts the non-eurocentric attitudes of the Jesuits, exemplified by their work both in China and in South America, which got them into conflict with most European powers and with the Church, and led to their order being outlawed in most of Europe. Here Justi continues a tradition started by Giovanni Botero (1544–1617) and lasting until after Christian Wolff, praising the wisdom of Chinese rule and Chinese philosophy. In 1723 Wolff was dismissed from the University of Halle for suggesting that in Chinese Confucianism one could find moral truths without the help of divine revelation. Wolff was subsequently ordered to leave Prussia within 24 hours, by punishment of the rope. (Drechsler 1997: 113–114). We suggest that Justi here is a late example of a Renaissance ethnographic tradition, typified by Giovanni Botero (1622), which celebrates the diversity, uniqueness and inventiveness of human cultures in response to different climatic conditions worldwide. (See Roscher 1878: 280 for the connection between Botero and Wolff in this tradition)

We see Botero's tradition as the ethnographic counterpart of Sombart's **activistic-idealistic** tradition in economics, which from Adam Smith on gradually yields to a **passivistic-materialistic** traditon, although pockets of activistic-idealistic economics survive well into the 20th Century with the creation and defense of the welfare state. During the 1770's, the decade of Adam Smith's *Wealth of Nations*, a gestalt-switch takes place in the attitudes of the Europeans on both sides of the Atlantic towards non-European cultures. The Jesuits, who were the protectors of South American aboriginals and of Chinese philosophy, are suppressed by Pope Clement XIV in 1773. The draft of the United States Constitution, dated 1775, discusses the relationship of the Federal Government to 'the Indian Nations'. One year later, in the Constitution itself, these are reduced to 'Indian tribes'. In the periphery of Europe, in Trondheim in Norway, the *Seminarium Lapponicum,* established to teach priests aboriginal Saami language and culture, is closed in 1774. From now on the Saami people of Norway lose their rights to land, and are forcefully integrated into Norwegian society. An important contributor to the philosophical foundation for the **passivistic-materialistic** traditon, both in economics and in anthropolgy, is John Locke (1632–1704). Locke's *Two Treatises of Government* (1690) establishes the legal foundations for taking over aboriginal land (discussed in Oskal 1995). Justi's study of China and Peru is worthy of a study in itself.

In June 1756 Justi's wife Gertrud leaves him, 'because her husband no longer maintained her'. A maid claims she has not been paid for five years' service to Justi in Vienna, Saxony and Göttingen. The legal divorce proceedings are long, and the reciprocal accusations are strong. The court allows Gertrud to sell Justi's books in order to cover alimony, but Justi accuses her of plotting, with her lawyer and lover, Bergmann – by whom she is pregnant – to steal his belongings. Justi's characterisation of his former wife is 'the craziest and most disgraceful woman under the sun' ('*die allerschändlichste und verrückteste Weibesperson unter der Sonne*'). The court allows Justi's wife to auction off his books, so when he writes his important work on Manufactures (Justi 25), he has no access to his library. The court papers put the wife in a bad light, and it is remarkable that the couple's children stay with their father. Of Justi's children we know that a daughter was an early proponent of women's suffrage. Both Justi and his wife remarry, his wife marries her lawyer Bergmann.

At this point, Justi moves to Denmark. We have devoted the whole of section 2 of this article to Justi's Danish interlude, which only lasted from 1757 to 1758. This is the part of his life which is the least covered so far in German and English literature, and for which there are good Danish sources.

After his stay in Denmark, Justi keeps his residence in the Northern town of Altona, outside Hamburg, not far from the Danish-German border at the time. Here, for the first time, he concentrates his writings around political issues (Justi 24, 26, 27 & 28). Judicious national rule – Justi uses the term *Staatsklugheit* – had since Botero's time been part of the same social science umbrella as economics. In his work on the political equilibrium in

Europe, from 1758, *Die Chimäre des Gleichgewichts von Europa* (Justi 24), Justi is of the opinion that when King William III of England originally promoted the idea of political equilibrium in Europe, this was just an excuse for war. Equilibrium is a preposterous idea, it corresponds neither to Justice nor to *Staatskunst,* says Justi. He takes the opportunity to define the real wealth of a nation in mercantilist terms, praising Colbert. 'Every nation has the right to carry its perfection and happiness as high as at all possible' says Justi. In 1759 follows *Die Chimäre des Gleichgewichts der Handlung und Schiffahrt,* also published by Iversen in Altona (Justi 28).

In 1759 Justi continues his journal 'Neue Wahrheiten' (Justi J1) under a new title: *Fortgesetzte Bemühungen zum Vorteil der Naturkunde und des gesellschaftlichen Leben der Menschen,* where the place of publication is Berlin and Stettin. Again Justi's lack of political correctness gets him into trouble during the Seven Years' War. In one of the issues Justi criticizes the 'hitherto unknown cruelties' committed during warfare under the allied Empresses of Austria and Russia, Maria Theresa and Catharine, 'disgracing their gender'. This causes a protest by the Imperial Austrian Ambassador, and when Russian troops occupy Berlin for ten days in October 1760, Justi's publication, with many others, are burned in public by the hangman. His two Unites States imprints (Justi 26 & 42), are also protests against what Justi saw as an uncivilized form of warfare.

Commencing in the spring of 1760, the most productive of all Justi's years of publishing, his books are published with a Berlin imprint. Justi is in the service of Frederick the Great, which has long been his goal (Frensdorff 1903/1970: 81). In Berlin, he takes the opportunity to start fresh studies of chemistry (Justi 36), history (Justi 58), and the natural sciences again (Justi 58, 59, 61, 62), in part responding to the price essays offered by the scientific academies.

Several important publications see the light during his Berlin years, among them his two-volume textbook on the 'Principles of Economics Policy', *Die Grundfeste zu der Macht und Glückseeligkeit der Staaten; oder ausführliche Vorstellung der gesamten Policey-Wissenschaft'* (Justi 45). A second edition is published in 1774, three years after Justi's death. Justi is also active as a translator, and between 1762 and 1765 he is the editor of the first four volumes of *Schauplatz der Künste und Handwerke* (Justi 56), a serial publication on practical matters of arts, crafts, and industry, with illustrations. The *Schauplatz* is a translation of parts of a work published by the French Academy of Sciences, a typical publication of the time in most European countries. The series continues to be published in Germany until 1805.

The high cost of living in Berlin with his new family and the children from the first marriage, a total of six children, drives the restless Justi to take up residence in Bernau, north of the city. For the rest of his life, however, he will stay in Prussia and in the Brandenburg and Neumark area, mostly east of Berlin in what is now Poland. With his income from book publishing and a pension of 200 *Thaler,* Justi lives in modest welfare. He buys property, and near the town of Soldin, present-day Mysliborz, he starts constructing factory buildings.

About this time Fredrick the Great, the Prussian King, receives Justi in an audience, and Justi gains his trust. In 1765 Justi is called back to public service, with the position of *Berghauptmann* in Landsberg an der Warthe, the present-day Gorzów Wielkopolski. His annual salary is now 2000 *Thaler,* ten times his previous pension. He moves to Landsberg and engages in a project to start producing metal sheets and plates, probably a project of his own design. This project is to cause his demise.

Justi has been in his new position less than a year when the first conflicts start. Two merchants in Berlin take him to court for the payment of a debt of 42 *Thaler.* Justi's extremely arrogant behaviour in this and other incidents creates him many enemies. His eyesight starts failing, and his increasing aggressiveness and paranoia with diminishing eyesight recalls the fate of another German economist, Eugen Dühring, more than 100 years later.

In June 1767 Justi declares to the king that his work on producing metal sheets is so well advanced that he will soon be able to satisfy the demand of the whole Prussian territory for such products. The King promptly orders a 30 per cent import duty on these products. More serious than the protracted legal quibbles over *42 Thaler* is soon the fact that Justi's factory fails to deliver on its promises, and complaints about his administration pour in from all sides. The Prussian administration decides to make an audit of Justi's administration.

Justi immediately complains that the two-member commission appointed to investigate his case consists of two of his sworn enemies. His complaints are to no avail, and in January 1768 the case is passed on to the courts. As Justi previously saw the commissioners plotting against him, he now sees the judges doing the same thing. His untiring and at times creative journalism is now focused on producing complaints against the courts. In February he is placed in domiciliary arrest, but is later transferred to Fortress Küstrin, today's Kostrzyn, where he is to spend the rest of his life.

Justi claims he is no richer than before, and that he has had to decide on the construction of the factories without any assistence from his superior. In June 1768, however, Justi is sentenced to pay back to the state 2878 *Thaler* and 6 *Groschen* (As a comparison his salary in 1765 was 2000 *Thaler*). Legal battles follow, and Justi is convinced of his own innocence. He continues to write and publish: a book on geology and the history of the planet Earth (Justi 66) and the third volume of the *Chymische Schriften* (Justi 36) are written in jail. The book on geology and the history of the planet Earth gets Justi into sharp polemics with his stepbrother Delius. His writings in jail, however, are not particularly marked by his condition. The foreword to the third volume of the *Chymische Schriften* is dated March 25, 1771, and published the same year.

On July 21, 1771, Justi dies in jail in Fortress Küstrin, actively dictating and writing until the last day, and being convinced that he will in the end be absolved. Justi was only 54 years old, and had been actively writing since 1744, for half of his life. He was the child of a century when it was normal to write and publish profusely, as did Christian Wolff. As Helge Peukert points to in this volume, Justi was an idealist, clearly belonging to the Renaissance-based **activistic-idealist** economic tradition, but he was a very pragmatic idealist. But at the same time he focused clearly on **principles;** economic policy was not to be the product of some haphazard gut feelings. Justi brings together qualities that are not commonly combined. He combines practical sense and pragmatism with a sense for the importance of principles – getting to the foundations of all issues – with a Germanic sense for systematization and order. In his short outline for the teaching of cameral sciences in Vienna (Justi 13), Justi's first publication on this issue, this powerful combination is succinctly brought together.

The most important label attached to Justi's life and work is that of a *Projectmacher* or *Projecteur* – a 'project maker'. There is nothing intrinsically pejorative in the term, but it is clearly being used as such by Justi's contemporary commentators. 'Finally he found the death of most *Projecteurs*, in jail on July 20, 1771' says Beckmann laconically about him (Beckmann 1770–1806, Vol. 10, 1779: 460). The main dictionary of the German language, which fills 110 cm on the shelves, reports the word *Projectmacher* used in 1755 (Grimm & Grimm 1889: Vol. 7, column 2164), but does not note that it has a pejorative connotation.

Justi himself comes to our assistance here: true to his fashion of writing himself out of personal problems, as with his failed marriage, in the *Gesammelte Politische und Finanzschriften* he has written a 25 page essay on 'Thoughts about Projects and Project Makers'; *Gedanken von Projecten und Projectmachern* (Justi 50, 256–281). Initially he defines Project Makers as something very positive: all human beings are – or ought to be – project makers, our lives are projects. He indicates that most people would benefit from having a much more conscious relationship to their lives being such projects. Justi here raises the issue of *conscientisation* that Brazilian educator Paolo Freire saw as a key element in overcoming poverty. People must see that their life is not only a result of the invisible hand of Providence shovelling them about – for the relationship between Adam Smith and Providence see Viner (1976) – but that they can actually affect the course of their own life. Such *conscientisation* is, of course, a necessary starting point for any act of entrepreneurship or innovation. People should, according to Justi, start seeing their lives as projects.

But, Justi says, changing the subject from private to public projects, some people make public projects that are no better than 'nice wishes'; they are completely unrealistic. And for this reason, and due to the many unserious projects presented, Justi informs us that the word *Projectmacher* has taken on 'a contemptuous and almost humiliating meaning' *('heut zu Tage eine gar geringschätzige und beinahe schimpfliche Bedeutung erlangen hat'.)*

'Project making is normally the last refuge of people whom one would call *adventurers'*, says Justi. (*Das Projectmachen ist gemeiniglich die letzte Zuflucht dererjenigen (sic), die man* Avanturiers *zu nennen pflegt*, p. 266). He then goes on to tell a story of a somewhat unfortunate and misunderstood *Projechtmacher* whose intentions were very good. This man's story has striking similarities to Justi's own, among other things he lived in Vienna, and the story towards the end develops into a defence of Justi's own actions. Justi's *Proyectmachen* made him an *Avanturier*, a *Staatsabenteuerer* or 'state adventurer' as he also calls this group of people.

The three most prominent German economists of Justi's time all had a career as *Staatsabenteuerer*. Justi's colleague Zincke, who was 15 years older, was jailed for three years on charges of economic embezzlement at the service of Duke Ernst August von Sachsen-Weimar. Pfeiffer, the great anti-physiocrat (Pfeiffer 1780), an economist one year older than Justi and almost as productive, was engaged in mining as was Justi. He founded a starch factory, but was later accused of embezzlement trading wood and spent some time in jail in Spandau.

There are important common elements between our German *Staatsabenteuerer* and the English Merchant Adventurers, like Sir Francis Drake. They were all working on behalf of their governments. But while the merchant adventurers were largely often pirates with a government licence in what most of the time in the end was a zero-sum-game – the gold of Spain changed hands and got English owners – Justi and the mercantilist *economist adventurers* were both theorising and putting into practice an economic theory where new learning and new institutions, producing under increasing returns, increased the size of the economic pie. In spite of their misfortunes, they represent a type of theorising and practice that was a necessary passage points for the development of modern Europe.

2. Justi's Influence in Denmark-Norway

As already noted, we have located 67 books written by Justi and 7 periodicals written and edited by him. Eight of his books have been translated – in thirteen different translations – into five languages, French, Spanish, Dutch, Russian and English. Yet Justi probably had the most profound impact outside Germany and Austria in Denmark, a country whose language is not among those listed. Some of his most important works were published in German in Copenhagen (Justi 25 & 50). His presence in Copenhagen left clear traces in the Danish economic journal of the time, *Danmark og Norges Oeconomiske Magazin*, his *repertoire* of policies are all found in a posthumous work of Ludvig Holberg, the most famous Danish-Norwegian author of the 18the Century, and his strong influence on Danish economics at the time is well documented in a 1902 Danish doctoral dissertation (Bisgaard 1902). The Danish sources make it possible to reconstruct Justi's influence here, in the country where it was probably stronger than anywhere else outside the German-speaking area. Since these sources of Justi's life and work are locked into the Danish language, which is relatively inaccessible, we shall devote a section of this article to Justi's interlude in Denmark, although it lasted only about a year.

The reason we find Justi in Copenhagen in 1757, is that he was on his way to Norway, until 1814 part of what was then the Kingdom of Denmark-Norway. Justi's wife, from whom he was about to be divorced, also heard rumours that he was on his way to Norway (Frensdorff 1903: 60). On August 27 1757, Benjamin Dass, the former dean of the *Kathedralschule* in the Norwegian town of Trondheim, writes a letter to a compatriot, the historian Peter Fredrik Suhm, where he complains about the annoying German who, according to the rumours, is about to be named chief mining inspector in the Norwegian town of Kongsberg (Frensdorff 1903: 61). Justi probably never made it to Kongsberg. Frensdorff claims what he did in Denmark was to produce a treatise on the cultivation of the heaths of the western part of the country, Jutland. According to the main Danish dictionary, Justi worked as customs director in Copenhagen from 1757 to 1758 (Salmonsen 1922, Vol. XIII, pp.273–274) Both claims may well be true.

Although we do not know what was the cause and what the effect, the fact is that Justi's sojourn in Denmark coincided with an explosive interest in economic development and economic theory in Denmark-Norway. Before 1755 the only author of economics in Denmark-Norway had been Ludvig Holberg, but from the mid-1750's there came a wave of new interest in economics, 'like a cloudburst after a period of drought' (Bisgaard 1902: 16). Both in the spirit of the time and in the spirit of Justi, the Danish Crown in 1755 asked its subjects to write treatises on practical economics. In spite of German being a second official language in Denamrk, the works of Christian Wolff had been translated into Danish, and had an enormous influence there. This interest in practical economics resulted in an early economics journal, *Danmark og Norges Oeconomiske Magazin,* which was published from 1757, the year of Justi's arrival, until 1764. The editor of this journal was Erik Pontoppidan, who after a distinguished career as reverend of the royal castle of Fredriksborg and bishop of Bergen, Norway, had been named chancellor of the University of Copenhagen in 1755.

In the second volume of *Danmark og Norges Oeconomiske Magazin,* dated Copenhagen 1758, Pontoppidan lists recently published economic literature. As item 14 of a list of 22 new publications, we find a book that is almost certainly Justi's: *Patriotic Thoughts on Manufacturing and Factories (Patriotiske tanker over Manufactur- og Fabrik-Wæsenet).* This is the subject of the work Justi wrote while in Denmark, and also published there (Justi 25). 'The author', says Pontoppidan, 'who is a patriot not by birth, but by choice, has held weekly lectures over this and other economic subjects, thinks that he finds much contradiction (to his ideas), and does not forget to meet these with the refusal he finds appropriate' (*Danmark og Norges Oeconomiske Magazin*: 1757).

Just as in Austria and Germany, Justi's works are thus celebrated, while his abrasive personality is not. In Copenhagen he is regarded as 'our great author' and 'the great man' and the hope is expressed that 'we might see a Danish von Justi arise' (Bisgaard 1902: 26), but on the other hand his many contradictions are noted. The most conservative Danish economist at the time, O. D. Lütken, is of the opinion that Justi's writings about the tilling of new land, published in Justi's journal 'Neue Wahrheiten', or 'New Truths' (J2 in our Justi bibliography), ought to have been called 'Neue Unwahrheiten', or 'New Lies'. On the other hand, even Lütken, his fiercest critic in Denmark, admits that when Justi writes about luxury 'he shows common sense, much erudition, and much practice'. (Bisgaard 1902: 26)

Ludvig Holberg (1684–1754), the first economist in Denmark-Norway, is that nation's great literary figure of the 18th Century, with a field of publication almost as wide as Justi's, but whose literary works truly excel also on an international level to this very day. A list of ten best-selling books in Denmark-Norway towards the end of the 18th Century would have contained the Bible plus nine of Holberg's works. Like his contemporary Jonathan Swift, Holberg was using his authorship in order to mock the remnants of scholastic science still present in their days, also in matters of economics (see Reinert 2000a). Justi dedicates a chapter to the discussion one of Holberg's works in his *Historische und Juridische Schriften* (Justi 46, Vol. II, Chapter 3)

In the third and posthumous edition of Ludvig Holberg's work *Description of Denmark's and Norway's Ecclesiastical and Secular State (Danmarks og Norges Geistlige og verdslige Staat eller Beskrivelse)* (Holberg 1762), we find a whole new chapter (Chapter 16) on 'Those Means and Measures which have been Introduced for the Improvements of Manufactures and Trade since the last Edition of this Work or, more correctly, since the Commencement of His Majesty's Government' (i.e. since the ascent of Fredrik V in 1746). Holberg clearly did not write this chapter, since most of the dates referred to are after his death. In this chapter we find a *résumé* of the policy legacy that Justi left in Denmark.

This new chapter of 73 pages describes the whole arsenal of policy measures typical of the pre-Smithian 'National Innovation System' of Justi and his contemporaries; encouragement of entrepreneurship, cultivation of new land, the introduction of manufactures, mechanisation where possible, and the maintenance of competition. The importance of synergies and linkages between different economic activities, the fact that the presence of manufacturing promoted growth in agriculture – a most important discovery of the early 18th Century – was at this time reaching the periphery of Europe. This effect was soon to be subject of a session in the Swedish Royal Academy (Schönberg 1772) and of a Ph. D. thesis at Åbo Akademi, the university in present-day Turku, Finland (Gadd 1772). As we shall return to under section 6, this is one of the important early 18th Century discoveries that virtually died with Adam Smith.

In 1747 privileges are given to foreigners who put up new industries in Denmark-Norway. Holberg (or the person who writes in his name) analyses that in a country with little manufacturing industry, industrial goods are very expensive, even though food is cheap. Therefore foreigners are called for in order to establish manufactures. The argument is based on the importance of knowledge, a type of argumentation which is completely alien to Adam Smith: it will take too long 'to teach the children of our own country' (Holberg 1762: 617). At the same time, there is full awareness of the role of competition in order to render manufactures inexpensive: 'It is necessary to call in foreign manufacturers, in order to induce competition between these and Denmark's own manufacturers in order to achieve good buys for manufactured goods' (Holberg 1762: 617)

In 1752 the Danish King gives 10 years tax holiday for the cultivation of new land in Norway. In another decree the King informs the Norwegians about their duty to build manufactures, and at the same time Norwegian merchants who purchase goods from factories in Copenhagen, rather than from outside the Kingdom, are given extra credit as an incentive. Also when it comes to the role of luxury, ex-bishop Pontoppidan and Holberg come down on the pragmatic middle way between Mandeville's embrace of luxury because it creates jobs and the previous rejection of luxury as a sin. Luxury was accepted, in Justi's spirit, when it caused employment at home where there would otherwise be idleness.

No foreign economist was so influential in Denmark-Norway as Justi, says Bisgaard (Bisgaard 1902: 24). This was not because of his originality, he assures, but rather because of the accessibility of his work compared to the 'impenetrable' Zincke, his contemporary. Justi reflects the inclinations that are found in Danish literature at the time, says Bisgaard, 'relatively liberal, fairly humane, has a healthy scepticism towards monopolies, privileges and guilds, emphasises the role of agriculture for the economic well-being of the people, and continuously reminds the King about his duties towards the people' (Bisgaard 1902: 24).

In the 18th Century the enlightened king becomes the dictator of what we would call 'the developmental state'. This is Christian Wolff's ideal of the 'Philosopher King', expressed in a work that was also translated into English (Wolff 1750). In the Marxist analysis of Justi and his contemporaries this aspect was also emphasised: 'The apparent absolute ruler is thereby made responsible for the promotion of capitalism' (*'Der scheinbar absolute Regent wird somit eigentlich Beauftragter des Bürgertums zur Förderung der Kapitalismus'*) (Autorenkollektiv 1977: 190). In this perspective Justi appears as *Systematiker der (anti-) kameralistischen Ökonomie der Manufakturbourgeoisie* (Autorenkollektiv 1977: 513). While Bisgaard emphasises Justi as a promoter of agriculture, very much on the Danish agenda at the time, it is equally true that he was a promoter of manufacturing. Justi may correctly also be considered an anti-cameralist, in that he absorbed the important 18th Century elements into traditional cameralism. This will be discussed in section 5.

As already mentioned, what made Justi so influential in Denmark was not his originality, most of his economic policy measures were contained in other works and the majority had been in use around Europe since the late 1400's. But Justi was accessible: 'His language flows easily, his expressions are clear, his presentation of the single points is easy and penetrable, this becomes very clear when comparing his *Staatswirthschaft* with his contemporaries....Last but not least, (Justi) systemathises: he treats everything in one place. Everything that one otherwise had to look up in many different publications, with many different authors, was immediately at hand with von Justi. One did not look in vain in his works, that was the main thing. And when he even in his presentation, genuinely German as he was, piles together a whole range of subjects, material of the kind that one at that time, under the very extended meaning of the word, called economics, he *had to* impress our novices, who came to look upon him as a wonder of thoroughness and erudition' (Bisgaard 1902: 25).

Justi was the first author to gather together, systematize and make into a science the practice of economic policy and public administration. To use a sentence from *System des Finanzwesens* (Justi 60: 4) singled out by Priddat, this science comprises 'the sciences of trade, manufacturing, town and rural economy, and (it) contains all the principles which make all branches of economic life – the source of all wealth – to flower' (Priddat 1998: 22). An active and enlightened economic policy in 18th Century Denmark created a healthy industrial and agricultural basis that made it possible to pursue relatively liberal policies in the 19th Century.

3. Systematizing Justi's Writings

Justi had an immense literary production, on a variety of subjects. Johann Georg Meusel (Meusel 1802–15) lists 48 books by Justi published between 1741 and 1771. In the bibliography by Reinert & Reinert in this volume the number of publication attributed to Justi increases to 67 books and 7 journals. Roscher (1868: 82–84) classifies Justi's writings into six categories. In the following we have changed Roscher's classification to sort Justi's publications as much as possible in accordance with today's academic fields. This has resulted in ten categories rather than Roscher's six.

Justi is accused by Roscher of being contradictory and changing his mind, particularly on the role of the rulers. This is true, but in our view two elements should be considered here. First of all there is Keynes' argument that when one gets new information, changing one's mind is sometimes the only correct thing to do. Secondly, in the period Roscher so brilliantly describes as *aufgeklärter Absolutismus* or 'enlightened despotism' (Roscher 1868: 77), Justi lived in a period where 'political correctness' could literarily be a matter of life and death, rather than the petty idea conveyed by the same concept today. The enlightened ruler – the 'Philosopher-King' in Wolff's terms (Wolff 1750) – was in charge of a developmental dictatorship, and the job of cameralists like Justi was to assist, guide, correct and cajole the rulers to do their job properly. As we have already alluded to, the quiet and uneventful life of Adam Smith as a university professor and customs official contrasts sharply with the turbulent life of Johann Heinrich Gottlob von Justi and the other *Staatsabenteurer*.

Many of Justi's works are repetitive, which is equally true of Christian Wolff's works, and self-plagiarizing. However, we have to keep in mind that Justi lived a tumultuous life in very tumultuous times – including the Seven-Year War when Russian troops even occupied Berlin – and that the sale of books probably was economically very important for Justi every time he changed his operating base. He never engaged in teaching for longer periods, which emphasizes the probable role of books as an important source of income. Justi's change of publishing houses reflects his change of bases, when he moves to Copenhagen his books are also published there. Justi's many similar publications are probably also the result of a cost structure which is very different from today's book publishing: relatively much higher transportation costs, but low capital costs and low labour costs compared to the cost of paper. Added to the problems of war: this all means that small and frequent printing runs made sense. Tribe's comments on this matter are to a surprising degree only self-congratulatory on having unmasked Justi's 'ruthless self-plagiarism', and show no attempt to explain why publishing this way may have made economic sense in times of war when production costs were differently structured (Tribe 1988: 59).

Justi's reputation no doubt rests on his works on economics and the cameralist sciences. His publications on law and politics as well as on ethnography give us very interesting pictures of his time. While Justi's social science predecessors, Leibniz and Christian Wolff, combined first class philosophy with very practical matters, Justi was at his best at the lower levels of abstraction. Georg Heinrich Zincke, Justi's contemporary, published a translation of Xenophon's import book on state management, the *Poroi* (Zincke 1753), and thus reestablished the link between the economics of his age and Ancient Greece, a link that was very evident with the Italian Renaissance economists. Justi's inclinations were different, less purely intellectual and theoretical. Monadology was an important cosmological building block from Giordano Bruno (1548–1600) to Leibniz (1646–1716), and monads are again in fashion today in computer programming. Justi's book on the subject (Justi 5) was very negative to the concept, and received several rebuttals (Anonymous 1747) (Anonymous 1748). Justi's abstract and philosophical writings were very early in his career, up to 1748, so it looks like he specialized dynamically according to his perceived comparative advantage.

The fight over monadology was not Justi's only fight when he ventured outside the cameral sciences. He was initially on very friendly terms with his stepbrother Christoph Traugott Delius, who also contributed to the Deutsche Memoires (Justi 1). Later they came into disagreement over Justi's writings on geology. It is probably fair to say that Justi was a jack of all trades, but master only in the cameral sciences. Establishing the science of economic policy and public administration, as he did, is by no means a trivial contribution to economics, and his inaugural lecture in cameral sciences (his second) at the Vienna *Theresianum* in 1752 (Justi 13) is a masterpiece of translating important principles of economic policy into teachable and practical policy measures.

In the following examples the numbers refer to those of the Reinert & Reinert bibliography of Justi in this volume, where his books are listed chronologically by first printings. The numbers lead to the original title in German and to translations in the bibliography.

I. **Literary Works**. One example here is the 'Joking and Satirical Writings', published in 1860 in 3 volumes (Justi 38) and Justi 30. Here we may also group Justi's biographical work on his mentor Count von Brühl and his wife (Justi 33, 40 & 57).

II. **Philosophical Works**. To these belong his works on monadology (Justi 5) and, according to Roscher (Roscher 1868: 52), also the work on the education of children (Justi 8).

III. **Works in the Natural Sciences**. Justi's publications in this area are definitely part of a normal cameralist agenda: to discover and fully utilize the resources of the nation with a keen eye to the opportunities both for technological change and import substitution. His work on the new dyes from Saxony (Justi 11) reached at least 3 editions and a French translation. His works on mineralogy (Justi 21, 36, 59, 61 & 66) were apparently not all up to standards and item 21 made him 'ridiculous' to the mining profession, according to Roscher. We have not attempted to verify the quality of these works to today's standard.

IV. **Works on the Progress of Science**. Here is where we find the closest affinity between Justi and the Leibniz/Wolff tradition of human progress through scientific advancement, itself a continuation of the Italian Renaissance tradition. Justi's two inaugural lectures in the *Collegio Theresiano* in Vienna, were published in 1754 (Justi 13). The first part, his 1752 lecture, is a very succinct statement and synopsis of Cameral Science (pp. 1–44, see category IX), the second part, his 1750 lecture, is a speech 'On the inseparable connections between the flowering of the sciences and the happiness of a people, with those means which make a state powerful and happy' (Justi 13, pp. 45–82). This relationship was commonly discussed in cameralism at the time, and recalls the title of a book by Johann Gottfried Herder several years later: 'The influence of a government on the sciences, and the sciences on the government' (Herder 1781). Here we are at the core of an important difference between cameralism and English economics. English economics focuses on barter and exchange and science only enters English economics with Charles Babbage (Babbage 1830), to the extent that Babbage counts as an economist at all.

V. **Works on Technology**. To this very important category belong items 51, his two volume work on manufacturing and factories, and 56: *Schauplatz der Künste und Handwerke.* This second item, very voluminous, is a typical publication of the time, found in all European countries, focusing on the practical and theoretical problems of production in all areas. The work is a translation of portions of *Descriptions des arts et métiers* published by the *Académie des Sciences* in Paris. Justi edited the first four of a total of 21 volumes, of which the last appeared in 1805. Continuing Justi's focus on technology, Johann Beckmann – professor of economics in Göttingen – published an important book on technology that reached at least three editions (Beckmann 1787). Beckmann was also the editor of the third and last edition of Justi's work on manufactures and factories (Justi 51). Beckmann's works on technology were published in England as 'A History of Inventions and Discoveries' in three volumes with a total of almost 1.500 pages (Beckmann 1797). Putting technology at the core of German economics is a tradition that starts with Justi, is continued by Beckmann, and lasts through Marx and Schumpeter. Charles Babbage represents also this subject in English economics (1836).

VI. **Works on Agriculture.** Justi wrote two works focused only on agriculture (Justi 49 & 62). Again this is part of the standard cameralist agenda.

VII. **Historical Works**. These comprise Justi 9, 40, 46, 58 & 63. According to Roscher 'Without much real scholarship these (historical) works testify to much skillfulness and practical understanding (*Verstand*) for historical matters' (Roscher 1868: 82)

VIII. **Works on Law and Contemporary Politics**. There are many works in this 'law and economics' category, which is also an integral part of cameralism at the time. Here belong Justi 12, 19, 23, 24, 28, 34, 42 & 46. After his dramatic divorce, Justi writes a two-volume work on marriage law (Justi 23), tying also this issue to the 'happiness of a state'.

IX. **Works on Ethnology.** As already mentioned Justi's work on the 'so-called barbarian states', China and Peru (Justi 54), which are clearly not barbarian at all in his view, is most interesting in that it is a late example in the Renaissance tradition of ethnology, typified by Giovanni Botero's *Relazioni Universali* (Botero 1622). This pre-ethnocentric tradition celebrates the diversity of the experience of human tradition, enthusiastically emphasizing the achievements of every culture, rather than emphasizing its backwardness compared to Europe.

X. **Works on Economics and the Cameral Sciences.** These are, of course, the bulk of his works and the works for which Justi is remembered. Justi's inaugural lecture at the *Collegio Theresianio* in Vienna (Justi 13) contains a remarkably succinct and pragmatic résumé of academic cameralism of 44 pages, complete with an outline of the different faculties, plans for what should be taught every semester, and a large number of practical exercises for the students at the Vienna *Ritterakademie*. As with the other cameralists, Justi's writing is sometimes both laborious and repetitive – Schumpeter comments on 'a fair ration of ponderous triviality' – but this work proves that Justi was able to do the opposite. Here (Justi 13: pp. 11–12) he outlines the sub-fields of cameralism: a) One *Collegium* for *Policeywissenschaft*, the science of policy and good organisation of civic life, b) one *Collegium* for the sciences of commerce and manufacturing, c) one devoted to lectures and practical student exercises in cameralism ('Draft a Law to Attract

Foreigners', 'Draft a Project for Establishing a School of Anatomy and Surgery without incurring large costs'), d) one *Collegium* for public administration and public finance, *Oeconomie oder Haushaltungskunst,* for the nation and for the cities, and e) additional lectures on mining. This system was later enlarged, and Roscher gives us a list of 6 to 7 professorial chairs, that also includes chemistry, mechanics and construction (Roscher 1868: 83).

Of these categories, only category I can be said to lie outside the normal range of the writing of a cameralist, and – except the natural sciences – even to be outside the realm of the German Historical School. These are the sciences that were necessary in order to promote the well-being of Mankind. At the core of cameralism was Man and His Needs – *der Mensch und seine Bedürfnisse* – and knowledge from all the above categories was necessary in order to promote that end.

4. Justi as the Continuity of the Continental Renaissance Filiation of Economics

Out of Italy is the title of a work by French historian Fernand Braudel, carrying the subtitle *1450–1650* (Braudel 1989). Indeed the Renaissance inspiration that was to create and form European civilization – be it art, inventions or banking – came *out of Italy,* but with significant links back to Ancient Greece and an injection of creativity from the philosophers of the collapsing Byzantine Empire (Reinert & Daastøl 1997). When the counterreformation later stifled the developments on the Italian peninsula, the torch was carried north by people like Leibniz, Wolff and – we would include – Justi.

The early economic development that grew out of the Renaissance had a very strong urban bias, and the question arose as to why this was so. The causes of 'The Greatness of Cities' are the subject of several chapters of Giovanni Botero's great work (Botero 1590). Italian humanism was also accompanied by *civic humanism*, which created institutions, and in this perspective the greatness of the cities was seen as an example of *virtù*, or virtue. The 1500's were a period of true European cosmopolitanism, both in university and church life. Typically Giovanni Botero, who was born and lived in Italy's *Piemonte,* had his two first works published in Krakow in Poland and Würzburg in Germany (Firpo 1960).

Today there are still civic institutions in Florence that are more than 500 years old. At the time of Justi this institution-building, from banking to health care to fire insurance, and the accompanying legislation, was still the task of the economists. Behind their theories and *Praxis* loom the utopias of Francis Bacon and Tommaso Campanella as blueprints for a better world. The programme of the mercantilists and cameralists was to spread the wealth-creating synergies found in the cities to the whole of the national territory, and behind it all – fighting to wake up the lethargic population – Justi and his contemporaries created and aided the 'Philosopher-King' (Wolff 1750), creating a system of government Roscher later would call 'enlightened despotism' and which we would probably call 'development dictatorship'. Justi would treat the interest of the king as being identical to the interest of the people.

Antonio Serra (1613) would describe the mechanisms behind this urban bias in early economic development: The synergies originate in increasing returns in manufacturing and in a great degree of division of labour, neither of which is normally found in the countryside. This added theoretic acumen to Botero's description, but as usual practice preceded theory. In England already the first Tudor King, Henry VII, based on the observation of the wealth of the manufacturing cities in Europe, had initiated a policy of targeting and protecting manufacturing industry. This type of 'Schumpeterian Mercantilism' (Reinert 1999) became prevalent all over Europe. In France Barthélemy Laffemas (1597) laid the foundation for 17th Century economic growth in France and everywhere – very much in Werner Sombart's spirit – war, love and luxury gave rise to a manufacturing industry, also in Denmark-Norway (Nilsen 1943).

The economic policy tools of the time were many, and most of them may be traced back both to the Italian city-states and to Henry VII and the Tudor monarchs. Artisans and manufacturers were encouraged through subsidies, bounties, tax reductions, prizes, free tools and subsidized buildings. Inventors were supported through prizes and, starting in Venice in the 1490's, by patents. The welfare of society was not seen as being kept together by any invisible hand, but by what Justi would call *Staatsklugheit and Staatskunst* – the wisdom and art of state governing. .

A moving factor behind the poverty on the land is, to Justi and his colleagues, the lack of entrepreneurship and innovation: 'Agriculture is carried out in the same way as it was done by the forefathers several hundred years ago. Everything is kept in the same apathetic routine, and no one wishes to try anything new' (Justi 15: Vol. 2: 206). The mercantilist writers and the monarch joined in plotting to get the people out of this lethargy, and in this way got the snowball rolling which to others much later would look like the work of an invisible hand.

Philipp Wilhelm von Hörnigk's work *Österreich über alles wann es nur will* (Hörnigk 1684), was the state of the art in economic policy at the time Justi started writing on the subject. The book was in print until after Justi's death, the latest edition appearing in 1784. Hörnigk's nine principles of economic policy, translated by Monroe (1930), are reproduced below. When reading these rules, we must keep in mind the setting at the time: manufacturers are scarce, but are correctly defined as the starting points of the synergies from which wealth and division of labour spread. We must also recognize that foreign exchange is a scarce commodity, that 'windows of opportunity' for improving practices in production are overwhelmingly many, and that the country is operating very far from any neo-classical 'production-possibility curve'. There are many underemployed hands that can be better employed than they presently are.

These are von Hörnigk's principles of economic policy:

First, to inspect the country's soil with the greatest care, and not to leave the agricultural possibilities of a single corner or clod of earth unconsidered. Every useful form of *plant* under the sun should be experimented with, to see whether it is adapted to the country, for the distance or nearness of the sun is not all that counts. Above all, no trouble or expense should be spared to discover gold and silver.

Second, all commodities found in a country, which cannot be used in their natural state, should be worked up within the country; since the payment for *manufacturing* generally exceeds the value of the raw material by two, three, ten, twenty, and even a hundred fold, and the neglect of this is an abomination to prudent managers.

Third, for carrying out the above two rules, there will be need of people, both for producing and cultivating the raw materials and for working them up. Therefore, attention should be given to the population, that it may be as large as the country can support, this being a well-ordered state's most important concern, but, unfortunately, one that is often neglected. And the people should be turned by all possible means from idleness to remunerative *professions*; instructed and encouraged in all kinds of *inventions*, arts, and trades; and, if necessary, instructors should be brought in from foreign countries for this.

Fourth, gold and silver once in the country, whether from its own mines or obtained by *industry* from foreign countries, are under no circumstances to be taken out for any purpose, so far as possible, or be allowed to be buried in chests or coffers, but must always remain in *circulation*; nor should much be permitted in uses where they are at once *destroyed* and cannot be utilized again. For under these conditions, it will be impossible for a country that has once acquired a considerable supply of cash, especially one that possesses gold and silver mines, ever to sink into poverty; indeed, it is impossible that it should not continually increase in wealthy and property. Therefore,

Fifth, the inhabitants of the country should make every effort to get along with their domestic products, to confine their luxury to these alone, and to do without foreign products as far as possible (except where great need leaves no alternative, or if not need, widespread, unavoidable abuse, of which the Indian spices are an example). And so on,

Sixth, in case the said purchases were indispensable because of necessity or *irremediable* abuse, they should be obtained from these foreigners at first hand, so far as possible, and not for gold or silver, but in exchange for other domestic wares.

Seventh, such foreign commodities should in this case be imported in unfinished form, and worked up within the country, thus earning the wages of *manufacturing there.*

Eight, opportunities should be sought night and day for selling the country's superfluous goods to these foreigners in manufactured form, so far as this is necessary, and for gold and silver; and to this end, *consumption*, so to speak, must be sought in the farthest ends of the earth, and developed in every possible way.

Ninth, except for important considerations, no importation should be allowed under any circumstances of commodities of which there is a sufficient supply of suitable quality at home; and in this matter neither sympathy nor compassion should be shown foreigners, be they friends, kinsfolk, *allies,* or enemies. For all friendship ceases, when it involves my own weakness and ruin. And this holds good, even if the domestic commodities are of poorer quality, or even higher priced. For it would be better to pay for an article two dollars which remain in the country than only one which goes out, however strange this may seem to the ill-informed.

5. Economics at the Time of Justi: 'Laissez-faire with the Nonsense Left out'

Joseph Alois Schumpeter wrote what is certainly the most encyclopedic of all histories of economic thought (Schumpeter 1954). Schumpeter's analysis differs from most other such works in his lack of enthusiasm for the economics of Adam Smith. Schumpeter argues, quite correctly in our view, that Adam Smith's *Wealth of Nations* – the most famous economics book ever – 'does not contain a single *analytic* idea, principle, or method that was entirely new in 1776' (Schumpeter 1954:184).

Even the division of labour, Smith's engine of growth, can be traced back to Xenophon's *Poroi*, and William Petty, who died 99 years before the publication of *The Wealth of Nations,* describes the division of labour in a clock factory. The most remarkable, and at the same time most unknown precedent, however, is that of Ernst Ludwig Carl, a German economist in French service, who wrote a three volume work on economics more than 50 years before Adam Smith, using the pin factory as his example for describing the principle of the division of labour, the same example that made Adam Smith famous and is assumed to be his original idea (Carl 1722–23).

Schumpeter heads his section on Justi in the *History of Economic Analysis* with the title 'Justi: The Welfare State' (Schumpeter 1954: 170). Since Schumpeter was not particularly enthusiastic about the welfare state, his later praise of Justi is all the more significant. In the comment on Justi below, Schumpeter succinctly states a typical pre-Smithian attitude to technological change and economic policy. Justi was the first to establish economic policy and public administration as a separate science – as **Policey-Wissenschaft** – the science of policy. Previously economic policy had belonged in a trinity of politics, ethics, and economics. Schumpeter's description of Justi's economics gives us a flair of the Pre-Smithian mainstream, and indicates how Justi and his contemporaries integrated technology into their analysis:

> 'He (Justi) saw the practical argument for laissez-faire not less clearly than did A. Smith, and his bureaucracy, while guiding and helping when necessary, was always ready to efface itself when no guidance or help seemed needed. (Schumpeter's footnote here: 'This was not merely a dream. It will be pointed out below that the bureaucracy in the typical German principality actually tried to behave like this') Only he saw much more clearly than did the latter all the obstacles that stood in the way of its working according to design. Also, he was much more concerned than A. Smith with the practical problems of government action in the short-run vicissitudes of his time and country, and with particular difficulties in which private initiative fails or would have failed under the conditions of German industry of his time. His laissez-faire was a laissez-faire plus watchfulness, his private-enterprise economy a machine that was logically automated but exposed to breakdowns and hitches which his government was ready to mend. For instance, he accepted as a matter of course that the introduction of labour-saving machinery would cause unemployment: but this was no argument against the mechanization of production because, also as a matter of course, *his* government would find equally good employment for the unemployed. This, however, is not inconsistency, but sense. And to us who are apt to agree with him much more than we do with A. Smith,

his (Justi's) vision of economic policy might look like **laissez-faire with the nonsense left out**.'(Schumpeter 1954: 172, emphasis added)

Schumpeter's comparison of Justi with Adam Smith confirms that Smith did not represent the beginning of reason in economics, and, as the 19th Century 'mainstream' both in the US and in Germany was eager to point out, in some practical matters he represented retrogression. In the next section – section 6 – we shall discuss the economic factors that were recognised as being most important by Justi and his contemporaries, but were nevertheless subsequently left out of economics as this science was redefined by Adam Smith and David Ricardo.

German economic understanding had advanced enormously during the 17th Century, from the old *Hausvaterliteratur* and Jacob Bornitz' rather simplistic compendium of economics and political science (Bornitz 1608) to Johann Joachim Becher's (Becher 1668) and his father-in-law Hörnigk's works (Hörnigk 1684). The human, material and economic disasters of the Thirty Years' War (1618–48) (where also Bornitz suffered from the violence of the soldiers and lost all his books) ignited a public will to civilize society, and Leibniz and Christian Wolff were key persons in this quest for a more human and civilized society. Becher also makes this goal explicit in the title of his 1668 book, to create a true *Societatem Civilem.* It is on this background, a clear parallel to the Italian Renaissance project – and written in the economic tradition started by Giovanni Botero – that the growth of cameralist literature must be seen. We must keep in mind that in 1683, only one year before Hörnigk published his *Österreich über alles, wenn sie nur will,* Vienna had been besieged by the Turks. Hörnigk's work was to remain in print for 100 years, reaching a total of 16 editions.

In addition to the strong advances of the latter part of the 17th Century, the 18th Century brought several new elements into German cameralism, and to European economic understanding in general. We shall single out three such significant elements: The Mandevillean Revolution, the understanding of synergies between industry and agriculture, and the role of science in promoting welfare.

The writings of Bernard Mandeville came as a shock to early 18th Century Europe. His book *The Fable of the Bees; or Private Vices, Publick Benefits* (Mandeville 1724) – of which the first volume was published in 1714 – opened up for individual self-interest as a main engine of growth inside an economic system of laissez-faire. At the time Mandeville was accused of heresy, being a 'zealot of infidelity', of 'subverting order and discipline in the Church' and 'of recommending luxury, avarice, pride and all kind of vices as being necessary to public welfare' (Mandeville 1724: 383–385). Nevertheless, as the 18th Century progressed, Mandeville's basic message of the importance of self-interest came to be recognized. The message is simplified by the example provided by Adam Smith: It is not through the kindness of the baker that we get our daily bread, it is because he needs to make money.

The effect of Bernard Mandeville's *The Fable of the Bees* was like that of a torch to a pile of dry wood. Mandeville's claims that 'private vices could become public virtues' – indeed the whole basis for Adam Smith and today's mainstream – went totally against the previous idea of a society constructed on virtue, on the *virtù* of the Renaissance civic humanism. A German translation of Mandeville's work, only the second part, did not appear until 1761. But already in 1757, in Copenhagen, Erik Pontoppidan, the editor of *Danmark og Norges Oeconomiske Magazin*, made the following statement about Mandeville's theory:

> 'I know how an English author of the work *The Fable of the Bees* can argue for lasciviousness and luxury: that it creates labour for many hands. This can apply to policy when foreigners buy more of the work than we do ourselves, when the raw materials are our own, and when the hands of our labourers are more than those who can be employed at the plough, at the flail[4], and at the oars. I also know what has been replied to this writer, with good reason, that if his suggestions had been well founded, it would follow that a group of arsonists, to whom it occurred to set fire to all four corners of London, ought to be seen as the best of patriots, because they, more than anyone else, would do much for the trade and employment of many thousands of masons, carpenters and other artisans in the reconstruction of the town.' (*Danmark og Norges Oeconomiske Magazin*, Preface to Vol. 1, 1757).

In the same volume Pontoppidan comments on Justi's activities in Copenhagen, and the quote above is typical of the pragmatic response of Justi and the idealist cameralists in general. Luxury is accepted as long as it adds value to local raw materials and/or employs idle hands, and as long as it does not worsen the balance of payment. We must keep in mind that most nations at the time were far from the production-possibility frontier, had much underemployment, and serious balance of payment problems.

Count Pietro Verri, of Milan, whose main work was translated into German in 1774 (Verri 1774), condenses Mandeville's thesis into one sentence that elegantly meets Schumpeter's criterion of 'laissez-fair with the nonsense left out'. This is clearly also Justi's opinion:

> 'Because the private interest of each individual, ***when it coincides with the public interests***, is always the safest guarantor of public happiness.'(Verri 1771: 42, emphasis added).

Any greed and self-interest is obviously not compatible with public interest. George Soros has shown us that it may be as easy to make money ruining a country as by building it up, but as long as private interests coincide with public interest, which they tend to do when money is made in production rather than in finance, the power and importance of private interest is very strong. This goes to show that the continental European economics profession had accepted Mandeville's basic message before Adam Smith, who is the one who tends to get the credit for this.

A second important 18th Century 'invention', originally attributable to Leibniz, was the understanding of the synergies (linkages) between manufacturing and agriculture. Based on the late 16th Century policies of Barthélemy de Laffemas (Laffemas 1597), 17th Century Colbertism had strongly favoured manufacturing, in practice at

---

[4] Instrument used for threshing grain.

the expense of agriculture. Physiocracy was the 'scientific' reaction to this by the French landowning class, making the claim that agriculture was the only productive science, since in the end Man's living was based on eating the products of agriculture. The German attitude towards physiocracy is one of strong rejection, as is evident from the title of Pfeiffer's book *Der Anti-Physiocrat* (Pfeiffer 1780). Here the German economists are in line with their Italian counterparts, headed by Abbé Galliani. The only exception here is found in the Duchy of Baaden where the Margrave himself was an ardent physiocrat and which is probably the only state anywhere where physiocracy was tried out in actual policies.

The 18th Century provided a solution to the conflict between agriculture and industry, but already in Hörnigk's nine-point scheme we notice that the importance of agriculture is well covered in phase one. Since Germany had not suffered from the excesses of Colbertism, physiocracy found no fertile ground there. Yet, the message of the mutual dependency of the two main economic activities was a welcome one. Bisgaard rather poetically describes how this idea was received in Denmark:

> '....(the) teachings about the mutual dependence of agriculture and manufacturing, or, if you will, their solidarity, became generally accepted. Agriculture was, after all, our favorite child, and manufacturing our *enfant terrible*. It was only natural that a theory which told us that their welfare was so interconnected, so intimately intervowen, would find so much resonance here. It was a most timely word' (Bisgaard 1902: 28)

The same idea is clearly stated also by David Hume, who – in his *History of England* – claims that 'the best way to promote agriculture is to promote industry' (Hume 1767, Vol. 3: 65). This idea disappeared from classical economics with Adam Smith, but later formed the basis for the industrialisation ideology of the United States: 'The American System of manufactures'. Here Mathew and Henry Carey, father and son, stressed the message of the harmony of interest between agriculture and manufacturing from 1820 until well after 1850. In the early 1820's Mathew Carey managed to win the farmers of the United States to the cause of industrial protection and 'The American System of Manufactures' with a book title that reads like an 18th Century German cameralist textbook: *Essays on Political Economy; or, the most certain Means of promoting the Wealth, Power, Resources and Happiness of Nations. Applied Particularly to the United States* (Carey 1822).

The third new element was the role of science, the project led by Leibniz and Christian Wolff, which is described more in detail in Reinert & Daastøl (1997). In all these three key areas, Justi not only integrated the new ideas into the existing theoretical structure, but also systematized the whole theoretical edifice.

We would argue that by the 1760's and 70's mainstream European economics – exemplified by Johann Gottlob von Justi in Germany, Pietro Verri in Italy and James Steuart in England – had thoroughly understood the role of private interests and the benefits of the self-regulatory elements of a market economy, while at the same time they saw the limits to and possible breakdown of a system of self-regulation. This period combined the new Mandevillean insights with the beneficiary elements of previous economic doctrines – of the activistic-idealistic economic policies that had brought Europe out of the Middle Ages. To the 1750's mainstream, the beneficial forces of laissez-faire were there to utilise in public policy, but not all private profit-making was necessarily beneficial to the nation. In the economics of the 1750's, self-interest was there as a main force, but economics was not yet a *Harmonielehre* (Robbins 1952), a system where natural harmony is already built into the core assumptions of the theory. The 1750's was –as Schumpeter comments on Justi – 'laissez-faire with the nonsense left out'. Cameralism at this point combined the best of the Renaissance, idealism and virtù, with the best of the new teachings: clearly recognizing the key role of both private interests and self-regulatory markets as long as it was in line with public interest.

6. What Justi knew, but Adam Smith and David Ricardo later left out of Economics

Adam Smith is generally hailed as the father of modern economics, but when Smith redefined economics he left out many of the fields of knowledge that were previously considered part and parcel of the science, many of which we are again attempting to put back in today. Among these fields are some that formed an integral part of Justi's economics: geography, history, institutions, learning, technology, and law and economics: in effect the whole society in which economics is embedded. Adam Smith also left out the synergies and linkages in an economic system. On the macro level we lost the dynamic systemic effects that today is called a National Innovation System[5] (Lundvall 1992, Nelson 1993), which clearly underlie the whole body of Justi's writings on economics and the *Staatswissenschaften,* and on a less aggregate level, among other things we lost the important practical insight that agriculture is promoted and fomented if and when manufacturing is introduced in a nation.

At the time of Justi these important synergies between agriculture and manufacturing were well known, but they disappear with Adam Smith, whose *de facto* recommendation it is that other nations specialize in producing raw materials while England specializes in manufacturing. Justi's contemporaries would have claimed that only in an industrialized nation will agriculture be efficient. Justi's economics thus contains the elements of a wider and production-based – rather than barter-based – economics tradition which we have termed The Other Canon (www.othercanon.org).

In line with the Schumpeter quote in the previous section where Justi's economics is described as 'laissez-faire with the nonsense left out', we shall go through some aspects of Justi's economics and argue that many points in this experience-based economics indeed make sense, although they may not intuitively do so for someone from today's abstract and context-free mainstream economics. There are indeed several aspects of economics where Adam Smith does not represent the beginning of the science, but rather the narrowing in of a vast field of study. In the following we shall discuss some of the things Smith and his successors left out.

5 This term originates with Christopher Freeman.

Geography

An important casualty when pre-Smithian economics was converted to catallectics – essentially a science of barter and exchange – was geography and the importance of distance. When Paul Krugman recently rediscovered economic geography, he argued that both in international trade theory and in spatial economics 'there was a set of core ideas that make considerable sense in light of recent economic analysis, but that were unacceptable to mainstream economics because they could not at that time be modeled' (Krugman 1995: 37). We would argue that this applies to most of the academic fields we list in this section; these are things which make practical sense, but which cannot be modeled by mainstream economics which, paraphrasing Krugman, has advanced along the path of least mathematical resistance rather than according to demand or to perceived usefulness.

When rediscovering spatial economics, Krugman's main hero is German economist Heinrich von Thünen. In Justi's work on cities (item 50, Vol. 3 pp. 449 and following), Justi treats economic geography using concentric circles from the center to the periphery, the main tool used by von Thünen. Roscher recognizes Justi as being the inventor of von Thünen's concentric circles (Roscher 1868: 97). Geography had been important in economics since the times of Giovanni Botero (Botero 1590 & 1622) and Antonio Serra (Serra 1613), but Justi introduced an important tool.

International Trade Theory and Uneven Economic Development

Krugman also here, without being aware of it, rediscovered Justi's theories. An extremely important theoretical insight may be reached by coupling the Justi/van Thünen spatial theory with a trade theory with increasing returns. Increasing returns were, especially in Justi's days, only to be found in the manufacturing sector which was also the urban sector (see also 'Urban Bias' below). Diminishing returns were only to be found in the agricultural sector, which is by definition rural. This key insight of Antonio Serra (1613) is the starting point for his theory of uneven development; why Naples with all its resources stayed so poor, and Venice, without any raw materials which would lead them into diminishing returns, grew rich on manufacturing and long-distance trade.

Paul Krugman had all these elements and essentially reformulated mercantilist trade theory in the 'New Trade Theory' (Krugman 1990), which was also Justi's trade theory. In his work on international trade theory (1990) and economic geography (1995) Krugman was essentially reformulating the core elements of mercantilist theory at the time of Justi. In other words Krugman's 'New Trade Theory' of the 1980's (Krugman 1990) is the trade theory also of Justi and von Thünen. Both Justi and von Thünen understood that the development machine at the core of the concentric circles – the urban increasing return industries (manufacturing) – needed, for a time, both targeting, nurturing and protection. Krugman had all the elements at hand, but the logical consequence of this insight would have been to sacrifice economic equilibrium in order to gain relevance. However, Krugman lacked the political courage to arrive at the same logical consequence that Thünen and Justi drew. Sacrificing equilibrium would have meant sacrificing the Archimedean Point of mainstream economics, and also the device that gives economics a claim to being more 'scientific' that the other social sciences. By introducing a situation where some nations specialize in increasing return activities and others in diminishing return activities – which is the core both of colonialism and of today's Third World poverty problems – equilibrium and the generalized claims of economics would have to be abandoned.

Jagdish Bhagwati today triumphantly declares that Krugman's 'youthful surrender to irrational exuberance' in increasing/diminishing return models (Bhagwati 2002: 22) because 'the invisible hand may be frail, but the visible hand is crippled' '(Bhagwati 2002: 31). In other words, faced with the resurrected theories of Justi and his contemporaries, the economics profession of the 1990's collectively decided not to trust governments to do what governments had done as a normal course of affairs continuously, and largely very successfully, from 1485 until the reconstruction of post World War II Europe lasting until the 1960's. It is difficult to see this as anything but pure ideology masked as 'science'. During 500 years of political support for increasing returns industries, it is an irrefutable historical fact that never has a nation taken the step from poverty to wealth without passing through a temporary stage of protecting such increasing return activities. In terms of welfare destruction, the de-industrialisation of parts of the Third World since the 1980's has been devastating. As Justi would have predicted, this de-industrialisation also frequently reduced the productivity in agriculture. (See Reinert 2003 for a discussion and case study)

The Reason for the Urban Bias of Early Economic Development

Early in the *Wealth of Nations* Adam Smith asks himself why there is so little division of labour in agriculture (Smith 1776/1976: Book 1, Chapter 1, p.10). If the division of labour is the key to wealth, as Adam Smith claimed, it should have been possible for him to find an explanation for the urban bias of early economic development. However, he does not proceed down that path, but – as the physiocrats – he makes agriculture the preferred economic activity. One of the many contradictions in Adam Smith is how agriculture can be the preferred activity, if a) the division of labour is the key to economic wealth and b) there is very little scope for division of labour in agriculture.

The mechanisms behind this urban bias are first described by Giovanni Botero in 1588 (Botero 1590), in his book On *The Greatness of Cities* which was translated into English already in 1606. Already here the superiority of manufacturing is acknowledged, both in terms of demanding more skill, and therefore higher wages, and in terms of providing much greater windows of opportunity for human skills and imagination. This leads Botero into the study of political science: what are the policies that create this progress (Botero 1590). The best short introduction in English to the subsequent logic which developed into the mercantile system is found in Schmoller (1897/1967).

The real clue to the mystery of the urban bias of economic development comes when Antonio Serra describes the synergies of the city as originating in increasing returns in manufacturing, coupled with the high degree of division of labour which together are both the cause and the effect of the wealth-producing synergies observed (Serra 1613).

Indeed Serra suggests an acid test to judge the wealth of a city: by counting the number of different professions present in a city it is possible to rank the city compared to others.

How Economic Activities Differ & The Role of Skills and Human Learning

Ever since Botero and Serra, and all through the mercantilist and cameralist tradition of continental Europe, there is an intimate connection between the perceived need for an *increase in human knowledge* and the *promotion of manufactures*. This is the great plan of Leibniz and Justi, and the high valuation of human knowledge is clearly also found in Justi. He declares '*dass alle Fähigkeiten der im State lebenden Menschen, ja diese Menschen selbst zum Vermögen des Staates gehören*'; 'All the skills of the people living in a state, even the human beings themselves, count towards the assets of the state' (Justi 50, Vol. I, p.160).

The whole issue of knowledge being of value, and its intimate connection to manufacturing activity, however, comes to an end with Adam Smith. In opposition to the physiocrats, Justi explicitly treats skills and knowledge as part of national wealth. As Friedrich List would later point out, to the physiocrats, a person raising pigs (a *Schweinerzieher*) would count as being productive, whereas somebody teaching human beings, like a university professor (a *Menschenerzieher*), would count as being unproductive as relates to national wealth. Although Smith corrected some of the excesses of physiocracy in this area, in our view the pre-physiocratic and pre-Smithian definition of productive labour remains superior to the later ones.

Perhaps the least convincing part of the *Wealth of Nations* is where Smith attempts to convince his readers that all economic activities are of equal quality as carriers of economic growth. In order to create this proof, he has to make the creation of knowledge into a zero-sum game: 'the cost of apprenticeship accounts for the wages of manufacturers being higher than those of country labour.' (Smith 1776/1976: 114). There are therefore no advantages to manufacturing over agriculture, although the earnings in manufacturing 'may be somewhat greater, it seems evidently, however, to be **no greater than what is sufficient to compensate the superior expense of their education**' (emphasis added). In other words, the mercantilist tradition that nations who export the products from professions of higher skills will be wealthier than nations exporting products with low skills is here, really for the first time, strongly refuted. From the point of view of both society and the individual, adding knowledge to labour is, in Smith's system, clearly a zero-sum game (See Reinert 1999, section 9, for a discussion).

Here we are at another contradiction in Adam Smith. While the importance of knowledge is belittled throughout the *Wealth of Nations* – one of Smith's points of attack is against the apprentice system instituted by Elizabeth I – in this context, when it comes to convincing the world about the unimportance of manufacturing, the cost of knowledge, 'the superior expenses of their education' as Smith says, which is needed to get into manufacturing is so high as to make manufacturing unprofitable for other nations. When it comes to warfare, a similar contradiction appears. In one section of his great book, Adam Smith claims that only a nation with manufacturing capacities will be able to win a war, while in another sections he claims that an attempt by the American Colonies to get into manufacturing will not be to their advantage. No wonder Adam Smith's *Wealth of Nations* was viewed with healthy scepticism on the continent and in the United States throughout the 19th Century.

Context Matters

Economic policy must always be adjusted to the prevailing conditions of a state *(…nach der Natur und dem Zustande der Natur des Staates (gerichtet werden))* The Washington Consensus policies of the 1990's, where the same economic prescriptions were applied to all non-industrialised nations, would have been a totally foreign proposition to Justi and his contemporaries. This is, indeed, a tradition that is totally foreign to any economist before Adam Smith.

Agriculture & Forestry

As in Hörnigk's principles, the agricultural sector is of prime importance, but this sector will not flourish without the manufacturing sector. Both the policy of attracting as many inhabitants as possible, and a fear of food shortages meant to Justi that all available land had to be cultivated. Here Germany and Austria should learn from England, they should start an agricultural extension system (with *Oeconomie-Inspectoren*) in order to facilitate innovation and new practices with the farmers. When it comes to forestry, Justi has a theory parallel to that of Richard Cobden when he ardently supported free trade in corn in England. To Justi the high price of firewood increases the cost of labour subsistence, and therefore hurts trade and exports (Justi 50, Vol. I: 441). This is a complete and perfect parallel to Cobden's argument as to why England should introduce free trade in corn (Reinert 1998).

The Size of the Population & Population Density

At one point Justi claims that 'if one would want to reduce the main aim of the real cameralist, of which he would have to consider with all regulations and institutions, into one word, one would have to scream Population!: '*wenn man das Hauptaugenmerk des echten Cameralisten, worauf er bei allen Maßregeln und Anstalten zu sehen hat, in ein Wort fassen wollte, so muss man durchaus: Bevölkerung! ausrufen*'. (Justi 50, Vol. III: 379).

This reflects two different aspects. First the aim of all cameralist activity was directed towards Man(kind) and his needs, *der Mench und seine Bedürfnisse*. In this sense, cameralism was an anthropocentric science. The contrast to today's standard economics is considerable. In today's theory Mankind is reduced to a factor of production, whose rewards and standard of living are completely exogenous and carry no weight.

Secondly the size of the population was important to the cameralists and the mercantilists (see Stangeland 1904/1966 for an overview). Again we are tempted to say with Schumpeter, 'this is not inconsistency, but sense.' If wealth-creation is essentially an urban phenomenon, due to the fact that increasing returns at the time was only found in manufacturing, and that the division of labour is dependent on the size of the market (Adam Smith kept this insight), then it means that there are increasing returns to the size of the city itself. This argument is also found in Xenophon's *Poroi*, which was reintroduced in Justi's Germany with Zincke's translation and comments (Zincke 1753). In this system, the increasing returns to larger markets make an increasing number of human beings in a state part of the virtuous circle of growth. It is only with Robert Malthus and his friend David Ricardo (Ricardo 1817), with a minimal understanding of technical change and void of increasing returns, that economics becomes a 'dismal science' (as Carlisle called it) when additional human beings become a burden instead of an asset. (See Stangeland (1904) for a review of population theories before Malthus)

The Limitations to the Power of the Nobility

This is a common element in the modernization of Europe since the Reign of Henry VII in England (1485), and the start of the 'Tudor Plan' for the development of England. True to this tradition Justi wishes to get rid of hereditary nobility in favour of a personal nobility (Justi 29); an important step in the direction away from the rule of aristocracy towards the rule of meritocracy. The experiences of Spain in the preceding centuries had shown the disastrous results of a virtually tax-exempt and idle nobility, with its economic resources tied to backward activities like sheep-rearing rather than to manufacturing. Justi's work on transforming an outdated and parasitic 'war nobility' to a 'commercial nobility' is evident both in the translation and elaboration on the work on this matter (Justi 19) and it impermeates the whole structure of his teaching in Vienna (Justi 13), where the nobility was largely to be his students.

Inventions, Innovations and Technological Change

Justi is very much aware of the importance of inventions, but he is of the opinion that inventions should be rewarded by the State rather than through patent rights (Roscher 1868: 99). This is interesting, because Adam Smith's (very valid) argument at the time against patents was that instead of rewarding inventions, patents for trivial things (like the production of sweets), were sold by the king in order to raise money. In this area Justi solves Adam Smith's problem before Smith himself points to the problem.

Justi attaches much importance to the use of machinery (Justi 51), which is totally peripheral to Smith. On the question of 'technological unemployment', people losing their job as a result of mechanisation (not at all treated by Adam Smith), Justi is of the same opinion as James Steuart (Steuart 1767): the problem is important if the change is sudden, but is only serious if there is no other work at all to be found, which is not likely to be the case.

Colonies

To Justi the only useful colonies are those that are only engaged in agriculture. As other economists before Smith and Ricardo he is aware of the fact that such arrangements are not in the interests of the colonies themselves. Knowing that manufacturing is the key to wealth, this is an obvious part of the logic of the mercantilist system, and Justi realises that such trading arrangements 'always will be in danger as soon as the foreign people starts getting wiser' (Roscher 1868: 91). Adam Smith and David Ricardo represent a real watershed in economics, in that it is only with their barter-based, rather than production-based, economic theories that colonialism becomes morally defensible. Colonialism is only defensible within an economic theory where national wealth grows independently of what the nation produces.

'Dutch Disease', or, How Too Much Unearned Wealth Destroys an Economy

If a nation's treasure is too big, this will make the nation dirt poor, says Justi: *'Durch einen zu großen Staatsschatz würde das Land blutarm werden'* (Justi 50, Vol. II: 83). This is no doubt an insight gained from the 16th Century de-industrialisation of Spain through the inflow of treasure from Mexico and Peru. Justi's statement here is, in our view, most significant, in that it shows – to an extent not at all understood by mainstream economics – that Justi and his contemporaries were *not* mainly interested in treasure, as modern histories of economic thought still claim, virtually unanimously. Quite the contrary: Justi was aware of the fact that too much treasure would be harmful to the real wealth of a nation, i.e. to ***the productive system and apparatus*** which is at the core of any national wealth-producing system.

Without the experience of the de-industrialisation and impoverishment of Spain from the 16th and 17th Century, Justi's conclusion here does not correspond to intuitive common sense. It may clearly be seen as what is today called Dutch Disease, that the presence of riches crowds out other economic activities. A similar phenomenon is known in Australia as the 'Gregory effect', raw material wealth causes the currency to revalue and *produces de-industrialisation*. Justi sternly warns against the national Treasury being too wealthy in relationship to the money in circulation in the country, and he recommends using any surplus money for *außerordentliche Bauten*. In other words, superfluous treasure should be invested in public works.

This paradox, that monetary wealth (treasure wealth) crowds out real wealth (wealth from the productive system), was expressed by a Spanish economist at the time when this effect had strongly been felt in Spain (Cellorigo 1600):

> 'The cause of the ruin of Spain is that the wealth has been and still is riding upon the wind in the form of papers and contracts, *censos* and bills of exchange, money and silver and gold, instead of in goods that fructify and by virtue of their greater worth attract to themselves riches from abroad, sustaining our people at home. We see, then, that the reason why there is no money, gold, or silver in Spain is because there is too much, and Spain is poor because she is rich. The two things are really contradictory, but though they cannot fittingly be put into a singe proposition, yet we must hold both to be true in our single Kingdom of Spain'.

The belief that mercantilists were only interested in gold and treasure is one of the most destructive legacies left by Adam Smith. Still today this myth obliterates the extraordinary efforts, theoretical and practical, which were necessary in order to create the industrial civilisation, indeed it represents a historically important and very successful attempt by Adam Smith to strip the economists before him of any legitimacy. Indeed this myth, combined with Smith's 'proof' that all economic activities are qualitatively alike as carriers of economic growth (see Reinert 1999), are probably the most serous obstacle limiting the progress of poor Third World nations.

As Foucault says: 'The usual attitude towards what it has been agreed to call 'mercantilism' is double unjust: either it is denounced for comprising a notion it continually criticised (the intrinsic value of metal as the principle of wealth), or it is revealed as a series of immediate contradictions: it is accused of defining money in its pure function as a sign while insisting upon its accumulation as a commodity; of recognising the importance of quantitative fluctuations in specie, while misunderstanding their action upon prices; of being protectionist while basing its mechanism for the increase of wealth upon exchange. In fact, these contradictions or hesitations exist only if one confronts mercantilism with a dilemma that could have no meaning for it: that of money as a commodity or as a sign' (Foucault 2002: 192). Too long mercantilism and cameralism have been judged by people who have rarely read a single such text. Fortunately new research is attempting to get the record straight: emphasising that cameralism and mercantilism were systems attempting at maximising national wealth through production (Perrotta 1988 & 1991; Magnusson 1991)

7. Conclusion: Lost Relevance that Could be Regained

Johann Heinrich Gottlob von Justi belongs to an under-researched and highly relevant school of economics that laid the necessary foundations for the economic growth of Europe. Once the productivity explosions of the first industrial revolution had started snowballing across Europe, the painstaking groundwork of these economists – which had taken between two and three hundred years – was expelled from what became economic theory. The welfare, the institutions, the innovations, the popular attitudes towards progress, and the mechanisms of 'good governance' that these early economists had created, started to be taken for granted, as spontaneous products of an invisible hand. With Adam Smith economics became *catallectics*: the science of exchange, of supply and demand of something that has already been invented and produced outside what became the narrowly defined sphere of economics. After A. Smith converted production and trade into one category, by reducing everything to 'labour time' void of any skills or other qualities, economics became, as 19th Century German economists would complain, a science of barter consisting of *qualitätslose Größen,* quantities void of any qualities.

With Adam Smith the tools used in the painstaking process of creating the productive civilisation of Europe, slowly built brick by brick and institution by institution, were cancelled both from the toolbox and from the collective memory of the economics profession. As one economist put it in 1840: 'The delusion that security of life and property, the productivity of labor, and the consequent possibility of adquisition and enjoyment, and even the elevation of the spiritual and the ennobling of the moral nature – that these goods came to Man in the gift of gratuities, is itself a proof of the advanced stage of culture which the greater part of Europe at present occupies. As the grown man has long since forgotten the pains it cost him to learn to speak, so have the peoples, in the days of their mature growth of the State, forgotten what was required in order to free them from their primitive brutal savagery.' (Johann Gottfried Hoffmann, quoted in Cohn 1895: 60). In this process economists like Justi were the builders of the institutional foundation that made the Industrial Revolution possible. This revolution was in full swing as Adam Smith wrote his *Wealth of Nations*, but there is no indication that he was aware of it.

One generation after Hoffman, Gustav Cohn, another German economist, picks up his argument and continues: 'In point of fact, how significant was the involuntary testimony which the eighteenth Century, with its repudiation of the historic State and its yearning after the primordial state of nature, bore to the blessings of the inherited culture which it ungratefully enjoyed.'(Cohn 1895: 60–61) This description – written more than 100 years ago – also fits the Zeitgeist of today, and it constitutes a serious impediment for our understanding of the continued underdevelopment of large parts of the Third World. It is therefore very timely that in a recent work, *The Spirit of Capitalism. Nationalism and Economic Growth*, Liah Greenfeld of Boston University (Greenfeld 2001) again raises these issues and does a commendable job in tracing these by now forgotten roots of economic civilisation.

During the 19th Century, many economists were keen to distance themselves from the perceived errors of the past, in practice distancing themselves from policies which were necessary for catching up, but superfluous once the industrial revolution had taken firm roots in a country. This came to colour their opinions of the economists of the preceding century, the 1700's. In judging pre-Smithian economics we quite naturally gravitate towards the authority of economists who lived closer to their times. In doing this, however, we open up for serious mistakes. For example, our traditional main sources of information about the works of the Spanish mercantilists, Manuel Colmeiro (1818–1894), converted to liberalism and free trade during his career, and this very much colours his later mainly negative comments on the works of the Spanish mercantilists (Colmeiro 1880/1979). 20th Century authors, who have studied Spanish mercantilism, have come to very different conclusion. Earl Hamilton, the eminent US economic historian and historian of Spanish economic thought, draws very positive conclusions on the role of the Spanish mercantilist writers, as opposed to Spanish economic policy: 'History records few instances of either such able diagnosis of fatal social ills by any group of social philosophers or of such utter disregard by statesmen of sound advice' (Hamilton 1932: 237).

We suggest Wilhelm Roscher's view of Justi should be seen in a similar light. Roscher was probably the member of the German historical school who positioned himself closest to Ricardo and the English tradition, although he also contributed to The Other Canon by placing increasing returns again on the theoretical map. It is true when Peukert (in this volume) is of the opinion that Wilhelm Roscher 'downgrades' Justi's work. His article on Justi (Roscher 1868), which is largely repeated in his book on the history of economic thought in Germany (Roscher 1874: 444–465), Roscher starts out with a very negative description of Justi's character (*der eitle Mann, ohne Selbstbeherrschung,…würdeloser Überlaufer*) and his theories partly full of contradictions, and partly plain banalities. As the article advances, the positive comments increase and the negative ones diminish. In the end Roscher's articles on Justi reminds one of much of the academic economic writing in the former German Democratic Republic: the interesting and good stuff only comes after an initial mandatory lip service to the ruling ideology. This was particularly true of the communist writings in economic history.

With A. Smith, as Schumpeter consistently calls him, economics lost many of the key features that we are again trying to put back today: institutions, technology, innovations and processes of human learning being key elements. We tend to forget that these elements – and many more, most of them relevant – were part of economics at the time of Johann Heinrich Gottlob von Justi. After the failure of globalisation to deliver economic growth in large parts of the Third World, the focus of the Washington Institutions of institutional development is an unrecognised attempt to put back some pre-Smithian economics. What they fail to implement, however, is the *activity-specific* elements in Justi and his contemporaries: economic development is a process that has never ever taken root in the absence of increasing return activities, normally manufacturing. Schumpeter indeed discusses Justi's work under the heading of 'Justi: The Welfare State' (Schumpeter 1954: 179)

Indeed, we would claim that in terms of relevance for qualitatively understanding the multiple facets of the process of economic development when starting from scratch, the period between 1750 and 1775 was probably the highest point ever reached in the economic science. James Steuart's *Principles of Political Economy* (1767), highly influenced by German cameralism, is a manual for nations catching up. Adam Smith's becomes the manual for how hegemony wishes the world was working: the nations which monopolised industrial knowledge and increasing return industries, pretending these factors do not matter. When the same nations were catching up, they used a very different ideology. England clearly did this. The best example of such an ideological switch, however, is the extremely strong resistance to the theories of Adam Smith and David Ricardo in 19th Century United States – when the US followed a set of policies inherited from Justi and his colleagues – and the subsequent change to neoclassical theory when the United States had reached world industrial hegemony.

Interestingly Holland, the world hegemone before England, also had its own 'A. Smith' more than 100 years earlier: Jean de Wit, alias Pieter de la Court (de la Court 1662). As already Friedrich List pointed out, there is a strong historical tendency for nations that profit from strong oligopolies in manufacturing and monopolies in trade to produce theories, for export, in which *trade rather than production*, and *perfect competition rather than dynamic quasi-monopolies* are the true causes of wealth. The important elements that Adam Smith left out of economics – those which are necessary to create national innovation systems – are central to the economics of Johann Heinrich Gottlob von Justi, and, like Steuart and List, he should be required reading in the many small and medium sized nations who are presently only falling further behind in the process of globalisation.

Bibliography

Anonymous (1747), *Vertheidigung der Leibnitzischen Monaden und einfachen Dinge wider den Angriff des Herrn Justi: nebst eine Wiederlegung seiner erdichteten leidenden Natur so er jenen in seiner Untersuchung der Lehre von den Monaden und einfachen Dinge etc. entgegen setzet / entworfen von einem Kenner der neuern Weltweisheit,* Halle, Gebauer.

Anonymous (1748), *Sendschreiben an Herrn Justi von der Wiederbringung der Monaden in das Reich der Wirklichkeit*, Liegnitz, n.p.

Autorenkollektiv (1977), *Grundlinien des ökonomischen Denkens in Deutschland, Vol 1: Von den Anfängen bis zur Mitte des 19. Jahrhunderts*, Berlin (East), Akademie-Verlag, 1977.

Babbage, Charles (1830/1989), *Reflections on the Decline of Science in England and on some of its Causes - with a new appendix of correspondence by Charles Babbage & Peter M. Roget from the Philosophical Magazine*, Reprint, London, Pickering.

Babbage, Charles (1836/1986), *On the Economy of Machinery and Manufactures*, reprint from the 4th edition, New York, Kelley.

Becher, Johann Joachim (1668*), Politischer Discurs von den eigentlichen Ursachen des Auf- und Abnehmens der Städ (sic), Länder und Republicken, in specie, wie ein Land Volkreich und Nahrhaft zu machen, und in eine rechte Societatem Civilem zu machen*, Frankfurt, Zunners.

Bhagwati, Jagdish (2002), *Free Trade Today*, Princeton, Princeton University Press.

Beckmann, Johann (1787), *Anleitung zur Technologie, oder zur Kentniss der Handwerke, Fabriken und Manufacturen, vornehmlich derer, die mit der Landwirthschaft, Polizey und Cameralwissenschaft in nächster Verbindung stehn*, Third edition, Göttingen, Verlag der Vandenhoeckschen Buchhandlung.

Beckmann, Johann & Johann Heinrich Gottlob von Justi (1789) *Vollständige Abhandlung von den Manufacturen und Fabriken mit Verbesserungen und Anmerkungen von Johann Beckmann*, (Third edition of Justi 25)Berlin, Joachim Pauli.

Beckmann, Johann (1770–1806), *Physikalisch-ökonomische Bibliothek worinn von den neusten Büchern, welche die Naturgeschichte, Naturlehre und die Land- und Stadtwirthschaft betreffen, zuverlässige und vollständige Nachrichten ertheilet werden*, Göttingen, im Verlag der Wittwe Vandenhoeck und im Vandenhoek und Ruprechtschen Verlage. 23 volumes.

Beckmann, Joh(an)n (1797), *A History of Inventions and Discoveries*. Translated from the German by William Johnston, London, Printed for J. Bell. 3 volumes.

Bisgaard, H.L. (1902), *Den Danske Nationaløkonomi i det 18. Århundre*, København, Hagerup.

Bornitz, Jacob (1608), *Partitionum Publicarum, libri IV. In quibus ordine & summantim capita artis Politicæ designatur…*, Hanau, Wechel.

Botero, Giovanni (1590), *Della Ragione di Stato. Libri Dieci*, this work also contains *Delle Cause della Grandezza delle Città,libri tre*, Rome, Vicenzio Pellagalo.

Botero, Giovanni (1622), *Relazioni Universali*, Venice, Alessandro Vecchi.

Braudel, Fernand (1991), *Out of Italy. 1450–1650*, Paris, Flammarion.

Carey, Mathew (1822), *Essays on Political Economy; or, the most certain Means of promoting the Wealth, Power, Resources and Happiness of Nations. Applied Particularly to the United States*, Philadelphia, H. C. Carey & I. Lea.

Carl, Ernst Ludwig (1722–23), *Traité de la richesse des princes et de leurs etats, et des moyens simples et naturels pour y parvenir*, par M.C.C. d P. de B., allemand, Paris, Theodore Legras, 1722–23. 3 volumes.

Carpenter, Kenneth (1977), *Dialogue in Political Economy. Translations from and into German in the 18th Century*, Boston, Kress Library, Harvard Business School.

Carus-Wilson (1967), *Medieval Merchant Venturers*, 2nd edition, London. Methuen.

Cellorigo, Martín González de (1600), *Memorial de la política necesaria y útil restauración a la República de España*, Valladolid. Translated in Grice-Hutchinson, Marjorie (1993), *Economic Thought in Spain*, Aldershot, Elgar

Colmeiro, Manuel (1880/1979), *Biblioteca de los Economistas Españoles del los Siglos XVI, XVII y XVII, Madrid, Real Academia de Ciencias Morales y Políticas.*

Cohn, Gustav (1895), *The Science of Finance*, translated by Thorstein Veblen, Economic Studies of the University of Chicago, No. 1, Chicago, University of Chicago Press.

Court, Pieter de la (Jean de Wit) (1662), *Interest van Holland*, Amsterdam, n.p.

D.M. (1777), 'Précis Historique sur la vie de Mr. Justi par Mad. D.M', in Rozier, *Observations sur la Physique*, May.

Drechsler, Wolfgang (1997), 'Christian Wolff (1697–1754). A Biographical Essay', in *European Journal of Law and Economics*, Vol. 4, No. 4, pp. 111–128.

Firpo, Luigi (1960), *Gli Scritti Giovanili di Giovanni Botero. Bibliografia Ragionata,* Florence, Sansoni.

Foucault, Michael (1966/2002), *The Order of Things. An Archaeology of the Human Sciences,* London, Routledge.

Frensdorff, F. (1903/1970) *Über das Leben und die Schriften des Nationalökonomen J.H.G. von Justi,* reprint, Glashütten im Taunus, Auvermann.

Gadd, P.A. (1772), *Försök til en politisk och economisk avhandling om näringarnes samband och medvärkan på hvarandra,* Åbo (Turku), F. Brandell, Ph.D. Thesis, Åbo Akademi.

Greenfield, Liah (2001), *The Spirit of Capitalism, Nationalism and Economic Growth,* Cambridge, Mass., Harvard University Press.

Grimm, Jacob & Wilhelm (1854–1954), *Deutsches Wörterbuch,* Leipzig, Hirzel.

Hamilton, Earl (1932), 'Spanish Mercantilism before 1700', in *Facts and Factors in Economic History, Articles by former Students of Edwin Francis Gay,* Cambridge, Mass., Harvard University Press, pp. 214–239.

Herder, Johann Gottfried (1781), *Vom Einfluss der Regierung auf die Wissenschaften, und der Wissenschaften auf die Regierung,* 2nd edition, Berlin, Georg Jakob Decker.

Höck, J(ohann) D(aniel) A(lbrecht) (1794), *Lebensbeschreibungen und literarischen Nachrichten von berühmten Kameralisten,* Vol. I (all published), Nürnberg.

Holberg, Ludvig (1762), *Danmarks og Norges Geistlige og verdslige Staat eller Beskrivelse,* Copenhagen, Fridr. Christ. Pelt.

Hörnigk, Philipp Wilhelm von (1684), *Oesterreich über alles wann es nur will. Das ist: wohlmeinender Fürschlag Wie mittelst einer wolbestellten Lands-Oeconomie die Kayserl. Erbland in kurzem über alle andere Staaten von Europa zu erheben, und mehr als einiger derselben, von denen andern Independent zu machen. Durch einen Liebhaber der Kayserl. Erbland Wolfahr,* no place, no publisher.

Hume, David (1767), *The History of England,* London, A. Millar, 1767. 6 volumes.

Klaus, Joachim & Joachim Starbatty (1990), *Vademecum zu einem Universellen merkantilistischen Klassiker. Johan Joachim Becher 'Politischer Discurs' (1660),* Düsseldorf, Verlagsgruppe Handelsblatt.

Krugman, Paul (1990), *Rethinking International Trade,* Cambridge, Mass., MIT Press.

Krugman, Paul (1995), *Development, Geography and Economic Theory,* Cambridge, Mass., MIT Press.

Laffemas, Barthélemy (1597), *Reiglement (sic) general pour dresser les manufactures en ce rayaume, et couper le cours des draps de soye, & autres merchandises qui perdent & ruynent l'Estat: qui est le vray moyen de remettre la France en sa splendeur, & de faire gaigner les pauvres…,* Paris, Claude de Monstr'oil and Jean Richter.

Lundvall, Bengt-Åke, editor (1992), *National Systems of Innovations,* London, Pinter.

Magnusson, Lars (1991), *Merkantilismen. Ett ekonomiskt tänkande formuleras,* Stockholm, SNS Förlag, English edition (1994). *Mercantilism: The Shaping of an Economic Language,* London, Routledge.

Mandeville, Bernhard (1724), *The Fable of The Bees,* London, J. Roberts.

Meusel, Johann Georg (1802–1815), *Lexicon der vom Jahr 1750 bis 1800 verstorbenen Teutschen Schriftsteller,* Leipzig: Gerhard Fleischer. 15 volumes.

Monroe, Arthur Eli (1930), *Early Economic Thought, Selection from Economic Literature prior to Adam Smith,* Cambridge, Mass., Harvard University Press.

Nelson, Richard, editor (1993), *National Innovation Systems,* New York, Oxford.

Nilsen, Axel (1943), *Industriens Historie i Danmark,* Copenhagen, Gad, 1943. 4 volumes.

Ortiz, Luis (1558), Memorial del Contador Luis Ortoz a Felipe II, ('Memorandum to the King to prevent money from leaving the Kingdom'), Madrid, manuscript 6487, Biblioteca Nacional, Madrid. Reprinted 1998, Düsseldorf, Verlag Wirtschaft und Finanzen. Quoted in Hamilton, Earl J. (1932)

Oskal, Nils (1995), 'Liberalisme og urbefolkningsrettigheter', *Norsk Filosofisk Tidsskrift,* Vol. 2–3.

Perrotta, Cosimo (1988), *Produzione e Lavoro Produttivo nel Mercantilismo e nell'Illuminismo,* Galatina, Congedo Editore.

Perrotta, Cosimo (1991), 'Is the Mercantilist Theory of the favorable balance of Trade Really Erroneous?', in *History of Political Economy,* Vol. 23, No. 2, pp.301–336.

Pfeiffer, Johann Friedrich von (1764–1765 & 1777–1778), *Lehrbegriff sämtlicher oeconomischer und Cameralwissenschaften,* Stuttgart und Mannheim, Johann Christoph Erhard und C. F. Schwan, Eight parts, four volumes in five tomes.

Pfeiffer, Johann Friedrich von (1780), *Der Antiphysiokrat, oder umständliche Untersuchung des sogenannten physiokratischen Systems für eine allgemeine Freyheit und einzige Auflage auf den reinen Ertrag der Grundstücke*, Frankfurt am Main, Schäfer.

Pfeiffer, Johann Friedrich von (1781–1784), *Berichtigungen berühmter Staats- Finanz- Policei- Cameral- Commerz- und ökonomischer Schriften dieses Jahrehunderts, von dem Verfasser des Lehrbegriffs sämtlicher Ökonomischen und Cameralwissenschaften*, Frankfurt, Esslingersche Buchhandlung, 1781–1784. 6 volumes.

Pfeiffer, Johann Friedrich von (1783), *Grundsätze der Universal-Cameral-Wissenschaft oder deren vier wichtigsten Säulen nämlich der Staats-Regierungskunst, der Policey-Wissenschaft, der allgemeinen Staats-Oekonomie, und der Finanz-Wissenschaft*, Frankfurt, Esslingersche Buchhandlung, 2 volumes.

Priddat, Birger (1998), *Produktive Kraft, sittliche Ordnung und geistige Macht. Denkstile der deutschen Nationalökonomie im 18. Und 19. Jahrhundert*, Marburg, Metropolis.

Reinert, Erik S. (1996), 'Diminishing Returns and Economic Sustainability: The Dilemma of Resource-Based Economies under a Free Trade Regime.' In Hansen, Stein, Jan Hesselberg and Helge Hveem (editors), *International Trade Regulation, National Development Strategies and the Environment: Towards Sustainable Development?*, Oslo, Centre for Development and the Environment, University of Oslo.

Reinert, Erik S. (1998) 'Raw Materials in the History of Economic Policy; or, Why List (the Protectionist) and Cobden (the Free Trader) Both Agreed on Free Trade in Corn.', in Parry, G. (editor), *Freedom and Trade. 1846–1996.* London, Routledge.

Reinert, Erik S. (1999), 'The Role of the State in Economic Growth.', In: *Journal of Economic Studies*, vol. 26, No. 4/5, 1999. A shorter version published in Amatori, Franco (editor) *State-Owned Enterprises in the Western World*, Cambridge University Press.

Reinert, Erik (2000a), 'Full Circle: Economics from Scholasticism through Innovation and back into Mathematical Scholasticism. Reflections around a 1769 price essay: 'Why is it that Economics so Far has Gained so Few Advantages from Physics and Mathematics?'', in *Journal of Economic Studies,* Vol. 27, No. 4/5.

Reinert, Erik S. (2000b), 'Globalisation in the Periphery as a Morgenthau Plan: The Underdevelopment of Mongolia in the 1990's, in Lhagva, Sakhia, *Mongolian Development Strategy; Capacity Building,* Ulaanbaatar, Mongolian Development Research Center, 2000. Also downloadable on www.othercanon.org & in Reinert (editor), 2003.

Reinert, Erik S., editor (2003), *Evolutionary Income and Income Inequalities,* Cheltenham, Elgar.

Reinert, Erik & Arno Daastøl (1997), 'Exploring the Genesis of Economic Innovations: The Religious Gestalt-switch and the Duty to Invent as Preconditions for Economic Growth, in *European Journal of Law and Economics,* pp. 233–283.

Ricardo, David (1817), *The Principles of Political Economy and Taxation*, London, John Murray.

Rieter, Heinz et. al. (1993), *J.H.G. von Justi's 'Grundsätze der Policey-Wissenschaft',* Düsseldorf, Wirtschaft und Finanzen.

Robbins, Lionel (1952), *The Theory of Economic Policy in English Classical Political Economy,* London, Macmillan.

Roscher, Wilhelm (1868), 'Der sächsische Nationalökonom Johann Heinrich Gottlob von Justi', in Archiv für die Sächsische Geschichte, pp. 76–106.

Roscher, Wilhelm (1874), *Geschichte der National-Oekonomik in Deutschland*, Munich, Oldenbourg.

Salmonsens Konversationsleksikon (1915–1930), 2nd edition, Copenhagen, Schultz.

Schmoller, Gustav (1897/1967), *The Mercantile System and its Historical Significance,* New York, Macmillan, Kelley (translated from articles in *Schmoller's Jahrbuch*)

Schönberg, A. (1772), *Tal om näringarnes inbördes förbindelse, hållet för Kongl. Vetenskaps academien…,* Stockholm, Kongl. Vetenskaps academien.

Schumpeter, Joseph Alois (1954), *History of Economic Analysis,* New York, Oxford University Press.

Serra, Antonio (1613), *Breve trattato delle cause che possono far abbondare li regni d'oro e argento dove non sono miniere,* Napoli, Lazzaro Scoriggio.

Small, Albion (1909), *The Cameralists*, Chicago, University of Chicago Press.

Smith, Adam (1776/1976), *The Wealth of Nations*, Chicago, University of Chigago Press.

Sombart, Werner (1928), *Der Moderne Kapitalismus, Vol. 2, Das Europäische Wirtschaftsleben im Zeitalter des Frühkapitalismus*, München und Leipzig, Duncker & Humblot.

Stangeland, Charles Emil (1904/1966), *Pre-Malthusian Doctrines of Population. A Study in the History of Economic Theory*, New York, Kelley.

Steuart, James (1767), *An Inquiry into the Principles of Political Economy: being an Essay on the Science of Domestic Policy in Free Nations. In which are particularly considered population, agriculture, trade, industry, money, coin, interest, circulation, banks, exchange, public credit, and taxes.* London, A. Millar & T.Cadell. 2 Volumes.

Steuart, John (1769–1770), *Untersuchung der Grundsätze der Staatswirtschaft, oder Versuch über die Wissenschaft der innerlichen Politik in freyen Staaten…*, German translation. – Hamburg, Typografischen Gesellschaft, 1769–1770. 2 Vols. (one of two editions in German during the same years)

Tribe, Keith (1987), 'Justi, Johann Heinrich Gottlob von (1720–1771), in: *The New Palgrave: A dictionary of Economics*, London, Macmillan, Vol. 2, p. 1039.

Tribe, Keith (1988), *Governing Economy. The Reformation of German Economic Discourse 1750–1840*, Cambridge, Cambridge University Press.

Tribe, Keith (1995), *Strategies of Economic Order. German Economic Discourse (1750–1950)*, Cambridge, Cambridge University Press.

Verri, Pietro (1771), *Meditazioni sull'Economia Politica*, Genova, Gravier.

Verri, Pietro (1774), *Des Hrn Grafen von Veri, Kayserl. Königl. Kammerherrns, Geheimden (sic) und Präsidentens des Commerzwesen zu Mayland, Betractungen über die Staatswirtschaft*, Dresden, in der Waltherischen Hofbuchhandlung.

Viner, Jacob (1976), *The Role of Providence in the Social Order*, Princeton, Princeton University Press.

Wolff, Christian (1750*), The Real Happiness of a People under A Philosophical King Demonstrated*, London, Printed for M. Cooper, at the Globe.

Zincke, Georg Heinrich (1753), *Xenophon's Buch von den Einkünften, oder, dessen Vorschläge, wie das bereiteste Vermögen grosser Herren und Staaten nach ächten Grund-sätzen des Finanz-Wesens zu vermehren*, Wolfenbüttel & Leipzig, J.C. Meissner.

Zincke, Georg Heinrich, editor (1747–1767), *Leipziger Sammlungen von Wirthschaftlichen Policey-Cammer- und Finantz-Sachen. Erster (bis) Sechzehender Band (und) General-Register*, Leipzig, 1746–1767, 192 issues in 17 volumes.

Chapter Six

JACOB BIELFELD'S "ON THE DECLINE OF STATES" (1760) AND ITS RELEVANCE FOR TODAY

Erik S. Reinert[1]

The idea of economic decline has been with us for a very long time. The notion that human societies are bound to follow the cyclical patterns of nature – birth, life, decline and death – is found from the Greek philosophy of Plato to the Arab philosophy of Ibn-Khaldun. Only late Renaissance and Enlightenment *Entzauberung* – demystification – of the world picture view freed mankind from the cyclical vicissitudes of the blindfolded goddess Fortuna and opened up for rational economic policy to prevent booms and bust.[2] During the last century the theory of decline in the Westmanifested itself in German *Kulturpessimismus* with Oswald Spengler's *Decline of the West* (1918)[3], in the United States with Paul Kennedy's *The Rise and Fall of the Great Powers* (1987)[4], but also as harsh reality in the Great Depression of the 1930s.

The combined effects of the present economic crisis, which started as a financial crisis in 2007, and the rise of Asia – particularly China – have again put the subject of economic decline on the agenda in Western countries. In a now virtually forgotten economic bestseller, *Institutions Politiques*, German Economist Jacob Bielfeld (1717–1770), an advisor to Frederick the Great of Prussia, has a very comprehensive and – as opposed to Spengler's generalisations 150 years later – very concrete, detailed and specific list of the factors which cause the decline of nations. This paper brings the first ever English translation of this chapter with a brief discussion arguing for a renewed relevance not only of the factors and mechanisms pointed to by Bielfeld, but also of Bielfeld's fact-based and taxonomic approach to

---

1 I wish to thank Riaz Tayob of Tallinn University of Technology for his assistance in organising Bielfeld's arguments.

2 For a brief discussion of this, see Reinert, Erik *How Rich Countries got Rich..and why Poor Countrties stay Poor*, London: Constable, 2007.

3 *Untergang des Abendlandes*, first German edition of the first volume was published in 1918 (Vienna, Braumüller).

4 New York: Random House.

economic understanding. An important reason for republishing Bielfeld's chapter on the decline of nations is that it compares so favourably with the narrow focus of modern economic theory on the subject, exemplified in Daron Acemoglu and James Robinson's *Why Nations Fail*[5].

Europe at the time of Bielfeld presented a large number of nations from which to draw experiences. The 1648 Peace of Westphalia had produced around 400 independent states in Germany alone, although by 1760 the number had decreased considerably. Due to his position at the Court of Frederick the Great and in Prussia's Foreign Service, Bielfeld had unique access to information from many nations. Precisely because of this privileged access to information, Bielfeld's correspondence was published and translated (from French) also into German and English.[6]

The rich sample of different nations pursuing different strategies in different contexts allows Bielfeld a large number of national case-studies on which to draw. Closer to our time, The Great Depression also provided a setting where national strategies differed – e.g. whether to stay on the Gold Standard or not – from which nations could learn from each other.

With today's coordinated policies and one-size-fits-all approach of the European Union, the diversity from which Bielfeld and his contemporaries could draw is gone. Europe has lost a diversity which historically probably has been crucial to its success, becoming "standardised" and "homogenised" in a lot of areas from a single currency to bank supervision to standardisation of shapes of cucumbers to research policy. I suggest this chapter be read in the spirit of evolutionary economics, where the "market" is so much more than a mechanism setting prices. At the time of Bielfeld Europe was an arena where different ideas, in the form of laws, types of government, efficiency of armaments, and economic policy were continuously compared and tested against each other, attempting to arrive at a "best practice" from a huge number of cases. As opposed to a unified China, Europe at the time was a huge living laboratory. From an evolutionary perspective[7], rather than from one of equilibrium, today's Europe is facing decline where seemingly only one solution is considered, however poor the results may be, say, in a Greek rather than in a German context. Today's political approach inside the European

---

5 New York: Crown, 2012. For a good critique of Acemoglu and Robinson, see Vries, Peer "Does wealth entirely depend on inclusive institutions and pluralist politics?, *The Other Canon and Tallinn University of Technology Working Papers in Technology Governance and Economic Dynamics*, No. 43, 2012, downloadable at http://technologygovernance.eu/files/main // 2012092612501919.pdf

6 Bielfeld's Lettres familières et autres (1763), in two volumes, was translated into German in 1765. The 1768 English translation is entitled *Letters of Baron Bielfeld: Secretary of Legation to the King of Prussia; Preceptor to Prince Ferdinand; Chancellor of the Universitys (sic) in the dominions of his Prussian Majesty, F.R.A.B. &c. Author of the Political Institutes(sic): containing original anecdotes of the Prussian Court for the last twenty years*, London: J. Robson, 1768.

7 As in the perspective of Nelson, Richard & Sidney Winter, *An Evolutionary Theory of Economic Change*, Cambridge, Mass: Harvard University Press, 1982.

Union has reduced the possibilities of learning to a minimum. From this perspective alone, Bielfeld's account is interesting.

Oswald Spengler uses the concept *Gleichzeitigkeit*, or *simultaneity*, in the sense of processes taking place at the same stage in the historical cycle. This notion may also be employed in Carlota Perez' theories of sequential techno-economic paradigms, where new technological revolutions are often accompanied by hegemonic shifts between world powers. [8] From this point of view one could think of the simultaneity of the decline of the English Empire around 1900 and that of the United States today, i.e. the US today may be at the same stage in the maturity cycle as England was around 1900. From this perspective of simultaneity one might expect the United States soon to repudiate the benefits of free trade as England did in the early 20th century.

From a perspective of simultaneity and technological shifts, Bielfeld's account is interesting also because of a possible technological simultaneity of the period up to 1760 with that of today. His account was written towards the end of a period when Europe's most prosperous city-states, from Venice to Amsterdam, experienced relative, even absolute, economic decline. The First Industrial Revolution, one of Perez' economic paradigms, had benefitted the large nation states England and France at their expense. The present period may be one where the exhaustion of the Mass Production Paradigm in a similar way coincides with a transfer of industrial and economic power from the West itself to Asia and China. In this perspective we shall see that many of Bielfeld's factors contributing to decline are at work.

German Economics: Jacob Bielfeld and his contemporaries

Of four great German Enlightenment economists, Bielfeld is probably the most forgotten. These are, in order of year of birth, Georg Heinrich Zincke (1692–1769), Jacob Bielfeld (1717–1770), Johann Heinrich Gottlob von Justi (1717–1771), and Johann Friedrich von Pfeiffer (1718–1787)[9]. All published profusely, but – importantly – of the four only Jacob Bielfeld makes it to Ken Carpenter's honours list of *Economic Bestsellers before 1850*[10].

Bielfeld's main work made it into 12 editions, including two translations each into German and Spanish, and one each into Italian and Russian. One reason for Bielfeld's greater international fame at the time is probably that his *Institutions Politiques* was first published – in 1760 – in French, rather than in German. French being the main

[8] Perez, Carlota, Technological Revolutions and Financial Capital: The Dynamics of Bubbles and Golden Ages, London: Elgar, 2002.

[9] For a discussion of Justi's life and work, also comparing him to Zincke and Pfeiffer, see Reinert, Erik S. 'Johann Heinrich Gottlob von Justi (1717–1771): The Life and Times of an Economist Adventurer', in Backhaus, Jürgen (ed.), *The Beginnings of Political Economy: Johann Friedrich Gottlob von Justi*, New York: Springer, 2009, pp. 33–74. I leave out a fifth important economist, Johann Beckmann (1739–1811) here because his is a slightly later generation.

[10] Carpenter, Kenneth, *Economics Bestsellers before 1850*, Boston: Harvard Business School, 1974. Downloadable on www.othercanon.org

academic and political language in Europe of the period, Bielfeld's work was more internationally accessible than that of the others. Bielfeld's background as part of the Court of Fredrick II of Prussia was very different from that of the other authors. Zincke, Justi, and Pfeiffer were all state employees with a military background. They were all what at the time somewhat derogatorily was called *Projektmacher* (project makers) and *Staatsabenteuerer* (state adventurers),[11] and all three ended up spending time in jail accused of embezzlement

This contrasts sharply with the faith of Jacob Bielfeld who, as a childhood friend of Frederick II (the Great) of Prussia (1712–1786) spent his life close to European courts, was employed in the Prussian Foreign Service, as tutor to Crown Prince August Ferdinand, and was ennobled. Bielfeld was therefore in a much better position to make international comparisons also of non-German states than our three other authors of Enlightenment Cameralism. This international perspective will be evident in the chapter of *Institutions Politiques* which is translated here.

But as economists Zincke, Bielfeld, Justi, and Pfeiffer still had much in common. They all covered a holistic subject which today would be split into different academic branches, and they contributed to the enormous growth of European economic literature which started around 1750[12]. They each published one main work which could be used as a textbook in German Enlightenment economics. Justi published animpressive 67 books[13], but his 13 translations into 5 languages are from 8 different books.[14]. Zincke was ahead of the trend with his two-volume work in 1742.[15] Zincke was also the one who consciously

---

[11] There are important common elements between our German *Staatsabenteuerer* and the English Merchant Adventurers, like Sir Francis Drake. They were all working on behalf of their governments. But while the merchant adventurers were often pirates with a government licence in what most of the time in the end was a zero-sum-game – the gold of Spain changed hands and got English owners – Zincke, Justi and Pfeiffer as Cameralist economist adventurers were both theorising and putting into practice an economic theory where new learning and new institutions, and manufacturing under increasing returns, increased the size of the economic pie. In a sense Zincke, Justi, and Pfeiffer were one-man research and development institutions and entrepreneurs on behalf of the state. In spite of their misfortunes, they represent a type of theorising and practice that was a necessary passage points for the development of modern Europe (see Reinert 2009).

[12] For a discussion, see Sophus Reinert, *Translating Empire*, Cambridge, Mass: Harvard University Press, 2011 and Carpenter, Kenneth, "Manufactures in European Economic Literature of the Enlightenment", in Backhaus, Jürgen, *Physiocracy, Antiphysiocracy and Pfeiffer*, New York: Springer, 2011, pp. 5–21.

[13] For a bibliography of Justi, see Reinert, Erik S. and Hugo Reinert, 'A Bibliography of J.H.G. von Justi' in Backhaus, Jürgen (ed.) *The Beginnings of Political Economy: Johann Friedrich Gottlob von Justi*, New York: Springer, 2009, pp. 19–31.

[14] The languages were French, Spanish, Dutch, Russian and English. Justi's editions and translations are spread among so many different works that no single one qualifies for Carpenter's bestseller list.

[15] Zincke, Georg Heinrich, *Grund-Riß einer Einleitung zu denen Cameral-Wissenschafften, in welchen die ersten Vorbereitungs- und Grund-Lehren, so in der wirthschafftlichen Policey-Wissenschafft abzuhandeln, in einem kurzen Zusammenhang zum Behuff seiner Academischen Vorlesungen vorgestellet werden. Nebst einer vorläufigen Abhandlung von der Art und Weise junge Leute auf Universitäten nicht nur darinn theoretisch*

kept the links to the economics of Ancient Greece by translating and publishing Xenophon's *Poroi*[16].

Justi has several works aiming at being a general textbook, but the main one is his *Grundsätze der Policey-Wissenschaft* first published in 1756.[17] Pfeffer's main textbook was published between 1764 and 1778, eight parts in five volumes.[18] With a third volume published posthumously, Bielfeld's *Institutions Politiques* ran into three volumes.

In addition to writing books, all four main German Enlightenment economists ran their own economic journals. Zincke's *Leipziger Sammlungen von Wirthschafftlichen- Policey- Cammer- und Finantz-Sachen* (Leipzig Papers on Police, Economic and Finance Matters) ran from 1742 to 1767. Bielfeld's weekly *Der Eremit* (*The Hermit*) ran only from 1767 to 1769. Due to his itinerant activities, partly caused by war, Justi ran a total of seven different journals published in eight different German cities. The one with the longest life span, from 1754 to 1768 was the *Physikalisch-oeconomische Real-Zeitung*.[19] Pfeiffer's journal, *Vermischte Verbesserungs-Vorschläge und freie Gedanken über verschiedene, den Nahrungszustand, die Bevölkerung und Staatswirthschaft der Deutschen betreffende Gegenstände*, was only published between 1777 and 1778.[20]

Jacob Bielfeld – a brief account of life and work

As an important advisor to Frederick the Great of Prussia, Bielfeld is frequently mentioned in the literature, but there is not much on Bielfeld himself. The literature is limited to two relatively slim theses (*Inauguraldissertationen*) on him, by Gerda Voss from the University of Berlin in 1928[21] and by Friedel

zu unterrichten, sondern auch denenselben zur würcklichen Ausübung Anleitung zu geben, Leipzig: Caspar Heinrich Fuchs, 1742. The two total more than 1000 pages.

16 Zincke, Georg Heinrich, *Xenophons Buch von den Einkünften, oder dessen Vorschläge, wie das bereiteste Vermögen grosser Herren und Staaten nach ächten Grund-Sätzen des Finanz-Wesens zu vermehren, aus dem Griechischen ins Teutsche übersetztet, und mit historisch-politischen Anmerkungen, sonderlich aber von Oeconomischen- Policey- Cammer- und Finanz-Sachen versehen*, Wolfenbüttel & Leipzig: Meitzner, 1753 (a massive volume of 564 pages)

17 *Grundsätze der Policey-Wissenschaft in einem vernünftigen, auf den Endzweck der Policey gegründeten Zusammenhange und zum Gebrauch Academischer Vorlesungen abgefasset*, 2nd enlarged edition, Göttingen: Verlag der Wittwe Vandenhoeck, 1759. This work was translated into Italian and Spanish.

18 Pfeiffer, Johann Friedrich von *Lehrbegriff sämtlicher oeconomischer und Cameralwissenschaften*, Stuttgart und Mannheim: Johann Christoph Erhard und C. F. Schwan, 1764–1765 and 1777–1778.

19 Initial full title: *Physikalisch-oeconomische Real-Zeitung, aus denen von der Natur- und Haushaltungs-Wissenschaft, Feld-Bau, Heilungs-Kunst, Cameralwesen, Policey, Künsten, Manufacturen und Handlung handelnden Schriften zusammen gelesen und mit neuen Stücken, Versuchen und Anmerckungen versehen nebst einer allgemeinen Anzeige alles dessen, was bisher in diesen Sachen geschrieben worden.* Continued under different titles.

20 Continuing this tradition Johann Beckmann's journal, the *Physikalisch-oeconomische Bibliothek*, ran in 23 volumes from 1770 to 1807.

21 *Baron von Bielfeld; ein Beitrag zur Geschichte Friedrichs des Grossen und des ausgehenden Rationalismus*, Berlin: Curtis, 1928. 62 pages.

Stössl[22] from the University of Erlangen in 1937. We also have an *Eloge* published after he passed away.[23] A brief outline of his life follows here.

Born into a family of merchants in Hamburg in 1717, Jakob Friedrich von Bielfeld's life was international already from an early age. In 1732 he started his university studies in Leyden, Holland. In 1735 he travelled in Holland, France, and England. In 1738 he met and befriended then Crown Prince Fredrick of Prussia. Like Frederick, Bielfeld was a freemason. With Fredrick's ascent to the Crown in 1740, Bielfeld started his diplomatic career as Counselor to the Prussian Consulates in Hannover, later in London and Berlin. In 1745 he became tutor to Prince August Ferdinand, in 1747 he became curator of Prussia's universities and director of Berlin's famous Charité hospital. In 1748 Bielfeld was ennobled as Baron, and after 15 years of service to Prussia – at the age of 38 – he withdrew from a *vita attiva* to a *vita contemplativa* at his properties in Altenburg in the Eastern part of Germany in 1755. Due to the Seven Years' War Bielfeld had to leave Altenburg in 1757 for his native Hamburg, returning only in 1763. He died in Altenburg in 1770, at the age of 53.

With the exception of his short-lived journal *The Hermit*, published towards the end of his life, Bielfeld wrote in French. Another important and equally forgotten German economist who wrote in French was Ernst Ludwig Carl (1682–1742).[24] In addition the *Institutions Politiques* (1760) – from which this translation is taken – and his correspondence and the journals – all already mentioned above – Bielfeld also wrote an interesting work on the recent progress of Germany[25] and an encyclopedic work in the Enlightenment tradition: *L'érudition universelle, ou Analyse abrégée de toutes les sciences, des beaux-arts et des belles-lettres* in four volumes.[26] The English edition is entitled *The elements of universal erudition: containing an analytical abridgment of the sciences, polite arts, and belles lettres*.[27]

These publications all fall within the realm of the normal for economists of Bielfeld's generation and importance. His only atypical publications are comedies, which were first staged in Berlin. One comedy is entitled *The Germans in Paris*.[28]

---

22 *Jakob Friedrich von Bielfeld: sein Leben und Werk im Lichte der Aufklärung*, Forchheim: O. Mauser, 1937. 87 pages.

23 Fournay, Johann Heinrich Samuel, "Eloge de M. de Bielfeld», in *Nouveaux Mémoires de l'Académie royale des sciences de Berlin*, Berlin: Voss, 1772.

24 Carl, Ernst Ludwig, *Traité de la Richesse des Princes, et de leurs etats: et des moyens simples et naturels pur y parvenir*, Paris: Theodore Legras, 1722–1723. Carl is the first to introduce the pin factory as an example to illustrate the division of labour, which more than 50 years later was to be made famous by Adam Smith.

25 *Progrès des allemands dans les sciences: les belles-lettres & les arts, particulièrement dans la poésie & l'eloquence*, Amsterdam: F. Changuion, 1752.

26 Berlin: n.p., 1768.

27 London: G. Scott, for J. Robson, 1770, Dublin edition: Printed for H. Saunders, J. Potts, etc, 1771. Three volumes.

28 *Comédies nouvelles, par M. le baron de Bielfeld*, Berlin: E. de Bourdeaux, 1753. *Amusemens* (sic) *dramatiques de Monsieur le Baron de Bielfeld*, Leyden: Sam. et Jean Luchtmans, 1768. *Les Allemands à Paris, comédie*, no place, no publisher, no date.

The volumes of *Institutions Politiques* from which the present chapter on the decline of states is taken, are written in the venerable *Fürstenspiegel* – of "King's Mirror" – tradition. Going back to Greek (Aristotle) and Roman (Pliny the Younger) this type of work lists the virtues and duties of ruler and princes, establishing the necessary wisdom and principles for good governance. An important German predecessor was Veit Ludwig von Seckendorff's *Teutsche Fürstenstaat* published in 1656 which was continuously in print for 100 years, the last edition being printed in 1754.[29] Seckendorff and Bielfeld were both employed by men who represented the best intellectualism of Enlightened Despotism: Ernest the Pious of Gotha and Frederick the Great of Prussia respectively.

Frederick the Great's *Antimachiavel* (1740), his criticism of Nicolò Machiavelli, represented a curious incident inside the *Fürstenspiegel* tradition. This book was the result of Frederick's correspondence with Voltaire from 1736 to 1740. Also Bielfeld corresponded with Voltaire.

Bielfeld's approach is taxonomic and typical of his time. Like Linnaeus (1707–1778) did in the world of plants and animals, Bielfeld attempts to create order in the economic and political world by creating the necessary categories of forces at work. The first person to create a scientific economic treatise, Antonio Serra (1613)[30], also used a taxonomic approach, and the same approach was found in English economics before Adam Smith.[31] In contrast with his predecessors, Smith eliminated important taxonomies as found e.g. in King (1721) – that of "good" and "bad" trade among them – and insisted on the counterintuitive proposal that all economic activities are qualitatively alike as agents of economic wealth.[32] Portugal having neglected its manufacturing sector, Bielfeld here (1760) sees that nation's position vis-à-vis Britain as one of unfortunate dependency. This of course contrasts sharply with Adam Smith's (1776) and David Ricardo's (1817) use of Portugal as an example of the blessings created by free trade.

Bielfeld's emphasis on avoiding inequity is noteworthy. This was strongly emphasised in pre-Smithian economics all over Europe: In Germany by Seckendorff and Justi, in France by Marquis de Vauban (1633–1707), and in Italy by Pietro Verri (1728–1797). Both Vauban's and Verri's main works made it to Carpenter's bestseller list; *Projet d'une dixme royale* (1707), *Meditazioni sulla economia politica*, (1771). Indeed the issue of equity seems to be remarkably similar, but cyclical, across culture and time. The advice of General and Governor Thahir Ibn al Husein (775–822) on this issue is equally relevant in Western politics today, 1.200 years later: "Distribute (taxes) ..among all taxpayers in a fair, just and equitable manner and make them general, not exempting anyone because

29 On Seckendorff, see Reinert, Erik S., "A Brief Introduction to Veit Ludwig von Seckendorff (1626–1692)" in *European Journal of Law and Economics*, Vol. 19, 2005, pp. 221–230.

30 Reinert, Sophus A., ed. Antonio Serra, *A 'Short Treatise' on the Wealth and Poverty of Nations (1613)*, London: Anthem, 2011.

31 King, Charles, *The British Merchant; or, Commerce Preserv'd*, London: John Darby, 1721. 3 volumes.

32 For a discussion of this, see Reinert, Erik S. "The Role of the State in Economic Growth", in *Journal of Economic Studies*, vol. 26, No. 4/5, 1999, pp. 268–326.

of his noble rank or great riches.. and do not levy on anyone a tax which is beyond his capacity to pay".[33]

The experience-based knowledge and wisdom contained in Bielfeld's work reminds one of the teachings and wisdom of Benjamin Franklin's *Way to Wealth*, which was first published in 1757. Franklin aimed his wisdom at the common man, Bielfeld's *Institutions* aimed at the rulers and administrators of Europe, while his works on *General Erudition* had been aimed at the common man. Contrary to what could be expected, Benjamin Franklin's *Way to Wealth* – not Adam Smith's *Wealth of Nations* – is the most published economics book in history, judged by the number of different editions.[34] It is certainly dramatic that this kind of economics – both at the macro and micro levels – has now virtually disappeared from economic science. The aim of The Other Canon Foundation is to revive this experience-based economics tradition. The translation and publication of this chapter from Bielfeld are part of this effort.

The Chapter 'On the Decline of States'

The following is an attempt at a résumé of the chapter, paraphrasing and citing Bielfeld (italics are mine). Numbers in brackets refer to the relevant paragraph in the translation itself which follows after the résumé.

In sharp contrast to today's equilibrium economics, Bielfeld starts out his chapter on the decline of states with the basic assumption that everything in the world is characterised by instability: "The most formidable empires are subject to the law of change and inconstancy". When change occurs in "great bodies" (like empires) these are called revolutions, Bielfeld states, that is when the "face of the universe is changed".

A "universal history of the world" investigates both the causes and effects of revolutions, Bielfeld says. He distinguishes between two kinds of revolutions, the natural and the political. The former are "grievous effects of nature, such as earthquakes, floods, plagues and like scourges". The latter revolutions are "caused by men, and alters only the system of states, by changing the form of their government, or by subjecting their peoples to alien laws", which is the subject of Bielfeld's inquiry.

Bielfeld's taxonomy starts by distinguishing between *internal* and *external* causes of decline. The power of the state may be *real* or *relative*, as is shown by external threats to the state. The internal power of the state may also be founded upon "the *local situation*, or on *opinion*, or *accessory*." The local situation may be affected by natural disasters, and responses to it may be strengthened or weakened given the circumstances of the country. On opinion (or ideology) Bielfeld states that, "The power of opinion becomes

---

33 The quote comes from the *Prolegomena* of Ibn-Khaldun (1332–1406), quoted in Neumark, Fritz, "Zyklen in der Geschichte ökonomischer Ideen", in *Kyklos*, Vol. 28, 1975, No. 2, p. 274.

34 More than one thousand editions of Benjamin Franklin's *Way to Wealth* in 22 different languages were published before 1851. A forthcoming work by Harvard's Kenneth Carpenter will be documenting these editions.

weaker, and falls into decline, in proportion as the opinion upon which this power is based dissipates in the mind of men; and as a consequence one must not find it at all strange that those who are at the head of such a state seek to perpetuate this opinion, whether it be true or false."

There are also direct and indirect causes of decline, "Among the great number of direct or indirect causes that can abbreviate the life of a government, change the system of states, and overturn empires, we will only indicate the principal causes, and those that produce the most sudden effects.

Bielfeld's taxonomy distinguishes between 8 *external* (alien) and 17 *internal* (intrinsic) causes of decline. In this résumé we have numbered the external factors from E-1 to E-8 and the internal ones from I-1 to I-17. One can imagine using these categories today for a summary diagnosis of national problems. The United States may presently be seen as suffering from E-4 (imperial overextension), I-8 (neglect of production and science, de-industrialisation), I-15 (debt), increasingly I-16 (constant internal wrangling) and probably also I-7 (too much freedom destroying social cohesion). From Bielfeld's perspective many Arab countries may be seen as suffering from E-2 (war), E-5 (dependency), probably I-1 (unwise constitutions), I-2 (defective public administration), I-5 (excessive religion), sometimes bordering on I-6 (oppression), and definitely I-8 (decline of production and science).

E-1. Migration

It is remarkable that, writing during the 18th century, Bielfeld would put migration as the top external danger to a nation. At the time, the Indian Nations of North America were being ruined by migration from Europe, but as expected this was not what Bielfeld had in mind: "Among the alien causes one can count first of all **the great migrations of peoples**, such as the spectacle that the fourth and fifth centuries offered Europe. Now hordes of Goths, Vandals and other Barbarians stream from the depths of the north to flood Europe, extending their conquests to Spain, to Italy and even Africa; now the peoples who inhabit the most northerly countries attack their neighbours towards the south, forcing them to leave their home. These last are then constrained in turn to fall upon other peoples who were their southern neighbours; and so, little by little, move around each other in turns, constantly pushing towards the most equable climates. (paragraph 5)

"...Indeed, each nation changed place, kingdoms, empires and republics were destroyed, or founded, or transported to other lands... **Is it unthinkable that one day there will arise from the Australian lands, from the almost unknown African interior, from Ethiopia, from the depths of Asia, from the upper Americas, an innumerable swarm of men, stronger, more robust, more indefatigable than the Europeans, and put to rout all the skill, all the facility of the latter in the art of war, and all their policy?** (5) I concede that such a revolution seems far removed, but it is not impossible; and without wishing to **anticipate remote evils**, there are dangers in this respect that are much closer to us". (6)

E-2. War

"War, unjust or equitable, can cause the decline of states. Wars may result in states declining by degrees rather than through one-off battles. All the writers on the rights of peoples maintain that the right of conquest is a legitimate right; but even if it were not, the greatest part of the changes occurring in empires, and in the world since its origin right up to the present day, have they not been occasioned by force of arms? Fortunate wars elevate states, just as the unfortunate ruin them. **It is however a rarity that one war alone destroys at once an empire.**

"… Princes, ministers, generals need to be persuaded of a Divine Providence ruling all, but act as if they do not believe this, and as if good or bad outcomes depend upon their own prudence; for indeed experience proves that all incidents of war, as in all other affairs of the world, derive always from natural causes. It is only visionaries, or spirits too slothful or stupid, who attribute each accident to the immediate and miraculous guidance of the Supreme Being; if they open their eyes, if they examine properly, then they will find this cause to be a side effect". (7)

E-3. Excessive demands from neighbouring states

"When a neighbouring power makes excessive advances in all objects of policy, its expansion can become the third cause, whether proximate or more remote, of the decline of another state. "

Excessive demands between states, in a context of a zero sum game, may lead to the decline of a state. Setting strategic long term objectives is crucial, and prudent negotiations can forestall war. "Europe's political system is today in general such that one state is not able to raise itself except at the expense of another, whether it be by conquest, or by commerce etc. Each degree of real power which it acquires gives it at least one more degree of relative power, and the degree that it gains is a loss for its rivals. Ultimately, going from strength to strength, it comes imperceptibly to engender terror among the other sovereigns, finally setting their measure. Nearly all statesmen have felt this truth. The lengthy disputes between the Austrian and Bourbon Houses, between the northern powers etc. have been ruled by no other principle; but cabinets only too rarely adopt the most fitting measures to prevent this excessive elevation of powers which is capable of inspiring in them a proper jealousy. Such cabinets can be seen to favour minor interests over major, ceding the most essential, constant advantage to a passing one, and sometimes concluding alliances with rivals which not only serve in turn to fortify the latter against themselves, but also against their natural allies, with whom they should make common cause by opposing in concert the expansion of these same rival powers. The Latin tag which is so true, and so politic, *obstare principiis*, that it is necessary to act quickly if not to be acted upon, is too much neglected by those who conduct affairs of state, and **sometimes a century of war is needed to gain what one could have been able to forestall by a few strokes of the pen.**"

E-4. Imperial over-extension

"The over-extension of an empire nearly always becomes a cause of its decline."

Bielfeld here makes the same point about Imperial overstretch which Paul Kennedy was to make about the United States more than 200 years later. To Bielfeld, uniting all lands under one empire is a "chimerical undertaking" because a central power cannot know what is happening in the distant parts of the empire. The governance structures of the empire in far off places are susceptible to breaking at any moment. Rebellions and internal wars are viewed as more dangerous than external ones. The local senates that have to be established in the provinces form so many, almost independent, states; and the loose relationship they enjoy with the principal government can break at any moment. Rebellions and internal wars are more dangerous than external wars, hence the dismembering of provinces, and the decline, fall, destruction of the state. (9)

E-5. Dependency

Bielfeld here raises the questions which, starting in the 1960s, created such a huge debate in Latin America: dependency. The contemporary example he uses, that of Portugal vis-à-vis Britain, seems very well taken. The absolute dependence of a state on another power is yet another cause of its gradual weakening, says Bielfeld: "The dependency of one nation upon another, may be for reasons of idleness or because of the need for protection ("vice of police") or regarding its basic needs (foodstuffs, manufactures and other primary needs).

The origin of dependence may be the result of bad policy. The dependent state may become way too entangled with its powerful ally. It may sell all or most of its produce to it and rely too much on the "subsidies" it receives. Bielfeld warns that, "These are involvements which go further than one thinks."

This dependence can come from **national idleness**, or from a **vice of police (policy) such that for most foodstuffs, manufactures and other prime needs** the country is compelled to provide for itself through another strong people, not being able to do otherwise in this regard. Portugal is almost in this situation vis-à-vis Britain. However, this dependence finds its origin in an inferior system of policy embraced by the government, in which it espouses all the disputes of a powerful ally, taking its part too deeply, attaching its fortune to that of that same ally through almost indissoluble links, and above all when it sells to this ally more or less all its forces and in return becoming too reliant on subsidies. **These are involvements which go further than one thinks.** Sailing in a stormy sea, one's barque is attached to a first-rate vessel with chains which one would not know how to break when this vessel is imperilled, and the barque is dragged with it into the abyss. (10)

E-6. Grandiosity of Independence

"The decline of the state may also be occasioned by the affectation of a great independence and an authority capable of casting into shade other sovereigns."

A state that becomes over-confident in its ability to be independent may raise the ire of other states that may result in other states uniting against it. It may also lead to undertakings that are beyond the means of the state. Power ought to be exercised judiciously and avoid excess.

A state that wishes to concern itself entirely with itself, breaking all liaisons, whether of commerce or of friendship with the rest of Europe – such a state revolts all other powers. **There is an art in hiding all the power that is possessed, and policy demands that that one never makes use of it on small occasions, but reserves it for major occasions.** (11)

If the state can enfeeble itself through the excessive indolence of those who govern it and who do not know how to make use of all its advantages, render its laws valued, render it respected by its neighbours, it can also be plunged into irreparable misfortune by a sovereign who embarks upon vain, chimerical, perilous undertakings that are absolutely beyond his powers. If he ventures upon commerce that he would not be able to protect, if he seeks justice with armed force for a power that can crush him, if he demands prerogatives and extraordinary honours, if he conceives projects of conquest that are too extensive. This point is obviously also relevant for modern democracies.

E-7. Division of Empire (or "Balkanisation")

This is another issue which has remerged in Europe, reinforced by the financial crisis. "The state also suffers loss by the monarch dividing his empire. Splitting up of territories weakens the state, this is in terms of pursuit of the 'good life' in the nation, and more especially as regards external threats. Splitting up the empire is against natural law and leaders should not be allowed to whimsically divide up territory"

There is a difference between what constitutes the Empire's possessions and that of its sovereign. The latter may be divided up, but division of the former needs to be thought of in different terms. Saxony, the richest and most extensive province of Germany, lost all of its unity through the territorial divisions and subdivisions which were successively made between the different lines of the House of Saxony and the diverse branches of each line. **This division of states is both unjust and futile. The least reflection on the origin of peoples and of civil government reveals that men are united in the body of society so that they might be stronger, and only consent to be ruled over by a sovereign so that they might be happier by their union, and to be able to oppose the attentions of their enemies with greater vigour under a common chief.** But this chief has no right to partition a country and a people that the ancients have once brought together, and for which providence has conferred upon it a government with the tacit and express condition that it maintain the country and people as entire as it is able.

All the deference that peoples show to their sovereigns is given only on the condition that they do not break the knot that binds them, and which keeps them in a *corps d'état*.

Ultimately natural law, the rights of peoples, and the founding constitutions of the greater part of countries are opposed to such partitions. One most essential part of the happiness of peoples must not depend on the caprice of a sovereign, and once a province is incorporated into the state, it can only be detached by *force majeure*, which silences all consideration of equity, and all policy. **But policy, whose principal object is that which is useful, does not lose sight of that which is equitable.**

There is also a great difference to be made between the succession of sovereigns and that of private persons. One cannot divide up men and people as one divides up other goods of fortune; and considering the matter closely, sovereignty is not a good over which its possessor has disposal, but rather a responsibility, an office with which he is endowed. (14). Here Bielfeld's discussion of luxury and on the roles of princes is also most interesting.

E-8. Single sovereign (or Sovereignty is indivisible)

There cannot be two sovereigns for the same state. Such attempts can become a direct cause for decline of a state. The political axiom stating that sovereignty is indivisible, since power divided is power enfeebled, also shows us why two princes cannot simultaneously occupy the same throne. Such an arrangement thus becomes a very direct cause for the decline of a state.

The following represent Bielfeld's internal (or intrinsic) factors of decline.

I-1. Unwise Constitutions leading to inequity

Again it is interesting what Bielfeld choses as his first cause of decline, in this case internal: **constitutions which lead to inequity**. "Similar states, seemingly defective edifices where burdens and support are poorly distributed and the proportions irregular, **crumble of themselves and succumb under their own weight**. The ancient Greeks, who groped unceasingly for the best form of government for their republics, fell into bad hands, and their legislators, lacking theory and experience, made monsters of republics which destroyed themselves whereas their citizens performed prodigies of valour against their external enemies".

I-2. Insane Sovereign

Insane sovereigns can lead to the decline of the state and should be removed or replaced by a guardian acting in his stead. "The constant mistakes committed by an extravagant prince occasion the decline of his state before the wisest ministers are able to remedy them."

I-3. Requirements of state (Public Administration)

In Bielfeld's discussion here we see the outlines of a description of a Weberian bureaucracy. The state needs to be supported by loyal ministers. It is not sufficient for the state to be regular, certain, and predictable and the leader wise. Loyal ministers are also needed. It is not enough that the form of a government be regular, and the prince wise; *for the preservation of the state one also needs loyal ministers.*

As only God can do everything, even the greatest king has need of support in governing, and in carrying out his wishes. Imagine a state that falls into the hands of incompetent, or ill-intentioned, ministers. Every occasion to do good for the country is missed, all the misfortunes that can befall a country are not forestalled. Success will never follow the wisdom or generosity of a prince's resolve, for it will sour in execution; such failures unsettle the prince, and make him uncertain of the measures that he should take in future. (22)

I-4. Relaxation of morals (importance of morals and Rule of Law)

"The *relaxation of moeurs*, in the maintenance of good order and of society, in the observance of laws – these are all once again a direct and intrinsic cause of the decline of a state."

Mediocre laws that are observed are preferable to wiser laws that are neglected. It is the people which make up the state; if this people abandon itself to all sorts of vices, only one or two generations is needed for it to become debilitated; this is a fact based upon centuries of experience.

Laws are not promulgated as a vain speculation, to occupy doctors and schoolmen, but to be put into practice. Well-observed, but somewhat mediocre, laws make the state stronger than wiser laws that go neglected. The impunity with which crimes are committed becomes the source of a thousand evils in the state, and as a consequence of its decay

I-5. Excessive Religion

"Those who argue that *religion* is of no use in the government of a state, and that cunning and the gallows is sufficient to deter malefactors and maintain good order, are talking claptrap."

Religion is important to a state. However religion has to subordinate itself to the king, and do so wisely. Religion should not be too dominant. Let us beware! As soon as positive religion spreads in a country, taking the place of natural religion, too speculative and too uncertain for the multitude, since each man is different in sentiment and insight – then this country is on the way to decline.

"This nation [England], the most political of all, recognises that its happiness, its tranquillity, the maintenance of its power, depend to a great extent upon the maintenance of its religion. Here **religion has subordinated itself to the king, and does so wisely**. (24) But as much as it is necessary for the good of the state for religion and a solid piety to prevail in the nation, **it is fatal if the state *allows it to become too ascendant***. A people of devotees, of whatever religion, would be a people both ridiculous and feeble. The reasons for this are so palpable that they require no elaboration. **External devotion too easily leads to enthusiasm, to superstition, to fanaticism, to idleness, to indolence**, to a disregard for worldly matters which is so harmful to the progress of the arts, talents and commerce." (25)

I-6. Oppression / Limits on Liberty (or Despotism)

Where despots limit the liberty of the people, the state cannot be powerful as there is not a time when the ruler is not at risk of losing the rulership. The means used to maintain domination and obedience of the people weakens the state. In other words, oppression is not a sustainable form of government

In countries where the natural liberty of men is oppressed by a purely despotic yoke, the state cannot be very powerful. There is not one moment when the despot is not in danger of perishing on his throne, and it costs a thousand-fold more to achieve obedience to absolute power than to the power of the Law. **The measures that such a despot is obliged to continually take to maintain the people in a state of obedience, and to prevention sedition, absorb half of the natural forces of the state**; each popular riot, which occurs despite all precaution, weakens it all the more, and each revolution that overthrows the monarch shakes the state to its foundations. Hence the unimaginable weakness of the Ottoman Empire, and other Asiatic monarchies which would, in the absence of this vice, shake all Europe. **It appears that slavery renders men at once worthless.**

I-7. Excess of liberty

Too much liberty and freedom can limit the need for restraint that is essential for the creation of social cohesion and the "general good" (*ben commune*). In modern terms this could be translated as a focus on individual rights at the expense of the correlative obligations that flow from such rights, to both individuals and collectives/communities. Likewise it could be expressed as an exclusive focus on *freedoms to* (e.g. to carry a gun), at the expense of *freedoms from* (e.g. from being shot).

"A people which seeks to become too free gives to its neighbours the means to forge its chains. To make men combine for the general good there is need of a restraint that will render them obedient, and a power that will make them all subjects". (27)

I-8. Decline of Production. Neglect of agriculture, commerce, sciences, useful arts and passion for liberal arts and frivolity

"When a nation neglects to perfect agriculture, commerce, the sciences and the useful arts (i.e. handicraft and manufactures), giving itself with too great a passion to the liberal arts and frivolous objects, it can only become weak, and the state languishes" (28) This point is obviously extremely relevant for Europe and the United States at the moment, and how the present (2013) crisis is handled.

I-9. Arrogance, pride, and idleness

This is an argument much in line with economist Thorstein Veblen's *Theory of the Leisure Class* (1899). "Another very direct cause of the weakness and decline of a state is **the**

pride and idleness of the nation. It was a great political idiot who was the first to seek to persuade the nobility into believing that they demean themselves through honest employment of their own hands. The author of the *Persian Letters*[35] admirably depicts the arrogance, the indolence, and the dislike of labour in the Spanish nation, especially among the nobility. He writes that nobility is acquired through sitting around."

"The nobility sets a dangerous example for the people. Their inactivity introduces idleness to that class of citizens whose work buttresses the state. Nobody has ever told me that the nobility are sufficiently occupied by warfare. Wars are short and the peace is long". (29)

I-10. Senseless laws

Laws need to be wise in and of themselves but also take into account the context in which they are applied or made. "We remarked above all that laws must not only be full of wisdom in themselves, but also quite appropriate to the countries for which they are made." In other words: context is very important. What use is it if, while the state is well-founded, the prince wise, ministers excellent, *moeurs* good, **the laws are ridiculous**? (31)

Here follows criticism of other religions, Catholicism and Jewry (32 & 33). Bielfeld's ugly anti-Semitism is unfortunately rather typical of the period, and is similar to that of Voltaire (with which, as reported, Bielfeld corresponded).

I-11. Excessively large colonies

Compared to the mechanistic understanding of trade in David Ricardo, Bielfeld in this paragraph (indirectly) explains why colonial trade differs from symmetrical trade among equal nations. "**Excessively large colonies** which the state establishes in distant provinces, and above all in other parts of the world, enfeeble the state, and moreover become an intrinsic cause of its decline." Large colonies need to be managed to gain the advantages from them without it becoming a cause of decline.

"I say **excessively large**, since one should not imagine that my remarks bear upon the colonies that Holland, England and France, for example, maintain, and almost constantly refresh in their Asian and American possessions. For apart from these nations being extremely numerous in themselves, and that they enrol as many foreign subjects as they can for their transport, it has to be considered that these colonies procure to the metropole five significant advantages which abundantly repay the losses incurred by the citizens removed, and who remain dependent on the state, constantly contributing to the good of the state. These advantages are 1. a much greater consumption of the products of the land which the metropole sends there; 2. the addition of a greater number of manufacturers, artisans etc. who serve the needs of the colonies; 3. the augmentation of navigation and of all workers contributing to it; 4. the export of a greater quantity of foodstuffs that are

---

35 I.e. Montesquieu.

necessary in these colonies; 5. a much greater superfluity of foodstuffs and merchandise which these colonies provide, and which the metropole provides to other peoples, which leads to the continual growth of its commerce."

I-12. Epidemics and occupational Health

"**Epidemics** greatly ravage the people and weaken the state, depriving it for a considerable period of the resources necessary to defend itself against an unjust aggressor."

Failing to maintain the people, and the armies, in good health enfeebles the nation.

"If one persists in establishing some good citizens in a country where the air is bad, sending them into mines which exhale sulphurous vapours, employing them in the cultivation of rice which grows only in mires constantly inundated with stagnant water and so on; such action constantly enfeebles the state's people, and as a result slowly leads, almost unfailingly, to the decline of the state". (35)

I-13. Abuse of Spirits and Strong Liquors

"The abuse the people make of spirits and other strong liquors; we add here that liquors can weaken a nation if they are made use of without due moderation."

As example Bielfeld uses the excess of alcohol consumption in England in 1734 and 1735, before wise legislation make the English again turn to "healthy beer".

I-14. Relaxation of military discipline

"The **relaxation of military discipline** also leads a state into unfailing loss." Women who have such influence over the hearts of men, priests, merchants, manufacturers, artisans, cultivators – they all desire peace, and look upon it with the greatest happiness. They are right in one sense, but they do not at all see that a lengthy peace corrupts the soldiery, relaxes discipline, allow the officer and the soldier to become unpractised in their art, and softens them. One would wish that in time of war the entire army would be composed only of lions, and in time of peace of sheep; but this is to ask for a contradiction, to want a chimera. Many people find military discipline too harsh in a peacetime garrison; it seems much too gentle when they march on the enemy. Men are never in agreement with themselves. They learn that peace is made to accustom officer and soldier to war, that discipline must be constantly upheld in an army, that the most skilful princes set up exercise encampments, carry out manoeuvres, marches, reviews, all to keep their troops up to the mark, making them practised, and not allowing them to forget the fatigue of serious campaigns, nor the art of winning." (37)

I-15. Debt

Bielfeld distinguishes between two kinds of debt: sovereign debt and debt accrued in commercial transaction. "..a state can have two kinds of debt: one whose real value is employed in manufactures, commerce, and all sorts of useful establishments for the relief of the people; the other in which the fund is consumed by the sovereign in frivolous expenditure. The excess of this latter kind of debt can only enervate the state, and lead it into a certain ruin." Today we can observe that also democratic governments may engage in *frivolous expenditure* and assume large debts.

"If the country in question has no kind of equivalent for the debt contracted upon its credit, if it has insufficient means to regain through the balance of its commerce the interests which the state pays annually on the borrowed capitals, not long is needed before it falls into decline." (38)

I-16. Constant internal wrangling

"The **continual wrangling between ministers, generals and others** in monarchies, and in republics the divisions between Senate and People, between magistrates and the heads of government – both can easily lead the state into decline, and from decline to fall."

Constant wrangling between ministers, generals and others in monarchies, and senate and people in republics, can lead to state decline because "that **every kingdom divided against itself will be reduced to a desert, and every city or house divided against itself cannot persist".** However it is recognised that 'real boats rock', and that divisions are "a necessary consequence of the republican state".

While one can of course imagine the most perfect form of government and set out the wisest maxims of policy, it is always necessary to place conduct of the diverse branches of government in different departments, which is to say, in the hands of men who are full of passion. If these passions blind them, if their views of matters are too diverse, if they are divided among themselves, their actions will unfailingly be at cross-purposes, and the state will fall into anarchy. Such divisions are more frequent and more dangerous in republics, for there is not an authority either as great or as active as in monarchies capable of reuniting all employees under the banner of the public good, and making everyone to address their own tasks in spite of themselves. Divisions are a necessary consequence of the republican state; they always have been, and always will be. Sovereign power cannot make itself felt too quickly to suppress disunion and bring its progress to a sudden halt, even with the greatest rigour. (39)

I-16. Interfering with fundamental laws of government

"When a republic interferes with the fundamental laws that regulate the constitution of its government the state runs a very great risk of running to ruin.

I know that different times call for different ways, and that laws have to follow those changes that occur in the world's state of affairs; but the constitution of the state must never alter, and the laws bearing upon this must remain as far as possible immutable. Every political arrangement has its disadvantages, and it is better to deal with those that arise from an established system than to change a system that has long supported a state. Experience is here in agreement with theory and principles." (40)

I-17. Regicide or assassination of the sovereign

The killing of the sovereign is an indirect cause that can bring about the decline or overthrow of a state, weakening its resilience. One thinks that these evil deeds, whose seed was sown in the works of Machiavelli and his disciples, have been stifled by the philosophical spirit which has, over the last few centuries, improved Europe's police, and it has been said, made Europe more virtuous.

"... all the citizens of a country, in submitting themselves to monarchical government, feel that their individual wills are united in the single person of the sovereign, to whom they accord an authority necessary to this end, and related powers to set it to work; that the person of the monarch has been rendered sacred and inviolable by the universal consent of all civilised nations, and the king is endowed with the title of "majesty" to impress upon the hearts of all men a greater veneration for their dignity. One also sees that it is not permissible for any member of society, of whatever estate, and whatever degree he might be, to believe his own interest, or that of the state in general, to be hurt in any particular, or betrayed by the decrees of his sovereign, such that he acquires the slightest trace of a right to make an attempt on the monarch; for on the contrary, each citizen is individually wounded by this same *attentat.* (41)

Bielfeld, *Institutions Politiques*, volume 2

Ch. XV. On the Decline of States[36]

§1. We have throughout this work reviewed the means by which states arise and sustain themselves; our work would be left imperfect if we did not undertake some investigation of the causes of their decline and of their fall. To such we devote this chapter, which will perhaps not be the least interesting. Policy will here discover the principal reefs against which the State is in danger of running. Princes and Ministers, true pilots at the helms of empires, will find here a chart of soundings and of the most dangerous places. Having seen what they have to do, they will now see what they have to avoid. How happy for them if, in noting the hazards, these hazards serve as lessons and examples which prevent their being suffered!

§2. The quintessence of everything in the world is *instability*. The most formidable empires are subject to the law of change and inconstancy. The Roman monarchy, a true colossus of power, as M. Montesquieu says, *ends like the Rhine which is no more than a brook when it loses itself in the ocean.* When change comes for great bodies, when kingdoms or empires are dismembered, weakened, destroyed, when nations are extinguished, when in

[36] Translated by Keith Tribe. Copyright 2013 The Other Canon Foundation, Norway. In the original 1760 edition (The Hague: Pierre Gosse, 1760) this chapter comprises pages 309 to 338 of volume (part) two. This second and last volume closes with a chapter *Conclusions* (pages 339–344) and a subject index to volume two. The footnotes from this point on are those of Bielfeld.

other words the face of the universe is changed, these are called *revolutions*. The tissue of these revolutions forms the *universal history of the world*, which not only accounts for that which has happened, but also investigates the causes, and explains their effects. It is this history that the statesman unceasingly studies. (Part I Ch. II §§13, 14). He finds there the practice of a science for which we shall give him the theory; he sees there the theatre of the world opened up, and all of our rules set in train.

§3. But all the particular changes that occur in the world seem made only to concur in the maintenance of the general system, which is immutable. Revolutions do not change countries at all, and rarely their inhabitants. A country with fertile soils never lacks for men to cultivate them. The land is not destroyed, nor are all the citizens exterminated in the revolutions which occur in states and which overturn empires. One must therefore distinguish two kinds of revolution that a country can suffer, the one *natural*, the other *political*. The first are occasioned by the grievous effects of nature, such as earthquakes, floods, plagues and like scourges. It is easy to see that we do not at all talk here of those natural causes in the destruction of states. The second kind of revolution is caused by men, and alters only the system of states, by changing the form of their government, or by subjecting their peoples to alien laws. It is the latter whose sources we seek to discover.

§4. History teaches us (§2.) that, from the origins of the world right up to our present days, no empire has maintained itself in the same condition, nor under the same form of government. The most powerful monarchies have been overwhelmed by the weight of their own grandeur. Numerous and martial nations have left their native lands, the resting place of their ancestors, to found kingdoms beneath other skies and distant climes. All of the empires of which we know are newcomers, including our own; the most enduring has been that of China. Whether we follow the dubious chronology of the Chinese, or whether we adopt that of the Europeans which has little more certainty, the era in which this empire was founded goes back so far that we lose sight of it. It was however conquered by the Tartars, who adopted some of China's laws and customs, and which in return introduced into this country some of their own. The descendants of the Tartar conquerors still reign in China; but the Chinese empire, in spite of the 22 families that have successively occupied the throne, in spite of internal wars, and in spite of the conquest of the Tartars, preserves itself in the grandest style. This extended period of time is a political phenomena and will seem incomprehensible enough to us, if we do not allow that the situation of China at the extreme orient of the known world contributed a great deal to making the country great, and that for the entire time it was governed by philosophers, or rather, the philosophical spirit which does nothing without principle and reason, which does not involve prejudice, which respects the dominant religion without however allowing it to enter into the affairs of state, which excludes from counsel all trace of fanaticism, and which turns the greatest amount possible in every situation to public utility. One can only seek the causes for the endurance of states in principles founded upon truth and reason, which are eternal and always uniform. How- ever, the greatest perfection of the constitution of a state consists in its endurance, as we have seen in Vol. I Ch. III §14.

§5. Among the great number of direct or indirect causes that can abbreviate the life of a government, change the system of states, and overturn empires, we will only indicate the principal causes, and those that produce the most sudden effects. These causes are either *alien*, or *intrinsic*. Among the alien causes one can count first of all the great migrations of peoples, such as the spectacle that the fourth and fifth centuries offered Europe. Now hordes of Goths, Vandals and other barbarians stream from the depths of the north to flood Europe, extending their conquests to Spain, to Italy and even Africa; now the peoples who inhabit the most northerly countries attack their neighbours towards the south, forcing them to leave their home. These last are then constrained in turn to fall upon other peoples who were their southern neighbours; and so, little by little, move around each other in turns, constantly pushing towards the most equable climates. The same thing happens with the Scythians, the Saracens and other peoples both numerous and poor, and so in consequence bellicose. In all of the revolutions it cannot be other than that the face of Europe and a part of Africa was entirely altered. Indeed, each nation changed place, kingdoms, empires and republics were destroyed, or founded, or transported to other lands. It will be perhaps said that *this cause of the destruction of states is no more than ideal, and no like revolution now need be feared*. With that I cannot entirely agree. So many countries of which we know nothing are contained in the map of the world, and there are so many others that we know badly; similar events are neither physically nor morally impossible. Is it unthinkable that one day there will arise from the Australian lands, from the almost unknown African interior, from Ethiopia, from the depths of Asia, from the upper Americas, an innumerable swarm of men, stronger, more robust, more indefatigable than the Europeans, and put to rout all the skill, all the facility of the latter in the art of war, and all their policy?

§6. I concede that such a revolution seems far removed, but it is not impossible; and without wishing to *anticipate remote evils*, there are dangers in this respect that are much closer to us. One only needs to cast one's eyes over the Mappa Mundi to see the immensity of the land under the domination of the Russian and Ottoman Emperors. It is true that up until the present these nations have enjoyed the extravagance of possessing such extents of territory without necessity or use; but can they not change their customs, their inclinations, their policy and their talents? Can the spirit of conquest not seize their leaders? We will not deal any further with a matter of which we have already spoken in Ch. IV §31. It is a dangerous sea on which our political helmsmen (*Palinures Politique*) slumber with too much self-assurance.

§7. *War is the second alien cause* that can occasion the decline of states; whether this war be undertaken by an unjust conqueror, or whether it be founded upon equity. All the writers on the rights of peoples maintain that the right of conquest is a legitimate right; but even if it were not, the greatest part of the changes occurring in empires, and in the world since its origin right up to the present day, have they not been occasioned by force of arms? Fortunate wars elevate states, just as the unfortunate ruin them. It is however a rarity that one war alone destroys at once an empire. Three Punic Wars were needed to ruin Carthage; but as the least reverse suffered by a power at first weakens it, and reinvigorates its enemy, or its rival, states ordinarily move from decline to fall by degrees. Any reversal in war is therefore to be feared by a state; and the sovereign must not betray a careless indifference when he survives it, but do his all to prevent them. A monarch is not fit to reign who receives news of the taking of one of his most important fortresses while taking amusement playing an instrument, continues playing and says, with a revolting indolence, *ha, they say it was a pretty little town*. Sangfroid of this sort is culpable. I consider that the kind of war, like that of empires, is in the hands of Providence, but it makes use of men to execute its decrees. Princes, ministers, generals need to be persuaded of a Divine Providence ruling all, but act as if they do not believe this, and as if good or bad outcomes depend upon their own prudence; for indeed experience proves that all incidents of war, as in all other affairs of the world, derives always from natural causes. It is only visionaries, or spirits too slothful or stupid, who attribute each accident to the immediate and miraculous guidance of the Supreme Being; if they open their eyes, if they examine properly, then they will find this cause to be a side effect.

§8. When a *neighbouring power makes excessive advances in all objects of policy, its expansion can become the third cause, whether proximate or more remote, of the decline of another state*. (See Ch. IV §8. & §26.) Europe's political system is today in general such that one state is not able to raise itself except at the expense of another, whether it be by conquest, or by commerce etc. Each degree of real power which it acquires gives it at least one more degree of relative power, and the degree that it gains is a loss for its rivals. Ultimately, going from strength to strength, it comes imperceptibly to engender terror among the other sovereigns, finally setting their measure. Nearly all statesmen have felt this truth. The lengthy disputes between the Austrian and Bourbon Houses, between the northern powers etc. have been ruled by no other principle; but cabinets only too rarely adopt the most fitting measures to prevent this excessive elevation of powers which is capable of inspiring in them a proper jealousy. Such cabinets can be seen to favour minor interests over major, ceding the most essential, constant advantage to a passing one, and sometimes concluding alliances with rivals which not only serve in turn to fortify the latter against themselves, but also against their natural allies, with whom they should make common cause by opposing in concert the expansion of these same rival powers. The Latin tag which is so true, and so politic, *obstare principiis*, that it is necessary to act quickly if not to be acted upon, is too much neglected by those who conduct affairs of state, and sometimes a century of war is needed to gain what one could have been able to forestall by a few strokes of the pen.

§9. *The over-extension of an empire nearly always becomes a cause of its decline*. All of the ancient monarchies are so many examples of this truth. The grandeur that was Alexandria brought about its destruction after the death of its founder. Rome crumbled under the weight of its own forces. Most useful instruction on this matter can be drawn from the excellent work of M. Montesquieu on the causes of the Romans' greatness and of their decline. He there describes with an admirable sagacity all that served to strengthen the nerves and springs of the empire when it advanced to greatness, and to weaken it once it had achieved greatness. I think it impossible to say anything better, more profound, and more true on this subject than that which he has said; and so that I can avoid here repeating his ideas, I recommend the reading, or rather study, of this incomparable treatise to all those destined to public affairs; and I allow myself to add only one remark. The wish to unite all lands under one empire is in my opinion a most vain and chimerical undertaking, for its government would be morally impracticable. Despite communication by letter and its swiftness, it is impossible that the sovereign, who would have established his seat at the centre of such a monarchy, could learn soon enough of everything that occurred in distant provinces, and communicate to such distant parts his commands. Human vision does not extent beyond its horizon, and the vision of the most perfect government cannot extend to the end of the world. The local senates that have to be established in the provinces form so many, almost independent, states; and the loose relationship they enjoy with the principal government can break at any moment. Hence rebellions and internal wars more dangerous than external wars, hence the dismembering of provinces, and the decline, fall, destruction of the state.

§10. *The absolute dependence of a state on another power is yet another cause of its gradual weakening.* This dependence can come from national idleness, or from a vice of police such that for most foodstuffs, manufactures and other prime needs the country is compelled to provide for itself through another strong people, not being able to do otherwise in this regard. Portugal is almost in this situation vis-à-vis Britain. However, this dependence finds its origin in an inferior system of policy embraced by the government, in which it espouses all the disputes of a powerful ally, taking its part too deeply, attaching its fortune to that of that same ally through almost indissoluble links, and above all when it sells to this ally more or less all its forces and in return becoming too reliant on *subsidies.* These are *involvements which go further that one thinks.* Sailing in a stormy sea, one's barque is attached to a first-rate vessel with chains which one would not know how to break when this vessel is imperilled, and the barque is dragged with it into the abyss.

§11. The decline of the state may also be occasioned by *the affectation of a great independence and an authority capable of casting into shade other sovereigns.* A state that wishes to concern itself entirely with itself, breaking all liaisons, whether of commerce or of friendship with the rest of Europe – such a state revolts all other powers. There is an art in hiding *all the power* that is possessed, and policy demands that one never makes use of it on small occasions, but reserves it for major occasions. Allowing it to erupt too soon, and for trifles, this will attract the attention of other princes to one's disadvantage, succour envy and enemies without necessity, and prompt them to unite themselves in opposition to us. More than one state has been halted in the midst of its advance for having neglected this maxim.

§12. If the state can enfeeble itself through the excessive indolence of those who govern it and who do not know how to make use of all its advantages, render its laws valued, render it respected by its neighbours, it can also be plunged into irreparable misfortune by a sovereign who embarks upon vain, chimerical, perilous undertakings that are absolutely beyond his powers. If he ventures upon commerce that he would not be able to protect, if he seeks justice with armed force for a power that can crush him, if he demands prerogatives and extraordinary honours, if he conceives projects of conquest that are too extensive, if he undertakes works comparable to those of the Romans, or buildings such as graced ancient Greece and Egypt, if he wishes to possess an army, a navy, a Court, fortified places, canals, Appian Ways, and a thousand similar things for which his country lacks resources; far from strengthening the state, he casts it into lethargy. The plans of Charles XII were too great for Sweden; and this kingdom was a hairsbreadth from loss when the death of the Prince put a stop to their execution.

§13. The state also suffers loss by the monarch dividing his empire. The monarchy founded by Philippe, King of Macedonia, and which his son rendered almost universal, was broken up in the hands of Alexander's successors, who shared it out between themselves. The division that Theodosius made of the Roman Empire between his sons Arcadius and Honorius was the real cause of its decline. The formidable Western Empire which Charlemagne re-established with so much effort was dismembered, or rather shattered, by the division that this emperor made between his sons. Saxony, the richest and most extensive province of Germany, lost all of its unity through the territorial divisions and subdivisions which were successively made between the different lines of the House of Saxony and the diverse branches of each line. This division of states is both unjust and futile. The least reflection on the origin of peoples and of civil government reveals that men are united in the body of society so that they might be stronger, and only consent to be ruled over by a sovereign so that they might be happier by their union, and to be able to oppose the attentions of their enemies with greater vigour under a common chief. But this chief has no right to partition a country and a people that the ancients have once brought together, and for which providence has conferred upon it a government with the tacit and express condition that it maintain the country and people as entire as it is able. God himself brought together the twelve tribes of Israel, and when this people divided itself, forming themselves into two distinct kingdoms, the Jewish nation was extremely enfeebled by this, and this division became the source of its decline. All the deference that peoples show to their sovereigns is given only on the condition that they do not break the knot that binds them, and which keeps then in a *corps d'état*. Each partition that a prince undertakes in his state is a manifest injustice committed against his subjects. It is even necessary to include under this rule those provinces of which he has made armed conquest; for such conquests have been made with the forces of the hereditary state, with the money and the blood of subjects; once incorporated into the state, they cannot be dismembered on the whim of a prince, giving institutions to his children, seeking to form different sovereignties, give them away, and reduce the established state, which has itself been substantially weakened in conquering them. Ultimately natural law, the rights of peoples, and the founding constitutions of the greater part of countries are opposed to such partitions. One most essential part of the happiness of peoples must not depend on the caprice of a sovereign, and once a province is incorporated into the state, it can only be detached by *force majeure*, which silences all consideration of equity, and all policy.[37]

---

[37] See what we have already said on this matter: This volume, Ch. I §§44, 45.

§14. Nothing is therefore wiser, nor more just, than the establishment of the *right of primogeniture*, which is founded on the principles established above, since reason and experience have demonstrated that indivisible succession, passing through the male first-born, preserves the state as much as the division of the country serves to ruin it. But policy, whose principal object is that which is useful, does not lose sight of that which is equitable. It might seem that sons born to the same father have an equal right to his succession, and that the younger siblings have cause to complain if the eldest inherits all, while they remain indigent. Policy has therefore forestalled this difficulty, establishing (1) that the younger siblings participate in succession to the allodial goods, whether moveable or immoveable, which are not incorporated to the crown but separated from it; (2) that the eldest who inherits sovereignty be obliged to show due *privilege* (*apanage*) to the other princes of his house, sufficient to provide for the maintenance of the dignity of their birth; or (3) that the sovereign provides a suitable establishment for each of his sons by buying at his own cost lands and seigneurages which place them beyond absolute dependence upon the head of the family. The late King of Prussia adopted this course; but his lands, or seigneurages, cannot involve any right of sovereignty, which has always to remain indivisible. With these safeguards, or similar, no prince provided with dispensations has a right to complain; other than that this right of primogeniture be introduced in all fiefs. There is also a great difference to be made between the succession of sovereigns and that of private persons. One cannot divide up men and people as one divides up other goods of fortune; and considering the matter closely, sovereignty is not a good over which its possessor has disposal, but rather a responsibility, an office with which he is endowed. We have already noted in the first chapter §§44 & 45 that the utility of young princes even finds itself in the institution of primogeniture and privileges: for, supposing a king ruling over a vast monarchy, and the division among a numerous family, that each branch retained this right of division; at the end of four or five generations the subdivided portions would be so small that the princes, descended from so considerable a stem, would be no more that little rulers of miniature states which were of little more significance than the fortune of a well-to-do gentleman. As sovereigns they would no longer have any real grandeur, and as a result no consideration at all among the other European sovereigns, and would be obliged to entirely concede precedence to the privileged princes of large houses. On the other hand, the state loses nothing by contributing to the privileges of the princes, since they are obliged to spend their money provided to them for their upkeep in the same country; on the contrary, their luxury places a much greater value in circulation, and this money percolates into the total mass of public wealth; without taking into account that many courts, or houses of princes of privilege, make a country more radiant and attracts strangers. If they possess lands, they possess them as subjects, and prosperous subjects, who are able to ameliorate and improve these lands, make cultivators and other inhabitants happy, and profit the state by their increased spending. And so from whichever side one considers the establishment of privileges and of primogeniture, it is one of the most agreeable inventions of policy.

§15. The political axiom stating that sovereignty is indivisible, since power divided is power enfeebled, also shows us why two princes cannot simultaneously occupy the same throne. All such imperial associations, of which one can find many examples in the history of emperors, erred grievously against sound policy. Placed together on the Russian throne the imbecile Ivan and the wise Peter I would have done inexpressible harm to this empire if the co-regency had lasted any longer. Such an arrangement thus becomes a very direct cause for the decline of a state. History furnishes us with a thousand proofs, and the simple lights of reason are able to convince us *a priori*. But this thought supposes that the sovereigns reign with an equal authority; for when the monarch becomes enfeebled with age, or by infirmity, a princess overwhelmed by the burden of public affairs, if associated through a regency with a son, a husband, a brother, transferring to them the cares of government, then the case is not the same, and the consequences are not at all so dangerous. This associate prince is merely a species of a Grand Vizier, a prime minister who can be deposed, and who must account to the sovereign for his actions.

§16. We have stated (Ch. IV §§5, 9, 10 & 11) that the power of a state is either *real*, or *relative*, founded upon the *local situation*, or on *opinion*, or *accessory*. Having expounded the principal causes which concur in the decline of the two first species of power, let us briefly examine the how latter three can be enfeebled by alien causes. When Nature breaks the barriers that serve to shield a country, when seas and rivers are rendered impracticable by the sandbanks that are raised there, when the countryside is under water, when mountains crumble, in a word, when there is a considerable change in the land itself, a country loses the advantages of an original situation, and the power of the state goes into decline through like disasters. It is for a wise sovereign to foresee, as much a human powers are able, the effects of like scourges, and to repair the hurts that they cause. But happily such accidents are rare, and one sees most often that the power of situation is enfeebled either by the commerce of neighbours; or by the efforts made by neighbours to render this situation ineffectual, substituting Art for Nature, or by putting themselves in a condition of surpassing the country once favoured. It is therefore necessary that the government of a powerful state neglect not the slightest means to preserve this same advantage to its greatest extent, and be able to force, if need be, all those who seek to deprive it of such advantage to desist from their projects by armed might. On this principle is founded all the efforts that England constantly makes to preserve a maritime empire, by employing immense sums for the upkeep of its navy and of its ports.

§17. The power of opinion becomes weaker, and falls into decline, in proportion as the opinion upon which this power is based dissipates in the mind of men; and as a consequence one must not find it at all strange that those who are at the head of such a state seek to perpetuate this opinion, whether it be true or false. Suppose for a moment that the religion of Christians began to lose some part of its credit, or faded away like so many before, or that the Roman Church ceased to be as triumphal as it has been over one thousand years, or that Protestantism became universal; it is clear that the power of the Pope would fall together with the entire hierarchy of the Roman Church. Is it therefore surprising to see the trouble taken in Rome to maintain, by persuasion or by force, the Catholic religion in full vigour, and to crush all those who would raise their head against it? Would not policy itself connive a little in the establishment of the Inquisition if this tribunal did not agitate on behalf of maxims so odious, and if it was not in the hands of the most culpable villains on earth? It is not for nothing that the ingenious author of the *Henriade* put the seat of policy in Rome;[38] for one would not know how to sufficiently admire the art and the amount of skill with which this court maintains its authority, and conserves the resources on which it has lived for centuries. If all the European powers believed that the establishment of the Knights of St. John on the island of Malta gave them a fortress useless against the Turks and African pirates, and that on the basis of this prejudice abandoned this order to the hatred of the Ottoman Empire, all their institutions would soon be destroyed; and it is important for them to maintain this favourable opinion of their utility among commercial nations in particular, for the fate of Christianity in general, and of navigation in particular, in purging the seas of corsairs and vigorously opposing the undertakings of infidels.

§18. Finally, *accessory power* is lost when distant provinces are taken by a foreign force and pass into other hands, or when their possession becomes more of a burden than a service to the state which holds them under its domination. If Portugal came to lose Brazil and its Asian possessions, if the islands and continental provinces that had belonged to Venice were also taken, these powers would find themselves very much enfeebled; and as a result the metropolis has to make much greater efforts to ensure their preservation, for their loss would immediately bring about their own decline. But there are provinces whose preservation itself becomes so onerous that this charge weakens the state, and so becomes the source of its frailty. A remarkable example is supplied by the island of Corsica, whose restless, malcontent and seditious inhabitants twenty-five years ago drove their sovereign, the Genoese Republic, to despair. If rebellion continues in the kingdom it is certain that the state of the Genoans will pass from decline to its annihilation. In a similar case the sovereign must carefully seek the true cause that renders retention so difficult, let fall no view on the preservation of ancient maxims, but when at last he has the means ready, he must change the system, abolish grievances, and seek all possible expedients to ameliorate the yoke upon those for whom he seeks to re-establish peace.

§19. Such are the general foreign causes in the decline of states; let us now consider those that can be intrinsic causes. It cannot be gainsaid that the first is *a vicious constitution of the state itself.* A monstrous form of government, that lacks the essential properties that we have developed in Ch. III of the first part, will not be able to maintain itself. Similar states, seemingly defective edifices where burdens and support are poorly distributed and the proportions irregular, crumble of themselves and succumb under their own weight. The ancient Greeks, who groped unceasingly for the best form of government for their republics, fell into bad hands, and their legislators, lacking theory and experience, made monsters of republics which destroyed themselves whereas their citizens performed prodigies of valour against their external enemies. We will not say more on this matter, so

[38] Henriade, Song Four where he says: "In the heart of the Vatican there reigns Policy…".

that we do not go back on ourselves and repeat the remarks made at the beginning of this work.

§20. But *the best regulated state can run to ruin when governed by an insane sovereign.* The constant mistakes committed by an extravagant prince occasion the decline of his state before the wisest ministers are able to remedy them. It is an evil, it is a scourge which it is difficult to prevent and hinder. It is Providence that bestows good and bad kings upon nations. The most suitable and dexterous counsellors can mitigate the follies of the latter, but not eradicate the fatal traces that always remain. When a sovereign prince suddenly succumbs to dementia the sensible course is for him to be removed from society; the presumptive heir, supported by the parents closest to the throne, ministers, generals and the various estates of the country, can take care of him, maintain the prince under the watch of those he can trust, place him in the most honourable and commodious prison possible, strip him of all power and assume the reins of government. This successor becomes the guardian of the insane prince, and state regent until recovery is complete, or until the death of the prince. However inviolate sovereignty may be, the rights of the people, which have for their object their safety, are far more sacred, and millions of men must not suffer the extravagances of one individual whose deranged mind is made manifest.

§21. It is written in Ecclesiastes Ch. 10 verse 16: "Woe to thee, O land, when thy king is a child". This statement is decreed by Divine Wisdom. Natural and positive law remove, it is true, regency from kings and minor princes, placing them under wise tutelage. This instance has been foreseen everywhere, and there is hardly a land in which such laws do not determine the age at which a sovereign can rule in his own right, and the persons upon whom the guardianship and regency of the state is conferred until he reaches his majority; but these periods of a sovereign's minority visit evils and distress upon people and provinces. These are stormy times when all passions become inflamed, with terrible effect. The history of modern France provides us with more than one example. There is not one minority that has not threatened to shake this great monarchy to its foundations. What evils occurred under those of Charles IX, Louis XIII, Louis XIV, and even if one wishes, Louis XV! These latter, it is true, do not approach those which prevailed during the rule of the first three; at least no blood was spilled; the confusions brought about in the system, far from having fatal consequences, could be turned to the advantage of the state, and the chicanery occasioned by the Papal Bull of 1713 belonged rather to the genre of theatre than to that of policy. This is an Italian farce which can be ended with a thrashing, and statesmen are wrong to take it seriously. The reason that the distress of this last period of minority has been neither as terrible nor as bloody as those before is that the regency is in the hands of a clever prince, and that supreme authority was not in any respect divided. The tribulations of guardians and regents are caused by the competition of too many eminent persons for sovereign power. Such persons, blinded by their new authority, and quite certain that they will retain this for only a short time, abuse their power; and only three consecutive periods of minor sovereigns suffice to place the kingdom in desperate straits. Policy therefore seeks, where guardianship becomes inevitable, to place it in the hands of a prince of the house closest to the throne, or to sovereignty, having the greatest interest in governing wisely, and there are a thousand precautions to take so that all his authority is returned to his pupil as soon as he attains that age at which he can rule.

§22. It is not enough that the form of a government be regular, and the prince wise; *for the preservation of the state one also needs loyal ministers.* We have learned of the importance of this in the second chapter of this part. As only God can do everything, even the greatest king has need of support in governing, and in carrying out his wishes. Imagine a state that falls into the hands of incompetent, or ill-intentioned, ministers. Every occasion to do good for the country is missed, all the misfortunes that can befall a country are not forestalled. Success will never follow the wisdom or generosity of a prince's resolve, for it will sour in execution; such failures unsettle the prince, and make him uncertain of the measures that he should take in the future. Eccentric resolutions, or approaches either false or tyrannical, will by contrast succeed, and assume the appearance of utility. This is how bad ministers can corrupt the most well-intentions sovereign. If they call for support on the charms of a cherished mistress the state is unfailingly set on a downward path, and more than a sage and fortunate ruler is needed to restore its ancient vigour.

§23. The *relaxation of moeurs*, in the maintenance of good order and of society, in the observance of laws – these are all once again a direct and intrinsic cause of the decline of a state. It is the people which make up the state; if this people abandons itself to all sorts of vices, only one or two generations is needed for it to become debilitated; this is a fact based upon centuries of experience. As soon as *moeurs* were corrupted among the Assyrians, the Persians, the Greeks, the Romans, and in all modern empires, their states soon went into decline. It is impossible to maintain society without order, and the maintenance of society requires that the population is the foundation of all fortunate policy (See Part One Ch. V). Laws are not promulgated as a vain speculation, to occupy doctors and schoolmen, but to be put into practice. Well-observed, but somewhat mediocre, laws make the state stronger than wiser laws that go neglected. Above, the impunity with which crimes are committed becomes the source of a thousand evils in the state, and as a consequence of its decay. The strange constitution of the government of Poland makes laws that are insufficiently observed, and criminals have too many ways of sheltering themselves from the pursuit of justice. It would however be difficult to imagine a nation so numerous, brave, spiritual, living in a fine country that was as frail as the Polish nation.

§24. Those who argue that *religion* is of no use in the government of a state, and that cunning and the gallows is sufficient to deter malefactors and maintain good order, are talking claptrap. Are all infringements of the law of such a nature to merit death, or corporal punishment, or such punishment that serves to ruin the citizen? Would one prefer to arrive by violence and by cruelty at an end to which one could find a way as gentle, as likeable, as the cult of the divine? Will a legislator be sorry to have this brake to keep men to their duty? Let us beware! As soon as positive religion spreads in a country, taking the place of natural religion, too speculative and too uncertain for the multitude, since each man is different in sentiment and insight – then this country is on the way to decline. There is no country in Europe that can be thought more open to the Christian religion than England, and which has greater respect abroad. The temples are superb and numerous, the clergy well-paid and well-regarded, the bishops rich and at the head of the nation, the divine cult practised with dignity and with all external marks of devotion, Sunday and feast days are observed with a rigour not found anywhere else, all commerce, all work, all play, all music prohibited on those days consecrated to religious practice. This nation, the most political of all, recognises that its happiness, its tranquillity, the maintenance of its power, depend to a great extent upon the maintenance of its religion. Here religion has subordinated itself to the king, and does so wisely.

§25. But as much as it is necessary for the good of the state for religion and a solid piety to prevail in the nation, it is fatal if the state *allows it to become too ascendant.* A people of devotees, of whatever religion, would be a people both ridiculous and feeble. The reasons for this are so palpable that they require no elaboration. External devotion too easily leads to enthusiasm, to superstition, to fanaticism, to idleness, to indolence, to a disregard for worldly matters which is so harmful to the progress of the arts, talents and commerce. One only has to glance at a map of Europe and run through all the countries in which Roman Catholicism reigns with an excessive authority to which the people too blindly submit; one will see everything without spirit and without vigour. A short time ago we read some *Mémoires*[39] which contained many anecdotes concerning the reign of Louis XIV. The statesman able to read quickly over the more frivolous passages and meditate on that which is essential will find here many reasons for the good and the bad fortune of this great monarch. Religion appears to have become the prime motivation. The affairs of France prospered as long as the king had mistresses and favourites who furthered his sense of glory and the pleasures of his heart; Louis supported efforts for a united Europe, triumphed, and made conquests; until a lady who portrayed herself in her letters and her actions as a penitent prostitute seized the heart of this king and led him through devotion to love, and through love to devoutness, to confessors, directors, Jesuits, bishops, religious and other persons belonging to the clergy involved in affairs, occasioning schisms, the formation of cabals, preoccupying the monarch with petty troubles and turning his attention away from the larger matters which were proper to him. Ministers were by turns appointed and dismissed through the intrigues of priests, or on suspicion of the purity of their belief. Skilled generals, but accused of Jansenism, were no longer allowed to command armies; instead these armies were entrusted to inept, but orthodox, officers. Confessors made the king a weak and ridiculous personage, making him slave to all kinds of mummery. The whole Court was at prayer while heretical enemies were in action. Troops were everywhere vanquished, cities taken, fleets wrecked, and France found itself in total decline. As the king reduced his godliness, and the credit of priests diminished, so political and military talents once

39 Laurent Angliviel de La Beaumelle, *Mémoires pour server à l'Histoire de Madame de Maintenon, & à celle du Siècle passé*, Amsterdam 1755–1756.

more had the right to be employed, so godliness waned at St. Cyr, God blessed France's armies, and re-established its affairs.

§26. In *countries where the natural liberty of men is oppressed by a purely despotic yoke, the state cannot be very powerful.* There is not one moment when the despot is not in danger of perishing on his throne, and it costs a thousand-fold more to achieve obedience to absolute power than to the power of the Law. The measures that such a despot is obliged to continually take to maintain the people in a state of obedience, and to prevent sedition, absorb half of the natural forces of the state; each popular riot, which occurs despite all precaution, weakens it all the more, and each revolution that overthrows the monarch shakes the state to its foundations. Hence the unimaginable weakness of the Ottoman Empire, and other Asiatic monarchies which would, in the absence of this vice, shake all Europe. It appears that slavery renders men at once worthless.

§27. *Too much liberty* also becomes the cause of the decline of a state. All is lost if this liberty descends into libertinage. This is the most dangerous excess into which a nation can fall. The extreme weakness of the Kingdom of Poland and the lethargy of the Dutch Republic have virtually no other source. A people which seeks to become too free gives to its neighbours the means to forge its chains. To make men combine for the general good there is need of a restraint that will render them obedient, and a power that will make them all subjects.

§28. *When a nation neglects to perfect agriculture, commerce, the sciences and the useful arts, giving itself with too great a passion to the liberal arts and frivolous objects, it can only become weak, and the state languishes.* There is not one page in the first part of this work that does not indicate the reasons for this. The inhabitants of the countryside of Portugal come down from the mountains to bring into the towns fruits which the land there produces quite naturally. They carry a guitar or a lute under a small cloak into Spain, they strum them delicately, are born lyrical poets, compose airs and lyrics, sing them, accompanying themselves, and do no other work with their fingers. The other half of the nation lives in churches, kneeling at the foot of an image of one or other saint; the Inquisition stultifies the remainder. Portugal finds all its manufactures and meets nearly all its needs through the wise English, who enfeeble them by taking Portugal's specie, and rendering this kingdom incapable of making the least progress, nor even the least defence without its support. It is very easy to discover the cause of such decline.

§29. I am unable to turn my eyes upon Italy without feeling private distress. This country, so celebrated, and still so beautiful, has very much declined from its ancient splendour. Today the French, the Germans, the Spanish and other peoples seem to meet there to fight, and to divide its provinces among themselves. The reason for this is that the nation is degenerating, the whole day is spent idling, at spectacles, in pleasure, and in too great an application to the fine arts. All cities in Italy have become much like Capua. Augustus I King of Poland, being once again merely Elector of Saxony, travelled to this country, and stayed for a time in Venice. There he saw a play in which the Germanic nation was very badly abused. Piqued by this outrage, he sketched a little comedy which he had performed in his palazzo. It was *Caesar's Dream*. This great man, from the very first scene, returned to the land, and appeared to be delighted to find himself in Italy, but is very astonished to hear cries of "Who goes there?" in the German language. He replies "Caesar", questions the sentry, and learns to his great astonishment that the Germans, whom he had otherwise treated as barbarians, are the masters of such beautiful provinces in this country. He examines the soldier, admires his armour and most of all his musket, which goes off and frightens him; but recovering from his initial surprise, the sentry tells him that the Germans had invented this weapon and the lethal powder with which it was charged. What, he cried! Has Prometheus stolen the fire from the skies and given it to savages, or even Jupiter given them his thunder! He continued questioning the soldier on the progress of his nation, and considered all that he saw and heard. During the ecstasy of his astonishment and of his admiration the German left, and there appears on the scene an inhabitant of ancient Cisalpine Gaul, carrying a hurdy-gurdy which he played to make a monkey dance; he is followed by a singer, the barbarity of whose parents has made him a eunuch, by a crowd of masked Venetians, by a troop of Arcadian poets crowned as laureates of Apollo, by several *monsignors* and Roman abbots, some painters and other artists. Only with extreme grief does Caesar learn that all these personages are Italian; that the Capitol is inhabited by a Pontiff who has in Rome taken the place of the Scipios, Pompeys, the Luculluses, that his country is prey to foreign nations, and that the descendants of the warriors who had in days of yore brought him so many victories now concern themselves with spectacle and music, have become soft with gallantry, or serve the amusement and luxury of other peoples. He dies a second time, of grief. This dramatic fiction tells us, in jest, everything that policy might reveal to us through serious argument concerning the causes of the decline of Italy.

§30. Another very direct cause of the weakness and decline of a state is *the pride and idleness of the nation*. It was a great political idiot who was the first to seek to persuade the nobility into believing that they demean themselves through honest employment of their own hands. The author of the *Persian Letters* admirably depicts the arrogance, the indolence, and the dislike of labour in the Spanish nation, especially among the nobility. He writes that nobility is acquired through sitting around. The nobility sets a dangerous example for the people. Their inactivity introduces idleness to that class of citizens whose work buttresses the state. The word "derogate" should be banned from the French language as it has been from others, or at least uniquely attached to vile employments. The vice itself is dishonouring, and idleness lends it support. Nobody has ever told me that the nobility are sufficiently occupied by warfare. Wars are short and the peace is long. The officer is not sufficiently useful in times of peace. He can do something other than exercise his men, and a numerous nobility will not always find openings in an army.

§31. What use is it if, while the state is well-founded, the prince wise, ministers excellent, *moeurs good, the laws are ridiculous*? We spoke in Ch. VI of the first part of laws and legislation; we believe to have there shown the principal rules that must be observed, and the most necessary precautions that the legislator must take in promulgating new laws, and we remind our readers of these arguments. We remarked above all that laws must not only be full of wisdom in themselves, but also quite appropriate to the countries for which they are made. A single senseless law, especially when it bears upon something relating to the constitution of the state, can engender inexpressible evils. Montesquieu remarks[40] with great justice that Constantine made a cardinal error when he transferred the capital of the empire to Constantinople, and wishing that his new city would resemble in all respects the older one, he decreed that grain would also be distributed there to the people, and that the grain of Egypt be nevertheless sent there. This law became one of the causes of the decline of the Eastern Empire.

§32. Of all senseless laws the most fateful are those which tend directly, or indirectly, to the *depopulation of the state by promoting, or even decreeing, celibacy*. When a Christian sect prohibits what the Holy Scripture allows in clear and simple terms, or when they decree what Divine Law prohibits, it is a culpable error; but when positive religion makes laws, prescribes rules founded upon futile casuistic subtleties, or upon theological interpretations repugnant to Natural Law, to the manifest aim of the Creator, or even that of society, to the happiness of the state, one can boldly say that such a religion is unworthy of God and men, and that such dogmas must be proscribed. A thousand passages and a thousand examples can be found in the Bible which authorise the marriage of priests and of the people of the Church; natural law and the well-being of society demand it; the dogmas of the Roman Catholic religion oppose it; what conclusion must one draw from this contradiction? What does sound policy say here? One is not content to prohibit marriage to persons who serve the Church, as with bishops, curates etc., one also condemns to celibacy numberless persons of the two sexes who devote themselves to the religious condition and idleness, like monks, religious persons, canons, abbots, knights of military orders, and all the rest; for whether one buries expectations of family in monasteries, or such persons are constrained to violate their vows, this gives rise to scandal, and leads to subjects who, through the disgrace of their birth, and by their poor educa- tion, are more a charge on the state than of use to it.

§33. For, once again, it is not a matter of indifference to the state with what kind of subjects the country is populated. If it were only a question of numbers, one could help matters by, for example, establishing in the more deserted provinces a throng *of Jews*, a nation which is among men as rabbits are to quadrupeds, who multiply themselves with a surprising fecundity, and ruin the countries that they people. Being not at all proper to agriculture, nor to any necessary art, one can tolerate the Jews, but not make them a source for population. (See Part One Ch. VIII §35). All of them are born with a usurious mind, their children are as useless to the state as are their parents, and their excessive number ruins commerce. Here experience serves as our guide, and shows that a commercial state can only tolerate a small number of Jews, as one finds in England, in Holland, in Hamburg and elsewhere; whereas too great a number, as in Poland, in Prague

40 *Considérations sur les causes de la grandeur des Romains et de leur décadence*, Paris 1734 Ch. XVII.

etc. is more detrimental. But whatever may be the received state maxims in a country on the tolerance of Jews, it is barbarous to use them as does the Inquisition in Spain and Portugal, and unjust to burden them with the vexations such as they sometimes bear in Germany, or in Poland.

§34. *Excessively large colonies* which the state establishes in distant provinces, and above all in other parts of the world, enfeeble the state, and moreover become an intrinsic cause of its decline. I say *excessively large*, since one should not imagine that my remarks bear upon the colonies that Holland, England and France, for example, maintain, and almost constantly refresh in their Asian and American possessions. For apart from these nations being extremely numerous in themselves, and that they enrol as many foreign subjects as they can for their transport, it has to be considered that these colonies procure to the metropole five significant advantages which abundantly repay the losses incurred by the citizens removed, and who remain dependent on the state, constantly contributing to the good of the state. These advantages are 1. a much greater consumption of the products of the land which the metropole sends there; 2. the addition of a greater number of manufacturers, artisans etc. who serve the needs of the colonies; 3. the augmentation of navigation and of all workers contributing to it; 4. the export of a greater quantity of foodstuffs that are necessary in these colonies; 5. a much greater superfluity of foodstuffs and merchandise which these colonies provide, and which the metropole provides to other peoples, which leads to the continual growth of its commerce. We do not here have in mind those large colonies, these forms of emigration, such as that in which Spain engaged to America shortly after the discovery of the New World. All the wealth of Peru and Chile has not hitherto been able to repair the enfeeblement that Spain has drawn from them; and when a state seeks to found a colony it is of ultimate importance to establish the principles upon which one will work, to make laws of consequence, and to make use of the greatest possible sobriety in the transport of subjects thence.

§35. *Epidemics* greatly ravage the people and weaken the state, depriving it for a considerable period of the resources necessary to defend itself against an unjust aggressor. These scourges have been discussed in the first part of this work (Ch. V §§18, 21 & Ch. VII §13.) together with the remedies which a prudent police can introduce. Sometimes these maladies (which, without being the plague itself, carry off no fewer subjects) are caused by an unhealthy climate, infected air, mortal exhalations which prevail in certain marshy areas, which attack inhabitants and, through contagion, spread their venom far and wide. There are several border cities in Flanders that are in this unfortunate position, and where the air is so impure that the Republic finds it necessary to renew the garrison every year, for the regiments stationed there are reduced by one half during this period. This inconvenience obliges the Estates General to replace all its garrison troops at least every two years, before each regiment, in turn, undergoes this dreadful year, the burden of which cannot be borne by just one regiment. But this constant turnover of troops causes much disorder, and costs for the army; it tires the soldiers, and ruins the officers. I do not know whether it would be better to leave the worst places without a garrison, at least in times of peace, or to find there such expedients as might diminish the evil by some means; but it is certain that humanity and policy prohibit sovereigns from consigning their subjects to an almost inevitable evil. If one persists in establishing some good citizens in a country where the air is bad, sending them into mines which exhale sulphurous vapours, employing them in the cultivation of rice which grows only in mires constantly inundated with stagnant water and so on; such action constantly enfeebles the state's people, and as a result slowly leads, almost unfailingly, to the decline of the state.

§36. Some remarks would already have been found (Part I Ch. VIII §26.) *regarding the abuse the people make of spirits and other strong liquors*; we add here that liquors can weaken a nation if they are made use of without due moderation. During the years 1734 and 1735 England was about to undergo a distressing experience if the wisdom of the government had not forestalled it. All sorts of vile distillations were sold at such a low price that the people drank to the greatest excess. The father of a family was no longer master of his servants, a tradesman of his workers, the officer of his soldiers, the captain of a ship of his sailors. All the common people were drunk before the hour for dinner, and in their drunkenness they assumed an insupportable insolence. The health of the English was disappearing, the same with manufactures, industry, commerce, navigation, military discipline etc. In 1736 an Act of Parliament prohibited almost entirely the use of brandy and gin, or at least raised their price so that the quantity was reduced; people were obliged to give them up and return to beer, the ancient and healthy beverage of the people. In northern countries, and most of all in Russia, there is again an excessive consumption of strong liquors, which might bring about fatal consequences for these nations. In truth, the rigours of the climate in those parts call for the use of spirits, but it is the abuse that has to be suppressed.

§37. The *relaxation of military discipline* also leads a state into unfailing loss. Nearly all monarchies, be they ancient or modern, have run upon this reef, all the more dangerous for being hidden. Women who have such influence over the hearts of men, priests, merchants, manufacturers, artisans, cultivators – they all desire peace, and look upon it with the greatest happiness. They are right in one sense, but they do not at all see that a lengthy peace corrupts the soldiery, relaxes discipline, allow the officer and the soldier to become unpractised in their art, and softens them. One would wish that in time of war the entire army would be composed only of lions, and in time of peace of sheep; but this is to ask for a contradiction, to want a chimera. Many people find military discipline too harsh in a peacetime garrison; it seems much too gentle when they march on the enemy. Men are never in agreement with themselves. They learn that peace is made to accustom officer and soldier to war, that discipline must be constantly upheld in an army, that the most skilful princes set up exercise encampments, carry out manoeuvres, marches, reviews, all to keep their troops up to the mark, making them practised, and not allowing them to forget the fatigue of serious campaigns, nor the art of winning. What is said here about the army applies also to the navy. A power formerly strong and much feared at sea enjoys a long peace. Warships remain tied up in harbour for half a century rotting away, their crews laid off, the admirals and skilful naval officers die; they are replaced by those without experience, the fleets only leave harbour for manoeuvres; war breaks out, the ships are armed and crewed, squadrons reappear at sea; all their undertakings fail; the commanders, for want of experience, give wrong signals, lacking discipline marines and sailors commit cowardly acts, all is despair, the state is in danger, there is surprise that ancient valour has been lost; sometimes matters do not go so badly given the pitiable circumstances.

§38. We have seen in Ch. X in Part One, dealing with public opulence, that a state can have *two kinds of debt*: one whose real value is employed in manufactures, commerce, and all sorts of useful establishments for the relief of the people; the other in which the fund is consumed by the sovereign in frivolous expenditure. *The excess of this latter kind of debt can only enervate the state, and lead it into a certain ruin.* If the country in question has no kind of equivalent for the debt contracted upon its credit, if it has insufficient means to regain through the balance of its commerce the interests which the state pays annually on the borrowed capitals, not long is needed before it falls into decline. Catholic countries are particularly subject to a kind of exhaustion which is more or less marked in proportion to the extent that its people, or its princes, are bigoted. I refer to ordinary and extraordinary contributions that the Court of Rome levies every year, and which it draws through the hands of the clergy of those countries in which the Catholic religion predominates. It is certain that these contributions, for very many years, must amount to quite considerable sums, the Protestant countries being in this regard at a great advantage over the others. In these latter, the modest salaries of the churchmen provide their maintenance, and it is spent, it circulates, and it always remains within the state. In the former, the immense incomes of the clergy are only partially spent, another part passes into the Treasury, and the third part takes the road to Rome and never returns. This is how the Holy See, whether nephews of the Popes, whether Roman princes, prelates, family, grow rich in Italy at the expense of other nations. Every sovereign must consider whether he weakens his state through the loss of all the money he allows the Pope to draw from his people; he must set limits to the superstitious liberality of his subjects, and not allow them to impoverish themselves in the Kingdom of the Earth for the sake of the Kingdom of Heaven.

§39. The *continual wrangling between ministers, generals and others* in monarchies, and in republics *the divisions between Senate and People, between magistrates and the heads of government* – both can easily lead the state into decline, and from decline to fall. The Mouth of Truth says that *every kingdom divided against itself will be reduced to a desert, and every city or house divided against itself cannot persist.* While one can of course imagine the most perfect form of government and set out the wisest maxims of policy, it is always necessary to place conduct of the diverse branches of government in different departments, which is to say, in the hands of men who are full of passion. If these passions blind them, if their views of matters are too diverse, if they are divided among themselves, their actions will unfailingly be at cross-purposes, and the state will fall into anarchy. Such divisions are more frequent and more dangerous in republics, for there is not an authority either as great or as active as in monarchies capable of reuniting all employees under the banner of the public good, and making everyone to address their own tasks in spite of themselves. Divisions are a necessary consequence of the republican state; they always have been, and always will be. The author of the *Causes of the Greatness and Decline of the Romans*[41] has quite rightly written:

> Whenever one sees that everything is tranquil in a state that calls itself republican one can be assured that there is no liberty. What is called union in a body politic is something quite equivocal. It is possible to have union in a state where there seems to be no disorder, that is to say, a harmony from which results happiness which is alone true peace. This is like those parts of the universe linked eternally by the action of the one and the reaction of the other. But in the accord of Asiatic despotism, that is to say, every government that is not moderate, there is always a real division. The labourer, the man of war, the merchant, the magistrate, the noble, they are united only in oppressing each other without resistance; if one sees here union, it is not the citizens themselves who are united, but corpses entombed side by side.

When these real divisions break out into open ruptures, or degenerate into civil wars, the state is not far removed from loss; and sovereign power cannot make itself felt too quickly to suppress disunion and bring its progress to a sudden halt, even with the greatest rigour.

§40. *When a republic interferes with the fundamental laws that regulate the constitution of its government* the state runs a very great risk of running to ruin. I know that different times call for different ways, and that laws have to follow those changes that occur in the world's state of affairs; but the constitution of the state must never alter, and the laws bearing upon this must remain as far as possible immutable. Every political arrangement has its disadvantages, and it is better to deal with those that arise from an established system than to change a system that has long supported a state. Experience is here in agreement with theory and principles. I never glance at the history of Rome, I never reflect on the causes of the various revolutions in this monarchy, but find my way to the *people's tribunes.* The introduction of these magistrates, which altered quite essentially the original constitution of the Roman Republic, became the source of all its ills. The Dutch Republic was founded under the auspices of a *stadhouder*, and the establishment of the *Stadhouderat* became an essential part of its government. Each time this republic has sought to do without such a head it has fallen into manifest decline; and when close to extinction, it has been rescued by the re-establishment of the *Stadhouderat*, which I allow does have its difficulties, but which will always undergird the United Provinces.

§41. Among the one thousand indirect causes which bring about the decline and overthrow of states, shaking their constitution, weakening their resilience, one can count regicide, or assassination committed against the person of the king, sovereign, prince, or head of the republic. One feels an inner repugnance in dealing with a crime so horrible; and one would voluntarily turn one's eyes away from something so revolting to humanity, if the monsters vomited up by hell had not recently awoken the idea of such a frightful *attentat.* One thinks that these evil deeds, whose seed was sown in the works of Machiavelli and his disciples, have been stifled by the philosophical spirit which, over

[41] Montesquieu, *Considérations sur les causes de la grandeur des Romains et de leur décadence*, Ch. IX.

the last few centuries, has improved Europe's police, and it has been said, made Europe more virtuous. One flatters oneself that, since the time of the Gérards, the Clémens, the Ravaillacs, the daggers in the hands of parricides, and the poisons of false, cruel, bloody and cruel policy, are no longer those of rational beings. We do not even intend to talk about the matter in this book, so that we do not have to recall the memory of names and such odious crimes; but since the life of the two best kings on earth,[42] who were the delights of their people, who merited all of their love, and whose names are dear to posterity, were not secure from *attentats* committed by cowardly assassins, we are constrained to portray all the horror of this crime, and to inform how much it seems detestable to true and healthy policy. The murder of a simple child born into the most vile class of citizens is a crime abominable in the eyes of the Supreme Being, and the laws of all civilised [*polices*] peoples punish it with death; oh! what would it be if the murderous knife, or the poison, is placed in the breast of a personage of the kind placed at the helm of government to watch over the security, and to contribute to the welfare of the whole nation? But the peak of all abomination is when a parricidal hand attacks the purple, and lands its blows on the throne. The Holy Scripture and the lights of reason are in agreement in recounting the horror of such an action. The first teaches us in a thousand places that Christians should submit themselves to the temporal authority that God has established for his people, should respect it, and that it is the greatest of crimes to strike against he who is anointed by the Eternal; the second tell us that no man of merit, no wise man, would wish to take on the tiresome job of governing the state, or to contribute to its happiness, if the law did not render his days secure against the bloody vengeance of a malcontent, or a guilty subject. Ministers and magistrates would live in perpetual danger and the state would soon be prey to villains. And as we have proved in Ch. III of the first volume, that all the citizens of a country, in submitting themselves to monarchical government, feel that their individual wills are united in the single person of the sovereign, to whom they accord an authority necessary to this end, and related powers to set it to work; that the person of the monarch has been rendered sacred and inviolable by the universal consent of all civilised [*polices*] nations, and the king is endowed with the title of "majesty" to impress upon the hearts of all men a greater veneration for their dignity. One also sees that it is not permissible for any member of society, of whatever estate, and whatever degree he might be, to believe his own interest, or that of the state in general, to be hurt in any particular, or betrayed by the decrees of his sovereign, such that he acquires the slightest trace of a right to make an attempt on his monarch; for on the contrary, each citizen is individually wounded by this same *attentat*. It is for these reasons, and for a thousand others, that the laws set no limit to the rigour of the torments appropriate for punishing a regicide; and if it is true that the humanity of the judges appointed to hand down a cruel sentence in respect of such a cruel assassin tells them that mercy is moving, and that the heart suffers when having to impose such horrible torments upon an unfortunate, it is no less certain that the safety of many thousands of citizens, and even of the human race, must prevail over compassion, which must set an

[42] Louis XV of France and Joseph, King of Portugal.

example of rigour in regard to other crazed villains, and that the love of Justice must in such moments stifle in one's heart the voice of nature and feelings of pity.

§42. But if a determined tyrant, a Nero, a Basilowitz, is unfortunately on the throne, whose rage attacks and destroys true religion, or reverses the essential constitution of the state so as to introduce extreme despotism, exercising the cruellest tyranny and bathing his best subjects in blood; if, I say, in such a case, the leaders of the people, the most eminent magistrates, princes of the blood all agree that for the preservation of the state the reins of government should be torn from such a monster, that he should be deposed, imprisoned and perhaps, for want of an alternative, put to death to preserve the life and fortune of so many innocent citizens, it seems that such an action should not be strictly included under the name and idea of regicide, or of the assassination of a sovereign. But it is very rare to see a tyrant so determined, with such a taste for blood, on the throne; ancient and modern history provides us with very few examples. Tyranny has to be so extravagant, so clearly established, in sum, so notorious, that it is almost impossible to foresee, or at least determine, a case where such a conspiracy would become legitimate. Policy has for its object the preservation of states; all its maxims must contribute to this end; but its silence is eloquent when such a delicate question is presented for decision; it is too accustomed to treat the person of the sovereign as inviolable.

§43. Such are in general the principal causes of the decline of states. There are more, and more particular, ones; but they are so indirect, and of such great number, that the limits of this work preclude their elaboration. We are hurrying to its conclusion, and we will end with a brief reflection on the characteristics by which one can establish whether a stating is rising or declining. These characteristics, similar to symptoms of health or of sickness in the human body, can be either internal, or external. The growth or the diminution of public revenue is the surest thermometer for the prosperity of a country; but to form a good judgement it must be assessed in peacetime and by the ordinary means of collection, without special exactions, without new taxes, without arbitrary levies, capitation payments, or other charges or compulsory payments. The augmentation of the number of inhabitants, best judged by careful personal assessment, or by examining the consumption of wheat, tells one more than other calculations whose principles are uncertain; the progress of luxury, which progresses without effort, the growth of commerce, which can be known from simply going through the customs records, the rise of manufactures, whether old or new, the increase of capital, the construction of new buildings or the repair of the old, the success of art and of artisans, the contended humour of the people, the good condition of the army and of the navy, the relative cost of necessities, the rates of exchange, the arrival of strangers who come to settle in the country, the prevalence of liberty and good order, all of these advantages form the visible marks of the prosperity of the state, as do the opposing disadvantages testify to its decline. The influence that the sovereign gains in the general affairs of Europe, the celerity with which other princes seek his alliance, the glory and success which he establishes in feats of arms, the advantageous treaties that he concludes, wither for political ends or for the commerce of his subjects, his flag that flies on all seas and in all foreign ports, the friendly welcome and distinctions offered his ministers in other courts; it is by these conspicuous marks that the cabinets of other kings and foreign nations can recognise the degree of prosperity, of greatness, or of weakness, in which each state finds itself. These are the characteristics that make themselves manifest from afar. The busy statesman never ceases to keep his eye on all these matters, on both the state for which he works, as well as the position it holds in relation to others in the general system of Europe. A true Argonaut, he can never fall asleep but with one eye open. If he follows the lessons of policy such as contained here, he can hope to make himself useful to his prince and to his country; but he has no hope of general approbation, and criticism cannot deflect him from the path of reason and probity. The world will never lack for troublemakers who attack good ministers just as they attack good books.

Chapter Seven

RAW MATERIALS IN THE HISTORY OF ECONOMIC POLICY; OR, WHY LIST (THE PROTECTIONIST) AND COBDEN (THE FREE TRADER) BOTH AGREED ON FREE TRADE IN CORN

Erik S. Reinert

It's the eternal paradox – the poor live in nations which are rich from Nature's bounties.

(José Cecilio del Valle, economist and vice president of the short-lived Central American Republic, about 1830)[1]

The higher the civilization of a people, the less does it depend on the nature of the country.

(Wilhelm Roscher, German economist and inspirer of Marx and Schumpeter, founder of the New Historical School of economics in Germany, about 1860)[2]

The commemoration of the repeal of the Corn Laws in 1846 presents an opportunity to look at the place of raw materials in what is virtually a non-existent field of academic enquiry: the history of economic policy. The history of economic thought has, to a large extent, become a study of the genealogy of neoclassical economics, which leaves out the history of an alternative tradition of economic policy which was not based on classical or neoclassical thought.[3] In this alternative economic tradition – which I call

[1] Valle's works are published as *Obras de Don José Cecilio del Valle,* Ciudad de Guatemala, Tipografia Sanchez & de Guise, 1930, 2 volumes.

[2] Roscher's four-volume *Grundlagen der Nationalökonomie* appeared in 26 editions, the first edition in 1854. This work formed a school of thought which was to dominate German economic and industrial policy until World War II. Roscher was the first economist to incorporate increasing returns and mass production in an economic textbook. His dynamic world view formed a platform for later dynamic theories, of economists with such diverse views as Marx and Schumpeter. The quote is taken from one of the two US editions of his textbook: *Principles of Political Economy,* Chicago, Callaghan and Co., 1882, volume 1, p. 137.

[3] It can be argued that the last history of economics which gave good coverage of the history of economic policy was Othmar Spann's *Die Haupttheorien der Volkswirtschaftslehre* which first

production-centred economics (as opposed to the barter-centred classical and neoclassical tradition) – raw material production alone cannot, in the absence of manufacturing, lead to national wealth. A genealogy of the alternative production-centred economic tradition over the last 500 years is shown in Figure 7.1.

The main debate on economic policy in the nineteenth century [was between barter-centred English classical theory on the one hand, and **[275]** production-centred economic theory, represented by Germany and the USA, on the other. Later, into this century, the same line of reasoning is found in Canada[4] and Australia.[5] These later developments, however, will not be discussed here. The aim of this chapter is to show that the repeal of the Corn Laws was a policy measure where both classical barter-based economics in England – represented by Richard Cobden – and production-based economics – represented by Friedrich List – fully agreed that free trade in corn was to the benefit of England. Free trade in corn being agreed upon both by the free traders and the protectionists at the time, I shall argue that the repeal of the Corn Laws should not be seen as a victory of the principle of free trade, but rather as the final demise of English feudal privileges.

The debate around the Corn Laws calls the attention to one important stylized fact in the history of economic policy: All presently industrialized countries have, in the early stages of industrialization – from fifteenth-century England to twentieth-century Japan and Korea – been through a period where economic policy was heavily discriminatory against raw material production, and/or heavily favouring manufacturing. The particular mix of anti-raw materialism and pro-manufacturing policies varied, depending on the special circumstances of each nation.

Throughout the chapter I shall attempt to show why this discrimination against raw materials was a necessary stage to go through – why production-based economics was right in seeing the exclusive specialization in the production of raw materials as 'bad trade'. I shall argue that the understanding of this point is a necessary step in order to comprehend an important aspect of the problem of world poverty and of sustainable economic development.

PRODUCTION-CENTRED VS. BARTER-CENTRED ECONOMIC THEORY

In the fundamentally barter-centred classical and neoclassical economic tradition there is, of course, no difference between raw materials and manufactured goods. I shall argue

---

appeared in 1911 and by 1936 had reached 24 editions and a total of 120,000 copies printed in German. The US edition is *The History of Economics,* New York, Norton, 1930. In England the book was published under the title *Types of Economic Theory.*

4 See, for example, Innis, Harold, *Staples, Markets, and Cultural Change. Selected Essays,* Daniel Drache (ed.), Montreal, McGill-Queen's University Press, 1995.

5 This type of thinking was reflected in Brigden, J.B. *et al., The Australian Tariff: An Economic Inquiry,* Melbourne, Melbourne University Press, 1929. Vernon, J. *et al., Report of the Committee of Economic Inquiry,* Canberra, Commonwealth Government Printing Office, 1965.

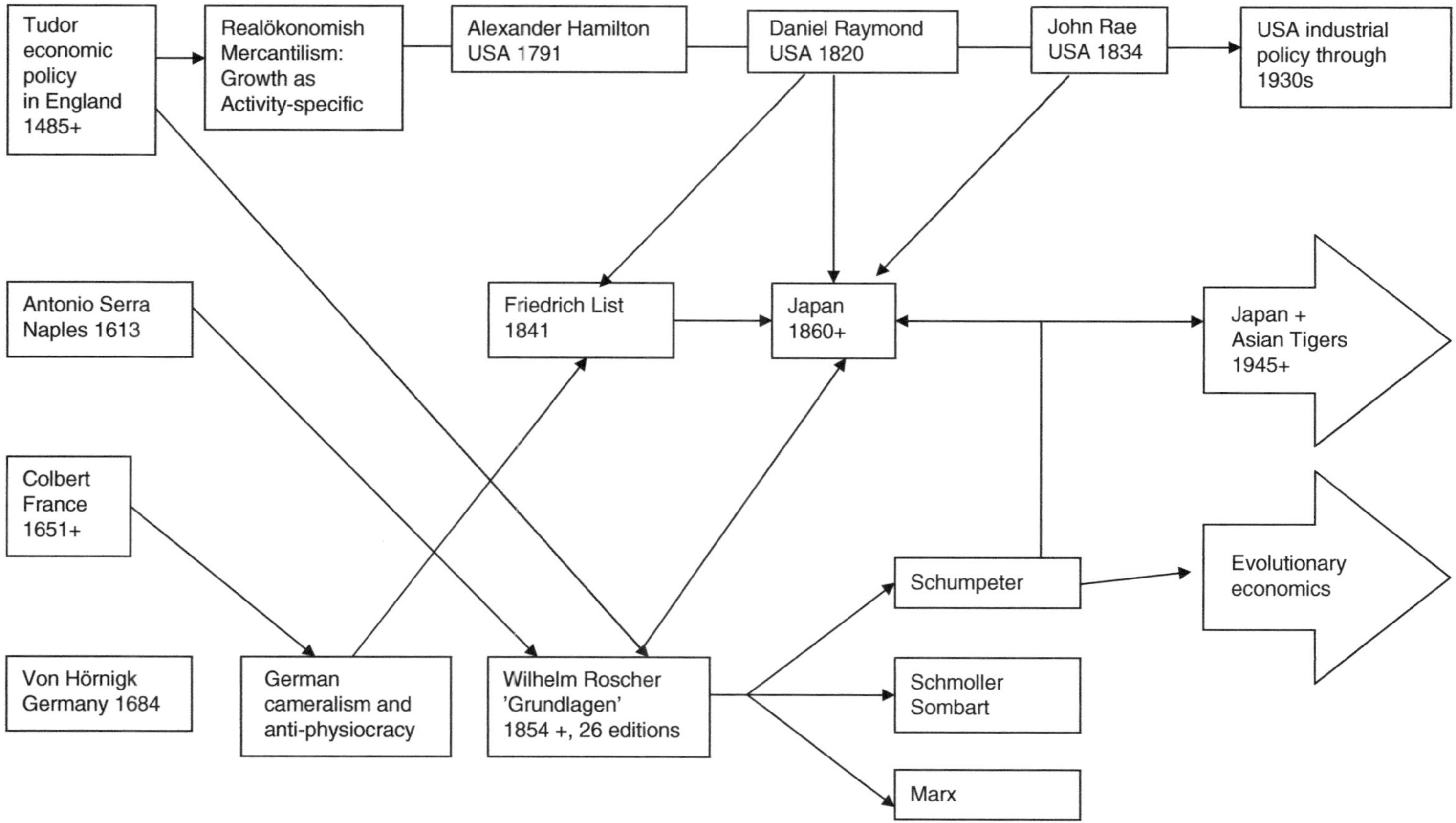

Figure 7.1 The knowledge- and production-based canon of economic theory.

that there exists a very long alternative line of economic theory – which I shall refer to as production-centred (as opposed to barter-centred) – where an economy based on raw materials, in the absence of a manufacturing base, almost by necessity will be poor. I shall argue that all presently industrialized nations – the UK, USA, Germany and Japan – went through an important stage of production-centred economics, where the output of raw materials was seen as an inferior economic activity. Only after having completed the process of industrialization did the economic policy of these nations come more in line with the classical or neoclassical paradigm.

Neoclassical economics sees physiocracy (from *physio* = nature, *-cracy* = rule) as the starting point of its family tree. At the root of neoclassical **[276]** economics there lies a preference for raw materials – for agriculture – over manufactured goods; not only in the name physiocracy, but also since, as Adam Smith pointed out, agriculture corresponds more closely to the 'natural' state of perfect competition. Raw materials behave 'more naturally' than manufactured goods. Neoclassical economics has also taken diminishing returns from Ricardo's corn economy to characterize its production functions, and, indeed most surprisingly, applies this constraint to a society of industrial mass production, which in reality is characterized by the opposite effect – by important increasing returns to scale. Here the problems created by general equilibrium analysis forced Alfred Marshall, although most reluctantly, to throw out of his model the increasing returns that he himself had observed as being perhaps the main characteristic of industrial society.[6] This is an early example of economic theory developing along what Paul Krugman has called 'the perceived line of least mathematical resistance'.[7]

The nature of neoclassical economists' tools and the quest for equilibrium forced them to stick to physiocracy – to the economic behaviour of the products of nature, not industry – as the basis for their science. As a consequence of this, the economic theory of the whole historical period whose main characteristic was industrial mass production – the 'Fordist techno-economic paradigm' – was accompanied by an economic theory deeply entrenched in the assumptions of pre-mass production: the absence of any scale effects (in trade theory) and diminishing returns in the production functions.

In the alternative production-based economic tradition, there is a 'curse of the resources' underlying the theory. Specialization in raw materials – without a parallel manufacturing base – causes poverty for a nation. In this chapter we shall argue that this argument belongs to a very old school in economic theory, which goes back to the Renaissance, a school that heavily influenced economic policy for centuries, but which all but died out with World War II. This alternative tradition differentiates itself by being oriented around production and knowledge ('mind') – in contrast with the classical and neoclassical traditions which are centred around barter (supply and demand) and matter (goods). A family tree of production-based economics is provided in Figure 7.1.

---

6 This process is narrated in Hart, Neill, *Increasing Returns and Economic Theory: Marshall's Reconciliation Problem,* University of Western Sydney, Discussion Paper Series no. E9004, 1990.

7 *Rethinking International Trade,* Cambridge, Mass., MIT Press, 1990, p. 4.

The 1846 repeal of the Corn Laws was a case where both these schools agreed – both pre-Smithian production-centred economics and barter-centred classical economics viewed free trade in corn as being beneficial to England. Free import of corn was also seen as being beneficial in the pre-Ricardian *ancien regime* trade, under the set of policies we shall refer to as King's Taxonomy.[8]

We shall therefore argue that the repeal of the Corn Laws should not be seen as a victory of free trade, but merely as a final demise of the power of the British landed aristocracy.

This is the reason why Friedrich List – the famous protectionist – and Richard Cobden – the famous free trader – were fully in agreement on the **[277]** case of the Corn Laws. By 1846 Friedrich List had in fact been suggesting for more than twenty years that, in their own interest, the English move towards free trade in corn.

The core argument of 400 years of production-centred economics can be reduced to the statement that the circumstances of production of goods and services are the fundamental determinants of national economic wealth. These circumstances are determined by dynamic increasing returns – what Schumpeter called historical increasing returns – by diminishing returns, by the slope of the learning curve, and by the different levels of capital and skill which can profitably be absorbed by different economic activities at any point in time. The varying degrees of imperfect competition, and of barriers to entry which result from these factors, cause national differences in wage levels.

By essentially studying barter Adam Smith and his neoclassical descendants miss the influence of the circumstances of production national wage levels – which constitutes around 70 per cent of GNP in a modern nation. The alternative theoretical tradition – which was very strong both in the USA and Germany in the nineteenth century – argues that this influence is so powerful that, when trade takes place between nations of very different skill levels, free trade is frequently a decidedly suboptimal option. We have argued elsewhere that the take-off stages into industrialization of all presently industrialized countries – in a sequence started by England around 1485 – have been based on these production-centred and not barter-centred economic theories,[9] and that barter-based classical and neoclassical economics have replaced the production-based theories only when a competitive manufacturing base had been achieved. This pattern holds true both for England (pre-Smith), for the USA, Germany and Japan.

On 'good' and 'bad' trade

Historically the economic policies recommended in production-based economics follow two alternative lines of argument. The first concerns the risks and perils of a

[8] After King, Charles, *The British Merchant or Commerce Preserv'd,* London, John Darby, 1721, 3 vols.

[9] Reinert, Erik S., 'Catching-up from way behind, a Third World view perspective on First World history', in Fagerberg, Jan *et al., The Dynamics of Technology, Trade, and Growth,* London, Edward Elgar, 1994.

resource-based economy – being specialized in economic activities not requiring high labour skills and subject to diminishing returns. These two effects may combine into a lock-in effect trapping a nation in poverty (the 'Bolivia syndrome'), which technical change will not solve. Exporting natural resources constituted 'bad trade' in the orthodoxy of English economic policy until long after Adam Smith and David Ricardo. The most clear statement of this orthodoxy is contained in three volumes published by Charles King in 1721.[10] In King's Taxonomy exporting raw materials was 'bad trade'. We later find this same line of argument in nineteenth-century Germany, Japan and the USA and in twentieth-century Australia and Canada. The 'curses' of economies based on natural resources[11] are five: **[279]**

- diminishing returns;
- low skills/low wages;
- perfect competition;
- price volatility;
- lack of ability to create national synergies/linkages.

The latter point is emphasized by Gerschenkron: 'the hope that industry in a very backward country can unfold from its agricultural activities is hardly realistic';[12] and by Hirschman: 'agriculture certainly stands convicted on the count of its lack of direct stimulus to the setting up of new activities through linkage effects: the superiority of manufacturing in this respect is crushing'.[13]

The second line of arguement concerns the benefits of concentrating a nation's economic activities in mechanizable, skill-absorbing activities, subject to increasing returns – a cluster of characteristics which for a long time could be efficiently short-handed as manufacturing. Exporting goods from these activities qualified as 'good trade' in King's Taxonomy – the English orthodoxy which built its national strength. The Canadian and Australian arguments later added to this by showing that the presence of a national manufacturing base upgraded skills in the resource-based activity and prevented these from going into diminishing returns – making raw material exports from a manufacturing country a viable strategy. In a previous paper we have argued that what today is called competitiveness reflects the pursuit of dynamic imperfect

---

10 King, Charles, *The British Merchant or Commerce Preserv'd,* London, John Darby, 1721, 3 vols.

11 These problems are discussed in Reinert, Erik, 'Diminishing returns and economic sustainability: the dilemma of resource-based economies under a free trade regime', in Hansen, Stein *et al., International Trade Regulation, National Development Strategies and the Environment: Towards Sustainable Development?,* Oslo, Centre for Development and the Environment, University of Oslo, 1996.

12 Gerschenkron, Alexander, *Economic Backwardness in Historical Perspective,* Cambridge, Mass., Harvard University Press, 1962, p. 215.

13 Hirschman, Albert O., *The Strategy of Economic Development,* New Haven, Yale University Press, 1959, pp. 109–10.

competition which in previous centuries was sought under the names of 'good trade' or 'national productive powers'.[14]

In this chapter we shall concentrate on the first part of the argument and try to explain the risks and perils of resource-based economies, why 'bad trade' was more than a primitive pre-Smithian superstition. This will also explain why protectionist Friedrich List so clearly saw the benefits accruing to England from the repeal of the Corn Laws.

On the differing capacity of economic activities to absorb skills and capital

In order fully to comprehend the argument underlying the philosophy of 'good' and 'bad' trade, it is important to understand how economic activities differ as potential carriers of economic growth. At any point in time different economic activities can profitably absorb very different quantities of human knowledge and capital, they present different windows of opportunity. You cannot upgrade the level of skill and salary of a person picking lettuce to that of a computer engineer by educating the lettuce picker, because the absorption capacity of human skills for the two professions are different. The absorption capacity for capital and skill of lettuce picking will only change at the point in time when lettuce picking is mechanized. Upgrading the economic situation of the lettuce picker can only take place by his changing **[280]** his job. That this fact applies to a nation as well as to an individual was the core argument of US economist Daniel Raymond in 1820.[15] Raymond laid the foundation for 'the American system of manufactures' and heavily influenced Friedrich List.

As long as there is a demand for goods produced with both high and low skills, economic growth – left to the market – will be very uneven and strongly history dependent. That vicious and virtuous economic circles originate in this fact was already indicated by Antonio Serra in 1613,[16] and also underlies nineteenth-century opposition to English classical theory both from Germany and the USA, and later from Japan. Only by producing a theory of economic barter – leaving out the production aspects – neoclassical trade theory proves that the wage earners in a nation making a living picking lettuce will be equally as rich as the wage earners in a nation of computer engineers.[17] If production is introduced, the theory would by valid only if one introduces the counterfactual assumption that all economic activities have the same capacity to profitably absorb skills and capital (i.e. that a barber shop profitably can be made as capital intensive as a nuclear power plant, and that picking lettuce profitably can be made as skill intensive as developing new computers). A fundamental difference between barter-based and

[14] Reinert, Erik, 'Competitiveness and its predecessors – a 500-year cross-national perspective', *Structural Change and Economic Dynamics* 6, 1995, pp. 23–42.

[15] Raymond, Daniel, *Thoughts on Political Economy*, Baltimore, Fielding Lucas, 1820. Raymond's work appeared in four editions from 1820 to 1840.

[16] Serra, Antonio, *Breve trattato delle Cause che possono far abbondare li Regni d'Oro e Argento dove non sono miniere*. Con applicazione al Regno di Napoli, Napoli, Lazzaro Scorriggio, 1613.

[17] Paul Samuelson's factor-price equalization.

production-based economics is therefore that in the latter the process of economic development is activity specific – it can only take place in certain economic activities at any point in time. Historically we tend to name historical periods according to the activities where economic development took place – in the stone age industry in the stone age, in the bronze age industry in the bronze age, and – in the machine age – in the economic activities which were being mechanized at any point in time.

To nineteenth-century Americans this point was brought home by looking at the cotton growing industry. The observable fact that cotton picking was only profitable with slave labour made any English hint that the USA would be better off producing cotton and leaving manufacturing industry to the English not very convincing outside the circle of slave-owners.[18] The US Civil War was therefore also a war between barter-centred English free trade theory, supported by the South, and production-centred economic theory, supported by the North.

In both Germany and in the USA there was a general feeling that England had achieved her wealth by going into skill- and scale-intensive manufacturing. By attempting to export a barter-centred economic theory which excluded these factors England was attempting to 'draw up the ladder' behind itself, in order to achieve a world monopoly in manufacturing. As we shall see, the writings of Richard Cobden all but confirm this. **[281]**

THE 'RAW AND THE 'COOKED' – THE DIFFERENT PHILOSOPHICAL UNDERPINNINGS OF BARTER-CENTRED AND PRODUCTION-CENTRED ECONOMICS

In 1964 Claude Lévi-Strauss– a famous French anthropologist – published a book called *The Raw and the Cooked,* carrying the subtitle *Introduction to a science of mythology.*[19] Lévi-Strauss suggests that 'the cooked' among 'primitive' peoples symbolizes the realm of the human, whereas 'the raw' symbolizes nature. The myths, drawn chiefly from the Amazon Indians, but also from countries like France, can be interpreted as 'cooking' being what differentiates man from beast. The domination of fire can be seen as the watershed between the ape and man. The main distinctions between man and beast in primitive societies were associated with the use of fire: man cooked his food, and he 'cooked' his pottery. 'Unlike the deer, the Tarahumara (tribe) does not eat grass, but interposes between the grass and his animal hunger a complicated cultural cycle involving the care and use of domestic animals … Nor like the coyote does the Tarahumara avail himself of meat torn from a scarcely dead animal and eaten raw. The Tarahumara interposes between his meat and hunger a cultural system of cooking.'[20]

---

18 The most complete account of the economic theory of the slave-owners is contained in *Cotton is King, and Pro-Slavery Arguments,* Augusta, Georgia, Pritchard, Abbot & Loornis, 1860. This is a massive tome of 908 pages, where the core of the economic arguments against the industrialization of the USA is found on pages 19–226.

19 New York, Harper, 1975.

20 Zingg, M., 'The genuine and spurious values in Tarahumara culture', *American Anthropologist 44* (1), 1942, p. 82. Quoted in Levi-Strauss, op. cit., p. 336.

Primitive tribes seem to have had a need to emphasize what differentiates man from other animals. Man interposes his knowledge and social organization between himself and nature – and 'cooking' is an early and powerful image of what characterizes this knowledge. Primitive myths therefore often tell stories on the origin of fire, the origin of cultivated plants or the origin of pottery – the watersheds that made *Homo erectus* into *Homo sapiens.* The distinction between the raw and the cooked turns into the distinction between nature and culture. Lévi-Strauss supports this view with many examples from all over the world. To this very day, 'to sleep in the raw' is a colloquial English expression meaning 'to sleep naked'. In eighteenth-century France, *danser á cru* would mean 'to dance barefoot', and *monter á cru* would mean 'to ride bareback'.

In the nineteenth century there was a strong conflict between English economic thought – representing barter and matter – on the one hand, and German and US thought – representing production and mind – on the other. As a philosophical basis of this economic debate, we find – as in the myths of the Amazon indians – that the participants feel they have to define what differentiates man from beast: man the trader or man the producer and innovator. The replies to this question seem to distinguish the barter-centred from the production-centred economic theory (see Figure 7.2).

The different answers to this question from Adam Smith and Abraham Lincoln typified two kinds of trade policies: protectionism in Germany and the USA until a necessary skill level in production has been reached that enables the nation to compete fairly with England versus free trade under any **[282]** circumstances – regardless of skill level – in English theory. No doubt Adam Smith also saw the general tendency of things to improve but, we would argue, this was not at all at the core of his system. At the core of his system was the division of labour, which he saw as resulting from a propensity to barter (from matter), not from a propensity to discover and invent (from the mind). We shall see below that this counterpoint between matter and mind was the essence of an important economic controversy in England in 1622–3. We would argue that today's mainstream economics carries the inherent weakness of an excessive focus on barter and matter – not on production and mind – from its founding father Adam Smith.

However, in the case of the repeal of the Corn Laws, both barter-centred and production-centred theories agreed. Friedrich List, who comes down in economic history as the incarnation of protectionism, fully agreed with free trader Richard Cobden that the repeal of the Corn Laws was in the interest of England. This seemingly curious agreement between protectionists and free traders indicates that the pre-twentieth-century protectionist debate **was** very much along the lines of 'matter' vs. 'mind' – 'raw' vs. 'cooked'. The German and American economists insisted that free trade in 'raw' goods – Friedrich List's *Urprodukte* – was something completely different from free trade in 'cooked' goods: goods where the human mind had added its skills. The industrial battle between nations is, in essence, the continual upgrading and adding of human skills to raw materials. Venetian glass blowers added value to sand, silicone chip producers add even more value per unit of sand. The nations which specialize in providing the 'raw' sand will inevitably lag behind in skills and, consequently, in the value

The reply from barter-centred economics

The division of labour arises from a propensity in human nature to ... truck, barter and exchange one thing for another... It is common to all men, and to be found in no other race of animals, which seem to know neither this nor any other species of contracts ... Nobody ever saw a dog make a fair and deliberate exchange of one bone for another with another dog.

(Adam Smith (1776) *Wealth of Nations*, Chicago: University of Chicago Press, 1976, p. 17)

The reply from production-centred economics

... Beavers build houses; but they build them in nowise differently, or better, now than they did five thousand years ago ... Man is not the only animal who labours; but he is the only one who *improves* his workmanship. These improvements he effects by *Discoveries* and *Inventions.*

(Abraham Lincoln, Speech of the 1860 presidential campaign)

Unlike the deer, the Tarahumara (a tribe) does not eat grass, but interposes between the grass and his animal hunger a complicated cultural cycle involving the care and use of domestic animals ... Nor like the coyote does the Tarahumara avail himself of meat torn from a scarcely dead animal and eaten raw. The Tarahumara interposes between his meat and hunger a cultural system of cooking.

(M. Zingg (1942) 'The genuine and spurious values in Tarahumara culture', in *American Anthropologist* 44 (1): 82. Quoted in Levi-Strauss, op. cit.: 336)

Man's ability to harness and use to his advantage the forces of nature. (E. Peshine Smith, US economist, 1814–82)

Man's ability to use tools.

(Karl Marx, German economist, 1818–83)

Man's rational will and ideas.

(Christian Wolff, German philosopher and economist, 1679–1754)

Figure 7.2 What differentiates man's economic activity from that of beasts? **[283]**.

of their manpower. As a result they will, as Marx put it, 'increasingly have to give up more hours of labour in exchange for less hours of labour'.

In the next part of the chapter, we shall see that in the long tradition of production-based economics, wealth was seen as being created by adding knowledge and social organization to the raw produce of nature, much as in the myths of Lévi-Strauss. Adding knowledge to nature was not only a better paid economic activity, this 'cooking' of raw materials was seen as being the very essence of man, the activity which separated man from beast. Man added 'mind' to raw materials, which without his interference was only 'matter'. Any economic theory that did not take man's mind into consideration was, in the German tradition, *Entgeistet* – void of spirit.

ECONOMIC THEORY: FROM 'PHYSICS ENVY' TO 'BIOLOGY ENVY' AND FROM 'MATTER' TO 'MIND'

Economic theory has, since its inception, carried with it an underlying counterpoint of 'raw' vs. 'cooked' – a counterpoint between the raw produce **[284]** of nature and the products where Man had added his 'mind' to the products of nature. In today's economic theory we find this tension reflected in the movement of economic theory from 'physics envy' towards 'biology envy', and in the increasing importance of innovations – the creativity of man's mind – added to the physical matter of the products being exchanged.

This way of thinking originates with the Renaissance, when man redefined his relationship with creation as we shall briefly discuss below. The distinction between 'raw products of nature' (what List 300 years later characteristically calls *Urprodukte* – giving them a connotation of something primitive and prehistoric as in *Urmensch,* prehistoric man) and the products which have had value added by human creativity shows up in the earliest non-scholastic economic literature, in Italy in the 1580s and in England in mercantilist tracts of the 1620s. This is clearly an issue in the prolonged nineteenth-century conflict between English economic theory, especially trade theory, on the one hand, and German and US economic theory on the other. We shall argue that this was the reason why Richard Cobden, the champion of free trade, and Friedrich List, the protectionist, agreed that protecting raw materials was not a good economic policy.

The Renaissance was essentially a period where man became conscious of the legitimacy of being creative. Mediaeval man was the caretaker in the world that God had created; creation was definitely complete and trying to understand it or to tinker with it was decidedly off-limits to man. To Aristotle, mining was one such violation of the creation. Oxford philosopher Roger Bacon was imprisoned for his experiments in 1271, standing accused of making 'suspect innovations'. Starting with the influx of neo-Platonist ideas from the Byzantine empire to the Academy of Florence in the early fifteenth century, man came to see himself in a different light. The new argument went like this: man was created in the image of God. What characterizes God above anything else had to be his enormous creativity. But – if man was created in the image of God – then man should also be creative.

Out of this line of reasoning man's duty to invent and to create new knowledge is born. But this duty was a pleasurable one. The argument seems to have gone like this: it is man's duty to people the earth, therefore God made the duty of procreating a joyous one. Similarly, because it was man's duty to create, to invent and to discover was also a joyous duty. In England, Francis Bacon – statesman under Elizabeth I – was the carrier of these ideas and wrote 'An Essay on Innovations' around 1605. In Germany the philosophers Leibniz and Wolff later represented the same philosophical tradition. 'Some people collect knowledge like other people collect money', says Christian Wolff. In a recent paper, 'Exploring the genesis of economic innovations: the religious gestalt-switch and the duty to invent as preconditions for economic growth', we explain this process in detail.[21]

Out of this changed attitude to knowledge, man's activities moved further and further away from the 'raw' and into the realm of the 'cooked'. Bartering **[285]** raw materials gave way to the production of manufactured goods, in a process where the value added to the raw materials was imputable to human knowledge – to 'the soul of man' which distinguished him from beasts. Importantly – to the observers of the day – these new and

---

21 Reinert, Erik and Daastøl, Arno, Norwegian Institute of International Affairs, Working Papers, no. 540, December 1995 in *European Journal of Law and Economics*, 1997, vol. 4, pp. 233–283.

knowledge-based economic activities were seen as bringing more wealth, as being more profitable, than the old resource-based activities. Therefore, in a truly Schumpeterian move, Renaissance economic policy supported the manufacturing industries at the expense of resource-based industries – of encouraging and protecting new knowledge. These economic policies included the establishment of a patent system (in sixteenth-century Venice), of bounties paid to new manufacturers, of the prohibition of export of machinery (in force in England until the 1830s), of the prohibition of migration of skilled workers (in Venice under the penalty of death), on the export duty of raw materials (to increase the value to the producing nation of this inferior good, and to ensure foreign industry a higher price of raw materials than local industry).

One of the earliest bestselling books on economics was *Delle Cause del la Grandezza delle Città*[22] written by the Italian Giovanni Botero (1543–1617). The English translation, published in London in 1606, is entitled *The Cause of the Greatnesse of Cities.* What, Botero asks, is more important for making a nation wealthy, the fertility of its soil or industry? No doubt, industry, argues Botero, first of all 'because the things produced by the able hands of man are many more, and have a much higher price, than the things produced by nature.[23] Nature gives the material, but the object… is the work of man. Wool is a simple, coarse material of nature. How many beautiful objects, varied in form and shape, the Arts can produce from this.' The best practical example showing the benefits of manufacturing industry over activities based on raw materials was Venice – a city where half of its inhabitants were engaged in manufacturing. A Venetian legislative poster from the eighteenth century fixed the punishment for bringing bread into the city as 'a fine of fifty ducats to be paid immediately and every time and three pulls of the cord'.[24] At roughly the same time the imports of all types of corn into Venice were freed definitely in 1782. The 'raw' could enter freely, the 'cooked' was to be produced nationally. Friedrich List, in my view correctly, saw the repeal of the Corn Laws as just a continuation of this very old policy of protecting 'the cooked' (bread) and letting 'the raw' (corn) have free entry.

Following Venice, England presents the most spectacularly successful use of the strategy of turning a nation's exports from 'the raw' to 'the cooked'. Daniel Defoe describes the English strategy, and praises the Tudor monarchs who carried it out, in his *Plan of English Commerce* in 1728.[25] In the early fifteenth century England was a poor country, heavily indebted to its Italian bankers. The chief export was raw wool. Henry VII, who came to power in 1485, had lived in exile in wealthy Burgundy where English wool was being spun into cloth. The Tudor strategy which started with him was to bring **[286]** England

---

22 Roma, Vincenzio Pellagallo, 1590.

23 Ibid., p. 362. All translations are the author's.

24 'pena di Ducati cinquanta da esser tolto subito ogni volta. .. oltre tre tratti di Corda', Title: *Noi, sopra proveditore…alle Biaue.* This refers to a form of torture – also called *strappado* – where the victim's hands are tied behind his or her back and suspended by a rope attached to the wrists, typically resulting in dislocated shoulders. Venice, no date, Stampato per Gio: Pietro Pinelli, Stampatore Ducale.

25 London, C. Rivington, 1728. Palgrave regards Defoe as 'an important authority for economic history'. Higgs, Henry (ed.), *Palgrave's Dictionary of Political Economy* (1926), New York, Kelley, 1963, vol. 1, p. 535.

into the wealth-creating downstream activities in wool manufacturing that Henry had observed abroad. The English strategy was gradual, starting with import substitution. In 1489 tariffs on cloth were increased and local cloth manufacturing was encouraged. The Crown paid for foreign workers to be brought in and businessmen were paid bounties for establishing textile manufacturing firms. When sufficient manufacturing capacity had been achieved, England prohibited all export of raw wool. As the wave of mechanization extended from wool to other areas of manufacturing, these new industries were in turn given the same preferential treatment initially given to the production of woollen cloth. Friedrich List later put it this way: 'The principle *sell manufactures, buy raw material* was during centuries the English substitute for an (economic) theory.'[26]

The logic of early economic policy seems to have worked by abduction – by a process similar to Kaldor's 'stylized facts'. Everybody could observe that the wool producers in England and the miners in Hungary were poor, just as they could observe that the manufacturers in Venice were rich, as were manufacturers everywhere. In fact, the establishment of the first textile industry in England under heavy protection was based on such a line of reasoning. The English economist Edward Misselden, in 1623, describes very well how economics passes from abductive and intuitive gut feelings to science: 'Wee felt it before in sense, but now wee know it by science.'[27]

In England the conflict between the 'raw' and the 'cooked' is clearly reflected in the main economic debate of the early seventeenth century, in 1622–3 between Gerard De Malynes[28] and Edward Misselden.[29] In the history of economic thought, this debate is interpreted as being about exchange controls and the balance of trade.[30] However, by going back to the sources one finds that the main line of attack by Misselden against Malynes is his 'mechanical' view of man – Malynes has left out man's 'art' and 'soul'. Misselden essentially accuses Malynes of not seeing the difference between 'the raw' and 'the cooked': the difference between stones and timber on the one hand and a house on the other. 'An [sic] House is not an house in respect of the matter whereof it is made; for then all other stone & timber should be a house: but in respect to the *Forme* of it, whereby it is known to be a house', states Misselden. This Forme was the 'cooking process' added by man to the natural 'matter' provided by nature. To Misselden, man creates value by, through his *Mind,* adding *Forme,* not by collecting *Matter.* According to Misselden, Malynes makes a crucial mistake by reducing commerce and economics only to its

---

26 *Das Rationale System der politischen Oekonomie* (1844), Basel, Kyklos, 1959, p. 12. My translation.

27 Misselden, Edward, *The Circle of Commerce,* London, Nicholas Bourne, 1623.

28 Malynes, Gerard, The Maintenance of Free Trade, According to the three essentiall [sic] Parts... Commodities, Moneys and Exchange of Moneys, London William Sheffard, 1622. The Center of the Circle of Commerce, or, A Refutation of a Treatise ... lately published by E.M., London, Nicholas Bourne, 1623.

29 Misselden, Edward, Free Trade and the Meanes [sic] to Make Trade Flourish, London, Simon Waterson, 1622. The Circle of Commerce or the Ballance [sic] of Trade, London, Nicholas Bourne, 1623.

30 Schumpeter discusses the controversy between the two men in his *History of Economic Analysis,* New York, Oxford University Press, 1954, pp. 344–5. See also their respective entries in *The New Palgrave.* In all cases these references are purely to the mechanics of money and exchange.

matter, merchandise and money. Without man's art and soul 'there would be no traffique amongst men, not withstanding the materials of trade', states Misselden.[31]

The conflict between the two economists Malynes and Misselden thus anticipates by some 250 years the nineteenth-century German critique of the *Entgeistung* ('the taking away of the human mind') in English classical economics and by some 350 years the present debate on 'physics envy' of neo-**[287]**classical economics. Misselden argues for a place of *the mind* – what man's creativity adds to the raw materials of nature – in economic theory. His equivalent of *Entgeistung* and 'physics envy' was – and he quotes Aristotle on this – *privation:* 'Privation is not Ens or Beeing, because it is not in the subiect which is made by it.' To Misselden, economics is not in the 'Commodities, Money and Exchange', these are merely 'matters thereof.

In the late seventeenth century William Petty (1623–87) invents both 'the division of labour' – using a clock factory rather than Adam Smith's pin factory – and 'political arithmetic': 'the art of reasoning by figures upon things "relating to government'.[32] Petty, following the trend of virtually all pre-physiocratic and pre-Smithian economics, observes how the relationship between primary production and manufacturing evolves over time: 'There is much more to be gained by *Manufacture* than *Husbandry* ... Now here we may take notice that as Trades and Curious Arts increase; so the Trade of Husbandry will decrease.' As other English writers of his day, Petty was commenting on the high standards of living in Holland, which he saw as the natural effect of so many Dutchmen being engaged in manufacturing and trade. In a nation involved in manufacturing and trade, agriculture would lose out, since it was everywhere observable that agriculture paid lower wages than manufacturing and trade. He found proof of his thesis in Holland because "there is little Ploughing and Sowing of Corn in Holland and Zealand, or breeding of young Cattle'. The Dutch imported much of their food.

The 'mechanical' views of Malynes and Locke were soon to win the day through the barter-centred economic theory of Smith and Ricardo. Other than on the intuitive and philosophical level, the early economists contributed relatively little as to explaining why the production of raw materials was an 'inferior' or 'bad' economic activity. The honour of explaining this goes to Antonio Serra.[33] Serra was the first economist who showed the mechanisms through which the nations producing raw materials stayed poor and the nations producing manufactured goods were wealthy. Serra explains the wealth

---

31 Ibid, p. 11.

32 *Political Arithmetick, or a Discourse concerning the Extent and Value of Lands, People, Buildings; Husbandry, Manufacture, Commerce, Fishery, Artizans, Seamen, Soldiers; Publick Revenues, Interests, Taxes, Superlucration, Registries, Banks; Valuation of Men, Increasing of Seamen, of Militias, Harbours, Situation, Shipping, Power at Sea &c. As the same relates to every Country in general, but more particularly to the Territories of His Majesty of Great Britain, and his neighbours of Holland, Zealand, and France*, London, Robert Clavel, 1691.

33 Serra, Antonio, *Breve trattato delle Cause che possono far abbondare li Regni d'Oro e Argento dove non sono miniere. Con applicazione al Regno di Napoli,* Napoli, Lazzaro Scorriggio, 1613. Serra's remarkable dynamic 'model' shows how wealth is created without the benefit of natural resources (Venice) on the one hand, and poverty remains in the midst of great natural resources (Naples) on the other. The parallel to modern Japan is interesting.

of Venice which had virtually no raw materials and the poverty of Naples which was extremely fertile. The key mechanisms at work in Serra's system are increasing returns to scale in the manufacturing industry of Venice, and diminishing returns and price volatility in the raw materials production in Naples. Serra explains how the volume of manufacturing production in Venice brings costs down and serves to create barriers to entry for other producers. In Serra's system, increasing returns to scale enable the Venetians to sell their products cheaper, while still paying higher wages to their workers than other nations. We shall return to Antonio Serra later in this chapter.

By generally grouping all mercantilists together in the history of economic thought and by reading them almost exclusively secondhand – invariably filtered through the lenses of a neo-classical *Weltanschauung* – we **[288]** have lost sight of both the process of historical policy formation and of a vast number of valuable insights into our own profession.

COBDEN AND LIST: THE REPEAL OF THE CORN LAWS IN KING'S TAXONOMY

In 1766 Carl von Linne, in the twelfth edition of his book on the natural system, completed his taxonomy of plants and animals by including man, *Homo sapiens,* in the binomial classification system. Linne's taxonomy is still the standard taxonomy in use for the plant and animal kingdoms. Ten years later Adam Smith effectively brought the long-lasting taxonomy of economic activities – of which ones were good and which ones were bad for a nation – to an end in economic theory but not in economic practice. The old taxonomy was, in England, most clearly stated by Charles King in his three-volume work from 1721.[34] Under King's Taxonomy importing raw materials and exporting manufactures was 'good trade' for a nation. Importing manufactured goods and exporting raw materials was 'bad trade', while, interestingly enough, trading by buying and selling manufactured goods with the same foreign nation was also good trade.

This system makes sense under certain assumptions:

- if we associate manufacturing with Schumpeterian historical increasing returns (continuous technical change coupled with increasing returns), that creates a dynamic national rent seeking where the rent is split between capital, labour (which continuously has to upgrade their skills) and government;
- if we associate raw materials with perfect information, perfect competition, diminishing returns and no demand for high levels of human skills.

The world today is still divided into an industrialized First World which, up to and including the Asian Tigers, has been through a successful period of economic policy based on King's Taxonomy, and the Third World, whose poverty is based on specialization in providing the world with raw materials. The support and protection given to

[34] King, Charles, *The British Merchant or Commerce Preserv'd,* London, John Darby, 1721, 3 vols.

innovations and to hi-tech industries in today's industrial countries – what the French call *neo-colbertisme* – is only a proof of the continuing validity of the pre-Smithian taxonomy: economic welfare is increasing only by adding more and more human skills to the 'raw' products of nature. The nations which capture the economic activities where the newest and most sophisticated skills can be profitably employed – at the frontier of human knowledge – become the world leaders.

The repeal of the Corn Laws, which today is generally seen as a victory of the 'new' ideology was, in fact, completely compatible with the old theory **[289]** based on Charles King's Taxonomy. The repeal of the Corn Laws in England was not the watershed in the history of free trade as we tend to see it today, and as it was sold to the rest of the world by the English of the period. There are two main aspects to this argument:

1 The repeal of the Corn Laws was fully consistent with the trade theory of the *ancien regime,* with Charles King's Taxonomy and the mercantilist tradition of what constituted good and bad trade. On the corn issue, pre-Ricardian trade theory and Ricardo's free trade theories were in complete agreement. One sign of this was that Friedrich List – who in the Anglo-Saxon world tends to be looked upon as a protectionist of the mercantilist school – had argued for many years already that free trade in corn would be in the interest of England.
2 The Corn Laws were seen at the time essentially to be a monopoly of the great landowners, and their repeal was much more a political victory of democracy over feudal privileges of the aristocracy than a victory of free trade. No doubt the repeal of the Corn Laws was used as an argument to open up foreign markets to British manufactures, and this was clearly an issue in the debate. However, French economist Leon Say seems to have pinpointed the essence of Cobden's movement to repeal the Corn Laws: 'Richard Cobden was, above all things, a thorough democrat and his followers trusted before everything else that he would establish de-mocracy upon the ruins of aristocracy, and that he would destroy whatever was left to the great landowners of their feudal privileges.'[35] Say's essay was published exactly 100 years ago, in connection with the fiftieth anniversary of the repeal of the Corn Laws in 1896.

The repeal of the Corn Laws can be seen as representing the decisive confrontation in a Schumpeterian battle, where industrial entrepreneurs, eager to join the upper strata of society, as a byproduct of their own success, came to overturn the old social order.[36] After the repeal 'industrial and commercial success [became] the nearest approach to medieval lordship possible to modern man', in the words of Schumpeter.[37] We shall argue that

---

[35] Léon Say in a speech on 'State socialism in England', 15 January 1884, quoted in *Richard Cobden and the Jubilee of Free Trade,* London, Fisher Unwin, 1896, pp. 131–2.

[36] For a description of this, see Schumpeter, Joseph Alois, *The Theory of Economic Development,* Cambridge, Harvard University Press, 1934, pp. 90–94, 156.

[37] Schumpeter, ibid., p. 93.

the repeal of the Corn Laws was primarily a result of this economic and political power struggle, and that the trade theoretical issues were of secondary importance, other than as arguments used by England to make other nations stop protecting their manufacturing industry. In other words: the English used the fact that they no longer protected 'the raw' as an argument for other nations to stop protecting 'the cooked'.

This was seen as a bluff and called such by the most influential German and American economists of the time, but it has convinced mainstream economics of today. We would argue that this represents a major issue behind the continuing poverty of most Third World nations. **[290]**

Almost forty years after the repeal of the Corn Laws, we find the same issue raised in the US tariff debate. Now King's Taxonomy has achieved a higher level of sophistication: raw materials were, as in the old logic, to enter the country free of duty, but tariffs on manufactured goods were to be gradually increased with increasing skill level of the workers. A very clear statement of this principle is found in a resolution which was passed by the Democratic National Convention in Chicago in 1884:

> First – the abolition of all duties on raw materials, such as wool, iron, and other ores, coal, jute, hemp, flax, dye stuffs, etc., in order that we may compete in home and foreign markets with other, manufacturing nations, not one of which taxes raw materials. Second – the adjustment of the tariff, so that manufactures approaching nearest to the crude state will pay a lower rate, and manufactures that are further advanced, requiring more skill and labour, will pay a higher rate of duties.[38]

Eight years later, one author remarks that 'these views … [now] form the credo of that party'.[39]

Cobden: free trade in corn in order to achieve cheapness of manufactures

The article on Cobden in the *New Palgrave Dictionary of Economics* strongly emphasizes that 'Cobden's reason [for agitating against the Corn Laws] was peace.' This is certainly one of the reasons, but the main reason was a powerful economic reasoning which is missed in the Palgrave entry.[40] Going through Cobden's own writings, it is clear that his main economic argument is that free trade in corn would strengthen manufacturing in Britain. Cobden's arguments are in many respects similar to those of Friedrich List. Although today we tend to see them as two opposite extremes, they shared a common pre-Ricardian view on what created national wealth. Both to Cobden and to List, this was not agriculture, not 'the raw', but 'the cooked'.

---

38 Quoted in Schoenhof, Jacob, *The Economy of High Wages. An Inquiry into the Cause of High Wages and their Effect on Methods and Costs of Production,* New York, Putnam's, 1892, p. 5

39 Ibid., p. 5.

40 Eatwell, John, Milgate, Murray and Newman, Peter, *The New Palgrave. A Dictionary of Economics,* London, Macmillan, 1987, vol. 1, p. 462.

Cobden views the English economy essentially as a Ricardian corn economy or a Sraffian economy producing 'commodities by means of commodities'. One basic input into English manufacturing was corn to feed the workers for their daily bread. The price of that corn heavily influenced the price of labour. By reducing the price of corn, one would reduce the subsistence cost of labour. For this reason, Cobden says, 'to restrict the import of corn into a manufacturing nation, is to strike at the life of its foreign commerce'.[41]

Richard Cobden pays homage to free trade, not as a lofty human principle, but because were it not for the Corn Laws, the industrialization of the USA and Germany could have been avoided. Cobden sees the high price of corn as the basic reason why England has not been able to hold on to its **[291]** near-monopoly of world manufacturing: 'The factory system would, in all probability, not have taken place in America and Germany; it most certainly could not have flourished, as it has done, both in these states, and in France, Belgium, and Switzerland, through the fostering bounties which the high-priced food of the British artisan has offered to the cheaper fed manufacturer of those countries.'[42]

In line with Cobden's pro-manufacturing stance for England and his anti-manufacturing stance for the rest of the world, he also favoured the South in the US Civil War. When evaluating any economic theory, we tend to forget the basic ethnocentric bias which I would claim, to varying degrees, underlies all economic theory. Lionel Robbins reminds us to keep in mind that English classical economists were in effect first of all Englishmen, and then economists: 'We get our picture wrong if we suppose that the English Classical Economists would have recommended, because it was good for the world at large, a measure which they thought would be harmful to their own community.'[43]

Today this bias lies in the assumptions of neoclassical theory. One example is that the economic theory of the nations which make their wealth under mass production and increasing returns excludes the possibility that only some economic activities are subject to increasing returns, while others are subject to diminishing returns. This kind of ethnocentrism is in some sense reflected when new trade theory only resurrects one half of Frank Graham's 1923 article,[44] dealing with the effects of increasing and diminishing returns in international trade. Only the half which deals with problems of interest to the industrialized world – increasing returns – is brought back. Using the rather heroic assumption that all economic activities are equally subject to increasing returns, this factor of course becomes yet another argument for universal free trade. Graham, on the other hand, also specifically raises the problem of nations whose exportables are subject to diminishing returns and provides an important clue leading to the understanding of

---

41 *The Political Writings of Richard Cobden,* London, William Ridgway, 1868, vol. I, p. 140.

42 Ibid., vol. l,p. 150.

43 Robbins, Lionel, *The Theory of Economic Policy in English Classical Political Economy,* London, Macmillan, 1952, pp. 10–11.

44 Graham, Frank, 'Some aspects of protection further considered', *Quarterly Journal of Economics* 37, 1923, pp. 199–227.

the 'curse of the resources'. In a previous publication I have explained the gap between the First and Third Worlds as a result of increasing and diminishing returns, and of the cumulative effects of uneven learning potential and imperfect competition over time.[45]

Cobden says that 'if a wise modification of our corn laws had been affected at the close of the Napoleonic wars, the official value of our exports would have exceeded by one third its present amount'. And further: 'Under such an assumed state of things, this country, we believe, by this time, would have acquired an increase to its present wealth, to the extent of 350 Millions – nearly one-half the amount of the national debt.'[46] The wealth of the nations clearly lies in manufacturing – in 'the cooked' – corn is only important in order to feed the workers and make their labour cheaper.

Throughout Cobden's writings, he emphasizes the importance of cheapness. Here we find old-fashioned price competition, in contrast to Cobden's **[292]** contemporary English writer on economics, Charles Babbage, who emphasized not the price of labour, but the role of the use of machinery and of science.[47]

Both Cobden and List sensed the crucial importance of the industrial system. To both of them the industrial system, and the need for change of economic policy which it carried with it, were at the core of their theories: 'The cardinal fact that struck his [Cobden's] eye was the great population that was gathering in the new centres of industry in the North of England … which the magic of steam had called into such sudden and marvellous being', states Cobden's biographer, John Morley.[48]

Cobden also saw the evils of the manufacturing system, and he was decidedly a man of peace. To quote from his biography: ' "But the factory system, which sprang up from the discoveries in machinery, has been adopted by all the civilised nations in the world, and it is in vain for us to think of discountenancing its application to the necessities of this country; it only remains for us to mitigate, as far as possible, the evils which are perhaps not inseparably connected with this novel social element." To this conception of the new problem Cobden always kept very close. This was always to him the foundation of the new order of things, which demanded a new kind of statesmanship and new ideas upon national policy.'[49] Richard Cobden saw, more clearly than most, the demands of the new techno-economic pradigm. By removing the last vestiges of the old feudal order – the duty on corn which subsidized the old nobility – Cobden decisively brought England into the age of industrialism.

At the time of his death there was little doubt that Cobden had achieved his goal of strengthening English manufacturing industry by lowering the price of provisions. On the day after his death, Monday 3 April 1865, his sometime foe, Lord Palmerston, rose in

---

45 Reinert, Erik, *International Trade and the Economic Mechanisms of Underdevelopment,* Ann Arbor, University microfilm, 1980.

46 *The Political Writings of Richard Cobden,* London, William Ridgway, 1868, vol. l, pp. 150–51.

47 *On the Economy of Machinery and Manufactures,* London, Charles Knight, 4th edn, 1835. *Reflections on the Decline of Science in England and some of its Causes,* London, B. Fellowes, 1830. Babbage is best known for his 'calculating machine', celebrated as the first computer.

48 Morley, John, *The Life of Richard Cobden,* London, Chapman and Hall, 1881, vol. 1, p. 96.

49 Ibid., vol. 1, p. 97.

Parliament and 'amidst breathless silence' held a speech in the honour of Cobden. In his speech Lord Palmerston emphasized the great achievements of Mr Cobden: 'in the first place, the abrogation of those laws which hindered the importation of corn, which gave a great development to the industry of the country'.[50]

Both List and Cobden understood the superiority of the manufacturing industry over unindustrialized agricultural pursuits. List, like his US contemporaries, saw clearly that a nation which had reached the stage of manufacturing power of England could 'graduate' to a world of free trade. There was no doubt in List's mind that both Germany and the USA would one day reach a stage where free trade was to their benefit, but only after their level of knowledge and industrial strength were on equal footing with the English.

List's argument can be seen as one where children with the knowledge of second grade education cannot fairly compete with college graduates. Free trade would only be beneficial to both parties when the laggard nation had also received its college degree. The German counterpart of duties for 'infant **[293]** industry protection' is therefore, in line with this reasoning, *Erziehungszoll* – carrying the double meaning of educational and upbringing duties.

List: why protecting agriculture is entirely different from protecting industry

In 1825 Friedrich List was banned from Germany and went to the USA. List tells us that one important event in his life, which converted him from being a free trader into an advocate of the protection of manufacturing, was the extreme poverty he witnessed in France with the collapse of French manufacturing that followed the fall of Napoleon. The second important event which influenced his view was no doubt his meeting with American political economy, particularly with the thoughts of Alexander Hamilton and, even more, of Daniel Raymond.[51] There are indeed whole passages in List's *National System* which follow, argument by argument, the 1820 book of Raymond.

Two years after his arrival in the USA, on 24 April 1827 List published an article on the English Corn Laws, 'Die englische Kornbill' in the German-language American newspaper, *Readinger Adler*, of which he was editor. In the same year Frederick [sic] List's *Outline of American Political Economy* was published in Philadelphia.[52] In this work List also raises the issue of the English Corn Laws, and asks what would happen to the American farmer if England should open up her corn trade. List foresees a rise in the price of US corn, but already in 1827 is fully in line with Richard Cobden on the main effect of the

---

[50] Quoted in McGilchrist, John, *Richard Cobden, The Apostle of Free Trade, His Political Career and Public Services. A Biography*, London, Lockwood, 1865, p. 259.

[51] Raymond, Daniel, *Thoughts on Political Economy*, Baltimore, Fielding Lucas, 1820.

[52] Printed by Samuel Parker. Reproduced in List's collected works in 10 volumes, 12 tomes, *Gesammelte Werke*, Berlin, Reimar Hobbing fur die List-Gesellschaft, 1931, vol. II, pp. 96–156. All translations of German texts are mine.

repeal of the Corn Laws: 'England would increase her manufacturing power immensely, and monopolise the Southern and all other markets.'

List clearly shows that a repeal of the Corn Laws, nineteen years before the event, would be a move which would benefit England, but could hurt American manufacturing. A US dependence on the export of raw materials to England would provide a 'destructive effect' on the USA. England could easily again exclude grain from the USA: 'by giving preference to the produce of Prussia, Poland, etc. etc. as it was the case last year respecting the English possessions in the West Indies. Certain is it that from the day of such an economical dependence the majority of the inhabitants of the United States would have to tremble before every new opening of the English Parliament, having more to fear and to expect from the proceedings and regulations in Westminster than from those in Washington, and that the independence of interest of the Unites States would be lost... Would it not be better if we had not sold a single grain of corn to Eng-land?'[53] In his articles on this issue List also made a point that the high transportation costs for corn gave the local English producers a big advantage over US farmers. List here presents himself as a forerunner of the *dependencia* school. In List's analysis, however, terms of trade are not the key economic issue, but the inferior nature of depending on the 'raw' rather than the 'cooked'. **[294]**

In 1830 Friedrich List received his US citizenship and – much to the dislike of some of the German states – President Jackson appointed him Consul General of the USA for Saxony, Bavaria, Hesse-Cassel and Alsace, with a seat first in Hamburg and then in Leipsic [Leipzig]. As a US Consul, List informed his Secretary of State, John Forsyth, about the future development of the English Corn Laws. In a long dispatch dated 'Leipsic, May 15, 1835', List foresees that 'the repeal of the corn laws must become soon one of the principal objects of a reforming ministry, in which they will have to encounter powerful personal interests and prejudices'.[54]

In 1839 List wrote an article on 'The English Corn Laws and the German Protective System' *(Die englische Kornbill und das deutsche Schutzsystem)*.[55] List is often not clear about the mechanisms which cause the protection of manufactures to have such a different effect than the protection of raw material. He explains how 'the olive growers will lose out to the machine producers', but his message of why this is so does not always come across completely. Daniel Raymond is in some ways more explicit on how the mechanisms at work under the protection of manufactures raise real wages, in spite of an initial increase in the price of imports. But, in this article, List states his case clearly:

> The Protective System, as we understand it, can only be applied to the cultivation *(Pflanzung)* of manufacturing power. Any limitation on the import of. raw materials and agricultural (food) products will in the long run hamper the development of manufactures, and is therefore against the interests of the Protective System. This is the case even if such measures stimulate

[53] *Gesammelte Werke,* vol. II, pp. 146–7.

[54] Original in the files of the Department of State, Washington DC. Reproduced in *Gesammelte Werke,* vol. II, p. 326

[55] Reproduced in *Gesammelte Werke,* vol. V, pp. 112–21.

> certain branches of agriculture and certain areas for some time … . The development of Manufacturing Power follows completely different laws than the development of Agricultural Power … To make this clear, we shall for the moment only outline how differently import duties influence prices of the two branches [manufacturing and agriculture]. When manufacturing is being cultivated, the prices of manufactured goods will rise, but as a result of the growing national manufacturing power and the increased competition resulting from this, the prices will, in time, be lower than they would have been through foreign imports.

Daniel Raymond's 1820 book strongly improves this argument by pointing to the fact that wages will rise considerably more than the prices of manufactured goods. It was an observable fact already since William Petty in the seventeenth century that agricultural wages were everywhere much lower than manufacturing wages. 'Applying import duties to agricultural products, on the other hand, does not have this invigorating power; such duties do not lead to lower prices later on. This flaw in their reasoning *(Denkfehler)*, like the **[295]** mixing up of cosmopolitical with political economy, the [English] school has inherited from the physiocrats.'

The year of the repeal of the Corn Laws was the last year of Friedrich List's life – he died on 30 November 1846. Since 1835 List had spent most of his time in Europe, losing all his US assets in 1837 and leaving the service of the USA. In connection with the repeal in 1846, List made his 'Final Reckoning with the English Free Traders' *(Letzte Abrechnung mit den englischen Freihandelspredigern)*.[56] This powerful essay is indirectly directed at Richard Cobden, but more particularly against his *Knecht Freitag* (his Man Friday), that is, James Wilson, the founder of *The Economist*, who had started 'a kind of a crusade' against List: 'Had Mr. Wilson read [our previous publications] he would have found that we have defended the complete freedom of trade with food and raw materials, before any Corn League existed, before one Sir Robert [Peel] was a minister, and before Richard Cobden started protesting against the Corn Laws.'[57] List's frustration lies in the fact that *The Economist* used the repeal of the Corn Laws to convince other nations to give up their protection of manufactured goods.

Again List attacks the barter-based theories of Adam Smith, and their physiocratic nature: 'Adam Smith claims that only work which produces exchangeable value is to be considered productive.' In this system, says List, the person who raises pigs (*ein Schweineerzieher*) is considered productive, the person who raises the level of knowledge of human beings (*ein Menschenerzieher*) is unproductive. In this essay we find the argument of 'the raw' and 'the cooked' again. Superior standards of living can only be achieved by adding productive power to nature. 'Only a harmonious development of the powers of [art and science] can lead to a higher degree of power and civilisation.'[58]

In England we find that List's basic views on what caused human progress were expressed by Charles Babbage,[59] and followed there in practical policy. This made a

[56] Reproduced in *Gesammelte Werke*, vol. IX, pp. 160–64.

[57] Ibid., p. 160.

[58] Ibid., p. 163.

[59] *On the Economy of Machinery and Manufactures*, London, Charles Knight, 4th edn, 1835. *Reflections on the Decline of Science in England and some of its Causes*, London, B. Fellowes, 1830. Babbage is best known for his 'calculating machine', celebrated as the first computer.

member of the US Congress, Henry Baldwin, observe that English trade theory 'like most English manufactured goods, is intended for export, not for consumption at home'.[60] A perusal of the works of Richard Cobden confirms that Baldwin's point was well taken. Both Cobden and List argued for the superiority of manufacturing over agriculture – of the 'cooked' over the 'raw'. The arguments behind the repeal of the Corn Laws were not concerning a lofty principle of free trade, but rather that England should get out of 'inferior' agriculture in order to lower the prices of a basic industrial input– corn for the daily bread of its working masses. However, England skilfully used the fact that it no longer protected 'the raw' as an argument for other nations to stop protecting 'the cooked'. **[296]**

[60] Quoted in List, *Gesammelte Werke*, vol V, p. 338.

Chapter Eight

COMPENSATION MECHANISMS AND TARGETED ECONOMIC GROWTH: LESSONS FROM THE HISTORY OF ECONOMIC POLICY

Erik S. Reinert

8.1 Introduction

The history of economic policy is curiously absent as an economic discipline. Economic history, history of economic thought and Schumpeter's *History of Economic Analysis* all touch on policy issues, but longitudinal analyses focusing on policy are scarce. We would claim that this is somewhat of a blind spot in academic economics. The size of this blind spot increases because most history of economic thought today is limited to presenting a genealogy of today's standard theory. The economic theories that formed the basis for successful economic policy in the past are, at best, treated peripherally. The works of Charles Babbage on the roles of machinery and manufactures (Babbage, 1835) and of science (Babbage, 1830) in economic life, influenced English thinking on economic policy at the time more than did the work of his contemporary David Ricardo. At the time, a member of the US House of Representatives actually made the comment that, like so many other English products, the theories of David Ricardo seemed to be intended for export only. Yet, today's textbooks in the history of economic thought are filled with Ricardo, but do not refer to Babbage. No doubt the absence of a long term policy perspective is further aggravated because ours is a time when – as Jacob Viner put it – 'economists have succeeded in being as ahistorical as an educated man can perhaps possibly be'. (Viner, 1991 (1957): 192)

For most of modern history, economic policy has been based on theories with assumptions fundamentally differing from today's standard theory. One important difference is that for most of the last 500 years national economic policies have been based on theories where economic activities have been seen as *qualitatively different*. In other words, economic growth and welfare were seen as *activity-specific* – as being present in some economic activities rather than in others. Consequently, economic policy was for centuries successfully targeted to activities with certain characteristics. Building the European market economies – with the necessary institutional and financial scaffolding – took centuries of conscious construction, and the *activity-specific* nature of economic growth was a crucial aspect of the policies that first built Europe, and then the United States.

The fact that the economics profession does not possess a coherent history of economic policy contributes to our collective unlearning of 'how the rich nations got rich'. As a consequence we have also unlearned how the problem of technological unemployment was treated in economic policy. In my opinion, the understanding of technological unemployment is intimately connected to the understanding of the process of economic growth itself. Out of a qualitative understanding of the process of economic development – particularly of its activity-specific nature – also came the approach to solving technological unemployment. The term *compensation mechanisms* referring to mechanisms reducing technological unemployment seem to originate with Babbage (1835: 231). *(See also* Chapters 2 and 3 of this book.)

In a comment on the influential German economist Johann Heinrich Gottlob von Justi (1717–71) (given below) Schumpeter succinctly states a typical pre-Smithian attitude to technological unemployment. Justi was the first to establish economic policy as a separate science – as *Policey-Wissenschaft* – the science of policy. Previously economic policy had belonged in a trinity of politics, ethics and economics. Schumpeter's description of Justi's economics gives us a taste of the pre-Smithian mainstream, and indicates how Justi and his contemporaries saw the problem of technological unemployment. Schumpeter's comparison of Justi with Adam Smith confirms that Smith did not represent the beginning of reason in economics, and – as the nineteenth century 'mainstream', both in the US and in Germany, were eager to point out – in some practical matters he represented a retrogression:

> He [Justi] saw the practical argument for laissez-faire not less clearly than did A. Smith, and his bureaucracy, while guiding and helping when necessary, was always ready to efface itself when no guidance or help seemed needed. {*Schumpeter's footnote here:* This was not merely a dream. It will be pointed out below that the bureaucracy in the typical German principality actually tried to behave like this.} Only he saw much more clearly than did the latter all the obstacles that stood in the way of its working according to design. Also, he was much more concerned than A. Smith with the practical problems of government action in the short-run vicissitudes of his time and country, and with particular difficulties in which private initiative fails or would have failed under the conditions of German industry of his time. His laissez-faire was a laissez-faire plus watchfulness, his private-enterprise economy a machine that was logically automated but exposed to breakdowns and hitches which his government was ready to mend. *For instance, he accepted as a matter of course that the introduction of labour-saving machinery would cause unemployment: but this was no argument against the mechanisation of production because, also as a matter of course,* his *government would find equally good employment for the unemployed.* This, however, is not inconsistency, but sense. And to us who are apt to agree with him much more than we do with A. Smith, his {Justi's} vision of economic policy might look like laissez-faire with the nonsense left out.
>
> (Schumpeter, 1954: 172, emphasis added)

8.2 The *invention of innovation* and the targeting of economic growth

> *There is a startling difference between the life of men in the most civilised province of Europe, and in the wildest and most barbarous districts of New India. This difference comes not from the soil, not from climate, not from race, but from* the arts (i.e. from the differences in economic activities).
>
> (Francis Bacon, *Novum Organum,* 1620)

How could Justi so confidently predict that government policy would be able to compensate technological unemployment? In Justi's world, the spirit of the Renaissance had already laid the foundations for the extraordinary economic growth Europe has experienced during the last 500 years. In a previous paper (Reinert and Daastøl, 1997) we have argued that the beginning of economic growth lies in 'the invention of innovation'. The complete turnabout in the meaning of the word 'innovation' symbolises the changing attitude to novelty, to new knowledge and to inventions. Whereas before the Renaissance 'innovation' stood for religious heresy – Roger Bacon was arrested for 'suspicious innovations' in 1277 – in the Renaissance innovations came to be the very material from which progress was made. Francis Bacon's 'An Essay on Human Learning' and An Essay on Innovations' – written around 1605 – are typical for the preoccupations of this period. Typically, one of Francis Bacon's biographies carries the subtitle 'The First Statesman of Science' (Crowther, I960). On the continent, the philosophers Leibniz and Wolff played the same role Bacon had done in England. There Justi's recipe for combining continuous improvements with continuous employment contained all these elements, including the cultivation of *science* and of *machinery.*

Figure 8.1 gives a shorthand version of the type of economic policy, promoting innovation and new knowledge, which was typical in the centuries before Adam Smith. We have labelled this economic policy *Schumpeterian Mercantilism.* Defoe (1730) has a detailed account of the early use of many of these policies in the UK, starting with the reign of Henry VII in 1485.

Starting in the Renaissance, economic policy was formed at two levels: at the level of philosophy and at the level of economics and political science. The philosophers of the time – like Bacon in England and Leibniz and Wolff in Germany – strongly stressed the role of *learning* in human societies.

Bacon gave the idea to the first research council in his *New Atlantis.* Justi made the important relationship between the 'blooming of sciences and the power and happiness of the state' the subject of his inaugural lecture at the Theresanium University in Vienna in 1750 (Justi, 1754). In Goethe's Weimar the philosopher Herder published an influential book on the relationship between science and good government (Herder, 1781). Babbage's 1830 work on the same subject represents the continuity of the important role played by science in developing government economic policy. This knowledge dimension was largely lost in classical and neo-classical economics, but was very much kept alive in the nineteenth-century German and US 'anti-classical' tradition in economics.

The establishment of scientific academies
- Bacon's 'New Atlantis': Salomon's House.
- Leibniz: Inspires the establishment of the academies of Berlin, Vienna and St. Petersburg.

Encouragement and assistance to inventors
- Bacon: 'Upon every invention of value we erect a statue to the inventor, and give him a liberal and honourable reward'.
- Wolff: 'We should forbid mockery of inventors.'

Diffusion of new knowledge/education
- Bacon: 'We have circuits of visits, of divers principal cities of the kingdom; where as it cometh to pass we do publish* such new profitable inventions as we think good.'
- Wolff as the 'educator of the German Nation'

Establishing an apprentice system
- In England under Elizabeth I (1533–1603)
- In Germany as a result of the teachings of philosophers like Leibniz and Wolff.

Patent protection for new inventions
- Showing a sophisticated understanding of the *appropriability problem* of new knowledge.

State-owned manufactures as 'places of learning'
- Emphasised by Werner Sombart.

Subsidies to firms in industries new to the nation or region
- Serra (1613): the number of different professions as a key factor in explaining the wealth of a city.

Tax breaks and bounties to firms bringing in new technology
- Systematically applied in England starting under Henry VII in 1485.
- Import of skilled labour

Travel restrictions for skilled labour
- Under penalty of death for certain skills in Venice.

Prohibition against the export of machinery
- In force in England until the 1830s.

Prohibition against the use of machinery in the colonies
- The heritage of this economic policy is still felt in many Third World countries, which are specialised in the economic activities which have not yet been mechanised.

Export duties on raw materials
- Ensuring that local manufacturing industries have lower prices on raw materials than foreign competitors.

Import duties on manufactured goods, which national competition insured
- Machines were seen as an indicator for new knowledge, and this policy measure maximises the flow of capital and labour to activities producing with machines, not manual power.

Strengthening the navy
- Taking advantage of 'the economies of scale in the use of force'.

*'Publish' here in its meaning of 'to make generally accessible, to disseminate, offer to the public'.

Figure 8.1 Schumpeterian mercantilism: promoting and protecting new knowledge in the economic policy of the Renaissance.

Historians of economic thought have mostly neglected this stress on the science base in pre-Smithian philosophy, economics and political science. Schumpeter – in his *History of Economic Analysis* – leaves out 'the great name of Leibniz and that of his faithful henchman, Christian Wolff' as making 'no contribution to our subject'. In my opinion, this is a grave error. By not understanding the cultivation of learning and new knowledge *per se* which permeated both philosophy and political science, it is impossible to appreciate the *systematic targeting* of new activities employing new knowledge and new machinery that was at the core of European economic policy for centuries.

A key point in the strategy of Justi and his contemporaries was to capture – in every European nation – the economic activities where (a) new knowledge was being developed (e.g. through the scientific academies) and (b) which were being mechanised (Justi, 1758 and 1761, 1760). It was intuitively obvious to these economists how the increased output achieved through mechanisation increased the 'common weal' of a nation. Already in 1613 Antonio Serra explained the wealth of Venice referring to the increasing returns to scale in manufacturing, and the virtuous circles which originated in this sector (see Reinert 1997 for a discussion of this). To the rulers of the time, product innovations were needed for two important purposes: warfare and luxury. Werner Sombart has written two brilliant books on the role of warfare and luxury in the development of capitalism (Sombart, 1913a and 1913b). If necessary, in addition to other encouragement this type of economic activity would also receive tariff protection. In our understanding of 'protectionism' today, we have lost the intimate ties of this kind of policy to the development of knowledge and the development of mechanisation. What originally was protected was not *any* economic activity, but the economic activities at the frontier of innovation.

Wilhelm Roscher is one of the few historians of economic thought who analyses the relationship between the level of philosophy and the level of trade policy. Leibniz – the great philosopher – likened a people who export raw materials, later to buy their own goods back in the form of manufactures, to a person gullibly buying back his stolen horse from the thief at a high price (Roscher, 1874: 336–7). The cultivation of the *manufactured* rather than the *raw* produce was based on an understanding that developing manufacturing industry was synonymous with adding to the national knowledge base – building manufacturing industries was synonymous with development. (See Reinert 1998 for a discussion of this.) In this system, Charles Davenant remarks (around the year 1700), money is needed 'to keep the wheels of the machine in motion'. As early as in 1622 one English economist, Misselden, scolded his colleague Malynes for not understanding the difference between a *heap of stones and logs* and a *house*. The house is a product of Man's knowledge and being, and thus much more valuable than a heap of raw materials.

Innovations, science and technology were also important parts of the economists' toolbox up until Adam Smith. James Steuart's work (Steuart, 1767) – in many ways the crowning work of mercantilism – uses the term *innovation* nine times. Two translations into German of Steuart's volumes within a few years testify to his influence in continental Europe, where industrial development lagged England's. However, the word innovation or its derivatives are completely absent from Adam Smith's *Wealth of Nations* which appeared seventeen years later. On the one hand, Adam Smith broke very clearly with the economics of his day by insisting that *all economic activities were alike* (see Reinert 1997 for a discussion of this). On the other hand, Adam Smith clearly approves of *the use in the past* of mercantilist, targeted and activity-specific economic policy that England had carried out through the Navigation Acts. Adam Smith calls these protectionist laws 'as wise ... as if they had all been dictated by the most deliberate wisdom' (Smith (1776) 1976: 486) and 'the wisest of all the commercial regulations of England' (ibid.: 487). A frequent criticism from German and US economists in the nineteenth century was that English classical economics – by ignoring the historical *activity-specific* strategy which had brought England to power – was, in effect, 'pulling up the ladder' for nations who were industrial laggards.

Friedrich List is no doubt correct when he states that 'the principle *sell manufactured goods, buy raw materials* was for centuries the English substitute for an [economic] theory' (List (1841) 1959: 12).[1] By targeting the production of manufacturing goods, England reaped both the Schumpeterian profits from innovations and the higher wages paid to skilled workers. By focusing on the mechanisation taking place at any point in time, this was a system that systematically 'picked winners'. From a learning perspective, this type of economic policy made sure that exports were made of the goods that exhibited the steepest learning curve. Since only a part of the technological advances were passed on to the foreign trading partners as price reductions, this policy slowly but surely 'jacked up' real wages in the industrial countries compared to the rest of the world. This was, in a sense, an early version of the Fordist mechanisms which will be discussed later.

Charles King's taxonomy of 'good' and 'bad trade' (King, 1721) was for a long time the most important tool of economic policy, not only in England, but also in the rest of Europe. 'Good trade' consisted in importing raw materials and exporting manufactured goods, 'bad trade' consisted in importing manufactured goods and exporting raw materials. Exchanging manufactured goods for other manufactured goods was also considered 'good trade'. From a fiscal point of view this policy was also a success: the people working with machinery were able to pay higher taxes than the artisans could. Charles King's taxonomy makes sense if manufacturing is associated with increasing returns and raw materials are associated with diminishing returns, as in Frank Graham's 1923 model (Graham, 1923) and in parts of Krugman's 'new trade theory'.

In nineteenth-century US tariff policy, King's taxonomy achieved a higher level of sophistication: raw materials were, as in the old logic, to enter the country free of duty, but tariffs on manufactured goods were to be gradually increased with increasing skill level of the workers. A very clear statement of this principle is found in a resolution which was passed by the Democratic National Convention in Chicago in 1884, and which came to dominate US tariff policy:

> *First* – The abolition of all duties on raw materials, such as wool, iron, and other ores, coal, jute, hemp, flax, dye stuffs, etc., in order that we may compete in home and foreign markets with other manufacturing nations, not one of which taxes raw materials.

---

1 My translation. This part of the foreword has not been translated in the English translation of 1885.

> *Second* – The adjustment of the tariff, so that manufactures approaching nearest to the crude state will pay a lower rate, and manufactures that are further advanced, requiring more skill and labour, will pay a higher rate of duties.
>
> (Quoted in Schoenhof, 1892: 5)

In this world-view – which dominated for centuries – wages in the agricultural sector were seen as a reflection of the wages in the manufacturing sector. The research of Thomas Cliffe Leslie – an important economist of the English Historical School – confirms this: 'the chief causes of high agricultural wages are proximity to great industrial centres' (Leslie, 1888: 377). This was partly because the proximity of a manufacturing sector advanced agricultural techniques, partly because of the additional demand created, and partly because the higher industrial wages increased the wages in agriculture. Today we can observe the same relationship between the manufacturing sector and the traditional service sector, as well as in cases where manufacturing has had no effects on productivity. In the spring of 1999 in Quito, Ecuador, a normal haircut is priced at the equivalent of 35 US cents. In Oslo, Norway, the same quality haircut would be priced at around 30 US *dollars.* This confirms what the mercantilists already knew: the wage level in agriculture and in the service sector are essentially set in the manufacturing sector.

Historically, the targeting of economic growth into specific areas was also applied in reverse. The activity-specific view of economic growth cannot be fully appreciated without this other side of the coin – preventing 'good trade' in the colonies. Prohibition of the use of machinery in the colonies was one important and common policy measure. The English prohibition of the very successful cotton textile production in Ireland, starting in 1699, is an outstanding example of the negative targeting – the *winner killing* rather than the *winner picking* aspect of mercantilism. Export of cotton textiles from Ireland was prohibited, and Ireland was assigned the much more labour intensive production of linen. One of the pamphlets lobbying for legislation prohibiting the export of woollen textiles from Ireland, argues that since Ireland was able to produce woollen manufactures cheaper than England, woollen manufacturers in England would be unemployed and would have to go to Ireland for work, 'which means that in time the whole trade would most probably be established there, and lost here' (Clement, 1698: 3). Because the colony threatened the manufacturing base of the mother country, manufacturing had to be shut down in the colony. In order to defend this *targeted underdevelopment,* Clement lists the measures of the other European colonial powers in order to show that these countries in no way treated their colonies better than the English treated Ireland. The full title of this pamphlet gives important clues to the essence of colonialism, which even today is not well understood (see Clement, 1698, bibliography).

8.3 The *activity-specific* nature of economic growth and of the possibility for creating compensation mechanisms

> I agree in particular that the 'residual' and growth in general are industry-specific. That has seemed clear to me since I was a graduate student in the Thirties and read the Kuznets and Burns books …
>
> (Moses Abramowitz in a letter to the author, dated August 16, 1996, quoted with permission)

In a world dominated by Schumpeterian *creative destruction* it is not obvious that *creation* and *destruction* take place in the same geographical area. As regards cotton textiles, the creative part of this industry took part in Manchester, and the destructive part in Bengal, whose weavers had previously supplied these textiles to the English market. Marx quotes the English Governor General reporting from India in 1834–5: 'The misery hardly finds a parallel in the history of commerce. The bones of the cotton-weavers are bleaching the plains of India' (Marx (1867) 1969: 389). My contention is that mechanisms compensating for the loss of jobs can only be created in the geographical areas – or rather, within the labour markets – where the *creative* part of creative destruction are located. Compensation mechanisms, just as economic growth, are highly *activity-specific* (see Chapter 2 of this volume for a complete treatment of the compensation theory).

In 1956, Moses Abramowitz found that only about 15 per cent of US economic growth could be accounted for by changes in factor inputs – capital and labour (Abramowitz, 1956). The rest – the 'residual' of around 85 per cent – he dubbed 'a measure of our ignorance' about the causes of economic growth. The work of Abramowitz and a contemporary work of Robert Solow unleashed a generation of 'growth accounting', attempting to separate the contributions to economic growth of increases in the quantity of labour and capital from those of technological change and other factors. However, very little attention has been paid to the fact that – as Abramowitz himself points out in the quote above – *different economic activities embody widely different amounts of 'residual'*. If the productivity of cutting hair has not changed for the last 50 years, then there is no real 'residual' in haircutting at the moment. In the late 1990s it is obvious that there is much more 'residual' in the type of industries inhabiting Silicon Valley than in the coal mines of England. The size and distribution of the 'residual' among different economic activities must necessarily reflect the *windows of opportunity* for new learning and for technological change at any point in time – reflecting the 'focus' of technological change.

In my view, compensation mechanisms can only be fully understood in the light of economic change and economic welfare being activity-specific. I would claim that compensation mechanisms work under two conditions: (a) that the economic activities of the nation in question also include non: commodity activities with a large potential for creating 'residual' (see Figures 8.2 and 8.3 below) *and* (b) that demand is kept up by ensuring that wages get a large share of the increase in the size of the pie. These are the conditions under which the Kaldorian mechanisms of cumulative growth come into effect (see Chapter 4 in this volume).

There is a crucial link between the Kaldorian mechanisms and the mercantilists: a mercantilist economist like Justi or Steuart would intuitively have grasped the activity-specific nature of compensation mechanisms. As Sombart says about the mercantilists: 'The wealth of nations was to them not the sum of goods, but a sum of *possibilities* for the production of goods' (Sombart, 1928: vol. 2, 918). From around 1800, these possibilities came to be called *the productive powers* of a nation. These possibilities – these windows of opportunity – vary enormously from one industry to the next, and out of this variation in windows of opportunity arises the activity-specific nature of the residual. The core of the mercantilist national strategies was to ensure that *their* nation was also engaged in the economic activities where these *possibilities* – these windows of opportunity – were the largest at the time.

If they were here today, it would have been obvious to the production-based mercantilists, and to the nineteenth-century national strategists like List and Carey that, in the late 1990s a successful software company like Microsoft adds much more to the *residual* of a nation than the world's most successful coal mine. They would have identified the productive powers of information technology, just as we associate high-tech industries with competitiveness. Productive powers were associated with new demand in industries producing product innovations, not with increased productivity from process innovations in agriculture. The importance of new demand industries – from the national point of view – does not principally lie in the profitability of the companies, but in the contribution to the increase of the size of the economic pie, in presenting an incredibly steep learning curve of human labour, combined with the creation of employment. A key factor in this mechanism is referred to by the French regulation school as Fordism: the fruits of technological change spread to a large degree in the local labour market in terms of higher wages. Not only are the wages spread to the manufacturing sector itself, but also to agriculture and to the service sector as we have previously discussed. In spite of the scarce possibilities for productivity increases, the barbers and bus drivers of the first world have had their wages increased in step with the wage increases of industrial workers. In this way their standard of living has been increased enormously compared to that of their equally efficient colleagues in the third world.

The 'quality' of an economic activity lies not alone in its possibilities for productivity increase, it lies in a combination of this possibility and the potential for appropriation of a large share of this increase by the producing nation (i.e. in the possibility of a 'Fordist' distribution of productivity increases) and its potential for rising or, at least, of maintaining employment. In Figure 8.2 I have attempted to list the factors causing 'high' and 'low' quality economic activities. At the top of the 'quality index' we find the products requiring new skills and presenting windows of opportunity for large entrepreneurial profits. With time, all economic activities fall – with varying gravity – towards the bottom of the index. Here at the bottom conditions close to those of a neo-classical 'perfect competition' rule. The quality index thus ranks economic activities according to their ability to promote economic growth. In my view, successful mechanisms compensating for technological unemployment are created if the national portfolio of economic activities also contains activities with a score on the quality index: new products responding to new needs, demanding scarce and valuable new knowledge in industries with increasing demand, steep learning curves and Schumpeterian competition.

At the top of the quality index we find high-tech industries paying very high wages, most importantly the activities carrying the techno-economic paradigm of the time. Also less sophisticated industries sharing labour market and technical knowledge with the paradigm carrying activities are 'pulled up' by a proximity to these activities. The mechanisms at work here are similar to the relationship observed in earlier centuries between manufacturing industry and agriculture as already described. At the bottom of the quality index we find for example the world's most efficient producers of baseballs for the US sport who – in Haiti and Honduras – make 30 cents per hour. The poverty

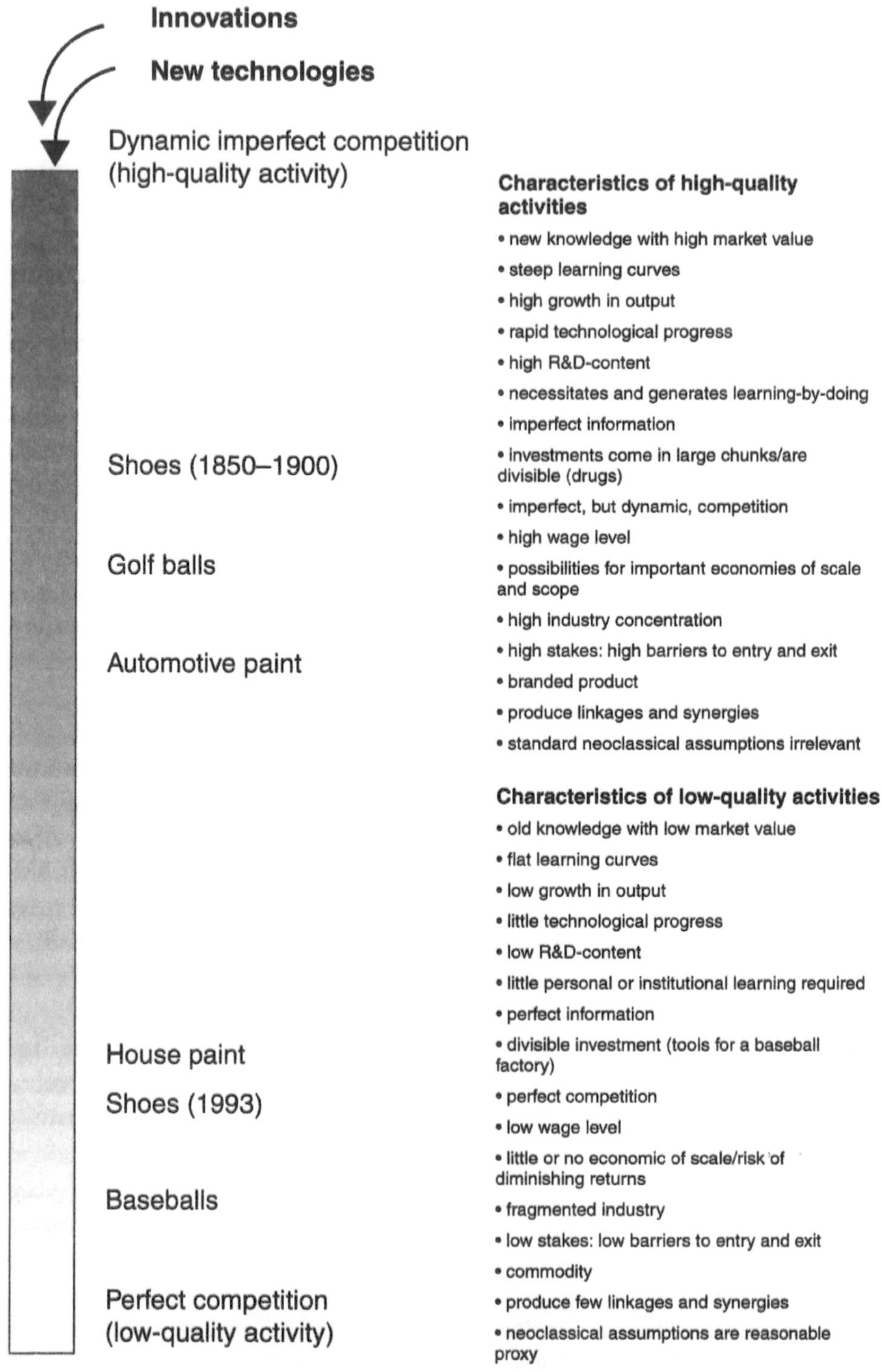

Figure 8.2 The quality index of economic activities.

of these people – the world's most efficient in an industry that all the capital of the US has not been able to mechanise – is intimately tied to the characteristics of the economic activity in which they engage. This is a piece of centuries old common sense that has been gradually lost since World War II.

Through the centuries the term 'manufacturing' and 'industry' have been used as shorthand for 'high quality' economic activities. This was also understood in the periphery of Europe, in the Kingdom of Denmark-Norway: 'Manufacturing is one of the noblest means, through which empires and nations grow, and welfare is created', states a document from the reign of Christian V, 1670–99 (quoted in Christensen, 1943: 129). The king himself confirms the importance of war, luxury and love singled out by Sombart as driving forces of capitalism. In 1693 Christian V states his main passions as 'hunting, love, warfare, and maritime affairs'. In the next century we find the continuation of the same strategies in Denmark – now inspired by Justi – in the works of Ludvig Holberg (Holberg, 1762).

Of course, we are not claiming that manufacturing industry *per se* is 'good', rather that a cluster of 'good' characteristics (see Figures 8.2 and 8.3) has been more frequently found in manufacturing than in agriculture. No doubt bulb production in Holland, in spite of being an agricultural activity, gets a very high score on the quality index. Also some service industries (e.g. finance, insurance, real estate) exhibit 'manufacturing-like' qualiries, whereas certain unmechanisable manufacturing activities (e.g. baseballs) do not qualify as 'good' activities. A key to economic policy-making in the United States, Australia and other resource-rich nations was that the presence of a manufacturing industry – even though this industry was not 'world class' – would fundamentally change the nature of agriculture. An industrialised nation was seen as being able to live well from exporting primary products, a nation without manufacturing industry could not (see Reinert, 1980 for a discussion of the mechanisms at work).

Figure 8.3 shows how the 'quality index' materialises in a measurable way in an economy. This figure is the result of a large project carried out by The National Bureau of Economic Research, in which Moses Abramowitz was also working at the time (Fabricant, 1940). Figure 8.3 shows how fifty-one industries in the United States differed, measured by three important characteristics – output, employment and productivity (wage earners per unit of product) – between 1899 and 1937. We can clearly see Verdoorn's law at work – the close relationship between an increase in *demand* for a product and the increase in *productivity* for the same product. Verdoorn's law strongly contributes to the activity-specificity of compensation mechanisms: nations not active in industries with increasing demand are unlikely to achieve increases in employment. It is important to note that this was true also *within* the United States. This trend will be much more pronounced in nations that were further away from the technology, markets and capital of the United States.

As can be observed in Figure 8.3, out of fifty-one industrial sectors technological change outpaced demand in twelve – creating 'technological unemployment'. With the exception of the cigar industry (no. 13), these industries were all characterised by decreases or very small increases in total output. Clearly both technological change and mechanisms compensating for technological unemployment will be extremely difficult to achieve in nations specialising in industries on the right hand side of Figure 8.3. This

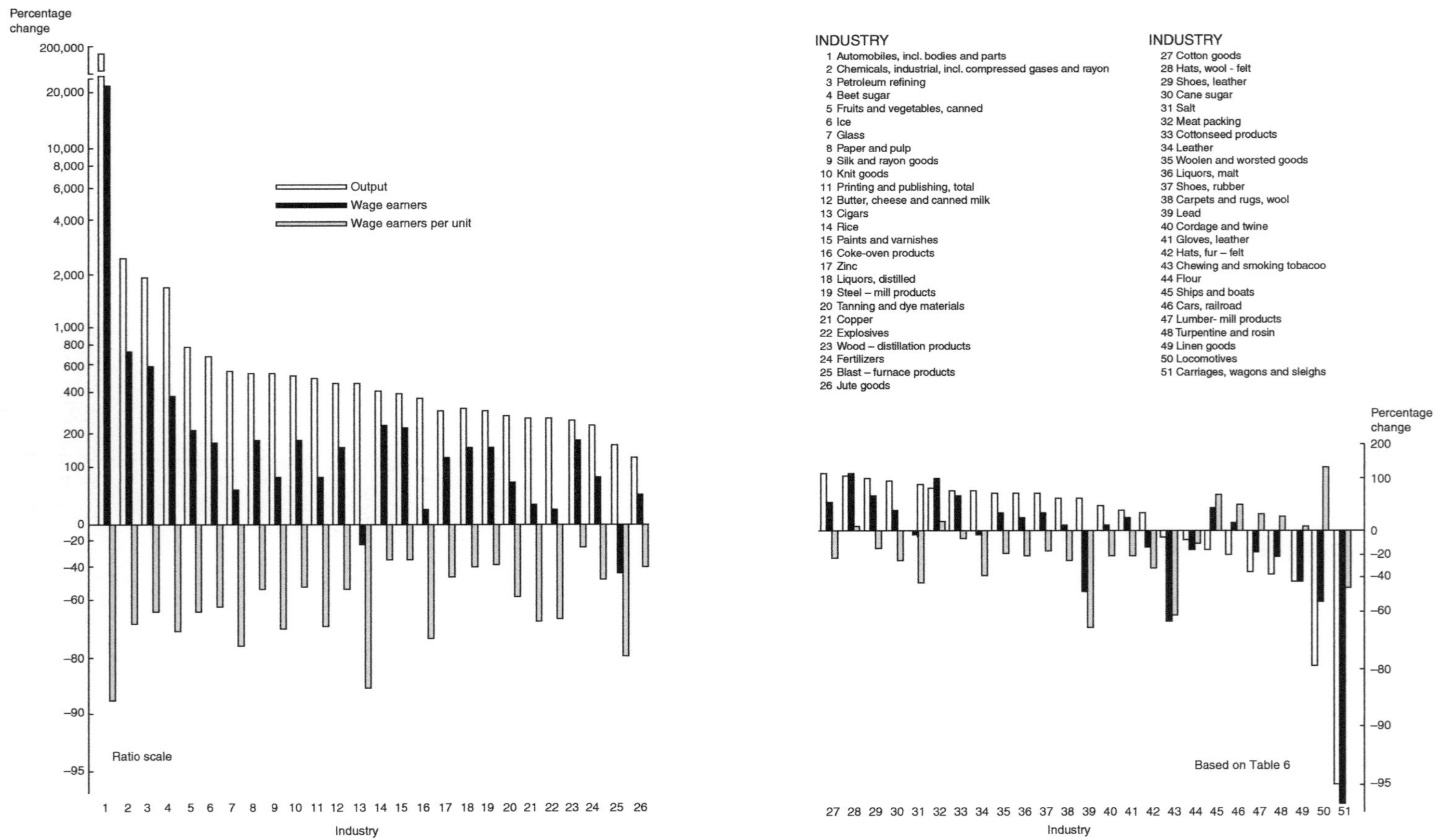

Figure 8.3 United States: individual manufacturing industries; change in physical output, wage earners employed and wage earners employed per unit of product, 1899–1937.

is a key to the activity-specific nature of economic welfare. In another work, Fabricant (1942) focuses exclusively on the employment effects in this project. This book contains a wealth of statistical material on the relationship between technological change and employment in the early 'Fordist' era.

It is worth noticing that to a nation engaged in the high quality industries (on top in Figure 8.2 and far left in Figure 8.3), the operation of the compensation mechanisms will tend to appear as the result of 'an invisible hand'. However, these compensation mechanisms, seemingly created by 'the market', are really a result of the momentum created by virtuous circles set in motion by previous activity-specific targeting. Regardless of what economic theory might say, the indisputable historical fact is that no nation larger than a city-state has ever achieved any degree of development without first having gone through a period protecting manufacturing industry. My reading of Adam Smith is that he agrees with this view. In the *Wealth of Nations,* Smith mentions the invisible hand only once: when it *leads people to support domestic rather than foreign industry* (Smith 1976 (177'6): I, 477). In this same chapter - within the same line of reasoning – Smith extols the extreme wisdom of mercantilist protectionism of the Navigation Acts. The 'other' Adam Smith – the misunderstood mercantilist – uses the metaphor of the invisible hand to describe a snowballing effect that has been set in motion by centuries of targeted economic policy.

Today the information and communication industry would have all the characteristics exhibited by the automotive industry in Figure 8.3 (far left), whereas the coal mining industry would show all the characteristics of the 'carriages, wagons and sleighs' industry (far to the right). Figures 8.2 and 8.3 are connected in an important way: the characteristics of a 'high quality industry' at the top of the quality index will show up in the statistics as an industry far to the left in a historical table like Figure 8.3. Of course, *within* the 'high quality' industry we find strong competition and industry shakeputs. Out of more than 250 car manufacturers of the United States early this century, only about four survived. Already in the early nineteenth century the slogan of the young United States was protection *and* competition.

The proximity to the paradigm carrying industries to the far left also radically changes the nature of the activities to the right within the same innovation system. The hat industry in the United States – being part of the same innovation system, knowledge base and labour market as the steel and auto industry – will have developed very differently in this period from the hat industry of Ecuador, home of Panama hats. These qualitative linkages or synergies between clusters and between industries are - in spite of their elusive nature – no doubt of great importance.

Historically one other important condition seems to be necessary in order to create compensation mechanisms protecting against technological unemployment. To Marx, mechanisation inevitably led to an increase in the capital employed per head of labour employed in production. It was therefore not obvious that the labourers would be able to buy the increased output produced with the aid of the growing volume of capital. Under these circumstances the compensation mechanism may very well be halted through a process of underconsumption, of lack of demand (Marx (1867) 1969: chapter 13). It is entirely possible to agree with Marx in this analysis – as many economists did at the time – but without seeing this as the one inevitable outcome. Demand could be maintained through political means.

About one hundred years after Marx' criticism of the compensation mechanism, the Director of the Swedish National Labour Market Board commented on this same problem. 'To distribute the result of production to all groups in the community and to do so in such a way that a high demand is maintained is an economic-political problem which must be solved by political means. Countries which do not solve these problems will also be unable to solve the problems of technological change' (Olsson 1963: 200).

Judging from the development of the third world after the fall of the Berlin Wall, Marx himself, somewhat paradoxically – through the spectre of a communist world revolution – contributed in a very important way to the establishment of efficient compensation mechanisms. Based on the very healthy intuition that wealthy workers are unlikely communists, the areas bordering on the communist world – East Asia and Europe – were encouraged during the Cold War by the United States to continue and to expand a highly 'mercantilist' protection of national industries. In Europe this reconstruction of 'national productive powers' was carried out through the Marshall Plan. When free trade was gradually introduced during the 40 years following World War II, the transition from protectionism through economic integration was almost out of Friedrich List's textbook.

8.4 Technological unemployment in early economic thought

In early economic thought, a high density of population was seen as a symptom of good 'statecraft' – of *Staatsklugheit* ('state wisdom') as Justi calls it. Before Malthus, the 'lack of people' was a much more frequent complaint than unemployment or idleness. Populousness, national wealth and popular welfare tended to be seen as highly interdependent. Justified or not, what we would label 'unemployment', would then tend to be classified as 'idleness' or 'vagrancy'. In England idleness and vagrancy were severely punished

James Steuart in his 1767 work dedicates a chapter (XIX) to technological unemployment: 'Is the Introduction of Machines into Manufactures prejudicial to the Interest of a State, or Hurtful to Population?' Although 'some moderns' – Steuart mentions 'the great Montesquieu' – 'find an abuse in bringing mechanisms to perfection', to Steuart innovations and the improvement of machinery are evidently an advantage. But, he clearly sees how mechanisation causes frictions and inconveniences. Almost like a criticism of the economic shock therapy fashionable in the 1990s, Steuart's main worry is the 'suddenness' of the introduction of machinery, which makes adjustment difficult (see Chapter 4 in this volume). 'A room cannot be swept without raising dust', Steuart says, 'neither can a machine which abridges the labour of men, be thrown *all at once* into an extensive manufacture, without throwing many people into idleness.'

Just as in the case of Justi, Steuart sees it as the job of the government both to ease the transition and to find new industries responding to new demands that employ the idle workers. Steuart states clearly: 'I constantly suppose a statesman at the head of government, systematically conducting every part of it, so as to prevent the vicissitudes of manners, and innovations, by their natural and immediate effects or consequences, from hurting any interest within the commonwealth'. If the machine proves hurtful, it is just because the state is not doing its job, says Steuart. It is important, however, to keep in mind that available to Justi, Steuart and their contemporaries was a powerful set of tools – including tariffs – which enabled them to capture the economic activities which at the time had the steepest learning curves and the fastest growth of demand.

T. H. Aschehoug – a Norwegian economist active early this century – indirectly invokes what later became known as Verdoorn's Law in defence of the use of machinery. In spite of the enormous productivity increases taking place in the British textile industry between 1870 and 1895, he says, employment in this very industry rose from 907,000 to 1,076,000 in the same period (Aschehoug, 1905: 2, 451). In the nations which reaped the productivity increases from being industrialised, machinery could not have harmed labour. Although in most places there was a constant shortage of labour in agriculture, Aschehoug says, workers from the countryside still poured into the cities where the machines were working.

Whereas the mercantilists saw a never-ending frontier of knowledge, the *Zeitgeist* of Malthus and Ricardo was much more one of a static zero-sum game. The changing attitude towards a large population – from being a blessing to being a threat – was just one manifestation of economics changing from being (in Sombart's terms) *activistic-idealistic* to being *passivistic-materialistic*, from a clear focus on *production* to a focus on *trade* and *barter*. The lost focus on production and innovation made economics into what Carlisle dubbed 'the dismal science'. In this spirit Marx quotes Ricardo as saying that 'machinery and labour are in constant competition' (Marx: 470). To a mercantilist, this phrase would have made no sense at all. At the core of the old economics was *Man and His Needs (Der Mensch und seine Bedürfnisse)* How could the machine – a tool which was there to help Man satisfy his needs – be in competition with Man himself? Can a hammer be in competition with the carpenter, they would have thought.

8.5 Unemployment and the death of Fordism in a historical perspective

The task of this chapter is to provide a historical background to the present debate. In this section, some comments will be added interpreting the present-day changes in light of the historical record. We have recently witnessed the break-down of the Fordist growth model, and have entered a new technological paradigm, based on information and communication technologies (ICTs). The following analysis combines Carlota Perez's work on the nature shifts in technological regimes with a historical record which in this chapter could only be sketched (see Perez, 1983; Perez and Soete, 1988).

In the works of Carlota Perez, shifts in techno-economic paradigms have two main features:

> First, the new paradigm is visible as a powerful cluster of new and dynamic technologies, products and industries. These new industries, selling new products, show an explosive growth and cause major structural change in the economy. They are economic activities with all the characteristics of 'high quality activities' in Figure 8.2. In Figure 8.3, which shows

> the development of Fordism, these same activities appear to the left. These activities are *paradigm carriers,* and the basis for their activities are *product innovations.*
>
> Secondly, paradigm shifts appear as an interrelated set of generic technologies and new organisational principles. These new technologies make possible a quantum jump in potential productivity for most industries. These activities are *paradigm users,* where innovations tend to take the form of *process innovations.* The *product* innovations of the *paradigm carriers* are used to make *process* innovations of the *paradigm users.*

The data from the National Bureau of Economic Research on the first period of Fordism in the US shows how the new industries – to the left of Figure 8.3 – were the industries which created new employment. These were the *paradigm carriers* of Fordism. The sector shedding most employment at the time – agriculture – is not part of Figure 8.3.

Fordism brought forward *product innovations,* in manufacturing industry – new products tied to fundamental innovations in the automotive industry, in steel, in a myriad of products using electricity and in the chemical industry. Starting with Ford's production of tractors, Fordism also caused very important *process innovations* in the agricultural sector. Indeed, the massive displacement of employment from the agricultural sector into the industrial sector was one of the main characteristics of the Fordist era.

Pianta (1999 and in Chapter 5 of this book) surveys recent works on the relationship between technology, growth and unemployment. Using the European Community Innovation Survey (CIS), Pianta looks at the effects of product innovations and process innovations on employment. For the early 1990s, he finds the same pattern which we observed in the historical data in Figure 8.3, based on data from the US from 1899 to 1937. Industries dominated by *product innovations* create employment (industries with Schumpeterian competition), whereas traditional industries where *process innovation* prevails (industries with price competition) shed labour. Today's mature industries exhibit many of the characteristics of agriculture under Fordism, the most important of which are a weak increase in demand, strong price competition, and the use of labour-saving technologies supplied by a new paradigm. In other words, in the *paradigm-carrying industries,* the new techno-economic system again causes product innovations, Schumpeterian competition, huge demand increases, and new employment. In traditional economic activities the new technology tends to cause labour-saving process innovations, price competition, little increase in demand and a consequent loss of jobs: German economist Adolph Lowe (1893–1995) has a good analysis of types of innovations, technological unemployment and economic policy (Lowe, 1988, chapter 6).

Pianta finds that Europe's industries are dominated by what I have referred to as *paradigm users* rather that *paradigm carriers,* by mature industries using the new technology more to save labour than to create new products. These activities are, in our view, comparable to agriculture under Fordism. Largely as a consequence of this, Europe in the 1990s continues to lose jobs, whereas the United States gains jobs. Europe seems to withdraw 'to a strategy of active price competitiveness dominated by labour saving process innovations' (Pianta, 1999) The *composition effect* of manufacturing industry – what we have called the

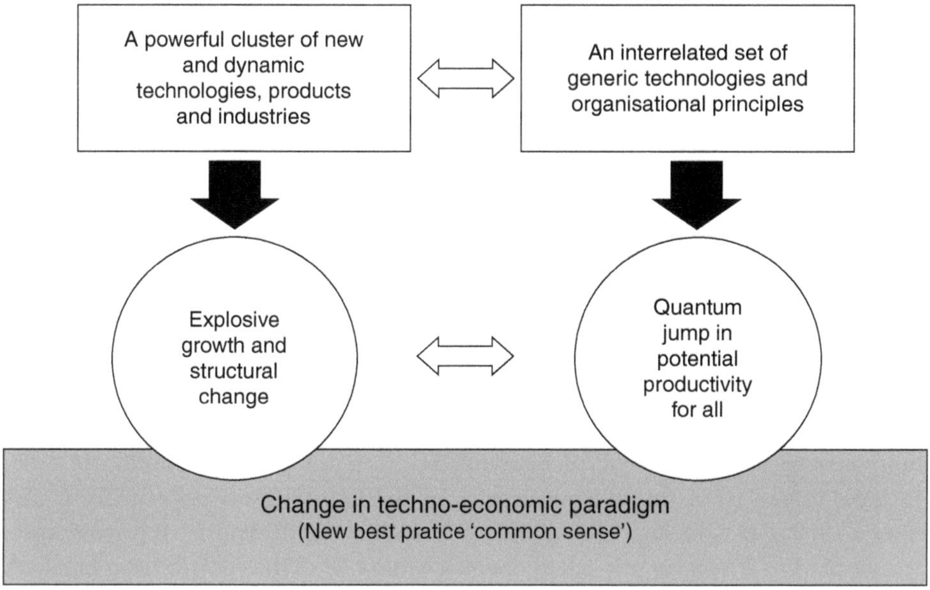

Figure 8.4 What is a technological revolution?
Source: Carlota Perez.

activity-specific aspects of economic growth – to a large extent explains why Europe loses jobs compared to the US and Japan.

What would be the strategy to follow under these circumstances? The literature is dominated by a focus on the labour market, on skills, rigidities and regulations (OECD, 1994). It is clear that a flexible labour market is of utmost importance to the nation where the new paradigm dominates. This in order to overcome the inevitable mismatch of skills created by the presence of a workforce trained in the old paradigm. In my view it is not at all clear, however, that *wage flexibility* will solve the problems of the nations who are weak in the new paradigm industries. These would be the nations who use the new technology essentially for process innovations and price competition. I shall give two relatively recent historical examples showing ruinous effects of wage flexibility, under conditions where a new paradigm – with its booming demand and its Schumpeterian and oligopolistic competition – is *absent.* One example below is from the US in the in the 1930s, the second from Latin America in the 1990s.

One of the key features of Fordism was the ratchet wheel effect[2] – wages (and consequently also to some extent prices) could only move one way: up. This is the phenomenon that Galbraith refers to as 'stickiness' of prices and wages. The ratchet wheel effect was the result of institutional and political arrangements made possible under the umbrella of the huge economies of scale typical of the paradigm carriers of Fordism. 'The social

[2] A toothed wheel constructed with a catch so as to move only in a single direction.

question' was for decades the main subject for economists, and the solution to the social question was a Galbraithian 'balance of countervailing powers' – an oligopolistic structure of both industry and labour.

During the Great Depression in the United States we can study the benefits of the ratchet wheel effect, of the downward inflexibility of wages. In the industrial sector, the crisis was taken out in the form of unemployment. Sheltered by its oligopolistic structure, industry could to a large extent keep up prices and absorb the shock of the crisis through unemployment. The share of labour in US GDP actually rose during the early 1930s. In agriculture, on the other hand, labour costs show the same flexibility which some economists now wish to see in Europe's labour markets. The result was acute poverty.

In the US, the relationship between the industrial and agricultural sector tended to be measured through the ratio of *farm prices* to *farm costs* – the so-called parity price relationship 'which farmers and farm organisations came to regard as having a natural, almost theological origin. The farmer is entitled to the parity price' (Galbraith, 1994: 83). The basic value 100 of this index was given by the ratio of farm prices to farm costs between 1909 and 1914. In 1918 – partly as a result of World War I – this relationship had increased to 200: farm prices had doubled compared to the costs of farm inputs. In 1929 the ratio was down to 138, in 1932 it was down to 'a dismal, even murderous 57' (Galbraith, 1984). In other words, the 'perfect markets' and resulting flexibility in agriculture had reduced the price of farm products by *more than 70 per cent* compared to the costs the farmers had. Those who have read Steinbeck's *Grapes of Wrath* will have captured some of the *Zeitgeist* in US agriculture at the time.

The second example is from the 1990s. The pressures from the 'Washington Consensus' during the 1990s have lead to a dramatic de-industrialisation of most of the former second world and of the third world. The latest figures show that ninety countries of the world were poorer in 1997 than in 1990, thirty-seven of them poorer in 1997 than they were in 1970. Real wages in a country like Peru are down by more than 50 per cent since the early 1980s. De-industrialisation forces these nations back into almost solely producing raw materials, which – as Europe has known for 500 years and the United States for 200 years – alone, in the absence of a manufacturing sector, has never made a nation wealthy. This de-industrialisation disconnects any compensation mechanisms at work, and produces Myrdalian vicious circles. The high unemployment and underemployment caused by the closing of industries leads to a downward pressure on wages, which again contributes to the falling prices of raw materials, causing terms of trade for raw material producers to deteriorate. Not by coincidence the times of import substitution in Latin America were also times of improving terms of trade: a typical case of positive cumulative causations (see also Chapter 9 in this book).

Also in the United States, the partial dismantling of the ratchet wheel has had serious effects on income distribution. Real wages peaked in the US in 1972–3 (Peterson, 1994), and since then the share of wages in GDP has shrunk considerably. A new techno-economic paradigm seems to start a new Kuznets curve, but not only that. The countervailing oligopolies of Fordism – industry and labour – appear to have created a unique system which made it possible to increase the share of wages as a percentage of GDP, and thus to create a welfare state. The emerging new paradigm seems less predisposed for such mechanisms. This is partly due to a trend towards economies of *scope* in networks, rather than on Fordist economies of *scale* in hierarchies. This tends to produce less solidarity and more 'winner takes it all' type of markets (Frank and Cook, 1995). Maintaining social cohesion under these circumstances means, in my view, to consciously maintain the ratchet wheel of wages created by Fordism, but pragmatically adjusting the institutions surrounding it to the new technological reality.

If Europe is not sufficiently present in the industries where new demand is greatest, opening up for downward wage flexibility will simply make things worse by unleashing a downward spiral of contracting demand, contracting production and contracting real wages. The experiences both of the US in the Great Depression and of Latin America during the 1990s amply testify to this. Indeed, both Latin America and Russia in the late 1990s seem to prove David Ricardo's point: if left to the market, in the long term real wages are determined by the prevailing minimum subsistence cost. Historically, only political interference in labour markets has prevented this from happening.

8.6 The future: innovations or a backward-bending supply curve of labour?

Early European colonisers overseas frequently complained about a phenomenon which economists named 'the backward-bending supply curve of labour'. The Europeans observed that once the 'natives' had earned enough money to buy what they found useful from European civilisations, for example knives or fishing hooks, they quit working and went back to their former way of living. This resulted in a 'backward-bending' supply curve of labour; the higher the wages, the less hours the natives worked.

We may ask ourselves if – at some point – society as a whole will not exhibit such a backward-bending supply curve of labour. In this century, daily working hours have been cut from about 12 hours to less than 8. Why don't we continue taking out the technological advances in the form of more spare time? In 1890 – like today, a period of fast and discontinuous technological change – an influential US economist, Francis A. Walker, reflected on this very subject in his address to the Fourth Annual Meeting of the American Economic Association. Walker – at the time President both of the American Economic Association and of MIT – explains the fundamental mechanism behind *compensation mechanisms:*

> To-day, having been born into a world comparatively simple in its organisation and requirements, we find ourselves … harassed, fatigued, and at times despondent, under the pressures of cares, obligations, engagements and labors innumerable, almost intolerable [Walker says. He then briefly entertains the thought of surrendering into a sybaritic existence, amid ease and comfort and perpetual music, but pulls himself together.] *We know that it is of the very essence of social progress that as fast as we are released by arts, inventions and improved organisation from cares and labors which have worn and wearied us, we should create for ourselves new wants which will take up all the time and strength thus set free;* and that it is not rest man needs, but work.
>
> (Walker, 1891: 9–10, my emphasis)

This philosophy was typical of the nineteenth century. Abraham Lincoln, in a well-known election speech in 1860, explains the difference between men and animals in that both work hard, but that only Man *innovates* and *invents*. Lincoln supports his analysis with a number of quotes from the Bible (Lincoln, 1860). The roots leading back to the Renaissance are very clear – it was this new interpretation of the Bible that unleashed the creative revolution of the Renaissance: God created the Universe in seven days, and then rested. Since Man is created in the image of God, it is Man's duty to continue His creation (Reinert and Daastøl, 1997). In this view, Man is doomed to eternal innovation – to pushing forward the never-ending frontier of knowledge almost in the manner of a Sisyphus, with the exception that the task is not repetitive, but always new. Here lies the origin of compensation mechanisms.

Compared to the Fordist age, the future will no doubt open up for more diversity of behaviour in the labour market. Individuals who use their spare time in ways that require little cash, will be able to exercise an option of letting their supply curve of labour periodically tilt backwards. Possibilities also open up for having consecutive multiple careers, where possibly only the period of a decade or so will be associated with the stress which the President of MIT associated with modern life in 1890.

Over time the economy does seem to function like a chain letter or pyramid game. We are doomed to innovate – to create new needs creating new employment – in order to compensate for the job losses created by continuous process innovations. The 'stationary state' which the classical economists like Smith and Ricardo envisioned somewhere on the horizon, was probably there only because they saw history in terms of one techno-economic paradigm. When the perfect set of stone tools had been produced, people tended to see not only the end of the Stone Age, but the end of history. In times of technological transition, people frequently fail to see that history then starts all over again founded on a new basic technology.

Some important lessons may be learned from the history of economic policy. Central to historically successful compensation mechanism is the strategy that every nation-state – really every *labour market* - should have paradigm-carrying activities within their borders. Only the presence of both *production* and *consumption* of the new products near the technological frontier, produced under Schumpeterian competition, secures sufficient new demand to offset jobs lost to continuous labour-saving new technologies. As textile production was mechanised, every ruler in Europe knew his realm would benefit from the employment of the new machines. Historically, this is the only recipe ensuring a tolerably balanced growth between nations, as best exemplified by European history over the last 500 years.

References

Abramowitz, M. (1956) 'Resource and Output Trends in the United States since 1870', *American Economic Review,* Papers and proceedings, No. 46, May, pp. 5–23.

Aschehoug, T.H. (1903–8) *Socialökonomik,* Christiania (Oslo): Aschehoug, 3 vols.

Babbage, C. (1830) *Reflections on the Decline of Science in England,* London: B. Fellowes.

Babbage, C. (1835) *On the Economy of Machinery and Manufactures,* 4th edn, enlarged, London: Charles Knight.

Christensen, A.E. (1943) *Industriens Historie i Danmark. Tiden indtil 1730,* Copenhagen: Gad.

Clement, S. (1689) 'The Interest of England, as it stands with the trade of Ireland, considered; the arguments against the bill for prohibiting the exportation of woolen manufactures from Ireland to forreign parts, fairly discusst, and the reasonableness and necessity of Englands restraining her colonies in all matters of trade, that may be prejudicial to her own commerce, clearly demonstrated', London: John Attwood.

Crowther, J.G. (I960) *Francis Bacon, The First Statesman of Science,* London: Cresset Press.

Defoe, D. (1730) *Plan of English Commerce, being a Compleat Prospect of the Trade of this Nation:* London: Riverton, 2nd edn.

Fabricant, S. (1940) *The Output of Manufacturing Industries, 1899–1937,* New York: National Bureau of Economic Research.

Fabricant, S. (1942) *Employment in Manufacturing, 1899–1937, An Analysis of Its Relation to the Volume of Production,* New York: National Bureau of Economic Research.

Frank, R.H. and Cook, P.J. (1995) *The Winner-Take-All Society,* New York: Penguin.

Galbraith, J.K. (1994) *The World Economy Since the Wars. A Personal View,* London: Manolazin.

Graham, F. (1923) 'Some Aspects of Protection further considered', *Quarterly Journal of Economics,* vol. 37, pp. 199–227.

Herder, J.G. (1781), *Vom Einfluss der Regierung auf die Wissenschaften, und der Wissenschaften auf die Regierung,* Berlin: Georg Jakob Decker, 1781.

Holberg, L. (1762) *Danmarks og Norges Geistlige og Verdslige Staat eller Beskrivelse,* 3rd edn, Copenhagen: Pelt.

Justi, J.H.G. von (1754), 'Vernünftigen Zusammenhange [sic] und practischen Vortrage aller Oeconomischen und Kameralwissenschaften wobey zugleich zur probe die Grundsätze der Policeywissenschaft mit denen darzu [sic] gehörigen praktischen Arbeiten vorgetragen werden, benebst einer Antrittsrede von dem Zusammenhange eines Blühenden Zustandes der Wissenschaften mit denjenigen Mitteln, welche einen Staat mächtig und glücklich machen', Leipzig, D.E. v. K.

Justi, J.H.G. von (1758 and 1761), *Vollstdndige Abhandlung von denen Manufacturen und Fabriken,* Copenhagen: Auf Kosten der Rothenschen Buchhandlung, 2 vols.

Justi, J.H.G. von (1760) *Die Grundsetze [sic] zu der Macht und Glückseeligkeit der Staaten, oder ausführliche Vorstellung der gesamten Policey-Wissenschaft,* Königsberg and Leipzig: Hartungs Erben.

King, C. (1721) *The British Merchant; or, Commerce Preserv'd,* London: John Darby, 3 volumes.

Leslie, T.E.C. (1888) 'The Movements of Agricultural Wages in Europe', *Essays in Political Economy,* Dublin: Hodges, Figgis & Co.

Lincoln, A. (1860/1978) 'Discoveries and Inventions', reprinted in A. Salisbury, *The Civil War and the American System,* New York: Campaigner Publications.

List, F. (1841/1959) *Das Rationale System der Politischen Okonomie* (1841), Basel: Kyklos Verlag.

Lowe, A. (1988) *Has Freedom a Future,* New York: Praeger.

Mansfield, E. *The Economics of Technological Change,* New York: Norton.

Marx, K. (1867/1959) *Das Kapital,* vol. 1, Frankfurt: Ullstein.

OECD (1994) *The OECD Jobs Study. Part I; Labour Market Trends and Underlying Forces of Change,* Paris: OECD.

Olsson, B. (1963) 'Policy Implications of Technological Change in Western Europe', in G. Somers, E. Cushman and N. Weinberg (eds) *Adjusting to Technical Change,* New York: Harper & Row.

Perez, C. (1983) 'Structural Change and the Assimilation of New Technologies in the Economic and Social Systems', *Futures,* vol. 15, No. 5, pp. 357–75.

Perez, C. and Soete, L. (1988) 'Catching-up in Technology: Entry Barriers and Windows of Opportunity', in G. Dosi, C. Freeman, R. Nelson, G. Silverberg and L. Soete (eds) *Technical Change and Economic Theory,* London: Pinter.

Peterson, W.C. (1994) *The Silent Depression,* New York: Norton.

Pianta, M. (1999) 'Innovation, Demand and Employment', in P. Petit and L. Soete (eds) *Technology and the Future of European Employment,* Cheltenham: Elgar.

Reinert, E. (1980) *International Trade and the Economic Mechanisms of Underdevelopment,* Ann Arbor: University Microfilm.

Reinert, E. (1995) 'Competitiveness and its Predecessors – a 500 Year Cross-national Perspective', *Structural Change and Economic Dynamics,* vol. 6.

Reinert, E. (1997) 'The Role of the State in Economic Growth, Centre for Development and the Environment', University of Oslo, *Working Paper No. 5.*

Reinert, E. (1998) 'Raw Materials in the History of Economic Policy; or, Why List (the Protectionist) and Cobden (the Free Trader) Both Agreed on Free Trade in Corn', in Gary Cook (ed.) *The Economics and Politics of International Trade,* London: Routledge.

Reinert, E. and Daastøl, A. (1997) 'Exploring the Genesis of Economic Innovations: The Religious Gestalt-switch and the Duty to Invent as Preconditions for Economic Growth', *European Journal of Law and Economics,* vol. 4, No. 2/3.

Roscher, W. (1874) *Geschichte der National-Oekonomik in Deutschland,* Munich: Oldenbourg.

Schoenhof, J. (1892) *The Economy of High Wages. An Inquiry into the Cause of High Wages and their Effect on Methods and Costs of Production,* New York: Putnam's.

Schumpeter, J.A. (1954) *History of Economic Analysis,* New York: Oxford University Press.

Serra, A. (1613) *Breve trattato delle cause che possono far abbondare li regni d'oro e argento dove non sono miniere,* Naples: Lazzaro Scoriggio.

Smith, A. (1776/1976) *Wealth of Nations,* Chicago: University of Chicago Press.

Sombart, W. (1913a) *Krieg und Kapitalismus,* Munich and Leipzig: Duncker & Humblot.

Sombart, W. (1913b) *Luxus und Kapitalismus,* Munich and Leipzig: Duncker & Humblot.

Sombart, W. (1928) *Der Moderne Kapitalismus,* Munich and Leipzig: Duncker & Humblot.

Steuart, J. (1767) *An Inquiry into the Principles of Political Economy: being an Essay on the Science of Domestic Policy in Free Nations,* London: Millar and Cadell, 2 vols.

Viner, J. (1991) *Essays in the Intellectual History of Economics,* Princeton: Princeton University Press.

Walker, F.A. 'The Tide of Economic Thought', reprint from American Economic Association Publication. (Speech delivered in Washington DC, December 26 1890.)

Chapter Nine

KARL BÜCHER AND THE GEOGRAPHICAL DIMENSIONS OF TECHNO-ECONOMIC CHANGE: PRODUCTION-BASED ECONOMIC THEORY AND THE STAGES OF ECONOMIC DEVELOPMENT

Erik S. Reinert

'In every inquiry concerning the operations of men when united together in society, the first object of attention should be their mode of subsistence. Accordingly as that varies, their laws and policies must be different'
William Robertson (1721–1793), *The History of America, 1777*

1. The Idea of Stages — from Tacitus to Karl Bücher and Carlota Perez

History – it has been said – was created to prevent everything from happening simultaneously. History implies that events happen in sequence. Stage theories are attempts, based on different criteria, to organise history in sequential stages. In their most general form, stage theories postulate *that a key factor in the process of socio-economic development is the mode of subsistence,* i.e. what, how, and with which tools a society produces. Stage theories are tools that can be used to study both the qualitative changes in the division of labour over time, and the processes of institutional design and change which accompany these changes. Stage theories point towards areas where the focus of human learning is concentrated at any point in time, and as such they serve as a basis for a qualitative understanding of processes of techno-economic change and of income inequality. **[177]**

Theories of periods and stages have been used in most of the social sciences. In the history profession the material from which Man's tools were made (e.g. stone or bronze) has become universally accepted as the basis for establishing early historical periods: the Stone Age (Mesolithic, Neolithic), the Bronze Age. Other criteria could have been used, e.g. based on social organisation, but *the technology variable* was chosen. Not only in the history profession, but also in anthropology the idea that technology is an important determinant for society is an old one; the discussion of the relationship between irrigation and centralised government being a classical example. In political science, the idea of stages of Man's development is born – with Jean Bodin's (1530–1596) study of the

Republic – with the commencing of the science itself. If we define sociology as starting with Auguste Comte (1798–1857), the idea of stages was there from the very beginning of that science as well. In economics, theories of stages were central both to the important French economist and statesman Robert Jacques Turgot (1727–1781) and in the teachings of Adam Smith (1723–1790). In his book on the early stage theories from 1750 to 1800, Ronald Meek goes so far as to suggest that 'there was a certain sense…in which the great eighteenth-century systems of 'classical' political economy in fact *arose out* of the four stage theories.'[1] In spite of this, today any idea of economic stages is peripheral, almost alien, to the economics profession. In this paper we shall explore stage theories as they relate to economics, and discuss their usefulness from the point of view of understanding human welfare.

Incipient ideas of stage theories are found in antiquity, both in Greece and in Rome. One may read Tacitus' (55?– after 117 AD) *Germania* in such a way that 'the relative degree of civilisation of the different German tribes depended upon the extent to which agriculture and pasturage, rather than hunting, preponderated in their mode of subsistence'.[2] The idea of stages grew out of the idea of *cycles,* which in political history is an old one. Cycle theories are **[178]** given importance both by the influential Arab historian Ibn-Khaldun (1332–1406) and by Machiavelli (1469–1527). With Jean Bodin, one of the path breakers of the Renaissance, comes the idea that historical cycles may have a cumulative and upward trend: the idea *of progress.* With Bodin, the idea of *progressive stages* is born as a child of the optimistic spirit of the Renaissance. Bodin at the same time discusses the embryonic nation-state (the Republic), its institutions, laws and taxation.

Whereas Bodin puts much emphasis on geographical and climatic conditions, Francis Bacon (1561–1626), in his *Novum Organum* gives a different explanation when discussing the startling difference between the conditions of life in the various parts of the world. Bacon postulates that 'this difference comes not from soil, not from climate, not from race, but from the arts.'[3] Bacon is probably the true founder of what we shall label the *production-based and activity-specific theory of welfare.* As we shall see, his idea *that the material condition of a people is determined by its arts* – i.e. by the professions exercised – is central to the 19the Century German and North American conflict with England over economic theory and industrial policy.

During the Enlightenment, particularly between 1750 and 1800, stage theories were – so to say – at centre stage, particularly in England and France. During the expansion and geographical extension of industrial society from the 1840's onwards, stage theories again became part of the economists' toolbox – this time particularly in the US and in Germany. At the time, the fundamental changes which could be observed made it obvious that the world was entering a historical period that was *qualitatively different* from all previous ones.

---

1 Meek, Ronald, *Social Science and the Ignoble Savage,* Cambridge, Cambridge University Press, 1976, p. 219. Emphasis in original.

2 *Ibid.,*p 12.

3 *The Works of Francis Bacon,* quoted in Meek, *op. cit.* p. 13.

The stage theories born during the First Industrial Revolution – those of Turgot and of the early Adam Smith teaching in the 1750's – follow Man first as a hunter and gatherer, then as a shepherd of domesticated animals, then as a farmer, finally to reach the stage of *commerce*. Most significantly, English classical economists tended from the late 18th Century on to concentrate their analysis on the last stage of evolution, on *commerce* – on supply and demand and on **[179]** prices – rather than on *production*. During the 19th Century, German and US economists insisted on a very different interpretation of the development stages. To them the previous stages were all built on ways *of producing* goods, and they saw it as a grave mistake to classify the next stage of development in terms of *commerce* rather than in terms of *production*. This theoretical difference of opinion essentially laid the foundation for how 19th Century German and US economic policy came to differ from that prescribed by English theory:

English Stage Theories (18th Cent.)	*German/US Stage Theories (19th Century)*
(Adam Smith)	(Friedrich List/Richard Ely)
1. Age of Hunters	1. Age of Hunting
2. Age of Shepherds	2. Age of Pasturage
3. Age of Agriculture	3. Age of Agriculture
4. Age of *Commerce*	4. Age of Agriculture and Manufacturing

This kind of stage theories is useful also in order to understand the important issues of population and sustainable development. The pre-Columbian population of North America – consisting essentially of hunters and gatherers – has been estimated at 1–2 million people, whereas the pre-Columbian population of the Andes, having reached the agricultural stage, has been calculated at 12 Million. This gives a population density 30–60 times higher in the apparently inhospitable Andes than on the fertile prairies. The concept of sustainability is not very meaningful until the technology variable is introduced.

Because the focus of analysis was to be trade and commerce, and not production, English and, later, neo-classical economic theory slowly came to see all economic activities as being *qualitatively alike*. Theories of production which were later added into this Anglo-Saxon tradition of economics – today's standard theory – essentially came to regard production as a process of adding capital to labour in a rather mechanical way, similar to that of adding water to genetically identical plants growing under identical conditions. In this theoretical **[180]** tradition no considerations are made as to how the availability of technology varies the potential which different activities – at any point in time – present in terms of adding capital to labour in a potentially profitable way. The standard economics tradition also came to disregard completely the 'soil' in which the process of adding water to the plant (capital to labour) took place, i.e. the historical, political and institutional context of the process of development. Standard economic theory considers neither the obvious focusing of technical change at any point in time, nor the extreme variation in 'windows of opportunity' between different economic activities which is the result of this focusing effect, nor the context in which this process takes place. In our view this blind spot of conventional economic theory is a major cause of our failure to come to grips with the extremely inequitable distribution of income on a world scale.

Classical, neo-classical and today's standard economics all stand in sharp contrast to the German/US tradition – which lasted until and including the theories of Simon Kuznets (1901–1985) – in which economic growth is seen as *activity specific*, i.e. the potential to create wealth varies enormously between economic activities. In this setting, stage theories serve as a focusing devise which singles out the area of human activity where learning was focused at any point in time, pointing at where the frontier of human learning is located.

In 1949 Paul Samuelson – using the standard assumptions of neoclassical economic theory – showed that international trade would lead to an equalisation of wages all over the world (factor-prize equalisation). In the alternative German/US production-based tradition, the equalisation of wages between a society solely specialised in herding animals – in pasturage – trading with one specialised in advanced industrial production is an absurd proposition. *Because the core of its theory was based on barter rather than production,* neo-classical economics created a *Harmonielehre,* where free trade automatically creates the equalisation of wages throughout the world economy, regardless of the economic activity in which the nation specialises. In our opinion it is difficult to overestimate the fundamental importance of the late 17th Century schism in economic theory which was created by the two different interpretations of the next stage in Man's evolution. Whether one saw this next stage as the *Age* **[181]** *of Commerce* — thus creating barter-based theory – or as the *Age of Agriculture and Manufacturing* — creating a production-based theory -result in completely different *Weltanschauungen* and in completely different ideas on what causes economic development and welfare.

Francis Bacon was essentially right: the choice of profession still determines the way of life more than do geography, climate, race or religion. A Tanzanian agricultural economist residing in Norway recently told me that he found many similarities between Tanzanian tribes who base their subsistence on herding animals and Norwegian Lapps whose subsistence base is herding reindeer. A stockbroker in Lima, Peru will have a lifestyle that has much more in common with a stockbroker in New York than with a Peruvian who makes his living cutting sugar cane. This *activity-specific* aspect of economic life has, however, been completely lost in today's economic theory. Today's world economic order essentially functions on the assumption that in a world of free trade, a nation of cane cutters will be as wealthy as a nation of stockbrokers. As already indicated, we feel that the loss of Bacon's insight accounts for our inability to understand the unequal distribution of wealth on a world scale. In other words, our incomplete understanding of production is at the core of our inability to understand income inequalities.

Stage theories are 'ideal types' in a Weberian sense. In Kaldor's terminology each stage would constitute a cluster of 'stylised facts' about one particular type of society. Fixed points of transition between stages are, of course, not easily established. Points of transition between childhood, adult life and old age are equally difficult to establish, but few would argue that this problem makes 'childhood' and 'old age' useless concepts. Stage theories are not iron laws, and there are no automatic mechanisms that carry nations from one stage to the next. During the 19th and early 20th century both conservatives and Marxists saw the spread of industrial society across the globe as an inevitable process. The last 50 years have taught us otherwise. Not only is there no automatic upgrading and promotion in the system, the possibilities of being downgraded, of 'falling behind', are definitely present. There are also instances when the historical sequence is different: before having tamed animals, American Indian women of some tribes were growing a few plants of corn around their dwellings. Keeping all the limitations of stage theories in mind, they constitute an instrument which deserves being put back into the tool-shed of economic theory.

Understanding the qualitative differences between economic stages – the relationship between technology and wealth – is a prerequisite for understanding, designing and implementing appropriate institutions and mechanisms for income distribution in a society. This point is emphasised by Schumpeter, who sees stage theories as 'a simple explanatory device for impressing upon beginners (or the public) the lesson that economic policy has to do with changing economic structures and therefore cannot consist of a set of unchanging recipes.'[4] Schumpeter is otherwise not very positive to the use of stage theories, perhaps because for a long time the very idea of stages and 'modes of production' was associated exclusively with Marxist economics.

Today the world economy is in a transition from a society based on Fordist mass production to a society where information technology sets the standard on which a new organisational common sense is being created. With their concept of techno-economic paradigms Carlota Perez and Christopher Freeman offer us an analysis within what List and Ely would call the manufacturing stage. Alternatively, it may be argued that the incipient information society with its dematerialisation of consumption represents a brand new fifth stage in the history of mankind. Karl Bücher treated the geographical dimension of this transition – globalisation – in his 1893 book *Die Entstehung der Volkswirtschaft*.

2. Stages, Postmodernity, and Harmony in Economic Theory

Profound changes in the structure of society seem, then, to create a demand for broader perspectives, for a qualitative and dynamic understanding of 'the bigger issues'. In the history profession, the present paradigm shift has again recently awoken interest in 'global history'. Although the idea of global history is easy to dismiss from **[183]** the depths of archival studies, long term history has a professional tradition in history dating back to the Renaissance and is still seen as compatible with the tools that historians use. During the 19th Century process of industrialisation, also in the economics profession

---

[4] Schumpeter, Joseph Alois, *History of Economic Analyisis,* New York, Oxford University Press, 1954, p. 442.

theories of economic stages *(Wirtschaftsstufen)* were seen as 'an indispensable part of the tool box of economics'.[5]

From the standpoint of today's standard theory, however, stage theories bring together three key aspects which were the most important casualties of the neo-classical process of formalising economic theory, i.e. the three conspicuously absent factors: *time, space* (geography) and *human knowledge.* In today's economics there is no longer such a compatibility with stage theories as can be found in the history profession. Standard economic theory is fundamentally quantitative, static and unhistorical, and the historical school of economics – which had produced the 19th Century stage theories – virtually died out with the 1950's. In the first section of this paper we have already pointed to a most important watershed in economic theory: how and when the English classical school – by no longer defining stages according to *production* – separates itself from previous economic tradition and from 19th Century US and German economic theory and policy. We would claim that this schism is of great importance in order to understand the economics of 'leader' and 'laggard' nations to this very day.

Stage theories are typically not products of Anglo-Saxon economics. They are all children of a dynamic and holistic, all-inclusive view of economics as involving all social sciences. Stage theories are dynamic and *modernist* in the sense that the Renaissance philosophers, like Francis Bacon in England and Leibniz in Germany, were modernists. A stage theory in the neo-classical tradition of Paul Samuelson and Milton Friedman would be a contradiction in terms, **[184]** because theirs is a theory void not only of time (and consequently of any historical sequence), but also of empirical facts.[6]

As opposed to *modernist* dynamism and its resulting 'stages' -cumulative, progressive, retrogressive or cyclical – neo-classical economics, containing no learning and no novelty, has clear *postmodernist* qualities[7]. Neo-classical economics with its innumerous equilibrium points takes on a quality of indeterminacy, of 'undicidability' which is seen as typical also of postmodernist poetry; of Gertrude Stein and Ezra Pound.[8] Like postmodernist poetry, the neo-classical world view seems to describe a world where 'innovation no longer seems possible, or 'even desirable'.[9] When their extreme static generalisations and determinacy – like factor-price equalisation – are queried, today's standard economists tend to retreat to the opposite standpoint, to the extreme unpredictability of theories of complexity and chaos theory. From the safe haven of a theory predicting and proving automatic universal harmony in the equalisation of factor

---

[5] 'Die Aufstellung solche "Wirtschaftsstufen" gehört zu den unentbehrlichen methodischen Hilfsmitteln', Karl Bücher, *Die Entstehung der Volkswirtschaft,* 11th edition, Tübingen, Laupp, 1919, p 87.

[6] It could be argued that diminishing returns is the only piece of historical evidence in neo-classical theory.

[7] I am indebted to Wolfgang Drechsler for the idea of connecting neoclassical economic theory with postmodernism.

[8] For a discussion of postmodernism and indeterminacy, see Hoover, Paul (Editor), *Postmodern American Poetry,* New York, Norton,1994, p. xxxix.

[9] Art critic Suzi Gablik, quoted in Hoover, *op. cit.,* p. xxxix.

prices – a 'Harmonielehre' as Lionel Robbins so fittingly calls it[10] – standard economic theory retreats to the opposite extreme, to a model with a complete lack of predictability. In other words, modern economics tends to treat all economic activities as either being qualitatively *all alike* or *all different*. The intermediate levels of abstraction – where 'some economic activities are more equal than others'[11] – offer clues to understanding world income distribution, is conspicuously absent. **[185]**

Today's equivalent of the 'invisible hand' is that 'the economy is like the weather', or like hurricanes and earthquakes.[12] These two types of metaphors are in a sense opposites – the automatic harmony and predictability created by the 'invisible hand' on the one hand and the chaotic complex diversity created by the weather on the other. What is interesting from the point of view of economic policy is that these counterpart metaphors lead to the same policy conclusions: in both cases Man is at the mercy of some uncontrollable force. Both in the case of the invisible hand and of hurricanes and earthquakes, human will, skills, knowledge, intuition and leadership can do preciously little to change the course of history. Adam Smith's invisible hand and Paul Krugman's metaphor about the economy being like the weather at their very core share the role of man as a passive being in the hands of 'Providence', as is discussed in Jacob Viner's interesting book on this subject.[13]

In contrast to this strategy, where a passive Man is at the mercy of external forces – be they invisible hands or the forces of the weather – stand the stage theories, where history is 'the result of human action, but not the execution of any human design.'[14] The contrast with Krugman, when he describes the great depression, is clear: '…most booms and slumps have had no obvious external cause. Most notably, the mother of all economic slumps, the contraction from 1929 to 1933, came as it were out of a clear blue sky. But then, so do hurricanes'. Krugman's alternative metaphor, if there is no such thing as a 'typical recession', is that 'recessions are more like earthquakes than like hurricanes.'[15] Its seems that Krugman considers economic slumps to be outside the influence of human beings, just like hurricanes or earthquakes. Just like with Adam Smith's invisible **[186]** hand, Mankind is again in Krugman's world view at the mercy of a pre-Renaissance type of 'Providence' or 'Faith'.

The idea that neoclassical economics is postmodernist is not new. According to McCloskey, Friedman's 1953 essay 'was more postmodernist than one might suppose from slight acquaintance with the text'[16], or, as another author puts it: 'Postmodernism

10 Robbins, Lionel, *The Theory of Economic Policy in English Classical Economics*, London, Macmillan, 1952, pp. 22–29.

11 With apologies to George Orwell.

12 Krugman, Paul, *The Self-Organizing Economy,* Cambridge, Mass, Blackwell, 1996.

13 For a discussion of this intellectual tradition, see Viner, Jacob, *The Role of Providence in the Social Order,* Philadelphia, American Philosophical Society, 1972.

14 Adam Fergusson (1793), quoted in Meek, op. cit. This is close to the idea of history previously expressed by Neapolitan philosopher Giambattista Vico (1668–1744).

15 Krugman, *op. cit.,* p. 5.

16 McCloskey, D., *The Rhetoric of Economics,* Madison, University of Wisconsin Press, 1985, p. 9.

is immanent in modern economics'.[17] Postmodernism and standard economics indeed seem to meet in their quality of static 'undicidability' – in contrast with the cumulative dynamics of the historical school of economics. Krugman's latest books are now making economics into *dynamic* undicidability. The contrast between this 'postmodernist' standard economics of today and the 'modernist' historical school can be traced back through the centuries to their very origins; to the Renaissance and the Enlightenment respectively.[18] Standard economic theory is a product of the mechanical and quantifiable *Weltanschauung* of the *Enlightenment,* where aporia (indecision) is a result of a rationality which, in the absence of novelty, 'will eventually enslave us to rules'[19]. Stage theories, on the other hand, are products of the *Renaissance* where new ideas, knowledge and leadership move history along, building and unbuilding structures and stages in a Schumpeterian process of creative destruction.

Stage theories are typical products of German economic theory[20], of a type of theory which Werner Sombart (Sombart 1929) calls *verstehende,* as opposed to *ordnende* economic theory, of what Nelson and Winter (Nelson & Winter 1982) call *appreciative economics.* **[187]** These theories exerted their influence in Germany, but also in the United States in the period when US economics was heavily influenced by German economics, a period which ended after WWII. Stage theories are framed in an attitude of *Zuerst war die Ganzheit:* in the beginning there was 'the whole', from a time where reality still was interpreted as obviously being interdisciplinary, from before Man started fragmenting his approach to the world around him into different professions with scant communication between them. In this holistic approach to economics, whatever seems relevant -regardless of what academic tribe a particular fact narrowly belongs to – is part of that profession. If, for example, it seems that nutrition in a particular time and place seems important for economic development, then the relevant part of nutritional theory is most obviously a part of economics. As is readily admitted by philosophers of economics today, this type of qualitative understanding has been lost in post-WW II economics: 'Scientism has damaged the ability to understand'.[21]

The stage theories – as well as traditional German economics in general – also internalise what Alfred Chandler[22] put on the map of business economics in 1990: scale and scope. Stage theories are fundamentally theories of non-equilibrium economics. They

---

17 Wendt, Paul, Comment on Amariglio's 'Economics as a Postmodern Discourse', quoted in McCloskey, D., *Knowledge and Persuasion in Economics,* Cambridge, Cambridge University Press, 1994, p. 72.

18 For a more general discussion of these issues, see Reinert, Erik, and Arno Daastøl, 'Exploring the Genesis of Economic Innovations: the religious gestalt-switch and the duty to invent as preconditions for economic growth,' in *European Journal of Law and Economics,* Vol. 4, June 1997, pp. 233–283.

19 McCloskey, D., *ibid,* p. 72.

20 For an overview of German stage theories, see Kalveram, Gertrud, *Die Theorien von den Wirtschaftsstufen,* Leipzig, Hans Buske, 1933.

21 McCloskey, D., *ibid.,* p. 50.

22 Chandler, Alfred, *Scale and Scope. The Dynamics of Industrial Capitalism,* Cambridge, Mass. Harvard University Press, 1990.

are fundamentally histories of various aspects of the cumulative growth of human knowledge – of novelty – and its impact on *division of labour and its impact on scale, scope and geography* of economies over time.

It would probably be correct to say that stage theories are all *economic interpretations of history,* although they may not all be *materialistic interpretations of history* in the Marxian sense. Edwin Seligman, the American social scientist, defined the economic interpretation of history as follows: 'We understand, then, by the theory of the economic interpretation of history, not that all history is to be explained in economic terms alone, but that the chief considerations in human progress are the social considerations, and that the important factor in the social change is the economic factor. The economic **[188]** interpretation of history means, not that the economic relations exert an exclusive influence, but that they exert a preponderant influence in shaping the progress of society.'[23] Marx and Engels focused on one particular aspect of the economic stages, on the conflict between social classes. As we shall see, this is only one of many aspects of which stage theories lend themselves to analysis.

We personally tend to look at both the economics profession and political development in general as having been stuck now during more than 100 years in an unrelenting fight between what with time no doubt will be seen as two very strange and unproductive theoretical angles. One set of theories, what we call today's 'standard theory', which, because it was fundamentally based on barter, created a static Harmonielehre – *a theory of automatic social and economic harmony.* In this theoretical model all economic activities are alike and all wage earners of the world will be equally wealthy. The other set of theories – the Marxist ones – focused on one particular aspect of the economic stages, on the fight between the social classes, and on a perceived inherent *impossibility of social and economic harmony,* except in a hypothetical stage following the dictatorship of the proletariat. During the 19th Century a third set of economic theories claimed that it was not primarily the economic system that causes social injustice, but rather the extra-economic, political and social factors that intervene in all economic processes. Existing property relationships, and the consequent class struggles, were seen to be the result of historical-political development, not an automatic outcome of the mode of production itself. *Social and economic harmony could be created* under any mode of production, but this required conscious design of economic institutions, of trade policy and of elaborate mechanisms of income distribution. Main theorists in this third, now defunct, type of economic theory were Henry Carey in the United States and Friedrich List and Eugen Dühring in Germany. Their view corresponds today to Carlota Perez' interpretation of the social challenges as the world economy moves away from the Fordist mass-**[189]**production stage of economic development and into a new stage based on information technology.[24]

---

[23] Seligman, Edwin, 'The Economic Interpretation of History', in *Political Science Quarterly,* Vol. XVII, 1902, p. 76, quoted in Ely, Richard, *Evolution of Industrial Society,* New York, The Chautauqua Press, 1903, p 25–26.

[24] Perez, Carlota, 'The Social and Political Challenge of the Present Paradigm Shift', in Reinert, Erik (Ed.), *Evolutionary Economics and Income Inequality,* Aldershot, Edward Elgar, 2000.

The alternative 19th Century economic theories – the 'Third Way' – which refused both English classical, Anglo-Saxon neo-classical economics, and Marxism became in very short supply during the cold war period following World War II. As often happens, the moderate reformers are the first casualties in a conflict – they are being shot at from both sides. Engels' *Anti-Dühring* is one such vehement attack on a set of theories that aimed at making capitalism a just and equitable society. Eugen Dühring, who was most sympathetic to the aims of Marx and Engels, but not to their methods, was perceived as their most dangerous enemy. Alternative 'Third Way' theories continued to live on in the pragmatic economic policies of social democracy, but the economic *theory* of social democracy most unfortunately became neo-classical economics. This made it virtually impossible to export practically functioning social democracy to the Third World -the theories which were at the roots of the political 'Third Way' had been unlearned by the economics profession.

3. *Anthropocentric Economics:* Man and his Needs *as the core of Economics*

Karl Bücher's book *Die Entstehung der Volkswirtschaft* addresses the geographical dimension of economic stages. *Die Entstehung* is a collection of essays around this same subject, and was first published in 1893. In his memoirs Bücher makes it clear that his preference was not for large texts, but rather for small essays. His publisher started typesetting his books long before the author had finished writing, and Bücher tells us that he worked best when the typesetter was just catching up on his writing. 'Not even half of the works I have published in my lifetime', he says in his memoirs, 'would have existed if my publisher had demanded that all the text be finished **[190]** before he started typesetting.'[25] Historians of literature similarly point to the fact that his publisher, who needed to get the books out, paced Henrik Ibsen's production to an important degree.

Chapter 3 of *Die Entstehung,* which is the core chapter presenting the stage theory, goes back to a lecture by Bücher at the University of Basel in 1885 (p. V). The book appeared in one volume in 10 printings, being reprinted in 1897, 1900, 1904, 1906, 1908, 1909, 1911, 1913, and 1917. A second volume of essays was added with the 11th printing in 1918, both volumes carrying the same title. This second volume, coinciding with the end of WW I, seems to have renewed the interest in the first volume, because both the 12th and 13th edition of the first volume were published in the first six months of 1919.[26] There is a US edition in English – *Industrial Evolution* – published in New York in 1901, and a Canadian edition published in Toronto in 1904 (Entitled *Industrial Society*).

---

[25] *Lebenserinnerungen,* Tübingen, Laupp, 1919, p. 199. (Title reads *Erster Band, 1847–1890,* but this is apparently the only volume to have been published).

[26] The latter information can be found in the advertising pages, following page 462, in Bücher's Memoirs, *Lebenserinnerungen,* Tübingen, Laupp, 1919.

Bücher's *Die Entstehung der Volkswirtschaft* (*The Genesis (*or *Formation) of the National Economy*) is, in its core aspects, a classical book written in the German tradition. On fundamental points this book is in strong conflict with the world view represented by today's standard Anglo-Saxon economics, the brand of economics which completely dominates in 'the global village' of today. While public opinion today is increasingly worried about maintaining the biological diversity of the planet – opposing cloning – few seem to care about the lack of diversity in approaches to economics. In their core assumptions about what their profession is all about, virtually all of today's living economists are cloned in a mode of thinking which is fundamentally different from that of Karl Bücher and the production-based tradition. We shall here briefly contrast Bücher's conception of economics with that of today's barter-based economics.

First of all, the very title of the book – The Genesis of the National Economy – is an affront to English economics at the time **[191]** (and even today, as in Margaret Thatcher's phrase 'There is no such thing as society.') In German economics, the Volkswirtschaft – the National Economy – is a fundamental unit of analysis, while, as Friedrich List pointed out, English economics is *cosmo*political economics. The factors which cause the nation state to be of any importance tend to be assumed away in English economic theory as well as later in neo-classical and in today's standard theories. The core assumptions of Anglo-Saxon economics create – in Lionel Robbins' felicitous term – an automatic *Harmonielehre* between all players, be it states or individuals. One basic mechanism creating a social harmony in neo-classical theory, is the fact that neo-classical economics made all economic activities qualitatively alike as carriers of economic development. This is what Buchanan calls *the equality assumption,* without which mainstream economics would lose its analytical power. Like all stage theories, Bücher's theory functions at a different, and lower, level of abstraction. Bücher is *praxisnah* – near to reality. He scorns what he sees as 'die verschimmelte Schulweisheiten' – the mouldy school truths – of theoretical economics.[27]

Secondly – as is so often pointed out by German economists up until W II – English economics was fundamentally a theory of *barter,* and not of *production.*[28] Very early in his *Wealth of Nations* Adam Smith defines 'his propensity to barter' as the main difference between Man and other animals.[29] Bücher goes very clearly against Smith on this: 'Primitive Man, rather than having an innate propensity to barter, has – to the contrary – a propensity against bartering. (Eine Abneigung). In the old language, Bücher says, the verbs for *barter* (tauschen) and *cheat* (täuschen) are the same. There is plenty of evidence to support the idea that trading was an occupation of very low prestige in many ancient cultures. On discovering that his wife owned a ship trading grain, one Byzantine emperor had the whole ship and its cargo burned in order to distance himself as much as possible from such 'vulgar' activities.[30] We can assume that since no standard method

---

[27] *Lebenserinnerungen,* p. 197.

[28] Bücher says to this: 'Die englische Nationalökonomie ist darum im wesentlichen Verkehrstheorie.', *Die Entstehung,* p. 89.

[29] On p. 17 in the 1976 Chicago edition.

[30] This story is told in Nicol, Donald M., *Venezia e Bisanzio,* Milan, Rusconi, 1990.

for measuring value existed, early bartering carried with it a high risk of being cheated. Anthropological research into processes of barter points at stable value relationships existing over long periods of time; e.g. 'a sheep for a sack of potatoes'. Bücher mentions, however, von Thünen as a German economist who in his *Isolierte Staat* starts from the assumption of a barter economy.[31] This could account for the fact that von Thünen – out of a huge number of German economists who wrote on economics and geography – is the only German economist which is quoted in Paul Krugman's papers on economics and geography.

To Adam Smith, then, *'in the beginning there were barter and markets'*, to Karl Bücher *'in the beginning there were production and social relations'*. To Bücher – as well as later to Karl Polanyi[32] who was inspired by him – during the early stages of civilisation the processes of production and consumption are so intertwined that the concept of barter makes no sense. As already mentioned, we consider the neglect of production – combined with *the equality assumption* discussed above – to be the main reason why Anglo-Saxon economics produces theories of harmony, like Samuelson's factor-price equalisation. Standard economic theory ignores a) the difference between production processes in their ability to absorb new knowledge and b) the historical increasing returns which are created by this new knowledge, producing a 'national rent' to economies engaged in the economic activities which carry the new economic stage or paradigm.

Thirdly, Bücher squarely places himself in the German tradition since Christian Wolff, in which *Man and his Needs* (Der Mensch und seine Bedürfnisse) are at the core of economic theory. This contrasts with English theory which came to be built around a utility maximising Homo Economicus. Bücher's definition of *Volkswirtschaft,* which includes also all institutional aspects of economic life, shows this **[193]** clearly: 'Die Gesamtheit der Veranstaltungen, Einrichtungen und Vorgänge, welche die Bedürfnisbefriedigung eines ganzen Volkes hervorruft, bildet die Volkswirtschaft[33], which I would attempt, not quite literally, to translate as 'The totality of institutions, measures and processes which are called upon to satisfy the needs of a nation form the National Economy.' It is evident that both policy and law – founded in national institutions, measures, and processes – are at the core of the National Economy in Bücher's system. The recent concept of a National Innovation System would then fit neatly into Bücher's conception of a Volkswirtschaft.

This third contrast is why we call classical German economics *anthropocentric* economics, rather than the *barter- and capital-centred* English political economy. In the Anglo-Saxon tradition Man is generally reduced to being a factor of production – an input. In the German tradition meeting the needs of this factor of production was the whole object of the exercise of economics, whereas in Anglo-Saxon tradition the reward to Man the factor of production is not an issue at all.

---

[31] *Die Entstehung,* p. 90.

[32] Polanyi, Karl, *The Great Transformation,* New York, Rinehart & Co., 1944.

[33] P. 85, all references to pages alone are to the 11th Edition of *Die Entstehung.*

4. Stage Theories and Economic Development: An Overview

4.1 Early Theories – from Cycles to Stages

When trying to put order in the concept of time, the idea of ordering history chronologically obviously suggests itself. A system of ordering periods according to the rulers of the reign also seems a 'natural' system. The idea that human history alternatively may be divided into *qualitatively different periods* or *stages* has been with us since the Bible. Mankind's first stage, Paradise, gives way to a period when Man shall only eat his bread 'in the sweat of his face' (*Genesis* 3, 19). In this first 'stage theory' there is no natural improvement from one stage to the next, there is indeed a qualitative retrogression. Only towards the end of his stay on Earth may Mankind again aspire to **[194]** repossess the qualities which he was forced to leave behind in the first stage.

As we have already mentioned, the idea of dividing human history into qualitatively different stages was essentially born with the idea of progress itself, with the Renaissance. The idea of the Renaissance – Rebirth – was itself a consequence of an acute awareness of retrogression: Mankind, compared to previous achievements, had 'fallen behind', but could 'forge ahead' if a social system encouraging and ordering Man's creativity could be created. Jean Bodin (1530–1596), French, and Hugo Grotius (1583–1645), Dutch – both lawyers – share a historical view emphasising changing division of labour in different historical periods.[34] The first division of labour, as Bücher would point out, was that inside the household, between husbandry and what was for a long time called housewifery. The very name 'economies', of course, comes from a Greek word describing this 'household management'. The idea of a further division of labour is found in Plato's *Republic* and *Laws* and, less spelt out, in Aristotle's *Ideal City*.[35] To Grotius the first division is between agriculture and husbandry: 'Hierbey ging bereits eine Art Theilung vor.'[36]

Stage theories of history differ from their predecessors – cyclical theories of history – in that they offer continuous improvement as a possibility, but not as a necessary outcome. In all stage theories it is understood that different areas of the world will normally be at different stages, and some of them specify the possibility for retrogression.

The 14th Century is considered a 'dark' age in most of Europe, except for an early Renaissance blooming in Sienna. This century produced a prolific Muslim historian and philosopher, Ibn-Khaldun (1332–1406, called Abenjaldún in the Spanish literature). Born in Tunis, and serving various of the potentates who divided Moslem North Africa and Spain between them, Ibn-Khaldun served as a professor of law and a judge in Cairo. Based on the studies of the Arab peoples, he emphasises the distinction between nomads and town dwellers, but – typically of pre-Renaissance thought – he saw history developing in cycles, advancing only to later fall back to the previous stage.

---

[34] For a discussion of this, see Kuczynski, Jürgen, *Studien zu einer Geschichte der Gesellschaftswissenschaften*, Berlin, Akademie-Verlag, 1978, Vol. 8, pp. 69–71.

[35] The relevant original texts are found in M. L. W. Laistner's translation in his *Greek Economics*, London, Dent, 1923. (The Library of Greek Thought).

[36] Quoted in Kuczynski (1978), p. 71.

Ibn-Khaldun describes the nomadic tribes of the desert, organised in clans originating in blood relationships. The entry on him in the Encyclopaedia of Social Sciences further describes the cycle of human societies as follows: 'The need for justice in the clan causes leaders to arise, and when the groups become sufficiently numerous, they migrate to fertile lands and ultimately change into town dwellers or subdue already existing town communities, adopting the previously established civilisation. The town dwellers become luxurious and lose their capacity for self-defence. The rulers, as their wants increase, must resort to constantly increasing taxation; and resenting the claims of their clansmen to equality with themselves they rely for aid on foreign supporters, who become necessary moreover because of the decline of clansmen as warriors. Thus the state grows decrepit and becomes the pray of a fresh group of nomads, who undergo the same experience.'[37]

Ibn-Khaldun fixes the duration of the cycle of human societies to 120 years, or 4 generations of 30 years. In the 14th Century Ibn-Khaldun describes societal retrogression based on a mechanism similar to the one described by Michael Porter in his 1990 book 'The Competitive Advantage of Nations'. Porter's cycle of retrogression is described below. The Perez-Freeman framework of techno-economic paradigms also expressly includes the possibility that a paradigm shift not only opens windows of opportunity for improvement, but also opens 'a back door' which let some nations to fall behind. In today's process of globalisation, the possibilities of retrogression merit, in our view, a much closer scrutiny.

Pre-Renaissance Europe was acutely aware of the historical cycles of violence that would operate. During the Renaissance, therefore, an important argument was that economic growth was a way of channelling Man's energy away from warfare and destruction and into **[196]** wealth creation.[38] Created in the image of God, it was Man's pleasurable duty to invent, to continue the creation that the Lord had initiated.[39] Today's Africa reminds us of the possibility of retrogression: we observe genocides of shattering cruelty, the collapse of nation-states and 'Somalisation' of nations into fiefdoms run by warlords. In a way we are reinventing 'private colonialism', with today's mining companies operating in ways similarly to Sir Walter Raleigh during the times of Elizabeth I.

Underlying all stage theories is a more or less well-expressed tendency towards an ever-increasing division of labour. Within this framework, the stage theories focus on different aspects, which we shall discuss in detail later. Friedrich List focused on the type of production, Karl Bücher on the geographical dimension, Karl Marx on the social conflicts, Bruno Hildebrand on a trend towards a more abstract system of payments, and Carlota Perez and Christopher Freeman today focus on the technological aspects.

---

37 Margoliouth, David S., in *The Encyclopaedia of Social Sciences,* Vol. 7, New York, Macmillan, 1932, p. 564–565.

38 This is excellently argued by Hirschman, Albert O. *The Passions and the Interests. Political Arguments for Capitalism before Its Triumph,* Princeton N. J., Princeton University Press, 1977.

39 Reinert, Erik S. & Arno Daastøl (1997) 'Exploring the Genesis of Economic Innovations: The Religious Gestalt-Switch and the Duty to Invent as Preconditions for Economic Growth', in *European Journal of Law and Economics,* Vol. 4, Nr. 2/3, s. 233–283.

As Richard Ely[40] (1903) and Franz Oppenheimer[41] (1927) points out, these approaches are highly complementary and correlated; they focus on different aspects of the same process of development or 'modernisation'.

Stage theories, then, are theories chartering the *degree of division of labour* over time. Until the fall of Fordism it is probably fair to say that this degree of division of labour was accompanied by ever-increasing scale of production in ever-larger units of production. Post-Fordism opens up a potential for increasing returns in very small niches, thereby simultaneously reducing the scale of operations and increasing variety through flexible specialisation. However, if our unit of analysis is division of labour – not scale – post-Fordism **[197]** continues the trend from the ancient household economy until today.

By tracing the degree of division of labour as human knowledge advances, stage theories also trace the *minimum efficient size* of human societies, from the household economy, via town economies and national economies, to the global economies. The division of labour – although it is probably the most celebrated of all Adam Smith's concepts – find no place whether in classical nor neo-classical economics. As we shall discuss later, we have today no theory of the division of labour. In our view, this is because the division of labour is essentially a tool of production-based economics, of mercantilism. As early as in 1613 Antonio Serra[42] used the division of labour in order to divide activities into those subject to increasing returns -which caused wealth – and other activities, which kept states in poverty. To Serra increasing returns and a high degree of division of labour were both at the basis of the synergy which mercantilist economists called *The Common Weal* (Das Gemeinwohl, il bene comune).

The division of labour is fundamentally based on the existence of fixed costs – either in tools or in human knowledge – which create synergies. Mercantilists would all the time refer to economic policies, e.g. the establishment of factories, which was done to 'promote the common weal'. The increase in the common weal was, in our view, caused by increasing returns from an ever-larger division of labour driven to a large extent by mechanisation. The assumption of constant returns to scale – which in practice denies the existence of fixed costs – is at the core of the individualist Anglo-Saxon approach to economics. The inclusion of the division of labour *and also its consequences* causes German economics to naturally include society as well as the individual in economic theory.

To Bücher, stage theories are 'the only way that economic theory may make use of the research of economic history'. But, these stages of development must not be confused with the periods in which the historian divides his material. The historian must not in any period **[198]** forget any important aspects of the period he studies, whereas the stages of the theoretician only has to cover what was normal, and confidently leave out what was confidential.' In these aspects it seems to me that Bücher's stages have a lot in common with Perez' and Freeman's techno-economic paradigms. Bücher also mentions what Perez and Freeman calls paradigm shifts as 'the so called periods of transition (*Übergangsperioden*) when everything is in flux (wenn alle Erscheinungen sich im Flusse befinden).'

---

40 Ely, *op. cit.*

41 Oppenheimer, Franz, *System der Soziologie*, Vol. 3, Tome 1, 5th edition, Jena, Gustav Fischer, 1923.

42 Serra, Antonio, Breve trattato delle cause che possono far abbondare li regni d'oro e argento dove non sono miniere, Napoli, Lazzaro Scoriggio, 1613.

4.2 Friedrich List and Bruno Hildebrand – the First Modern Stage Theories (1840's)

Bücher himself lists two alternative stage theories, those of List and Hildebrand.[43] The first stage theory in German economics was that of Friedrich List, who, as already mentioned in the introduction, divides history in the following stages 1. The hunting period, 2. The pastoral period, 3. The farming period, 4. The agricultural-manufacturing period and 5. The agricultural-manufacturing-trading period. Another similar early stage theory was that of Carl Rodbertus-Jagetow.[44]

Bruno Hildebrand – an economist held in high esteem by Bücher[45] – in his theory uses the *mode of exchange* as his criterion for the establishment of stages. His stages are: natural economy, money economy, and credit economy.[46] The theory as such was published in **[199]** 1864, but the fundamental ideas are already in Hildebrand's 1848 book 'Die Nationalökonomie der Gegenwart und Zukunft'. The date 1848 puts his theory into the right perspective; it was a contribution to address the social problems of the day. Whereas Engels tries to destroy the bourgeoisie, Hildebrand wants to make *Bürger* out of the workers. In this sense his agenda is very similar to that of Dühring some years later, who also sees the de-proletarisation (*Entproletarisierung*) of the workers as the only solution to the social problems of the day.

Hildebrand sees the natural economy as a system that keeps Man to the cultivation of the soil. The creation of a money economy was a necessary condition for a division of labour, and consequently for the market economy which freed Man from toiling the ground. This development would not have been possible if money had not been available as a way to store value (*ein aufbewahrungsfähiges Gut*) and as a common denominator of value. To Hildebrand, the modes of exchange (*die Umsatzformen*) are the fundamental powers which enables economy, society and culture to change. The money economy allowed for improvements, but in the long run the advantages of the money economy developed into disadvantages. The worker, freed from the land, became vulnerable in the ensuing competition in an atomistic society in which the ties of family and kinship that kept people together tended to break up. To Hildebrand the credit economy would solve this problem by re-establishing trust and human interaction in qualitatively better relationships in the processes of exchange and investment.

---

43 *Entstehung*, p. 88.

44 For a discussion of early 19th Century German stage theories, see Sommer, Artur: 'Über Inhalt, Rahmen und Sinn älterer Stufentheorien (List und Hildebrand), in Salin, Edgar (Editor), *Synopsis. Festgabe für Alfred Weber*, Heidelberg, Lambert Schneider, (1948), pp. 534–565.

45 He makes this clear in the *Erinnerungen*.

46 Hildebrand's two articles on stage theory – 'Natural-, Geld- und Kreditwirtschaft' and 'Die Entwicklungsstufen der Geldwirtschaft' – appeared in *Jahrbücher für Nationalökonomie und Statistik*, Vol. II, 1864, pages 1–24 and in Vol. XXVI, 1876, p. 15–26, respectively. Both articles are reprinted in Gehrig, Hans (Ed.), *Die Nationalökonomie der Gegenwart und Zukunft und andere gesammelte Schriften von Bruno Hildebrand*, Jena, Gustav Fischer, 1922.

4.3 Richard Ely – the Main US Stage Theorist – and his Comparison of Stages (1903)

US economist Richard Ely – a student of Karl Knies in Heidelberg – has a good survey of stage theories in his 1903 book *Studies in the Evolution of Industrial Society*.[47] Ely (1854–1943) was one of several German-educated Christian US Economists who were very influential in the United States up until, and including, The New Deal. According to The International Encyclopaedia of Social Sciences, Richard Ely 'probably exerted a greater influence upon American economics during its vital formative period than any other individual.' The fact that he is normally labelled a Christian socialist shows how the mental forces that built US society were very far away from what today is standard Anglo-Saxon economics. Rather than dividing economics in macro and micro, Ely seems to have *income creation* and *income distribution* as the two important facets of economics.

THE ECONOMIC STAGES

From the Standpoint of Production	From Bucher's Standpoint	From Hildebrand's Standpoint	From the Labor Standpoint	From Giddings's Standpoint
1. Hunting and Fishing	Independent Domestic Economy	Truck Economy	Slaughter of Enemies, Woman's Labor, and Beginning of Slavery	Luck Magic Sacrificial
2. Pastoral				
3. Agricultural			Slavery and Serfdom	Slave Labor
4. Handicraft	Town Economy	Money Economy	Free Labor governed by Custom	Trade
5. Industrial (1) Universal Competi-tion as an ideal (2) Concentration (3) Integration	National Economy (World Economy)	Credit Economy	Individual Contract with Increasing Regulation by Statute Group Contract and Regulation by Statute	Capitalistic

Source: Ely 1903.

[47] New York, Chautauqua Press, 1903.

Ely's own stages are similar to those of List: 1: The hunting and fishing stage, 2. The pastoral stage, 3. The agricultural stage, 4. The handicraft stage, and 5. The industrial stage. More interestingly, however, Ely provides a comparative chart of five different types of stage theories, all displaying different aspects of the societal development of **[201]** Mankind: from the point of view of production (his own stage theory), from Bücher's standpoint, from Hildebrand's stand-point, from labour's standpoint, and from Gidding's standpoint. Gidding's main stages are Ceremonial and Business economics. These both have three sub-stages: Luck, magic and sacrificial economies, and slave, trade and capitalistic economies. These different types of stages, would, of course, often not overlap in time. In this framework – reproduced on the next page – Carlota Perez' techno-economic paradigms fit like a natural sixth type of stage theory, based on the fundamental technologies carrying each period. Taken in conjunction, these stage theories emphasise different aspects, each of them representing a *necessary but not sufficient* condition for the progress of mankind.

4.4 Oppenheimer's Typology of Typologies

In the third volume, tome one, of his *System der Soziologie* from 1923, Franz Oppenheimer[48] has an excellent and systematic discussion of stage theories from several angles. Oppenheimer starts by discussing two factors which contribute to the stages: *Die Differentierung* (i.e. the division of labour), *Die Integrierung* (i.e. the integration), which he both divides into their political and trade aspects. Oppenheimer introduces a special chapter on what he calls *Transportwiderstand* – i.e. the resistance to integration that is formed by geographical distance and consequent coasts in terms of time and transportation cost. His *Transportwiderstand* lends itself perfectly as a concept through which the role of infrastructure may be introduced into the discussion of techno-economic stages.

Oppenheimer thoroughly discusses the combined effects of his two main factors (division of labour and integration) on the evolution of the following types of stages of societies: 1. The Stages of Division of Labour, 2. The Stages of Integration (essentially Bücher's), 3. The Phases of Evolution (scale of operation seen from the business point of view; i.e. handicraft, manufacturing, factories **[202]** and trusts), and finally 5. Phases of Means of Circulation (the stages of monetary sophistication, i.e. Hildebrand's stages). One interesting aspect of previous stage theories in the light of the present transition into a new techno-economic paradigm is that the 'natural' tendency towards an ever-increasing scale of operation seems to have ceased with the Fordist mass-production paradigm.

4.5 Rostow's Non-communist Manifesto (1960)

One of the latest stage theories to gain prominence was the five-stage theory of development presented by W. W. Rostow his book *The Stages of Economic Growth*[49]. The subtitle *A*

48 Oppenheimer, *op. cit.,* pp. 254–309.

49 Rostow, W. W., *The Stages of Economic Growth,* Cambridge, Cambridge University Press, 1960.

Non-communist Manifesto hints at an agenda for the book that is clearly spelled out on the dust jacket: 'to offer a comprehensive, realistic and soundly based alternative to Marx' theory of how societies evolve'.

Rostow's stages are 1. The traditional society, 2. The preconditions for take-off, 3. The take-off, 4. The drive to maturity, and 5. The age of high mass-consumption. However, he fundamentally traces these stages as they are reflected in the relationship between two ratios: the proportion of income saved (the savings ratio) and the productivity of new investments (the output-capital ratio). His model is typical for the rather simplistic views about economic growth which were prevalent for many years following World War II, and which are still deeply embedded in the world economic order. Rostow's model clearly represents what Schumpeter calls 'the pedestrian view that it is capital per se which propels the capitalist engine'. Rostow is silent on the mechanisms whereby society converts savings to investments and to production: on Man's intuition, skills, tools, will and leadership, on Nietsche's *Geist- und Willenskapital.* **[203]**

4.6 Porter and the Possibility of Regression (1990)

As already mentioned, Michael Porter's book *The Competitive Advantage of Nations*[50] contains an interesting example of a stage theory where the possibility for retrogression is clearly present -almost unavoidable if great care is not taken to prevent it. The model is clearly of a Schumpeterian brand, where society passes through the following stages of progress: 1. The factor-driven stage, 2. The investment-driven stage, and 3. The innovation-driven stage. The 4th stage – representing retrogression – Porter calls the wealth-driven stage.

This stage of decline sets in when the wealth created in the past is not able to create new wealth. The motivation of investors, managers, and individuals in general shifts in ways that undermine sustained innovation. Powerful companies are able to protect themselves – often with the help of government – from the need to innovate. Management-labour relations harden as each side strives to keep its share of a shrinking pie. At the same time the social burdens increase, and ultimately outgrow society's ability to sustain them.

Porter's book received world-wide attention in the early 1990's, much as Rostow's book had in the early 1960's. However, Porter's ideas of industry clusters – already known under different names from Marshall, Perroux and from Swedish economist Erik Dahmén – received most of the attention. His Schumpeterian stages deserved much more attention than they got.

4.7 Techno-economic Paradigms – Perez and Freeman (1983/1991)

As mentioned in the introduction, historians traditionally divide the early history of Mankind into historical periods named after the technologies that dominated the period: e.g. stone cutting technology in the Stone Age and iron technology in the Iron

[50] London, Macmillan, 1990, pp. 545–573.

Age. Carlota Perez and Christopher Freeman have broken down the historical period **[204]** since the industrial revolution into different periods: *techno-economic paradigms.*[51]

These periods are in may ways a continuation of Bacon's insight that the arts – the professions – are the most important factor determining Man's conditions of life. These periods may be looked upon as different modes – different methods – of increasing Man's material standard of living. Towards the end of each period it becomes increasingly clear that the previous technology is 'used up', its potentials are exhausted. There is no more room for improvements along the previous technological path – the world does not change anymore without fundamental changes to the technological base. Such periods are closely related to the long waves in economic history.

Techno-economic paradigms are clearly stage theories in the same way that Bucher's is, but focusing on the basic technologies driving the economy. They can be interpreted as a continuation of List's and Ely's stage theories. In modern history, Perez and Freeman distinguish between five such different ways of increasing the standard of living, all of which dominated a long historical period. Below we show, after Perez and Freeman, an overview of the characteristics of these periods, the industries which carry the paradigm, the inexpensive resources which become available in seemingly unlimited supply at rapidly falling prices, and the necessary infrastructure which is needed to reduce the *Transportwiderstand.*

The Perez/Freeman model is easily compatible with Porter's stages – both models are fundamentally Schumpeterian and innovation-driven. In both cases the risk of falling behind is acknowledged – the process of creative destruction may be easily develop in such a way that the creation takes place in one nation and the destruction in another. **[205]**

The historical techno-economic paradigms

Period from-to	*Name of Period*	*Important Industries*	*Inexpensive Resource*	*Infra-Structure*
1. 1770–1840	Early mechanisation	Textiles Wool	Water power Cotton	Canals Roads
2. 1830–1890	Steam and railway	Iron Transportation	Steam Coal	Railroad Steam ships
3. 1880–1940	Electricity and Ships	Electr. machinery heavy industry	Chemical ind.	Electricity Steel Roads
4. 1930–1990	Mass production (Fordism)	Cars Synthetic mater	Oil	Roads, Planes Cables
5. 1990-?	Information and communication	Data/Software Biotechnology	Microelectronics	Digital telecom Satellites

[51] See Perez, Carlota, 'Structural Change and the Assimilation of New Technologies in the Economic and Social System', in *Futures,* Vol. 15, 1983, No. 4, pp. 357–375, Freeman, 'The Nature of Innovation and the Evolution of the Productive System', in *Technology and Productivity. The Challenge for Economic Policy,* Paris, OECD, 1991.

The fundamental driving force behind the changing techno-economic paradigms is the changing level of Man's knowledge. Only by assuming away this factor, neo-classical economics produces factor price equalisation. Part of an alternative theory based on this vision is also the fact that nations exporting products based on old and commonplace knowledge will have a lower standard of living than nations exporting products containing advanced, new and scarce knowledge – regardless of their relative efficiency. The world's most efficient producers of baseballs for the American sport, who are in Haiti, make 30 US cent per hour. They are the world's most efficient producers in an industry that all the capital of the United States has not managed to mechanise. Baseballs are sown by hand everywhere. The world's most efficient producers of golf balls – made by machines – have a nominal wage which is about 30 times higher. The uneven advance of mechanisation produces huge inequities in world income, and locks many poor nations into a comparative advantage **[206]** of being poor and ignorant. This fact was not lost on US economists and politicians of the 19th Century, but today its absence forms the most important blind spot on the cornea of mainstream economic theory. Until we include knowledge – Man's 'wit and will' – as a factor into economic theory, we shall continue, in vain, to throw money at the *symptoms* of poverty, rather than address its *causes*.

5. Bücher's Four Techno-Geographic Economic Stages

Karl Bücher's *Die Entstehung der Volkswirtschaft* studies *the geographical dimension* of techno-economic stages. Changing technologies carry with them qualitative changes in many aspects. Technologies and technological systems create particular spheres of gravity. They have their own geographical 'footprints': each different technology creates its own geographical sphere much like each fluvial basin has its unique area of precipitation. This geographical dimension is the subject of Bucher's study.

Techno-economic stages develop according to Adam Smith's fundamental insight that the division of labour is dependent on the size of the market. Underlying this statement from Smith is an understanding that the division of labour is influenced by *scale*. The size of the market cannot be of importance for any other reason than scale: the division of labour is concomitant with increasing fixed cost and consequently with increasing returns to scale. Neo-classical economics, based on constant or diminishing returns to scale, has never been able to incorporate Adam Smith's basic insight about the extent of the market in it's theory – no theory of the division of labour exists in modern economics. As George Stigler says: 'Almost no one used or now uses the theory of division of labour, for the excellent reason that there is scarcely such a theory …

There is no standard, operable theory to describe what Smith argued to be the mainstream of economic progress.'[52] The constant-return assumptions of standard economics have erected a barrier preventing standard economic theory **[207]** from absorbing what Adam Smith – as well as William Petty 100 years earlier – saw as the fundamental source

[52] Stigler quoted in McCraw, Thomas, 'The Trouble with Adam Smith', in *The American Scholar*, Vol. 61, Summer 1992, p. 362.

of progress. Karl Bücher's framework, however, is able to trace the geographical dimension of increased division of labour over time.

5.1 Family Economy (Hauswirtschaft)

In Bücher's system, the first geographical sphere of human development is the family economy, or Hauswirtschaft. In the *Hauswirtschaft* the whole cycle from production to consumption takes place in the closed circle of family and kin. In this stage it is not possible to distinguish production from consumption, they 'fliessen in einander über'. Exchange is by *gegenseitige Hilfeleistung* – what modern anthropologists call *reciprocity*. The income distribution systems in such a society – described by Karl Polanyi – who was clearly much inspired by Bücher: 'In nonmarket economies these two forms of integration — reciprocity and redistribution – occur in effect usually together.'[53]

Bücher's view on primitive society was clearly much influenced by his meeting with a Belgian scholar, Emile de Lavelene from Liege, at the 1875 meeting of the *Verein für Sozialpolitik* in Eisenach. Lavelenes's *De la proprieté et de ses formes primitives* was first published in 1874. Bücher translated this book into German as *Das Ureigentum,* published in Leipzig in 1879. In his memoirs Bücher emphasises the importance of his connections with Lavelene, although he later found that his work 'needed both to be broadened and revised in many places.'[54]

At this stage society is very dependent on the soil[55], and collective labour (*Arbeitsgemeinschaft*) is important, rather than division of labour (*Arbeitsteilung*). This *Arbeitsgemeinschaft* is a subject of another of Bücher's books *Arbeit und Rytkmus* [56]. The basic political units are clans (*Sippen*), where property is collective (*Gesamteigentum*). Houses are common (*Gemeinschaftshäuser*). Bücher here refers to Africa at the time of his writing. The lack of individualism is very clear, in some societies even death penalty can be taken over by another member of the tribe. Specialised labour – like a village shepherd – works for everybody and is fed by everybody (as is still the case today in the Alps).

Within the same tribe, food is almost common property[57] (The term used is *Gütergemeinschaft*). Some long distance trade exists, e.g. in salt. As Polanyi has shown with the long-distance traders in pre-Colombian Mexico, the little trade that existed was to a large extent done on behalf of the clan. There is no industry outside the household at this stage in Bücher's system, artisans are household slaves (Handwerkssklaven). Bücher emphasises that this system opens up for a large amount of division of labour – he names

[53] Polanyi, **Karl,** The Economy as an Instituted Process', Polanyi, Arensberg and Pearson (eds.), *Trade and Markets in the Early Empires,* Chicago, Gateway, 1971, p. 253.

[54] *Erinnerungen,* p. 197–198.

[55] P. 94.

[56] Sixth edition, Leipzig, Emmanuel Reinicke, 1924. First edition 1896.

[57] P. 62.

a lot of professions within the same Roman household – but this division of labour is not accompanied by trade.

5.2 Town Economy (Stadtwirtschaft)

The next evolutionary stage is the town economy. This stage is characterised by trade without intermediaries between specialised artisans and the public at town markets. The towns were often built around castles which provided refuge for the townspeople and people from the surrounding countryside in times of war. A person enjoying this privilege was a *Burger* (Burgensis). The need arose for economic institutions, for codifying laws and regulations for exchange, which were not needed in earlier types of societies. Town markets required standards for weight and measure. In Mediaeval Europe the towns had different standards of measurements, and an important part of early economic manuals was to list these weights and measures and to give their equivalents in the weights and measures of other towns. Still **[209]** today these local standards of measurement are found on the old church walls in Italian towns.

Towns arose in ports, at river crossings, at trading posts for an increasing trade in goods like salt and iron. Markets grew in symbiosis with religious celebrations: accumulation of people always favours trade. The town specialises in arts and crafts and exchanges this for food from the surrounding countryside. Infrastructure is improved to reduce what Oppenheimer calls the *Transportwiderstand*.

5.3 National Economy (Volkswirtschaft)

This stage is characterised by a slow transfer of the institutions and synergies which had been seen as productive at the town level to a whole nation. This stage involves large-scale manufacturing, and trade is no longer direct between producer and consumer, but through intermediaries.

Bücher clearly sees the importance of mercantilist policies in order to create a national economy: 'Mercantilism is not a dead dogma, but the living *praxis* of all statesmen of any importance, from Charles V to Friedrich The Great. The typical economic policy of mercantilism was that of Colbert.' It is worth noting that no nation of any size – with the exception of tiny states like San Marino – has created a high standard of living without going through a stage of economic policy of the Colbert type.

The national economy became a very important unit for income distribution through labour mobility, and through common education, language, skills and values. Wages and – after the gold standard was abandoned – also money supply, were increased at the pace of physical productivity of the economy. The barber raised his prices at the rate of productivity increase in the economy, and in this way the service workers in the industrialised countries came to have a much higher living standard than their Third World counterparts. This way of distributing the fruits of technological progress is what the French regulation school in economics refer to as 'Fordism' – a corollary to Fordism as a system of mass production in the theory of Perez and Freeman. This mechanism is what we have referred to as a *collusive* **[210]** spread of the gains from technological change – a spread that to a large extent takes place inside a national labour market. The national economy became a *Burg* for the defence of a high living standard, just like the *Burg* in the town economy defended the *Burger* from enemy attacks.

5.4 The Global Economy

When reading Bücher's *Entstehung* today, one is struck by the thought that this book gives the account of Mankind's road toward a globalised economy. Bücher himself hints at the possibility of a *Weltwirtschaft*, but he sees it far into the future.[58] Using Bücher's framework in his *Studies in the Evolution of Industrial Society*, Richard Ely makes the point about globalisation very clear already in 1903: 'We are now in this stage (of national economies); and one may add, the next stage, according to this view, would be world economy. The money market is truly a world market.'[59]

As in the previous stages, trade and technology leads the way, and the necessary human institutions are slowly following. Today, we still have different 'economies' operating in all Bücher's extended four spheres. We make sandwiches and brush our teeth in the Family Economy, we shop and buy services from the plumber in the Regional Economy, we participate in an educational and health system which is part of the National Economy, and buy computers and watch movies which are part of the Global Economy. The global economy opens a new set of challenges for human institutions to create the 'good' society. In our view there are particular problems in the area of income distribution, to which we shall return below. **[211]**

6. Income Distribution Issues in the Four Stages

Stage theories open up insights into both international trade theory and to a better understanding of world income distribution. Friedrich List's theory of international trade – which set the standard for non-English trade policy in the 19th century – was based on his understanding of the stages of human evolution. Richard Ely says the following about List's 'National System of Political Economy':

> 'He (List) was interested especially in the problem of the protective tariff, holding that the policy which was suitable for one period in a nation's growth could not be safely followed in a subsequent period. In other words, he taught clearly that no one could properly describe himself either as a free trader or a protectionist. A man might be rationally a free trader at one period of development (of a nation), a protectionist at a later period, and again, at a subsequent period … a free trader.'[60]

In this perspective any nation dominating the new stage or paradigm would benefit from free trade, but nations risking to get stuck specialised in the activities of the former

---

[58] P. 149.

[59] Ely, *op. cit.*, p. 68–69.

[60] Ely, *op. cit.*, p. 21–22.

paradigm would need temporary protection. The 19th century common sense was that free trade was beneficial to nations at the same level of evolution, but only in the interest of the richer nations if trade was between nations at different stages of evolution.

All Bücher's stages also have their own mechanisms of income distribution. On the chart on the following page we have tried to summarise the stages and their respective mechanisms of income distribution. In all stages the regional or national labour market – in a system of free labour mobility – has provided what was probably the most important mechanism of income distribution. The income of the barber in the United States rose at the pace of productivity increase of the whole US economy – not at the pace of increase of productivity of the barber. For this reason the income of barbers, bus drivers, waiters, and of most traditional service workers are so much higher in the First World than in the Third. This in spite of the fact **[212]** that the barbers and bus drivers in the Third World are just as productive and efficient as their colleagues in the First World.

The global economy as we know it today differs fundamentally from all previous stages of economic geography in that labour mobility is – for the first time – restricted inside the prevalent sphere of the economic system. Since free labour mobility is not part of the globalised economy, it is – in our opinion – even more important than before to distribute productive activities of the new paradigm between nations. If not, the globalised economy we will risk – even more than in the Fordist paradigm – that a large number of nations specialise in being poor and ignorant in the international division of labour.

Bücher's Stages of Development of Economics and Geography

Type of economy	*Mechanisms of income distribution*
I. Household Economy	Family: According to need 'social relations' not 'markets'.
II. Town/regional Economy	Family + labour mobility in small area + church.
III. National Economy	All of the above + distributing paradigm-carrying activity (= "the industrial system")to all nations + State (taxation, schooling, health, 'welfare state')
IV. Global Economy	None of the above (except intra-EU) but 'development aid'

7. Are Stages 'Obligatory Passage Points' – or are Short-cuts Possible?

As already discussed, stage theories do not pretend to present iron laws. Bücher clearly describes their passage as 'what is normal' – they are, says Oppenheimer, 'ideal types' in the Weberian sense. Stage theories do not represent the Whig conception of history that everything invariably improves. In my view they tend to conform to **[213]** Carlota Perez' view that all stages or modes of production both socially and economically present a wide range of options according to what values society promotes.

There are, however, several aspects of stage theories that suggest that their *sequence* is mandatory, although retrogression – both self-induced and induced from the outside – is clearly possible. This is what Carlota Perez sees as a paradigm shift not only opening new windows of opportunity, but also opening back doors to retrogression. The whole idea of the Renaissance was to catch up to a previous stage which had been lost after what was – at the time – clearly perceived as a long period of retrogression.

All authors tie the stages to a cumulativeness of human knowledge that carries with it an increasing division of labour. Both Bücher and other authors are very conscious about the role of an *increasing division of labour* in the historical stages. As already mentioned, Oppenheimer calls the degrees of division of labour *The Stages of Differentiation*, which he ties to the geographical dimension (Bücher's stages) in *The Stages of Integration.*

Clearly, the duration of paradigms and stages can be drastically cut in time. Korea's 'leap-frogging' over a brief period of 40 years is perhaps the most remarkable example of how an industrial revolution may be compressed in time. In Korea having eliminated a feudal landholding pattern seems to have been a prerequisite for this leapfrogging. The elimination of most of the feudal land holding structure in Bolivia after 1952 and in Peru after 1968 proves, however, that this is only one of many necessary conditions for 'take-off.'

The following two aspects would – in our view – point to stages being what historians of technology call 'mandatory passage points' -points which the evolution seemingly have to go through:

1. The *cumulative nature* of human knowledge. This cumulative aspect is evident when it comes to education; most people start in grade one and follow every grade up through university, although short-cuts – skipping one grade – is sometimes possible, but still the exception rather than the rule. In the same manner there seems to be a natural sequence of technological change. Motorised land transport (cars) is, for example, likely to precede motorised air **[214]** transport just like an age based on nature's materials, like the stone age, is likely to precede an age dominated by a material produced by Man, like the iron age. However, I would not like to push the 'naturalness' of any sequence too far, I believe – in the spirit of Paul David's Economics of QWERTY – that there are a wide range of possible trajectories, and that many end up not being optimal. This, however, does not subtract from a degree of cumulativeness: the Stone Age is not likely to follow an age of aluminium.

   Human knowledge may be seen – as Leibniz saw it – as a conscious climbing in a hierarchy of monads towards ever-higher levels of knowledge. In the Renaissance world view, since Man was created in the image of an incredibly creative God, it was his pleasurable duty to climb the hierarchy of monads towards ever higher levels of knowledge. Leibniz' monadology in this sense points to the cumulative aspect of the growth of human knowledge.
2. There are clearly connections between the stages of economic evolution and Man's *hierarchy of needs.* The German stage theorists make it very clear that an agricultural surplus was an absolute 'mandatory passage point' for human evolution to pass on to a further stage. The agricultural revolution was the first one, providing Man with food, his most basic need. Next came the industrial revolution, where production of textiles and clothing carried a succession of techno-economic paradigms – from the early industrialisation of Venice in the 14th Century all the way through 19th Century Manchester. A hierarchy of human needs must, through the demand

mechanism, to some extent determine the sequence of technological change: it is not feasible to think of a paradigm carried by sophisticated consumer services if people have not covered their basic needs for food, shelter and clothing.

There is then, something organic in the process of evolutionary stages, whatever the criteria for the stages may be. This does, in our view, apply also to Perez/Freeman's techno-economic paradigms. In our view there are particular reasons to believe that Fordism is a mandatory passage point in order to create a post-Fordist society **[215]** with an equitable income distribution. There seem to be two basic reasons for this:

1) In our view the Fordist paradigm was, and may remain, unique in its potential for large-scale income distribution within labour markets. The large scale of operations and the political power of a large number of workers allowed a rapid increase in the price of labour compared to the price of capital. This speeded up mechanisation, which – in a virtuous circle – again increased the price of labour, and so on. This is what we have referred to as *collusive* distribution of the gains from technical change, in a three layer rent-seeking where both capitalists, workers and the government in the producing nation 'collude' and keep a large share of the technological gains in their own nation. This contrasts with the classical distribution of gains from technical change as it is assumed in economic theory: to the consumer as lowered prices. The smaller scale of operations in the network society of post-Fordism seems to make collusive distribution of gains from technical change much more difficult than before: we now get richer more from lower prices than from higher nominal wages. This tendency is reinforced by the sheer size of global markets, creating a new situation of 'the winner takes it all' markets. In our opinion it is therefore likely that societies going directly from semi-feudalism to post-Fordism will maintain the feudal structure of income distribution, albeit based on other criteria. We are much in agreement with Carlota Perez' view that all stages and techno-economic paradigms open for a whole range of possible types of societies. However, we fear that the establishment of a nation-wide distributive justice will be very difficult without passing through the nation-state based Fordist mass production society as an obligatory passage point. The scale of operations under the mass production paradigm may have had as its most important effect that labour was needed on such a large scale that their bargaining power for the first time in history made a more equitable income distribution politically feasible.
2) One important aspect of Fordism was – as Carlota Perez points out – that, influenced by the technologies of mass production, **[216]** large categories of objects became standardised and 'alike'. The typical example of this age is Henry Ford's statement that 'You can have your car any colour you want as long as it is black'. In Northern European social democracies it was stressed that human beings are equal. Under Maoism all individuals were even supposed to dress equally. Even under Hitler all Aryans were seen as being alike, as well as all Jews and Gypsies in their categories. All human beings, or groups of human beings, came to be seen as 'equal' and 'alike'. Most societies now face a transition from seeing all human beings as being

alike, to a stage where – if all goes well – all human beings are seen as being different – unique – but *of equal value.* Is it likely that cultures which have not passed through this stage of 'all human beings are equal' are able to build a consensus that all Men are different, but of equal value? Can such a consensus be built in places where native Indians are still considered not much higher than animals – like in parts of the Amazon? Is, in some cumulative sense, a notion that 'all Men are equal' an obligatory passage point in order that the idea that all Men are different – but of equal value – may be created?

8. Conclusions and Brief Policy Implications

Common to all stage theories during their 'golden age' from the 1840's to the 1930's is a view that, at any point in time, different geographical areas live in different stages. This may not be so obvious today, when most consumers consume in the global supermarket. However, if we, in the tradition of Bücher, focus on *production* rather than *consumption,* it will be clear that although consumers in Somalia or Haiti – if they can afford it – have access to state-of-the art goods, their own system of production is, to a large extent, locked into a specialisation in activities operating under previous technological paradigms. Haiti is the world's largest exporter and most efficient producer of baseballs, a product that all the capital of the United States so far has not managed to mechanise. All baseballs are hand-sewn, steeped in a techno-economic paradigm which otherwise died out centuries ago. Because they are specialised in leftover activities **[217]** from former paradigms, the Haitians are increasingly reinforcing their comparative advantage in international trade: they are specialised in being poor and ignorant.

We would claim that the study of economic stages – keeping the *caveats* of such generalisation in mind – is indeed useful for understanding today's world. Today agricultural labour performed by women is a main characteristic of African economies. Keeping in mind today's agricultural production in Africa and the horrid description of the slaughtering of Tutsies in Rwanda, US economist Richard Ely's 1903 description of one stage of the development of Mankind is striking. 'The slaughter of enemies and woman's labour are characteristic features of the early stage in the development of labour.'[61] Africa's problems are clearly not within the range of the (admittedly now slightly changing) policies of the World Bank. These are problems which are too fundamental to be solved in the sphere of 'fiscal restraint' and monetary economics, of 'openness' of the economy and of 'free trade' and of 'getting the prices right'.

We would suggest that *what* the disintegrating and desperately poor African nations produce, and *how* they produce it – as the stage theories suggest – are important elements which today have been unlearned in the policies of the World Bank and the IMF. Perhaps, by insisting that these nations specialise according to their comparative advantage in raw materials, we are preventing them from entering into the creative processes that brought wealth elsewhere. Perhaps, by attacking symptoms rather than causes of poverty, and

---

[61] Ely, *op. cit.*, p. 72.

by putting Africa 'on the dole' in line with our own unemployed, we have played an important role in the process of retrogression? Perhaps, by focusing on their needs as *consumers* we have prevented them from developing as *producer*? Perhaps a Renaissance-type gestalt-switch -fundamentally changing a society's view on the importance of new knowledge – is the *mandatory passage point* which Asia has been through, but Africa not?

If these are factors of any importance, they are clearly not included in the policies of the 'Washington Consensus' on development policies. Present policies are, as is neo-classical economics, **[218]** essentially based on a view of Man as an animal which has learned to *barter*, rather than an animal which has learned to *produce*.[62] Our policies towards the South today are heavily biased towards monetary aspects, we forget that money is only 'the veil behind which the action of real economic forces is concealed'.[63] The focus on *monetary* and *consumption* aspects, rather than on *the real economy of goods and services* and on *production*, is an invitation to treat symptoms rather than causes of poverty. Perhaps we may regain lost insights by attempting to internalise the intuitions and the factual knowledge behind long lost stage theories, theories which allow us to strip off the monetary veil which prevents qualitative understanding.

Stage theories are generalisations, and as any kind of generalisation they are subject both to misuse and to easy criticism. Without generalisation or abstractions, however, there is no science. Neo-classical economics, as well as today's standard economics, is a case of such an abstraction carried to the extreme. This theory is based on a seed on a very special case where the forces causing 'progress' are assumed away, creating what Schmoller called 'dead equilibrium'.

The present world economic order is based on a type of economic theory which has not managed to formalise the activity-specific aspects of human knowledge – and its relationship both to human welfare and to ecological sustainability – and which is therefore of solving the problems of nations which are stuck in past evolutionary stages and techno-economic paradigms, like Haiti. Because their theories are based on the assumption that all economic activities – regardless of evolutionary stage or paradigm – have the same potential for creating welfare, these institutions do not see that their fundamental demand on immediate 'openness' to international trade under all circumstances may cause whole nations to disintegrate and retrogress in the stages of evolution. The core assumptions of economic theory are irrelevant and harmless to the nations carrying the next techno-economic paradigm, but they are irrelevant and very harmful to the welfare of societies that are lagging in the evolution. **[219]**

In the 1960's many people wished to see 'one, two, many Vietnams'. Now we risk a breakdown of civilised society in an increasing number of states which are absolutely uncompetitive and unemployable – at any wage level – in the globalised economy. Liberia, Rwanda, and Somalia are recent examples of total collapse of the nation-state, and of a step back into tribal economies, back into Karl Bücher's clan economies.

---

62 See Reinert, Erik S. (1997) *The Role of the State in Economic Growth*, SUM Working Paper No. 5, 1997.

63 Pigou, A. C, *The Veil of Money*, London, Macmillan, 1949, p. 18.

By reintroducing what Bücher saw as the 'indispensable tool' of stage theories – *of production-based (as opposed to barter-based) economic theories* – will we be able to better understand why globalisation on the one hand is producing unprecedented wealth in some nations, but also has the power to create 'one, two, many Somalias'.

References

Bücher, Karl. *Arbeit und Rythmus.* Sixth edition, Leipzig: Emmanuel Reinicke, 1924.1st edition 1896

Bücher, Karl. *Lebenserinnerungen.* Tubingen: Laupp, p. 199, 1919 (Title reads *Erster Band, 1847–1890,* but this is apparently the only volume to have been published)

Bücher, Karl. *Die Entstehung der Volkswirtschafi.* 11th edition, Tubingen: Laupp, 1919

Chandler, Alfred. *Scale and Scope. The Dynamics of Industrial Capitalism.* Cambridge: Mass. Harvard University Press, 1990

Ely, Richard. *Studies in the Evolution of Industrial Society.* New York, Chautauqua Press, 1903

Freeman, Christopher. "The Nature of Innovation and the Evolution of the Productive System". In: *Technology and Productivity. The Challenge for Economic Policy.* Paris: OECD, 1991

Hildebrand, Bruno. "Natural-, Geld- und Kreditwirtschaft". In: *Jahrbücher für Nationalökonomie und Statistik,* Vol. II, pages 1–24, 1864. Reprinted in Gehrig, Hans (ed.), *Die Nationalökonomie der Gegenwart und Zukunft und andere gesammelte Schrifien von Bruno Hildebrand,* Jena: Gustav Fischer, 1922

Hildebrand, Bruno. "Die Entwicklungsstufen der Geldwirtschaft". In: *Jahrbücher für Nationalökonomie und Statistik.* Vol. XXVI, p. 15–26, 1876. Reprinted in Gehrig, Hans (ed.). *Die Nationalökonomie der Gegenwart und Zukunft und andere gesammelte Scbriften von Bruno Hildebrand.* Jena: Gustav Fischer, 1922

Hirschman, Albert O. *The Passions and the Interests. Political Arguments for Capitalism before Its Triumph.* Princeton N.J.: Princeton University Press, 1977

Hoover, Paul (ed.). *Postmodern American Poetry.* New York: Norton, 1994

Kalveram, Gertrud. *Die Theorien von den Wirtschaftsstufen.* Leipzig: Hans Buske, 1933

Krugman, Paul. *The Self-Organizing Economy.* Cambridge: Mass, Blackwell, 1996

Kuczynski, Jiirgen. *Studien zu einer Geschichte der Gesellschaftswissenschaften.* Berlin: Akademie-Verlag, vol. 8, 1978

Laistner, M. L. W. *Greek Economics.* London: Dent, 1923. (The Library of Greek Thought).

Margoliouth, David S. "Entry on Ibn-Khaldun". In: Seligman, Edwin (ed.). *The Encyclopaedia of Social Sciences.* Vol. 7, New York: Macmillan, 1932

McCloskey, D. *The Rhetoric of Economics.* Madison: University of Wisconsin Press, 1985

McCraw, Thomas. "The Trouble with Adam Smith". In: *The American Scholar.* Vol. 61, Summer 1992

Meek, Ronald. *Social Science and the Ignoble Savage.* Cambridge: Cambridge University Press, 1976

Nicol, Donald M. *Venezia e Bisanzio.* Milan: Rusconi, 1990

Oppenheimer, Franz. *System der Soziologie.* Vol. 3, Tome 1, 5th edition, Jena: Gustav Fischer, 1923

Perez, Carlota. "Structural Change and the Assimilation of New Technologies in the Economic and Social System". In: *Futures.* Vol. 15, No. 4, 1983

Perez, Carlota. "The Social and Political Challenge of the Present Paradigm Shift". In: Reinert, Erik (Ed.). *Evolutionary Economics and Income Inequality.* Aldershot: Edward Elgar, 2000

Pigou, A. C. *The Veil of Money.* London: Macmillan, 1949

Polanyi, Karl. *The Great Transformation.* New York: Rinehart & Co., 1944

Polanyi, Karl. "The Economy as an Instituted Process". In: Polanyi, Arensberg and Pearson (eds.). *Trade and Markets in the Early Empires.* Chicago: Gateway, 1971

Porter, Michael. *The Competitive Advantage of Nations.* London: Macmillan, 1990 **[221]**

Reinert, Erik, and Daastøl, Arno. "Exploring the Genesis of Economic Innovations: the religious gestalt-switch and the duty to invent as preconditions for economic growth". In: *European Journal of Law and Economics.* Vol. 4, June, 1997

Reinert, Erik S. "The Role of the State in Economic Growth". *Journal of Economic Studies,* vol. 26 (4/5), 1999

Robbins, Lionel. *The Theory of Economic Policy in English Classical Economics.* London: Macmillan, 1952

Rostow, W.W. *The Stages of Economic Growth.* Cambridge: Cambridge University Press, 1960

Schumpeter, Joseph Alois. *History of Economic Analyisis,* New York, Oxford University Press, 1954

Seligman, Edwin. "The Economic Interpretation of History". In: *Political Science Quarterly,* Vol. XVII, 1902, p. 76, quoted in Ely, Richard, *Evolution of Industrial Society,* New York: The Chautauqua Press, 1903

Serra, Antonio. *Breve trattato delle cause che possono far abbondare li regni d'oro e argento dove non sono miniere.* Napoli: Lazzaro Scoriggio, 1613

Smith, Adam. *Wealth of Nations.* Chicago, 1976

Sommer, Artur. "Über Inhalt, Rahmen und Sinn älterer Stufentheorien (List und Hildebrand)". In: Salin, Edgar (ed.). *Synopsis. Festgabe für Alfred Weber.* Heidelberg: Lambert Schneider, 1948

Viner, Jacob. *The Role of Providence in the Social Order.* Philadelphia: American Philosophical Society, 1972

Wendt, Paul. "Comment on Amariglio's 'Economics as a Postmodern Discourse", quoted in McCloskey, D. *Knowledge and Persuasion in Economics.* Cambridge: Cambridge University Press, 1994

Chapter Ten

AUSTRIAN ECONOMICS AND THE OTHER CANON: THE AUSTRIANS BETWEEN THE *ACTIVISTIC-IDEALISTIC* AND THE *PASSIVISTIC-MATERIALISTIC* TRADITIONS OF ECONOMICS

Erik S. Reinert

AUSTRIAN ECONOMICS AND 'THE OTHER CANON'

The Austrians between the *activistic-idealistic* and the *passivistic-materialistic* traditions of economics

1. Typologies of Economic Theory and the Two Canons

We have recently argued that when focusing on very long-term longitudinal trends in economics, two ideal types of economic theory appear to have co-existed parallel over an extended period of time.[1] These ideal types can be seen as constituting two separate *filiations*[2] – to use Schumpeter's term – and they come into occasional methodological clashes. Werner Sombart fittingly calls the first tradition **activistic-idealistic,** a tradition born with the Renaissance. The second type of economic theory he calls **passivistic-materialistic**[3]**,** a tradition having its origins with Mandeville and Adam Smith and solidifying as the 'a-priori method' with David Ricardo. The purpose of this paper is to outline the characteristics of the two traditions – the tradition behind today's mainstream and 'The Other Canon' – and to discuss the position of Austrian economics in this context.

In most sciences, periodical and radical *gestalt-switches* terminate old theoretical trajectories and initiate new ones. In a Kuhnian paradigm shift the scientific world moves from a situation when everybody knows that the world is flat, to a new understanding when everybody knows that the world is round. This happens in a relatively short time. Lakatos' idea of 'degenerating scientific research programmes' that gradually shift to 'progressive' ones convey a similar idea. In this respect economics is different. In economics the theory that the world is flat has been living together with the theory that the world is round for centuries. We describe this apparent lack of paradigm shifts in economics by the co-existence of these two long-term parallel *filiations*, where weight and influence periodically tilt back and forth between two alternative *Weltanschauungen*.

Today evolutionary economics – based on a tradition founded by the Austrian Joseph Alois Schumpeter – represent the most important challenge to the mainstream. However, evolutionary economics has, in our view, so far had an unnecessarily limited scope. This tradition now focuses relatively narrowly on innovations, including neither Schumpeter's own interest in financial matters, nor addressing to any extent the broader issues of uneven economic growth and employment on a world level which are, at their origin, intimately tied to Schumpeterian mechanisms. And, by bringing simple 'Schumpeterian' variables into mainstream equilibrium models, his message is being domesticated and made innocuous. As in the case of Keynes, the mainstream again shows a great ability to usurp, absorb, and subdue threatening alternative theories.

As already indicated, the two different canons are based on fundamentally different *Weltanschauungen*. The lines of the two canons can be traced back to the period when

---

1 Reinert, Erik & Arno Daastøl, 'The Other Canon and Uneven Economic Development: Renaissance Economics as an Immaterial and Production-based Canon in the History of Economic Thought and in the History of Economic Policy', in Reinert, Erik (editor) *Evolutionary Economics and Income Inequality*, Aldershot, Edward Elgar, 2000.

2 'The relation of one thing to another from which it may say to be descended or derived; position in a genealogical classification', The Oxford English Dictionary, Oxford 1933, Vol. 4, p. 212.

3 Sombart, Werner, *Der Moderne Kapitalismus,* Vol. 2, *Das Europäische Wirtschaftsleben im Zeitalter des Frühkapitalismus,* München und Leipzig, Duncker & Humblot, 1928, p. 919.

the term economics was first used, to ancient Greece[4]. While today's standard economics is based on a mechanistic and barter-centred tradition, Renaissance economics – The Other Canon – is dynamic activistic-idealistic, and production-centred. The first tradition belongs to what Werner Sombart calls *ordnende Nationalökonomie*, which is concerned about *organising* the economic sphere. The second tradition is what Sombart calls *verstehende Nationalökonomie* [5], what Nelson and Winter refer to as *appreciative economics.*[6] The first tradition typically explains Man's economic activities in terms of physics (of dead matter), the second in terms of biology (of living matter *and* of Man's wit and will). The first tradition is represented by Malthus' *dismal science*, the second by Christopher Freeman's *Economics of Hope* [7] – by the *never-ending frontier of human knowledge.*

Present mainstream economic theory places itself solidly in a canonical sequence descending from the Physiocrats, via Adam Smith and Ricardo to the neo-classical tradition beginning with Jevons and Marshall. The sequence has been made clear to generations of economists as the 'Family Tree of Economics' featured on the inside back cover of many editions of Paul Samuelson's *Economics.* The alternative canon in economic theory runs parallel in time with the tradition of Samuelson's 'Family Tree'. We have named this alternative type of theory ***The Other Canon*** or ***Renaissance Economics***. The latter because never before and never after have the values which this canon represents dominated the world picture as they did during the Renaissance. The mainstream canon is clearly a product of the next philosophical period – The Enlightenment – which was in opposition to Renaissance values and outlook on important matters. Rationality and individuality during the Renaissance was based on an image of man as a spiritual being: creative and productive. The Enlightenment had a more materialistic understanding of human rationality and individuality: mechanical and consuming. Today the Renaissance canon – The Other Canon – tends to disappear in the history of economic thought, as this branch of economics more and more concentrates on the predecessors of neo-classical economics.

In 19th Century United States, The Other Canon dominated economic policy and the land-grant universities, while the standard canon dominated at the Ivy League universities. Typically Cornell University, as the only university that was both land-grant and Ivy League, was for a while teaching two kinds of economics: the British system and the American system. In all presently wealthy nations, an economic policy based on The Other Canon has served as a *mandatory passage point* in the history of economic policy. We would claim that the absence of the **History of Economic Policy** as a branch of Economics to some extent explains why The Other Canon has been brought into virtual oblivion.

---

4 See Reinert & Daastøl, *op. cit.*

5 Sombart, Werner, *Die Drei Nationalökonomien,* München & Leipzig, Duncker und Humblot, 1930.

6 Nelson, Richard and Sidney Winter, *An Evolutionary Theory of Economic Change,* Cambridge, Mass., Harvard University Press, 1982.

7 Freeman, Christopher, *The Economics of Hope,* London, Pinter, 1992.

As already mentioned, Renaissance economics is optimistic: the *never-ending frontier of knowledge* stands in sharp contrast with Malthus' *dismal science* and with the production theory of mainstream economics, the foundation of which is still today fundamentally a formalisation of Ricardo's static corn economy. Here the main agents of change, new knowledge and the entrepreneur, are both absent. In the middle of the Cold War, in 1955, Nicholas Kaldor made the extremely important point that 'the Marxian theory is really only a simplified version of Ricardo, clothed in a different garb'[8]. It was not at all obvious to most people at the time that the two political extremes were based on what were really only nuances of the same basic Ricardian economic theory. Only long after the fall of the Berlin Wall, in the late 1990's, arguments stressing the similarities of the two political extremes have again surfaced in books by Stiglitz[9] and Hodgson[10].

The cold war between what were in effect two versions of Ricardian economics led to the present crisis of The Other Canon. As it now is, the healthy Galbraithian balance of countervailing powers between the standard Anglo-Saxon theory and The Other Canon no longer exists. A hundred years ago the need for a balance of induction and deduction was generally recognised in all schools.[11] On this matter the neo-classical founder Alfred Marshall approvingly quotes the historicist Gustav Schmoller as saying that 'Induction and deduction are both needed for scientific thought as the right foot and left foot are both needed for walking'[12]. Induction has to a very large extent been lost, making mainstream economics tilt very heavily towards the left side of the brain. The essentially mechanical neo-classical economics now dominates the field, and – as we shall see – the prominent 'Other Canon' aspects of both of Alfred Marshall's early neo-classical economics and of Carl Menger's early Austrian economics have largely been lost.

Several observers have in fact pointed to the similarities between the economics of Alfred Marshall and of Carl Menger.[13] In this paper we argue that the theories that these

---

8 In 'Alternative Theories of Distribution', in *Review of Economic Studies*, Vol. XXIII, No. 2, 1955–6. Reprinted in Kaldor's *Essays on Value and Distribution*, Glencoe, Ill., Free Press, 1960, page 211.

9 Stiglitz, Joseph, *Wither Socialism?*, Cambridge, Mass., MIT Press, 1994

10 Hodgson, Geoffrey M, *Economics and Utopia*, London, Routledge, 1999.

11 At the time most economists have stressed the importance of having access to different theories at different levels of abstraction, see e.g. Aschehoug, T. H, *Socialøkonomik: En Videnskabelig Fremstilling af det Menneskelige Samfunds Økonomiske Virksomhed.*, Kristiania (Oslo), H. Aschehoug & Co. (W. Nygaard), 1903–1908, 3 Volumes. This was also one of Schumpeter's most important comments to the *Methodenstreit* in *Das Wesen und der Hauptinhalt der theoretischen Nationalökonomie*, Leipzig, Duncker & Humblot, 1908.

12 Marshall, Alfred, Principles of Economics, 9th (variorum) edition, London, Macmillan, 1961, p. 29.

13 Foss, Nicolai, 'Austrian and Post-Marshallian Economics. The Bridging work of George Richardson', in Foss, Nicolai and Brian Loasby (Editors), *Economic Organization, Capabilities and Co-ordination. Essays in Honour of G.B. Richardson,* London, Routledge, 1998. Erich Streissler looks at the common roots of Menger and Marshall in 'The Influence of German Economics on the Work of Menger and Marshall', in Caldwell, Bruce J. (Editor), *Carl Menger and his Legacy in Economics,* Annual Supplement to HOPE, Volume 22, Durham, Duke University Press, 1990.

two economists founded – neo-classical and Austrian – suffered a gradual and parallel loss of their Other Canon aspects over the course of the 20th Century.

The following are main characteristics of Other Canon economics: The fundamental cause of economic welfare is Man's productive creativity and morality; the *immaterial* production factors. In order for these ideas to materialise, capital is needed. Capital *per se* is in this tradition sterile. The Renaissance tradition can be contrasted with mainstream using Schumpeter's description of the economics of John Rae – a 19th Century US economist of the Renaissance canon: 'The essential thing is the conception of the economic process, which soars above the pedestrian view that it is the accumulation of capital *per se* that propels the capitalist engine'[14]. Whereas classical economics focused on barter, exchange, and the accumulation of material capital, the Renaissance tradition focuses on production based on human creativity. For this reason Renaissance economics emphasises education, science, incentives, and entrepreneurship.

Mainstream economics defines its origins in the French school of **physiocracy**[15] (i.e. 'the rule of nature'), where value is created by Nature, and harvested by Man. In Renaissance economics value originates through Man's wit and will (i.e. 'ideocracy' – 'the rule of ideas'). During the mechanisation of the world picture, which took place during the materialistically oriented Enlightenment, the defenders of the Renaissance tradition were the anti-physiocrats.[16] The Renaissance tradition is holistic and idealistic – not atomistic and materialistic. Nevertheless, at the core of the system is the individual, set in a complex web of synergetic interrelations. The beneficial effects of these interrelations first became evident in Renaissance towns giving birth to the Renaissance expression of the **common weal** (*il bene comune, das Gemeinwohl*) – a synergetic understanding of Society as being more than the sum of its parts.[17]

The growth of towns and cities brought these synergies into evidence. Towns permitted communication that unleashed individual freedom, creativity, diversification and synergies that together created unprecedented wealth. This was the fundamental observation of one of the earliest best-selling books in economics, *Delle Cause della Grandezza delle Città* [18] written by Giovanni Botero (1543–1617). The English translation, published

14 Schumpeter, Joseph A., *History of Economic Analysis,* New York, Oxford University Press, 1954, p. 468.

15 Of which Schumpeter says: 'Its analytical merit is negligible, but all the greater was its success', Schumpeter, *op.cit.*, p. 175.

16 In Germany the main anti-physiocrat was Johann Friedrich von Pfeiffer, in France Abbé Mably, Accarias de Serrionne, Necker, Forbonnais, Jean Graslin, Abbé Galiani – a Neapolitan envoy at the Court of Paris – and, most critical of them all: Simon-Nicolas-Henry Linguet. For a list of works by German anti-physiocrats, see Humpert, Magdalene, *Bibliographie der Kameralwissenschaften,* Cologne, Kurt Schroeder, 1937, p. 1031–1032.

17 The description of these synergetic effects is clear in Giovanni Botero (1589) and even more so in Antonio Serra (1613). To Serra these 'virtuous circles' have their origins in the increasing returns found in the manufacturing sector, which are absent in agriculture. Machiavelli is also clear on this point: 'Il bene comune è quello che fa grandi le città.'

18 Rome, Vicenzio Pellagalo, 1590.

in London in 1606, is entitled *The Cause of the Greatnesse of Cities*. This argument was to be discussed at great length by Antonio Serra in 1613.[19]

Later nation-building in this tradition tried consciously to reproduce the synergetic benefits of towns on a larger, national scale.[20] In order to achieve this, the sciences of law and administration had to be consciously cultivated and promoted. Renaissance economics emphasises the crucial role of nation-states and the duties of 'the ruler' – i.e. government – not only to regulate in order to provide incentives for the creation of welfare (in the old tradition of law and economics), but also the duty of 'the ruler' to initiate projects creating a *demand* for knowledge-based production. Thus, Renaissance economics has a strong emphasis on institutions. After all, the key enabling institutions of capitalism – like for example patents, banks and standards – were products of Renaissance Italy.

At the core of the Renaissance Other Canon is the observation that **some economic activities produce higher welfare than others**, a static and non-systemic observation of welfare being *activity specific*. (As if today: lawyers make more money than people picking lettuce; therefore a nation of lettuce pickers will be poorer than a nation of lawyers). Very soon – before 1500 – this argument is extended into one of synergies: Some economic activities are seen as being at the core of **systemic synergies** that produce and spread welfare locally or nation-wide ('where there are many people working with machines, **also the shopkeepers** are wealthier than in other places, where machines are not used'). There are degrees of understanding how these systemic synergies develop into **positive feedback systems**, but the top performance is that of Antonio Serra in 1613, who has a description of Venice as a true autocatalytic system, where ***increasing returns*** and ***diversity*** – the latter expressed *as the number of different professions in a nation* (i.e. *degree* of division of labour) – are identified as being at the core of virtuous circles which generate wealth[21]. Naples is the example of the opposite effect in Serra's system, because the production of raw materials is not subject to increasing returns. We also find Adam Smith in *The Wealth of Nations* asking himself: Why is there so little division of labour in agriculture? On the other hand agriculture is to him the only 'natural' activity. Smith fails, however, to make the connection that the 'unnatural' imperfect competition is a product of a sophisticated division of labour. Today these synergy-based arguments are found in the works on increasing return by authors like Paul David, W. Brian Arthur[22], and James Buchanan. [23]

---

[19] Serra, Antonio, *Breve trattato delle cause che possono far abbondare li regni d'oro e argento dove non sono miniere,* Naples, Lazzaro Scoriggio, 1613.

[20] For a discussion of this, see Reinert, Erik, 'Catching-Up From Way Behind. A Third World Perspective on First World History', in: Fagerberg, Jan et. al., *The Dynamics of Technology, Trade and Growth,* Aldershot, Edward Elgar, 1994.

[21] For a discussion of this, see Reinert, Erik, 'The Role of the State in Economic Growth.', in *Journal of Economic Studies,* vol. 26, No. 4/5, 1999.

[22] Arthur, W. Brian, *Increasing Returns and Path Dependency in the Economy*, Ann Arbor, University of Michigan Press, 1994.

[23] Buchanan, James and Yong J. Yoon (editors), *The Return to Increasing Returns,* Ann Arbor, University of Michigan Press, 1994.

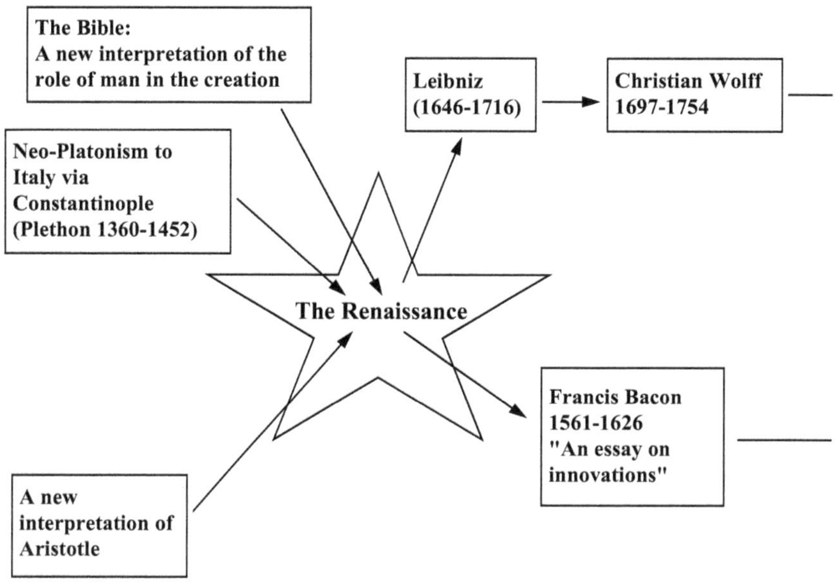

Figure 10.1

An integral part of the nation-building strategy was a notion that a national market had to be **created** – that such a marked did not appear spontaneously. For this reason, communication and state-initiated investments in large-scale infrastructure projects hold a very strong position in the Renaissance tradition, from the dams and irrigation canals of the Sumerian kingdoms via Colbert's canals to Kennedy's Interstate road projects. Using modern terms, we could say that the strategy of Renaissance economics was to create **perfect competition** within the national borders and **dynamic imperfect competition** in the export trade. Contrary to the common preconceptions of economics before Adam Smith, 'Competition was often artificially fostered (nationally)…in order to organise markets with automatic regulation of supply and demand'[24]. It was commonly agreed that a national competitive advantage had to be created in knowledge-intensive activities before free trade could be established with the most advanced nations.

This new world view of the Renaissance released enormous creativity in all sciences and arts – the new intellectual freedom gave us Leonardo da Vinci, Michelangelo, Rafael, Kepler and Copernicus. In all arts and sciences the people of the Renaissance still stand out in a heroic light in history, all but the statesmen and economists of the Renaissance. Still today these economists of the Renaissance, who made the modern world possible, come across as the gold-loving caricature that Adam Smith created of his mercantilist predecessors. These economists, however, are the true founders of evolutionary

[24] Eli Hecksher quoted in Polanyi, Karl, *The Great Transformation* (1944), Boston, Beacon Press, 1957, p. 278.

economics. In the spirit of the Renaissance Francis Bacon - Queen Elizabeth's Lord High Chancellor - wrote, around 1605, *An Essay of Innovations.* Bacon became the 'scientific leader of the new industrialist'[25] - urging the use of science to produce manufactured goods and profits. Up until and including James Stuart's 1767 two-volume *Inquiry into the Principles of Political Economy*[26] the term 'innovation' is frequently used, only to disappear with Adam Smith.

Bacon's spirit has often been evoked in order to argue against the mechanical world view of post-Ricardian economics. Richard Jones[27], the founder of the English historical school, and John Rae[28] were two economists who – as a reaction to the Ricardian system – consciously attempted to 'Baconise' economics again. Also Carl Menger quotes Francis Bacon against what we today would call 'physics envy' when he criticises 'the attempts to carry over the peculiarities of the natural-scientific method of investigation uncritically into economics.'[29]

Bacon's emphasis of scientific knowledge was very similar to that of Friedrich List more than 200 years later: 'Industry is the mother and father of science, literature, the art, enlightenment, useful institutions and national power... The greater the advance in scientific knowledge, the more numerous will be the new inventions which save labour and raw materials and lead to new products and processes.'[30] In this sense, there is a continuity of argument from the Renaissance, through Francis Bacon and Friedrich List to today's evolutionary economics that emphasises the role of Research and Development and of innovations for economic welfare. As to natural resources, List says that 'industrialisation will greatly increase the value of a country's natural resources.'[31] This thinking was the basis for economic policy in the resource-rich nations which have achieved general welfare: Canada, Australia, and New Zealand. A manufacturing sector – although one which was not seen as being competitive with that of England – was needed in order to transform the natural resources of a nation into national wealth.

---

25 Crowther, J.G., *Francis Bacon. The First Statesman of Science*, London, The Cresset Press, 1960, p. 97.

26 London, Millar and Cadell.

27 See Rashid, Salim, 'Richard Jones and Baconian Historicism at Cambridge', *Journal of Economic Issues,* Vol. XII, No. 1, March 1979, pp 159–265.

28 Rae, John, Statement of some new principles on the subject of political economy, exposing the fallacies of the system of free trade, and of some other doctrines maintained in the "Wealth of Nations", Boston, Hilliard, Gray & Co., 1834.

29 In the foreword to the *Grundsätze*: Menger, Carl, *Grundsätze der Volkswirtschaftslehre,* Vienna, Wilhelm Brauchmüller, 1871. In the English edition of the work, Menger's Latin quote from Bacon is translated as: 'similitudes and sympathies of things that have no reality, ...they describe and sometimes invent with great vanity and folly.' *Principles of Economics*, Glencoe, Ill., Free Press, 1950, p. 47.

30 List, Friedrich, *The National System of Political Economy* (1841), London, Longman, 1904, pp. 66–67.

31 *Ibid.,* p. 79.

The two types of economics that we have outlined should be seen as 'Ideal Types' in the Weberian sense. Through time there are several distinguishing features that clearly separates the two canons. A basic one is their different conceptions of the origin of wealth:

- In the *mainstream canon* wealth originates from ***material sources***: from nature, i.e. land, physical labour and capital. The accumulation of these assets takes place through ***trade*** and war. This accumulation is ***static***, i.e. more of the same.
- In the *Renaissance Other Canon* wealth originates from ***immaterial sources***: from culture, i.e. Man's creativity and morality. The accumulation of assets takes place through ***innovations*** cumulatively changing Man's stock of ***knowledge*** and his ***tools*** (technology). This accumulation is ***dynamic***, i.e. more of something new and qualitatively different. [32]

A second major distinguishing feature between the two canons is:

- In the *mainstream canon* the focus of analysis is ***barter, consumption*** and ***accumulation*** ('Man the Trader and Consumer').
- In *The Other Canon* the focus of analysis is on ***production*** and ***innovation; productivity*** being the pineal gland bringing together mind and matter ('Man the Creative Producer').

A third and fundamental difference between the canons is:

- The *mainstream canon* is – since the Aristotelian idea of the complete independence of politics from all other aspects of social life – fundamentally atomistic and mechanical in its analytical approach. The unit of analysis is the ***atomistic*** unit (in economics: the individual).
- *The Other Canon* – since Plato's *Republic* – is fundamentally ***holistic***, organic and synthetical (from *synthesis*) in its approach (*die Ganzheit*). The units of analysis include both individuals and their institutions in time and space.

At a very fundamental level, the two canons of economics are founded on two different views of how Man differs from other animals. We shall let Adam Smith represent the material and barter-based canon, and Abraham Lincoln represent Renaissance economics – the immaterial and production-based canon:

---

[32] For a discussion of this, see Reinert, Erik and Arno Daastøl, 'Exploring the Genesis of Economic Innovations: The Religious Gestalt-switch and the Duty to Invent as Preconditions for Economic Growth, in *European Journal of Law and Economics*, Vol. 4 (1997), pp. 233–283.

Adam Smith

> **'The division of labour arises from a propensity in human nature to... truck, barter and exchange one thing for another...It is common to all men, and to be found in no other race of animals, which seem to know neither this nor any other species of contracts...Nobody ever saw a dog make a fair and deliberate exchange of one bone for another with another dog.'**[33]

Abraham Lincoln

> **'...Beavers build houses; but they build them in nowise differently, or better, now than they did five thousand years ago...Man is not the only animal who labours; but he is the only one who *improves* his workmanship. These improvements he effects by *Discoveries* and *Inventions*....'**[34]

We also see a consistent pattern of application of the two canons in a ***catching-up*** framework:

No nation-state[35] has ever gone through a transition from poverty to affluence without practising a long period of the immaterial and production-based canon as the fundamental guide for economic *policy*. This is true in France (where a modern starting point for policy could be Louis XI, (1461); and Montchrétien, Jean Bodin, and Sully for theory), England (where a logical starting point for policy is the reign of Henry VII, in 1485), in Germany, the United States (Benjamin Franklin, Alexander Hamilton, Daniel Raymond, Henry Clay, Matthew and Henry Carey, E. Peshine Smith) and Japan (Meiji Restoration). Today we see the production-based economic strategy at work in East Asia. The Third World is essentially an area that has experienced neither a Renaissance-type creative awakening nor any production- and knowledge-based economic canon. Figure 10.2 shows the family tree of The Other Canon.

On the practical policy-level the two canons produce conflicting recommendations. This is due to the fact that whereas in the Renaissance theory different economic activities offer different potentials for achieving national welfare, in the barter-centred theory all economic activities become qualitatively 'alike'. If anything, in the standard canon superiority is traditionally awarded to agriculture, which is more 'natural' a) because it delivers Nature's produce, and b) because competition here is more 'natural'; atomistic and 'perfect.'

It is really only after 1960 that the economic policies of Smith and Ricardo have completely won the day in economic policy. The economists of alternative traditions who were crucial to the economic **policy** are almost completely left out of today's history of economic thought. The last history of economics to give a good coverage of the

---

33 Adam Smith, *Wealth of Nations* (1776), Chicago, University of Chicago Press, 1976, p. 17.

34 Abraham Lincoln, Speech of the 1860 Presidential Campaign.

35 With the possible exception of small city-states, like Hong Kong or San Marino.

theories behind the 19th Century economic policy was Ottmar Spann's *Die Haupttheorien der Volkswirtschaftslehre,* which first appeared in 1911. By 1936 this book had reached 24 editions and a total of 120.000 copies printed in German.[36] There were translations to several languages, and, interestingly, the UK edition was published under the title *Types of Economic Theory,* flagging Spann's awareness of diversity: that there are, indeed, different types of economics, not only one monolithic canon.

Of course, we do not imply that the world is a binary one, where all economists belong either to one tradition or the other. On the contrary, a key characteristic of several important economists is their at times schizophrenic allegiance to both sets of theory. One example of this is the conflict between the Marshall whose 'Mecca of the economist' lay in economic biology [37] and the Marshall of the appendices to his *Principles* which were deeply steeped in 'physics-envy'. In order to create the equilibrium that characterises today's physics-based standard economic theory, Marshall paradoxically had to restore to a *biological* metaphor. Increasing returns had been an important argument for industrial policy ever since Antonio Serra in 1613 [38] all through the 19th Century. In order to reconcile the existence of increasing returns with equilibrium, Marshall uses a lengthy metaphor of firms growing and dying like trees in the forests.[39] This evolutionary growth process supposedly counteracts the tendency towards uneven accumulation caused by increasing returns to scale.[40] The argument that killed all future biological analogies in neo-classical economics was a biological analogy. This biological analogy was important in making economics into what it is today, a profession where a physics-inspired equilibrium is the central gestalt.

Seen from this point of view, also Marx was caught between two paradigms which at one level are mutually exclusive. In terms of his emphasis on technology and economic dynamics, Marx – like Schumpeter – is a clear member of the Renaissance production-based canon. Marx' and Schumpeter's visions have a common basis in the German economic tradition. In Anglo-Saxon economics these two economists come across as extremely original, seen from the German side they are both firmly rooted in that alternative canon. The one aspect of Marx' theory which decidedly belongs to the Anglo-Saxon canon is his use of Ricardo's labour theory of value. The labour theory of value is out of place in the German tradition where entrepreneurship, ideas, knowledge, leadership, and management necessarily contribute importantly to the value added created by physical labour.

---

36 The US edition is *The History of Economics*, New York, Norton, 1930.

37 Marshall, Alfred, *Principles of Economics,* London, Macmillan, 1890, p. iv.

38 Serra, Antonio, *Breve trattato delle cause che possono far abbondare li regni d'oro e argento dove non sono miniere,* Naples, Lazzaro Scoriggio, 1613.

39 Marshall, *op.cit.*, pp. 315–316.

40 This problem is discussed in Hart, Neil, 'Increasing returns and economic theory: Marshall's reconciliation problem', University of Western Sydney, *Discussion Paper Series*, No. E9004, 1990.

Reality Economics: The Knowledge- and Production-Based Other Canon of Economics

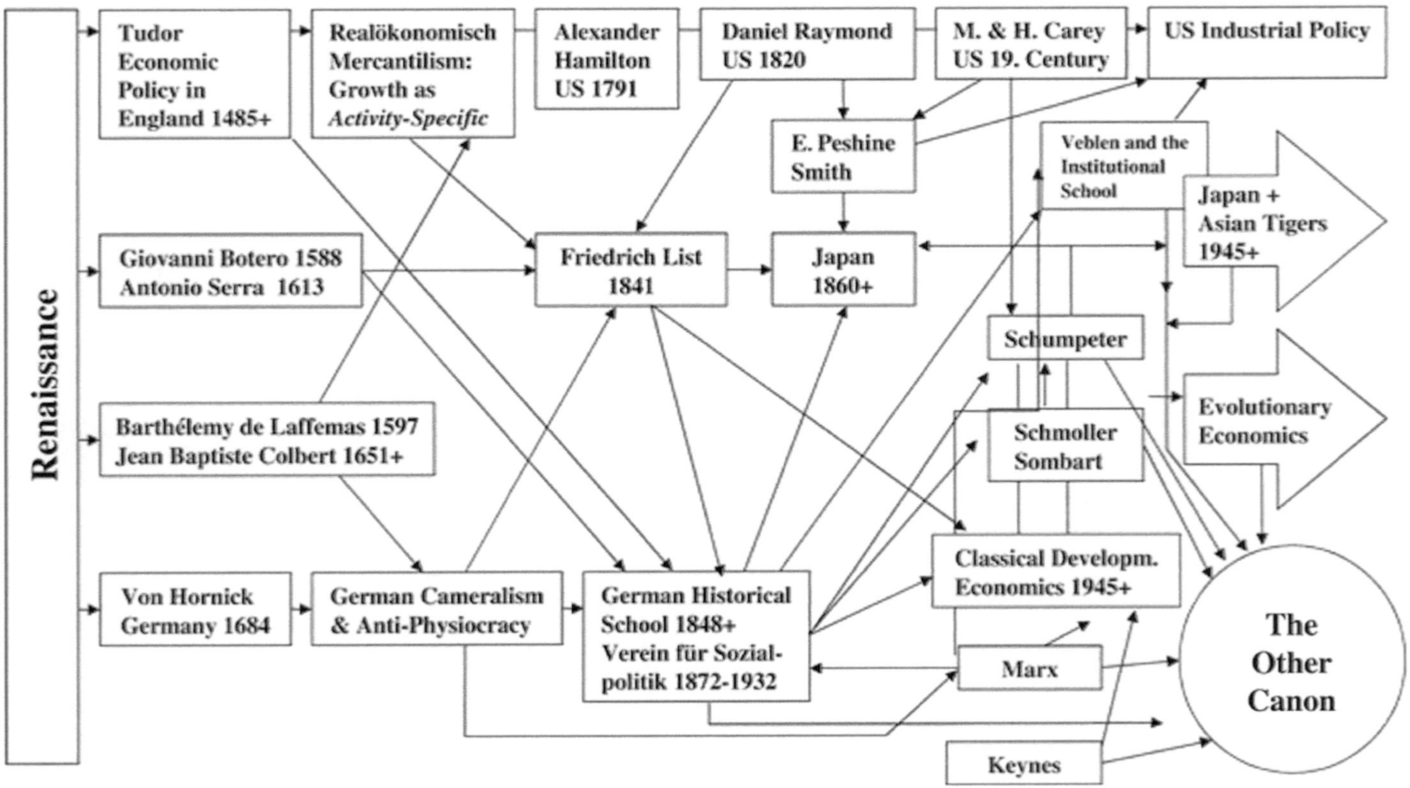

Figure 10.2

2. The Two Canons Contrasted as *Ideal Types*.[41]

STARTING POINT FOR THE STANDARD CANON:	**STARTING POINT FOR 'THE OTHER CANON':**
Equilibrium under *perfect information* and *perfect foresight*	Learning and decision-making under uncertainty (Schumpeter, Keynes, Shackle)
High level of abstraction	Level of abstraction chosen according to problem to be resolved
Man's wit and will absent	Moving force: *Geist- und Willenskapital:* Man's wit and will, entrepreneurship
Not able to handle *novelty* as an endogenous phenomenon	*Novelty* as a central moving force
Moving force: 'capital per se propels the capitalist engine'	Moving force: New knowledge which creates a demand for capital to be provided from the financial sector
Metaphors from the realm of physics	Metaphors (carefully) from the realm of biology
Mode of understanding: Mechanistic ('begreifen')	Mode of understanding: Qualitative ('verstehen'), a type of understanding irreducible only to numbers and symbols
Matter	*Geist* precedes matter
Focused on *Man the Consumer*	Focused on *Man the Innovator and Producer.*
A. Smith: 'Men are animals which have learned to barter'	A. Lincoln: 'Men are animals which not only work, but innovate'
Focused on static/comparative static	Focused on change
Not cumulative/history absent	Cumulative causations/'history matters'/ backwash effects (Myrdal, Kaldor, Schumpeter, German Historical School)
Increasing returns to scale and its absence a non-essential feature	Increasing returns and its absence essential to explaining differences in income between firms, regions and nations (Kaldor)
Very precise ('would rather be accurately wrong than approximately correct')	Aiming at relevance over precision, recognizes the *trade-off between relevance and precision* as a core issue in the profession
'Perfect competition' (commodity competition/price competition) as an ideal situation = a goal for society	Innovation- and knowledge-driven Schumpeterian competition as both engine of progress and ideal situation. With perfect competition, with equilibrium and no innovation, capital becomes worthless (Schumpeter, Hayek)
The market as a mechanism for setting prices	The market also as an arena for rivalry and as a mechanism selecting between different products and different solutions. (Schumpeter, Nelson & Winter)
Equality Assumption I: No diversity	Diversity as a key factor (Schumpeter, Shackle)
Equality Assumption II: All economic activities are *alike* and *of equal quality* as carriers of economic growth and welfare	Growth and welfare are *activity-specific* – different economic activities present widely different potentials for absorbing new knowledge

(*continued*)

[41] I am grateful the co-authors of this set of ideal types: Leonardo Burlamaqui, Ha-Joon Chang, Peter Evans and Jan Kregel.

STARTING POINT FOR THE STANDARD CANON:	**STARTING POINT FOR 'THE OTHER CANON':**
Both theory and policy recommendations tend to be *independent of context* ('one medicine cures all')	Both theory and policy recommendations highly *context dependent*
The economy largely independent from society	The economy as firmly embedded in society
Technology as a *free good*, as 'manna from heaven'	Knowledge and technology are *produced*, have cost and are protected. This production is based on incentives of the system, including law, institutions and policies
Equilibrating forces at the core of the system and of the theory	Cumulative forces are more important than equilibrating ones, and should therefore be at the core of the system
Economics as *Harmonielehre* II: The economy as a self-regulating system seeking equilibrium and harmony	Economics as an inherently unstable and conflict-rich discipline. Achieving stability is based on Man's policy measures (Carey, Polanyi, Weber, Keynes)
Postulates the representative firm	No 'representative firm'. All firms are unique (Penrose)
Static optimum. Perfect rationality	Dynamic optimization under uncertainty. Bounded rationality
No distinction made between real economy and financial economy	Conflicts between real economy and financial economy are normal and must be regulated (Minsky, Keynes)
Saving caused by refraining from consumption and a cause of growth	Saving largely results from profits (Schumpeter) and saving *per se* is not useful or desirable for growth (Keynes)

3. Canonical Battles: The Head-on Confrontations

Occasionally the two canons meet head-on in what we have labelled ***Canonical Methodenstreite.*** Below we describe five of these Methodenstreite:

Canonical Methodenstreit 1: Misselden vs. Malynes (1622–23)

The theoretical conflict between the forefathers of today's mainstream canon and the Renaissance canon has existed at least since the 1622–23 'English' debate between Gerard de Malynes [42] and Edward Misselden, [43] where Malynes represented

[42] Malynes, Gerhard, *The Maintenance of Free Trade, According to the three essentiall (sic) Parts... Commodities, Moneys and Exchange of Moneys*, London William Sheffard, 1622, and *The Center of the Circle of Commerce, or, A Refutation of a Treatise,...., lately published by E.M.*, London, Nicholas Bourne, 1623.

[43] Misselden, Edward, *Free Trade and the Meanes (sic) to Make Trade Flourish*, London, Simon Waterson, 1622, and, *The Circle of Commerce or the Ballance (sic) of Trade*, London, Nicholas Bourne, 1623,

a static theory rooted in *barter* and Misselden represented a theory centred around *learning* and *production*. Both Misselden and Malynes were Dutchmen from Antwerp working in London. In the history of economic thought, their debate is interpreted as being about exchange controls and the balance of trade.[44] The controversy between the two was an 'acrimonious, even abusive' one, in which 'ink was shed like water'[45].

However, by going back to the sources, one finds that the main line of attack by Misselden against Malynes is his 'mechanical' view of man – Malynes has left out Man's 'art' and 'soul'. Misselden quotes at length a paragraph from Malynes, where Malynes reduces trade to three elements, 'namely, Commodities, Money, and Exchange'[46]. Objecting to this definition, Misselden says: 'It is against Art to dispute with a man that denyeth the *Principles* of Art'. Misselden scorns Malynes for not seeing the difference between a heap of stones and logs and a house – because Man's productive powers and his soul, which produce the house, have been left out. A similar criticism can of course be made of neo-classical economics. Typically, after the Renaissance, the wealth of a nation was seen as lying in its capacity to produce, its 'productive powers.'

Misselden represents the acute Renaissance awareness of the enormous territory to be covered between Mankind's present poverty and ignorance, and the enormous potentials. This released enthusiasm and energy. The situation recalls Keynes' frustration with the suboptimal situation of the world under the Great Depression. Both the Renaissance philosophers/economists and Keynes were searching for the formula needed to liberate society from its obviously suboptimal position at the time. This is what Keynes called 'Salvation through Knowledge'[47]. This attitude is very different from Man as the passive victim of 'two sovereign masters, pain and pleasure'[48], which is the philosophical foundation of English classical economics.

Canonical Methodenstreit 2: Anti-physiocracy vs. Physiocracy & Adam Smith (ca. 1770–1830)

The second Methodenstreit between the knowledge-based Renaissance school and the predecessor of today's standard (neo-classical based) economic theory starts in the 1770's with the rise of the Physiocratic School in France. It may be said that the Physiocratic School in some sense was a reaction to the perversion of Colbertism into a policy of

[44] Schumpeter discusses the controversy between the two men in his *History of Economic Analysis*, New York, Oxford University Press, 1954, pp. 344–345. See also their respective entries in 'The New Palgrave'. In all cases these references are purely to the mechanics of money and exchange.

[45] Buck, Philip, *The Politics of Mercantilism*, New York, Henry Holt, 1942, p. 23.

[46] Misselden, *op. cit.*, (1623), p. 8.

[47] Ibid., p. 102.

[48] Jeremy Bentham, *An Introduction to the Principles of Morals and Legislation*, (1780), London, University Paperback, Ch. I, p.11.

indiscriminate taxation. It was also clearly a reaction of the landowners against Colbert's policy of systematically diverting resources from agriculture to manufacturing.

The physiocrats had an animalistic view of Man which was compatible with the philosophical foundations of English classical economics: '…sometimes (the physiocrats) regard man as a browsing animal, concerned only with his nourishment, the maximum production of the fruit of the earth as his social ideal.'[49]

The anti-physiocratic movement has received little attention in the history of economic thought. These authors, however, represented the true continuation of Renaissance economics. Interestingly, two of the main opponents of physiocracy in France were clergymen: Abbé Mably and Abbé Galiani, the Neapolitan envoy to the Court of Paris.[50] Galiani was to take a position which in many ways foreshadowed the position of the historical school in late 19th Century Methodenstreit: 'Abstract principles are no good for commercial policy. Corn laws which are good in one time or place may be bad in another. … The statesman who admired Colbert should not imitate him, but ask himself, "What would Colbert do if he were here now?" '[51] Abbé Galiani's criticism of a very abstract and context-free theory is very similar to the reaction of Reverend Jones, against the writings of Ricardo in 1820. Richard Jones was the father of the English historical school of economics, which became very influential during the latter half of the 19th Century. The insistence that economic theory and policy must be context-specific is a sure hallmark of Other Canon economics through the ages.

One of the main opponents of the physiocratic school[52] in France was Forbonnais, who refused to admit that trade and industry are sterile. Also to Forbonnais the main agent creating wealth is Man – not nature itself: without human agency **the land itself** is doomed to absolute or relative stability. Other contemporary French opponents of physiocracy were Accarias de Serrionne, Graslin, Necker, and Linguet.

Perhaps the most ardent anti-physiocrats were found in Germany. Under the heading 'Antiphysiokraten', Humpert's bibliography of the German cameralist school lists 25 works – published between 1771 and 1832.[53] The best known of these works is Johann Friedrich von Pfeiffer's ***Der Antiphysiokrat***.[54] Pfeiffer was also the author of the most influential economic work in Germany at the time. Other strong continental opponents of physiocracy were Johann Jakob von Moser, Dohm, and Sonnenfels.

---

[49] Higgs, Henry, *The Physiocrats*, London, Macmillan, 1897.

[50] A good description of Galiani and his unique standing in French society at the time is found in Pecchio, Giuseppe, *Storia della Economia Pubblica in Italia,* Lugano, Tipografia della Svizzera Italiana, 1849, pp. 80–86.

[51] Higgs, *op. cit.*, p. 117.

[52] The anti-physiocrats are discussed in Weulersee, Georges, *Le mouvement physiocratique en France*, Paris, Alcan, 1910, vol. 2, pp. 256–682, and in Higgs, op.cit., pp. 102–122.

[53] Humpert, Magdalene, *Bibliographie der Kameralwissenschaften*, Cologne, Kurt Schroeder, 1937, pp. 1031–1032.

[54] Pfeiffer, Johann Friedrich von, *Der Antiphysiokrat, oder umständliche Untersuchung des sogenannten physiokratischen Systems für eine allgemeine Freyheit und einzige Auflage auf den reinen Ertrag der Grundstücke,* Frankfurt am Main, Schäfer, 1780.

Canonical Methodenstreit 3: The American System vs. The British System (19th Century United States)

The US opposition to English classical economic theory started with Benjamin Franklin and continued with Alexander Hamilton's 1791 'Report on the Manufactures'. This *Methodenstreit* on the policy level lasted all through the 1930's, although on the theoretical level English classical economics was to be increasingly taught at the Ivy League universities during the late 19th Century. Important economists in this US tradition were Daniel Raymond, Matthew and Henry Carey, John Rae, E. Peshine Smith and many others. The last great economists of this tradition were Richard Ely and Simon Patten, who – like most US economists who studied abroad in the 19th Century – studied in Germany. After Thorstein Veblen, this economic tradition continued under the label of institutional economics. Both the general stance against Ricardian economics, and the mental affiliation with German-type economics, continued much as in the 19th Century tradition.

On the policy level, the nations industrialising in the 19th Century were to take up the example that had been set by England – and later abandoned by her when she had reached world hegemony. Economic thought and policy of all great industrial nations in their pre-take-off period share a core theme of the *activity-specific* nature of growth. Economic growth could only be achieved by including activities with fast technological change and a rapid growth in output in the nation's portfolio of industrial activities. This theme can be followed in economic writings from the early 1500 in Italy and England and France, a little later in the German cameralists. It is introduced to the United States through Alexander Hamilton and his favourite economist, the English mercantilist Malachy Postlethwayt[55]. Two path-breaking volumes in this school were published in 1820 by Daniel Raymond[56] and Mathew Carey[57]. Heavily influenced by Daniel Raymond, Friedrich List's involuntary exile in the US reinforces this already traditional way of thinking in the Germany of the Zollverein. In Meiji Japan the *doitsugaku* school – favouring the German model – came to be the most influential for the building of society, at least until 1945.[58] In Japan, after 1883, 'a stream of German teachers of political economy and related disciplines continually flowed in'.[59]

---

55 It has been shown that Hamilton knew his Adam Smith, but rejected particularly the free trade conclusion. Excerpts from Postlethwayt's *Universal Dictionary of Trade and Commerce* were scattered through Hamilton's Army pay book, see Morris, Richard B. *Alexander Hamilton and the Founding of the Nation,* New York, Dial Press, 1957, p. 285. Hamilton's view on the English classical economists was similar to that taken 80 years later by the Japanese, see Morris-Suzuki, Tessa, *The History of Japanese Economic Thought,* London, Routledge, 1989.

56 Raymond, Daniel, *Thoughts on Political Economy,* Baltimore, Fielding Lucas, 1820.

57 His pamphlet: *An Address to the Farmers of the United States.*

58 Yagi, Kiichiro, 'German Model in the Modernisation of Japan', in *The Kyoto University Economic Review,* Vol. 59, No. 1–2, April-October 1989, p. 29.

59 Sugiyama, Chuhei, and Hiroshi Mizuta, *Enlightenment and Beyond. Political economy comes to Japan,* Tokyo, University of Tokyo Press, 1988, p. 32.

A common thread of successful long-distance catching-up through the centuries is a shared distrust of generalised free trade until the nation is firmly established in what was seen to be the *right* economic activities – the *specific activities* which increased the nation's 'productive powers'. Through the dynamic imperfect competition (i.e. Schumpeter's 'historical increasing returns') in these specific activities, real wages could be raised: first in the 'engine' industry and subsequently spreading through the whole national labour market. In the US tradition, by adding skill to the labourer, his price or value (= wage) was increased. This tradition survived in the United States up until and including the economists who were taught by Ely's and Patten's generation. In a letter to the author, dated August 16, 1996, Moses Abramowitz comments: 'I agree in particular that the "residual" and growth in general are industry-specific. That has seemed clear to me since I was a graduate student in the Thirties and read the Kuznets and Burns books…' This certainly points to a 'filiation' between the old American school and present day 'economics of catching up'.

Canonical Methodenstreit 4: The Historical School vs. Marginalism (1883–1908)

The resounding success of Ricardian economics and its extreme laissez-faire policies during the 1840's provoked a theoretical countermovement following the political events of 1848. The international depression in1873 further increased the opposition against the classical economic tradition all over Europe. The stronghold of the opposition was in Germany, where the older historical school founded by Bruno Hildebrand – whose book was published in 1848[60] – Karl Knies and Wilhelm Roscher increasingly challenged both the theoretical foundations and practical conclusions of Ricardian economics. Later a new generation of historical economists led by Gustav Schmoller – the younger historical school – for a long time completely dominated German academic and practical economics.

Carl Menger, the founder of the Austrian marginalist school, in 1883 published his book: *Untersuchungen über die Methode der Sozialwissenschaften und der politischen Ökonomie insbesondere.* Menger had dedicated his first book to Wilhelm Roscher – the prominent German economist of the Historical School. Menger closed the preface praising recent German economics and hoping that his book 'be regarded …as a friendly greeting from a collaborator in Austria.' The reply from Germany to his books was not friendly. Schmoller reviewed the *Untersuchungen* unfavourably in his *Jahrbuch*, and Menger replied in a small book entitled *Errors of Historicism* in 1884.[61] Of all the *Methodenstreite*, this – the most famous one – is paradoxically the least fundamental of them all. Menger and Schmoller essentially shared the same critical attitude towards the mechanical and

[60] Hildebrand, Bruno, *Die Nationalökonomie der Gegenwart und Zukunft*, Frankfurt, Literarische Anstalt, 1848.

[61] Menger, Carl, *Die Irrtümer des Historismus in der deutschen Nationalökonomie,* Wien, Alfred Hölder, 1884. See also Ritzel, Gerhard, *Schmoller versus Menger*, Frankfurt am Main, n.p., 1950.

barter-based English theory. Their personalities and pride clashed, but compared to Ricardian economics the two are next of kin. This *Methodenstreit* created a debilitating civil war inside The Other Canon.

Schmoller wanted theory to be empirically founded, in opposition to the English classical tradition that founded theory on introspective assumptions, and deducing far-reaching practical conclusions from these abstract structures. This practice was what Schumpeter labelled 'the Ricardian vice'. Today's standard explanation of the *Methodenstreit* generally fails to point out how similar their criticism of Ricardian economics was. The New Palgrave describes the Methodenstreit as follows: '(Schmoller) rejected Menger's deductive method for three chief reasons: its assumptions were unrealistic, its high degree of abstraction made it largely irrelevant to the real-world economy, and it was devoid of empirical content. The theory was therefore useless in studying the chief questions of importance to economists; how have the economic institutions of the modern world developed to their present state, and what are the laws and regularities that govern them? The proper method was induction of general principles from historical-empirical studies'.[62] However, reading through Menger's *Errors of Historicism* with the perspective of what economics has become in the year 2000, it becomes clear how 'Other Canon' both Schmoller and Menger in fact were.

The historical school was deeply steeped in the German tradition of embracing *die Ganzheit* – the whole. This search for *die Ganzheit* forced the historical school to cross the boundaries into what in the English tradition were other – and to them unrelated – academic disciplines. In the German historical tradition it would be complete nonsense to exclude any information relevant to the question asked – be it from the realm of climatology, pedagogy or any other branch of human knowledge. In the German tradition economics was a science that integrated all the others. However, it is not at all clear that Menger disagreed with this. Menger drew up a picture – a model – of the economic forces at work, but, like Schumpeter later, he insisted that history was an 'indispensable' tool for the profession.

To Menger, the problem of the historical school was that they suffered from a kind of a 'case-study syndrome': they collected raw materials for a theory, but never got around to establishing a proper theory. This criticism is similar to that of Thorstein Veblen. However, this criticism is more appropriate to some members of the historical school than to others. It is indeed crucial to define what is meant by 'theory'. The marginalist tradition came to seek 'pure theory', a formalist kind of theory that excluded from economics all the forces that in the Renaissance tradition were the driving forces of history. However, of all the marginalists, Menger was clearly the closest to the historical school, as we shall discuss later he both 'invented' marginalism and, at the same time, went far beyond it.

62 Fusfeld, Daniel R, 'Methodenstreit', in *The New Palgrave Dictionary*, Macmillan, London 1987, p. 454.

The criticism of the marginalists from the historical school was that the very source of wealth – Man's wit and will – had disappeared. This had led to an *Entgeistung der Volkswirtschaftslehre,* the role of Man's wit and will had been left out of the science. The German ethical historical school – with its US followers like Richard Ely and Simon Patten – followed the Renaissance tradition of seeing economics as a normative science, setting out to transform society for the benefit of the common weal. Morality was, to them, rational, and part of the *Ganzheit* of the economics profession. In contrast, to British empiricist philosophy and classical economics, morality was irrational and based on sympathy (feeling) in the tradition of Hume and Smith. Accordingly, to the English school morality was totally separated from economics.

Canonical Methodenstreit 5. The US Institutional vs. The Neoclassical School (20th Century)

Institutional economics presents a continuation of the US and German 19th Century economics tradition. Institutionalism – a term originally coined only to describe the work of Norwegian-American economist Thorstein Veblen (1857–1929) – continued the radical trend of 'The American System' in opposing the abstract structures of English theory.

The institutionalists were very critical of the established economic doctrine, but most of them did not seek to throw it out completely. Since their theory was *praxisnah* – empirical and close to reality – the institutionalists attracted the attention of policy-makers. Academically and in terms of influence US institutionalism peaked in the troubled 1930's, and it may be argued that institutional policy-makers in the early 1930's anticipated the Keynesian policy prescription without his elaborate theoretical framework.

Although institutionalism declined rapidly after World War II – really during the years of McCarthyism – its influence on economic policy-making in Washington still lingers on. Two recent and informative books trace the demise of institutional economics in the United States: Yuval Yonay's *The Struggle over the Soul of Economics* [63], and a collection of papers: *From Interwar Pluralism to Postwar Neoclassicism.*[64]

Today Paul Krugman complains that 'It is not just that economists have lost control of the discourse; the kinds of ideas that are offered in a standard economics textbook do not enter into that discourse at all….'[65] If we ask ourselves *to whom* the economists have lost control, Krugman lists an alliance of 'policy makers, business leaders and influential intellectuals'.[66] These are the groups which today defend the common sense and pragmatism of institutional economics against the unmitigated rule of standard textbook

---

63 Yonay, Yuval, *The Struggle over the Soul of Economics*, Princeton University Press, 1998.

64 Morgan, Mary S. and Malcolm Rutherford (editors), *From Interwar Pluralism to Postwar Neoclassicism,* Annual Supplement to History of Political Economy, Volume 30, Durham, Duke University Press, 1998.

65 Krugman quoted in Reder, Melvin W., *Economics. The Culture of a Controversial Science,* Chicago, University of Chicago Press, 1999, p. 6.

66 *Ibid.*, same page.

economics. To the *Ricardian Vice* labelled by Schumpeter we may add the *Krugmanian Vice*: the vice of possessing more relevant economic theories – like e.g. new trade theory – but refusing to employ these principles in real world economic policy.

Thus, though neo-classicism won the day in academia and in our economic policy towards the Second and Third Words, the eclectic pragmatism of the institutional school lives on in the policy-making both in United States and in Western Europe. In academia, the proponents of this school are today mostly scattered in business schools, departments of governments, and of international affairs. As a result of the virtual eradication of Other Canon economists from departments of economics, the poor countries of the world are still treated to undiluted neo-classical economics as administered by the Washington Institutions.

4. The Austrians and The Other Canon

Austrian economics in many ways bridges the two canons. If the theory of economics is seen from the angle outlined in the first part of this paper, the founder of Austrian economics, Carl Menger, his pupil Richard Schüller, and Joseph Alois Schumpeter all stand out as economists whose fundamental attitudes make them Other Canon economists. In the other end of the historical spectrum – in a process clearly also influenced by the political agenda created by the Cold War – the modern US/Austrian School has, for most practical purposes, strongly approached what we here refer to as the standard canon of economics.

The central idea of Menger's *Grundsätze* [67] is to present a dynamic theory of economic development, which he presents in the fifth paragraph as 'The Causes of Progress in Human Welfare'. In this section we shall attempt to illustrate the similarities between Menger's approach and that of 19th Century Other Canon theorists in the United States, people like John Rae and E. Peshine Smith. Like Menger, these were economists writing in strong opposition to the English classical school.

When reading Menger, it soon becomes clear that this man went far beyond the marginalism he is noted for. As Erich Streissler says it: 'Menger is unique because he surpassed marginalism at the same time that he created it'. 'To him (Menger), his ideas beyond marginalism were the most precious.'[68] A re-reading of Menger makes it clear that Streissler is right when he explains: 'Menger.. is to a large extent now forgotten precisely because in the reign of his successors in Vienna, the co-reign of Wieser (1903–24) and Böhm-Bawerk (1904–14) – the latter pre-dominating during his life-time – much of what was genuinely Menger's tradition got lost.' We shall argue in this paper that both neo-classical economics and Austrian economics have followed similar paths away from the visions of their founders, Marshall and Menger, parallel paths away from a focus on production and methodological diversity towards a theory where barter/exchange and

[67] Menger, Carl, *Grundsätze der Volkswirtschaftslehre,* Vienna, Wilhelm Brauchmüller, 1871.

[68] Streissler, Erich, 'To what Extent was the Austrian School Marginalist', *History of Political Economy,* Vol. 4, No. 2, fall 1972, p. 430.

lack of diversity dominates. In our terminology, most important 'Other Canon' elements were lost both in neoclassical and in Austrian economics during the 20th Century.

Menger lived long enough to see that his successors were sliding back into 'old errors' of economic science. Menger told Schumpeter that 'The time will come when people will realize that Böhm-Bawerk's theory is one of the gravest errors ever committed'[69] Menger also charged Böhm-Bawerk directly in his obituary that he had relapsed into old doctrines. Schumpeter identifies these doctrines as the 'Ricardian roots' of Böhm's theories.[70] Already with Menger's first successor in the genealogy of Austrian economics, in 1903, Austrian theory is taking a decisive bend towards the English-based mainstream tradition. One recent book discusses this under the fitting heading of 'The progressive Neglect of Menger's Originality'.[71]

Typically, today's standard economic theory is what Lionel Robbins termed a *Harmonielehre*[72], a system where the resulting economic harmony is built into the very assumptions of the theoretical structure. There are two types of entrepreneurs in Austrian theory, who have opposite impacts in this respect:

1. The *Hayekian/Kirznerian entrepreneur* who produces equilibrium and economic harmony, and
2. The *Schumpeterian entrepreneur*, who produces disequilibrium and disharmony in the form of uneven economic development.

Of these two types of entrepreneurs, the Hayekian version is fundamentally a harmony-producing element of the standard economic canon, whereas the Schumpeterian entrepreneur is the destroyer of equilibrium, the element introducing the *novelty* and *new knowledge* that standard theory is essentially unable to handle. As we shall see, the young Schumpeter – as opposed to most other Austrians – also fundamentally disagreed with the notion of equilibrium.

Today the fundamental difference between modern US-Austrian and neoclassical economics seems to be that while neoclassical economics has a mechanical view of equilibrium, the Austrians focus on the process of *reaching* equilibrium, and the need for an entrepreneur to get there.[73] This may indeed have been a crucially important distinction in the debate between central planning and capitalism, but in a post-cold-war world, the differences in policy recommendations that can be derived from the two theories seem less important. Although the intellectual effort underpinning Hayek's *laissez-faire* towers above the mechanics of basic neoclassicism, the outcome on the policy level does

---

69 Schumpeter, *History of Economic Analysis*, p. 847.

70 *Ibid.*, p.846.

71 Gloria-Palermo, Sandye, *The Evolution of Austrian Economics From Menger to Lachmann*, London, Routledge, p. 37–75.

72 Robbins, Lionel, *The Theory of Economic Policy in English Classical Economics*, London, Macmillan, 1952, pp. 22–29.

73 This is the main argument in a recent book, Machovec, Frank M., *Perfect Competition and the Transformation of Economics*, Routledge, 1995.

not differ significantly.[74] Nicolai Foss pinpoints the problem: 'It is not only that modern Austrian economics asks different questions and gives different answers, it is perhaps more a fundamentally a matter of modern Austrian economics being unable to ask a number of interesting questions.'[75] Foss then lists the questions about which Austrian economics is silent: 'the process of technological change, its organization and economic consequences, strategic interaction between duopolists, oligopolists, etc., the firm, its organization and activities.' We could also add: diversity of all kinds, including the issue of world poverty, and novelty. The list of questions that are outside the reach of the modern Austrian and of the neo-classical paradigms overlaps to a large degree, although most of these questions were discussed both by Menger and Marshall. This is one reason we here refer to the parallel loss of Other Canon issues in both sets of theories.

One fundamental element causing this convergence between Austrian and Neoclassical economics seems to lie in the loss of the factor *time* in both theories[76]. Focussing on exchange rather than on production, and having accepted Walras' virtually instant equilibrium – the one-minute *tâtonnement* – modern Austrians and modern neoclassicals are both *Harmonielehren.* Here they stand in sharp contrast to Menger and Schumpeter. Menger's *tâtonnement* takes a century[77], and in a system with constant innovations equilibrium *will hardly ever be reached.* Here we find a most important difference between Menger on the one hand and the later Austrians and the neo-classical on the other: To Menger the theoretical structure was *a map of the forces at work*, but the final outcome of these forces could neither be fully described, nor quantified. Nor would the final result necessarily be harmonious. Menger thus opens up for an economic theory that analyses the world as it is, and where development is potentially an uneven process.

Menger's pupil Richard Schüller writes his two main works while Menger's influence dominates at the University of Vienna, before the 'backsliding'[78] of Wieser and Böhm is much felt. Schüller dedicates both his works to his teacher Menger: *Die klassische Nationalökonomie und Ihre Gegner* (Berlin 1895) and *Schutzzoll und Freihandel. Die Voraussetzung und Grenzen Ihrer Berechtigung* (Vienna 1905). There are reasons to believe that Schüller was one of the students who were closest to Menger. This is indicated when – much later, in 1923 – Menger's son, Karl Menger, asks Schüller to write the foreword to the second edition of his father's *Grundsätze*[79]. This edition is published two years after Menger's death at the age of 81, marking the 50's anniversary of the first edition. In his introduction, written just five months after Manger passed away, Karl Menger thanks 'his father's dear friend, Prof.

---

74 For an evaluation of Hayek and economic policy, see Streit, Manfred E. 'Constitutional Ignorance, Spontaneous Order and Rule-Orientation: Hayekian Paradigms from a Policy Perspective', in: Frowen, Stephen F. (Editor), *Hayek. Economist and Social Philosopher,* Basingstoke, Macmillan, 1997, pp. 37–58.

75 Foss, Nicolai, *The Austrian School and Modern Economics: Essays in Reassessment,* Copenhagen, Handelsøjskolens Forlag, 1994, p. 194.

76 With some exceptions in the Austrian tradition.

77 See Streissler, *op. cit.*, p. 440.

78 This is the term Streissler uses in describing Menger's successors.

79 Wien, Hölder-Pichler-Tempsky, 1923.

Dr. Richard Schüller', for his 'many valuable suggestions' and for agreeing to write the foreword to the book.

In Schüller, a Mengerian unpolluted by the 'backsliding' Austrians of the next generation, we find a typical Other Canon economist. When discussing the perennial question of free trade vs. protectionism, Schüller starts with a discussion of *how costs develop* as a nation specialises in a certain type of activity[80]. This discussion goes right to the core of the trade debate of The Other Canon from Serra's first description of increasing returns in 1613, limited to manufacturing, and all through the 19th Century debates in the US and Germany. Schüller's focus on production rather than on barter, and on increasing returns, makes him a typical Other Canon economist, whose system is one of uneven benefits from trade caused by the different development in costs structures according to a nations 'choice' of specialisation. Schüller's increasing returns are found not only in production, but also in finance, advertising and in 'travelling salesmen'[81]. Increasing and diminishing returns are, to Schüller, factors which cause uneven economic growth, and one of many factors which need to be evaluated before deciding whether a nation should protect its manufacturing industry or not.

Also in Schumpeter's world, economic development is an uneven process. To Schumpeter 'the upper strata of society are like hotels which are…always full of people, but people who are forever changing'.[82] In chapter 7 of the first edition of his *Theorie der wirtschaftlichen Entwicklung*, Schumpeter makes the following statement on economic equilibrium:

> 'It lies in the very foundation of our way of thinking that there is no such thing as a dynamic equilibrium. Economic development is in its very nature a disturbance of the existing static equilibrium, without any tendency whatsoever for the system neither to move back to the original point of equilibrium, nor to any other point of equilibrium.'[83]

By the time the second edition of this work appears, in 1926, the whole chapter containing this paragraph – *Das Gesamtbild der Volkswirtschaft* – is gone. This 'case of the missing chapter' contains some interesting elements. In his new foreword to the second edition, Schumpeter informs the reader that chapter 7 has been omitted. Then, later on in the same foreword he comments on the changes that have been made to chapter 7 – a chapter which is not in the book at all. The same mistake – referring to a chapter which is not there – is repeated in the otherwise carefully edited and commented French translation of 1935. In his foreword Schumpeter comments as follows on chapter 7, which he

---

80 Schüller, Richard, *Schutzzoll und Freihandel. Die Voraussetzung und Grenzen Ihrer Berechtigung*, Vienna, Tempsky, 1905, starting on page 9.

81 *Ibid*, p. 15.

82 Schumpeter, Joseph A., *The Theory of Economic Development*, Cambridge, Mass., Harvard University Press, 1934, p. 156. This part has been added since the first German edition, Leipzig, Duncker & Humblot, 1912.

83 Schumpeter, J., *Theorie der wirtschaftlichen Entwicklung*, Leipzig, Duncker & Humblot, 1912, p. 489. All translations, except where otherwise indicated, are our own.

must have decided not to publish at the last minute: 'as I reworked it, I agreed with (my) most severe critics, and excused others who did not understand the argument…'[84]

Following the other Austrians coming after Menger, here also Schumpeter moves towards a *rapprochement* with the standard canon. This *rapprochement* is also on an issue with almost religious significance: is there such a thing as equilibrium or not, or rather, what kind of questions can be usefully answered by the metaphor 'equilibrium'. In our view the postulate of an equilibrium severely reduces the scope of economic theory, leaving issues of great practical importance *outside* the paradigm. We can only speculate how much the different factors weighed in Schumpeter's decision to abandon his most fiercely anti-equilibrium stance; the weight of the criticisms, his admiration for Walras' system, or – and this is pure speculation – perhaps that fact that he wanted his work to appeal more to the Anglo-Saxon economic world, where he was to spend the last almost 20 years of his career. We must agree with Streissler that, in general, it is 'because he admired Walras so much that Schumpeter is such a bad guide to the real Austrian achievement, which has always been in complete contrast to Walras.'[85]

With a perspective of more than 100 years, the ties and similarities between the economics of Carl Menger and traditional German economics are many. This is particularly true when the development of mainstream economics since the Methodenstreit is taken into consideration. In commenting on the *Methodenstreit,* Carl Brinkmann wrote in the *Encyclopaedia of the Social Sciences* that both Schmoller's and Menger's economics were parts of 'the great reaction that had set in against the one-sidedly deductive methods of orthodox utilitarianism….' 'In fact', Brinkmann says, 'there is the same craving for realism, after an age of self-satisfied "pure" reasoning, in the opening pages of Menger's *Principles* as there is in Schmoller's contemporaneous work on the small crafts in Germany…'[86]

The fact that Menger dedicated his first work to Wilhelm Roscher now seems a natural choice, whereas the *Methodenstreit* appears as a fight between two fractions that had more elements in common against the English neoclassical school than what divided them. Based on this, one should have thought that once the personal animosity between Schmoller and Menger disappeared, the two schools should find each other again. If Austrian economics had followed the path embarked upon by Menger, the *Methodenstreit* would most likely have come down differently in history, less methodologically acute and more of a personal quibble between insiders of the anti-classical movement. The opposite seems to have happened. The more the second and third generation Austrians *moved away from Menger*, the more relentless became their criticism of the historical school. We suggest that the reason why the *Methodenstreit* worsened considerably over time – the most vitriolic attack ever on historicism being Mises' in 1959 – is that both Austrian economics and neo-classical economics, in a parallel fashion, moved away from all the Other Canon aspects which Menger and Schmoller shared. This will be discussed more in detail in Section 5 of this paper.

---

84 *Theorie der wirtschaftlichen Entwicklung*, Leipzig, Duncker & Humblot, 1926, p. xiii.

85 Streissler, p. 430.

86 Seligman, Edwin (editor), *Encyclopaedia of the Social Sciences*, New York, Macmillan, 1953 (1930). Vol. 1, p.167.

The rest of this chapter is dedicated to the discussion of concrete theoretical points where Menger and Schmoller were both on the Other Canon side, against what developed into the English-Walrasian theoretical mainstream.

In the foreword to the second edition of Carl Menger's *Grundsätze*, his son Karl Menger emphasises his father's belief that 'the starting point of all inquiry into theoretical economics is the needs of human nature'[87]. This is the classical starting point of German economics since the times of Leibniz and Christian Wolff: the profession is 'anthropocentric', i.e. centred on 'Man and his Needs'. The Germans always saw this as a sharp contrast to the English classical tradition, which is centred on barter, and where – in the end – Man is just a 'factor of production'. Menger's roots in German cameralism are discussed by Paul Silverman.[88]

Menger makes the very *Other Canon* statement that 'the quantity of consumption goods at human disposal is limited by the extent of human knowledge'[89], evoking the 'never-ending frontier of knowledge' which is so typical of the **activistic-idealistic** and optimistic alternative canon. Menger here appears to be inspired by the spirit of US economist Erasmus Peshine Smith[90], whose work was translated to German only in 1878[91]. To Peshine Smith there were two factors of production: 1. Nature, and 2. Man's wit and will. This is similar to Menger's view that the production in primitive societies depends solely on nature, 'it takes place independent of the wishes and needs of Mankind, and hence, so far as they are concerned, accidental'[92]. When human beings leave primitive society, and 'explore and research the causal mechanisms which produce consumption goods and take control over these processes, the production of consumption goods takes place as before, but their production is no longer coincidental to the wishes and needs of Man. Instead this is a process where Man is in charge and which is organised around Man's needs and purposes within the limits of nature's laws'[93].

Like John Rae in his 1834 book[94], Carl Menger sees the division of labour as being a necessary consequence of human innovations and inventiveness[95], not – like Adam

87 Menger, Carl, *Grundsätze der Volkswirtschaftslehre,* zweite Auflage mit einem Geleitwort von Richard Schüller, aus dem Nachlass herausgegeben von Karl Menger, Wien, Hölder-Pichler-Tempsky, 1923, p. ix.

88 'The Cameralist Roots of Menger's Achievement', in Caldwell, Bruce J. (Editor), *Carl Menger and his Legacy in Economics,* Annual Supplement to HOPE, Volume 22, Durham, Duke University Press, 1990.

89 Streissler's translation, in Streissler, *op. cit.*, p. 431.

90 The first of many US editions was: Smith, E. Peshine, *A Manual of Political Economy,* New York, Putnam, 1853.

91 Smith, E. Peshine, *Handbuch der politischen Ökonomie*, Berlin, Expedition des Merkur, 1878.

92 *Grundsätze*, p. 28.

93 P. 28–29.

94 Rae, John, *Statement of some new principles on the subject of political economy, exposing the fallacies of the system of free trade, and of some other doctrines maintained in the 'Wealth of Nations'*, Boston, Hilliard, Gray & Co, 1834.

95 See paragraph 5, 'Über die Ursachen der fortschreitenden Wohlfahrt der Menschen' in his *Grundsätze*, Menger, Carl, *Grundsätze der Volkswirtschaftslehre,* Vienna, Wilhelm Brauchmüller, 1871, pp. 26–29.

Smith – the other way around. Menger uses a whole section of his *Grundsätze* to refute Adam Smith on this point. This again is the 'anti-English/anti-barter' stance that is typical of The Other Canon.

Menger also represents the 'economics of time and uncertainty' which in many ways is the antithesis of neo-classical economics. However, as time has evolved, Austrian economics and neo-classical economics – particularly in their policy prescriptions – have converged on something that for all practical purposes is indistinguishable from that of the neo-classical synthesis. Hayek was, of course, sharply critical of any attempt to convert economics into a discipline similar to the natural sciences[96]. Yet, in a post-cold-war world, Austrian economics came to appear as neo-classical economics in words rather than in mathematics. Menger's great map of the forces at work that would hardly ever come even close to their resting position, became a map which was considered accurate enough to reach the same policy conclusions as mainstream neoclassicism.

One important criticism of The Other Canon tradition against neo-classical economics has traditionally been its emphasis on monetary aspects and the limited role of the real economy of goods and services (what Schumpeter and others called the *Güterwelt*). In 1936, just after Menger's works had been reprinted in German at the London School of Economics, one author saw this as the *key issue* separating neo-classical and Austrian economics. The author, Franz Wien-Claudi of the University of Prague, published a book which was an early attempt to introduce Austrian economics to an English-speaking public. Wien-Claudi claims at that point that 'Hayek's main objection to the modern English School of Economics was that these authors have overestimated the significance of monetary phenomena and undervalued the importance of the events in the world of goods.'[97] However, this point is not listed as one of Fritz Machlup's six ideas that separated Austrian economics from neo-classical economics before World War II.[98] Again, what was a typical 'Other Canon' feature of early Austrian economics seems to have been lost.

As the tradition was 'backsliding' into Ricardian and Walrasian economics, Austrian economics became increasingly 'schizophrenic', torn between a *verstehende* and a *mechanistic/ordnende* paradigm. Schumpeter emanated from the Renaissance tradition of the German historical school and spent his life on the hopeless task of formalising the creative essence of Renaissance economics – of entrepreneurship, novelty, and creative destruction – into the framework of dead equilibrium that is at the core of neoclassical economics. Schumpeter was, indeed, 'a living, breathing contradiction' as Mirowski puts it[99]. We would claim that this contradiction is an inevitable result of attempting to reconcile two paradigms that are irreducible to any common language.

---

96 Hayek, Friedrich von, *The Counter-Revolution of Science. Studies in the Abuse of Reason,* Glencoe, Ill., Free Press, 1952.

97 Wien-Claudi, Franz, *Austrian Theories of Capital, Interest, and the Trade-Cycle,* London, Stanley Nott/Allen Unwin, 1936, p. 7.

98 See Israel Kirzner's entry 'Austrian School of Economics' in *The New Palgrave,* London, Macmillan, 1987, Volume I, p. 148.

99 Mirowski, Philip, 'Doing what comes naturally: four metanarratives on what metaphors are for', in Mirowski (Ed.), *Natural Images in Economic Thought,* Cambridge, Cambridge University Press, 1994, p. 5.

John Bates Clark points to this 'schizophrenia' when he discusses Hayek's *Individualism and Economic Order.* The factors that create disequlibrium and, consequently, those that create the need for economic policy and government intervention are still there in the Hayek of 1949. However, these factors are being pushed more and more into the background as Austrian economics comes of age, 'slides back', and increasingly focuses on addressing the threat from communist central planning:

> 'Hayek's position on economic policy is baffling: stressing the function of the free market and the dangers of expanding public controls, admitting the necessity of a considerable measure of control, but avoiding adequate definition of the line between the controls he opposes and those he would approve. The present volume contributes little to clarification of this vagueness. This is partly because the volume is a collection of short essays and addresses, in which Hayek repeatedly excuses himself from systematic and specific elaboration on grounds of space; but it seems to be fundamentally a matter of Hayek's method of attacking the analysis of these problems.
>
> He starts with a principle, which he emphasizes as of dominant importance. **He then admits that an opposing principle has validity and some proper scope; but never comes to grips with the question how far the opposing principle may be properly carried, and how it may be kept down to sound methods and limits**. This is a fairly common theoretical method of analysis; and amounts to throwing the pragmatic emphasis, which generally accompanies the inevitable oversimplification of theory, in one direction or the other. If this direction is that in which the next step need to be taken, this pragmatic effect may be useful, as far as it goes and so long as only those steps are in consideration. If the emphasis is thrown in the opposite direction, as Hayek's is, its usefulness is limited to sounding a very general warning against possible excesses of wrong methods, but without yielding much useful guidance to those who are earnestly seeking it, aware of dangers but aware also of things that must be done.
>
> In general, Hayek seems to underrate amazingly the seriousness of the problem of assured employment, and the extent of the public intervention it makes inevitable. **He pitches the argument on a mechanistic economic level**, and seems intolerant of attitudes that do not fit that scheme, rather than recognizing their existence and seeking a viable adjustment with them. On this basis, he seems doomed to the role of Cassandra.[100], [101]

5. The 20th Century Closing of the Economic Mind.

In 1987 Richard Bloom's book *The Closing of the American Mind*[102] became an unlikely bestseller in the US. The aim of the book was to prevent American education – and the United States itself – from degenerating further into what the author perceived as an increasingly low and narrow mental horizon. Bloom describes American society's

---

[100] In Greek mythology, the woman whom Apollo granted the gift of prophecy, but – when she refused to return Apollo's love – made the gift useless by decreeing that no one would believe her predictions.

[101] Clark quoted in Hickman, C. Addison, *J. M. Clark*, New York, Columbia University Press, 1975, pp. 69–70. My italics.

[102] New York, Simon & Schuster.

loss of the foundations in the humanities that were once synonymous with civilisation itself. He holds up the Europeans as being better off than the Americans – whom he at one point refers to as 'big babies' – in this respect. However, the 20th Century as 'the American Century' has insured the diffusion of US values and attitudes also to Europe.

One important aspect of this development was thoroughly analysed already in the early 1960's, in Richard Hofstadter's *Anti-Intellectualism in American Life*[103]. Although the roots of this anti-intellectualism can be traced back to the Pilgrim Fathers, Hofstadter focuses on the 1950's, on McCarthyism, as being the decisive period for the growth of anti-intellectualism. McCarthyism and the Cold War created a demand for a kind of economics that the mechanical versions of neo-classical economics and Austrian economics could both provide. The neo-classical utopia of a market creating harmony and factor price equalisation was an important counterweight to the communist utopia and its omnipotent state that promised to wither away.

In this context the 'intellectuals' became a nuisance. The 'intellectuals' had historical and political qualifications and modifications to the clear message of an absolute superiority of the unmollified market economy. American pragmatism under the pressures of the Cold War degenerated into expediency and anti-intellectualism. History – also US history – cluttered the message of the near 'evilness' of state interventions under all circumstances and in all contexts. Removing economics' previously solid foundation in the humanities pried open for the rule and dominance of the mechanical models: clear conclusions, but conclusions which in their pure and undiluted form are only valid in a world void of diversity, of friction, of scale affects, and of time and ignorance. The one handed economist was created, freeing the profession from the nuisance of qualifications – 'on the other hand' – created by the inclusion of historical context and perspective. This new economist was created at the cost of severely limiting the use of experience-based cognition, intuition and *Fingerspitzgefühl* – of qualities that are normally associated with the right half of the brain. The one armed economist is to some extent also the 'left brain only' economist.

The pure neo-classical techniques in which economic harmony is already solidly built into the basic assumptions – providing results like Samuelson's *factor-price equalisation* – was the kind of theory that was ideologically and politically in demand. We are not suggesting that this kind of theory was created for political purposes. The theories had been there essentially since Ricardo, but the *demand* for this kind of theorising rose considerably during the Cold War, sharpening its focus and message, but conveniently leaving aside the mitigating counterarguments of history. John Bates Clark's criticism of Hayek's failure to come to grips with 'the opposing principles' is a case in point. In this way the 'technicians' crowded out the 'intellectuals' of the economics profession. Still today, when Paul Krugman complains that 'economists have lost control of the discourse', his villains are an alliance of 'policy makers, business leaders and influential

[103] New York, Knopf, 1963.

intellectuals'.[104] Some of Hofstadter's anti-intellectualism is still around when a technical economist like Krugman perceives the 'intellectuals' as being his enemies.

Both neo-classical economics and the Austrian economics of Hayek and Mises provided extremely useful defence mechanisms against what indeed was a communist threat. The question is what to do now, when this battle is won, and the problems of the world are essentially new, while the Cold War versions of neo-classical and Austrian economics are still the only games in town? We suggest that the need to re-establish the countervailing 'Other Canon' is urgent.

Both neo-classical and Austrian economics came to lose the kind of historical knowledge and experience that is required for the *Fingerspitzgefühl* necessary for difficult policy decisions. In this respect it is interesting to note that also typical neo-classical economists of the pre-WW II kind complained about the loss of historical knowledge. In pre WW II neoclassicism both theory and history were used as a matter course. Jacob Viner is one example of this. Viner was largely responsible for eliminating increasing returns from international trade theory on the account that it was *not compatible with equilibrium*[105], thus sacrificing the real world in order to keep the 'purity' of the model.

It was indeed a paradox that this happened in the middle of the 'Fordist' paradigm, where increasing returns were at the very core of the wealth-creating economy of the industrialised world. This severed the understanding of the relationship between manufacturing/industry and progress which had been at the core of European and North American economic policy for about 500 years. This is very different from the attitude of the founder of neo-classical economics, Alfred Marshall, who in the early editions of his celebrated *Principles of Economics,* clearly recognized that a nation could improve its position by subsidising economic activities subject to increasing returns, and tax those subject to diminishing returns (e.g. agriculture).[106] Just like Austrian economics, neo-classical economics was backsliding away from its founder into Ricardian and Walrasian models already before World War II.

Yet the very same Jacob Viner wrote a most interesting book on the problem of economic man as a passive being in the hands of 'Providence' – of the invisible hand being a metaphor for Providence, thus bringing laissez-faire and 'passivity as strategy' close to a primitive belief in faith and providence.[107] The same Viner who threw out increasing returns, also years later complains that 'economists have succeeded in being as ahistorical as an educated man can perhaps possibly be.'[108] This shows the dualism so typical of economists both of the Austrian and neo-classical school before World War II: the real

104 Krugman quoted in Reder, Melvin W., *Economics. The Culture of a Controversial Science,* Chicago, University of Chicago Press, 1999, p. 6.

105 In his *Studies in the Theory of International Trade,* New York, Harper, 1937, pp. 475–482.

106 Marshall, Alfred, *Principles of Economics*, London, Macmillan, 1890 (1st edition). p. 452.

107 Viner, Jacob, *The Role of Providence in the Social Order,* Philadelphia, American Philosophical Society, 1972.

108 Viner, Jacob, *Essays in the Intellectual History of Economics,* Princeton, Princeton University Press, 1991.

world was kept as a frame of reference that was to be continuously confronted with the theoretical map of 'the forces at work'.

What has been lost is primarily this important skill of going back and forth between the theoretical models and the real world, between theory and experience. The loss of this skill, and a general lack of historical knowledge, contributes to what Veblen calls the *contamination of instincts:* Today's standard education economics too often fails to communicate with what to practical people is 'common sense'. In this vein, a distinguished committee of the *American Economic Association* pointed in 1991 to the danger that 'graduate programs (in economics) may be turning out a generation of too many *idiots savants*, skilled in technique but innocent in real economic issues.'[109]

An Austrian parallel to Jacob Viner – very orthodox but still insisting on the role of history and of the real world – is Fritz Machlup. One of the founders, with Hayek, of the ideologically important Mont Pelerin Society, Machlup received his Ph.D. in Vienna in 1923 and came to the US in 1933. In spite of his orthodoxy, Machlup wrote extensively on 'Schumpeterian' subjects like 'The Supply of Inventors and Invention'[110] and 'The Production and Distribution of Knowledge in the United States'[111]. Machlup was also the supervisor for Edith Penrose's research for her Ph.D. thesis, a research that eventually led to the *Theory of the Growth of the Firm*[112]. This book is important as a key foundation for the microeconomics of The Other Canon. A recent publication on work of Edith Penrose comments that it is 'a fascinating paradox how Machlup, a doyen of neo-classical economics, should have been partially responsible for a work so far removed from the mainstream'[113]. We would suggest that this was much less of a paradox 40–50 years ago that it is now. This is yet another example of the loss of diversity of scope and tools in the profession.[114]

The economics of Edith Penrose was sharply at odds with textbook theory, but she would not engage in a *Methodenstreit:* 'Would anyone … try to reconcile a football game with a cricket match just because they are both ball games?'[115] Whereas the early Austrians and early neo-classicals were able to play 'both football and cricket', this ability was gradually lost, together with the multitudes of tools and approaches previously used.

In spite of what we today may perceive as a position against the use of history in economics in his *Irrtümer des Historismus,* Carl Menger really goes out of his way to emphasise the important role of history in economics[116]: 'A highly developed theory of economic

---

[109] 'Report of the Commission on Graduate Education in Economics', in *Journal of Economic Literature,* September 1991, pages 1044–1045.

[110] In *Weltwirtschaftliches Archiv,* Vol. 85, No. 2, 1960, pp. 210–254.

[111] Princeton, Princeton University Press, 1962.

[112] Oxford, Blackwell, 1959.

[113] Penrose, Perran & Christos Pitelis, 'Edith Elura Tilton Penrose: Life, Contribution and Influence', in *Contributions to Political Economy,* Vol. 18, 1999, p. 5.

[114] For a discussion of the loss of tools, see again Morgan, Mary S. and Malcolm Rutherford (editors), *From Interwar Pluralism to Postwar Neoclassicism,* Annual Supplement to History of Political Economy, Volume 30, Durham, Duke University Press, 1998.

[115] Ibid., same page.

[116] Menger, Carl, *Die Irrtümer des Historismus in der deutschen Nationalökomie,* Wien, Alfred Hölder, 1884, e.g. pp. 22, 26, 31, 35, etc.

phenomena is inconceivable without the study of economic history'[117], 'No reasonable person conceals the importance of historical studies for research in the field of political economy',[118] and history is 'indispensable' for theoretical economics.[119] Schmoller and Menger agree that both induction and deduction must be on board, and the *Methodenstreit* is seemingly about who is to be in the driver's seat. Which of the two is going to be the 'main science' and which should be the 'auxiliary science'. Menger's main objective seems to relegate history to the position as a *Hilfswissenschaft* (auxiliary science), a term to which he returns again and again. The contestants of the *Methodenstreit* discuss whether history – which they both see as indispensable to economics – should be an *Überbau* or *superstructure* (Schmoller) or an *Unterbau* or *foundation* (Menger). From this methodological angle, the *Methodenstreit* seems to fit the definition of a quibble: an unsubstantial argument based on playing with words.

As has been said by many commentators, this particular *Methodenstreit* seems like a waste of scholarly energy. Seen from today's perspective, Schmoller and Menger were very close in the role they saw for economics, and both were far from today's mainstream. In his first book – of which there is still no English translation – Schumpeter denounced such doctrinal as the Methodenstreit as a waste of time[120]. Each method had its concrete areas of application, and it is useless to struggle for universal validity. To the young Schumpeter, one should enter the theoretical edifice at a level of abstraction where one was likely to find answers to the questions posed. In this spirit we might say that the neoclassical structure is not 'wrong' under its assumptions. It becomes wrong only when – unmitigated by historical observations – it is applied to the real world, where entirely different assumptions are appropriate.

The cases when economists were able to keep both their theoretical models *and* refer back to the many dimensions and complexities of the real world became increasingly rare. Economics came to suffer from what Philip Mirowski calls 'physics-envy'.[121] Also the Austrians 'suffered to some degree from the effects of an intellectual world that expected all science to emulate the rigour of physics', as Allan Oakley puts it in his book on the Austrian.[122] John B. Clark's 1949 accusation, quoted above, that Hayek 'pitches the argument on a mechanistic economic level, and seems intolerant of attitudes that do not fit that scheme' is indicative of the same development.

We shall let the development of Ludwig von Mises' treatment of *historicism* – comparing his 1933 treatment and his 1957 treatment of the same subject – serve as the

---

117 *Ibid*, p. 22.

118 P. 26.

119 P. 36.

120 Schumpeter, Joseph Alois, *Das Wesen und der Hauptinhalt der theoretischen Nationalökonomie,* Munchen & Leipzig, Duncker und Humblot, 1908.

121 *More Heat than Light. Economics as Social Physics, Physics as Nature's Economics,* Cambridge, Cambridge University Press, 1989, see also De Marchi, Neil (editor), *Non-natural Social Science: Reflecting on the Enterprise of 'More Heat than Light'*, Durham, Duke University Press, 1993.

122 Oakley, Allen, *The Foundations of Austrian Economics from Menger to Mises,* Cheltenham, Elgar, 1997, p. 2.

last illustration of the development of Austrian economics over time. Mises' treatment of the *Methodenstreit* went from being a purely academic disagreement in 1933, to being an important ideological and political issue in Austrian economics after World War II.

In Mises' 1933 *Grundprobleme der Nationalökonomie*[123], the *Methodenstreit* is still very much alive, already in the introduction of the book. Mises here presents and caricaturises historicism in its 'pure' form. When Sombart is quoted as admitting that 'general economic concepts, which are valid for all economies' do exist, Mises does not take this as an invitation towards a compromise.[124] All through the book, Mises introduces a *Methodenstreit* type of debate that seems to know few concessions. For example on pages 56 to 59 Mises argues against Gunnar Myrdal that 'Myrdal knows neither the contemporary situation nor the history of our science, and is therefore fighting against windmills'. On page 129–134 he polemises again against Werner Sombart. However, the whole debate is apolitical and – though caustic – purely confined to academic economics.

When Mises again picks up historicism in his *Theory and History*, first published in 1957, the basic criticism is the same, but the treatment very different. (It may be noted that in the 1933 book the author was Ludwig Mises, in the US he is Ludwig *von* Mises). Mises comes to the treatment of historicism from a section called 'planning history', which ends as follows: 'It is possible that in a few years all nations will have adopted the system of all-round planning and totalitarian regimentation. The number of opponents is very small, and their direct political influence almost nil. But even a victory of planning will not mean the end of history. Atrocious wars among the candidates for the supreme office will break out. Totalitarianism may wipe out civilization, even the whole of the human race. Then, of course, history will have to come to its end too.'[125]

We shall quote extensively from Chapter 10, *Historicism*, which in a sense represents the last act to be performed in the *Methodenstreit* (bolds are mine):

1. The Meaning of Historicism

> 'Historicism developed from the end of the eighteenth Century on as a reaction against the social philosophy of rationalism. To the reforms and policies advocated by various authors of the Enlightenment it opposed a programme of preservation of existing institutions and, sometimes, even a return to extinct institutions. Against the postulates of reason it appealed to the authority of tradition and the wisdom of ages gone by. **The main target of its critique was the ideas that had inspired the American and the French Revolutions and kindred movements in other countries**. Its champions proudly called themselves antirevolutionary and emphasized their rigid conservatism. But in later years the political orientation of historicism changed. **It began to regard capitalism and free trade – both domestic and international – as the foremost evil**, and **joined hands with the 'radical' and 'leftist' foes of the market economy**, aggressive nationalism on the one hand and revolutionary socialism on the other. As far as historicism still has actual

123 Jena, Fischer, 1933.

124 Page 6.

125 Mises, Ludwig von, *Theory and History. An Interpretation of Social and Economic Evolution*, Auburn, Alabama, The Ludwig von Mises Institute, 1985, 197.

> political importance, it is ancillary to socialism and nationalism. Its conservatism has almost withered away…'
>
> If the historicists had been consistent, they would have substituted economic history for the – in their opinion counterfeit – science of economics. (…) But this would not have served their political plans. **What they wanted was to propagandise for their interventionist and socialist programs. The wholesale rejection of economics was only one item in their strategy**. It relieved them from the embarrassment created by their inability to explode the economists' devastating critique of socialism and interventionism. But it did not in itself demonstrate the soundness of prosocialist or interventionist policy. In order to justify their 'unorthodox' leanings, the historicists developed a rather self-contradictory discipline to which various names were given such as realistic or institutional or ethical economics, or the economic aspects of political science (wirtschaftliche Staatswissenschaften).'

The line of reasoning against historicism – most of it is not quoted here – is very much like Mises' 1933 treatment of the same subject. But in the 1957 book, the academic antagonism has yielded to what, in the eyes of this writer, comes very close to McCarthyist political propaganda. Historicism is vilified as being the root of most evils of history: not only of socialism. All reactionaries, enemies of 'reason', and also the enemies of the American Revolution, are by definition 'historicists'. Note that the institutional school is, according to Mises, just another name for these 'reactionaries'. Again this contrasts sharply with Menger, who – as Streissler points out – on many points 'was very close to the Institutionalists'.[126]

This piece of Cold War Americana is not complete without a brief account of the alleged 'ideological conflict' between Yale University Press – which originally published the book – and Mises. The disagreement between Mises and his publishers seems to originate in quality problems in the production of Mises' *Human Action*. The press apologises, and admits that it is not up to standards[127]. This printing problem is by the Mises interpreted as an 'ideological conflict between Ludwig von Mises and Yale University Press'. 'Who was it that wanted to harm my husband by producing a bad print, and in that way obstruct the reader?' 'Why did Lu's (Ludwig von Mises') lawyers, who had such a clear case in their hand, decide not to go to court, although Ludwig von Mises so obviously had the right on his side?' Not only does Mises insist that *historicism* is the incarnation of all evil across history from the 'conservative' opponents of the American Revolution to 'revolutionary socialism', but Yale University Press is seen as waging an ideological war against Mises. We have full understanding of an author who sees his press not doing a proper job. However, these kinds of interpretations are only understandable in the context of McCarthyism. Austrian economics had indeed come a long way from Carl Menger.

In many ways the 20th Century has witnessed a slow closing of the minds of the economics profession. More than before, economists became the 'eggheads' they were

---

126 Streissler, *op.cit.*, p. 433.

127 This account is found in Mises, Margit von, *Ludwig von Mises. Der Mensch und sein Werk,* Munich, Philosophia Verlag, 1981, pp. 155–163.

traditionally accused of being in the US: 'People who do not understand everything they know.' Probably the most dramatic event in this development is that the economics profession lost its base and points of reference in the humanities. The early Austrian and neoclassical economist used the theoretical structure as an inaccurate map which was constantly held up and evaluated against the real world history, and its philosophy and values were firmly embedded in the humanities. This approach created and allowed methodological diversity and pluralism, a diversity that was lost when the ties between economics and the humanities were slowly severed. We have already mentioned two recent volumes which trace this development in economics, and their titles are descriptive: *The Struggle over the Soul of Economics*[128], and *From Interwar Pluralism to Postwar Neoclassicism*.[129]

The founders of both the neo-classical school, Alfred Marshall, and of the Austrian School, Carl Menger, took great care in emphasising the importance of history in economics. In his preface to the *Principles of Economics*, Marshall spells out the chief influences common to all modern schools of economic thought as biology and history, whereas mathematics is seen as influencing the *form* of the theory.[130] 'It is the business of economics … to collect facts, to arrange and interpret them, and to draw inferences from them'[131], Marshall says, laying the foundation for economics as an *Erfahrungswissenschaft* (a science of practice), rather than the Ricardian science of *a priori* assumptions with categories established once and for all. Later Marshall approvingly quotes Schmoller as saying that 'Induction and deduction are both needed for scientific thought as the right foot and left foot are both needed for walking'[132].

Both neo-classical economics in general and modern Austrian economics in the United States seem to have taken on many of the characteristics that Bloom ('The Closing of the American Mind') and Hofstadter ('Anti-Intellectualism in American Life') associate with intellectual life in the United States, and spread this attitude to the rest of the world. In terms of economic policy and of belief in 'spontaneous order' Austrian and neo-classical economics seem, for all practical purposes, to be of one mind. The main difference between the two schools seems today to lie in the absence or presence of an equilibrium-making entrepreneur. The foundations of the theory in the humanities are difficult to locate in today's structures, and this economic theory – void of context and of institutions beyond that of the market – indirectly also becomes curiously ethnocentric. If institutions are assumed away in a theory void of time and history, this implicitly assumes that the institutions ruling in one's own country can be taken for granted and can be expected to arise spontaneously and instantly anywhere and in any context. The co-evolution of economic activities and their accompanying institutions is lost.

---

128 Yonay, Yuval, *The Struggle over the Soul of Economics*, Princeton University Press, 1998.

129 Morgan, Mary S. and Malcolm Rutherford (editors), *From Interwar Pluralism to Postwar Neoclassicism,* Annual Supplement to History of Political Economy, Volume 30, Durham, Duke University Press, 1998.

130 Marshall, Alfred, *Principles of Economics,* London, Macmillan, 1890, pp. ix–x.

131 This phrase marks the start of Chapter III, 'Economic Generalizations or Laws', Principles of Economics, 9th (variorum) edition, London, Macmillan, 1961, p. 29.

132 Ibid., also page 29.

The collective memory of the tremendous effort it took to build the institutions of civilisation was lost from the neo-classical and also to a large extent from the neo-Austrian schools. As a German economist put it in 1840: 'As the grown man has long since forgotten the pains it cost him to learn to speak, so have the peoples, in the days of their mature growth of the State, forgotten what was required in order to free them from their primitive brutal savagery.'[133] The policy implications of this proved devastating to the economic welfare in the former communist world and in Africa. A re-introduction of brutal savagery has, in some cases, been the result.

US pragmatism in its best sense is related to the *praxisnähe* in German social sciences: What is wanted is not theory for its own sake, but a practical theory where action is intimately tied to analysis. The same US pragmatism, however, may deteriorate into 'expediency', into going ahead without proper analysis of alternatives and of consequences. After World War II, Western Europe was given a period of 15 to 20 years to adjust to free convertibility of currency and free trade. Comparing the economic policy applied in Western Europe after World War II with the 'shock therapy' applied to the former communist world after 1990 provides a good example of how the praxis of economics degenerated from the first definition of pragmatism (operating with a 'practical' theory reflecting the real situation) to the second (going ahead without a proper analysis).

6. Understanding Human Cognition: Carl Menger and the King Who Wanted to Make the Perfect Map

In the previous section, we looked at Menger's *Irrtümer des Historismus* compared to mainstream economics during the latter half of the 20th Century. From this vantage point the *Methodenstreit* between Menger and Schmoller seems like two 'Other Canon' economists involved in a relatively minor quarrel. They both agreed on the fundamental importance of history as an indispensable building block for any economic theory. This point was later strongly emphasised also by Schumpeter. From this point of view, Marshall, Menger, Schmoller and Schumpeter all represent a theoretical tradition that is virtually dead in the year 2000.

Only in one aspect does there seem to be a fundamental disagreement between Menger and Schmoller. This disagreement is about the use of past experience in human cognition. In his disagreement with Schmoller, Menger here takes a position that finds its parallel in a short story by Argentine author Jorge Luis Borges about the king who wanted to make the perfect map. The perfect map was seen as one holding all conceivable details, and – obviously – the larger the map, the better it was. Borges tells the story through a fictitious 17th century book, *Viajes de Varones Prudentes*:

> 'In that Empire, the Art of Cartography achieved such perfection that the Map of one single Province occupied the whole of a City, and the Map of the Empire, the whole of a Province.

---

[133] Hoffmann, J.G., introduction to *Lehre von den Steuern*, quoted in Cohn, Gustav, *The Science of Finance*, translated by Thorstein Veblen, Economic Studies of the University of Chicago, No. 1, Chicago, University of Chicago Press, 1895, p. 60.

In time those disproportionate maps failed to satisfy, and the Schools of Cartography sketched a Map of the Empire which was of the size of the Empire and coincided at every point with it.'[134]

Norwegian author Tor Åge Bringsværd has a similar story about a man who wants to write world history, and starts with September 11[135] of one particular year. He found that so many things had happened in the world on that particular date, that his history of the world never advanced as far as September 12 of the same year.

Menger criticises the *Kleinmalerei* or *Mikrographie* of the German Historical School, the 'small paintings' they produce of apparently insignificant historical events. Schmoller' publications on the cloth production in Strasbourg are attacked by Menger as such a useless *micrography*. Menger quotes his colleague Emil Sax, and considers him optimistic when he claims that the historical research needed to create a sufficient basis for economics will take 'generations'. Says Menger:

> 'Should economic history be completed, in the spirit of Schmoller's micrography, before it could go on with theoretical economics, only aeons would suffice. Just think of the meat prices in Elberfeldt! In Pforzheim! In Mühlheim! In Hildesheim! In Germersheim! In Zwickau! And so on. As astronomers had to introduce the concept of light years in their science to measure enormous distances, we economists would at least have to start using the living spans of solar systems as time units, in order only to achieve an approximate idea of the amount of time needed to achieve a complete historical and statistical foundation for scientific research in Schmoller's meaning of the word.'[136]

Hopefully, the parallel between Menger's idea of historicism, Mr. Borges' mapmaking and Mr. Bringsværd's writing of history will now be clear. Menger creates the picture of a map in scale 1 to 1, a complete historical record of every price in every village in Germany (and presumable the rest of the world), which will have to be faithfully drawn in order to create the necessary theoretical foundations for a historical economics. The quote from Menger also gives a flair of the aggressive and personal, even insulting, style on both sides of the *Methodenstreit*. In continuation of the meat price argument, Menger accuses Schmoller of being 'naïve' and a 'dilettante', and – closing the book – claims that 'in the future only children and idiots will pay any attention to (Schmoller's) odd theoretical gestures'[137]. This tone was not that unusual among academic economists in Germany at the time. Eugen Dühring's debates with his opponents were possibly even more vitriolic.

The debate over the use of history in economics is fundamentally a debate on human cognition. Schmoller and the German Historical School come from a long tradition where

---

134 Borges, Jorge Luis & Adolfo Bioy Casares, *Extraordinary Tales*, New York, Herder & Herder, 1970, p. 123.

135 In: Bringsværd, Tor Åge, *Den som har begge beina på jorden står stille*, Oslo, Gyldendal, 1974.

136 Menger, *Historismus*, p. 38–39.

137 P. 87.

history was the raw material for human decision-making. Economics was, like conducting a business, an *Erfahrungswissenschaft* – a science of practice and experience. We shall see below that Schmoller directly inspired the man who created Harvard Business School, a place where management is still today successfully taught as an *Erfahrungswissenschaft* with the case method of the German Historical School.

This view of the role of history contrasts with the philosophical foundations of Adam Smith's economics, which lie in the philosophy of John Locke. In this philosophical tradition the human mind is a passive 'blank slate'. The philosophers behind The Other Canon – Gottfried Wilhelm von Leibniz and Christian Wolff – were in extreme opposition to John Lock's view of the mind as a 'blank slate' passively receiving impressions. To The Other Canon philosophers, the mind is fundamentally active, not passive. The mind perceives the world by incessant observations, continuously formulating and reformulating hypotheses based on pre-existing patterns, or schemata, of thought. Feedback mechanisms in this system – important parts of which is clearly subconscious – include intuition, vision and 'gut feelings'. Memorising series of numbers in large statistical databases, like Menger suggests, is not a part of this system.

In this tradition the mind produces 'clues'. In economics Keynes' biographers call it his 'intuition', while Schumpeter speaks about 'vision'. These theories of the mind are based on a mode of inference called *abduction,* or *phronesis*, Aristotle's third form of knowledge. The tradition was continued by Italian philosopher and historian Giambattista Vico (1668–1744), and continued in the 18th Century in German philosophy, and in the 19th Century both in German and US philosophy. To US philosopher C.J. Pierce '(Induction) can never originate any idea whatever. No more can deduction. All the ideas of science come to it by way of Abduction. Abduction consists of studying facts and devising a theory to explain them. Its only justification is that if we are ever to understand things at all, it must be in this way'. Pierce here continues the role played by the formation of hypothesis in the neo-platonic tradition of Leibniz and Christian Wolff.[138]

English economist Edward Misselden expressed the view that abduction anticipates 'science' in 1623: 'Wee felt it before by sense, but now wee know it by science.' W. Brian Arthur of the Santa Fe Institute is today working on economics and human cognition. Based on work in psychology, a scientific foundation for what was the 'sense' of the Historical School is again being established. In an article in Harvard Business Review, but without reference to economics, Arthur describes how the study of history builds qualitative *verstehen*:

> 'What counts to some degree (in hi-tech business) – but only to some degree – is technical expertise, deep pockets, will, and courage. Above all, the rewards go to the players who are first to make sense of the new games looming out of the technological fog, to see their shape,

---

[138] For a discussion of this, with references to Pierce, Leibniz and Wolff, see Reinert, Erik and Arno Daastøl, 'Exploring the Genesis of Economic Innovations: The religious gestalt-switch and the **duty to invent** as preconditions for economic growth', *European Journal of Law and Economics,* Vol 4, No. 2/3, 1997.

to cognize them. Bill Gates is not so much a wizard of technology as a wizard of precognition, of discerning the shape of the next game.'[139]

This is a description of the abductive, qualitative understanding (*verstehen*) that has been lost in economics. US pragmatism at its best is also 'abductive', and nowhere are the principles of the German Historical School being put so consciously to work as at Harvard Business School (HBS). Reading and discussing several cases from real business every day for two years, forcing people to make decisions from real-life cases, produces an 'artificial experience' which develops and fine-tunes the underlying and subconscious system of *production* and *constant and continuous modification* of hypotheses. The cases are full of figures, but thinking – like Menger did – that the training for decision making in real life consists of memorizing these numbers is completely missing the point.

There is a consistent discrepancy between how Harvard Business School is rated by the deans of other business schools ('not that brilliant') vs. what HBS graduates are paid (considerable above the graduates of all other business schools). The market is willing to pay a large premium for the systematic and focused artificial honing of abductive reasoning which is unique to this school. HBS students know that they are trained in 'management by gut feeling', there are T-shirts sporting a mock Latin translation of this slogan and the school's coat-of-arms.

The link from Schmoller's historicism to Harvard Business School is direct. The man who created the case method was a student of Schmoller, Edwin F. Gay (1867–1946). Gay is representative of a whole generation of US students who came back imbibed with the attitudes and values of the German Historical School, and whose careers formed the economic policy of the United States up until World War II. We shall therefore look at Gay's career in some detail, as a typical representative of those great American scholars who brought home both their scientific methods and their social consciousness from Germany.

After an MA in Michigan, Gay stayed more than 12 years studying in Europe, mainly in Berlin, Zürich and Leipzig. He studied under Schmoller and Adolf Wagner, receiving his Ph.D. in Economic History in Berlin in 1902. Studying under Wagner, Gay found himself losing the 'kind of fear of the encroaching action of the state' that he had carried with him from America. 'It was Schmoller, however, who really fired Gay's attentive interest and enthusiasm', says his biographer[140].

Gay joined the Harvard Faculty in 1902. He was a brilliant organiser and motivator of people, so when Harvard decided to set up a Business School in 1908, Gay was called upon to be its first Dean, a job he kept for 10 years. All through his life he was frequently handpicked to launch new ventures, and was constantly called upon for his advice. In spite of his vast knowledge of economic history, he therefore published very

139 W. Brian Arthur, 'Increasing Returns and the New World of Business', *Harvard Business Review*, July-August 1996, pp. 100–109.

140 Heaton, Herbert, *A Scholar in Action – Edwin F. Gay*, Cambridge, Mass., Harvard University Press, 1952. p. 38.

little. Although he was very proud of the achievements of the Business School, Gay later regretted giving up so much research and writing time for launching the HBS. However, among his students of economic history at Harvard were Julius Klein and Earl Hamilton, who were to become the foremost economic historians of Spain in the United States.

Gay held the job as Dean of HBS until 1918, but spent the war years in Washington organising US foreign trade, minimising international trade (maximising autarky!) in order to free as much tonnage as possible of ocean freighters for the war effort. It was here Gay met Herbert Hoover. From 1919 to 1923 Gay worked as the editor of the New York *Evening Post*, and started what became the *Saturday Reveiw of Literature*. From 1923 to 1933 Gay shared the direction of the National Bureau of Economic Research with Wesley Claire Mitchell. He was the first secretary-treasurer of the Council of Foreign Relations, and was the 'moving spirit' in launching *Foreign Affairs* in 1922.

Gay was also elected President of The American Economic Association. Today it is of course absolutely unthinkable that a former Dean of Harvard Business School should be elected President of the American Economic Association. This again goes to show how extremely different and more *praxisnah* mainstream US economics was before World War II, and how much more intimately the leading economists were integrated into the practical life of the nation.

Gay was very active in promoting better labour legislation and a new Factory Act. His colleagues emphasised that he always saw the 'altogetherness of everything' – the Faustian *Ganzheit* – and one comments that 'He is an exceedingly important part of the bridge between the social sciences and the humanities'. As a keen observer of economic history, Gay also saw successive waves of industrialisation: a sequence of techno-economic paradigms. Under the heading 'Swings of the Pendulum', a history of Harvard Business School states the following about its first Dean:

> '…he developed a dynamic vision of economic history: it was, he concluded, a record of swings of the pendulum between periods when social controls dominated, and periods dominated by the actions of aggressive individuals. The former periods were static, characterized by security and stability. The latter periods, ushered in by the introduction of new tools, weapons, or other forces, were controlled by the powerful individuals who introduced these forces. [141]

These dynamic periods, Gay felt, were crucial to economic development. The Industrial Revolution, for all its unwelcome side effects, had made possible new levels of productivity and prosperity. The role of the economic historian, as Gay perceived, was to study and comprehend these cycles, and to suggest ways of restraining their excesses'. In the famous and voluminous Hoover report – so optimistic before the 1929 crash – Gay's is the only paper that senses that something is not right in the economy.

At the root of the present problem of economics is the loss of the educational tradition that produced people like Gay. The practice lives on, like in the case method that Gay introduced at Harvard Business School – which is a tool right out of Schmoller's

---

[141] Cruikshank, Jeffrey L., *A Delicate Experiment. The Harvard Business School 1908–1945,* Boston, Harvard Business School Press, 1987, p. 29.

Historical School of Economics – and in the 'businessmen, politicians and intellectuals' who, as Krugman complains, do not listen to textbook economic theory. US history holds a treasure of 'Other Canon' personalities like Gay, they just become fewer and fewer in economics as the mechanical world view increasingly takes over economics after WW II, contaminating the healthy instincts of abductive reasoning in the profession. All founders of the American Economic Association had studied in Germany, and most of US economics essentially belonged to 'the Other Canon' until just after WW II.

7. Relevance Lost: The Parallel Paths of Austrian and Neo-Classical Economics

Neo-classical economics travelled a long way from Alfred Marshall's *Wanderjahre* in English industry to Paul Samuelson's *factor price equalisation* – from a *production-based* understanding of what creates differences in income, to a barter-based *Harmonielehre.* Young Marshall took pride in being able to estimate, with remarkable accuracy, any wage in the industries he visited by observing the skill requires for the job.[142] The path travelled by Austrian economics from Menger's insistence that 'the quantities of consumption goods at human disposal are limited only by the extent of human knowledge'[143] to the modern Austrian economics of the US South is equally long and changing.

The trajectories of the two schools of economics are in many ways parallel. Both founders – Marshall and Menger – built theoretical structures as *maps of the forces at work.* Particularly Menger insisted that his map was extremely inaccurate; he consistently refused attempts to derive 'high degrees of exactness' from a structure that was, by its very nature, sketchy.[144] Over time, their respective *maps of forces* became rigid structures where time, diversity, friction and complexity disappeared in an increasingly mechanical exercise. Both schools – Austrian and neoclassical – came to focus on barter/market rather than on production. In short, they lost the 'Other Canon' features of economics that make the structure *praxisnah* (close to the real world) and able to explain important features like uneven economic growth.

The rising threat from communism and the planned economy influenced both schools. The political element, we could even call it the propaganda elements, in the writings of Hayek and Miser is unmistakable. In many ways Samuelson's *factor price equalisation* is more insidious as a tool of propaganda, because the political elements are better hidden under a mathematical garb than in prose. Communism promised that every man should receive according to his needs; Samuelson 'proved' that under a market economy all wage earners would be equally rich! Samuelson here 're-invents' and widens the scope of the *Gesetz des Preisausgleiches* (law of the equalisation of prices) from 'second generation' Austrian economist Friedrich von Wieser, who – in sharp contrast to Menger – believed in 'perfect markets.' In both cases it seems to us that the conclusion – factor price

---

142 Pigou, A.C. (Editor), *Memorials of Alfred Marshall,* London, Macmillan, 1925, p. 358–359.
143 Streissler, *op.cit.*, p. 431.
144 For a discussion of this, see Streissler, p. 439.

equalisation – automatically results from the assumptions. Samuelson's journal articles on this matter were published during the height of the Berlin blockade.

Both neoclassical and Austrian economics lost their embeddedness in real economic life and in society in general: Both drifted away from production into barter and, each in their own way, became fascinated with Walrasian instant equilibrium. In the case of neoclassical economics, the system worked without an entrepreneur. In case of the Austrians the system needs a Hayekian equilibrium-making entrepreneur. But both theories became static and mechanical, as John Bates Clark pointed out about Hayek. Both types of theory came to produce automatic economic harmony, and both became useful propaganda tools in the Cold War. The Cowles Commission, for neo-classical economics, and the Mont Pelerin Society, for Austrian economics, each in their own way contributed to the development of harmonious economic utopias that were effectively pitched against the communist utopia. In this battle of utopias the *praxisnah* Other Canon became almost extinct.

Both the neo-classical and Austrian theories lost their ties to a different, and lower, level of abstraction. The *praxisnah* ('near to reality') Other Canon traditionally scorns what German economists Karl Bücher called 'die verschimmelte Schulweisheiten' – the mouldy school truths – of theoretical economics.[145] When these mouldy school-truths are driven through in economic policy unmitigated by any reference to history or to context – like in the case of the World Bank and the IMF during the 1990's – they may cause considerable harm.

Menger's economics was also disequilibrium economics, one of uncertainty and of increasing complexity over time. Menger introduces *monopoly theory* as the *general theory*. However, both neo-classical and Austrian economics became over time more simplistic and focused on frictionless perfect competition. Economics increasingly became *catallectics* – a science of exchange. Both traditions became more static and void of diversity, they became *Harmonielehren*. During the 20th Century theory stopped being only a starting point for analysis both in neoclassical and Austrian economics, a starting point that was continuously to be compared with historical reality. Theory was increasingly treated as if it were a description of reality itself.

Menger's original Austrian vision was a world of dynamic imperfect competition in a world pushing forward with 'the never-ending frontier of knowledge' as the engine of growth. If Menger was the prototype Austrian economist, Schumpeter was surely the most 'Austrian' of both the second and third generation Austrians. In our view the task in economics is now to reconstruct an appreciative economic theory based on the visions of Menger and Schumpeter, to resurrect an economics profession where 'subjective' theory finds an arena where it meets 'objective' facts.

In The Other Canon we have attempted to outline the characteristics of this type of theory, and how it contrasts with today's mainstream. The Austrian economics of Carl Menger and Joseph Schumpeter are valuable building blocks in this project. Like other *Erfahrungswissenschaften*, Menger's theory produced neither accuracy nor any positive

---

145 Bücher, Karl, *Lebenserinnerungen*, Tübingen, Laupp, 1919, p. 197.

theorems. Just like in The Other Canon and in the Historical School, 'truth' – and economic policy – will always be highly *context dependent.*

Menger, the original Austrian economist, was clearly an Other Canon economist. Echoing Other Canon criticism of mainstream economics since the publication of Ricardo's *Principles* in 1817, Menger chided Böhm-Bawerk – his successor to the Chair of Economics in Vienna – both for 'the obvious artificiality of his theoretical constructions' and for 'the contradictions between Böhm's fundamental ideas and the real world'.[146]

---

146 Streissler, *op.cit.*, p. 433.

Chapter Eleven

NIETZSCHE AND THE GERMAN HISTORICAL SCHOOL OF ECONOMICS

Sophus A. Reinert & Erik S. Reinert

1. Preface: Nietzsche and the late 19th Century Economic Agenda

From the viewpoint of modern mainstream economics, Nietzsche would hardly be considered as having made any contributions, directly or indirectly, to the economics profession. However, seen in the light of the German, and indeed Continental, tradition in economics – what we have labelled The Other Canon,[1] core parts of Nietzsche's writing have immediate relevance to economics. Today's standard theory is in effect a continuation of what some 19th Century economists suggested calling *catallectics,* 'the science of exchanges', rather than of production. In contrast to this mainstream body of barter-focused economic theory, the German tradition since the Renaissance has emphasized production, and particularly the role of what Nietzsche fittingly calls *Geist- und Willens-Kapital* (Nietzsche 2000:4722) – Man's wit and will – as a factor of production.

[1] See www.othercanon.org

Within a theory where man's wit and will – new knowledge, innovations and entrepreneurship – are considered a factor of production, Nietzsche has important things to say about economics. Indeed, as is argued in another paper in this volume ('Creative Destruction in Economics: Nietzsche, Sombart, Schumpeter'), Joseph Schumpeter and the growing paradigm of evolutionary economics may be said to have their immediate roots in Nietzsche's thoughts and in the *Zeitgeist* so much influenced by his work.

One important dividing line in 19th Century economics was the origin of the division of labour. This was in effect the tip of the iceberg of a profound philosophical debate as to the very nature of human beings (Reinert & Daastøl 1997). Adam Smith emphasised barter as the origin of wealth, highlighting Man's ability to barter as a main difference between Men and dogs (Smith 1976: Book 1, p. 17). This emphasis on barter rather than production as being the core of the economic activities of Mankind was the object of constant rebuttal from German and US economists all through the 19th Century. In the German-American tradition, the division of labor was the necessary consequence of the scale and diversity of human innovations and inventiveness, not the other way around. In the United States, the work of John Rae (1834) may serve as an early example, whereas in the German language Carl Menger, the father of the Austrian School of Economics, in fact uses a whole section of his *Grundsätze* to refute Adam Smith on this point (Menger 1871/1923: 26–29). [2] This is the 'anti-English/anti-barter' stance that is typical of Other Canon economics, to which we shall claim that Nietzsche has a strong affiliation. In this production-based tradition, economics is strongly tied to the science of statecraft, of the management of the state in order to maximise the welfare of a nation. We shall also point to some of Nietzsche's many references to the importance of economic institutions, and to similarities between the approaches of Friedrich Nietzsche and Thorstein Veblen, the founder of the American Institutional School of Economics.

While scholars previously have made judgments as to Nietzsche's political position on the right-left axis (e.g. Kashyap 1970), we will abandon this established political mould in favour of a lost, but historically significant, alternative tradition, The Other Canon. At the time of Nietzsche's writings this tradition was represented by a group of economists of the German Historical School of economics who came to be called *Kathedersozialisten*, Socialists of the Professorial Chair, a term coined by H. B. Oppenheim (Ingram 1967:206). The economists who were interested in social reform, Schumpeter says, were 'with singular infelicity dubbed *socialists of the chair*' (Schumpeter 1954:758). For the sake of simplicity we shall still use the term *Kathedersozialisten* to represent a diverse group of social reformers and statecrafters unified in the *Verein für Socialpolitik*. There personalities involved in these three institutions – *Verein für Socialpolitik*, *Kathedersozialisten* and the *German Historical School* – overlap to a large degree, in all cases the non-monolithic nature of these groupings facilitates a loose use of the terms.

In this paper, we shall look at Nietzsche's work, in particular *Human, All too Human*, written in Sorrento in 1876–77, as it relates to the economics of the great question of the time: The Social Question (*Die Soziale Frage*). The foundation of the *Verein für Socialpolitik*

2 Section entitled 'Über die Ursachen der fortschreitenden Wohlfahrt der Menschen'.

(literally 'The Association for Social Policy') in October 1872 had established the so-called *Kathedersozialist* program as a genuine Third Way between economic liberalism, where the market is seen as producing automatic harmony, and communism. We shall argue that in this ideological fight, which was to be prolonged until the fall of the Berlin Wall in 1989, Nietzsche comes out as a supporter of the Third Way of the *Verein für Socialpolitik*, of Other Canon economics.

The debate on the Social Question was a key issue not only in Germany, but all over Europe. On the Continent, the issue was central to the economics profession, whereas in England, the 'social reformers' were and are not considered economists in the strict sense.[3] Since what is presently taught as the history of economic thought basically covers the family tree of neo-classical economics plus Marx, this very important debate tends to get a marginal coverage.

1848 marks the political repercussions of the Social Questions, with revolutions in all major European countries except England and Russia, and the same year marks the birth of the German Historical School with the work of Bruno Hildebrand. In 1872, with the foundation of the *Verein für Sozialpolitik* under the leadership of Gustav Schmoller, the systematic work starts in order to create a solution to the Social Question. Barely a year earlier, Bismarck had forged the German state, and it was the joint efforts of Bismarck and the *Kathedersozialisten* – the political arm of the German Historical School of Economics – that built the welfare state as a viable alternative to liberalism and communism. By 1873 this debate and the agenda of the *Kathedersozialisten* had reached Italy, where an intense debate continued until 1876[4], the same year Nietzsche began working on *Menschliches, Allzumenschliches* in Sorrento. The fight to solve *la Questione Sociale* was intense in Italy up until World War I (Loria 1915 & 1920).

As Nietzsche wrote in Sorrento, it was against a backdrop, in Italy and internationally, of intense academic and political debate on liberalism, communism, and the Third Way attempted by the *Kathedersozialisten*, or *i socialisti della cattedra* as they were called in Italy. We therefore feel that it is appropriate to evaluate *Menschliches, Allzumenschliches* in the light of this debate. It is not at all clear that Nietzsche followed the academic debate in Italy on the pros and cons of the 'new' German theory which took place while he wrote *Menschliches, Allzumenschliches* in Sorrento. Nietzsche was not a linguist, but reports in his letters already in 1861 that he is studying Italian and reading Dante in the original language.[5]

---

3 John Stuart Mill is an exception here.

4 Cossa (1891/92:68–69) lists two pages of literature on the Italian debate on these issues. There we find titles like Francesco Ferrara's 'Il Germanismo economico in Italia' (1874), Salvatore Majorana Calatabiano's 'La scuola germanica e la scuola Adamo Smith in economia politica' (1875) and Constatino Baer's 'I socialisti della cattedra in Germania' (1875). The 'new' germanofile economists held an important congress in Milan in 1875.

5 In Nietzsche's letters he reports studying Italian and reading Dante in the original language. 'Augenblicklich studiere ich ja Italienisch....wo im Kränzchen Dante gelesen wird.' (Nietzsche 2000:9668). In his letters Nietzsche also reports speaking Italian with a ballerina from Milan on the train, and to conversing with a Spaniard in Italian.

Any inquiry into the possible political connotations of Nietzsche's philosophy must be accompanied by a certain restraint. His writings are notoriously confusing, and the sheer complexity of his vision leaves, as Conway has pointed out, his readers with an incredible freedom in reinterpretation:

> *Nietzsche's strategy of indirection has backfired egregiously and often. Rather than discourage unworthy readers from attempting to divine his Promethean wisdom, his rhetorical gyrations have in fact issued a blanket invitation to cranks and scholars alike. Encountering no insurmountable textual obstacles to their own interpretations of his elusive teachings, Nietzsche's readers regularly conscript him as the philosophical progenitor of their respective political schemes* (Conway 1997:119–120).

Indeed we find that anarchists, socialists, feminists, Nazis, and anti-clericalists of all sorts separately have found chimerical kinship in some aspect of Nietzsche's writings (Magnus 1996:125–138). It is thus in full awareness of the multiple pitfalls left us by his literary vicissitude that we make our case. Our focus will be on Nietzsche's view of the state, as it is expressed in the chapter "A Glance at the State", in his 1878 *Human all too Human*. Most readers with even a passing familiarity with Nietzsche's work will automatically recall the oft-quoted aphorism from *Thus Spake Zarathustra,* where Nietzsche calls the State "the coldest of the cold monsters", but his quote is far too often taken out of context. What should be seen as an attempt to liberate his contemporaries from the shackles of civic submission, to shock them from their decadent lifestyles, has become a general attack on inappropriate social constructs regardless of nature.

2. The *Kathedersozialist* Program.

In order to better illuminate our arguments on Nietzsche's sociopolitical views, it is necessary briefly to outline the *Kathedersozialist* program. Their economic tradition was a progression of mercantilist doctrines as they were defined by Gustav Schmoller: '[Mercantilism] in its innermost kernel… is nothing but state making – not state making in a narrow sense, but state making and national-economy making at the same time, state making in the modern sense, which creates out of the political community an economic community, and so gives it a heightened meaning' (Schmoller 1884/1967:50–51). Spearheaded by economists like Adolph Wagner, Gustav Schmoller and Lujo Brentano (Wittrock 1939) the movement reacted to reigning social conditions created by Ricardian doctrines and policies. Acknowledging Engels' terrible verdict of working class welfare under *laissez-faire* liberalism (Engels 1892) but unwilling to accept the Marxist alternative of a dictatorship of the proletariat, these economists sought to find a viable third alternative. State intervention in economic life was, on a general level, to follow the more active model of Friedrich List and what was later to become the American Institutional School, rather than the limited vision of Smith and the Ricardians. The *Verein für Socialpolitik* was established as a consequence of the growing profession's need for direction (Schumpeter 1954:756). Involving a definite pledge and a practical agenda stretching beyond the limits of quantification, the *Verein* functioned on a basis of large-scale coordination of research activities that in the end resulted in the 188 volumes of the *Verein's Schriften* published between 1872 and 1932.

The social question of the day, the *Soziale Frage,* was pressing. While the theory fuelling *laissez faire* liberalism already existed in praxis as public policy, the Marxist alternative did not. The Herculean task facing what was to become the Social Democrats was therefore to translate Marx' analysis of the ills of capitalism increasingly into a viable political system compatible with democracy. As Haselbach argues, the task facing liberal revisionism was even more daunting, namely explaining why liberal theory had not functioned in praxis, and why liberalism had failed to deliver on its political promises. "The question for liberal revisionism was thus, why liberalism, as a practical policy, had not succeeded in harmonising and ordering the economic and social world through the invisible hand of the market forces, but had, instead, brought about new social divisions and political turmoil, the Social Question"(Haselbach 2000:65). In other words, why was the gap between rich and poor growing every day, and why was Europe in this period threatened by the lingering possibility of anti-capitalist revolution, rather than lulled into perpetual sociopolitical harmony by the Mandevillian *private vices – public benefits* doctrine? This was the focal point of Germany's political debate from the mid-19th Century, and the uncertain foundation of the *Kathedersozialist* movement.

The *Verein für Socialpolitik* – created six years before Nietzsche wrote *Human, all too Human* – attempted to take the best of both worlds, allowing for individual creativity and *Geist* within a framework of social welfare. There was no use to, like the Jacobins, demand an overnight revolution to solve all of humanity's problems, so instead a "fundamental reconstruction of society was to come about in time, as a by-product rather than as the result of efforts directly aimed at it" (Schumpeter 1954:803). While attacked by their opponents due to their lack of scientific objectivity and empirical proofs, these highly normative economists

> *adopted a stance somewhere between the German free-trade party and the democratic socialists... whilst rejecting the socialist program, they called for the intervention of the state... for the purpose of mitigating the pressure of the modern industrial system on its weaker members* (Ingram 1967:205).

John Rae, writing in his 1901 book on *Contemporary Socialism*, judged their method to be as natural and legitimate a descendent from Adam Smith as the *laissez faire*-intensive German Manchester Party, and perhaps even more so, "for in science the true succession lies with those who carry the principles of the master to a more fruitful development, and not with those who embalm them as sacred but sterile simulacra" (Rae 1901:198–199).

The *Verein* was, however, not a proper 'School' per se, as its individual members disagreed on what course should be taken to achieve the intended reforms. A classic example can be found in the disagreements between Lujo Brentano and Gustav Schmoller on the role of the state in insuring the welfare of workers. Where Schmoller argued for direct state intervention in matters of the market, Brentano had faith in labour unions and the intrinsic mechanics of the commercial system (Kaku 2000:72–86). They all shared the final goal, but not the means of getting there. The diversity of its legacy greatly facilitates our task, as Nietzsche's idiosyncrasies fail to alienate him from their larger goal. The theoretical nature of the *Verein* in the end found its perfect match in Bismarck's pragmatism, and its work created the foundations for the European welfare states.

3. Nietzsche and Renaissance Individualism

So how do Nietzsche's principles of statecraft fit into this? Before we attempt to answer, we must first establish the *Zeitgeist* that bore them. In sharp contrast to the quantitative stasis of Newtonian Mechanics, Nietzsche's Protagorean world is one of constant, qualitative flux: "Our social order will slowly melt away, just as all earlier orders have done, as soon as the suns of new opinions shone with new heat over humanity" (Nietzsche 1995:239).[6] Perspectives on reality are relative, and so are morals. To Nietzsche, and indeed to the whole German economic tradition, the true engine of socio-economic growth is Man's wit and will, in Nietzsche's terms "The Will to Power". While the academic community fails to agree on the exact meaning of this elusive ideal (Magnus 1996: 41), we argue along the lines of Richardson and others that it reflects a basic need to master reality (Richardson 1996:148–157); an urge to fulfil our personal potential and reach for the divine within us (see also Reinert, H & E, in this volume).

This better part of human nature was, long before Nietzsche, defined by Benjamin Constant as: "that noble disquiet which pursues and torments us, that desires to broaden our knowledge and develop our faculties… it is to this self-development that our destiny calls us" (Constant 1816). Industry, innovation, and production are all keywords in this tradition. While the commercialist Smith saw Man as a dog bartering bones (Smith 1976: Book 1 p. 17) (Man the Trader), the German tradition saw Man as a dog learning to can dog food instead of chewing bones (Man the Innovator and Producer).

The close relationship between Nietzsche and his older University of Basel colleague Jacob Burckhardt, the famous Renaissance scholar, is well documented in Edgar Salin's *Jacob Burckhardt und Nietzsche* (Salin 1948), and more recently in Lionel Gossman's *Basel in the Age of Burckhardt* (Gossman 2000). Burckhardt was the eminent historian of the same time periods that fascinated Nietzsche: Ancient Greece (Burckhardt 1998) and the Renaissance (Burckhardt 1958). Werner Sombart gives Jacob Burckhardt the credit when he refers to the Renaissance as "an embryonic age for the interest in the individual: in portraits, in biographies, and in psychology"[7] (Sombart 1930:88). This was clearly also Nietzsche's view. The word Renaissance appears 76 times in Nietzsche's complete works, of which 14 times in *Human, all too Human.*

---

[6] *"Unsere gesellschaftliche Ordnung wird langsam wegschmelzen, wie es alle früheren Ordnungen getan haben, sobald die Sonnen neuer Meinungen mit neuer Glut über die Menschen hinleuchten"* (Nietzsche 2000:4689)

[7] *Es erwacht, wie das vor allem Burckhardt nachgewiesen hat, im Zeitalter der Renaisance das Interesse am Individuellen: am Porträt, an der Biographic, an der Psychologie…*

To Nietzsche the Renaissance with its birth of individualism was the main event of the second millennium:

> *To me the Renaissance will always mark the high point of this millennium; and what happened subsequently is the great reaction of all kinds of herd instincts against the individualism of that period.*[8]

Nietzsche's economics is today not easily recognised as such, because in many ways it belongs to the 'duty-based economics' of the Renaissance, what Werner Sombart calls *richtende Nationalökonomie.* In the new interpretation of the Bible that created the Renaissance, the duty to invent and to create emanated from Man being created in the image of God. As the most typical characteristic of the Lord was his creativity, innovations and creation were Man's pleasurable duties (Reinert & Daastøl 1997). Nietzsche's teachings retain the pleasurable and playful duty to create that characterises the Renaissance, but now as a duty towards an inner self: 'Yes to the game of creation, my brothers, requires a holy saying of yes' he says in Zarathustra.[9]

In the Renaissance tradition Nietzsche identifies a fundamental role played by the individual in society – an aspect which much later came to be associated with the economics of Joseph Schumpeter – namely the vital role of the individual entrepreneur in renewing society through 'creative destruction'. As an economist, Nietzsche upholds the Renaissance legacy of humanist creativity from Gottfried Wilhelm Leibniz and Christian Wolff, the founders of German economics. "The industry of men", as the term appears in the works of Molinaeus (Molinaeus 1546/1930:73), was born when Neo-Platonic influences during the Renaissance made creation itself self-conscious (Reinert & Daastøl 1997). Fuelled by what Nietzsche refers to as *Geist- und Willens-Kapital* (Nietzsche 1995:258), in this tradition Man's wit and will became the true engine of socio-economic growth. This is what Nietzsche complaints was being lost in the economics of his age: *Our age, which speaks so much of economics is wasteful, it wastes the most precious of all, the Geist.*[10] This is an echo from the complaints of German economists at the time against die *Entgeistung* of economic theory: that Man's *Geist*, his wit and will, was disappearing from economic theory as the barter-based English tradition of automatic economic harmony increasingly dominated the scene.

4. Nietzsche and the German Economic Tradition

Nietzsche accepts the standard goal of statecraft as "making life tolerable for the greatest number [of people]" (Nietzsche 1995:236).[11] This places Nietzsche in the

---

[8] *Die Renaissance bleibt mir immer noch die Höhe dieses Jahrtausends; und was seither geschah, ist die große Reaktion aller Art von Herdentrieben gegen den »Individualismus« jener Epoche.* Nietzsche's letter to Franz Overbeck, October 1882 (Nietzsche 2000:10228).

[9] *Ja, zum spiele des Schaffens, meine Brüder, bedarf es eines heiligen Ja-sagens: seinen Willen will nun der Geist, seine Welt gewinnt sich den Weltverlorene* (Nietzsche 2000:6373).

[10] *Unser Zeitalter, soviel es von Ökonomie redet, ist ein Verschwender: es verschwendet das Kostbarste, den Geist* (Nietzsche 2000:5579).

[11] *Überdies: wenn es sich nun einmal bei aller Politik darum handelt, möglichst vielen das Leben erträglich zu machen, so mögen immerhin diese Möglichst-Vielen auch bestimmen, was sie unter einem erträglichen Leben verstehen...* (Nietzsche 2000:4683).

anthropocentric German tradition of social sciences emanating from Leibniz and Wolff.[12] This tradition emphasizes the need to construct a theory around a core of 'Man and his needs'. This tradition is holistic, stressing the organic coherence of the social sciences, the *Strukturzusammenhänge.* This problem-oriented science finds no room for arbitrary distinctions between academic disciplines. The metaphysical instruments of philosophy, economics, and politics are all applied according to their relevance to the task at hand, in sharp contrast to the limited toolbox of neoclassical economics. Whereas modern economists tend to be tool-focused, in that they seek to apply a few axiomatic instruments to all problems they face, the statecrafters were problem-focused, finding or inventing the right tool for the right job. It is therefore impossible, and in fact anachronistic, to divorce the sphere of economics from the whole in Nietzsche's work; his arguments are synergical, the totality reflecting the State in its all-encompassing form of human coexistence.

In its origins, with Christian Wolff, German economics was based on duty. As already mentioned, Werner Sombart calls this type of economics a *richtende Nationalökonomie* (Sombart 1930). Symptomatically, in the collected works of Nietzsche the word *Pflicht* – duty – gets 167 hits. The word 'market' gets only 8.

Physiocracy marks the point where today's standard economics diverges from German economics and Other Canon economics. Physiocray, or 'the rule of Nature', stands in sharp contrast to the Renaissance tradition where the creative human being is the driving force. Most German economists at the time were ardent anti-physiocrats, and interestingly Friedrich Nietzsche comes out with an unusually strong praise of the greatest anti-physiocratic economist of all, the Neapolitan Abbé Galliani: 'the profoundest acutest… man of his century, he was far profounder than Voltaire' (Nietzsche 2000: 6909).

Corresponding to the German tradition, citizenship, according to Nietzsche, is a reward for dutiful sacrifices on the altar of common good; "We must ourselves, along with other people, have risked what is dearest to us, only this binds us firmly to the state, we must have the happiness of posterity in mind, in order to take the proper, natural interest in institutions and in their alteration" (Nietzsche 1995:245).[13]

This phrase in Nietzsche raises the issue of the many similarities between the Nietzsche and Thorstein Veblen, the founder of the US Institutional School of Economics. Two connecting points come to mind from the last phrase in the former paragraph: first of all, the active attitude towards institution building, and secondly the need to have 'the happiness of posterity in mind'. In a similar vein Veblen's term 'parental bent' signified Man's ties to and obligations towards posterity. In Veblen's system the 'good' production-capitalists had this trait as opposed to the 'bad' financial capitalists who were, at best, a necessary evil. The creative and constructive people, in Veblen's case the engineers, are the carriers of salvation for both Nietzsche and Veblen.

12 See Reinert & Daastøl 1997.

13 *Man muß selber mit den anderen sein Liebstes daran gewagt haben: das erst bindet an den Staat fest; man muß das Glück seiner Nachkommen ins Auge fassen, also vor allem Nachkommen haben, um an allen Institutionen und deren Veränderung rechten, natürlichen Anteil zu nehmen* (Nietzsche 2000:4700).

In a parallel fashion, Veblen's contempt for people making their living based on 'vendibility' clearly mirrors the perspectives of Nietzsche, and later of Sombart (Sombart 1915). In the Renaissance spirit, Veblen's basic driving force in the economy is Man's 'idle curiosity' which produces inventions that become innovations when they meet 'workmanship' and capital, and the duties and 'drives' he establishes for mankind are very similar to those of Benjamin Constant in the quote above. The connections between Nietzsche and Veblen seem to have caused even less academic interest than the connections between Nietzsche and Schumpeter. Of a selection of twelve biographies and works on Veblen, just four (Diggins 1978/1999, Tilman 1992, Eby 1998 and Jorgensen & Jorgensen 1999) seem to make references to Nietzsche, and all of them only peripherally and in passing, not connecting or comparing the analysis of the two authors. Veblen was interested in philosophical matters, his first publication was 'Kant's Critique of Judgement' (Veblen1884/1934).

Going back to Nietzsche's emphasis on the need to have risked something in order to properly qualify for citizenship, he clearly betrays his Classicist heritage in the sentence quoted above. Arguing here along the lines supported today by Raaflaub (1997), Ober (1996), Rahe (1994), and others, Nietzsche seemingly alludes to the birth of democracy with the ascension of Athenian rowers following the battle of Salamis. Politically alienated due to their material inability to participate in traditional *hoplite* battle – the martial progenitor of Western warfare characterized by high barriers to entry due to the high cost of bronze armaments (Hanson 2000) – the lower classes utilized their participation in the new naval activities as leverage in political disputes. The essential argument followed Nietzsche's earlier statement in the empowerment of people actively making sacrifices for the good of the state. Accentuating the need for a higher morality to seriously pursue long-term socio-political goals, Nietzsche clearly belongs to the movement revolting against the hedonistic nature of post-Mandeville economics (see Mandeville 1714/1924).[14] Nietzsche sees the need to sacrifice 'what is dearest to us' for the State, and he is conscious of the need to change and shape societies institutions. If we ask ourselves what Nietzsche means by 'risking what is dearest to us', risking one's life comes to mind, but, specifically in Nietzsche's case, it may be argued that what was dearest to him was 'individuality'.

In this one crucial phrase, quoted above, Nietzsche thus distances himself from right-wing liberalists on two important points, both of which place him squarely in the German economic tradition against unmitigated economic liberalism. First of all institutions matter and need 'proper, natural interest', careful attention and conscious design: the economy does not create a 'spontaneous order'. Secondly, people like Ayn Rand, who combine characters superficially similar to Nietzsche's *Übermensch* with a hatred for the state and for collectivity, have completely missed Nietzsche's point about the need *both* for heroic individualism *and* a solid state structure. As with the Athenian rowers, heroism could almost be seen as a precondition for the honor to participate in the affairs of the state.

---

14 For a discussion of Mandeville's 1714 *Fable of the Bee*, see Schumpeter (1954:184 and 325).

In terms of economic policy, this follows in the footsteps of Friedrich List. While not being part of any 'school' of economics, List is still a luminary in the German tradition and the history of economic analysis. A precursor to the Historical School and the *Verein für Socialpolitik,* List's writings were undoubtedly influential, laying the foundations for the late 19th Century policies which spread industrialization to continental Europe. List's emphasis was on organizing forces of production over accumulation of wealth, arguing that the power to produce wealth was infinitely more important than wealth itself (List 1909:109). His anthropocentric system was also quintessentially continental, in that it elevated the mind of Man to a position of primacy: "…all discoveries, inventions, improvements, perfections and exertions of all generations which have lived before us… form the *mental capital of the present human race*"(List 1909:113 discussed in Bell 1953:310). As we have already seen, this last term is also found in Nietzsche, a point to which we will get back.

5. Nietzsche: Social Justice and Welfare

So what does Nietzsche's socioeconomic construct actually look like? Most first-time readers of his works will approach the subject with a severely distorted 'vision' of a right-wing anti-Semitic *Übermensch* with Nazi sympathies, but even a preliminary study will uncover the fallacy of such a predisposition. It is on the Jews that he bestows the 'capital of spirit and will', and he argues:

> *it was the Jewish freethinkers, scholars, and physicians who held fast to the banner of enlightenment and of spiritual independence while under the harshest personal pressure and defended Europe against Asia, it is not least thanks to their efforts that… the ring of culture that now unites us with the enlightenment of Greek and Roman antiquity remained unbroken* (Nietzsche 1995:158).[15]

The Jews should, in Nietzsche's eyes, thus be respected as superior intellects, not defiled as racial inferiors. The further one reads, the further this castle of propaganda, started by Nietzsche's sister Elisabeth, crumbles under the weight of the evidence. Nietzsche harbours a deep-seated respect for the individual, and while most scholars would trace this back to his Homeric legacy of individual greatness, *Human, All too Human* takes a different stance; "Like every organizing political power, the Greek polis resisted and mistrusted the growth of culture… it did not want to allow any space in culture and education for history or 'becoming' (*Werden*)" (Nietzsche 1995:256).[16] The Greek polis

---

[15] *Überdies: in den dunkelsten Zeiten des Mittelalters, als sich die asiatische Wolkenschicht schwer über Europa gelagert hatte, waren es jüdische Freidenker, Gelehrte und Ärzte, welche das Banner der Aufklärung und der geistigen Unabhängigkeit unter dem härtesten persönlichen Zwange festhielten und Europa gegen Asien verteidigten; ihren Bemühungen ist es nicht am wenigsten zu danken, daß eine natürlichere, vernunftgemäßere und jedenfalls unmythische Erklärung der Welt endlich wieder zum Siege kommen konnte und daß der Ring der Kultur, welcher uns jetzt mit der Aufklärung des griechisch-römischen Altertums zusammenknüpft, unzerbrochen blieb* (Nietzsche 2000:4723–24).

[16] *Die griechische Polis war, wie jede organisierende politische Macht, ausschließend und mißtrauisch gegen das Wachstum der Bildung; ihr gewaltiger Grundtrieb zeigte sich fast nur lähmend und hemmend für dieselbe. Sie wollte keine Geschichte, kein Werden in der Bildung gelten lassen;* (Nietzsche 2000:4720).

did thus not supply enough cultural flux to allow for individual genius, a social condition that, as we mentioned earlier, only emerged in the Renaissance. The humanist veneration of the individual simultaneously explains Nietzsche's violent reactions both against the social conditions surrounding him, and against the collectivist solutions presented by the communists. Individuality is a pivotal characteristic of Nietzsche's state.

Nietzsche claims the greatest cost of government lies in the redirection of individual energy from personal creativity to macroscopic problem solving, but acknowledges a sacrifice has to be made to ensure public good. The 19th Century *Soziale Frage* – worries that created the *Verein für Socialpolitik* in 1872 and the *Kathedersozialismus* – clearly weigh heavily on Nietzsche; "Every day, new questions and concerns about the public welfare devour a daily tribute from mental and emotional capital of every citizen" (Nietzsche 1995:263).[17] There are several other instances where he seems incensed by issues of social justice, and he acknowledges the old truism that slaves were treated better than workers, as slaves had an inherent cost and a value to the owner:

> *Whereas everyone must concede that slaves live more securely and happily in every respect than the modern worker and that the work of slaves involves very little work compared with that of the 'worker'* (Nietzsche 1995:246).[18]

While giving room for entrepreneurial activities, the liberal *Laissez-Faire* doctrines that emerged from Ricardian economics created a system of institutionalised abuse of the lower classes, a social imbalance totally unacceptable to Nietzsche. Following the above discussed decline of the state,[19] we find that Nietzsche goes as far as distinguishing between a person and an individual: "The disregard for, decline, and *death of the state*, the liberation of the private person (I take care not to say: of the individual) is the consequence of the democratic concept of the state; herein lies its mission" (Nietzsche 1995:254).[20] An individual is unique, whereas a private person can be an undifferentiated part of the masses.

Nietzsche is fundamentally critical of the theoretical bases of liberal economics, of utilitarianism and of Spencer's social Darwinism. He particularly engages himself against the 'respectable but mediocre Englishmen: Darwin, John Stuart Mill and Herbert Spencer.'[21] The passive adaptation – *Anpassung* – of Darwinism is fundamentally opposed to Nietzsche's creative Will to Power as the driving force of history. To him it makes no

---

17 *die täglich neuen Fragen und Sorgen des öffentlichen Wohls verschlingen eine tägliche Abgabe von dem Kopf- und Herz-Kapitale jedes Bürgers* (Nietzsche 2000:4731).

18 *während jeder sich sagen muß, daß die Sklaven in allen Beziehungen sicherer und glücklicher leben als der moderne Arbeiter, daß Sklavenarbeit sehr wenig Arbeit im Verhältnis zu der des »Arbeiters« ist* (Nietzsche 2000:4701).

19 See footnote 22.

20 *Die Mißachtung, der Verfall und der Tod des Staates, die Entfesselung der Privatperson (ich hüte mich zu sagen: des Individuums) ist die Konsequenz des demokratischen Staatsbegriffs; hier liegt seine Mission* (Nietzsche 2000:4716).

21 achtbarer, aber mittelmäßiger Engländer - ich nenne Darwin, John Stuart Mill und Herbert Spencer [Curt Paul Janz: Biographie: XI. Erste Ernte, S. 60. Digitale Bibliothek Band 31: Nietzsche, S. 2285 (vgl. Janz-Nietzsche Bd. 2, S. 470) (c) C. Hanser Verlag].

sense to establish a secondary reactive adaptation at the core of the theory of human development, rather than the original force to which others then have to adapt.[22] As with Adam Smith's characterisation of human beings as dogs having learned to barter, English social theory again with Mill and Spencer leaves out Man's creative spirit in the foundations for the social sciences. In this criticism Nietzsche is truly in the mainstream of 19th Century German social science.

6. Nietzsche: Entrepreneurship, Gradualism and Uniqueness

So was Nietzsche then in the end a 'socialist'? Far from it. According to Nietzsche,

> *Socialism is the visionary younger brother of an almost decrepit despotism whose heir it wants to be, its aspirations are therefore in the deepest sense reactionary. For it desires an abundance of governmental power such as only despotism has ever had and indeed outdoes the entire past by striving for the outright annihilation of the individual* (Nietzsche 1995:255).[23]

Again we find Nietzsche absorbed by the historical significance of the present, mirroring the German Historical School. Like the *Kathedersozialisten*, Nietzsche did, however, acknowledge the value of socialist ideals and the need for social justice, but he distrusted their motivation: "By contrast, the *demand* for equality of rights made by socialists of the subjected caste never flows from a sense of justice, but instead from greed" (Nietzsche 1995:243).[24] He thus argues that extreme anti-bourgeoisie sentiments are derived from a deep-seated jealousy of the more 'successful' castes, rather than any sense of social welfare.

Again, the principal reason for Nietzsche's scepticism of extreme Socialism seems to be his opposite stance on the value of the individual. Nietzsche indeed claims Socialism strives for "the outright annihilation of the individual" (Nietzsche 1995:255), a goal quite contrary to his *will to power*. This remarkable distrust of the masses has clear Classical roots. Nietzsche's Homeric legacy saw no 'justice' in Socialism, and from Thucydides to Livy, 'mob' was consistently presented as a derogatory term, as a screaming, angry, easily agitated and directed mass of drones. And this is exactly what Nietzsche argues

---

[22] *Druck jener Idiosynkrasie die »Anpassung« in den Vordergrund, das heißt eine Aktivität zweiten Ranges, eine bloße Reaktivität, ja man hat das Leben selbst als eine immer zweckmäßigere innere Anpassung an äußere Umstände definiert (Herbert Spencer). Damit ist aber das Wesen des Lebens verkannt, sein Wille zur Macht; damit ist der prinzipielle Vorrang übersehn, den die spontanen, angreifenden, übergreifenden, neu-auslegenden, neu-richtenden und gestaltenden Kräfte haben, auf deren Wirkung erst die »Anpassung« folgt* (Nietzsche 2000:7323).

[23] *Der Sozialismus ist der phantastische jüngere Bruder des fast abgelebten Despotismus, den er beerben will; seine Bestrebungen sind also im tiefsten Verstande reaktionär. Denn er begehrt eine Fülle der Staatsgewalt, wie sie nur je der Despotismus gehabt hat, ja er überbietet alles Vergangene dadurch, daß er die förmliche Vernichtung des Individuums anstrebt* (Nietzsche 2000:4718).

[24] *Dagegen Gleichheit der Rechte fordern, wie es die Sozialisten der unterworfenen Kaste tun, ist nimmermehr der Ausfluß der Gerechtigkeit, sondern der Begehrlichkeit* (Nietzsche 2000:4696).

people under Socialism would necessarily become. Socialism "pounds the word 'justice' like a nail into the heads of the half-educated masses in order to rob them completely of their understanding" (Nietzsche 1995:256),[25] and furthermore unduly influences its subjects: "Someone who has money and influence can make the public share any opinion"(Nietzsche 1995:241)[26] summons visions of George W. Bush and Silvio Berlusconi. Socialist masses may be free of their materialistic fetters, but sadly their spiritual capital is lost along with their monetary one. 20th Century social democracy therefore saw mass education as a key task.

The bloody revolution proclaimed by the more ardent socialists also failed to convince Nietzsche, as his economic theory had no room for sudden revolts. Perhaps influenced by the 'Reign of Terror' following the French Revolution, as well as the general failure of the 1848 uprisings, he deeply distrusted limited truth in 'spontaneous order', both from the left and from the right:

> *There are political and social visionaries who ardently and eloquently demand the overthrow of all social order in the belief that the most splendid temple of beautified humanity would immediately be raised, as by itself…. Unfortunately, we know from historical experience that every such revolution brings with it a new resurrection of the most savage energies in the form of long-buried horrors and excesses of the most distant ages: that a revolution can therefore certainly be a source of energy when humanity has grown feeble, but never an organizer, architect, artist, perfecter of human nature* (Nietzsche 1995:248–249).[27]

Nietzsche's goal and the need for a gradual approach to get there is not only stated clearly, but also presented as a mirror image of the *Verein's* ideology:

> *What is necessary is not a forcible redistribution of property, but instead the gradual transformation of sensibility, the sense of justice must become greater in everyone, the instinct for violence weaker* (Nietzsche 1995:244).[28]

---

25 *Deshalb bereitet er sich im stillen zu Schreckensherrschaften vor und treibt den halbgebildeten Massen das Wort »Gerechtigkeit« wie einen Nagel in den Kopf, um sie ihres Verstandes völlig zu berauben (nachdem dieser Verstand schon durch die Halbbildung sehr gelitten hat) und ihnen für das böse Spiel, das sie spielen sollen, ein gutes Gewissen zu schaffen* (Nietzsche 2000:4719).

26 *Weil es beinahe sittlich gleichgültig erscheint, eine Zeile, noch dazu vielleicht ohne Namensunterschrift, mehr zu schreiben oder nicht zu schreiben, so kann einer, der Geld und Einfluß hat, jede Meinung zur öffentlichen machen* (Nietzsche 2000:4692).

27 *Es gibt politische und soziale Phantasten, welche feurig und beredt zu einem Umsturz aller Ordnungen auffordern, in dem Glauben, daß dann sofort das stolzeste Tempelhaus schönen Menschentums gleichsam von selbst sich erheben werde... Leider weiß man aus historischen Erfahrungen, daß jeder solche Umsturz die wildesten Energien als die längst begrabenen Furchtbarkeiten und Maßlosigkeiten fernster Zeitalter von neuem zur Auferstehung bringt: daß also ein Umsturz wohl eine Kraftquelle in einer matt gewordenen Menschheit sein kann, nimmermehr aber ein Ordner, Baumeister, Künstler, Vollender der menschlichen Natur* (Nietzsche 2000:4706).

28 *Nicht gewaltsame neue Verteilungen sondern allmähliche Umschaffungen des Sinnes tun, die Gerechtigkeit muß in allen größer werden, der gewalttätige Instinkt schwächer* (Nietzsche 2000:4697).

While Nietzsche here agrees with the need for greater justice in the distribution of wealth, in his opinion, the socialist formulas were too simple-minded:

> *When the socialists demonstrate that the division of property among present-day humanity is the consequence of countless acts of injustice and violence… they are seeing only one isolated thing* (Nietzsche 1995:243).[29]

As contemporaries Marx and Nietzsche share a perception of a *Zeitwende,* of the end of an era and the start of a new one. However, while Marx sees history moving as a result of material factors, Nietzsche's world is moved by the spirit and will of man. It may be argued, of course, that these are but two aspects of the same historical movement, at two different levels of abstraction: the material world being the result of Man's inventiveness.

Nietzsche reports having read Marx in a letter from Bonn dated May 1865[30]. This is two years before the first volume of *Das Kapital* is published, so the reference is likely to be to *Zur Kritik der Politischen Ökonomie* (1858). The Communist manifesto is unlikely to have qualified as a *Werk,* which is the term used by Marx. Other than in this letter, Nietzsche never refers to Marx by name. Nietzsche thoroughly dislikes the picturesque fanatics of history, those devoted to one single issue. To him these fanatics who appeal to the masses, he calls them 'Epileptiker des Begriffes' ('concept-epileptics')[31], form the antithesis to the strong and free spirit. Although Nietzsche so clearly sees the basic point of the need for social justice, it is likely that he may have considered Marx as having fallen into this category.

An interesting parallel between the two is the analysis of institutional inertia that makes sudden change difficult. Nietzsche presents a poetic version of Marx' idea of 'institutional mismatch': "The overthrow of institutions does not follow immediately upon the overthrow of opinions, instead, the new opinions live for a long time in the desolate and strangely unfamiliar house of their predecessors and even preserve it themselves, since they need some sort of shelter" (Nietzsche 1995:249–250).[32] In this case Nietzsche's ideas are far from utopian, as long as one can see through the masques of poetry that hide his realism.

---

[29] *Wenn die Sozialisten nachweisen, daß die Eigentums-Verteilung in der gegenwärtigen Menschheit die Konsequenz zahlloser Ungerechtigkeiten und Gewaltsamkeiten ist, und in summa die Verpflichtung gegen etwas so unrecht Begründetes ablehnen: so sehen sie nur etwas einzelnes* (Nietzsche 2000:4697).

[30] *Als Nebensache treibe ich jetzt Beethovens Leben nach dem Werk von Marx* (Nietzsche 2000:9712).

[31] *Die pathologische Bedingtheit seiner Optik macht aus dem Überzeugten den Fanatiker - Savonarola, Luther, Rousseau, Robespierre, Saint-Simon -, den Gegensatz-Typus des starken, des freigewordnen Geistes. Aber die große Attitüde dieser kranken Geister, dieser Epileptiker des Begriffs, wirkt auf die große Masse - die Fanatiker sind pittoresk, die Menschheit sieht Gebärden lieber, als daß sie Gründe hört* (Nietzsche 2000:8001).

[32] *Neue Meinungen im alten Hause. - Dem Umsturz der Meinungen folgt der Umsturz der Institutionen nicht sofort nach, vielmehr wohnen die neuen Meinungen lange Zeit im verödeten und unheimlich gewordenen Hause ihrer Vorgängerinnen und konservieren es selbst, aus Wohnungsnot* (Nietzsche 2000:4708).

7. Nietzsche in the Middle: *Kathedersozialismus* and the True Third Way

> *...the cleverness and self-interest of human beings are the best developed of all their characteristics; if the state no longer corresponds to the demands of these forces, chaos is the least likely thing to emerge; instead, an invention even more to the purpose than was the state will triumph over the state. How many organizing forces has humanity already seen die out... We ourselves are seeing the idea that attributes significant legal and political power to the family, which once held sway as far as the Roman way of life reached, becoming ever fainter and feebler. Thus, a later generation will likewise see the state become insignificant in certain areas of the world – an idea that many people today can scarcely conceive without fear and abhorrence. To work towards the diffusion and realization of this idea is admittedly something else: we would have to be quite arrogant about our rational capacity and hardly understand history halfway to put our hand to the plow right away – at a point when nobody can yet exhibit the seeds that later are to be strewn upon the rended earth. Let us therefore trust to "the cleverness and self-interest of human beings" that the state will still persist for a good while yet and that the destructive experiments of over-zealous and premature half-knowers will be repelled!* (Nietzsche 1995:255)[33]

Hidden in the bowels of this voluminous passage, we see the embryonic form of a *Kathedersozialist* ideology. While "the cleverness and self-interest of human beings" appear to be the next in kin to a certain invisible hand, Nietzsche's phrase seems to be of a different temperament. Where Classical economics saw the aggregate self-interest of Man usurping the idea of a state, as in an extreme *laissez-faire* system, Nietzsche's self-interest was of a more political nature. Social experimentation is to be avoided, as one should instead rely on nature's perpetual propensity to change, evolve, and mature. The role of the state in society is to be evaluated from a historical perspective, and not defined on the basis of a monolithic model.

One can thus see how Nietzsche is unwilling to sacrifice the creative genius of the individual to the avatar of communist collectivism. He demands social justice and improved conditions for the working classes, but also acknowledges that progress originates in

---

33 *Die Aussicht, welche sich durch diesen sichern Verfall ergibt, ist aber nicht in jedem Betracht eine unglückselige: die Klugheit und der Eigennutz der Menschen sind von allen ihren Eigenschaften am besten ausgebildet; wenn den Anforderungen dieser Kräfte der Staat nicht mehr entspricht, so wird am wenigsten das Chaos eintreten, sondern eine noch zweckmäßigere Erfindung, als der Staat es war, zum Siege über den Staat kommen. Wie manche organisierende Gewalt hat die Menschheit schon absterben sehen: - zum Beispiel die der Geschlechtsgenossenschaft, als welche Jahrtausende lang viel mächtiger war als die Gewalt der Familie, ja längst, bevor diese bestand, schon waltete und ordnete. Wir selber sehen den bedeutenden Rechts- und Machtgedanken der Familie, welcher einmal, so weit wie römisches Wesen reichte, die Herrschaft besaß immer blasser und ohnmächtiger werden. So wird ein späteres Geschlecht auch den Staat in einzelnen Strecken der Erde bedeutungslos werden sehen - eine Vorstellung, an welche viele Menschen der Gegenwart kaum ohne Angst und Abscheu denken können. An der Verbreitung und Verwirklichung dieser Vorstellung zu arbeiten, ist freilich ein ander Ding: man muß sehr anmaßend von seiner Vernunft denken und die Geschichte kaum halb verstehen, um schon jetzt die Hand an den Pflug zu legen, - während noch niemand die Samenkörner aufzeigen kann, welche auf das zerrissene Erdreich nachher gestreut werden sollen. Vertrauen wir also »der Klugheit und dem Eigennutz der Menschen«, daß jetzt noch der Staat eine gute Weile bestehen bleibt und zerstörerische Versuche übereifriger und voreiliger Halbwisser abgewiesen werden!* (Nietzsche 2000:4717–18).

individual innovations and individual initiative; "A higher culture can arise only where there are two different castes in society… the caste of those who are forced to work and the caste of those who are free to work" (Nietzsche 1995:237).[34] Mirroring the ideas Benjamin Constant proposed in his *The Liberty of Ancients Compared with that of Moderns* (Constant 1816), he simultaneously requests the freedom *from* need, and the freedom *to* be creative. While liberalism tends to emphasize the freedoms *to* (freedom as 'civil liberties'), communism tended to emphasize the freedoms *from* (hunger, illiteracy etc). The characteristics of the Third Way of the *Verein für Socialpolitik* and the successors have been a simultaneous attention to both of these freedoms.

Furthermore, it was important to Nietzsche that there was circulation between the two castes: "…it is even possible for some movement between the two castes to take place, so that the duller, less intelligent families and individuals from the upper caste can be demoted to the lower one and the freer people from the lower caste can in turn gain admission to the higher one…" (Nietzsche 1995:237–238).[35] Nietzsche's idea of social mobility was followed up by Vilfredo Pareto's 'Circulation of Elites' (Pareto 1916). Schumpeter's later metaphor that the economy is like a hotel where the persons inhabiting the luxury rooms always change also shows clear kinship to the same idea; "In fact, the upper strata of society are like hotels which are indeed always full of people, but people who are forever changing" (Schumpeter 1959:156).

Writers like Kashyap have already pointed out that Nietzsche was "as opposed to the socialist State as to the democratic one" (Kashyap 1970:91), but fail to elaborate on the argument. Nietzsche was thus left hanging in mid-air as a utopian renegade whose social criticisms were as disturbing as they were impractical. The general impression left us by the considerable body of secondary literature on Nietzsche's political philosophy is that of a diagnostic prophet, a social critic with a visionary analysis of his contemporary power structures. His writings are, however, seldom policy-centred, and hard to relate to the dichotomous political situation created by the Cold War. It can thus, in this day and age of bipolar socioeconomic systems, seem as if Nietzsche's goal indeed was utopian, that he simultaneously demanded socialism and liberalism; that he wanted to 'have his cake and still eat it'. This conclusion, however, is anachronistic in that it imposes modern Cold War values on history. Anthony Giddens writes "The ruling groups who set up the social insurance system in imperial Germany in the late nineteenth Century despised *laissez-faire* economics as they did socialism" (Giddens 1998) and it is indeed in this tradition, independent as it was from the right-left axis of the Cold War, that we find Nietzsche and the *Kathedersozialisten.*

---

[34] *Eine höhere Kultur kann allein dort entstehen, wo es zwei unterschiedene Kasten der Gesellschaft gibt: die der Arbeitenden und die der Müßigen, zu wahrer Muße Befähigten; oder mit stärkerem Ausdruck: die Kaste der Zwangs-Arbeit und die Kaste der Frei-Arbeit* (Nietzsche 2000:4685).

[35] *Findet nun gar ein Austausch der beiden Kasten statt, so, daß die stumpferen, ungeistigeren Familien und einzelnen aus deroberen Kaste in die niedere herabgesetzt werden und wiederum die freieren Menschen aus dieser den Zutritt zur höheren erlangen: so ist ein Zustand erreicht, über den hinaus man nur noch das offene Meer unbestimmter Wünsche sieht* (Nietzsche 2000:4685–86).

Also, 'As a political metaphor, the third path claims a larger field than just economics. Their path took the meaning to bridge the gap, or find an alternative approach beyond the dualism of modernity and tradition, of liberal democracy and authoritarian rule, of rationalism and *Heimat*' (Haselbach 2000:67).

Nietzsche's *Zeitgeist* was very different from the present one, resting on the intellectual ruins of the Cold War. As a consequence of the NATO-Soviet axis of hostilities, economics became divided in a system of binary opposites, but binary in the sense of a circle cut in two. Only recently did it dawn upon us that the Cold War was fought between two brands of Ricardian economics, while the Other Canon type theory of economics – represented by the *Kathedersozialisten* and the US institutionalist and pre-institutionalist counterparts – died out. The common Ricardian roots of both neo-classical economics and the planned economy of the communist counterparts have been emphasized by Geoffrey Hodgson (Hodgson 1999), Nicholas Kaldor (Kaldor 1955–1956), and Joseph Stiglitz (Stiglitz 1994). While confusing, shocking, and at times contradictory, Nietzsche's *Glance at the State* is more than the quixotic bile of a confused mind, and can indeed be read as a concrete statement of public policy.

8. Conclusion and Notes on Further Research

Marxist critique of Nietzsche often characterises him as an apologetic of liberalism and capitalism. We have attempted to show that this is a fundamentally wrong interpretation. Indeed, not only liberalism itself, but also its philosophical foundations are at cross-purposes with Nietzsche's basic philosophy. Typically, the appreciation of Nietzsche as a true Third Way social scientist in the German economic tradition has been lost in the prolonged crossfire between liberalism and communism.

While we now have joined ranks with countless 'cranks' in securing Nietzsche for one cause or another, we believe this to be one of the few occasions on which his writings have been evaluated from the perspective of an economist (Ottmann 1987 is one of them). This paper is, however, not intended as a final verdict on the matter, but rather as a prelude for further analysis. There are immediate questions whose answers remain beyond the scope of this essay, which would be interesting topics for future studies. We only analysed a very small portion of his substantial literary legacy, and the obvious continuation would be the task of testing our preliminary conclusion against this vast body of writings. Given Nietzsche's rhetorical gymnastics, this could be a monumental task. We have already noted Nietzsche's classicist heritage on several occasions – and from Thucydides to Aristotle, from Xenophon to Pericles, the intellectual echoes of ancient Athenians are indeed prominent in his writings – and the next logical step would be to connect the plethora of existing studies on this subject to our theory of Nietzschean *Kathedersozialismus*. Upon browsing though the vast body of secondary literature on Nietzsche, one clearly sees the uneven distribution of their topics. Countless scholars have discussed his connection to the Ancient Greeks, but few indeed have evaluated his contributions to the fields of economics and political science.

While Nietzsche for years has been thought to be a philosophical pariah, we have sought to establish his connection to the German tradition of appreciative and *verstehende* economics. Nietzsche's influence on his *Zeitgeist* was, as other papers in this volume have explored, considerable. While we have placed Nietzsche's economic policies under an overall heading, his political writings are still a unique amalgamation of two millennia of Western political theory, and what ideas he took from where remains contested. In the end our contribution has been to place Nietzsche's economic policies within the context of an existing school of political economy. His legacy remains that of an intrepid, if somewhat esoteric statecrafter.

As a final note it should be said that the *Kathedersozialist* agenda, and indeed the entire German tradition, has gained new relevance in the past years, as it becomes clear that our times also have a *Soziale Frage*. Haselbach's statement about the *Kathedersozialisten* seems highly relevant also for Nietzsche:

> [His] *work tried to re-write liberal economic theory with a distinctively anti-capitalist stance, albeit by reinvigorating the liberal utopia, and by reinterpreting the notion of capitalism. This theoretical approach can be characterised as a theory of a third path between capitalism and communism* (Haselbach 2000:64).

The gap between rich and poor has, however, this time increased in scale, as the task at hand is one of solving fundamental international discrepancies arising from globalisation, rather than re-evaluating domestic policy. The question to ask is therefore why most of the World's countries are poorer today than ten years ago, and what can be done about it. In our post-Cold War era, the true Third Way can perhaps provide us with the best tools for the job.

Bibliography

Bell, John Fred 1953: *A History of Economic Thought.* New York: The Ronald Press.

Burckhardt, Jacob 1958: *The Civilization of the Renaissance in Italy.* New York: Harper.

Burckhardt, Jacob 1998: *The Greeks and Greek Civilization.* London: HarperCollins.

Burckhardt, Jacob 1979: *Reflections on History.* Indianapolis: Liberty Fund.

Constant, Benjamin 1816: *The Liberty of Ancients Compared with that of Moderns.* Online version at http://www.uark.edu/depts/comminfo/cambridge/ancients.html

Conway, Daniel W. 1997: *Nietzsche & the Political.* London: Routledge.

Cossa, Luigi 1891/92: *Saggi di Bibliografia*, supplement to *Giornale degli Economisti.*

Diggins, John P. 1978: *The Bard of Savagery: Thorstein Veblen and Modern Social Theory.* New York: Seabury Press. Republished (1999) as *Thorstein Veblen: Theorist of the Leisure Class.* Princeton: Princeton University Press.

Eby, Clare Virginia 1998: *Dreiser and Veblen, Saboteurs of the Status Quo,* Columbia: University of Missouri Press.

Engels, Friedrich 1892: *Die Lage der arbeitenden Klasse in England.* Stuttgart: J. H. W. Dietz.

Giddens, Anthony 1998: *The Third Way – the Renewal of Social Democracy.* Cambridge: Polity Press.

Gossman, Lionel 2000: *Basel in the age of Burckhardt – a study in unseasonable ideas.* Chicago: University of Chicago Press.

Hanson, Victor Davis 2000: *The Western Way of War – Infantry Battle in Classical Greece.* Berkeley: University of California Press.

Haselbach, Dieter 2000: Franz Oppenheimer's Theory of Capitalism and of a Third Path in Koslowski, Peter (ed.): The *Theory of Capitalism in the German Economic Tradition.* Berlin: Springer.

Hodgson, Geoffrey 1999: *Economics and Utopia.* London: Routledge.

Ingram, John Kells 1967: *A History of Political Economy*. New York: Augustus M. Kelley.

Jorgensen, Elizabeth and Henry Jorgenson 1999: *Thorstein Veblen: Victorian Firebrand*, New York: Sharpe.

Kaku, Sachio 2000: 'Lujo Brentano on the Compulsory Insurance System for Workers in Germany' in Shionoya, Yuichi (editor): *The German Historical School – The Historical end Ethical Approach to Economics*. London: Routledge.

Kaldor, Nicholas 1955–1956: *Alternative Theories of Distribution* in *Review of Economic Studies XXIII(2)*.

Kashyap, Subhash C. 1970: *Unknown Nietzsche*. Delhi: National.

Kaufman, Walter 1974: *Nietzsche – Philosopher, Psychologist, Antichrist*. Princeton: Princeton University Press.

Krökel, Fritz 1929: Europas *Selbstbesinnung durch Nietzsche - Ihre Vorbereitung bei den französischen Moralisten*. München: Verlag der Nietzsche-Gesellschaft.

List, Friedrich 1909: *The National System of Political Economy*. London: Longmans, Green, and Co.

Loria, Achille 1915 & 1920: *Verso la giustizia sociale – Idee, battaglie ed apostoli*. (2 Vols.). Milan: Societa Editrice Libraria.

Mandeville, Bernard 1714/1924: *The Fable of the Bees: or, Private Vices, Publick Benefits*. Oxford: Clarendon Press.

Magnus, Bernd and Higgins, Kathleen M. 1996 (eds.): *The Cambridge Companion to Nietzsche*. Cambridge: Cambridge University Press.

Menger, Carl 1923, *Grundsätze der Volkswirtschaftslehre*, 2. edition, Vienna: Hölder-Pichler-Tempsky und G. Freytag.

Molinaeus, Carolus 1546/1930: *Tractatus Contractuum et Usurarum Redituumque Pecunia Constitutorum* in Arthur Eli Monroe (ed.), *Early Economic Thought – Selections from Economic Literature prior to Adam Smith*. Cambridge: Harvard University Press.

Nietzsche, Friedrich 1995: *Human, all too Human*. Stanford: Stanford University Press.

Nietzsche, Friedrich 2000: *Werke und Briefe*. Berlin: Hanser Verlag.

Ober, Josiah 1996: *The Athenian revolution: essays on ancient Greek democracy and political theory*. Princeton: Princeton University Press.

Ottmann, Henning 1987: *Philosophie und Politik bei Nietzsche*. Berlin: Walter de Gruyter.

Pareto, Vilfredo 1916, *Trattato di Sociologia Generale*, Florence: G. Barbèra, 2 volumes. (English edition *The Mind and Society*, New York: Harcourt, Brace and Company, 1935)

Raaflaub, Kurt A. 1997: *Democracy 2500?: Questions and Challenges*. Dubuque: Kendall/Hunt.

Rae, John 1834: *Statement of some new principles on the subject of political economy, exposing the fallacies of the system of free trade, and of some other doctrines maintained in the 'Wealth of Nations'*. Boston: Hilliard, Gray & Co.

Rae, John 1901. *Contemporary Socialism*. New York: Charles Scribner's Sons.

Rahe, Paul A. 1994: *Republics Ancient and Modern*. Chapel Hill: University of North Carolina Press.

Reinert, Erik 1994: Catching up from Way Behind – A Third World Perspective on First World History in Fagerberg, Jan (ed) The Dynamics of Technology, Trade, and Growth. London: Edward Elgar.

Reinert, Erik & Daastøl, Arno M. 1997: Exploring the Genesis of Economic Innovations: The religious gestalt-switch and the duty to invent as preconditions for economic growth in *European Journal of Law and Economics*, Vol 4, No. 2/3, 1997, and in *Christian Wolff. Gesammelte Werke, Materialien und Dokumente*, Hildesheim: Georg Olms Verlag.

Richardson, John 1996: *Nietzsche's System*. Oxford: Oxford University Press.

Salin, Edgar 1948: *Jacob Burckhardt und Nietzsche*. Berlin: Verlag Lambert Schneider.

Schmoller, Gustav 1884/1967: *The Mercantile System and its Historical Significance*. New York: Augustus M. Kelley.

Schumpeter, Joseph A. 1959: *The Theory of Economic Development*. Cambridge: Harvard University Press.

Schumpeter, Joseph A. 1954: *A History of Economic Analysis*. London: Routledge.
Shionoya, Yuichi 2001 (ed.): *The German Historical School*. London: Routledge.
Smith, Adam 1776/1976: *An Inquiry into the Nature and Causes of the Wealth of Nations*. Chicago: University of Chicago Press.
Sombart, Werner 1915: *Händler und Helden*, München & Leipzig: Duncker & Humblot
Sombart, Werner 1930: *Die drei Nationalökonomien*. Berlin: Duncker & Humblot.
Stiglitz, Joseph 1994: *Wither Socialism?* Cambridge: MIT Press.
Veblen, Thorstein (1884/1934): 'Kant's Critique of Judgement', in *The Journal of Speculative Philosophy*, Vol. XVIII, July. Reprinted in *Essays in our Changing Order*, New York: Viking Press.
Wittrock, Gerhard 1939: *Die Kathedersozialisten bis zur Eisenacher Versammlung 1872*. Berlin: Ebering.

Chapter Twelve

CREATIVE DESTRUCTION IN ECONOMICS: NIETZSCHE, SOMBART, SCHUMPETER

Hugo Reinert & Erik S. Reinert

Table of Contents

'From the heart of all matter
Comes the anguished cry -
'Wake, wake, great Siva,
Our body grows weary

Of its law-fixed path,
Give us new form.
Sing our destruction,
That we gain new life…'

Rabindranath Tagore, Indian Poet.

1. Creative Destruction in Vogue

The 1990's brought Joseph Alois Schumpeter (1883–1950) into the center stage of the economic debate. The Austrian-born economist had been teaching at Harvard from 1932 until his death. As the phenomena surrounding the 'New Economy' temporarily seemed to have cancelled the normal laws of economic gravity, Alan Greenspan heralded Schumpeter as the theoretician and prophet of the events[1]. At the core of the phenomenon was the process of creative destruction that had become associated with the name of Schumpeter. This concept seemed tailor-made to describe the process by which information and communication technology destroyed previous technological solutions and laid waste old companies in order to make room for the new.

In today's standard economic theory, Schumpeter stands out as being highly original. However, his great intellectual independence is generally misinterpreted as meaning that his ideas appear on the scene only with him. This is far from the truth (see Reinert 2002), also as it applies to the key concept of 'creative destruction'. This idea itself is a very old one. In this paper we shall argue that the idea of 'creative destruction' enters the late 19th Century *Zeitgeist* through the works of Friedrich Nietzsche. Going back further in time, the process of creation and destruction plays a central role in Hinduism, the religion which so inspired Nietzsche's *Erzieher* (educator) Arthur Schopenhauer. Nietzsche's own ideas about creative destruction, as popularized through his *Also Sprach Zarathustra*, had a profound and wide-ranging influence on generations of German-speaking artists and intellectuals (Sokel 1959). We shall further argue that – contrary to the firm beliefs of the economics profession – the term 'creative destruction' was brought into economics not by Schumpeter but by Werner Sombart (1863–1941), the economist who was probably most influenced by Nietzsche.

Nietzsche saw it as his task to bring about the regeneration of Western culture. This he sought to achieve by attacking its decadent institutions and philosophical foundations. Perceiving the impossibility of basing a modern moral system on God, and the imminent danger of nihilism, Nietzsche sought to set up an alternative, immanent morality of the 'super-human', or the *Übermensch*, to replace the old transcendental morality. In order to create this new morality, it was necessary for Nietzsche to destroy the old one: the new morality must quite literally stand on the ruins of the old. We shall argue that this new

[1] In speeches of April 4 and October 24, 2001.

morality is based on a concept of creative destruction, insofar as it demands of each individual human being that it 'write its own tablets', thereby destroying the 'old tablets'. Nietzsche's central work *Zarathustra* is thus at the same time both a meditation on creative destruction, because it presents this new 'morality of innovation', and a practical example of the same, insofar as it attacks the existing morality and seeks to replace it with this new morality.

To Hegel certain people epitomize the spirit of the age they live in. He cites Alexander the Great, Caesar and Napoleon as examples. Although he would himself strongly have disliked the reference, Nietzsche was decidedly one of these world-historical individuals who shaped the *zeitgeist* in a decisive way, individuals about whom Hegel says that their '*...own particular purpose contain the substantial will of the World Spirit'*. (Hegel 1953:39–40). The influence of such individuals on their time goes beyond references and footnotes.

Schumpeter was himself somewhat of an *Übermensch*, which was definitely also an image he wished to project. In his obituary to Schumpeter, his Harvard colleague Gottfried Haberler indeed quotes Nietzsche's laudatory remark on Schopenhauer: *'Seht ihn nur an – Niemandem war er untertan'* (Haberler 1950:344). At the age of 25 Schumpeter published a book on the methodology of the economics profession (1908), at 29 he wrote his celebrated *Theory of Economic Development* (1912) and at the age of 31 he published a history of the economics profession (1914). Schumpeter was never a beginner. The most popular anecdote about Schumpeter is that he is said to have remarked that he only had three ambitions in life: to be Vienna's best lover, Austria's best horseman, and the world's best economist. With hindsight he admitted having had some problems with the horses.

Schumpeter left no school of economics, and in spite of his encyclopedic writing on the history of economic thought and the filiations of economic ideas over time, he was himself very unclear as to the origins of his own ideas. He is therefore, somewhat mistakenly, generally seen as an isolated and highly original thinker. Although Schumpeter usually is classified as a member of the Austrian school of economics, in many ways his views were not those prevailing in Vienna at the time. Schumpeter did not wish to take sides in the famous *Methodenstreit* between Carl Menger and Gustav Schmoller; in fact, in his first book the 25-year-old Schumpeter solomonically attempts to settle the dispute by suggesting, in effect, that theories at different levels of abstractions ought to be seen as complementary rather than in conflict with each other (Schumpeter 1908).

Technological innovation and the role of the entrepreneur had been standard features of German economics since its inception with Gottfried von Leibniz and Christian Wolff (Reinert & Daastøl 1997). With Nietzsche's *Übermensch* and Zarathustra's 'creative destruction', however, these ideas were brought into focus in a wider societal context, and they acquired both new heroic dimensions and a new vocabulary. Indeed, the main features of Schumpeter's economics, both the entrepreneur, the instigator of change, and his 'will to power' and creative destruction, are truly Nietzschean creatures. In the social sciences, bestsellers like Oswald Spengler's *Untergang des Abendlandes (The Decline of the West*, 1939) – influencing the intellectual climate in the period between the World Wars – and Ayn Rand's *Atlas Shrugged* (1957) – influencing the Cold War debate – reflect the Nietzschean moral value of 'create or decay'. In contrast to Schumpeter, Oswald Spengler specifically mentions Nietzsche's influence on his *Decline*...(Spengler 1939:xiv).

2. Creative Destruction before Nietzsche

2.1. Creative Destruction as a Universal Idea

The idea that the birth of something new is founded on the destruction of previous existence is an old one. From the Egyptians, the Greek inherited the myth of Phoenix, the bird Bennu which was a symbol for the rising sun. This bird lived for five hundred years at a time, and at the end of that time it built its own funeral pyre and lightened it with the beating of its wings. Bennu or Phoenix was consumed to ashes, but out of the ashes grew a new Phoenix which, in time, repeated the 500 year cycle. In medieval Christian writings Phoenix was a symbol of the Resurrection of Christ, in itself a prime example of creative destruction.

Nowhere is the concept of creative destruction more clearly outlined than in Hinduism: here we find one of the most complex and certainly one of the richest cosmological illustrations of the dynamics of creation and destruction. At its heart are the three supreme godheads of the pantheon: Brahma the Creator, Vishnu the Preserver and Shiva the Destroyer. Brahma creates the universe; Vishnu protects what comes into being: his role includes rescuing mankind in times of need; Shiva, in turn, is the destroyer of the universe, fated to destroy it as it winds down in order to bring about its regeneration. After Shiva finishes his work of destruction, Brahma in turn begins the creation of the universe: thus the cycle is infinite.

In other traditions, Shiva is both the creator and the destroyer: in this capacity he is often represented as the *Shiva Nataraja*, the Lord of the Dance. His dance is the dance of the universe as it endlessly moves from creation to destruction, destruction to creation. It is in his nature to embody both, as one is not possible without the other. The reclusive philosopher-god was also said to reside in solitude on a mountaintop, from whence he gazed across the world with his eagle eyes sharpened by ascetic practices. It is said that his burning gaze once incinerated the young god of love, when the latter foolishly disturbed Shiva's meditations.

Echoes of these myths and their themes are easy to find in Nietzsche. Nietzsche himself never referred directly to the theme of creative destruction in Hindu mythology, but we know that Indian ideas and myths, including the myth of Shiva, were current and circulated in Nietzsche's intellectual milieu. Nietzsche's older colleague and close friend at the University of Basel, the historian Jacob Burckhardt discusses the regenerative role of Shiva: '*Not without cause do the Indians worship Shiva, the God of destruction. Filled with the joy of destruction, wars clear the air like thunderstorms, they steel the nerves and restore the heroic virtues, upon which states were originally founded, in place of indolence, double-dealing and cowardice.*' (Burckhardt 1979:217)

2.2. Creative Destruction as a 'German' Idea: From Goethe to Nietzsche and Sombart

'And the cobweb, shall it be eternal?
If the maid does not destroy it, the spider itself will tear it up.'[2]

Goethe, *Zahme Xenien VIII*

Johann Gottfried Herder (1744–1803) was the philosopher who first brought the Indian myths of creative destructions into German philosophy. Herder's very positive attitude towards Indian civilization and form of government appears in the context of a four-volume *Philosophy of History of Human History* (*Ideen zur Philosophie der Geschichte der Menschheit*) (Herder 1790–92). Among Herder's publications we also find a book on what we could call 'science policy', with the title *On the Influence of Government on the Sciences and Sciences on the Government* (Herder 1781). His very sympathetic treatment of India (Herder 1790–92:III 41–64) contrasts sharply with his negative views on what he calls oriental despotism (*Despotismus des Orients*) (1781:17). Herder's negative judgment also extends to the hierarchical forms of government of the Hebrews and the Egyptians (1790–92:Vol. III). Also the Roman Empire failed to satisfy Herder's standards for freedom and human rights (Kantzenbach 1970:103).

The man who brought Herder to the court of Archduke Carl August in Weimar was Johann Wolfgang von Goethe (1749–1832), and also in Goethe we find clear references to the need for destruction in order to create. If we are to explore intellectual filiations, in Schumpeter's tradition, the cosmology of Indian religions in all likelihood reaches Nietzsche through his 'educator' Arthur Schopenhauer (1788–1860) by way of the orientalist Friedrich Majer (1772–1818), himself a disciple of Herder.

In the following poem, Goethe powerfully relates the pain of creation, already on Day One of existence: the pain of overcoming what Nietzsche later would call the *vis inertiae*, the powers of inertia and status quo:

'As the world, deep down
lay at God's eternal breast,
He arranged for the first hour
With sublime joy of creation (Schöpfungslust),
And he spoke the word: let there be light!
Then a cry of pain sounded,
As reality with all its power
broke into being.'[3]

Goethe, *Divan, Buch Suleika.*

2 *'Und ein Gewebe, sollt es ewig sein?*
Zerstört's die Magd nicht, reißt die Spinne es selber ein.'

3 *'Als die Welt im tiefsten Grunde*
Lag an Gottes ewiger Brust
Ordnet er die erste Stunde

The key role of *Schöpfungskraft* – of the power to create – is reflected in German economics of the time, where the *productive powers* were seen as being the key to national wealth. Friedrich List (1789–1846), whose early works were written when Goethe was still alive, is a key example here. In 19th Century US economics, the term 'productive powers' is equally frequent. We have argued that during the 19th Century the term 'increasing productive powers' played a role similar to that of 'increasing competitiveness' in today's discourse: a way of increasing national wealth (Reinert 1995). The emphasis in German economics on what Werner Sombart calls '*das Werdende, das ewig wirkt und lebt*' (Sombart 1930:299) ('the becoming, which forever is active and lives') stands in sharp contrast with the English barter-based theories of the time, a fact frequently emphasized by German economists.

A necessary corollary to *Schöpfungskraft* (the power to create) is the term Goethe here uses about God's creation: *Schöpfungslust* (the *desire* and *joy* of creation). The power to create is intimately tied to joy of the process of creation. This reflects the Renaissance idea that Man is created in the image of God, and it is therefore his pleasurable duty to invent (Reinert and Daastøl 1997). In the 20th Century, this same idea was to be reflected in Schumpeter's entrepreneur as a 'routine breaker' who innovates, motivated not only by profit, but also by an inner urge that this is what he or she has to do. But, as in Goethe's poem, this act is painful: As God said 'let there be', a 'cry of pain' – of what must have been the original *Weltschmertz* – was heard as the world was created.

Another typical trait of Goethe and German philosophy at the time is the holistic emphasis, the role of *die Ganzheit,* of the *totality.* Again Werner Sombart is the economist who constructs the bridges which carry these ideas into the economics profession. The key work here is Sombart's *Die Drei Nationalökonomien* [4] ('The Three Types of Economics') (Sombart 1930), his main methodological work. In this book the many entries on *Ganzheit* are interwoven with references to Goethe and Nietzsche. In fact the Swedish economist Sven Helander, who worked and published in Germany between the two wars, refers to German economics as 'Faustian economics'. This carries over to the emphasis by German economists on their science extending to and including whatever is relevant for the working of the economy. The last chapter, chapter seven, of Schumpeter's *Theorie der wirtschaftlichen Entwicklung* was entitled 'The Economy as a whole'. Characteristically, Schumpeter left this chapter out of the second 1926 edition of the book, as he was

Mit erhabner Schöpfungslust
Und er sprach das Wort: Es werde!
Da erklang ein schmerzlich Ach!
Als das All mit Machtgebärde
In die Wirklichkeiten brach'

[4] Othmar Spann is another economist who particularly emphasizes *das Ganze*. His best-selling history of economic thought, which by 1929 has reached nineteen editions and 95.000 copies sold in German, was published in England as *Types of Economic Theory* and in the United States as *The History of Economics* (both in 1930). Notice the similarity of the English title of Spann's book and the title of Sombart's work ('The Three Types of Economics') published in the same year: in contrast to the present situation, there was at the time a generalised awareness that there were several *types* of economics.

developing an economic theory that was more compatible with the rising Anglo-Saxon and neoclassical tide (see *Industry & Innovation*, No.1–2, 2002 for discussions).

Qualitative understanding – *Verstehen*[5] – of the totality requires the understanding of structural connection (*Strukturzusammenhänge*) of the whole economy. In his book on economic methodology, *Die Drei Nationalökonomien*, Sombart quotes from Goethe's *Faust*:

> *'I acknowledge, what in the innermost*
> *Keeps the world together,*
> *Behold all will to power and seeds*
> *And do no longer poke around in words.'*[6]
>
> (Sombart 1930:106)

On the same page Sombart, using a quote from *Faust*, refers to Man's creation in the image of God, his *Gottähnlichkeit*, and the risk that Man may fear his own godlike qualities. Here Sombart uses the above quote from Goethe to express the core Renaissance insight of Man's pleasurable duty to invent as originating in his *Gottähnlichkeit*. Noble (1997) provides a fascinating discussion on this same subject – on Man's *Gottähnlichkeit* – as it relates to modern inventions and innovation.

In *Die Drei Nationalökonomien*, the heredity of German economics from the Renaissance via Goethe and Faust is neatly drawn in a few sentences on page 106. Goethe's *Willenskraft* as main moving force is closely related to Nietzsche's *Geist- und Willenskapital*, Man's wit and will, which is the most conspicuously absent factor of production in today's mainstream economics. It may indeed be argued that Sombart's *Drei Nationalökonomien* indeed has Zarathustra-like qualities; a somewhat rambling discourse around the essence of the creative nature of Man, filled with references to philosophers Greek and German.

2.3. Creative Destruction, Cyclicality, and German Economics

> '...*denn im irdischen Kreise ist denn doch alles wiederkehrend.*'
>
> Goethe, *letter to August von Goethe, 3.6.1808.*

The vision of creative destruction leads to a particular view of history. Just as with the bird Phoenix and its 500-year cycles, creative destruction leads to cyclical rather than linear patterns of history: an example is Schumpeter's 'clustering of innovations' as the basic cause of business cycles. Early theories of human history tended to consist of such cycles, as those of the influential Arab historian Ibn-Khaldun (1332–1406). Warrior tribes conquer a city, flourish and decay, only to lose the city to a new tribe.

---

5 See Drechsler (2002) in Reinert for a discussion.

6 *'Dass ich erkenne, was die Welt*
Im Innersten zusammenhält,
Schau alle Willenskraft and Samen
Und tu' nicht mehr in Worten kramen.'

We find a similar historical view in Niccolò Machiavelli (1469–1527). Only with Jean Bodin (1520–1596), one of the path-breakers of the Renaissance, comes the idea that historical cycles may have a cumulative and upward trend: the idea of progress (Reinert 2000).

Giovanni Battista Vico (1668–1744), an important philosopher of history, also emphasized the cyclical nature of history (Vico 1744/1984). The idea of 'creation as pain' as we quoted from Goethe, is also found in Vico. With him we also find other 'German' themes, as the Nietzschean need for Mankind to plunge himself into Man's original ignorance 'between angels and beasts' (Lilla 1993:16) in order to understand.

The birth of classical economics, also with the young Adam Smith, is tied to such cycles, to the notion of 'stages of development' (*Wirtschaftsstufen*) (Reinert 2000). In English economics, both history generally and the technical change that demolished the previous stages of history disappeared with Ricardo and his followers. In German economics, the role of stages in economic development continued to be an important feature of the historical schools. Inspired by the framework in Schumpeter (1939), today the idea of creative destruction lies at the heart of the cyclical theories of economic life associated with Carlota Perez (Perez 2002a, 2002b) and Christopher Freeman (Freeman & Louca 2001). Here history as progress as first seen by Bodin and his contemporaries is combined with the cyclicality of history that is associated with creative destruction.

A cyclical economic theory based on creative destruction is found in Vilfredo Pareto's idea of 'circulation of elites' (Pareto 1916/1935).[7] In fiction we find the same idea with Thomas Mann, who was an author considerably influenced by Nietzsche. In Mann's first important novel, *Buddenbrooks* (1901), we find the same circulation of elites that Pareto would later use on an aggregate level: the first generation entrepreneur makes the money, the second generation vacillates between entrepreneurship and *rentier*, and the third generation, only *rentier.* In the English edition of Schumpeter's *Theory of Economic Development*, published almost 20 years after the first German one, Schumpeter has made this view into one of his metaphors on capitalism: '*In fact, the upper strata of (a capitalist) society are like hotels which are indeed always full of people, but people who are forever changing*'. (Schumpeter 1934:156)[8]

3. Nietzsche and Creative Destruction

Clearly, it is impossible to do justice to the vast complexity of Nietzsche's thinking on the subject of creative destruction in a brief paper. What we will try to do is chart out a rough, introductory topology of some of Nietzsche's principal ideas on the subject, so as to better understand how he may have influenced subsequent writers: in this case, Sombart and Schumpeter.

---

7 The discussion of this subject is found in paragraphs 2233 and following.

8 This metaphor is not found in the original German text.

There is no doubt that creation and creativity, artistic or otherwise, were among the principal themes that occupied Nietzsche throughout his life: from his early essays on Greek art and *The Birth of Tragedy*, to his prolific writings on Wagner and his art, to the mystical experiences with music that he experienced prior to his nervous breakdown in Italy. Nietzsche's specific interest in the relationship between creation and destruction underpinned his 'genealogical' enquiry into the history of moral concepts (Nietzsche 1994), as well as many of his general ideas concerning history, morality, society and evolution.

This particular discussion centers on *Thus spake Zarathustra*, written in 1883–1885, because this text is probably the closest Nietzsche himself ever got to outlining a positive alternative to what he saw as the moribund system of Christian morality. Tragedies of interpretation[9] such as the insertion of the *Übermensch* into the racial ideologies of the Nazis have obscured the original context and meaning of the term, turning the *Übermensch* into a symbol of racial supremacy, eugenics and violence. This illicit[10] appropriation of the *Übermensch* makes it doubly important for us to understand at least part of the fabric of ideas to which the *Übermensch* originally belonged.

For simplicity and the sake of argument, we have organized our discussion around a series of key ideas extracted from the texts which, when put together, form the rough outline of a 'cosmology' of creation and destruction.

These 'principles', or central ideas, are:

1. **Creation and Destruction**
2. **The Opposite of Creation and Destruction is Stagnation**
3. **The Will to Power**
4. **Life is that which Constantly Overcomes Itself**
5. **Warfare is a Form of Therapy**

[9] There are well-known problems one encounters in reading Nietzsche. Some of these are inherent (his sprawling, rhetorical, aphoristic, ironical, contradictory style) and deliberate (hermetic arguments; complex use of literary personae, layered irony, rhetorical hyperbole): Nietzsche was categorically *not* writing for 'the masses'. Other difficulties arise from the long and troubled history of Nietzsche reception: his sister presided like a high priestess over his legacy after his breakdown, to the point of editing and falsifying letters and documents he left behind, enthusiastically offering her brother up as ideological fodder for the Nazi regime. Even before this, however, Nietzsche had been assimilated, ironically, by the ideologues of German nationalism: foreign commentators dubbed World War 1 the 'Euro-Nietzschean War'. These are all issues one must consider while reading Nietzsche. The most important demand Nietzsche places on the reader, however, is the suspension of immediate judgments, in favor of the willingness to investigate not just the immediate meaning of the text, but also the unspoken premises that may underlie and underpin it. Anything less, and the reader's response risks becoming merely a reflection of the 'intellectual baggage' each individual reader brings to the text. It is easy to violently disagree (or agree) with Nietzsche, but far more difficult to set aside one's initial reactions and investigate the complex web of the text.

[10] For a discussion of the complex relationship between Nietzsche and his sister, and of her influence on his intellectual reception, Peters (1977) is still a relevant source.

1st Principle: Creation and Destruction

'*Whoever must be a creator always annihilates*' (Nietzsche 1968a:59)[11]

Creation and destruction are inseparable to Zarathustra; the creator must always destroy. Thus it is axiomatic that new creation is always preceded by the destruction of old, existing forms. '*The man who breaks… tables of values, the breaker, the lawbreaker; …he is the creator*' (Nietzsche 1968a:23)[12]. In more general terms, the affirmation of one thing always implies the denial, even the destruction, of something else. As Nietzsche states elsewhere: '*affirmation requires denial and annihilation*'[13]. Zarathustra phrases this principle in specifically moral terms, but also indicates that it has a more general, 'cosmological' validity; the idea is also frequently echoed elsewhere in Nietzsche's work (ie. Nietzsche 1994).

One of the key moral ideas in Zarathustra is that the 'self' is (or can be) self-created: as a proto-existentialist, Zarathustra demands of his disciple that he take responsibility for who he is, for creating himself and his own laws. The obvious implication of this idea, considering it in the light of the above relationship between creation and destruction, is that the old 'self' must be destroyed in order to make way for the new 'self': '*You must wish to consume yourself in your own flame: how could you wish to become new unless you had first become ashes!*' (Nietzsche 1968a:64)[14]

A particularly important illustration of this doctrine of 'ego death' is the allegory of the Three Transformations of the Spirit, the first of Zarathustra's discourses. The allegory tells of how the noble spirit, through a series of transformations, comes to realise itself by becoming first a camel, then a lion, then a child. The first stage is that the camel wanders into the desert, carrying the heaviest burden of moral laws. In the desert the camel transforms into a lion and the moral laws it carries are transformed into a 'great dragon'. The lion defeats the dragon to make way for the child; the lion's role is the 'creation of freedom for oneself for new creation'[15]. With the dragon out of the way, the lion is free to transform into the creative child, who is a '*new beginning, a game, a self-propelled wheel, first movement, a sacred yes.*' (Nietzsche 1968a:27)

Creation is thus inseparable from destruction. This relationship exists only in one direction and does not function when reversed. Denial does not imply affirmation, destruction itself does not lead to creation; this to Nietzsche is the case of the anarchist or the nihilist. Following the allegory of the Three Transformations, these two qualities or processes – creation and destruction – are personified in the recurrent textual figure of *Der Edle*, the 'noble man' who embodies Zarathustra's moral and spiritual ideals. The

---

[11] '*Immer vernichtet, wer ein Schöpfer sein muß.*' (Nietzsche 2000: 6427)

[12] '*Den, der zerbricht ihre Tafeln der Werte, den Brecher, den Verbrecher - das aber ist der Schaffende*' (Nietzsche 2000: 6367)

[13] '*… im Jasagen ist Verneinen und Vernichten Bedingung*'. (Nietzsche 2000: 7884)

[14] '*Verbrennen mußt du dich wollen in deiner eignen Flamme: wie wolltest du neu werden, wenn du nicht erst Asche geworden bist!*' (Nietzsche 2000: 6435).

[15] '*Neue Werte schaffen - das vermag auch der Löwe noch nicht: aber Freiheit sich schaffen zu neuem Schaffen - das vermag die Macht des Löwen.*' (Nietzsche 2000: 6372)

'noble man' is Nietzsche's 'utopian' reply to what he perceives as the decadent spirit of the times; in his nobility and power he embodies Nietzsche's hopes for the future of humanity.

The 'noble man' possesses numerous attributes: he is generally physically healthy, self-aware, generous, un-resentful, 'innocent' and prone to laughter, both cruel and kind. His most important and defining attribute however, the one that marks him off as Zarathustra's hope for the future, is his capacity for extremes: for good and evil, worship and contempt, love and hatred, lust and revulsion, creation and destruction: 'The great despisers are the great venerators'[16].

To Zarathustra, the 'noble man' is primarily a creator: *'The noble man wants to create something new and a new virtue'* (Nietzsche 1968a:44)[17]. Creation demands destruction, and it is here that the capacity for extremes is at its most important: in the noble man the capacity for creation is mirrored by an equivalent potential for destruction. Driven as he is, he will never stoop to indifference: the risk is that if he cannot create he will turn to nihilism, destroying without creating: *'But this is not the danger of the noble man, that he might become of the good, but a churl, a mocker, a destroyer.'* (Nietzsche 1968a:44)[18]

An inner necessity drives the 'noble man' to create, but his most important creation is himself. To create himself he must destroy his old self, and since he must constantly create, he is in some sense never more than a stage: his *present* self will be the ashes on which his *future* self is built. The promise of the 'noble man' is that at some point in his chain of self-overcoming he will transcend the human and achieve the *Übermensch*, the 'super-human' or 'above-human'. The 'noble man' is therefore the prelude to the 'super-human'.

This driving necessity is the measure both of his nobility and his power. The 'noble man' is powerful, not necessarily in the physical sense but morally and spiritually, and the nature of this power is such that the more powerful he is, the more powerfully he is compelled to seek growth and grow even more powerful. This inner compulsion is his 'will to power'.

> *'And whoever must be a creator in good and evil, verily, he must first be an annihilator and break values. Thus the highest evil belongs to the highest goodness: but this is creative'* (Nietzsche 1968a:114)[19]

2nd Principle: The Opposite of Creation and Destruction is Stagnation

If creation and destruction are interlinked and embodied in the figure of the 'noble', they are in turn opposed by another principle, embodied throughout Nietzsche's writings in

[16] *'Die großen Verachtenden nämlich sind die großen Verehrenden."* (Nietzsche 2000:6794)

[17] *'Neues will der Edle schaffen und eine neue Tugend'* (Nietzsche 2000: 6400)

[18] *'...nicht das ist die Gefahr des Edlen, daß er ein Guter werde, sondern ein Frecher, ein Höhnender, ein Vernichter'.* (Nietzsche 2000: 6400).

[19] *'Und wer ein Schöpfer sein muß im Guten und Bösen: wahrlich, der muß ein Vernichter erst sein und Werte zerbrechen. Also gehört das höchste Böse zur höchsten Güte: diese aber ist die schöpferische.'* (Nietzsche 2000: 6520)

the figures of priests, ascetics, 'despisers of the body' and the numerous other 'unhealthy' examples of the human type we could dub the 'preserver type'. The main example of the 'preserver type' in Zarathustra is the human type he describes as 'the good and the just'. These characters are fundamentally pathological profiles and personify the idea of preservation, stagnation, paralysis and decline. Sick, pale, unhealthy and weak, they are unable to overcome the *vis inertiae*, the forces of status quo. They also tend to congregate and cluster. It is significant that Zarathustra consistently refers to the 'good and the just' in the plural and the 'noble man' in the singular. The tension between the two types thus also embodies the tension between the individual and the collective, a very important point to the hermit Zarathustra.

Unable to create, 'the good and the just' fervently cling to the existing and resist change. '*The good want the old, and that the old be preserved*' (Nietzsche 1968a:44).[20] This attitude leads them into paralysis, stagnation, decline and ultimately spiritual, even physical death. Their path thus leads to nihilism:

> '*The creative self created respect and contempt; it created pleasure and pain. The creative body created the spirit as a hand for its will.*
>
> *Even in your folly and contempt, you despisers of the body, you serve your self. I say unto you: your self itself wants to die and turns away from life. It is no longer capable of what it would do above all else: to create beyond itself. That is what it would do above all else, that is its fervent wish.*
>
> *But now it is too late for this: so your self wants to go under, O despisers of the body. Your self wants to go under, and that is why you have become despisers of the body! For you are no longer able to create beyond yourself.*' (Nietzsche 1968a:35)[21]

Their will to preserve is to Zarathustra both the function of a stunted and unhealthy life-force *and* a moral failure. In the sense that they are thwarting the unfolding of the life process and the promise of the *Übermensch,* the preserver types are both objects of pity *and* contempt, agents *and* victims of nihilism.

As we have seen so far, Nietzsche's human typologies are orientated around the question of health, and the healthy 'human animal'. Physical health is Nietzsche's main metaphor for cultural, intellectual and spiritual phenomena. Health is a moral, spiritual and intellectual quality as much as a physical one, and the spiritually unhealthy 'preserver type', represented in Zarathustra mainly by 'the good and the just', is merely the prelude to the worst of all human specimens, the 'most despicable man', the embodiment of decline: the 'Letzte Mensch' (the Last Man), or the dull post-human remains that litter

---

[20] '*Altes will der Gute, und dass Altes erhalten bleibe.*' (Nietzsche 2000: 6400)

[21] '*Das schaffende Selbst schuf sich Achten und Verachten, es schuf sich Lust und Weh. Der schaffende Leib schuf sich den Geist als eine Hand seines Willens.*

Noch in eurer Torheit und Verachtung, ihr Verächter des Leibes, dient ihr eurem Selbst. Ich sage euch: euer Selbst selber will sterben und kehrt sich vom Leben ab.

Nicht mehr vermag es das, was es am liebsten will - über sich hinaus zu schaffen. Das will es am liebsten, das ist seine ganze Inbrunst.

Aber zu spät ward es ihm jetzt dafür - so will euer Selbst untergehn, ihr Verächter des Leibes.

Untergehn will euer Selbst, und darum wurdet ihr zu Verächtern des Leibes! Denn nicht mehr vermögt ihr über euch hinaus zu schaffen.' (Nietzsche 2000: 6386)

the earth at the end of time. '*'What is love? What is creation? What is desire? What is a star?' thus asks the last man, and he blinks*' (Nietzsche 1968a:17)[22]. This quasi-human is Nietzsche's bleak projection of the decadent human animal of modernity, the ultimate outcome of the historical process whereby humanity condemns itself to stagnation and decline by embracing the comfortable mediocrity of the existing. The last man personifies the final extinction of human will and creativity.

Differences in health as well as in ability and drive to create thus poise the 'noble man' against 'the good and the just'. The tension between the two reflects the tension between the 'last man', the dead end of human history, and the *Übermensch*, the promise of a heroic future. If the 'noble man' threads the path to the *Übermensch*, compelled by the inner necessity constantly to overcome himself and eventually even his own humanity, 'the good and the just' thread the path towards the 'last man', bent on resisting the need for change. The two future types represent the two possible outcomes of the human life process as it either declines, in the former case, or ascends, in the latter. The force that governs this process, and which thus determines the future of humanity, is the 'will to power'.

3rd Principle: The Will to Power

In Nietzschean terms, the difference between these two types – the *letzte Mensch* and the *Übermensch* – must be understood in terms of their relative 'will to power'. Elaborating this difference requires us to examine, at least in passing, some of the elements that make up Nietzsche's notion of the 'will to power'.

The will to power is one of Nietzsche's most complex and contradictory concepts, easily subject to simplification or misrepresentation. It is often represented as a crude form of social Darwinism, a doctrine of 'survival of the fittest' that glories in power over other human beings and ruthless physical supremacy. It is primarily this interpretation, aided by simple assumptions about 'power' and the enthusiastic crudity of Nietzsche's sister's posthumous exegesis, that led Nietzsche to be incorporated into Nazi ideology (Peters 1977).

Against this reductive reading, we shall here mobilize a number of statements made by Nietzsche-Zarathustra that support a more complex, ambivalent interpretation, and suggest links between the doctrine of the 'will to power' and notions such as creativity and generosity.

Creativity, to Zarathustra, is a function of the will to power: *The will is a creator* (Nietzsche 1968a:141)[23]. The will to something is the will to bring something into being: '*To will liberates, for to will is to create: thus I teach. And you shall learn solely in order to create.*' (Nietzsche 1968a:206)[24]. Life and the will to power are dynamic forces that seek constantly to create,

[22] *"Was ist Liebe? Was ist Schöpfung? Was ist Sehnsucht? Was ist Stern?' - so fragt der letzte Mensch und blinzelt.'* (Nietzsche 2000: 6357)

[23] *'...der Wille ist ein Schaffender'* (Nietzsche 2000: 6562)

[24] *'Wollen befreit: denn Wollen ist Schaffen: so lehre ich. Und nur zum Schaffen sollt ihr lernen!'.* (Nietzsche 2000: 6663)

and – as in the German economics tradition – there is an imperative to *learn*. The acquisition of knowledge must be a means to future creation.

The will to power is subject to decline; when it does decline, the consequence is degeneration. When the will to power is too weak, it is unable to expand beyond itself and there is stagnation; the 'tide' turns back and there is stagnation, physical and spiritual decadence and ultimately nihilism, which Nietzsche dubs the 'symptom of a terminally exhausted soul'.[25] Nietzsche dedicated one of the chapters of his *On the Genealogy of Morality* to an analysis of the ascetic impulse as a nihilistic expression of the will to power as it turned on itself (Nietzsche 1994).

One of the consequences of decadence is the atrophy of the 'gift-giving spirit':

> '*Tell me my brothers: what do we consider bad and worst of all? Is it not degeneration? And it is degeneration that we always infer where the gift-giving soul is lacking. Upward goes our way, from genus to over-genus. But we shudder at the degenerate sense which says, "everything for me*'". (Nietzsche 1968a:75)[26]

Thus when life is abundant and the will to power in growth, these are expressed as generosity. Selfish greed is the product of the decline or distortion of the will to power.

The will to power can thus not be reduced to the mere will to dominion over others: primarily the will to power is not a social concept but a measure of health, in the broader sense described above[27]. As Nietzsche describes this, the 'health' of the organism finds expression in generosity, 'nobility' and the drive to create 'beyond oneself'. Amongst other creative processes, the will to power drives the creation (and re-creation) of the self. From this, and from the discussion in the above paragraphs, self-overcoming emerges as perhaps the most important creative expression of the will to power. The will to power is therefore the driving force behind all processes of change, progress and evolution, both in the individual, in the species, and in society.

4th Principle: Life is that which Constantly Overcomes Itself

This mechanism of the will to power governs both the individual and the species and, in a broader sense, all life processes: *'And life itself confided this secret to me: 'Behold', it said. 'I am that which must always overcome itself''*. (Nietzsche 1968a:115)[28]

---

[25] '*...anzeichen einer verzweifelnden sterbensmüden Seele.*' (Nietzsche 2000: 6878)

[26] *'Sagt mir, meine Brüder: was gilt uns als Schlechtes und Schlechtestes? Ist es nicht Entartung? - Und auf Entartung raten wir immer, wo die schenkende Seele fehlt. Aufwärts geht unser Weg, von der Art hinüber zur Über-Art. Aber ein Grauen ist uns der entartende Sinn, welcher spricht: 'Alles für mich'.'* (Nietzsche 2000: 6454–6455)

[27] There are obviously numerous possible interpretations of the will to power; for an introductory philosophical analysis of the history of the concept, and of its various academic interpretations, see Williams (2001)

[28] '*Und dies Geheimnis redete das Leben selber zu mir: 'Siehe', sprach es, 'ich bin das, was sich immer selber überwinden muß'.*' (Nietzsche 2000: 6519)

As we have seen the 'choice' lies between creation-destruction and preservation. One leads to greater heights, the other to decline. Even life itself is subject to this 'law', forced either to overcome itself or remain as it is, in slow decline. The 'choice' between growth and decline is essentially the same as the choice between the 'noble' and the 'the good and the just': both are aspects of the same underlying processes of the will to power.

Biological evolution is creative destruction put into practice. Life overcomes itself and creates new, higher forms for itself, passing through stages of biological evolution: man is in one sense only the 'over-ape', or the self-overcoming of the ape.

> *'All beings so far have created something beyond themselves; and do you want to be the ebb of this great flood and even go back to the beasts rather than overcome man? What is the ape to man? A laughingstock or a painful embarrassment. And man shall be just that for the overman: a laughingstock or a painful embarrassment.'* (Nietzsche 1968a:12)[29]

The human form is merely a stage, a transient animal that must either rise beyond itself or decline. To Zarathustra Man's implicit promise of self-transcendence and future greatness comes very close to being his essence: '*O my brothers, what I can love in man is that he is an overture and a going under.*' (Nietzsche 1968a:287)[30]

This broadly defined transcendence of the human can and must also be moral: *"Man must become better and more evil' – thus I teach'* (Nietzsche 1968a:288)[31]. Because the noble man and his indomitable will to power carry the promise of the *Übermensch*, and because nobility is measured by the capacity for extremes and the drive to create, 'goodness', which is the opposite of 'nobility', cannot be a measure of moral worth. The good must in fact be 'destroyed', because through their moral complacency and resistance to change they block the very mechanism whereby human life reaches beyond itself:

> *'O my brothers, who represents the greatest danger for all of man's future? Is it not the good and the just? Inasmuch as they say and feel in their hearts, 'We already know what is good and just, and we have it too; woe unto those who still seek here!' And whatever harm the evil may do, the harm done by the good is the most harmful harm… The good must crucify him who invents his own virtue. That is the truth!… The creator they hate the most: he breaks tablets and old values. He is a breaker, they call him lawbreaker. for the good are unable to create; they are always the beginning of the end…'* (Nietzsche 1968a:212–213)[32]

---

29 *'Alle Wesen bisher schufen etwas über sich hinaus: und ihr wollt die Ebbe dieser großen Flut sein und lieber noch zum Tiere zurückgehn, als den Menschen überwinden? Was ist der Affe für den Menschen? Ein Gelächter oder eine schmerzliche Scham. Und ebendas soll der Mensch für den Übermenschen sein: ein Gelächter oder eine schmerzliche Scham.'* (Nietzsche 2000: 6349)

30 *'O meine Brüder, was ich lieben kann am Menschen, das ist, daß er ein Übergang ist und ein Untergang.'* (Nietzsche 2000: 6793–6794)

31 *"Der Mensch muß besser und böser werden' - so lehre ich.'* (Nietzsche 2000: 6795)

32 The entire passage reads in German: *'O meine Brüder! Bei welchen liegt doch die größte Gefahr aller Menschen-Zukunft? Ist es nicht bei den Guten und Gerechten? -*

'The good and the just' are the greatest danger to Man's future, because they promise only the steady, mild, pleasant decline into spiritual paralysis, animal comfort and mediocrity of the 'last man'.

This is the sense of Zarathustra's plea: *'Break, break the good and the just! O my brothers, have you really understood this word?'* (Nietzsche 1968a:213)[33] His greatest fear for the future is that humanity, under the influence of the complacent and 'the good and the just', should become a dead end, rather than a stepping stone to a better future. To prevent this, Zarathustra (and Nietzsche) threw themselves into battle: *'Man is something that must be overcome'* (Nietzsche 1968a:37)[34]

5th Principle: Warfare is a Form of Therapy

Zarathustra is animated by a spirit of battle:

> *'Your enemy you shall seek, your war you shall wage – for your thoughts. And if your thoughts be vanquished, then your honesty should still find cause for triumph in that. You should love peace as a means to new wars – and the short peace more than the long.'* (Nietzsche 1968a:47)[35]

It is in the light of this 'dialectic' philosophy of ideas that Nietzsche can claim that to him, 'attacking is proof of good will'[36]. Life thrives on change, challenge and extremes; continuity leads to stagnation and decline. Challenge and hardship make it possible to grow stronger: *'What does not kill me makes me stronger'* (Nietzsche 1968b:23)[37]. Weak ideas must be pruned.

- als bei denen, die sprechen und im Herzen fühlen: »Wir wissen schon, was gut ist und gerecht, wir haben es auch; wehe denen, die hier noch suchen!«

Und was für Schaden auch die Bösen tun mögen: der Schaden der Guten ist der schädlichste Schaden!

Und was für Schaden auch die Welt-Verleumder tun mögen: der Schaden der Guten ist der schädlichste Schaden.

O meine Brüder, den Guten und Gerechten sah einer einmal ins Herz, der da sprach: »es sind die Pharisäer«. Aber man verstand ihn nicht.

Die Guten und Gerechten selber durften ihn nicht verstehen: ihr Geist ist eingefangen in ihr gutes Gewissen. Die Dummheit der Guten ist unergründlich klug. Das aber ist die Wahrheit: die Guten müssen Pharisäer sein - sie haben keine Wahl! Die Guten müssen den kreuzigen, der sich seine eigne Tugend erfindet! Das ist die Wahrheit! Der zweite aber, der ihr Land entdeckte, Land, Herz und Erdreich der Guten und Gerechten: das war, der da fragte: »wen hassen sie am meisten? «Den Schaffenden hassen sie am meisten: den, der Tafeln bricht und alte Werte, den Brecher - den heißen sie Verbrecher. Die Guten nämlich - die können nicht schaffen: die sind immer der Anfang vom Ende: -- sie kreuzigen den, der neue Werte auf neue Tafeln schreibt, sie opfern sich die Zukunft - sie kreuzigen alle Menschen-Zukunft! Die Guten - die waren immer der Anfang vom Ende.' (Nietzsche 2000: 6673–6674)

33 *'Zerbrecht, zerbrecht mir die Guten und Gerechten! - O meine Brüder, verstandet ihr auch dies Wort?'* (Nietzsche 2000: 6675)

34 *'Der Mensch ist etwas, das überwunden werden soll.'* (Nietzsche 2000: 6349)

35 *'Euren Feind sollt ihr suchen, euren Krieg sollt ihr führen, und für eure Gedanken! Und wenn euer Gedanke unterliegt, so soll eure Redlichkeit darüber noch Triumph rufen! Ihr sollt den Frieden lieben als Mittel zu neuen Kriegen. Und den kurzen Frieden mehr als den langen.'* (Nietzsche 2000: 6406)

36 *'Angreifen ist bei mir ein Beweis des Wohlwollens.'* (Nietzsche 2000: 7752)

37 *'Was mich nicht umbringt, macht mich stärker.'* (Nietzsche 2000: 7535).

Nietzsche perceived the Western world to be in the throes of nihilism and decadence: his project was to identify the causes of this and bring about the necessary regeneration. Zarathustra's teaching, intended as a cure for this degeneration, was a 'tonic', a doctrinal remedy to the comfort of modernity and the life-denying morality of obedience and subjugation that to him were obstacles to the higher man. Nietzsche was no mere 'amoralist' or 'immoralist'; rather he conceived of himself as a sort of 'dialectic therapist' of morality and culture: his cure was the 'highest fight'. The renewal and regeneration of culture was to be forged and achieved through a sort of cultural shock therapy:

> *'For earthquakes bury many wells and leave many languishing, but they also bring to light inner powers and secrets. Earthquakes reveal new wells. In earthquakes that strike ancient peoples, new wells break open.'* (Nietzsche 1968a:211)[38]

Christianity, because of its origins in the slave revolt, preached a metaphysic and a morality of submission, self-denial and subjugation, but at the heart of the structure of Christianity lay the dead body of God. Nietzsche's critique aimed to clear away the fragmentary remnants of the Christian system, destroying them[39] to make way for a new morality that replaced the transcendent with the immanent, Heaven with earth, God with Man:

> *'Let your spirit and your virtue serve the sense of the earth, my brothers; and let the value of all things be posited newly by you. For that shall you be fighters! For that shall you be creators!'* (Nietzsche 1968a:77)[40]

The obedient Christian man, 'the good and the just', and the morality that he slavishly obeyed had to be destroyed in order to make way for the possible future 'higher' man: *'Dead are all gods: now we want the overman to live'* (Nietzsche 1968a:79)[41]. This was the promise of the *Übermensch*, the 'man of the future':

> *'This man of the future, who will redeem us both from the reigning ideal and from that which was bound to grow out of it, from the great nausea, from the will to nothingness, from nihilism; this bell-stroke of noon and of the great decision, which again liberates the will and restores to the earth its goal and to man his hope; this Antichrist and antinihilist, this conqueror of God and of nothingness - he must come one day.'*[42]

---

38 *'Das Erdbeben nämlich - das verschüttet viel Brunnen, das schafft viel Verschmachten: das hebt auch innre Kräfte und Heimlichkeiten ans Licht. Das Erdbeben macht neue Quellen offenbar. Im Erdbeben alter Völker brechen neue Quellen aus.'* (Nietzsche 2000: 6672)

39 Perhaps ironically, perhaps not, Christian theology has survived, recuperated from and even grown stronger after Nietzsche and his onslaughts: theologians now submit doctorates on Nietzsche. Did Nietzsche secretly predict this?

40 *'Euer Geist und eure Tugend diene dem Sinn der Erde, meine Brüder: und aller Dinge Wert werde neu von euch gesetzt! Darum sollt ihr Kämpfende sein! Darum sollt ihr Schaffende sein!'* (Nietzsche 2000: 6457)

41 *'Tot sind alle Götter: nun wollen wir, daß der Übermensch lebe'* (Nietzsche 2000: 6460)

42 (*Zur Genealogie der Moral*, second essay, our translation) *'Dieser Mensch der Zukunft, der uns ebenso vom bisherigen Ideal erlösen wird als von dem, was aus ihm wachsen mußte, vom großen Ekel, vom Willen zum Nichts, vom Nihilismus, dieser Glockenschlag des Mittags und der großen Entscheidung, der den Willen*

Nietzsche's attacks against morality, culture, the German nation and institutions were in a very real sense attempts at creative destruction: not a negation so much as an affirmation of what *could* be or become instead; *Übermensch* rather than God, Europe rather than Germany, effort rather than complacency, genius rather than mediocrity:

> *'Whether we immoralists do virtue any harm? – As little as anarchists do princes. Only since they have been shot at do they again sit firmly on their thrones. Moral: one must shoot at morals.'* (Nietzsche 1968b:26)

Morality must be shot at: partly because challenge and opposition foster strength, partly because only through destruction can the new be brought into being. According to Nietzsche's own logic, the affirmation of one thing required the negation of another. His problem, however, was that he was generally far more eloquent, versatile and persuasive as a critic than he ever was as an architect. Destruction eclipsed creation: directions for change were drowned out by the sound of cannons.

Summary and Concluding Remarks about the Principles

We have seen so far that:

- Zarathustra's perspective on creative destruction can be meaningfully described as a tension between the three concepts of creation, destruction and preservation.
- These three terms are represented principally in the relationship between the two figures of the 'noble', who embodies creation and destruction, and 'the good and the just', who embody preservation, stagnation and decline.
- The difference between these two figures can be explained as a relative difference in the 'will to power': whereas the 'noble' is driven to create by his will to power, 'the good and the just' lack the ability to create, and consequently have a vested interest in maintaining the existing order.
- The idea of 'power' that underpins the doctrine of the 'will to power' is neither simple nor immediately evident; rather it is a complex 'metaphysical' concept constituted of distinct elements; in abundance, this power expresses itself as creativity and generosity.
- Because the nature of the will to power is that it is either in the ascendant or in decline, life must constantly overcome itself; the 'noble man', in overcoming himself, abides by this and consequently comes to represent the future hope of mankind overcoming itself.
- This purpose is aided by challenge and battle, but not necessarily in the simple physical sense. Nietzsche's 'higher' war is fought for symbols, values and ideals; the therapeutic function of his entire cultural enterprise is dependent on his general philosophy of creation and destruction.

---

wieder frei macht, der der Erde ihr Ziel und dem Menschen seine Hoffnung zurückgibt, dieser Antichrist und Antinihilist, dieser Besieger Gottes und des Nichts - er muß einst kommen...' (Nietzsche 2000: 7354)

'Like the sun, Zarathustra too wants to go under; now he sits there and waits, surrounded by broken old tablets and new tablets half covered with writing.' (Nietzsche 1968a:198)[43]

Nietzsche's project was never completed: perhaps it was by definition impossible to complete. Nevertheless we are left with the task of digesting his tablets, *'half-covered with writing'*, and his dwarfing legacy, both in the form of his writings and in the enormous body of texts that constitute the history of his intellectual reception.

To conclude this section, we might quote Williams:

'I agree with a remark made by Michel Foucault in a late interview, that there is no single Nietzscheanism, and that the right question to ask is 'what serious use can Nietzsche be put to?'' (Williams, in Schacht 1994:238)

Among the many uses to which Nietzsche has been put in the century since his death, some have indeed been very, very serious; others, however, have been playful or artistic: the ghost of Zarathustra dances equally through the arts, the sciences, the poetry and the war rhetoric of the 20th Century, from America to Japan, from Expressionism to post-structuralism.

For many reasons, this influence is sometimes disguised. In many circles, Nietzsche still carries the stigma of Nazism, of irrationalism, *Blut und Boden* mysticism and Superman eugenics. His influence is therefore often subterranean, particularly in discourses and disciplines that reject the values for which he is taken to stand. Keeping these things in mind, the question we lead into the next section with is this: is economics really as unfazed by Nietzsche as it generally claims to be?

4. Nietzsche in Economics: From Sombart to Schumpeter

'Creative destruction' has almost become the trademark of Joseph Schumpeter. However, the first use of the term 'creative destruction' in economics must be attributed to Werner Sombart: Here on the century-long shortage of wood in Europe through the mass destruction of forests; the destruction of the forests created the very foundation for 19th Century capitalism:

'Again, however, from destruction a new spirit of creation arises; the scarcity of wood and the needs of everyday life… forced the discovery or invention of substitutes for wood, forced the use of coal for heating, forced the invention of coke for the production of iron. That these events, however, made possible the enormous development of capitalism in the 19th Century, is beyond doubt for any well-informed person. Thus even here, in this decisive point, the invisible threads of commercial and military interests appear closely intertwined'. (Sombart 1913:207)[44]

---

[43] *'Der Sonne gleich will auch Zarathustra untergehn: nun sitzt er hier und wartet, alte zerbrochene Tafeln um sich und auch neue Tafeln - halbbeschriebene.'* (Nietzsche 2000: 6651)

[44] *'Wiederum aber steigt aus der Zerstörung neuer schöpferischer Geist empor; der Mangel an Holz und die Notdurft des täglichen Lebens drängten auf die hin, drängten auf die Auffindung oder die Erfindung von*

Werner Sombart (1863–1941) was the leading economist of the Younger German Historical School of economics (Backhaus 1996). During Schumpeter's most creative and, at the same time, formative period, Sombart held a dominating position in German-speaking economics. Sombart's path-breaking work on modern capitalism, *Der moderne Kapitalismus* (Sombart: First edition in two volumes in 1902, a later editions in four volumes in 1919, last edition in six volumes in 1927) was translated to Spanish and Italian, but no English translation has yet been published.

However, during the period after World War II, Sombart and all pre-war II German economics went into an eclipse. Part of the explanation for this was the rise of mathematization of the profession, which was very much against the German tradition. Another part of the explanation was that to a surprising degree what was a healthy scientific baby was poured out with what was perceived as the post-nazi bath-water. The German tradition in economics therefore came to be represented solely by Marx and Schumpeter, a feature which made these two economists seem much more unique than they in effect are when seen in their own historical context. As we have already mentioned, Schumpeter himself assisted in this process, also by systematically neglecting the philosophical foundations of German economics in his *History of Economic Analysis* (Reinert 2002).

Schumpeter's originality in the Anglo-Saxon environment was then to a large extent also a product of the ignorance, outside Germany, of the traditions on which he built. Part of what Schumpeter did was to filter Sombart's work and the economic debate in Germany between the world wars to the Anglo-Saxon world. Most Schumpeterians, especially non-Germans, would probably be surprised by a German book that describes Schumpeter's 1942 book *Capitalism, Socialism and Democracy* – the work that made him accessible to the layman – as essentially a reworking of a German debate which had taken place decades earlier, where, as the author carefully points out, Schumpeter neither refers to the debate itself, nor to its protagonist Werner Sombart.

> *'Without referring to Sombart or to the general literature of the twenties and thirties, (in' Capitalism, Socialism and Democracy') Schumpeter in essence presented only what had already been written and said decades earlier in the German discussion about 'the future of capitalism'.'* (Appel 1992:260) [45]

Of Schumpeter's biographers, only Shionoya (1997) and Swedberg (1991) mention Nietzsche, and both do so in connection with entrepreneurship, not with Schumpeter's core concept of creative destruction (Shionoya 1997: 173,321) (Swedberg 1991:192). The most elaborated article dealing with the relationship between Schumpeter and Nietzsche

Ersatzstoffen für das Holz hin, drängten zur Nutzung der Steinkohle als Heizmaterial, drängten zur Erfindung des Kokesverfahrens bei der Eisenbereitung. Daß dieses aber die ganze Großartige Entwicklung des Kapitalismus im 19. Jahrhundert erst möglich gemacht hat, steht für jeden Kundigen außer Zweifel. Sodaß auch hier, in diesem entscheidenden Punkte, unsichtbare Fäden die merkantilen und die militaristischen Interessen eng miteinander zu verknüpfen scheinen'

[45] *'Ohne auf Sombart und die allgemeine Literatur der zwanziger und dreißiger Jahre hinzuweisen, bot Schumpeter (in Kapitalismus, Sozialismus und Demokratie) im wesentlichen nur daß, was bereits Jahrzehnte zuvor in den deutschen Diskussionen über die 'Zukunft der Kapitalismus' geschrieben und gesagt worden war…'*

is written by two Italian economists, Enrico Santarelli and Enzo Pesciarelli (1990). Also this article focuses on the entrepreneur.

Nietzsche's influence on the work of Werner Sombart is well documented both through Sombart's many references to Nietzsche and through his biographers. Also the people who most influenced Sombart, some of which were his close friends, were strongly influenced by Nietzsche (Lenger 1994:141). Sombart was himself known to quote frequently from Nietzsche's *Zarathustra* (ibid.:247).

In his main methodological work, *Die drei Nationalökonomien*, Sombart often quotes Nietzsche when addressing the basic history and philosophy of economics and the evolution of Man. To Sombart the development of science and of the human *Weltanschauung* follows through the same stages as Nietzsche's does. The world is at first *entzaubert* (demystified) and the finally *entgottet* (de-deified) (Sombart 1930:102).

Sombart finds that what the social sciences can learn from the natural sciences in terms of the return of identical (or presumably also similar) situations, i.e. the cyclicality of history. In this connection he also quotes Nietzsche:

> *'The predictability of an event does not result from a rule having been followed, or a necessity having being complied with, or from a law of causality that was projected by us onto every event-: it lies in the recurrence of 'identical cases'.'* (Sombart 1930:118) (Nietzsche 2000:9384) [46]

At the end of his most important methodological book, Sombart uses Nietzsche to express the very purpose of economics:

> *'But science, and above all the social sciences, should 'serve life'. This is the demand that anyone will make today, after Nietzsche's admonition a couple of generations ago, which we all in the depth of our souls consider justified, more so today than ever. We want no armchair erudition, no peddling of petty antiquities, no 'dead' knowledge.* (In a footnote Sombart refers to the title of Nietzsche's work, 'Untimely Meditations'[47], 'which still today are most timely')' (Sombart 1930:334–335) [48]

It is in this sense that Nietzsche says: 'Wissenschaft ist die bestimmteste Form des Willens zur Macht'. (Science is the most definite form of 'the will to power'). The 'will to power' is essentially 'the will to create', and consequently the key driving force in economic development. This is clearly Werner Sombart's view, and he here groups Nietzsche with Francis Bacon (1930:333). Grouping Nietzsche and Bacon effectively clarifies the dividing line between the two camps in the battlefield of 19th and early 20th Century economics. The first anti-Ricardian economists – the Reverend Jones in England and John Rae in the United States, both writing in the in the early 1830's – wished to re-Baconise economics. Bacon's and Nietzsche's approach both stand for Man the Creator at the

---

[46] *'Die Berechenbarkeit eines Geschehens liegt nicht darin, daß eine Regel befolgt wurde, oder einer Notwendigkeit gehorcht wurde, oder ein Gesetz von Kausalität von uns in jedes Geschehen projiziert wurde -: sie liegt in der Wiederkehr 'identischer Fälle'.'*

[47] In the Stanford translation called 'Unfashionable Observations',

[48] *'Aber die Wissenschaft und gerade auf die Geisteswissenschaft soll doch 'dem Leben dienen'. Das ist die Anforderung, die heute jeder stellen wird, nachdem vor ein paar Menschenaltern Nietzsches Mahnruf erklungen*

centre of economics, thus following the tradition of what we have labelled The Other Canon or *Renaissance Economics*. Bacon's affinity to the philosophers and economists in our genealogy of the idea of creative destruction is further strengthened by the fact that also Johann Gottfried Herder, 'sought refuge' in Francis Bacon against the metaphysics of Kant (Kantzenbach 1970:20)

5. Nietzsche and Economics at the Centenary of his Death

5.1. Methodology

Nietzsche the Economist is generally to be found indirectly, through the influence he had on his time. However, he occasionally himself makes references to economics that show his familiarity with the debates of the profession. At one point Nietzsche comments negatively on the harmful effect of *laissez faire* economics on the morality of whole nations.[49] Without referring to him, Nietzsche also uses Mandeville's key concept from *The Fable of the Bees* (1714) with an amusing twist. Instead of Mandeville's 'private vices, public benefits' – which was a key factor in the transformation of economics from being duty-based to being based on self interest – Nietzsche coins the expression 'public opinions, private laziness' (Nietzsche 1994:172). The collectivisation of society will in the end create passivity, and passivity necessarily leads to decay.

A third example of Nietzsche entering the economics debate is that when criticizing modern science, he approvingly quotes English economist Walter Bagehot (1826–1877), in a phrase which is even more appropriate in 2002 than it was when Bagehot wrote it.

> *'Unproved abstract principles without number have been eagerly caught up by sanguine men and then carefully spun out into books and theories which were to explain the whole world. But the world goes totally against these abstractions....'*[50] (Nietzsche 1994:249)

---

ist [Sombart's footnote reads: *'die heute immer noch zeitgemäß ist'*], *den wir alle im Tiefsten unserer Seele für berechtigt halten und der heute mehr denn je am Platz ist. Wir wollen keine Stubengelehrsamkeit, keine Antiquitätenkrämerei, kein 'totes' Wissen.'*

49 *'Der Verkehr mit der Wissenschaft, wenn er durch keine höhere Maxime der Erziehung geleitet und eingeschränkt, sondern, nach dem Grundsatze »je mehr desto besser« nur immer mehr entfesselt wird, ist gewiß für die Gelehrten ebenso schädlich, wie der ökonomische Lehrsatz des laisser faire für die Sittlichkeit ganzer Völker'.* (Nietzsche 2000: 4008)

50 The original passage in German reads as follows: *'Wer ist nicht fast im voraus überzeugt, daß ihre Prämissen eine wunderbare Mischung von Wahrheit und Irrtum enthalten und es daher nicht der Mühe verlohnt, über die Konsequenzen nachzudenken? Das fertig Abgeschlossne dieser Systeme zieht vielleicht die Jugend an und macht auf die Unerfahrnen Eindruck, aber ausgebildete Menschen lassen sich nicht davon blenden. Sie sind immer bereit, Andeutungen und Vermutungen günstig aufzunehmen, und die kleinste Wahrheit ist ihnen willkommen - aber ein großes Buch voll deduktiver Philosophie fordert den Argwohn heraus. Zahllose unbewiesene abstrakte Prinzipien sind von sanguinischen Leuten hastig gesammelt und in Büchern und Theorien sorgfältig in die Länge gezogen worden, um mit ihnen die ganze Welt zu erklären. Aber die Welt kümmert sich nicht um diese Abstraktionen, und das ist kein Wunder, da diese sich untereinander widersprechen.'* (Nietzsche 2000: 4124–4125)

Also as regards methodology, on the fashionable subject of human cognition and objectivity in science, Nietzsche has something important to say to today's economists:

> *'Henceforth, my dear philosophers, let us be on guard against the old and dangerous myth that postulates 'a pure, will-less, painless and timeless knowing subject'. Let us take care not to get caught in the tentacles of such contradictory concepts as 'pure reason', 'absolute spirituality', and 'knowledge in itself'; these always demand that that we should think of an eye that is absolutely unthinkable, an eye which cannot be allowed to be turned in any particular direction, and in which the active and interpreting forces – through which seeing becomes seeing something – are supposed to be lacking; these always demand of the eye a contradiction and a nonsense. The only seeing which exists is a seeing in perspective, a seeing with perception; and the more feelings we allow to get involved about an issue, the more eyes – different eyes – that we mobilise to observe one thing, the more complete will our concept of this thing, our objectivity, be. Would not eliminating the will....be the same as to castrate the intellect?'*[51]

A crucial problem in standard economics is that it is focused on exchange – on supply and demand – rather than on production. Continental economists used to complain that Anglo-Saxon economics had become *catallectics* – just a science of exchange. Nietzsche's criticism of English philosophy is completely in line with this: '*Among the English, Nietzsche had found, he thought, the prototype of a morality and a politics of traders and peddlers: counting and reckoning, calculation and assessment not only as the key to the world of commerce, but also to the world of morality and politics. What disturbed him – nay, outraged him – about this, was the intrusion of this equalisation, necessary for exchange and economic calculation, into the realm of life, which should not obey such a logic of equivalences*' (Ottmann 1987:131) [52]. This is a central theme in Werner Sombart's nationalistic book *Traders and Heroes* (*Händler und Helden*), published in 1915. In this work Sombart quotes extensively from Goethe, Fichte, Schopenhauer and Nietzsche. In today's methodological discussion, the 'equality assumption' (Buchanan 1979:231),

---

[51] (*Zur Genealogie der Moral*, our translation): '*Hüten wir uns nämlich, meine Herren Philosophen, von nun an besser vor der gefährlichen alten Begriffs-Fabelei, welche ein 'reines, willenloses, schmerzloses, zeitloses Subjekt der Erkenntnis' angesetzt hat, hüten wir uns vor den Fangarmen solcher kontradiktorischer Begriffe wie 'reine Vernunft', 'absolute Geistigkeit', 'Erkenntnis an sich'; - hier wird immer ein Auge zu denken verlangt, das gar nicht gedacht werden kann, ein Auge, das durchaus keine Richtung haben soll, bei dem die aktiven und interpretierenden Kräfte unterbunden sein sollen, fehlen sollen, durch die doch Sehen erst ein Etwas-Sehen wird, hier wird also immer ein Widersinn und Unbegriff vom Auge verlangt. Es gibt nur ein perspektivisches Sehen, nur ein perspektivisches 'Erkennen'; und je mehr Affekte wir über eine Sache zu Worte kommen lassen, je mehr Augen, verschiedne Augen wir uns für dieselbe Sache einzusetzen wissen, um so vollständiger wird unser 'Begriff' dieser Sache, unsre 'Objektivität' sein. Den Willen aber überhaupt eliminieren, die Affekte samt und sonders aushängen, gesetzt, daß wir dies vermöchten: wie? hieße das nicht den Intellekt kastrieren?'* (Nietzsche 2000:7394–7395). This is an example of how the Kaufmann translation often makes a 'kinder' Nietzsche: 'Fangarme' was translated as 'trap' rather than 'tentacles'.

[52] *'Nietzsche hat bei den Engländern die, wie er meinte, prototypische Moral und Politik der Krämer und Händler vorgefunden, das Rechnen und Berechnen, Kalkulieren und Taxieren nicht nur als Schlüssel zur Welt des Geschäfts, sondern auch zur Welt der Moral und Politik. Was ihn daran störte, ja empörte, war das Übergreifen tauschnotwendiger Gleichheit und ökonomischen Taxierens auf Bereiche des Lebens, die solcher Logik der Äquivalenz gerade nicht gehorchen sollten.'*

the exclusion of factors irreducible to numbers and of qualitative 'verstehen' (Drechsler 2002) are still at the core of the debate.

In fighting to create a theory at an appropriate level of abstraction for their analysis, economists are necessarily forced constantly to compare and equate 'unequals'. This search leads to the creation of mental tools like Weber's 'ideal types', Kaldor's 'stylised facts', and Perez' and Freeman's 'techno-economic paradigms'. These concepts are put into use in order to create some order in a chaos of observations and facts. To this methodology, Nietzsche provides the following encouraging message:

> *'Every concept originates through our equating what is unequal. No leaf ever wholly equals another, and the concept 'leaf' is formed through an arbitrary abstraction from the individual differences, through forgetting the distinctions; and now it gives rise to the idea that in nature there might be something besides the leaves which would be 'leaf' – some kind of original form after which all leaves have been woven, marked, copied, coloured, curled, and painted, but by unskilled hands, so that no copy turned out to be a correct, reliable, and faithful image of the original form.... What then, is truth? A mobile army of metaphors, metonyms, and anthropomorphisms – in short, a sum of human relations, which have been enhanced, transposed, and embellished poetically and rhetorically, and which after long use seem firm, canonical, and obligatory to a people; truths are illusions about which one has forgotten that this is what they are; metaphors which are worn out and without serious power; coins which have lost their picture and now matter only as metal, no longer as coins.'* [53]

---

[53] ('Über Wahrheit und Lüge im außermoralischen Sinn', our translation): *'Denken wir besonders noch an die Bildung der Begriffe. Jedes Wort wird sofort dadurch Begriff, daß es eben nicht für das einmalige ganz und gar individualisierte Urerlebnis, dem es sein Entstehen verdankt, etwa als Erinnerung dienen soll, sondern zugleich für zahllose, mehr oder weniger ähnliche, das heißt streng genommen niemals gleiche, also auf lauter ungleiche Fälle passen muß. Jeder Begriff entsteht durch Gleichsetzen des Nichtgleichen. So gewiß nie ein Blatt einem andern ganz gleich ist, so gewiß ist der Begriff Blatt durch beliebiges Fallenlassen dieser individuellen Verschiedenheiten, durch ein Vergessen des Unterscheidenden gebildet und erweckt nun die Vorstellung, als ob es in der Natur außer den Blättern etwas gäbe, das »Blatt« wäre, etwa eine Urform, nach der alle Blätter gewebt, gezeichnet, abgezirkelt, gefärbt, gekräuselt, bemalt wären, aber von ungeschickten Händen, so daß kein Exemplar korrekt und zuverlässig als treues Abbild der Urform ausgefallen wäre. Wir nennen einen Menschen »ehrlich«; warum hat er heute so ehrlich gehandelt? fragen wir. Unsere Antwort pflegt zu lauten: seiner Ehrlichkeit wegen. Die Ehrlichkeit! Das heißt wieder: das Blatt ist die Ursache der Blätter. Wir wissen ja gar nichts von einer wesenhaften Qualität, die »die Ehrlichkeit« hieße, wohl aber von zahlreichen individualisierten, somit ungleichen Handlungen, die wir durch Weglassen des Ungleichen gleichsetzen und jetzt als ehrliche Handlungen bezeichnen; zuletzt formulieren wir aus ihnen eine qualitas occulta mit dem Namen: »die Ehrlichkeit«. Das Übersehen des Individuellen und Wirklichen gibt uns den Begriff, wie es uns auch die Form gibt, wohingegen die Natur keine Formen und Begriffe, also auch keine Gattungen kennt, sondern nur ein für uns unzugängliches und undefinierbares X. Denn auch unser Gegensatz von Individuum und Gattung ist anthropomorphisch und entstammt nicht dem Wesen der Dinge, wenn wir auch nicht zu sagen wagen, daß er ihm nicht entspricht: das wäre nämlich eine dogmatische Behauptung und als solche ebenso unerweislich wie ihr Gegenteil. Was ist also Wahrheit? Ein bewegliches Heer von Metaphern, Metonymien, Anthropomorphismen, kurz eine Summe von menschlichen Relationen, die, poetisch und rhetorisch gesteigert, übertragen, geschmückt wurden und die nach langem Gebrauch einem Volke fest, kanonisch und verbindlich dünken: die Wahrheiten sind Illusionen, von denen man vergessen hat, daß sie welche sind, Metaphern, die abgenutzt und sinnlich kraftlos geworden sind, Münzen, die ihr Bild verloren haben und nun als Metall, nicht mehr als Münzen, in Betracht kommen.'* (Nietzsche 2000:8591–8592)

5.2. Schumpeterian and Evolutionary Economics

Behind the contemporary highly fashionable Schumpeterian and evolutionary economics towers Nietzsche, his *Übermensch* entrepreneur and his creative destruction. Nietzsche the economist here comes to us filtered through Joseph Alois Schumpeter via Werner Sombart. As opposed to Sombart, who carefully documented the influence Nietzsche had on him, Schumpeter as usual has held the cards that would have revealed the origins of his own ideas very close to his chest. However, a closer look at the intellectual climate, the general *Zeitgeist,* and the work of the most influential continental European economist during Schumpeter's 'golden period', his own 20s, shows the overwhelming influence of Nietzsche on all three counts.

We are living at a time where standard neoclassical economics is entering a period of decline. In order to achieve any degree of relevance, whatever theory replaces this mechanical and barter-based view of economic will have to incorporate Nietzschean traits: without Man's wit and will, his incessant creative process, and the role of the human beings who push this forward, economics will – as neo-classical economics – always be like playing Hamlet without the Prince of Denmark.

Forty-five years of cold war marginalised Nietzsche and those economists who worked towards the authentic Third Way, those who – in the words of Anthony Giddens – hated communism as much as they hated liberalism (Giddens 1998). Nietzsche's own legacy was tarnished by the misuse and outright falsifications of his work by his sister, who made him appear like a nazi sympathizer. The economist whom Nietzsche read most closely was Eugen Dühring. By going back to the original sources, to Nietzsche's vigorous rebuttals of Dühring's increasingly anti-Semitic attitudes[54], and in the violent counter-attack attacks from Dühring's followers against Nietzsche as a friend and supporter of the cause of the Jews, we come to understand the absurdity of the attacks on Nietzsche as an anti-Semite.

We suggest it is time to go back to the pre-World War II understanding of Nietzsche. In the 1929 edition of *Encyclopedia Britannica*, Oscar Levy, editor of the authorized English translations of Nietzsche, gives the following account on how the understanding of Nietzsche had evolved:

> *'Nobody understood in the early days that his teaching against pity sprang from his love of a healthy life, against morality, from his love of a higher ethic, and against patriotism for a united Europe….Late and slowly the world began, or is beginning, to change its mind about 'the anti-antichrist' and to perceive that he was not mere 'anti'; but that the destroyer of the old tables of values was also a creator of new values.'* (Levy 1929:433)

At the core of Nietzsche, as well as at the core of any viable theory of the economic progress of human beings, lies Man the Creator, his wit and his will. As in the Renaissance

[54] Amongst other things, Nietszche describes Dühring as *'jenen Berliner Rache-Apostel Eugen Dühring, der im heutigen Deutschland den unanständigsten und widerlichsten Gebrauch vom moralischen Bumbum macht: Dühring, das erste Moral-Großmaul, das es jetzt gibt, selbst noch unter seinesgleichen, den Antisemiten.'* (Nietzsche 2000:7402)

tradition, to Nietzsche creation is the reason we are here on Earth, it is the way to free ourselves from pain:

> '*Creation – that is the great redemption from suffering, and life's growing light. But that the creator may be, suffering is needed and much change*' (Nietzsche 1968a:87)[55]

We have already mentioned the work of Oswald Spengler (1880–1936), whose work *The Decline of the West* strongly influenced the intellectual debate between the two world wars. This work was finished before WWI, in the same year as Werner Sombart finished his *Krieg und Kapitalismus,* where 'creative destruction' is first brought into economics. In his foreword to the revised edition of *The Decline of the West* (1939; first edition 1922) Spengler acknowledges his intellectual influences as follows:

> '*And now, finally, I feel urged to name once more those to whom I owe practically everything: Goethe and Nietzsche. Goethe gave me method, Nietzsche the questioning faculty – and if I were asked to find a formula for my relation to the latter I should say that I have made of his 'outlook'* [Ausblick] *an overview* [Überblick]. *But Goethe was, without knowing it, a disciple of Leibniz, in his whole mode of thought. And, therefore, that which has at last (and to my own astonishment) taken shape in my hands I am able to regard and, despite the misery and disgust of these years, proud to call a German Philosophy.*' (Spengler 1939:xiv)

We would argue that Spengler here describes intellectual filiations that he has in common with true Schumpeterian economics. Indeed, if Schumpeter had been as proficient in tracing his own intellectual filiations as he was in tracing those of other economists, he could have made Spengler's acknowledgements his own, just adding the name of Werner Sombart; the economist who brought the ideas of Leibniz, Goethe and Nietzsche back into economics.

Bibliography

Appel, M., 1992, *Werner Sombart. Theoretiker und Historiker des modernen Kapitalismus*, Marburg: Metropolis

Backhaus, J. (editor), 1996, *Werner Sombart (1863–1941), Social Scientist,* Marburg: Metropolis, 3 vols.

Buchanan, J., 1979, *What Should Economists Do?,* Indianapolis: Liberty Press

Burckhardt, J., 1979, *Reflections on History,* Indianapolis: Liberty Classics

Drechsler, W., 2002, 'Natural vs. Social Sciences: On Understanding in Economics', in Reinert E. (editor), *Evolutionary Economics and Income Inequality,* Cheltenham: Elgar

Freeman, C. & Louca, F., 2001, *As Time Goes By. From the Industrial Revolution to the Information Revolution,* Oxford: Oxford University Press

Giddens, A. 1998: *The Third Way – the Renewal of Social Democracy*. Cambridge: Polity Press.

Haberler, G., 1950, 'Joseph Alois Schumpeter, 1883–1950', in *Quarterly Journal of Economics,* Vol. LXIV, No. 3, August 1950, pp. 333–372

Hegel, G.W.F., 1953, *Reason in History – a general introduction to the philosophy of history,* New York: The Liberal Arts Press

---

[55] '*Schaffen - das ist die große Erlösung vom Leiden, und des Lebens Leichtwerden. Aber daß der Schaffende sei, dazu selber tut Leid not und viel Verwandelung*'. (Nietzsche 2000:6468)

Herder, J. G., 1781, *Vom Einfluss der Regierung auf die Wissenschaften, und* der *Wissenschaften auf die Regierung*, Berlin: Decker

——, 1790–92, *Ideen zur Philosophie der Geschichte der Menschheit,* Karlsruhe: Schmieder

Industry and Innovation, Vol. 9, Nos. 1–2, April-August 2002, Special Issue: Schumpeter's "Lost" Seventh Chapter, J. A. Mathews, editor.

Kantzenbach, F., 1970, *Johann Gottfried Herder*, Hamburg: Rowohlt

Lenger, F., 1994, *Werner Sombart (1863–1941) - eine Biographie*, Munich: Beck

Levy, O., 1929, 'Friedrich Wilhelm Nietzsche', entry in *Encyclopedia Britannica*, 14th edition vol. 16, London: Encyclopedia Britannica Company

Lilla, M., 1993, *G. B. Vico. The Making of an Anti-Modern,* Cambridge, Mass: Harvard University Press.

Nietzsche, F., 1968a, *Thus spoke Zarathustra*, (translated by W. Kaufmann), London: Penguin Books

——, 1968b, *Twilight of the Idols*, (translated by R. Hollingdale), London: Penguin Books

——, 1994, *On the Genealogy of Morality*, (translated by C. Diethe), Cambridge: Cambridge University Press

——, 1995, *Unfashionable observations*, (translated by R. Gray), Stanford: Stanford University Press

——, 2000, *Digitale Bibliothek Band 31: Nietzsche*, Berlin: Directmedia (CD-ROM)

Noble, D.F., 1997, *The Religion of Technology. The Divinity of Man and the Spirit of Invention,* New York: Knopf.

Ottmann, H., 1987, *Philosophie und Politik bei Nietzsche,* Berlin: de Gruyter

Pareto, V., 1916, *Trattato di Sociologia Generale,* Florence: G. Barbèra, 2 volumes. (English edition *The Mind and Society*, New York: Harcourt, Brace and Company, 1935)

Parkes, G., 1991, *Nietzsche and Asian Thought,* Chicago, University of Chicago Press

Perez, C., 2002, *Technological Revolutions and Financial Capital. The Dynamics of Bubbles and Golden Ages,* Cheltenham: Elgar

——, 2003, 'Technological Revolutions, Paradigm Shifts, And Socio-Institutional Change', in Reinert E. (editor), *Evolutionary Economics and Income Inequality,* Cheltenham: Elgar

Peters, H.F., 1977, *Zarathustra's Sister: The Case of Elisabeth and Friedrich Nietzsche*, York: Crown Publishers

Rand, A., 1957, *Atlas Shrugged*, New York: Random House

Reinert, E, 1995, 'Competitiveness and its predecessors - a 500 year cross-national perspective'. In *Structural Change and Economic Dynamics*, Vol. 6

——, 2000, 'Karl Bücher and the Geographical Dimensions of Techno-Economic Change', in Backhaus, Jürgen, (editor) *Karl Bücher: Theory - History - Anthropology – Non Market Economies,* Marburg: Metropolis.

——, 2002, 'Schumpeter in the Context of two Canons of Economic Thought', in *Industry and Innovation,* Vol. 6, No. 1.

——, 2003 (editor), *Evolutionary Economics and Income Inequality,* Cheltenham: Elgar

Reinert, E. & Daastøl, A., 1997 'Exploring the Genesis of Economic Innovations: The religious gestalt-switch and the duty to invent as preconditions for economic growth', in *European Journal of Law and Economics,* Vol 4, No. 2/3, 1997, and in *Christian Wolff. Gesammelte Werke, Materialien und Dokumente,* Hildesheim: Georg Olms Verlag, 1998.

Santarelli, E. and Pesciarelli, E., 1990, 'The Emergence of a Vision: The Development of Schumpeter's Theory of Entrepreneurship', in *History of Economic Policy*, Vol. 22, Winter 1990, no. 4

Schacht, R., 1994, *Nietzsche, Genealogy, Morality*, London: University of California Press

Shionoya, Y., 1997, *Schumpeter and the Idea of Social Sciences,* Cambridge: Cambridge University Press. (Original edition, Tokyo 1995)

Schumpeter, J. A., 1908, *Das Wesen und der Haupteinhalt der Theoretischen Nationalökonomie,* Leipzig: Duncker & Humblot

——, 1912, *Theorie der wirtschaftlichen Entwicklung,* Leipzig: Duncker & Humblot.

——, 1914, *Epochen der Dogmen- und Methodengeschichte,* Tübingen: Mohr

——, 1939, *Business Cycles*, New York: McGraw-Hill, 2 volumes
——, 1942, *Capitalism, Socialism and Democracy*, New York: Harper
Sokel, W., 1959, *The Writer in Extremis*, Stanford: Stanford University Press
Sombart, W., 1913, *Krieg und Kapitalismus*, Leipzig: Duncker & Humblot
——, 1902 / 1927, *Der moderne Kapitalismus*, München & Leipzig: Duncker & Humblot
——, 1915, *Händler und Helden*, München & Leipzig: Duncker & Humblot
——, 1930, *Die drei Nationalökonomien*, München & Leipzig: Duncker & Humblot
Spann, O, 1930, *Types of Economic Theory*, London: Allen & Unwin, published in the US as *The History of Economics*, New York: Norton.
Spengler, O., 1939, *Decline of the West*, New York: Alfred A. Knopf
Swedberg, R., 1991, *Schumpeter. A Biography*, Princeton: Princeton University Press
Vico, G., 1984, *The New Science*, Ithaca: Cornell University Press.
Williams, L. L., 2001, *Nietzsche's Mirror: The World as Will to Power*, Lanham: Rowman & Littlefield

Chapter Thirteen

SCHUMPETER IN THE CONTEXT OF TWO CANONS OF ECONOMIC THOUGHT

Erik S. Reinert

"Seht ihn nur an—Niemandem war er Untertan" says Gottfried Haberler in his obituary to Schumpeter, quoting Nietzsche. "Just look at him. He was inferior to no one" (Haberler 1950: 344). Schumpeter certainly deserves his reputation as a truly powerful independent and original égure in economics. Yet, as I shall argue in this paper, when seen in the context of pre-World War II and of German economics, Schumpeter's economic thinking was less original than we perceive it to be today. One part of Schumpeter was deeply rooted in a knowledge- and production-based academic tradition that today is only supported by a minority of economists; it is what I call the "Other Canon" of economics. However, the tension between this economic tradition and Schumpeter's admiration for the logic, accuracy and elegance of the emerging mathematics-based economics was an important factor in producing the many paradoxes and contradictions of the man.

Both to his contemporaries at Harvard and in the context of the history of economic thought as studied today, Schumpeter's towering égure is perceived as being unique among 20th-century economists on three counts: the originality of his thought; his perceived independence of the 20th-century political axis from left to right; and the perceived contradictions and paradoxes of his teachings.

My contention is that these three phenomena are closely interrelated, and can be better understood in their entirety by studying the philosophical and historical roots of non-Anglo-Saxon economic thinking. Both Schumpeter's originality and his political independence from the standard 20th-century political axis from right to left are, to an important degree, explained by examining the Other Canon economic tradition in which Schumpeter, the Austrian, had his intellectual roots. I argue that Schumpeter's academic schizophrenia was caused by his attempt at unifying two fundamentally incompatible world-views, as they are contrasted in this paper.

Schumpeter wished to be original, and wanted to be perceived as being independent of environmental inèuences. Haberler comments on his "absolute refusal to be swayed by current fashions in science and politics" and his "almost perverse pleasure in being unpopular and standing alone" (Haberler 1950: 344). This solitary intellectual life of Schumpeter—paradoxically as usual—was combined with an unusual capacity to understand other people's views, a skill which is apparent both in his biographical essays and in the *History of Economic Analysis*. Schumpeter was uniquely skilled in following the mental éliations of economic thought through history. In fact he states this as the main purpose behind the monumental *History of Economic Analysis* (Schumpeter 1954: 6). Schumpeter's reluctance to state *his own* intellectual éliations and sources makes him appear to posterity more singular than he really was. As an example, the concept which today has almost become Schumpeter's trademark—"creative destruction"—was first used by Werner Sombart, a German economist of the Historical School.

In the first section of the paper, I point to Marx and Schumpeter as being the only well-known economists from a long and distinguished tradition in economics. The surprising similarity of these two economists who were located at the two extremes of the traditional political spectrum—a similarity Schumpeter himself pointed to—is, in my opinion, the outcome of their common heritage in the German Historical School and in strong opposition to the English economic tradition. In section two I discuss Schumpeter's "theoretical schizophrenia", by which I mean his immersion in the German historical tradition and his admiration for a different philosophical tradition. In part three I discuss Schumpeter's theoretical duality in the context of a typology of economic theories. In part four I discuss the intriguing legacy of Schumpeter and the German historical school in the work of the Harvard Business School, and in particular its case method of teaching and research. While biographical analyses of Schumpeter's Harvard years (Allen 1994; Shionoya 1997; Stolper 1994; Swedberg 1991) have focused on his work in the Economics Department, I draw attention to his activities at the Harvard Business School and at the Research Center in Entrepreneurial History. In these institutions, as opposed to the Harvard Economics Department, Schumpeter found researchers, traditions and institutions which were much closer to the *verstehende* ("appreciative") Germanic historical tradition in economics. This includes the first Dean of Harvard Business School, Edwin Gay—an enthusiastic student of Gustav Schmoller—who anticipated Schumpeter's key notion of the clustering of innovations and entrepreneurship as the forces behind the cyclical movements of capitalism. The concluding remarks put Schumpeter's merited ascent as an economic theorist in a context where his thoughts are not quite as original as they appear today, again making the point that the less understood part of Schumpeter's work was a direct extension of a long and noble economic tradition which has now fallen into oblivion.

SCHUMPETER AND MARX: LOST SAILORS IN A SEA OF ANGLO-SAXON ECONOMICS

Over the last 150 years Karl Marx and Joseph Schumpeter stand out among the economists usually studied today as being particularly original. The axis from left to right that was created by the cold war places Marx and Schumpeter on opposite ends of the political spectrum. But in terms of *type of economic theory*, Marx and Schumpeter solidly belong in the "The Other Canon" German tradition of economics. In the foreword to the Japanese edition of *The Theory of Economic Development*, Schumpeter himself clearly states his own mental affiliation to Marx. They both share "a vision of economic evolution as a distinct process generated by the economic system itself" (Schumpeter in Clemence 1951: 160), but the similarities between Marx and himself are "obliterated by a very wide difference in general outlook" (ibid.: 161).

The fact that Schumpeter "managed to shock and antagonize Philistines on the right and on the left at the same time" (Haberler 1950: 344) is largely explained by the fact that his intellectual roots lay in the soil of a tradition which was quite independent of the Ricardian intellectual tradition that during the 20th century gave birth to both the political left and the political right. German economics was situated in a position outside this right–left axis. Schumpeter's intellectual roots were close to those of the German Historical School and the economists that formed the *Verein für Sozialpolitik* and—with the political backing of Bismarck—created the welfare state. Schumpeter's perceived originality in the Anglo-Saxon environment is, in our view, largely a product of the ignorance, outside Germany, of this tradition. Features that we today tend to associate with Marx and Schumpeter, the importance of technology, innovations and learning, indeed form a strong intellectual thread in all German economics from Gottfried Wilhelm von Leibniz and Christian Wolff (Reinert and Daastøl 1997), through 18th-century economists like Georg Heinrich Zincke, Johann Heinrich Gottlob von Justi and Johann Beckmann, and in the 19th century to Friedrich List and to the two generations of the Historical School.

The focus of this German school of economics was very different from that of English economics. Simultaneously with Adam Smith's writings, focusing on *Man the Trader*, Johann Beckman, a professor of economics in Göttingen, wrote and edited voluminous works on technology, on *Man the Innovator and Producer* (Beckmann 1780). His journal on practical economics ran continuously from 1770 to 1806. Some of his work was published in English as *A History of Inventions and Discoveries* in three volumes (Beckmann 1797), but—as later with the economics of Charles Babbage—such works tend to fall outside what in the English tradition is classified as economics. This is also the tradition on which Marx's analysis of the industrial revolution builds. Marx, however, added to this analysis Ricardo's "labour theory of value". Marx's adoption of this very un-German idea from Ricardo made German economists in general favourable to his historical analysis, but in deep disagreement with his solutions to the problems at hand.

In contrast to English economics, an emphasis on the key role of the entrepreneur had been a standard feature of German economics all through the 19th century. The role of the entrepreneur was also at the core of the works of Werner Sombart (1863–1941), undoubtedly the most influential 20th-century German economist in the period between the two world wars. It is a scandal that his monumental work on the history of capitalism has still not been published in English (Sombart 1902, 1928). In 1913 two books by Sombart appeared, in which he discussed, respectively, the role of war and the role of luxury in promoting technological development and innovations in capitalism (Sombart 1913a, b). The concept that people today would see as the main heritage of Schumpeter—creative destruction—was first used here by Werner Sombart. On the last page of his *Krieg und Kapitalismus* [*War and Capitalism*] the idea of a "creative destruction", as far as I have been able to judge, appears for the first time in economics.[1] This idea, now so closely linked to Schumpeter's economics, is originally not his own. We have elsewhere argued that the idea of creative destruction was already part of a wider German intellectual tradition, found in both Johan Wolfgang von Goethe (1749–1832) and Friedrich Nietzsche (1844–1900), already colouring the *Zeitgeist* of the early 20th century (Reinert and Reinert, in Backhaus and Drechsler (eds.)).

To someone familiar with the German tradition in economics, Schumpeter's originality is considerably reduced. One of Sombart's biographers, harshly but correctly, describes Schumpeter's 1942 book *Capitalism, Socialism and Democracy* as essentially a reworking of a German debate which had taken place decades earlier, where Schumpeter neither refers to the debate itself, nor to its protagonist Werner Sombart (Appel 1992: 260). Schumpeter's *Capitalism, Socialism and Democracy* has been characterized as brilliant after-dinner discussion, much in the tradition that Johnston (1972) describes as typically Austrian in Schumpeter's generation.

THE "SCHIZOPHRENIA" OF SCHUMPETER'S THOUGHT

Schumpeter emanated from the Renaissance tradition of the German Historical and *Staatswissenschaftliche* (State Science) Schools, a tradition always torn between the importance of the creative individual and the collective need to build society (Reinert and Daastøl 1997; Reinert 1999). Whereas traditionally the economists of this school had fought the use of static equilibrium theory and barter-based English economics, Schumpeter could not only see the advantage of both approaches, he tried to unite them. He spent his life on the hopeless task of formalizing the creative essence of Renaissance economics—of entrepreneurship, novelty, and creative destruction—into the framework of dead equilibrium which is at the core of neo-classical economics.

The fundamental paradox of Schumpeter's dual vision of economics can be illustrated by contrasting his view of French economist Leon Walras with Alfred Marshall's view of the same French economist. Marshall, the founding neo-classical, wished to see economics as an evolutionary science, and he therefore disdained Leon Walras' mechanistic approach to economics as sterile. To Schumpeter, who today is hailed as the founder of evolutionary economics, Leon Walras was the greatest economist ever. Marshall's own theory in effect came to be based on the mechanical model, while Schumpeter's vision was clearly evolutionary. Schumpeter was to spend most of his life attempting to close the gap between his dynamic vision and Walras' statics. He strove in vain to unite two essentially incompatible world-views; his goal was to include his dynamic and essentially organic vision into the mathematical mechanics of Walras. In a sense both Marshall and Schumpeter ended up precisely in the spot they initially did not want to be, although Schumpeter often skilfully managed to be simultaneously in two places.

---

1 "Schöpferischer Zerstörung" is the original German term for "creative destruction", and here the two words appear in the same form: "Wiederum aber steigt aus der Zerstörung neuer schöpferischer Geist empor" ["But again out of the destruction, new creative spirit rises"].

The last 300 years of economic theory in Europe have produced two entirely different types of economic theories, which—in my view—are mutually exclusive. Briefly put, the type of theory one would choose depends on one's view of the human constitution. Type A. If you believe that the human brain is a passive *tabula rasa* inhabiting a pleasure-calculating machine, avoiding pain and maximizing pleasure—a dog that has learned to barter—then you will favour a hedonistic and barter-based economics with corresponding value system and incentive system. If however you believe in type B, that the essence of humans lies in their potentially noble spirit with an active brain, constantly registering and classifying the world around them according to set schemata, then you will believe in an economy whose central feature is that humans produce, not that they barter. The driving force of the second type of economy is not capital *per se*, but what Nietzsche calls *Geist- und Willens-Kapital*, i.e. humans' wit and will. If one believes in theory type A, then theory type B becomes irrelevant, and vice versa. The first view of humans makes it possible to produce a simple, calculable and quantifiable static economic theory. This second type of theory, of a much more complex kind of human, also needs a much more complex and dynamic theory, the core of which is *irreducible to numbers and symbols* (Drechsler 2002). The first view calls for what Sombart calls an *ordnende* economic theory (i.e. related to *organization*), while the second calls for a *verstehende* economic theory (i.e. an "appreciative" theory), interspersed with the older *richtende*—or duty-based—economic system (Sombart 1930). These contrasts are further elaborated below.

Schumpeter frequently provides brilliant insights into the weaknesses of *Type A* theory, yet he spends his life trying to remould and fit the richness of *Type B* economics into the barren tools of *Type A* economics. This task calls to mind something like the boiling down of an ox into a bouillon cube, and then expecting all the vitality of the ox still to be there. Of Ricardo's highly abstract construction he says: "It is an excellent theory that can never be refuted and lacks nothing but sense" (Schumpeter 1954: 473).

In his first book, *Das Wesen und der Hauptinhalt der theoretischen Nationalökonomie* (Schumpeter 1908, no English translation), Schumpeter denounces the *Methodenstreit*—partly a doctrinal battle between type A and type B view of Man—as a waste of time. To Schumpeter, different models of research are needed for different purposes. To him each method has its concrete areas of application, and it is useless to struggle for universal validity. Schumpeter suggests pragmatically that we should first state the question we want to address, and then enter into the theory at a level of abstraction where an answer is likely to be found.

In his foreword to Zeuthen (1930), Schumpeter makes this argument even clearer. The economist and the reader, he says, "will have to make up his mind, whether he wants simple answers to his questions or useful ones—in this as in other economic matters he cannot have both". Type A economics gives us Paul Samuelson's factor price equalization, which is very simple and elegant, but in practice totally irrelevant and harmful to human welfare in the economic periphery. Schumpeter sees the basic problem in principle, yet he fails to draw the practical consequence that the complexities of Type B theory are incompatible with Type A tools.

TYPOLOGIES OF ECONOMIC THEORY AND SCHUMPETER'S DUALITY

When focusing on very long-term trends in economics, two ideal types of economic theorizing appear to have coexisted over an extended period of time (Reinert and Daastøl 2002). These ideal types can be seen as constituting two separate *filiations*— to use Schumpeter's term—and they come into occasional methodological clashes.[2] Werner Sombart calls the first tradition *activistic-idealistic*, a tradition born with the Renaissance. The second type of economic theory he calls *passivistic-materialistic* (Sombart 1928: Vol. 2, 919), a tradition having its origins with Mandeville and Adam Smith and solidifying as the "*a priori* method" with David Ricardo. As a historian of economic thought, Schumpeter shows an uncanny ability to grasp and to explain the thought of his fellow economists of both filiations.

In most sciences, periodical and radical *gestalt-switches* terminate old theoretical trajectories and initiate new ones. In a Kuhnian paradigm shift the scientific world moves from a situation when everybody knows that the world is flat, to a new understanding when everybody knows that the world is round. This happens in a relatively short time. Lakatos' idea of "degenerating scientific research programmes" that gradually shift to "progressive" ones conveys a similar idea. In this respect economics is different. In economics the theory that the world is flat has been living together with the theory that the world is round for centuries. We describe this apparent lack of paradigm shifts in economics by the coexistence of these two long-term parallel *filiations*, where weight and influence periodically tilt back and forth between two alternative *Weltanschauungen*.

Today evolutionary economics—based on a tradition founded by Schumpeter—represents the most important challenge to the mainstream. However, evolutionary economics has, in my view, so far had an unnecessarily limited scope. This tradition now focuses relatively narrowly on innovations, including neither Schumpeter's own interest in financial matters, nor addressing to any extent the broader issues of uneven economic growth and employment on a world level which are, at their origin, intimately tied to Schumpeterian mechanisms. And, by bringing simple "Schumpeterian" variables into mainstream equilibrium models, his message is being domesticated and made innocuous. As in the case of Keynes, the mainstream again shows a great ability to usurp, absorb, and subdue threatening alternative theories.

The two different canons are based on fundamentally different *Weltanschauungen*. The lines of the two canons can be traced back to the period when the term economics was first used, to ancient Greece (Reinert and Daastøl 1997). While today's standard economics is based on a mechanistic and barter-centred tradition, Renaissance economics—The Other Canon—is dynamic, activistic-idealistic, and productioncentred. The first tradition belongs to what Werner Sombart calls *ordnende Nationalökonomie*—concerned with *organizing* the economic sphere. The second tradition is what Sombart calls *verstehende*

[2] Filiation: "The relation of one thing to another from which it may be said to be descended or derived; position in a genealogical classification", *The Oxford English Dictionary*, Oxford, 1933, Vol. 4, p. 212.

Nationalökonomie (Sombart 1930)— concerned with *comprehending* the economic sphere, or what Nelson and Winter (1982) refer to as *appreciative economics*. The first tradition typically explains human economic activities in terms of physics (of dead matter), the second in terms of biology (of living matter *and* of human wit and will). The first tradition is represented by Malthus' *dismal science*, the second by Christopher Freeman's *The Economics of Hope* (Freeman 1992)—by the *never-ending frontier of human knowledge* which Schumpeter shared. "Schumpeter was an optimist in his belief in the boundless progress of the inquiring mind" said Schumpeter's Harvard colleague Wassily Leontief in his obituary (Leontief 1950: 110).

Present mainstream economic theory places itself solidly in a canonical sequence that starts with the Physiocrats, the French school of *physiocracy* (meaning literally, "rule of Nature"), where Value is created by Nature and harvested by humankind. It then descends via Adam Smith and Ricardo to the neo-classical tradition beginning with Jevons and Marshall. The sequence has been made clear to generations of economists as the "Family Tree of Economics" featured on the inside back cover of many editions of Paul Samuelson's *Economics*. The alternative canon in economic theory runs parallel in time with the tradition of Samuelson's "Family Tree". I have termed this alternative type of theory *The Other Canon* or *Renaissance Economics* (Reinert and Daastøl 2002). The latter term derives from the observation that never before and never after have the values which this canon represents dominated the world picture as they did during the Renaissance. The mainstream canon is clearly a product of the successor philosophical period—The Enlightenment—that was in opposition to Renaissance values and outlook on important matters. Rationality and individuality during the Renaissance were based on an image of man as a spiritual being: creative and productive. The Enlightenment had a more materialistic understanding of human rationality and individuality: mechanical and consuming. Today the Renaissance canon—The Other Canon—tends to disappear in the history of economic thought, as present-day scholarship increasingly concentrates on the genealogy of the predecessors of neo-classical economics.

The "cold war" between what were in effect two versions of Ricardian economics led to the present crisis of The Other Canon. As it now is, the healthy Galbraithian balance of countervailing powers between the standard Anglo-Saxon theory and The Other Canon no longer exists. A hundred years ago the need for a balance of induction and deduction was generally recognized in all schools. On this matter the neo-classical founder, Alfred Marshall, approvingly quotes the historicist Gustav Schmoller, as saying that "Induction and deduction are both needed for scientific thought as the right foot and left foot are both needed for walking" (Marshall 1961: 29). In the beginning of the 20th century most observers seemed to consider these two approaches as *alternative* sets of binoculars through which to observe the world. Schumpeter's frustration seems to have originated in an attempt to produce one single set of binoculars from two views that to most others were seen to be incompatible. Since then induction has to a very large extent been lost in economics, making mainstream economics tilt very heavily towards the left side of the brain. The essentially mechanical neo-classical economics now dominates the field, and the prominent "Other Canon" aspects of both Alfred Marshall's early neo-classical economics and Carl Menger's early Austrian economics have largely been lost (Reinert).

The following are the main characteristics of Other Canon economics. The fundamental cause of economic welfare is humankind's productive creativity and morality; the *immaterial* production factors. In order for these ideas to materialize, capital is needed. Capital *per se* is in this tradition sterile. The Renaissance tradition can be contrasted with mainstream using Schumpeter's description of the economics of John Rae—a 19th-century US/Canadian economist of the Renaissance canon: "The essential thing is the conception of the economic process, which soars above the pedestrian view that it is the accumulation of capital *per se* that propels the capitalist engine" (Schumpeter 1954: 468). Whereas classical economics focused on barter, exchange, and the accumulation of material capital, the Renaissance tradition focuses on production based on human creativity. For this reason Renaissance economics emphasizes education, science, incentives, and entrepreneurship.

In the USA, The Other Canon dominated 19th-century economic policy and the land-grant universities, while the standard canon increasingly dominated at the Ivy League universities. Typically Cornell University, as the only university that was both land-grant and Ivy League, was for a while teaching two kinds of economics: the British system and the American system. In all presently wealthy nations, an economic policy based on The Other Canon has served as a *mandatory passage point* in the history of economic policy. The absence of the "History of Economic Policy" as a branch of Economics to some extent explains why The Other Canon has been brought into virtual oblivion.

Mainstream economics defines its origins in the French school of *physiocracy*, where, as noted above, value is created by Nature, and harvested by humankind. In a true "Other Canon" frame of mind, Schumpeter says about physiocracy that "Its analytical merit is negligible, but all the greater was its success" (Schumpeter 1954: 175). In Renaissance economics value originates through Man's wit and will (i.e. "ideocracy"—"the rule of ideas"). During the mechanization of the world picture, which took place during the materialistically oriented Enlightenment, the defenders of the Renaissance tradition were the anti-physiocrats. The Renaissance tradition is holistic and idealistic—not atomistic and materialistic. Nevertheless, at the core of the system is the individual, set in a complex web of synergetic interrelations. The beneficial effects of these interrelations first became evident in Renaissance towns giving birth to the Renaissance expression of the *common weal* (*il bene comune, das Gemeinwohl*)—a synergetic understanding of Society as being more than the sum of its parts (see Reinert 1999 for a discussion).

Renaissance economics is optimistic: the *never-ending frontier of knowledge* stands in sharp contrast with Malthus' *dismal science* and with the production theory of mainstream economics, the foundation of which is still today fundamentally a formalization of Ricardo's static corn economy. Here the main agents of change, new knowledge and the entrepreneur, are both absent. In the middle of the cold war, in 1955, Nicholas Kaldor made the salient point that "the Marxian theory is really only a simplified version of Ricardo, clothed in a different garb" (Kaldor 1955/1960: 211). It was not at all obvious to most people at the time that the two political extremes were based on what were really only nuances of the same basic Ricardian economic theory. Only long after the fall of the

Berlin Wall, in the late 1990s, arguments stressing the similarities of the two political extremes have again surfaced in books by Stiglitz (1994) and Hodgson (1999). As we shall see below, one of the first economists to renounce David Ricardo as the root of both the evils of communism and of liberalism was Herbert Foxwell, the creator of the Kress Library at Harvard Business School, where Schumpeter conducted his research for the *History of Economic Analysis.*

SCHUMPETER AND THE OTHER CANON AT HARVARD

The Charles River divides the Harvard University campus in two. From the point of view of the world of economics, the river also divides the two canons of thought. The Economics Department with its increasingly mechanical and *ordnende* approach to economics is on the Cambridge side, while Harvard Business School with a *verstehende* approach to the economic world rests on the opposite bank, technically in Boston. Disenchanted "with his colleagues in the economics department Schumpeter turned elsewhere for inspiration", says Swedberg (1991: 168). We shall argue that at Harvard Business School Schumpeter found the time and opportunity to focus on the "verstehende" economics in the German tradition. Schumpeter was a co-founder and active participant in the Harvard Center for Entrepreneurial Studies. This centre technically had an independent status under the Faculty of Arts and Sciences (Research Center in Entrepreneurial History 1949: vii), but the centre's executive director, Arthur Cole, was based at the Business School.

It was at the Kress Library at the Harvard Business School that Schumpeter, "spent the war years almost as a monk" (Allen 1994: 2, 158) researching for what was to become his monumental *History of Economic Analysis*. To Schumpeter and his second wife, Kress was "a scholar's paradise" (McCraw 1991: 386). We shall focus our analysis around three persons whose spirit and/or personality were present at the Harvard Business School in Schumpeter's time, influencing the anti-Ricardian "Other Canon" part of Schumpeter's paradoxical economics: Herbert Foxwell, Edwin Gay, and Fritz Redlich.

Herbert Somerton Foxwell (1849–1936): The spirit of Kress Library

Few people today are aware of the strong ties that existed between Harvard Business School and the German—and even English—anti-Ricardian "Other Canon" economic tradition at the time Schumpeter worked at Harvard. Going up the steps to the Kress Library inside the large Baker Library at Harvard Business School, Schumpeter would pass the life-size portrait of Herbert Somerton Foxwell, the Cambridge University economist who assembled what are still today the two largest and most comprehensive libraries of economics, Kress Library at Harvard and The Goldsmiths' Library at the University of London.

We know Herbert Foxwell through a thorough and sympathetic obituary by Keynes, first published in the *Economic Journal* in 1936 (Keynes 1972). Like his German counterparts at the time, Foxwell argued strongly against the abstract economic methods of David Ricardo, and like the members of the German Historical School, he equally disliked liberalism and communism. Foxwell wrote several pieces on the history of English socialist economics and 19th-century economics in general. Together with Edwin Seligman of Columbia University (another serious collector of economics books), Foxwell is a main source of information on minor English economists, both socialists and anti-Ricardian, of the 19th century. Importantly, Foxwell focused his criticism of Ricardo's negative influence on economics on two accounts (Foxwell 1899): Ricardo both gave the whole course of mainstream economics a "wrong twist", making it unhistorical and unrealistic, and his "crude generalisation" gave "modern socialism its fancied scientific basis".

Foxwell thus very early saw the point that lately has been made by Stiglitz (1994) and Hodgson (1999) that both communism and liberalism have the same intellectual roots in David Ricardo. So strong was Foxwell's dislike of Ricardo, that he refused to deliver his Presidential Address on Ricardo to the Royal Economic Society "on the ground that his onslaught of the man, who had convinced the world of the dreadful heresy of a necessary conflict between the interests of capital and labour, would have been too provocative" (Keynes 1972: X, 270). Foxwell also wrote on finance and banking, emphasizing the advantages of the continental banking practices over the English.

It was indeed Foxwell who spelt out the danger of what Schumpeter later labelled "The Ricardian Vice" in economics:

> Ricardo, and still more those who popularised him, may stand as an example for all time of the extreme danger which may arise from the unscientific use of hypothesis in social speculations, from the failure to appreciate the limited applications to actual affairs of a highly artificial and arbitrary analysis. His ingenious, though perhaps over-elaborated reasonings became positively mischievous and misleading when they were unhesitatingly applied to determine grave practical issues without the smallest sense of the thoroughly abstract and unreal character of the assumptions on which they were founded. (Foxwell 1899: xli)

Foxwell's collection of economics books—still today the core of Kress Library—reflects the collector's understanding that economics must be studied in its economic and social context, and Foxwell's "special sympathy for all heretics against the bondage of economic orthodoxy" (Keynes 1972: 281). Schumpeter's own defiance of economic orthodoxy—of the normally uncontested superiority of the canonical writings from the Physiocrats to "A. Smith"—is very much in the spirit of Foxwell and of his book collection. It is on the basis of this that Schumpeter wrote the *History of Economic Analysis*. Schumpeter's well-known scepticism towards "A. Smith" is paralleled in Foxwell's critical attitude towards the English tradition. Schumpeter is indeed open to see positive aspects of most economic ideas, perhaps with the exception of the German Romanticists. This may again be related to our discussion in section two of this paper.

Being an English economist, Foxwell was unique in his intuitive closeness to the German philosophical and economic approach from which Schumpeter came. Against the backdrop of Foxwell's own economics and his book collection, Schumpeter stands out as a kindred spirit. He refers to Foxwell five times in the *History of Economic Analysis*, but—somewhat surprisingly—always only as a collector or editor, never as an economist and historian of economic thought in his own right.

Edwin Francis Gay (1867–1946): Gustav Schmoller and the Harvard "case method"

At Harvard Business School (HBS) Schumpeter met an academic tradition that is no longer associated with business schools. Here he encountered the intellectual heritage of Gustav Schmoller, the founder of the younger German Historical School, brought to the Business School by Edwin Gay (1867–1946) (Copeland 1958; Cruikshank 1987; Heaton 1952), a student and great admirer of Schmoller. Gay, an economic historian, was crucial in establishing the Business School and was its Dean during its first 10 years of existence (1908–19). How different both the economics profession and business schools were before World War II compared to now, is illustrated by the fact that Gay—an economic historian and former dean of a business school—was elected President of the American Economic Association.

Edwin Gay was one of those American scholars who brought home both their scientific methods and their social consciousness from Germany. He was an inspired teacher, and his former students edited a massive *Festschrift* in his honour (*Facts and Factors* 1932) and commissioned his biography (Heaton 1952). After an MA at Michigan, Gay spent 12 years studying in Europe, mainly in Berlin, Zürich and Leipzig. Studying under Adolf Wagner and Gustav Schmoller, he received his PhD in Economic History in Berlin in 1902. All the founders of the American Economic Association had studied economics in Germany, so Gay's *Wanderjahre* at German and Swiss universities was the rule rather than the exception at the time.

Edwin Gay developed the famous case method of HBS, supported by economist and trade theorist Frank Taussig. Together with his colleagues Arthur Cole (a student of Gay's) and Edward Mason, Schumpeter was later to praise this method of teaching in Taussig's obituary in the *Quarterly Journal of Economics* (Schumpeter et al. 1941). The man who inspired Gay and the case method was Gustav Schmoller, a key economist in the Other Canon tradition. Says Gay's biographer: "It was Schmoller … who really fired Gay's attentive interest and enthusiasm" (Heaton 1952: 38).

The case method at HBS fits the description of the German tradition as discussed above—building qualitative understanding (*verstehen*) from a myriad of details combined, collected, and interpreted with a view to arriving at a fair understanding of the whole. At HBS, the focus of analysis in most cases was the firm. In fact HBS case-studies can only be read successfully in Leibniz' spirit as Roscher describes it: "No manure was to him too dirty, no trash too small, no list of courses too dry and boring, no bookkeeping too unpoetic" (Roscher 1874: 330).

In Gay we find Schumpeter's idea that innovations and innovators are clustered in time (Schumpeter 1939), giving rise to the business cycles:

> … he [Gay] developed a dynamic vision of economic history: it was, he concluded, a record of swings of the pendulum between periods when social controls dominated, and periods dominated by the actions of aggressive individuals. The former periods were static, characterized by security and stability. The latter periods, ushered in by the introduction of new tools, weapons, or other forces, were controlled by the powerful individuals who introduced these forces. (Cruikshank 1987: 29)

Without stretching our interpretation too much, we could say that Edwin Gay here bridges the discrepancy between Schumpeter's two types of entrepreneurs, the individualist of his first writings and the *functional* entrepreneur of the later writings. Gay very sensibly seems to identify two types of management as belonging to different stages of each techno-economic paradigm. In the famous Hoover Report edited by Gay (1929)—so optimistic before the 1929 crash—his is the only paper that senses that something is not right in the US economy.

Gay held the position of Dean of HBS until 1919, but spent the war years in Washington organizing US foreign trade, minimizing international trade (maximizing autarky!) in order to free as much tonnage as possible of ocean freighters for the war effort. It was here Gay met Herbert Hoover, who later put him in charge of the 1929 Hoover Report (Gay 1929). From 1919 to 1923 Gay worked as the editor of the New York *Evening Post*, and started what became the *Saturday Reveiw of Literature*. From 1923 to 1933 Gay shared the direction of the National Bureau of Economic Research with Wesley Claire Mitchell. He was the first secretary-treasurer of the Council of Foreign Relations, and was the "moving spirit" in launching the journal *Foreign Affairs* in 1922.

Fritz Redlich (1892–1978): The Center for Entrepreneurial Studies at Harvard

Of Schumpeter's main biographers, Swedberg (1991: Chap. 8) devotes the most space to Schumpeter's work at the Center for Entrepreneurial Studies, which operated until 1958. While Swedberg, correctly, points out that Schumpeter's ideas were far from being generally accepted at the Center, the point is that there was a connecting thread between the Center's approach and that of HBS and German and Other Canon economics (see Schumpeter 1949). Herbert Foxwell and his Kress Library, Edwin Gay and his students, and Fritz Redlich and the historical study of entrepreneurship all synergetically kept alive The Other Canon of economics that was slowly being lost in the Harvard Economics Department during the latter part of Schumpeter's stay there.

During my own time at HBS in the mid-1970s there were still reminiscences of Schumpeter around. Across the River Charles, in the Economics Department, Schumpeter's former student and probably closest friend in Cambridge at the time of his death, Arthur Smithies, taught my course in the history of economic thought. The course developed into a course in Schumpeterian economics more than anything else, and my interest was fired. This happened, however, during the ebb years of attention to Schumpeter's writings, as measured by the publications referring to his work (Augello 1990: 22). When attempting to buy a copy of *The Theory of Economic Development* at the Harvard University Press store, I was directed to drive to a far-away deposit, where a reprint was found.

The Center for Entrepreneurial Studies at HBS had closed already in 1958, but the person from the Center whose background was the closest to Schumpeter's own was still on campus. Fritz Redlich, who was, like Schumpeter, of a *Grossbürgerlich* (high bourgeoisie) German-speaking background, almost daily visited the Kress Library where Schumpeter had spent most of the World War II years researching the history of economic thought.

To the two young European librarians in Kress, Redlich's *gestalt* and manners brought flashbacks of a culture that had ceased to exist in Europe. Ken Carpenter, the Kress curator, phoned Redlich daily to ascertain that he was in good health. (See Carpenter 1975, 1977 for his important work in Schumpeter's "filiation tradition" in the history of economic thought.) Schumpeter had been vividly interested in the work of Redlich on business and entrepreneurial history "which would create the foundations for his own theories" (Redlich 1964: 21).

Although they were both in one sense in exile from Nazi Austria and Germany, Schumpeter and Redlich were both equally atypical as German scholars in exile. Neither of them had been persecuted by the Nazi regime; they could both probably have continued their work in Germany or Austria undisturbed. Hans Jaeger, Redlich's biographer in Hagemann and Krohn (1999: Vol. 2, 553) states his reason for leaving Germany in March 1936 as his "disgust with the system that made it impossible for him to stay in Germany". Already in the early 1940s, while teaching at the University of Georgia, Redlich established contacts at Harvard, where Schumpeter and Taussig encouraged him to continue his historical studies on entrepreneurship. In 1943 he received his US citizenship and moved to Boston, where he held various non-academic positions while continuing to publish, mostly on entrepreneurship. From 1950 to 1958 he was Senior Associate of the Center for Entrepreneurial Studies. His work was later acknowledged also in Germany, where—in the 1960s—he received honorary doctorates at the University of Erlangen and at the Free University of Berlin.

My wife Fernanda worked as a librarian in the Kress Library during my 2 years at Harvard. In this way I came both to know this "scholars' paradise" very well, and to meet and discuss economics with Redlich. Already then it was clear to me that with Fritz Redlich I had a unique chance to get to know a last member of an otherwise extinct economic species of the same German *Grossbürgerliche*—high bourgeoisie— pre-war academic tradition as Schumpeter represented.

Three impressions stand out today from my conversations with Redlich: First of all his profound sigh of disappointment when he discovered that I, a young European who had studied economics in a German-speaking university (albeit in Switzerland) had never heard the name of Werner Sombart, who was clearly a towering figure in German economics. I have never felt as ignorant as I did right then under the eyes of the old Fritz Redlich, aged 84 at the time. This led me to study Sombart, and I consequently came to find the strong, but mostly unacknowledged, influence of Sombart on Schumpeter's writings. My second recollection is his despair that US students and scholars of entrepreneurship would take for granted that the great achievers in society necessarily would go into *business*. That might be logical in the US tradition, but in other traditions—as Redlich's own work had shown—the entrepreneurial type could dedicate his or her skills to other than moneymaking activities. My third recollection is his deep regret that he had lost the productive 30s of his own life in business rather than in research and in academia. (This is the important decade following what Schumpeter referred to as the "sacred" third decade of a scholar's life.) I often came to recollect his regrets as I followed exactly the same path, though with fewer regrets of my own.

An indication of Redlich's own intellectual debts may be found in his own references. In a collection of his articles (Redlich 1964) there are 14 references to Gustav Schmoller, 21 to Werner Sombart, and 40 to Joseph Alois Schumpeter. Another tie to the old German tradition is that Redlich's book was published with the financial assistance of the List-Gesellschaft, the society which published the books and articles of and about Friedrich List.

Fritz Redlich went to the very roots of entrepreneurship and innovation in the history of economic thought when he published an article on Francis Bacon's 1625 *Essay of Innovations*: "The role of innovations in a quasi-static world. Francis Bacon and his successors" in *Explorations in Entrepreneurial History* (Redlich 1954). Redlich here links Bacon's early piece on innovations with later writings on innovations by scholars such as Daniel Defoe and Malachy Postlethwait in England and Johann Joachim Becher and Jacob Marperger in Germany. Francis Bacon indeed represents an important starting point in Other Canon economics (Reinert and Daastøl 1997). The movements against Ricardian economics in the 1830s, by Reverend Jones in England and John Rae in the USA, were both attempts to re-Baconize economics. One link between Redlich and recent work at the HBS in the unacknowledged tradition of Other Canon economics is that he published two articles jointly with Alfred Chandler Jr in *Business History Review*.

The quarterly journal of the Research Center in Entrepreneurial History—*Explorations in Entrepreneurial History*—where Redlich published the Bacon article, only existed for 10 years, from 1949 to 1958. As a printed publication, the journal is not very impressive, often produced with the inexpensive duplication technology of the time on cheap paper. The bindings, sometimes made with the kind of metal mechanisms which were normally used to bind letters in a file, point to a fairly small circulation. However, the range of authors which contributed to this humble publication indicates its importance at the academic intersection point between economic history, business history and economics: Alfred Chandler, James Duesenberry, Alexander Gerschenkron, Bert Hoselitz, David Landes, Douglass North, Henry Rosovsky and Paul Sweezy.

Even today, it can be argued that the spirit of the research at HBS is closer to the methods of the German Historical School than to that of mainstream economics, in that the research is pragmatic and problem-driven rather than tool-driven. Scholars like Bruce Scott, Michael Porter and Thomas McCraw work and publish in the huge and largely uninhabited field of meso-economics, at a level of abstraction between economics and the real world of business. This is the area where the loss of the German Historical School has left a vacuum in academic economics. The following statement from a 1991 HBS folder on "Intellectual Innovation at the Harvard Business School" is illustrative of this type of research at its best:

> After constantly observing and studying and thinking, you stumble across something and think 'I don't understand that. There's some mismatch of existing theory and my observation of reality. It doesn't fit. I think it's important—and either I've got it wrong, or they've got it wrong. I want to find out.'

CONCLUDING REMARKS: SCHUMPETER ASCENDING AND IN CONTEXT

Schumpeter's life was haunted by paradoxes. Schumpeter was, indeed, "a living, breathing contradiction" as Philip Mirowski puts it (Mirowski 1994: 5). We have tried to throw light on Schumpeter's apparent paradoxes and contradictions by showing that these may be better understood as a result of Schumpeter being steeped simultaneously in two mutually exclusive mind-sets. While other economists of the German type saw the basic incompatibility between the two approaches, Schumpeter attempted to unite them.

"I give up Harvard. In this soil no more do any of my roses blossom" wrote Schumpeter in his diary in the 1940s (Allen 1994: 2, 237). As equilibrium mathematics and the Cowles' Commission increasingly set the agenda for the Harvard Economics Department, we have tried to show that several intellectual currents associated with HBS provided a sanctuary where Schumpeter encountered the *verstehende* meso-level economics that was an important part of his intellectual upbringing. While most of the elements have been known, we have tried to show the synergies between these elements and their common roots in non-neoclassical Other Canon economics: Herbert Foxwell, his economics and his library, Edwin Gay, his vision of the clustering of innovation and his many students, among them Arthur Cole and Abbot Payson Usher, who became Schumpeter's friends and colleagues, and Fritz Redlich, another idiosyncratic "German" economist, an equally atypical academic refugee as Schumpeter, and the Center for Entrepreneurial Studies.

"Schumpeter ascending" is an appropriate title of a 1991 article by Thomas McCraw of HBS (McCraw 1991). The present Schumpeter boom started in the early 1980s and "Schumpeterian" variables slowly started creeping into equilibrium models. As with Keynes' theory, mainstream economics absorbed and usurped essential features of Schumpeter's vision, but left out most of the spirit of the argument. A truly evolutionary model is achieved only when all static and restrictive assumptions are lifted simultaneously, not when a "Schumpeterian" variable is simply included in an equilibrium model. At the core of a true Schumpeterian vision in the Other Canon tradition lies what Nietzsche called *Geist- und Willens-Kapital*—Man's wit and will— as the true engine of capitalism. This "Man the Producer"—essentially what separates human beings from other animals, not the ability to barter—is the unquantifiable nucleus of economics. The two *Weltanschauungen* remain as incompatible as they were in Schumpeter's time.

REFERENCES

Allen, Robert L. 1994: *Opening Doors. The Life and Work of Joseph Schumpeter.* New Brunswick, NJ: Transaction Publishers.

Appel, Michael 1992: *Werner Sombart. Theoretiker und Historiker des modernen Kapitalismus* [*Werner Sombart. Theoretician and Historian of Modern Capitalism*]. Marburg: Metropolis.

Augello, Massimo 1990: *Joseph Alois Schumpeter. A Reference Guide.* Berlin: Springer-Verlag.

Beckmann, Johann 1770–1806: *Physikalisch-ökonomische Bibliothek* [*Physical-Economic Library*], 23 vols. Göttingen: im Verlag der Wittwe Vandenhoeck und im Vandenhoek und Ruprechtschen Verlage.

Beckmann, Johann 1780: *Anleitung zur Technologie, oder zur Kenntniss der Handwerke, Fabriken und Manufacturen* [*Technological Instructions; or Knowledge on Handicrafts, Factories and Manufactures*], 2nd edn. Göttingen: Wittwe Vandenhoeck.

Beckmann, Johann 1797: *A History of Inventions and Discoveries*, translated from the German by William Johnston, 3 vols. London: J. Bell.

Carpenter, Kenneth 1975: The economic bestsellers before 1850, *Bulletin of The Kress Library of Business and Economics*, No. 11. Boston: Harvard Business School.

Carpenter, Kenneth 1977: *Dialogue in Political Economy*. Boston: Kress Library of Business and Economics, Harvard Business School.

Clemence, Richard V. (ed.) 1951: *Essays. Joseph A. Schumpeter*. Cambridge, MA: Addison-Wesley.

Copeland, Melvin T. 1958: *And Mark an Era. The History of Harvard Business School*. Boston, MA: Little, Brown.

Cruikshank, Jeffrey L. 1987: *A Delicate Experiment. The Harvard Business School 1908–1945*. Boston: Harvard Business School Press.

Drechsler, Wolfgang 2002: Natural vs. social sciences: on understanding in economics, in Erik S. Reinert (ed.), *Evolutionary Economics and Income Inequality*. Aldershot: Elgar.

Facts and Factors in Economic History. Articles by Former Students of Edwin Francis Gay 1932: Cambridge, MA: Harvard University Press.

Foxwell, H.S. 1899: Foreword to Menger, Anton, *The Right of the Whole Produce of Labour*. London: Macmillan.

Freeman, Christopher 1992: *The Economics of Hope*. London: Pinter.

Gay, Edwin (ed.) 1929: *Recent Economic Changes in the United States* ("The Hoover Report"). New York: McGraw-Hill.

Haberler, Gottfried 1950: Joseph Alois Schumpeter, 1883–1950, *Quarterly Journal of Economics*, 64(August): 333–372.

Hagemann, Harald and Krohn, Claus-Dieter (eds.) 1999: *Bibliographisches Handbuch der deutschsprachigen wirtschaftswissenschaftlichen Emigration nach 1933* [*Bibliographical Handbook on the Emigration of German-speaking Economists after 1933*], 2 vols. Munich: Saur.

Heaton, Herbert 1952: *A Scholar in Action—Edwin F. Gay*. Cambridge, MA: Harvard University Press.

Hodgson, Geoffrey M. 1999: *Economics and Utopia*. London: Routledge.

Johnston, William M. 1972: *The Austrian Mind. An Intellectual and Social History 1848–1938*. Berkeley, CA: University of California Press.

Kaldor, Nicholas 1955: Alternative theories of distribution, *Review of Economic Studies*, XXIII(2): 1955–1956. (Reprinted in *Essays on Value and Distribution*. Glencoe, IL: Free Press, 1960.)

Keynes, John Maynard 1936/1972: Herbert Somerton Foxwell. *The Collected Writings of John Maynard Keynes*, Vol. X. London: Macmillan, pp. 267–296.

Kress Library 1940–1967: *The Kress Library of Business and Economics. Catalogue*, 4 vols. Baker Library, Harvard Business School.

Leontief, Wassily 1950: Joseph A. Schumpeter (1883–1950), *Econometrica*, 18(2) (April): 103–110.

Marshall, Alfred 1890/1961: *Principles of Economics*, 9th (variorum) edn. London: Macmillan.

McCraw, Thomas 1991: Schumpeter ascending, *The American Scholar*, 60(3): 371–392.

Mirowski, Philip 1994: Doing what comes naturally: four metanarratives on what metaphors are for, in Mirowski (ed.), *Natural Images in Economic Thought*. Cambridge: Cambridge University Press.

Nelson, Richard and Winter, Sidney 1982: *An Evolutionary Theory of Economic Change*. Cambridge, MA: Harvard University Press.

Redlich, Fritz 1954: The role of innovation in a quasi-static world. Francis Bacon and his successors, *Explorations in Entrepreneurial History*, VII(1) (October): 12–25.

Redlich, Fritz 1964: *Der Unternehmer. Wirtschafts- und Sozialgeschichtliche Studien* [*The Entrepreneur: Studies in Economic and Social History*]. Göttingen: Vandenhoeck & Ruprecht.

Reinert, Erik S. 1999: The role of the state in economic growth, *Journal of Economic Studies*, 26(4/5): 268–326. (A short version of this paper is published in Toninelli, Pier Angelo (ed.), *The*

Rise and Fall of State-owned Enterprises in the Western World. Cambridge: Cambridge University Press, 2000.)

Reinert, Erik S. (ed.) 2002: *Evolutionary Economics and Income Inequality.* Cheltenham: Elgar.

Reinert, Erik S. 2005: Austrian economics and *The Other Canon.* The Austrians between the activistic-idealistic and the passivistic-materialistic traditions of economics, in J. Backhaus (ed.), *Modern Applications of Austrian Thought.* London: Routledge.

Reinert, Erik S. and Daastøl, Arno 1997: Exploring the genesis of economic innovations: the religious gestalt-switch and the duty to invent as preconditions for economic growth, *European Journal of Law and Economics,* 4(2/3): 233–283.

Reinert, Erik S. and Daastøl, Arno 2002: The Other Canon and uneven economic development: Renaissance economics as an immaterial and production-based canon in the history of economic thought and in the history of economic policy, in Erik Reinert (ed.), *Evolutionary Economics and Income Inequality.* Aldershot: Edward Elgar.

Reinert, Erik S. and Reinert, Hugo 2006: Creative destruction in economics: Nietzsche, Sombart, Schumpeter, in Jürgen Backhaus and Wolfgang Drechsler (eds.), *Friedrich Nietzsche: Economy and Society,* The European Heritage in Economics and the Social Sciences, Vol. 4. Dordrecht: Kluwer.

Research Center in Entrepreneurial History, Harvard University 1949: *Change and the Entrepreneur. Postulates and Patterns for Entrepreneurial History.* Cambridge, MA: Harvard University Press.

Roscher, Wilhelm 1874: *Geschichte der National-Ökonomik in Deutschland* [*History of Economics in Germany*]. Munich: Oldenbourg.

Schumpeter, Joseph Alois 1908: *Das Wesen und der Hauptinhalt der theoretischen Nationalökonomie* [*The Essence and Principal Contents of Economic Theory*]. Leipzig: Duncker & Humblot.

Schumpeter, Joseph Alois 1939: *Business Cycles.* New York: Macmillan.

Schumpeter, Joseph Alois 1942: *Capitalism, Socialism and Democracy.* New York: Harper.

Schumpeter, Joseph Alois 1949: Economic theory and entrepreneurial history, in Research Center in Entrepreneurial History (ed.), *Change and the Entrepreneur. Postulates and Patterns for Entrepreneurial History.* Cambridge, MA: Harvard University Press.

Schumpeter, Joseph Alois 1951: *Essays,* Richard V. Clemence (ed.). Cambridge, MA: Addison-Wesley.

Schumpeter, Joseph A. 1954: *History of Economic Analysis.* New York: Oxford University Press.

Schumpeter, Joseph Alois, Cole, A.H. and Mason, E.S. 1941: Frank William Taussig, *Quarterly Journal of Economics,* 55(May): 337–363.

Shionoya, Yuichi 1997: *Schumpeter and the Idea of Social Science.* Cambridge: Cambridge University Press.

Sombart, Werner 1902: *Der moderne Kapitalismus. Der Genesis des Kapitalismus & Die Theorie der kapitalistischen Entwicklung* [*Modern Capitalism. The Genesis of Capitalism and the Theory of the Development of Capitalism*], 2 vols. Leipzig: Duncker & Humblot.

Sombart, Werner 1913a: *Krieg und Kapitalismus* [*War and Capitalism*]. Munich and Leipzig: Duncker & Humblot.

Sombart, Werner 1913b: *Luxus und Kapitalismus* [*Luxury and Capitalism*]. Munich and Leipzig: Duncker & Humblot.

Sombart, Werner 1928: *Der moderne Kapitalismus* [*Modern Capitalism*], 6 vols. Munich and Leipzig: Duncker & Humblot.

Sombart, Werner 1930: *Die drei Nationalökonomien* [*The Three Types of Economics*]. Berlin: Duncker & Humblot.

Stiglitz, Joseph 1994: *Wither Socialism?* Cambridge, MA: MIT Press.

Stolper, Wolfgang E. 1994: *Joseph Alois Schumpeter. The Public Life of a Private Man.* Princeton, NJ: Princeton University Press.

Swedberg, Richard 1991: *Schumpeter. A Biography.* Princeton, NJ: Princeton University Press.

Zeuthen, F. 1930: *Problems of Monopoly and Economic Warfare, with a Preface by Professor Joseph A. Schumpeter.* London: Routledge.

Chapter Fourteen

THE ROLE OF TECHNOLOGY IN THE CREATION OF RICH AND POOR NATIONS: UNDERDEVELOPMENT IN A SCHUMPETERIAN SYSTEM

Erik S. Reinert

Introduction[1]

There is a growing awareness of the role of technology in creating economic growth. A large research programme by the OECD — TEP (Technology and Economy) — recently brought this issue, and the underlying evolutionary theory of economic growth, into focus. However, the insights of Schumpeterian or evolutionary economics have so far not been used to study the problems of underdevelopment, only to study the growth problems of the industrialized nations. This paper is, as far as this writer is aware, the first attempt to use Schumpeterian analysis of technological change to explain poverty and underdevelopment. 'Schumpeterian poverty' indeed sounds like a contradiction in terms.

The aim of this paper is to show that the dynamics of Schumpeterian economics, in addition to explaining the creation of wealth, also implicitly contain the elements of a theory of relative poverty. It attempts to explain the role of technological change in the creation of what is labelled 'Schumpeterian underdevelopment'. It is argued that the German tradition of economics, of which Schumpeter is a part, has always encompassed the necessary elements of a theory of *uneven* growth. List, Marx and Schumpeter have all emphasized different aspects of this uneven growth. To all of them, technological change was at the core of their theories. This contrasts sharply with the Anglo-Saxon tradition, where technological change has been neglected. As a consequence of this, particularly since the 1890s, Anglo-Saxon economics has produced theories of growth and trade which imply *even* growth, a converging distribution of world activity and income (factor-prize equalization).

---

[1] This paper draws heavily on a paper presented at the 5th Conference of the Joseph Alois Schumpeter Society in August 1994, in Münster, Germany. Helpful comments provided by Keith Smith and the editor of this volume are gratefully acknowledged. The usual disclaimer applies.

The organization of the paper is as follows. The next section contrasts Anglo-Saxon and German economic traditions from the point of view of theories of *uneven* growth vs theories of *even* growth. Then the question of the relationship between technological change and underdevelopment is raised, and two key mechanisms which create uneven distribution of the gains from technological change are identified. These are: the consequences of the extremely uneven advance of the 'technological frontier'; and classical and collusive spreads of technological gains. The next section shows how these mechanisms work to create three cases of 'Schumpeterian underdevelopment' in the Caribbean. The following section claims that the aspects of technological change identified earlier may create conflicting interests between the two parts that every individual plays in economic life, that of producer and that of consumer. It is claimed that these are identical only under the assumptions of neoclassical economics and in special cases of what is labelled *symmetrical* trade. Finally, the policy conclusions of these findings are discussed. It is shown how the conflicting interests of man-the-consumer and man-the-producer, produced by classical and collusive spreads of technical change, were central to the creation of US industrial policy in the early nineteenth century.

Anglo-Saxon vs German economics: theories of *even vs* theories of *uneven* growth

Friedrich List, Karl Marx and Joseph Alois Schumpeter are the German economists who have had major influence on economic policy outside the German-speaking area. The theories of Marx and Schumpeter are deeply rooted in the traditions of the German historical school of economics, and although Friedrich List antedates what is generally seen as the starting point of the older historical school, his approach is clearly that of a 'proto-historical school'. The roots of this line of thought go back to the times of the cameralists, at least as far back as Wilhelm von Hörnigk (1684).[2] All three authors — List, Marx and Schumpeter — share an essentially very similar dynamic view of economic development. This is especially evident when their theories are contrasted with the Anglo-Saxon economic tradition, that which provides the foundation for our present world economic order. The German tradition produces theories of *uneven* growth; Anglo-Saxon neoclassical economics tends to produce theories of *even* growth. This is particularly true when neoclassical economics is translated into international economic policy, and the finer points of the theory are lost. In terms of economic policy, a key difference between these two bodies of thought is that whereas in Anglo-Saxon economic theory the location of production in space is not an issue, this location is often crucial

---

2 Von Hörnigk's important work appeared in sixteen editions between 1684 and 1784, all in German. This was considerably more than the most famous English economists at the time. Mun's *England's Treasure* from 1664 reached eight editions in English and six in translations, Child's *Brief Observations* of 1690 reached ten editions in English and two translations. For a study of economic policy making under the 'proto-historical' school after Hörnigk, see Tribe (1988).

to economic wealth in German economic policy. Anglo-Saxon economics is primarily a theory of *exchange,* whereas German economic theory to a much larger extent involves *production.* In German theory, differences in circumstances of production translate into differences in wealth.

Before Adam Smith many English theories of growth were also theories of uneven growth. I have argued elsewhere (Reinert 1994) that the mercantilist view was that economic growth was *activity-specific,* that it took place in some economic activities and not in others. It should also be noted that in the nineteenth-century US the economic theories which served as guidance for economic policy (as opposed to what was often taught at 'ivy league' universities) were 'German-type' theories. Friedrich List's prolonged stay in the US in the 1820s clearly provided a cross-fertilization of German theories and US Hamiltonian thoughts on the matter of economic policy. Similarly, in Japan, the economic theories adopted after the Meiji restoration were specifically based on German *national*ökonomische theories, openly rejecting the *cosmo*political aspects of English economic theory.

The similarities between Marx and Schumpeter are readily admitted by Schumpeter, most clearly so in the foreword to the Japanese version of the *Theorie der wirtschaftlichen Entwicklung* (Schumpeter 1912; 1934). Schumpeter explains here how he was looking for 'a source of energy within the economic system, that would of itself disrupt any equilibrium that might be attained …It was not clear to me at the outset…that the idea and the aim are exactly the same as the idea and the aim which underlie the teachings of Karl Marx'. The similarities in the two systems are, Schumpeter says, 'obliterated by a very wide difference in general outlook'. Clemence (1951) translates and reproduces the Japanese foreword. Many authors, starting in the late 1940s, have compared Marx and Schumpeter. A bibliography of 'Works on Schumpeter' lists 77 works — of a total of 1916 entries — treating both Marx and Schumpeter (Augello 1990).[3]

In spite of their similarities, the 'wide difference in general outlook' between the two economists has continued with their modern disciples. A special division of labour of Schumpeter's *creative destruction* has taken place between Schumpeterians and Marxists: the Schumpeterians explain the *creative* part, e.g. the growth of the English cotton textile industry, whereas the Marxists concentrate on the *destructive* part: the bones of the Bengali weavers, the previous suppliers of the same product to the English and Indian markets, 'whitening the plains of India'. Schumpeterians produce theories of *development;* Marxists produce theories of *underdevelopment.* Both these sets of theories, however, intrinsically contain the elements of the opposite view. Marxian economics (as distinguished from Marxist economics) produces a dynamic theory of development, albeit uneven, where the 'bourgeoisie cannot exist without constantly revolutionising the instruments of production'. Rosenberg (1976, 126–38) comments on Marx's view of technology, where the uneven distribution of wealth is kept up by, among other factors, the imperfect competition produced by constant innovations.

[3] The largest numbers of publications comparing Marx and Schumpeter have appeared in Italian books and journals, a total of 23. The second most frequent nation is Japan.

A similar picture of Schumpeter's *dynamic income inequalities* can be found in his *Theory of Economic Development:* Schumpeter recognizes that 'the upper strata of society are like hotels which are always full of people, but people who are forever changing.' (Schumpeter 1912; 1934, 156).[4] As opposed to Marx, Schumpeter's interest in the fate of the groups not living in this upper-class hotel, however, is very limited. The key factor which unites Marx and Schumpeter — and distinguishes both these approaches from Anglo-Saxon economic theory — is that theirs is essentially a theory of *uneven* growth. For this reason, in any 'German-type' theoretical approach, problems of income distribution are implicit in the system, whereas this type of problem is non-existent at the paradigm level in Anglo-Saxon economics.

If we compare the world of today with the world in which Marx wrote, two important developments have taken place, especially since the Second World War. These developments have changed the geographical setting of distributional problems, from being essentially *national* to being *international* problems: first, successful mechanisms for income redistribution in most industrialized countries have alleviated national problems of income distribution; and second, 'globalization' has substituted the present international division of labour for the previous national one, also in manufacturing goods. In this way the distributional conflicts have been moved more and more from the national (between 'classes') to the international arena (between nations). National problems of income distribution, in the sense of poverty alleviation, have to a large extent been solved in many industrial countries, particularly in some European countries and in Japan. The enormous costs involved in this redistribution within the industrial nations are rarely debated, least of all on a theoretical level.

Since Adam Smith, Anglo-Saxon economics has been cosmopolitical. In English classical theory distributional issues were not a core issue — but, as Lionel Robbins (1952) has shown, in practical economic policy distributional issues were indeed considered on the national level. In neoclassical theory, national and international distributive issues have been assumed away through the inclusion of simplifying assumptions. Over time these simplifications crystallized into the two key assumptions of neoclassical economics: perfect information and the absence of increasing returns. It is the inclusion of these two assumptions — both counterfactual — which has created the blind spot of neoclassical economics: the inability to account for the extremely different levels of development between the nations of the world. With the assumptions of perfect information and constant returns to scale in place, any theory of economic growth automatically becomes a theory of *even* growth. These assumptions seem to remove the reasons for a Smithian 'division of labour': differences in human knowledge and fixed costs in specialized machinery. Perfect information seems difficult to reconcile with a notion of 'human capital'. Constant returns to scale seems difficult to reconcile with the existence of fixed costs, which create varying degrees of 'minimum efficient size'. These two assumptions — implicit or explicit — turned English economics into a *cosmo*political school of economics. As a reaction to this, nineteenth-century German economics

---

4 This part is not found in the 1912 German edition.

became *Nationalökonomie* and *Volkswirtschaft* — terms which stick to this very day both in Germany and in Scandinavia. Here, less restrictive assumptions were made.

What Marx and Schumpeter have in common are strong roots in the German historical school of economics. These roots are not clear to the observer of today, for at least two reasons. First of all the German historical tradition is hardly known outside the German-speaking world; very few works have been translated. Exceptions are Roscher (1882) and Sombart (Backhaus 1995). Second, the followers of both Schumpeter and Marx have, for different reasons, consciously and/or unconsciously cultivated the originality of their leading man. In the communist bloc Marx's doctrine was cultivated as being the product of what in another religion is called an 'immaculate conception': Marx could not be seen as having borrowed from despicable bourgeois economists. The fact is that Marx borrowed heavily from the founder of the German historical school, Wilhelm Roscher (1854).

Together with Charles Babbage (1832) and Andrew Ure (1835), both of whom he quotes several times, Roscher was probably the first economist to understand fully the economics of technological change and mass production: 'He [Roscher] created the image of large-scale industry whose essential feature is increasing returns or decreasing costs' (Streissler 1994, 1). Roscher also specifically pointed to the existence of increasing returns in research. Whereas Babbage and Ure wrote specialized treaties on the economics of large-scale industry, Roscher incorporated these insights into a holistic economic theory. Roscher's work was to be the standard textbook for a generation of Germans, appearing in 26 editions. Marx differed from the rest of the German school by subscribing to Ricardo's labour theory of value, which to Roscher and to the German historical tradition was un-German and 'typically English'. The importance given to economies of scale in German economics goes back before Roscher to previous works by Hufeland (1807) and Hermann (1832). Roscher also refers several times to Serra (1613), whose treatise was the first to associate national welfare with increasing returns, and national poverty with the lack of it.

Schumpeter's originality in the Anglo-Saxon environment was clearly to a large extent also a product of the ignorance, outside Germany, of the traditions on which he built. Most Schumpeterians, especially non-Germans, would probably be surprised by a recent German book that describes Schumpeter's *Capitalism, Socialism and Democracy* (Schumpeter 1942) as essentially a reworking of a German debate which had taken place decades earlier, where, the author carefully points out, Schumpeter neither refers to the debate itself, nor to its protagonist Werner Sombart (Appel 1992).[5]

All of this is in sharp contrast to the Anglo-Saxon tradition. Adam Smith provided the great insight of the importance of 'division of labour', but he failed to see its

---

[5] 'Ohne auf Sombart und die allgemeine Literatur der zwanziger und dreissiger Jahre hinzuweisen, bot Schumpeter (in *Kapitalismus, Sozialismus und Demokratie)* im wesentlichen nur dass, was bereits Jahrzehnte zuvor in den deutschen Diskussionen über die "Zukunft der Kapitalismus" geschrieben und gesagt worden war, wobei er freilich die gesellschaftlich konservativen Folgerungen, die bei Sombart in der Forderung nach Reagrarisierung und Autarkie gipfelten, nicht übernahm' (Appel 1992, 260).

organizational implications. He assumed markets would continue to function as perfectly as the agricultural markets of his time. On the other hand, he specifically states that the lack of progress of agriculture at the time of his writing was probably due to the 'lack of scope for the division of labour'. Adam Smith goes half-way to seeing the connection between 'lack of division of labour' and perfect competition, but not all the way. The differences in organization of production have been left out in neoclassical theory, as has any follow-up of the consequences of various degrees of 'division of labour'. Neoclassical economics is essentially a theory of the exchange of goods already produced, taking no account of the diversity of conditions of production and their influence on pricing behaviour. Neoclassical theory is, it seems, one which cannot accommodate the existence of fixed costs, since these create increasing returns. We are, seemingly, still victims of Adam Smith's inability to see the necessary organizational consequences of his key insight into the importance of division of labour. The division of labour will create firms organized around the combining of tasks into which the manufacturing, assembly and sale of a final product have been divided. The fixed costs invested in machinery and equipment will by definition create a minimum efficient size, increasing returns, barriers to entry and imperfect competition. The understanding of this is traditionally part of German economics but, since the early 1890s, definitely not of the paradigm of Anglo-Saxon economics. Rosenberg (1994, 24–46), referring to Charles Babbage, has an interesting discussion of 'division of labour' in the history of economics.

For this reason, a most significant long-term pattern of economic policy emerges: 'German-type' theories of uneven growth dominated the take-off stage of all industrialized countries, including England from the late 1400s up until the late 1800s. The economic policies of these nations have gradually changed to 'English-type' theories as they, one by one, reached the 'technological frontier'. At that point increasing returns in industrial activities turn from being a barrier to growth (for nations not engaged in such activities) into a mechanism where international trade is beneficial to both trading partners. In the early stages, increasing returns create a barrier to development and an obstacle, but as the economy industrializes they become an important ally. As a consequence of this, to a poor country with an economy based on natural resources, free trade was seen as a poverty trap (due to the existence of diminishing returns and perfect competition). To a nation engaged in increasing return activities, the existence of these factors becomes yet another reason for free trade. The earliest treatment of this is probably that found in Charles King (1721, I, 3). In a successful strategy, increasing returns must be part of economic growth theory in the early take-off stage. Therefore a 'German-type' theory has always been present at an early stage in all industrialized countries. Once a nation is established in a virtuous circle of increasing return activities and dynamic imperfect competition, leaving increasing returns out of economic theory is not harmful on a short-term basis. Consequently, the successful former laggard countries all convert to Anglo-Saxon-type theories — especially with respect to international trade — without any short-term damage.

In Anglo-Saxon economics all economic activities are 'alike': they are all equally suited to promote national welfare. In German economic theory some economic activities are 'better' than others: those exhibiting dynamic imperfect competition produced by 'historical increasing returns'. Engaging in these 'better' activities is a necessary requirement if a country is to 'catch up' with the leading nations of the world.

'German' economic theory has been the basis of the economic policies of the 'laggards', including England when it was one. Anglo-Saxon economics has been the theory of the 'leaders' — the theory embarked upon when 'German' theory has brought a nation into international leadership. For this reason, all rich countries have attempted to export 'Anglo-Saxon' ideas, whereas they themselves have stuck to 'German' ideas. The policy of the US in imposing free trade on Japan and Latin America, while still engaged in extremely heavy-handed protection of national industry at home, is but one example. Today's *managed free trade* is an attempt to achieve the same thing: the advantages of 'German' theories for home use combined with Anglo-Saxon for the rest of the world.

The basic difference between a rich and a poor nation in the world of today is that whereas *all* rich nations — except some small city states — have been through a long stage of 'German' economic policy, in most cases lasting at least one hundred years; it is difficult to find a poor nation which has been through this stage. The key feature of this 'German' economic policy is the combination of competition *and* protection of manufactures. The thinking of the times is well reflected in the title of Whatley (1774): *Principles of Trade. Fredom* [sic] *and Protection are its best Suport* [sic]: *Industry, the only Means to render Manufactures cheap.* This second edition incorporates laudatory notes by Benjamin Franklin on the subject.

Technological change and Schumpeterian underdevelopment

As stated in the previous section, in German economic theory, some economic activities are 'better' than others, in the sense that they produce dynamic technical change and increasing returns. English economic theory tended to neglect these factors and, for this reason, for the purposes of economic growth, all economic activities became 'alike'. This was a necessary condition for equilibrium. Increasing returns were, however, still important in the first edition, but not in the later, of Alfred Marshall's *Principles.* Marshall, consequently, is able to give us a formula for an excellent industrial policy: 'A tax ...on the production of goods which obey the Law of Diminishing Return, and devoting the tax to a bounty on the production of those goods with regard to which the Law of Increasing Returns acts sharply' (Marshall 1890, 452). This insight had to be sacrificed in later editions, since the existence of increasing returns was incompatible with equilibrium. What in Marshall's early writings starts out as a 'Law' (with a capital 'L') of increasing returns, is reduced to being a 'tendency' in subsequent editions, later to disappear from mainstream theory altogether with John Hicks. Today, new trade theory and new neoclassical growth theory are about to rediscover the impact of increasing (but not diminishing) returns. An excellent survey of these models is found in Verspagen (1992); see also Romer (1994). Today's policy conclusions from new trade theory and new growth theory are no different from Marshall's in 1890, Roscher's in the 1850s, or Serra's in 1613.

Schumpeter's dynamic system, with the role of 'historical increasing returns', retains the characteristics of other authors of the German school, and therefore of a system which produces uneven growth. My notion of Schumpeterian underdevelopment relates to two aspects of technological change, discussed below. Both of these mechanisms are based on the existence of increasing and diminishing returns, imperfect information, barriers to entry, and resulting imperfect competition.

The uneven advances of the 'technological frontier'

It is often visualized that technological knowledge moves forward in the form of a technological 'frontier' of knowledge. The word 'frontier' conveys a notion of a fairly orderly and even progress, where a borderline is being pushed ahead, somewhat reminiscent of the 'frontier' being pushed from the east to the west coast in US history. I feel our understanding of wealth and poverty is hampered by this vision of an orderly 'frontier'. The historical pattern of technological change looks more like a scatter diagram than an orderly frontier. Technical change happens very fast in some areas, dragging with them others, but in some areas the 'frontier' hardly moves at all for centuries. At any particular time both the search for new technologies, and technological change itself, are — in Nathan Rosenberg's word — 'focused' (Rosenberg 1976, Ch. 6) on specific areas of technological problems and opportunities. In the stone age, technical change was concentrated in the stone implements industry, in the bronze age in bronze implements, and in the machine age in the activities which were being mechanized. Even today, two hundred years into the machine age, some activities are still not mechanized — cutting hair, picking strawberries or sewing baseballs.

'If improvements in all the arts were to take place *at the same rate,* they would obviously have no effect to alter the exchangeable value of things', said US economist Henry Vethake (1844, 95). In a system with perfect information and constant returns to scale, the sequence of technological change makes no difference to the distribution of wealth. Vethake's insight has been almost completely neglected in neoclassical economic theory. A paper by Robert Lucas (1988) provides an exception. In this paper Lucas presents a formal model in which learning takes place at different rates in different sectors of the economy. As to the practical consequences of uneven learning, Lucas provides an unusually candid remark from a formal economist: 'The consequences for human welfare involved in questions like these are simply staggering: Once one starts to think about them, it is hard to think about anything else'.

The two ways in which the benefits from technical change spread

Under perfect competition, the advances from technical change will spread in the economy in the form of lowered prices to the end user. In Reinert (1994) I argue that this is the assumption made already by both Adam Smith and David Ricardo. In the same paper — contrary to the assumptions of both of classical and neoclassical economics — I propose that in order to capture the mechanisms of national wealth and poverty, it is necessary to understand how the benefits from technological change can be distributed in one of two ways: one which creates wealth and one which merely preserves the *status quo:*

- *To the customers* buying the product in the form of lowered prices and/or better quality. I call this the *classical* form of distribution of the gains from technological change, because Adam Smith and David Ricardo both state that this will be the effect of technical improvements. This mechanism will operate when conditions of production and markets are similar to those assumed in neoclassical theory.
- *To the owners and workers* in the producing firm, and later to the *government* of the producing country in the form of higher taxable income. I call this the *collusive* form of distribution of the gains from technical change, because the forces of the producing country (capital, labour and government) in practice — although not as a conspiracy — 'collude' to appropriate these gains. This mechanism will operate if the technical change is accompanied by the creation of barriers to entry, where increasing returns are a key mechanism.

A typical example of the *collusive* form is Henry Ford's decision to increase the wages of his workers from an average of $2.34 for a nine-hour day to $5 for an eight-hour day in January 1914 (Raff 1988, 387). A typical example of a *classical* distribution would be the employment of bar code readers in supermarkets. This technological improvement would not show up as higher wages to the store staff. Harvard's Zwi Griliches uses this case to show what I call 'invisible economic growth', those cost-cuts and quality improvements which never show up in any statistics *(Business Week* 1994).

Most technical changes contain an element of both *classical* and *collusive* distribution of the benefits from technical change. What we measure as economic growth is largely the collusive mode. Collusive technical change is accompanied by the creation of higher barriers to entry, more imperfect competition, and it normally affects the minimum efficient size of an operation. The effects of classical technical change 'fall through' the producing organization without changing the structure of the firm or the industry, and are visible mainly as lower prices of the end product. This classical technical change does not affect the bargaining power of labour. Classical technical change takes place under conditions that do not strongly violate the neoclassical assumptions of perfect competition, and is most frequently found in agriculture and in the traditional service sector. Typically an invention initially creates a temporary monopoly which allows for a collusive spread of benefits, but as the technique in question becomes commonplace, its benefits will spread more and more as lower prices, not as higher wages and profits. Table 14.1 illustrates the characteristics of classical and collusive spread of technical change.

In a typical industrialized country 70 per cent of GNP is accounted for by factor payments to labour in the form of wages. What we measure historically as growth in GNP is to a large extent the impact of technical change on monetary wages. Classical technological change tends to leave fewer traces. When, as in the last decade, an increasing percentage of GNP growth takes place in the service sector — following Petty's Law — the classical-type spread of technical change becomes more dominant in the economy. Because of the decentralized nature of service production (the classical definition is that a service product must be produced where it is consumed), economies of *scope* in multisite operations are more of a success factor in the service industry than traditional economies of *scale,* typical of a Fordist-type factory. This, combined with the use of technology to *replace* and not to *enhance* labour skills in the traditional service sector, allows for a classical rather than a collusive spread of the benefits of technical change in this sector. An important part of the explanation of the 'Solow paradox' — that computers are visible everywhere except in government statistics — clearly lies in the combination of the huge measurement problems in the service sector combined with the classical spread of technological change in this area.

The two phenomena — the classical spread of technological gains and the measurement problems — are closely intertwined. A considerable portion of the lower growth in what we measure as GNP in most industrialized countries over the last decade is most likely the result of increasing employment in the traditional service sector which produces 'invisible growth' (lowered transaction costs in grocery purchases due to checkout scanners, etc.). However, the subject of this paper is not the measurement problems of GNP caused by technical change, but the effects of technical change on income distribution among nations.

In the collective bargaining process, the collusive mode is traditionally seen as being 'fair'. If a company improves its labour productivity, part of the benefits of this should go to labour *in that firm.* The phenomena which I describe as the classical and collusive modes of distributing the proceeds from technical change were thoroughly discussed in a 'comprehensive series of investigations of the relation of the distribution of income to economic progress' by the Brookings Institution (Bell 1940, 3). These investigations led to the publishing of a series of books between 1935 and 1940 (Bell 1940; Moulton 1935; Nourse and Drury 1938), several of which directly address the way benefits from technological change spread in the economy. In the framework of the Brookings Institution, my classical spread is called 'distributing income through price reductions' and the collusive spread is called 'distributing income through raising money wages'. In general, the Brookings studies find that, although the classical way of distributing gains from technological progress is the preferred one from the point of view of society as a whole, the imperfectly competitive markets for goods and labour in industry make this impossible to achieve. These studies point, however, to the serious problems of income distribution caused (within the US) by the collusive spread of the benefits from technical change in industry and the classical spread in agriculture. In a paragraph entitled 'The conflict between wage earners and farmers' Moulton (1935, 124–5) has the following comments as to the national income distribution resulting from collusive spread of gains. We ask the reader also to study the paragraph substituting for the US farmers a Third World nation producing raw materials or mature industrial products under conditions of near-perfect competition:

> In considering the price-reduction method [our classical mode] as an alternative to wage increases [our collusive mode] attention should also be called to a broad social consequence of the latter that has apparently seldom been recognized. The disparities in the income and purchasing power of the industrial and agricultural populations resulting from the wage increasing method create a basic maladjustment between two great divisions of our economic life and imposes a serious barrier to economic progress. It is apparent that there would be a growing disparity in the economic position of the agricultural and industrial populations

Table 14.1 Characteristics of the two modes of diffusion of productivity improvements

Characteristics of mode	The collusive mode	The classical mode
Divisibility of investment	Indivisible, comes in *chunks*	Divisible
Degree of perfect information	imperfect (e.g. patents, internal R&D)	Perfect (competitive market for technology itself)
Source of technology from user company point of view	Internal, or external in *big chunks* = high degree of economic of scale	External
Barriers to entry	Incraese	No change
Industry structure	Increases concentration	Neutral
Economies of scale	Increase	No Change
Market shares	Very important	Unimportant
How benefits spread		
GNP as measured	Highly visible	Tends not to appear ('Solow paradoxes')
Profit level	Increases stakes: possibility for larger profits or losses	No change
Monetary wages	Increase	No change
Real wages (nationally)	Increase	Increase
Price level	No change	Decreases
Terms of trade	No change	Turns *against* industry experiencing technological progress
Examples of innovation in the two groups	New pharmaceuticals, mainframe computer production, automotive paint production	Electricity, telephones, sewing machines, use of PCs, dispersion paint production, containers
Where found	Mainly in industry, in recent products and processes	In primary and tertiary industries, use of new basic technologies, mature industry

even if prices of industrial products showed no tendency to rise as wages rose:[6] the income of the urban population would be increasing while that of the agricultural population would be stationary. In practice there is, however, a tendency for industrial prices to rise somewhat as wages are increased, and the consequence is that the purchasing power of the farm tends to be actually reduced. The consequent inability of the agricultural population to buy ever increasing quantities of industrial products limits the scale on which industrial establishments can operate.

The struggle to obtain higher living standards through the medium of higher money wages has been the cause of a long and deep-seated conflict between the agricultural and

6 This statement should be compared with the terms-of-trade debate following the PrebischSinger argument in the early 1950s. Moulton shows a mechanism where one group grows rich and the other poor with terms of trade unchanged. My collusive spread and Moulton's argument reflect the views of Singer rather than Prebisch: see Singer's 1949 paper 'The Distribution of Gains between Investing and Borrowing Countries', reproduced in Singer (1964).

> urban population. The people of the cities have fought for higher wages even though it has meant somewhat higher prices for industrial products. The farmers have long fought for lower prices on the commodities they have to buy. The struggle underlies the so-called granger movement of the seventies; it explains the traditional opposition of the agricultural South to high protective tariffs; and it lies at the basis of farmer opposition to trusts, monopolies, and combinations in all their forms.

These paragraphs describe the problems of income distribution between two groups within the same nation who both produce at what was then the *technological frontier:* both the US farmers and the US industrial population were the most productive in the world. Yet, one group got rich and the other group stayed poor. At about the same time another American author tried to explain the same phenomenon from a leftist point of view in a book called *Why Farmers are Poor* (Rochester 1940). I would argue that the reason for this poverty *of the world's most efficient farmers on the world's probably most fertile soil is* as follows.

The productivity increases of the farmers are taken out in the form of lowered prices, in the classical way, whereas the productivity increases of their trading partners producing industrial goods are taken out collusively, in the form of higher wages. In a neo-classical world of perfect information and no economies of scale, this would of course not be a problem, because the individual farmers would all produce the tractors and all the other industrial implements in their own backyard without any loss of efficiency compared to industrial production. In real life, however, the farmers were facing high barriers to entry — the 'perfect information and constant returns to scale option' is of course non-existent. The farmers of the US in the 1930s suffered from 'Schumpeterian underdevelopment'.

If we now place these two groups in two different countries, an industrial country and an agricultural country, and open for trade, we would have achieved a much bigger gap in the standard of living than the one which so much worried the Brookings Institution in the late 1930s. Placing the two groups of producers in two different countries would have eliminated important distributive mechanisms that existed within the US. Migration of surplus labour from the farms to the industrial districts as fanning demanded less labour and more capital was an important distributive mechanism, as was the pressure from alternative employment in the cities on farm wages. The government tax base was much larger in the cities and in industrial areas, so infrastructure, schools, and other government services in the farming areas were clearly heavily subsidized by the industrial districts. Last but not least, the farmers, in spite of their steadily declining numbers, did have political power. Moulton mentions the granger movement which started just after the Civil War, whose activities served as the basis for later legislation affecting income distribution within the US: for example, railroad and public utility regulations, antitrust laws and measures establishing a postal savings bank and parcel post on government hands. Our basic point is that had the industrial population and the agrarian population in the US been living in two different nations, we would have found a deeply impoverished agricultural nation and an extremely wealthy industrial nation. Both would have been the world's most efficient, but one would still have suffered from Schumpeterian underdevelopment.

This is but one example. Using other examples from the Caribbean later in the paper, I shall argue that wealth is not caused by relative efficiency but by *imperfect competition*. From the point of view both of an individual and of a nation, the choice of economic activity is much more important than the degree of efficiency. There is, for nations as well as for individuals, an optimization process available.

Over time, labour mobility inside the industrialized nations tends to contribute to a more equitable division of industry rent *within* nations. Typically, the government sector — a gigantic redistributive machinery — represents more than 50 per cent of GNP in an industrial nation. Within the EU, similar transfer mechanisms are at work, particularly in the agricultural sector. Typical of these redistributive measures are that they are carried out as a matter of political necessity, and that, in spite of the huge numbers involved, no one ever asks *why* the maldistribution occurs in the first place. Joan Robinson was correct in pointing out that neoclassical economics does not have any theory of uneven distribution of wealth, but what is so surprising is the apparent lack of articulated demand for such a theory.

Three cases of Schumpeterian underdevelopment in the Caribbean

The case of serious maldistribution of income in the US between the agricultural and industrial sectors — both the world's most efficient at the time — demonstrates that being wealthy is not so much a matter of being efficient, it is more *what one chooses to be efficient in*. Schumpeterian underdevelopment happens if a nation chooses to be efficient *in the wrong sector*. This mechanism works similarly with individuals: the most efficient dish-washer in the country has a much lower income than the most efficient lawyer.

There are two mechanisms which come together to cause this: the uneven advance of the phenomenon which by a misnomer is called the *technological frontier*, and the *collusive* vs *classical* spread of the benefits from technical change. These mechanisms are able to operate because of what Schumpeter called 'historical increasing returns' — the fact that the technological change that we measure as economic growth has been accompanied by higher fixed costs creating greater economies of scale. This 'visible' (as opposed to the often invisible growth in the traditional service sector) technological change consequently operates under very imperfect competition protected by two important sets of barriers to entry: scale-based and knowledge-based, which interact and cumulate in creating Myrdalian vicious circles.

One important feature of neoclassical economies is that, under its standard assumptions, all economic activities become 'alike'. In neoclassical economics, a faster technological change in one industry than in another is neutralized by instant adjustment, provided by 'perfect information', 'perfect foresight', and 'constant returns to scale'. In real life the existence of huge differences in knowledge and information, 'bounded vision' and huge increasing returns to scale combine to chain nations to the trajectories they have historically embarked upon, or in the case of the Caribbean, those they *have been* embarked upon. In the following examples we shall observe how, in the case of three Caribbean islands, Schumpeterian underdevelopment occurs. In all three cases the choice of economic activity, rather than the efficiency, determines wealth or poverty.

Cuban counterpoint of tobacco and sugar

In 1940 the foremost Cuban social scientist in this century, Fernando Ortiz, published a book (Ortiz 1940) with a fascinating account of how Cuban society and history have been shaped in very different ways by tobacco and sugar, 'two gigantic plants, two members of the vegetable kingdom which both flourish in Cuba and are both perfectly adapted, climatically and ecologically, to the country. The territory of Cuba has in its different zones the best land for the cultivation of both plants. And the same happens in the combinations of the climate with the chemistry of the soil' (Ortiz 1947, 7).

From an economic point of view, Cuba clearly has an absolute advantage in the production of both crops. But to Cuba, one crop — tobacco — produced wealth; the other — sugar — poverty. The counterpoint between tobacco and sugar is a parallel to the uneven wealth creation we witnessed in a previous paragraph, between the industrial and agricultural sectors in the US. Both in the US and Cuban cases we are studying *the most advanced production in the world,* both in the activities which produced wealth and the activities which produced poverty. The difference here is that we are studying two agricultural products which are both being transformed into an industrial product. We must, then, go beyond the standard categorizations of agriculture as being 'bad' and industry as being 'good', to find the mechanisms at work.

In Cuban society tobacco was the hero, sugar the villain. Tobacco — predominantly grown on the western part of the island — created a middle class, a free bourgeoisie. Sugar — grown on the rest of the island — created two classes of people: masters and slaves. The cultivation and picking of tobacco created a demand for specialized skills: tobacco leaves were harvested individually, and the market price of the product depended on the skill of the picker. Tobacco bred skills, individuality and modest wealth. 'Sugar was an anonymous industry, the mass labor of slaves or gangs of hired workmen, under the supervision of capital's overseers' (Ortiz 1947, 65). Where tobacco required skill, care and judgement, sugar only required brute force in cutting the cane. Tobacco was individuality and division of labour; sugar was bulk and commodity. Tobacco carries its origins with it as a brand name, 'sugar comes to the world without a last name, like a slave.' Tobacco is stable prices; sugar is wildly fluctuating prices. A skilled tobacco selector can distinguish 70 or 80 different shades of tobacco, but all saccharose is the same. Timing is crucial in the harvesting of tobacco; for the cutting of cane timing is not important. Tobacco is delicately cut leaf by leaf with a small sharp knife, making sure that the rest of the plant survives. The sugar plant is brutally slashed with a big machete. Working with sugar is a trade; working with tobacco an art.

As a result of this, Ortiz says, the tobacco worker is not only wealthier than the destitute sugar workers; 'he is better mannered and more intelligent'. Tobacco is wealth and intelligence; sugar is poverty and ignorance. Sugar is foreign capital; tobacco is predominantly national capital. 'In the history of Cuba sugar represents Spanish absolutism; tobacco, the native liberators… Sugar has always stood for foreign intervention'. 'Sugar has always preferred slave labour; tobacco free men. Sugar brought in Negroes by force; tobacco encouraged the voluntary immigration of white men.'

Differences in barriers to entry are clearly a key factor producing the differences in production and marketing which created the Cuban counterpoint. Cuban tobacco was one of the few cases of brand name products from the Third World. Cuba had an absolute advantage in the world in both products, but one brought wealth and the other poverty. This is a parallel case to the Brooking Institution study from the US in the 1930s, which showed a US 'counterpoint' similar to the Cuban: the US had both the world's most efficient farmers and the world's most efficient industry. But the farmers stayed poor and the industrial workers got rich. Both in the US and in Cuba world level efficiency led to wealth for those who specialized in one product, and poverty to those who specialized in another. We are facing cases of *classical* spread of the gains from technological change in the case of the US farmer and the Cuban sugar workers, and *collusive* spread in the case of US industry and Cuban tobacco production. It is also worth noting that in spite of a much larger technological change in sugar refining than in cigar making, the cigar makers were consistently wealthier than their sugar-producing colleagues. From the point of view of the nation involved, imperfect competition and no technical change is infinitely better than technical change and perfect competition. Farming in the US and sugar in Cuba led to Schumpeterian underdevelopment; industry and tobacco did not.

Fifty years after the original publication of *Cuban Counterpoint,* a Cuban author in exile dedicated his book *La Isla que se repite (The Island which Repeats itself)* to its author, Fernando Ortiz (Benìtez Rojo 1989). The title of the book says it all: in spite of a change in political paradigm, the qualities inherent in sugar production — not only in Cuba but anywhere — continue to shape Cuba and determine its economic faith.

Two years ago two US political scientists and Latin-Americanists published a study of the political and economic structure of two Caribbean islands: the Dominican Republic and Jamaica (Hillman and D'Agostino 1992). In spite of the extremely different historical and administrative backgrounds of the two islands, one coming from the Spanish tradition and one from the English, the authors found both nations had very similar political and economic structures and the same set of problems. Again, their conclusion is, without referring to Ortiz, that the fate of both islands is shaped by the economic forces of sugar production. No matter what your past, producing the same thing will make you alike.

Many modern studies point to the extreme poverty of the world's most efficient sugar producers. The titles indicate the social concerns which prompted their publication: *The Hunger Crop. Poverty and the Sugar Industry* (Coote 1987) and *Bitter Sugar* (Lemoine 1985). The policies of the industrialized countries subsidizing their own inefficient sugar production — beet sugar in Europe and cane sugar in the US — plus the increased competition from corn-based sweeteners just add to the desolation of this 'lock-in effect'. Some years ago, *The Economist* dedicated a cover story — 'Enslaved by Subsidies' — to the sugar policies of the industrialized nations, calling it 'a case study in taxing the rich to ruin the poor' *(The Economist* 1985).

Haiti — economic counterpoint in baseballs and golf balls

Today the unchallenged position at the bottom of the sugar hierarchy is held by the Haitian seasonal workers in the sugar fields of the Dominican Republic (Lemoine 1985). But the Republic of Haiti also dominates the world market for a manufactured product: baseballs, produced mainly for the US market, provide a classic case of Schumpeterian underdevelopment.

Economists make sense of the enormous variations of industries by placing them in groups according to a standard industrial classification. Even seemingly homogeneous groups, however, may contain enormous diversity in the economic conditions individual products create in the country of production. The world's most efficient golfball producers are located in industrialized countries and make a normal industrial wage of 9 dollars per hour. The world's most efficient baseball producers are in Haiti, working 10 hours per day for an hourly wage of 30 US cents. The wage ratio between the two groups of workers, both in the same industry and both being the most efficient in the world, is about 30 to 1.

Why is there no factor price equalization with the industry producing balls for various sports? The technological explanation is: the machine age has not yet reached the production of baseballs; they have to be hand-sewn, even in the US. The currents of creative destruction have not yet penetrated this little industry. The baseball-producing industry is a relic from an otherwise extinct technoeconomic paradigm, to use the terms of Perez and Freeman.

As in sugar production, the characteristics of the product 'baseballs' themselves contain the elements of poverty and underdevelopment. No new skills are developed because there is no *demand* for new skills. No learning-by-doing takes place in Haiti, because there is no learning taking place in baseball production *anywhere.* The Haitians are not working with capital and with machines, because not even all the capital of the US has managed to mechanize baseball production. The mercantilists told us that economic growth was *activity-specific* — it happened in some industries and not in others. And they were right.

When Haiti sells baseballs to the US and buys golfballs back, one hour of labour in the US is exchanged for 30 hours of labour in Haiti. This in spite of the fact that US baseball sewers are *not* more efficient than the Haitians. These are the 'unequal exchange' effects of Schumpeterian underdevelopment.

The Dominican Republic and technological change in pyjama production

The Dominican Republic scores considerably higher in terms of GNP per capita than Haiti. As we have seen, the Dominican Republic can afford to import labour which is even cheaper than her own for the *zafra* — the sugar harvest. Over the last decade more than 400 000 new manufacturing jobs have come to the Dominican Republic. Most people expected economic growth and higher wages to result from manufacturing. After all, wasn't the wealth of the US built on manufacturing?

Much to the surprise of everybody, the 400 000 manufacturing jobs did not increase welfare to any measurable extent. The explanation lies in the way the market mechanisms of Schumpeterian underdevelopment assign production processes with and without technical change. The Dominican Republic produces garments, made from imported fabrics. Pyjamas bought in the US fifteen years ago would have a label reading: 'Fabric made in the US, cut and assembled in the Dominican Republic.' About ten years ago, the labels were changed. They now read: 'Fabric made *and cut* in the US, assembled in the Dominican Republic'. What had happened?

It was at this time that a new technology — laser cutting — hit the garment industry. As a result, the labour content in the operation fell dramatically, and the cost of labour was no longer a strategic factor in the cost of the final product. The cutting operation was therefore taken back to the US when the new technology appeared.

As long as the frontier of technological change moves forward extremely unevenly in a world with imperfect competition, free trade will lead to Schumpeterian underdevelopment in parts of the world economy. Production processes with no technological development, with no creative destruction, will, by the logic of the market, be farmed out to the poor nations. In some cases, where a huge closed market absorbs one small and relatively poor nation, this 'farming out' of products with less technical change may have beneficial effects to both trading partners. The inclusion of small and relatively poor Portugal in the EU can prove beneficial to all, just as the import of a few Third World citizens to wash dishes in the First World can be to the benefit of all parties.[7] However, the number of poor compared to the number of rich in the world today makes this 'absorption', this attempt to make the poor nations rich, not a viable strategy. The extremely high costs faced by West Germany in absorbing the relatively rich and much smaller East Germany testify to this.

The circular flow and the two economic roles of man

If the world is a stage where each must play his part, we are all — in an economic sense — playing two different roles: that of the producer and that of the consumer. On the one hand, we produce goods (man the producer), and on the other hand we consume goods (man the consumer) which are exchanged for the ones we produce. What counts as GNP is limited to production where these roles are *separated,* where the producer is not the consumer. The economics profession has abdicated from the study of situations where the roles of producer and consumer of a good are played by the same person. These cases of household economies have been left to economic anthropology. It is the *exchange,* and not the production, which is at the very heart of modern economics.

A special feature of neoclassical economics is the perfect harmony of interest between these two roles of man (or woman). This is one aspect of what Lionel Robbins (1952) refers to as the *Harmonielehre* resulting from the assumptions of economic theory. Man the producer never has any conflict of interests with his other self — man the consumer. Individual human beings, during their life span, face a similar situation as that of society as a whole. But individuals have possibilities to optimize their strategies, a path which

---

7 During 1994, the Tamil refugees in Switzerland, who were threatened with expulsion, proved to have only one political ally: the association of restaurant owners who depend on them for dishwashing.

today is difficult for a nation. For the individual, who consciously or unconsciously selects a profession, the two roles of consumer and producer imply trade-offs. The individual can embark on a path which optimizes his income. One can easily imagine man the consumer rejecting the suggestions of his producer self that present consumption has to be reduced in order to attend law school. A reasoned discussion between man the consumer and man the producer, both inhabiting the same individual, may lead to the conclusion that the individual in question would be better off quitting the job as a dishwasher and going to law school, i.e. foregoing consumption now for more prestige and consumption in the future. Among thousands of different professions, individuals are able to *optimize* their situation. Normally this optimization carries with it a trade-off between present and future income. The optimization between professions is clearly recognized also by economists, on a practical level or in the guise of 'human capital'. Certainly no economists, not even traditional trade theorists, tell their children to stick to the job washing dishes because 'factor-price equalization is just around the corner — the time when people washing dishes will make the same amount of money as lawyers'. Indeed, it would be easy to produce a convincing Ricardian-style argument for the would-be lawyer, that the world would be richer if he stuck to washing dishes and did not try to become a lawyer.

Why does this optimization option apply to individuals and not to nations? We all agree that our children should rather become lawyers than wash dishes in a restaurant. Why is it conceptually impossible for an economist to extend this argument to apply to a nation specializing in dishwashing trading with a nation of lawyers? Why is a certain path obviously an optimizing path to an individual, but not to a collection of individuals like a region or nation? Why do economists make opposite recommendations to one individual than to a group of individuals facing the same options? Why would we never dream of recommending to nations whose part in the international division of labour is similar to washing dishes that they can optimize by changing into a different profession?

The answer is relatively simple: neoclassical theory has abstracted from — assumed as not existing — all the characteristics which distinguish the job of washing dishes from the job of being a lawyer. Under conditions of perfect competition and perfect information with constant returns to scale, lawyers and dishwashers would make the same salaries. Under these conditions all individuals in an economy would have the same salaries; no trade-offs and no optimizations would be possible.

Individual wage differences as well as differences in industry profitability are caused by a package of factors which carry the collective label 'barriers to entry' — fixed costs and increasing returns, imperfect competition, speed of technological change, and many others which are listed in Figure 14.1. The quality index represents a continuum from perfect competition to monopoly, on which any economic activity conceptually can be plotted. The score on this index reflects the degree to which an activity can support a high wage for the individual and a high standard of living for the nation exporting this good.

In other words, the score of the quality index shows the degree of 'industry rent' available to the individual or to the nation. Schumpeter's 'historical increasing returns' — the interplay of scale and technological change over time — are an important factor creating

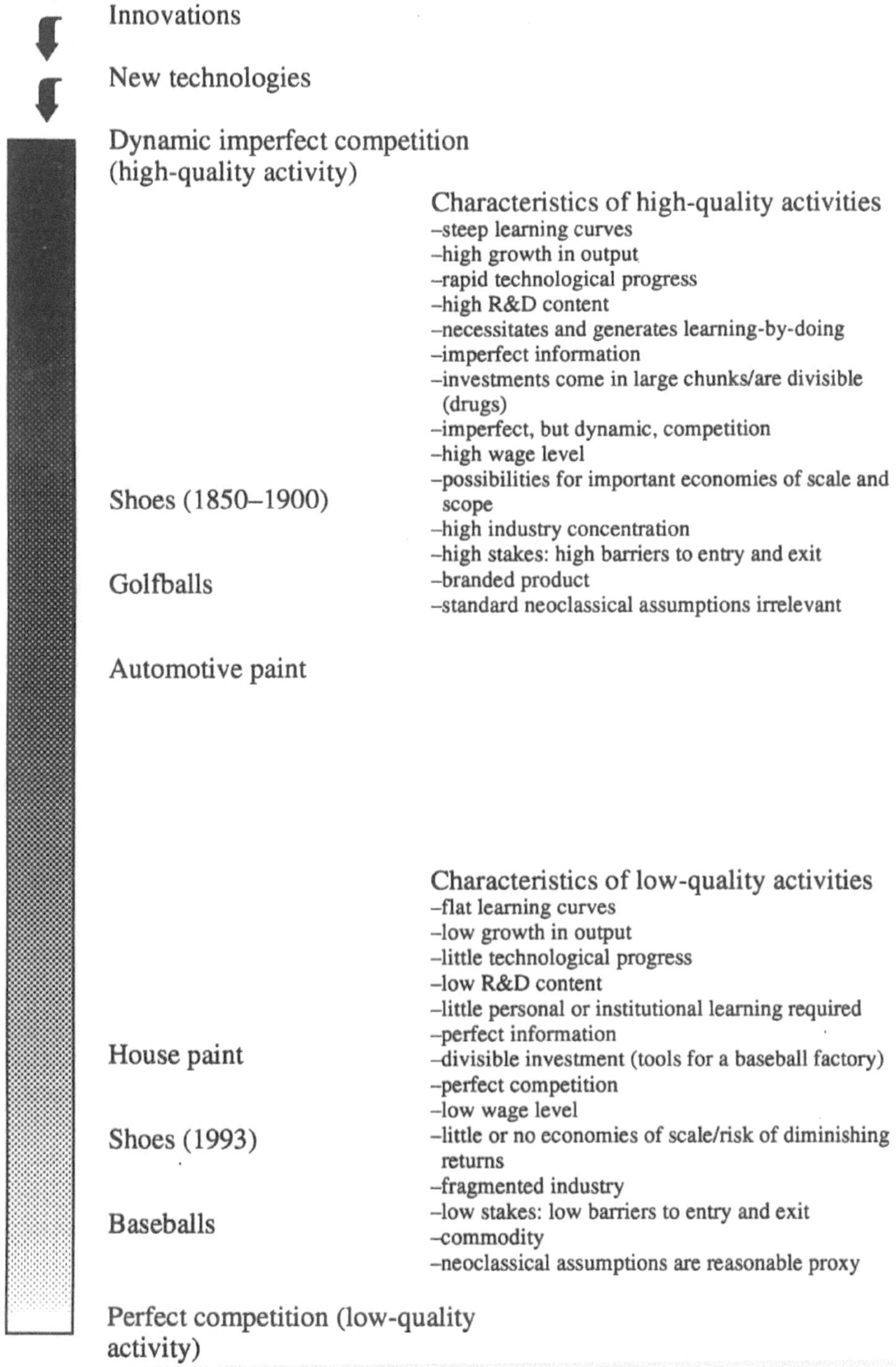

Figure 14.1 The quality index of economic activities.

high-quality activities.[8] Schumpeterian underdevelopment is the result of a specialization, within the international division of labour, in activities with a low score on the quality index of economic activities.

The national strategies under mercantilism and cameralism shared the view of economic growth being *activity-specific:* it took place in some economic activities and not in others (Reinert 1994). In order to get rich, a nation had to engage in the activities which gave the nation *productive powers* or *nationale Produktivkraft,* the equivalent of today's 'competitiveness', as discussed in Reinert (1995). This was the core of English economic policy from the late 1400s and in the economic policies of France (starting in the 1600s), Germany (from its cameralist past and with the Zollverein in the 1830s), the US (starting in 1820), and Japan (after the Meiji Restoration). In practical terms this meant engaging in the economic activities which at any point in time were in the process of being mechanized, through bounties, subsidies and protection. By singling out the activities which at any point in time were in the process of being mechanized, this 'mercantilist' trade policy developed a 'national innovation system'. Seen from a slightly different angle, the slope of the national learning curves were maximized. The scale effects and the barriers to entry created in these activities secured the creation of 'industry rent', which produced the gap in standards of living between the European countries and their colonies. The exceptions were formed by the 'white' colonies — those which in the early UN statistics were grouped under the heading 'areas of recent settlement'. These nations followed the former strategies of the metropolis countries, protecting and supporting local industry even from that of the mother country.

The Ricardian trade theory excludes all the factors which cause 'industry rent'. Our personal 'gut feelings' when we give our children or others advice on what profession to seek takes the industry rents in our own economies into account. When we analyse the relationship between nations, this tacit knowledge is automatically blocked off, and we return to Ricardo and a world where all the factors creating uneven wealth within a nation are assumed not to exist. But why are Ricardo and Samuelson able to convince us that a nation of dishwashers will be equally rich as a nation of lawyers when we intuitively know that each individual lawyer will be much richer than each individual person making a living washing dishes?

In a world where the division of labour causes different degrees of imperfect competition, scale effects and — in general — a different market value on different types of knowledge, an uneven income distribution is bound to be found. It is not the existence of increasing returns and barriers to entry *per se* that causes this maldistribution, but the fact that different economic activities embody these characteristics to varying degrees. Relative wealth and poverty are created by the asymmetry between different degrees of imperfect competition, not by imperfect competition in and of itself. In the very hypothetical case that all activities had the same degree of imperfect information and increasing

---

[8] The 'quality index' can be seen as an attempt to explain Robert Reich's 'high-quality jobs' and low-quality jobs'. A nation specializing in 'low-quality jobs' — like Haiti — will suffer from Schumpeterian underdevelopment.

returns, we could still have an even income distribution. On the quality index this would correspond to persons or nations trading in professions with the same score on the quality index — the case of the lawyer going to the doctor. This case was specifically recognized in the most important work on 'national strategy' in eighteenth-century England, when Charles King explicitly lists among 'good trade' the exchange of manufactured goods for other manufactured goods (King 1721). Paul Krugman's conversion from free-trade scepticism after he rediscovered increasing returns — and consequently an important mechanism of uneven development — in the late 1970s (Krugman 1979; 1981) to virtually advocating free trade across the board today (Krugman 1994) seems to be based on this 'special case': when nations trade at the same degree of increasing returns — or at the same degree of imperfect information for that matter — the existence of increasing returns and imperfect information is correctly seen as an additional argument for free trade. This is, however, only a special case — e.g. that of Germany and France trading large cars, or that of the lawyer visiting the doctor: both benefit mutually from the specialization of the other (essentially from the saving of fixed costs and from having better information), and income distribution is not affected. This case — lawyers and doctors exchanging services in activities with the same score on the quality index — we shall refer to as *symmetrical* trade. However, if two nations previously under autarky, both consisting of lawyers and people washing dishes, suddenly open up for trade so that one country specializes in legal matters and the other specializes in washing dishes, we have the case of an *asymmetrical* specialization which will have serious effects on income distribution: one nation will be much richer than before and one will be much poorer. This, in a very simplified form, is what has caused the GNP per capita in Eastern Europe to fall between 30 and 50 per cent in three years. This is what Friedrich List saw happening in France after the fall of Napoleon, and what converted him from being a free trader to being a promoter of industrialization and of the somewhat vague concept of *nationaler Produktivkraft,* normally as ill-defined as the concept of 'competitiveness' today.

The nation at the losing end of this deal, the nation specializing in the activity with no 'historical increasing returns' and no 'industry rent', will be poor. Adam Smith's 'division of labour' is free of distributional effects on income only when all the economic activities created by the division of tasks are 'alike', when they have the same degree of scale effects, imperfect information, barriers to entry, etc. The spectrum of economic activities which surrounds us is clearly extremely divergent in terms of these characteristics, and consequently an increasing division of labour also opens up for increasing divergence of income levels, both inside nations and between nations.

Conclusion: Schumpeterian underdevelopment — policy conclusions past and present

The rediscovery of the effects of increasing returns in new trade theory and new growth theory are made without any reference to the economic thinking and to economic policies of past centuries. The new theories open up for an understanding of uneven growth, but they are hardly translated to practical policy, least of all in the policies of the First World towards the Third World, which is where they would have had the most impact.

The editor of the Papers and Proceedings of the 1993 Annual Meeting of the American Economic Association appropriately heads the section on new trade theory: 'Free Trade: A Loss of (Theoretical) Nerve?' *(American Economic Review* 1993, iv).

One basic reason for this is the unwillingness to test the theoretical models in economics with observable economic facts. The practical relevance of a theoretical economic model is hardly ever tested with actual observations of how the world economy operates. Paul Krugman's 1981 paper, quoted in the previous section, actually contains a relevant description of how international trade creates wealth on one side and poverty on the other. Without knowing it, Krugman rediscovered and mathematized the principal nineteenth-century argument for protection of industry which made his own country rich. This is only one of Krugman's models. Another earlier model is in 'a clever paper on interstellar trade, where goods are transported from one stellar system to another at speeds close to that of light; the resulting relativistic correction to time entails different interest rates in different frames of reference' (Dixit 1993, 173). One of these theories is very important to human welfare; the other is not. As long as verification in the real world is not part of economic modelling — and cleverness and not relevance tends to be a main criterion for success — both these theories are part of what essentially is a purely theoretical intellectual game. On one level, there is nothing wrong with this. Playing simulation games, like chess, is perfectly legitimate. Problems arise only if the general public, in particular those responsible for the economic policy of the Third World, are led to believe that there is any direct relationship between economic modelling and what goes on in the world economy.

Here the laments of Colin Clark, in the foreword to his book *The Conditions of Economic Progress* (Clark 1940, vii–viii) are even more valid now than at the time of his writing:

> I have left the academic world with nothing but regard for the intellectual integrity and public spirit of my former colleagues in the … Universities; but with dismay at their continued preference for the theoretical rather than the scientific approach to economic problems. Not one in a hundred — least of all those who are most anxious to proclaim the scientific nature of Economics — seem to understand what constitutes the scientific approach, namely, the careful systematisation of all observed facts, the framing of hypotheses from these facts, prediction of fresh conclusions on the basis of these hypotheses, and the testing of these conclusions against further observed facts. It would be laughable, were it not tragic, to watch the stream of books and articles, attempting to solve the exceptionally complex problems of present-day economics by theoretical arguments, often without a single reference to the observed facts of the situation. …The hard scientific discipline has yet to be learned, that all theories must be constantly tested and retested against observed facts, and those which prove wrong ruthlessly rejected.

The observed or 'stylized' facts are that an increasing international division of labour is accompanied by an increasing gap in income between poor and wealthy nations, with little movement between the two groups. The same effect is also found within the EU: larger markets require more redistribution. Every year the European Union increases the amount of money flowing through its enormous redistributional machinery, which adds to the redistribution which already absorbs around 50 per cent of GNP — the government sector — in the industrialized nations. Another key stylized fact is that economic welfare seems to be much less a product of the *efficiency* of a nation in its specialization, but much more the product of the *choice* of economic activity. The cases where nations are efficient in their production compared to world 'best practice', but are still poor, I have labelled as cases of Schumpeterian underdevelopment.

The policy implications which slowly emerge from new neoclassical growth theory and new trade theory are in principle not different from those of Serra, Roscher, or the early Marshall, authors writing from 1613 to 1890. These new theories rediscover the essence of mercantilist industrial policy: in a world inhabited by economic activities with different potentials for raising national income, there are optimizing paths. These insights are being used in the industrial policies of the First World, but they are absent from the policy of the First World towards the Second (previously communist) and the Third World, which is where they would have the most effect.

In any country, a mediocre lawyer has a much higher income than the most efficient dishwasher in a restaurant. For a person washing dishes, studying to become a lawyer is an optimizing path, one which will maximize future income compared to a do nothing *(laissez-faire)* option: 'My comparative advantage in society, due to my low wages, is to wash dishes.' A similar situation faces nations stuck in Schumpeterian underdevelopment. Haiti could, instead of exchanging 30 hours of labour producing baseballs for export for one hour of US labour in imported golfballs, optimize national welfare by producing golfballs less efficiently than the US. Even if the US managed to stay ten times as efficient as Haiti producing golfballs, the Haitian would, in terms of balls at today's prices, still be three times as rich under autarky in golfballs than under specialization and free trade. Under autarky in sporting balls, Haiti could improve its position compared to free trade. How would Haiti get the capital? Presumably the same way our law student will: taking up a loan and paying it back from his future 'industry rent'.

In any system with differing degrees of increasing returns and a mixed pattern of collusive and classical distribution of gains from technical progress, some nations will be better off under autarky than under free trade. This is the basic reason why most of the German historical economists, including the dean of the historical school, Werner Sombart, were fundamentally critical of free trade between nations at different levels of development. The Haitian example, far from being a far-fetched theoretical argument, was at the core of the optimizing path embarked upon by the US in the 1820s: the American system of industrial protection, which in a period of less than 100 years made the US into the world's powerhouse.

The economist who, next to Alexander Hamilton, was the spiritual father of the North American protection of industry, Daniel Raymond, compared the situation of individuals to that of nations: 'If an individual can do this, so' may a nation' (Raymond 1820, 115). The core of Raymond's argument was one of optimization: the increased prices paid in the US for industrial products under protection would be more than compensated by the increase in wages, since industrial workers everywhere had so much higher wages than farm labour.[9] In the case of the nineteenth-century US economy, the trade-off between man the consumer and man the producer led to the conclusion that, there and then, free trade was a suboptimal option. Both the Second (former communist) World and the Third present many cases of Schumpeterian underdevelopment where there are similar optimizing paths to be explored. Exploiting these requires more 'theoretical nerve' from economists, and a conscious move into what Colin Clark would have called 'factual and scientific investigations' to complement the theoretical ones which dominate today.

References

American Economic Review, 83 (2), May 1993.

Appel, M. (1992), *Werner Sombart. Theoretiker und Historiker des modernen Kapitalismus*, Marburg: Metropolis.

Augello, M.M. (1990), *Joseph Alois Schumpeter. A Reference Guide*, Berlin: Springer-Verlag.

Babbage, C. (1832), *On the Economy of Machinery and Manufactures*, London: Charles Knight.

Backhaus, J. (1995), *Werner Sombart (1863–1941): Social Scientist*, 3 vols, Marburg: Metropolis.

Bell, S. (1940), *Productivity, Wages, and National Income*, Washington, DC: The Brookings Institution.

Benitez Rojo, A. (1989), *La isla que se repite*, Hanover, New Hampshire: Ediciones del Norte.

Business Week (1994), 'America's New Growth Economy', 16 May.

Clark, C. (1940), *The Conditions of Economic Progress*, London: Macmillan.

Clemente, R.V. (1951), *Essays of J.A. Schumpeter*, Cambridge, Mass.: Addison-Wesley.

Coote, B. (1987), *The Hunger Crop. Poverty and the Sugar Industry*, Oxford: Oxfam.

Dixit, A. (1993), 'In Honor of Paul Krugman: Winner of the John Bates Clark Medal', *Journal of Economic Perspectives*, 7.

Hermann, F.B.W. (1832), *Staatswirtschaftliche Untersuchungen*, Munich: A. Weber.

Hillman, R.S. and D'Agostino, T.J. (1992), *Distant Neighbours in the Caribbean. The Dominican Republic and Jamaica in Comparative Perspective*, New York: Praeger.

Hufeland, G. (1807), *Neue Grundlegung der Staatswirthschaftskunst, durch Prüfung und Berichtigung ihrer Hauptbegriffe van Gut, Werth, Preis, Geld und Volksvermogen mit ununterbrochener Rücksicht auf die bisherigen Systeme*, Giessen and Wetlar: Tasche & Miiller.

King, C. (1721), *The British Merchant or Commerce Preserv'd*, 3 vols, London: John Darby.

Krugman, P. (1979), 'Increasing Returns, Monopolistic Competition, and International Trade', *Journal of International Economics*, 9.

Krugman, P. (1981), 'Trade, Accumulation, and Uneven Development', *Journal of Development Economics*, 8.

Krugman, P. (1994), *Peddling Prosperity. Economic Sense and Nonsense in the Age of Diminished Expectations*, New York: Norton.

Lemoine, M. (1985), *Bitter Sugar*, London: Zed Books.

Lucas, R. (1988), 'On the Mechanisms of Economic Development'. *Journal of Monetary Economics*, 22.

Marshall, A. (1890), *Principles of Economics*, London: Macmillan.

Moulton, H.G. (1935), *Income and Economic Progress*, Washington, DC: The Brookings Institution.

[9] This wage difference is well documented in Clark (1940), where he finds, e.g. that in Norway agricultural wages were only 8 per cent of industrial wages (presumably leaving out the value of room and board).

Nourse, E. and Drury, H. (1938), *Industrial Price Policies and Economic Progress*, Washington, DC: The Brookings Institution.

Ortiz, F. (1940), *Contrapunteo Cubano del Tabaco y el Azúcar*, Havana: Jesus Montero. Second edition: Caracas: Biblioteca Ayacucho, 1978. English translation by H. de Onis (1947), *Cuban Counterpoint. Tobacco and Sugar*, New York: Alfred A. Knopf, with an introduction by Bronoslaw Malinowski.

Raff, D.M.R. (1988), 'Wage Determination Theory and the Five-Dollar Day at Ford', *The Journal of Economic History*, 43.

Raymond, D. (1820), *Thoughts on Political Economy*, Baltimore: Fielding Lucas.

Reinert, ES. (1994), 'Catching-up from way behind: a third world view perspective on first world history', in J. Fagerbcrg et al. (eds), *The Dynamics of Technology, Trade and Growth*, Aldershot: Edward Elgar.

Reinert, ES. (1995), 'Competitiveness and its Predecessors - a 500 year Cross-national Perspective', in *Economic Dynamics and Structural Change*, March.

Robbins, L. (1952), *The Theory of Economic Policy in English Classical Political Economy*, London: Macmillan.

Rochester, A. (1940), *Why Farmers are Poor. The Agricultural Crisis in the United States*, New York: International Publishers.

Romer, RM. (1994), 'The Origins of Endogenous Growth', *Journal of Economic Perspectives*, 8.

Roscher, W. (1854), *Die Grundlagen der Nationalökonomie*, Stuttgart: Cotta.

Roscher, W. (1882), *Principles of Political Economy*, Chicago: Callaghan & Company.

Rosenberg, N. (1976), *Perspectives of Technology*, Cambridge: Cambridge University Press.

Rosenberg, N. (1994), *Exploring the Black Box. Technology, economics, and history*, Cambridge: Cambridge University Press.

Schumpeter, J.A. (1934), *The Theory of Economic Development*, Cambridge, Mass.: Harvard University Press. Original German edition: *Theorie der wirtschaftlichen Entwicklung*, Berlin: Duncker & Humblot, 1912.

Schumpeter, J.A. (1942), *Capital, Socialism, and Democracy*, New York: Harper.

Serra, A. (1613), *Breve trattato delle cause che possono far abbondare li regni d'oro e argento dove non sono miniere*, Napoli: Lazzaro Scoriggio.

Singer, H. (1949), 'The Distribution of Gains between Investing and Borrowing Countries', reproduced in Singer (1964).

Singer, H. (1964), *International Development. Growth and Change*, New York: McGraw-Hill.

Streissler, E.W. (1994), 'Increasing Returns and the Prospects of Small-scale Enterprise', paper presented at the Sixth Annual Heilbronn Symposium in Economics and the Social Sciences, 'Wilhelm Roscher (1817–1894). A Centenary Reappraisal', June 1994.

The Economist (1985), 'Enslaved by Subsidies', 10 August.

Tribe, K. (1988), *Governing Economy. The Reformation of German Economic Discourse 1750–1840*, Cambridge: Cambridge University Press.

Ure, A. (1835), *The Philosophy of Manufactures, or, an exposition of the scientific, moral, and commercial economy of the factory system of Great Britain*, London: Charles Knight.

Verspagen, B. (1992), 'Endogenous Innovation in Neo-classical Growth Models: A Survey', *Journal of Macroeconomics*, 14.

Vethake, H. (1844), *Principles of Political Economy*, 2nd edn, Philadelphia: J.W. Moore.

von Hörnigk, W. (1684), *Österreich über alles wann es nur will*, Nürnberg: n.p.

Whatley, G. (1774), *Principles of trade. Freedom and protection are its best suport. Industry, the only means to render manufactures cheap*, London: Brotherton and Sewell.

Chapter Fifteen

TOWARDS AN AUSTRO–GERMAN THEORY OF UNEVEN ECONOMIC DEVELOPMENT? A PLEA FOR THEORISING BY INCLUSION

Erik S. Reinert

Abstract

Based on Meir Kohn's distinction between research programmes based on 'value' and 'exchange' (2004), this paper argues for a 'production' paradigm based on the tradition of Menger and Schumpeter. It is suggested that this production-based programme could use, as its starting point, Schumpeter's (Wesen und Hauptinhalt der theoretischen Nationalökonomie, 1908) attempt to mediate in the *Methodenstreit* by arguing that different types of economic problems require theories at different levels of abstraction. This opens up for 'theorising by inclusion', an approach combining key elements both of traditional German economics and of Austrian economics in the Mengerian tradition.

Keywords Uneven economic development. Mengerian–Schumpeterian economics. Production-based economics

JEL codes B4. B5 . O1

1 Introduction

Meir Kohn's thoughtful and thought-provoking essay on the impasse of mainstream economic theory – in particular, the fact that 'on the great issues of today, it has been virtually silent' (Kohn 2004, p 306) – highlights the need for alternative approaches. Kohn himself identifies two alternative paradigms, one based on 'value' (Walrasian) and one based on 'exchange' (Mengerian). This paper adds to the discussion by introducing a third category – which very well may be considered a version of the Mengerian one – a paradigm based on 'production'. This paradigm emphasises the

Menger–Schumpeter line of Austrian thought, while at the same time retaining key features of the German economics tradition as it relates to the understanding of uneven economic development (Reinert 2005a). I have previously argued that the Menger–Schumpeter line of Austrian thought also retained key features of traditional German economics, in particular the core importance of context-specificity and history (Reinert 2005b). This paper is, then, an attempt to reconcile the two sides of the late 19th century *Methodenstreit*, in particular, as the two sides of this debate coincide in sharp contrast to the Walrasian paradigm and to the Hicks–Samuelson research programme. This, I feel, is also very much in the spirit of Schumpeter's first book (Schumpeter 1908); the one which still has no English translation.

This approach would create an Austro–German evolutionary economic approach to the problems of Third World development, based on production rather than on value or exchange. Here, the clues to the problems of economic development would be found by studying differences in the structures and systems of production. I find the Austro–German label particularly fitting also because of the solid German roots – in Werner Sombart and Friedrich Nietzsche – of Schumpeter's production-based *creative destruction* so much in vogue today (Reinert and Reinert 2006). I will attempt to show that this approach can be compatible with, and enriched by, insights and elements from pre-Smithian economics, from the history of economic policy, and from classical development economics (post-World War II). This is particularly important when policy recommendations are introduced into new contexts where institutions and circumstances that can be taken for granted in the First World are not necessarily present. The paper argues that a dynamic theory of economic change requires that all neo-classical assumptions be relaxed at the same time, while re-introducing the many factors that used to be recognised long ago as contributing to the unevenness of economic development.

Sometimes, new approaches are stifled by the mainstream's ability to usurp and absorb them, while at the same time neutralising their most novel aspects. Keynesian economics was one example of this. 'New institutional economics' is another. This approach became neo-classical economics with some static institutions (mainly property rights) added, which is a very different type of theory from a much broader 'old' institutional school tracing its roots back to Thorstein Veblen[1]. As I see it, there is presently a risk of a similar development within evolutionary economics that a 'new' evolutionary theory is created consisting essentially of standard economics with an added 'Schumpeterian' variable. This risk of blending neo-classical and evolutionary elements is evident today in the European Union. The Lisbon Strategy – in its conception, an evolutionary theory – is increasingly becoming a Schumpeterian icing on a solidly neo-classical cake. The same danger is present when applying evolutionary theories in the Third World, where – in its simplest form – we risk that 'evolutionary economics' is created by substituting 'investment' for 'innovation' in an otherwise standard neo-classical approach. I suggest here going in another direction: that a

1 For a discussion of institutions in this perspective, see Reinert (2006).

series of old insights – particularly as these are brought together systemically – are both useful and necessary to complement present approaches. As I see it, by bringing in underlying technological elements, evolutionary economics may sometimes even reinforce old arguments and explain why both mercantilists and classical development economists were often right. This will be illustrated by a discussion by Schumpeter's student Hans Singer's seminal article (Singer 1950) below. This paper attempts to map the most important of these factors which, alone and cumulatively, add to the complexities of Austro–German development economics.

2 Economics as theorising by exclusion

'Zuerst war die Ganzheit'; 'in the beginning there was the totality': This is a typical statement from the German historical tradition in economics. This wish to embrace and qualitatively understand 'the whole' necessarily yields a large toolbox for the profession and, on the other hand, not a very abstract theory. 'The economy as a whole' (*Das Gesamtbild der Volkswirtschaft*) is also the title of the last chapter of Joseph Schumpeter's *Theory of Economic Development* (Schumpeter 1912), the chapter he left out of all subsequent editions and translations, arguably to anglo-saxonise his theory when embarking on a career in the USA[2]. Economics, Schumpeter says, presents us with an eternal trade-off of accuracy vs relevance: 'We must make up our minds whether we want *simple* answers to our questions or *useful* ones – in economic matters we cannot have both'.[3] As a very young man, Schumpeter's Salomonic solution to the fierce *Methodenstreit* of the economics profession was to have theories at various levels of abstraction, and then go into the theory at a level of abstraction where one is likely to find an answer to the question at hand (Schumpeter 1908). A main contention of this paper is that today's standard economics operates at a level of abstraction that is too high to capture key factors responsible for uneven development. Patching this up by adding a 'Schumpeterian' variable is not possible. 'The whole' must be considered.

Until the mid-18th century, the trade-off between accuracy and relevance was generally solved by using holistic theories favouring relevance rather than abstraction. Although the writers all considered their field a 'science', compared to the present situation one could almost call these pre-disciplinary approaches. Whatever was relevant was part of the theory. As an example: to the extent that malnutrition affects economic performance, nutrition is part of economics. Early attempts at reaching higher levels of abstraction through the use of mathematics – by Italian 18th century economists – were rapidly abandoned because, as mathematician Ignazio Radicati warned his economist friends in 1752, 'You will do with political economy what the scholastics did with philosophy. In making things more and more subtle, you do not know where to stop' (Tubaro 2000, p 15; S. Reinert 2005).

2 The chapter is both reproduced in German and translated into English in Backhaus (2003).

3 Schumpeter in the foreword to Zeuthen (1930).

When, with Adam Smith and later with David Ricardo, economics increased its level of abstraction, this was done at the cost of excluding a number of factors that were integral parts of economics in the 1750s: the importance of synergies and of balancing different economic activities in a country, institutions, the role of increasing returns combined with a large division of labour, the role of innovations and technical change [for example, Francis Bacon[4], Cary (1695), and Steuart (1767)], and the fact that economic activities are qualitatively different as carriers of economic growth. For most of the history of the profession, these are all factors that have been seen as important in explaining why economic development is such an uneven process. Achieving a higher degree of abstraction was made at the cost of reducing complexity and excluding variables. In economics, this is a process which moves back and forth over time almost as 'fashions'. It is possible to see the history of economic thought as consisting of long and almost monotonous sequences of the same economic factors entering the theory, later to be thrown out, and later to be included again: Increasing returns as an economic factor were described by the Greeks and codified into a theory of uneven growth by Antonio Serra in 1613, forgotten but resurrected in Italy in the 1750s, abandoned again by Smith and Ricardo, only to be rediscovered by German economists in the 1840s and 1850s, kept by Alfred Marshall[5], formally developed by US economist Graham (1923), thrown out again by Jacob Viner in the 1930s on the account that it was incompatible with equilibrium, reintroduced by Paul Krugman in the 1980s, and its importance again dismissed by Jagdish Bhagwati as Krugman's 'youthful surrender to irrational exuberance' (Bhagwati 2002, p 22).

The guiding insight of French philosopher Jacques Derrida's deconstruction is highly relevant to economics: every structure – be it literary, psychological, social, economic, political or religious – that organises our experience is constituted and maintained through such acts of exclusion. In the process of creating something, something else inevitably gets left out. These exclusive structures can become repressive – and that repression comes with consequences. In a manner reminiscent of Freud, Derrida insists that what is repressed does not disappear but always returns to unsettle every construction, no matter how secure it seems (Taylor 2004). We suggest that a 'new and improved' development economics must keep Derrida's caveat in mind. Over the last years, the immense economic and political weight of The Washington Institutions have created a series of single-issue fads, factors that – added to standard economics – shall solve the problems of poverty: institutions, property rights, 'competitiveness', governance, and so forth.[6] Care should be taken that 'innovation' does not become yet another buzzword with which neo-classical economics is kept alive by adding new factors in the margin. My suggestion for creating an evolutionary development economics requires an inclusive approach where long-existent and still relevant notions would be re-introduced in the

4 For a discussion on the introduction of the concept of innovation into the social sciences, see Reinert and Daastøl (1997).

5 See, particularly, Marshall (1890, p 201) for a policy statement.

6 This is discussed in the foreword to Reinert (2004a).

theoretical structure. I have referred to this alternative type of economics as The Other Canon (Reinert 2004a).[7]

3 A study in the history of theorising by inclusion: why economic development requires 'manufacturing'

From the point of view of the Third World, the most salient feature of standard economics since Adam Smith is probably that a theory of the international economy as a harmony-making machinery has been constructed. This was achieved at the time of Adam Smith mainly by introducing two fundamental changes in the way economic theory was built, effectively through the exclusion of factors that previously had been deemed important for economic growth. Successful catching up – from that of the United States and Continental Europe to East Asia – has therefore all retained key elements of pre-Smithian economics: among them insisting not to join the world economy fully until industrialisation had been achieved. In this section, I shall look at how the understanding of the need for manufacturing for development has evolved over time, and suggest how evolutionary economics can improve this very long sequence of analysis.

The fundamental changes introduced by Adam Smith to economics were:

1. From Emperor Justinian's codification of Roman Law around AD 400 until Adam Smith, the metaphor for human society had been the *human body*, with its diversity, synergies and division of labour (Reinert and Reinert 2005). Starting with Adam Smith, physics-based metaphors have dominated economics, leading both to methodological individualism (the exclusion of society as such as a unit of analysis) and an underlying 'equality assumption' in the profession (Buchanan 1979), leaving out the diversities, complexities and synergies of real life that, in the end, contribute decisively to making the process of economic growth, by its very nature, a very uneven process.
2. Adam Smith unified 'production' and 'trade' into 'labour hours' (Biernacki 1995). As a result of this, economics abdicated from studying the complexities and vicissitudes inherent in the world of production, and – with David Ricardo – trade theory could consequently be reduced to an exercise in bartering of labour hours. These labour hours and the theory itself are void of any qualitative attributes of understanding of production (skills, innovations, learning, increasing and diminishing returns, technology, and so forth).[8] Human knowledge, wit and will were excluded from economics and the profession came to focus on the *accumulation of capital* rather than on the *diffusion of knowledge* (Nelson 2006).

---

7 http://www.othercanon.org

8 Technology continued to play an important role in the Continental European and, particularly, German economic tradition continuously through Marx and Schumpeter. Economics professor Johann Beckmann published his seminal work on technology the year after Smith's *Wealth of Nations* (Beckmann 1777). For an overview of this tradition, see Reinert (2005a).

It is interesting to note that the theoretical insights that point to wealth as a product of *systemic factors* – as in today's National Systems of Innovation approach – are among the oldest of the important economic insights. This view was 'mainstream' from the 1200s, with Florentine chancellor Brunetto Latini (ca.1210–1294) and his concept of wealth being a result of a *ben comune*, a *common weale* (Baron 1966; Latini 1993).[9] However, as physics-based metaphors came to dominate economics, such systemic elements tended to disappear because theory lost the tools with which to handle them.

However, the most serious consequence of the adoption of physics-based models in economics was the creation of the 'equality assumption';[10] abandoning the common sense notion that not all activities are qualitatively alike as promoters of growth and development. As a consequence, the whole debate on increasing and diminishing returns was silenced, although these clearly are at the core of the vicious and virtuous cumulative effects in economics. The elegance of economics was achieved at the price of ignoring the different conditions and contexts in which wealth creation takes place, and with it, some of the most crucial insights of the mechanisms that cause wealth and poverty were lost. In the same century when humanity created order in our world through taxonomic systems – that of Linnaeus being the most famous – Adam Smith gave birth to an equality assumption that rid economics of all taxonomies. The irony in this is that England's own economic policy was based on a simple taxonomy: 'buy raw materials, sell manufactured goods', a formula which, as Friedrich List acutely observed, for centuries took the place of a whole economic theory in England.[11]

Diminishing returns has been with us as an economic fact and factor since the Bible, where it explains why Abraham and Lot parted because 'the land was not able to bear them that they might dwell together' (*Genesis* 12: 6). Diminishing returns happens when, at some point, each additional labourer will add relatively less output than his/her predecessor did because he/she has less and less of the fixed amount of land to work with and/or when more marginal land has to be brought into production.[12] Antonio Serra, whom Schumpeter names 'the first to write a scientific treatise in economics', explained the increasing gap between the wealth of Venice and the poverty of Naples by juxtaposing the increasing returns, falling costs, increasing 'barriers to entry', and increasing standard of living in Venice with the poverty of Naples' production of raw materials where diminishing returns produced an opposite effect (Reinert and Reinert 2003). Although diminishing returns are counteracted by technological change, in deindustrialised countries, population pressures combined with diminishing returns to this very day can produce disasters of almost biblical proportions.[13]

---

9 When Machiavelli, 300 years later, explains why cities are rich, he echoes Latini: *il ben comune* fa grandi le città (Reinert and Daastøl 1997).

10 See James Buchanan's chapter on 'Equality as Fact and Norm' (Buchanan 1979, pp 231–252).

11 In the foreword to List (1841). I have not found this observation in the English translation.

12 Genuine diminishing returns are only found in economic activities where one factor of production has been 'produced' by nature, in agriculture, mining or fisheries. In other activities, all factors of production are essentially expandable at the same or better quality.

13 See Reinert (2004b) for a case study of such developments in Mongolia. See also Reinert (1996b).

Although conceptually clearly separable, Schumpeter noted the difficulty of separating increasing returns and technical change in practice. Because Henry Ford's production technology was not available in the scale previously employed in car production, it was impossible to separate the effects of the two factors. Schumpeter therefore coined the term *historical increasing returns* to cover both phenomena (Schumpeter 1996, p 263).[14] This insight is even more important today, when the growth of intangibles, services and intellectual value added have become such a major feature of the so-called knowledge society. At the same time, the process of segmentation and differentiation in manufacturing markets, as the total market grows, creates scale and barriers to entry in smaller and smaller niches. Some types of agricultural production may acquire characteristics that were previously associated with manufacturing, while some manufactured goods may behave more like commodities (although with constant rather than diminishing returns). This development blurs the traditional distinctions between sectors.

Nevertheless, in both cases – the growth of intangible value and the differentiation processes – a key question remains whether the fruits of production can be retained thanks to having control over the sources of productivity and the prices to market. This traditionally happened in manufacturing through having control of technical change and through the barriers to entry created by increasing returns.

A key insight from classical development economics was Hans Singer's seminal paper discussing how the fruits of technological change spread differently in the manufacturing industry of the First World and in the raw materials production of the Third World (Singer 1950). This was an important part of the Prebisch–Singer thesis, which contained important discussions of technology and development that, at the time, were obliterated by the general preoccupation with the terms of trade.

Evolutionary economics potentially brings new insights to the terms of trade debate and the Prebisch–Singer thesis of classical development economics. This thesis is based on the idea that developing countries' terms of trade are determined by asymmetries in the operation of the labour markets in the country of the centre and of the periphery (Ocampo and Parra 2006, p 169). Evolutionary economics may, in fact, move this analysis one step further back, by analysing the technological variables – such as product and process innovations – that contribute to the asymmetries in the labour markets. In commodity agriculture, the fact that the sources of innovation tended to be outside the sector itself – in Ford's tractor factory or in Monsanto's seed factory – coupled with the low barriers to entry, diminishing returns, climatic volatility and perfect competition together explain why agriculture has failed to retain the fruits of technical change. A proper analysis of technological change will, in many ways, be able to supplement and enrich the explanations as to why the perceived differences between 'manufacturing' and 'agriculture' actually came about.

Table 15.1 puts together this historical process of trying to understand the sources of wealth and prosperity of nations by understanding the contrast between manufacturing and agriculture, the city and the countryside, the self-propelled growth of technology-intensive activities under increasing returns and the constricted potential for wealth creation of land restrained commodity production under diminishing returns. These

[14] Schumpeter attributes this insight to Scottish economist Anderson (1777).

Table 15.1 Theorising by Inclusion: The Qualitative Differences Between Manufacturing and Agriculture as Perceived Over Time as *Ideal Types* or *Stylised Facts*

'Manufacturing'	'Agriculture'
Generalised wealth only found in cities with artisans and manufacturing, and explained as a systemic effect: *il ben comune* (Florence, 1200s)	Traditionally very little systemic effects, no *ben commune* (common weale)
The experience of 1500s Spain: The real gold mines are the manufacturing industries because the gold from the Americas ends up in the manufacturing cities outside Spain (generalised knowledge, 1600s)	The experience of 1500s Spain: de-industrialisation and return to agriculture creates increased poverty: a nation is better off with a relatively ineffective manufacturing sector than with none
Windows of opportunity for innovation concentrated in few activities (all urban: Botero 1589) (Perez and Soete 1988)	Few windows of opportunity for innovation (until very recent history)
Generalised wealth caused by a large diversity/large division of labour/maximising the number of professions (Serra 1613)	Traditionally only a minimum of diversity and very little division of labour
International specialisation leads to increasing returns/economies of scale, producing falling costs, barriers to entry and higher profits (Serra 1613)	Specialisation will meet the flexible wall of diminishing returns and increasing costs/falling productivity (from the Bible's Genesis to Ricardo and John Stuart Mill)
Increased population a necessity to create scale/markets for manufactures (European pre-Malthusian population theory)	Increased population a problem because of diminishing returns and no new land (Malthus)
Important synergies between city and countryside: Only farmers near manufacturing cities produce efficiently (Europe 1700s to George Marshall 1947)	Only farmers who share a labour market with manufacturing activities are wealthy: market for products, market for excess labour, access to technology (USA/Europe 1800s)
Export of manufactured goods and import of raw materials, but also exchanging manufactures for other manufactures, is 'good trade' for a nation (King 1721)[a]	Export of raw materials and import of manufactured goods is 'bad trade' for a nation (King 1721)
Dynamic imperfect competition	Perfect competition (*commodity competition*)
Activities with high growth in demand as income grows/Verdoorn's law ties increase in demand to increase in productivity	Activities with low income elasticity of demand
Subject to 'productivity explosions' since the 1400s	Slow growth in productivity until after World War II
Stable production that can be fine-tuned to demand. Overproduction avoided by storing raw materials and semi-manufactures	Cyclical production/overproduction (no possibility of storing semi-manufactures)
Stable prices	Large price fluctuations. Timing of sales often more important for income than production skills

'Manufacturing'	'Agriculture'
Creates a middle class and conditions for democracy ('city air makes free')	Generally creates a feudal class structure
Creates bargaining power for labour and irreversible wages: 'stickiness' of wages in money	Reversible wages and payment in kind
Dominated by product innovations which, when products mature, turn to process innovations	Dominated by process innovations, product innovations for agriculture are made outside the agricultural sector (Ford's tractors, Monsanto's seeds, biotechnology)
Technological change leads to higher wages, profits and taxes in the producing countries ('a Fordist wage regime')	Technological change leads mainly to lower prices in the consuming countries (Singer 1950)
Terms of trade tend to improve over time compared to agriculture	Terms of trade tend to deteriorate over time compared to industrial products
Creates large synergies (linkages, clusters)	Creates few synergies

a If we assume that manufactures are produced under increasing returns and raw materials under diminishing returns, this is perfectly compatible with Krugman's new trade theory (Krugman 1990)

elements work together cumulatively creating both path dependence and lock-in effects (Arthur 1989, 1994).

It is important to keep in mind that it is not manufacturing per se and agriculture per se that produce these effects, but a bundle of characteristics that for centuries – and with reasonable accuracy – have been perceived as typical of the two types of economic activities.[15] Today, there are many manufacturing segments and types of services that live under constant returns to scale, few barriers to entry and almost under commodity competition. On the other hand, there are both knowledge-intensive services and some niches in agriculture that can behave like high-tech manufactures. Therefore, the insights and the understanding of the contrast between manufacturing and agriculture still hold, as long as one keeps in mind who has the levers of productivity and pricing as growth proceeds.

It must also be emphasised that, at the time, great care was generally taken to differentiate purely administrative cities – like Madrid or Naples – from the manufacturing cities like Milan or Venice. It was the typical urban activities – subject to increasing returns and a great division of labour in synergy – that created wealth, not the agglomeration of people per se. How the benefits from innovation spread is a key question for evolutionary development economics today.

To understand wealth and poverty outside the already industrialised First World, it is necessary to go beyond the promotion of innovation per se to understand in which cases innovation benefits the producing country or the consuming country or both. Evolutionary economics has, as I see it, not paid sufficient attention to how different

[15] The discussion of 'good' and 'bad' trade in the 1700s is a particularly sophisticated version of this type of analysis (King 1721; Reinert and Reinert 2005)

types of innovations affect different businesses. For example, information technology creates very different results around Microsoft's headquarters in Seattle than what the same information technology does in the hotel industry in Venice or on the Costa del Sol. In the hotel business, as well as in the used book business across Europe, new technology has caused more perfect information that leads to falling margins and increased downward pressures on wages and profits. If we use the standard definition of the term 'competitiveness' – its ability to create higher real wages – recent innovations in these industries, seen in isolation, have caused *decreased* rather than *increased* competitiveness. Innovations have made people in those activities poorer.[16] Innovations may also create pressures towards de-skilling, as when the fast food industry created new cash registers that could be operated by illiterate workers.

Although it is well known in innovation economics that product innovations and process innovations often have different effects on employment (see Vivarelli and Pianta 2000; Reinert 2000; Pianta 2005), not enough emphasis has been given to the fact that innovations actually may reduce the realised value added in certain industries and geographic areas. When extending innovation economics to the Third World, these types of considerations become much more important than they are in the First World.

Perez (2002) considers that each major technological revolution has two complementary but very different aspects: (a) a cluster of new basic innovations creating distinct dynamic inter-related industries and (b) a techno-economic paradigm that defines the way in which these new generic technologies will transform how the other activities in the economy will go about their businesses in the most effective and efficient manner. Figure 15.1 illustrates these two aspects of paradigm shifts.

The two aspects of the paradigm shift explain two very different types of innovations. The paradigm carrying industries generally produce *product innovations* that create dynamic imperfect competition. In the rest of the economy, the paradigm shift tends to produce *process innovations* that either do not shift the degree of imperfect competition or – as in the case of the airline industry – may unleash a price and productivity competition that will benefit consumers rather than producers. Such innovations may produce lower rather than higher monetary wages in the industry affected, but will result in higher *real* wages for the people consuming their services. Should one group of nations specialise in product innovations while the other specialises in process innovations, the standard of living is very likely to rise much faster in the *product-innovating* compared to the *process-innovating* country, where it might actually fall.

The increased wealth produced by innovations may reach us in two different ways, either through increased monetary wages or through lowered prices for what we consume. To the classical economists, productivity improvements would show up in the economy as lowered prices for the goods that experienced these improvements (Smith 1976, p 269; Ricardo 1817, pp 46–47).

---

[16] It may be argued that those hotels that transformed their offer into a special niche product through service innovations and segment differentiation may have escaped this fate. However, the essential point holds for the great majority, which obviously encompasses the majority of those employed in the sector.

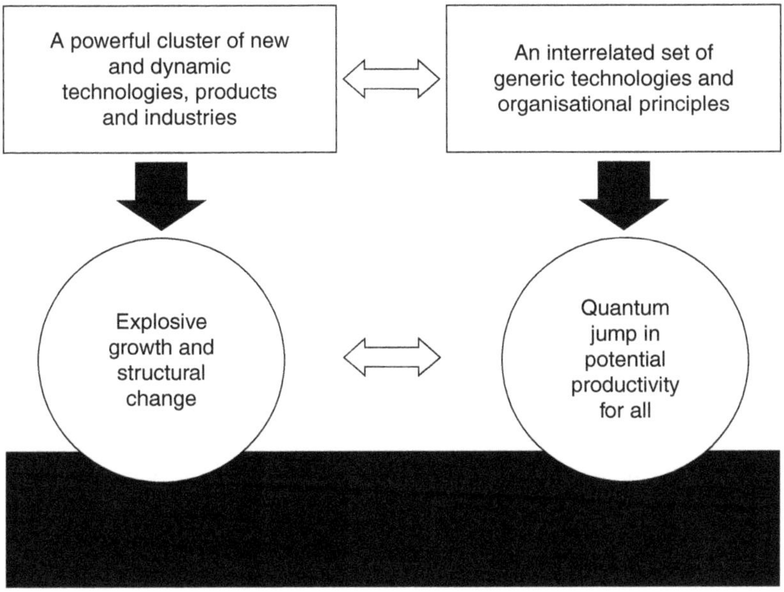

Figure 15.1 The Two main Aspects of a Techno-economic Paradigm Shift.
Source: Carlota Perez.

At the time of Smith and Ricardo, the gold standard facilitated the result they predicted. In a closed economy, holding velocity of circulation constant, the increase of goods in the economy resulting from technological progress would chase only the same amount of bullion. Prices *would have to fall*. Rapid technological progress would therefore lead to deflation – which it, in fact, often did until the gold standard was abolished.

Once without the gold standard, people in the industrialised countries got rich in a different way. Instead of seeing the price of industrial goods fall, they now saw their monetary income rise in *nominal* terms. Previously, deflation had caused awkward social problems: it was difficult to convince people who had to take continuous pay cuts that, in spite of these pay cuts, they were still getting richer because the price of the goods they purchased fell at an even faster rate than their wages. From the point of view of the industrialised nations, the monetary policy that followed after abolishing the gold standard was a more sensible one: money supply kept rising with the amount of goods in the economy, or slightly faster, creating a small inflation which seems to have served to lubricate the machinery of development. Now the producer in an activity not exhibiting productivity improvements – for example, the barber – got rich by raising his/her prices at the rate that everybody else had their salaries raised, not only by having the price of manufactured goods lowered.

A monetary policy that increased supply at par with productivity improvements not only prevented deflation, combined with the new-won power of labour unions, it made possible what the French regulation school calls 'Fordist wage regime': the regime which dominated wage formation in all the developed world, particularly after World War II, where it was accepted that nominal wages to industrial workers would roughly correspond to the productivity increases in industry. This was the underlying cause of the asymmetry in the labour markets in Singer's analysis. This Fordist wage regime could not be copied in the Third World because these countries generally failed to have the market power required to achieve this effect, created as it was by the First World 'countervailing powers' of imperfect oligopoly competition of industry and labour union power. This mechanism increased the wage differential between the First and the Third World significantly during most of the twentieth century.

A previous paper (Reinert 1994) elaborates a number of factors which determine whether innovations and productivity improvements spread in the economy as lower prices to the consumers (which I call a 'classical' spread[17]) or as higher prices to the producers (a 'collusive' spread). When bringing evolutionary economics to the Third World, this type of analysis is, in my view, crucial, particularly because what little there was of a Fordist wage regime in the Third World has now completely broken down. This is shown dramatically by the percentage of wages and salaries falling rapidly as a percentage of GDP in most Third World countries. While wages and salaries constitute close to 70% of GDP in Norway, in Peru this percentage had dropped to around 23% in 1990 when the statistical office stopped calculating this figure.

Adding the technology element brings new perspectives to the terms of trade debate. History shows that the terms of trade *do not* move against the industrialised countries with the most technology-intensive production. If the terms of trade – the relationship between the relative prices of exports and imports – remain unchanged over time, this must mean in practice that, on the average, every nation can 'pocket' its own average productivity improvements in the form of higher welfare. Faced with a large diversity between economic activities, a world with fixed terms of trade would bring with it a new logic. If the potential – the windows of opportunity – for productivity improvements are much higher in some economic activities than in others, national welfare may be increased by imposing an import duty on the product with the high-productivity potential. This would make it possible to capture what we could call a Schumpeterian rent. This argument becomes even stronger if the presence of the high-tech industries, their high wages, their potential for creating jobs, the markets and the technologies they bring with them are each and all a necessity to create an efficient agricultural sector (as was accepted common sense in the 18th and 19th centuries).

Schumpeterian economics also bring new perspectives on colonialism. From an innovation economics point of view, colonialism was – and is – in its very essence a technology policy. In 1729, English economist Joshua Gee described 'Colonialism 101' in a nutshell:

> That all Negroes shall be prohibited from weaving either Linnen or Woollen, or spinning or combing of Wooll, or working at any Manufacture of Iron, further than making it into Pig or Bar iron: That they be also prohibited from manufacturing of Hats, Stockings, or Leather of any Kind...Indeed, if they set up Manufactures, and the Government afterwards shall be

[17] Because this is the effect assumed by classical economists Smith and Ricardo.

> under a Necessity of stopping their Progress, we must not expect that it will be done with the same Ease that now it may.[18]

Colonialism made the metropolitan country benefit doubly from technological change. On the one hand, the colonial power pockets the fruits from technological change at home through the Fordist wage regime, a *collusive* spread of the fruits of technological change. On the other hand, the colonial power also benefits from the productivity improvements in the colonies because the fruits of the improvements hit the mother country as lowered prices (*classical* spread). Technologically, the colonial power wins doubly while the colony loses doubly. The transfer of technological dead-ends, bereft of any scale effects, to poor countries (*maquila*-type industries) is a variant of the same system.[19] Once the world has been divided into a high-wage area and a low-wage area, the market logic will automatically assign the technological dead-ends to the poor.

4 Increased poverty as the result of the break-down of the Fordist wage regime

High wages in a country are the result of combined effects of technological change and Schumpeterian imperfect competition, of market power exercised both by industry and labour unions under technical change. This increases both wages and purchasing power, which feeds back to more growth in a virtuous circle aided by Schumpeter's historical increasing returns. A core problem of standard economics and of the economics of the Washington Institutions is that they see 'perfect competition' as a goal, not realising what every businessman knows, that perfect competition is a formula for not making money and not being able to pay high wages. The havoc created in the world coffee market is just one example of how the Washington Institutions have produced a race to the bottom. This section will look at some of the mechanisms that made this race almost the only game in town.

What we call 'development' is, in a sense, a gigantic Schumpeterian rent which a relatively small percentage of the world population has achieved. It is not understood that today's policies may lead into a depression spiral built up through the cumulative interaction of falling wages and falling demand into a 'classical' overproduction crisis of the capitalist system. The 2.5 billion Chinese and Indians – rapidly upgrading technologically but less in wages – added to the global labour market only fuel these pressures. Why do economists seem to assume that the famous factor–price equalisation should be upwards? More perfect competition in labour markets would make it most likely that factor–price equalisation will be *downwards*. Both the United States and core European Union countries are experiencing falling real wages (often through longer hours for the same pay) in Europe for the first time since the 1930s.

The break-down of the Fordist wage regime is clearly an important element in the vicious circles of faltering demand and jobless growth in many Third World countries

[18] Quoted in Reinert and Reinert (2005).

[19] I have referred to this as Schumpeterian Underdevelopment (Reinert 1996a).

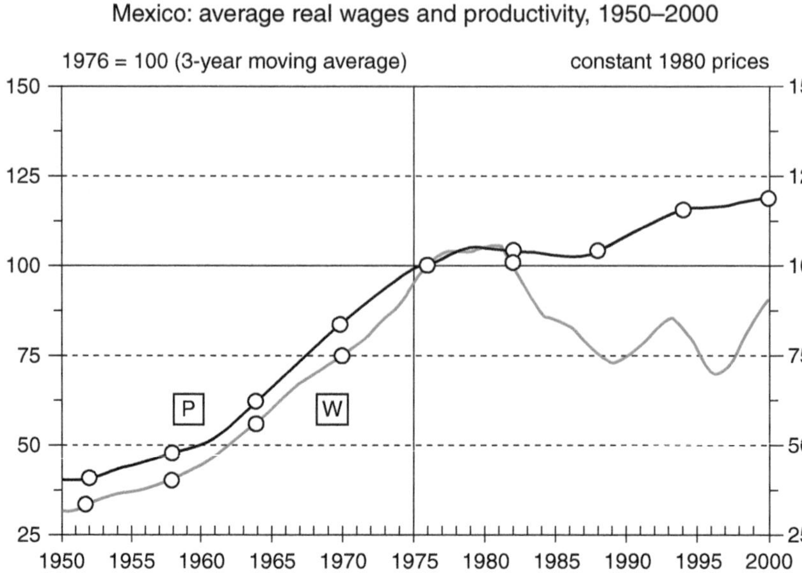

Figure 15.2 The Break-down of the Fordist Wage Regime: the Case of Mexico.
Source: Palma (2002).

(Cimoli et al. 2005). The world is shifting to a 'classical' form of distribution of the gains from technological change, which means that rich countries will get richer through cheaper imports and improving terms of trade while poor countries see their exports rise while their real wages fall.

Import substation policies in Latin America brought with it elements of the Fordist wage regime. In fact, real wages in most Latin American countries where I have had access to data peak some time in the 1970s. Freer trade at the wrong time did not necessarily bring with it a lowering of GDP, but it did bring with it falling real wages and salaries for the common folk. The percentage of GDP 'reserved' for wages, which English classical economists thought was fixed for eternity at a very low level (the wage fund doctrine), collapsed, as discussed above. Figure 15.2 shows how the Fordist wage regime collapsed in Mexico in the late 1970s; wages and productivity split up: productivity continues up while wages fall. The resulting lack of demand is a key element in the 'jobless growth' that followed through what is called 'the lost decades' in Latin America. Falling real wages prevent the growth of the high end of the service sector, which is so important in the developed world.

Figure 15.3 shows a similar development in Peru, but focusing on exports and wages. The export figures show a resounding success, which is combined with falling real wages and, in most years, with a big trade deficit. The global economy has crated a system that maximises international trade (and accompanying transportation costs and pollution) while decreasing the real wages of a majority of the population in many countries. Wages and salaries compose a sharply falling percentage of national GDP. The finance,

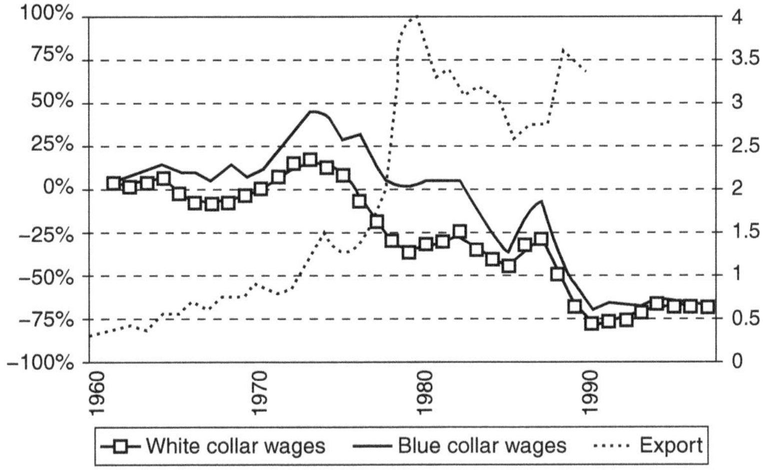

Figure 15.3 Peru 1960–1990: Diverging Paths of Real Wages and Exports. The Export Figures are in Current US Dollars, Exaggerating the Visual Effect.

insurance and real estate sector appropriates not only all that is registered as economic growth, but also an increasing share of what used to go to wages and salaries. We have established a type of winner-take-all globalisation (Frank and Cook 1995).

An increased focus on innovation alone will not solve these structural problems. If the fruits of innovation all go to the customers abroad, a poor nation must look for other alternatives where it is possible to create a 'collusive' distribution of technology rents. The long list of arguments in Table 15.1 will still prove to be valid, adapted to today's context.

5 Conclusion – creating an Austro-German development economics

'He who heals is right' goes an old saying in medicine. This paper has made a plea for returning to the type of analysis that has successfully 'healed' poverty and created wealth from 15th century England to Korea in the 1970s. In this tradition, economic development is *activity-specific*, tied to certain economic activities exhibiting high-productivity growth and increasing returns in a synergetic system formed by the presence of a large division of labour (Reinert 1994), in short, what German economist Werner Sombart called 'the industrial system'. That only the presence of such an industrial system will create efficient agriculture was a key insight of the 1700s. Historically, successful processes of catching-up have created copies of the economic structures dominating in the wealthy countries at any time; that is the same balance between manufacturing and agriculture and the same paradigm-carrying industries. Initially, for a variety of reasons, these copies are necessarily less efficient than the original economic structure they try to emulate and, therefore, need some form of targeting and protection.

Werner Sombart defined capitalism as consisting of (1) *the entrepreneur*, (2) *the modern state*, and (3) *the industrial system* (Sombart 1928). By this definition, the production system of the colonies was never capitalism. As we have argued, from an evolutionary point of view, colonialism was, for centuries, in effect, a technology policy aimed at keeping industrial dynamics out of the colonies. Today's world order has kept a similar pattern, with the new element that some manufacturing industries with little technological change and void of scale effects are farmed out to poor countries (*maquila*-type assembly activities). Changing this centuries-old path-dependence will require strong policies.

The economics of innovation today brings together elements describing what Sombart calls *the industrial system*, a system similar to what Friedrich List in 1841 called the *national system of political economy*, what we today would call national innovation systems, associated with the names of Christopher Freeman, Bengt-Åke Lundvall and Richard Nelson. As has been pointed out (Lundvall et al. 2002, p 226), one of the greatest challenges facing this body of theory is that much of the work done on national systems of innovation is post facto, in the sense that most research is done on systems that are already mature, already diversified and successful. Theories and concepts that work wonders in countries with an industrial tradition dating back centuries, may, however, become much less productive – if not downright destructive – in the context of developing countries unless filtered through a historical lens.

In this paper, I have argued that a necessary part of the solution to this problem lies in the introduction of a number of factors, some of which have been part of the economic discourse for centuries, but also elements (like the different effects of process and product innovations) that are part of evolutionary economics itself, but which will be much more central to a Third World discourse. To create a qualitative understanding of the factors polarising the world in growing wealth and growing poverty, we need to create *economics by inclusion*, a system where all relevant factors are considered simultaneously. This will bring back the historical/institutional approach to economics that died after World War II. This economics by inclusion will also open the way for *policies of inclusion*, a system that will put the accent on the wellbeing of the majority and not on the growth of the export sector.

An Austro–German development economics could enrich new development economics (Chang 2003; de Paula and Dymski 2005; Jomo and Fine 2006) by enlarging its toolbox and historical scope. Doing so would bring back the key insights from classical development economics, and also insights from the only laboratory that economists have: the history of economic policy (Jomo and Reinert 2005). The resulting synergy would create *economics without equilibrium* (to use Nicolas Kaldor's term), something very close to the approach of the now extinct historical schools of economics where relevance was the only criterion by which the economists' tools were chosen. Instead of equilibrium, we would have an *optimum* as a moving target ahead of us as the never-ending frontier of knowledge is pushed ahead, but with the fruits of technological change distributed in a more equitable way by re-distributing production rather than by redistributing income in the form of aid.

References

Anderson, J. (1777). *Observations on the means of exciting a spirit of national industry; chiefly intended to promote the agriculture, commerce, manufactures, and fisheries, of Scotland. In a Series of Letters to a Friend.* Edinburgh: T. Cadell.

Arthur, B. (1989). Competing technologies, increasing returns and lock-in by historical events. *Economic Journal*, 99, 116–131.

Arthur, B. (1994). *Increasing returns and path dependence in the economy*. Ann Arbor: University of Michigan Press.

Backhaus, J. (Ed.) (2003). *Joseph Alois Schumpeter. Entrepreneurship, style and vision*. Boston: Kluwer.

Baron, H. (1966). *The crisis of the early Italian Renaissance*. Princeton: Princeton University Press.

Beckmann, J. (1777). *Anleitung zur Technologie, oder zur Kenntniss der Handwerke, Fabriken und Manufacturen, vornehmlich derer, die mit der Landwirthschaft, Polizey und Cameralwissenschaft in nächster Verbindung stehen.* Göttingen: Wittwe Vandenhoeck.

Bhagwati, J. (2002). *Free trade today*. Princeton: Princeton University Press.

Biernacki, R. (1995). *The fabrication of labour: Germany and Britain, 1640–1914*. Berkeley: University of California Press.

Botero, G. (1589). *Della ragione di stato. Libri dieci*, also containing *Delle cause della grandezza delle città, libri tre*. Rome: Vicenzio Pellagalo.

Buchanan, J. (1979). *What should economists do?* Indianapolis: Liberty Press.

Cary, J. (1695). *An essay on the state of England in relation to its trade, its poor, and its taxes, for carrying on the present war against France*. Bristol: W. Bonny.

Chang, H.-J. (Ed.) (2003). *Rethinking development economics*. London: Anthem.

Cimoli, M., Correa, N., & Primi, A. (2005). *Crecimiento y estructura productiva en economías abiertas: lecciones de la experiencia de América Latina*. Santiago: CEPAL.

de Paula, S., & Dymski, G. (Eds.) (2005). *Reimagining growth. Towards a renewal of development theory*. London: Zed.

Frank, R., & Cook, P. (1995). *The winner-take-all society*. New York: Free Press.

Graham, F. (1923). Some aspects of protection further considered. *Quarterly Journal of Economics*, 37, 199–227.

Jomo, K. S., & Fine, B. (Eds.) (2006). *The new development economics. After the Washington Consensus*. New Delhi: Tulika.

Jomo, K. S., & Reinert, E. S. (Eds.) (2005). *The origins of development economics. How schools of economics have addressed development*. New Delhi: Tulika.

King, C. (1721). *The British merchant; or, commerce preserved. 3 volumes*. London: John Darby.

Kohn, M. (2004). Value and exchange. *Cato Journal*, 24(3), 303–339.

Krugman, P. (1990). *Rethinking international trade*. Cambridge: MIT Press.

Latini, B. (1993). *The book of the treasure (Li livres dou tresor)*. New York: Garland.

List, F. (1841). *Das nationale System der politischen Ökonomie*. Stuttgart: Cotta.

Lundvall, B.-Å., Johnson, B., Andersen, E. S., & Dalum, B. (2002). National systems of production, innovation and competence building. *Research Policy*, 31, 213–231.

Marshall, A. (1890). *Principles of economics*. London: Macmillan.

Nelson, R. R. (2006). Economic development from the perspective of evolutionary economic theory. In *The Other Canon Foundation/Tallinn University of Technology Working Papers in Technology Governance and Economic Dynamics. No 2*. Retrieved from http://hum.ttu.ee/tg.

Ocampo, J. A., & Parra, M. A. (2006). The commodity terms of trade and their strategic implications for development. In K. S. Jomo (Ed.), *The Long Twentieth Century: Globalization under Hegemony* (pp. 164–194). New Delhi: Oxford University Press.

Palma, G. (2002). *The Mexican economy since trade liberalisation and NAFTA: on the 'de-linkaging' of a dynamic export expansion and the collapsing of an export multiplier.* Cambridge: Cambridge University.

Perez, C. (2002). *Technological revolutions and financial capital. The dynamics of bubbles and golden ages.* Cheltenham: Elgar.

Perez, C., & Soete, L. (1988). Catching up in technology: entry barriers and windows of opportunity. In G. Dosi, C. Freeman, R. Nelson, G. Silverberg, & L. Soete (Eds.), *Technical change and economic theory* (pp. 458–479). London: Pinter.

Pianta, M. (2005). Innovation and employment. In J. Fagerberg, D. Mowery & R. Nelson (Eds.), *The Oxford handbook of innovation* (pp. 568–598). Oxford: Oxford University Press.

Reinert, E. S. (1994). Catching-up from way behind. A Third World perspective on first world history. In J. Fagerberg, B. Verspagen, & N. von Tunzelmann (Eds.), *The dynamics of technology, trade and growth* (pp. 168–197). Aldershot: Elgar.

Reinert, E. S. (1996a). The role of technology in the creation of rich and poor nations: Underdevelopment in a Schumpeterian system. In D. Aldcroft, & R. Catterall (Eds.), *Rich nations—poor nations. The long run perspective* (pp.161–188). Aldershot: Elgar.

Reinert, E. S. (1996b). Diminishing returns and economic sustainability: The dilemma of resource-based economies under a free trade regime. In S. Hansen, J. Hesselberg, & H. Hveem (Eds.), *International trade regulation, national development strategies and the environment: Towards sustainable development?* (pp. 119–150). Oslo: Centre for Development and the Environment, University of Oslo.

Reinert, E. S. (2000). Compensation mechanisms and targeted economic growth: Lessons from the history of economic policy. In M. Vivarelli, & M. Pianta (Eds.), *The employment impact of innovations* (pp. 182–206). London: Routledge.

Reinert, E. S. (Ed.) (2004a). *Globalization, economic development and inequality: An alternative perspective.* Cheltenham: Elgar.

Reinert, E. S. (2004b). Globalisation in the periphery as a Morgenthau plan: The underdevelopment of Mongolia in the 1990's. In E. S. Reinert (Ed.), *Globalization, economic development and inequality: An alternative perspective* (pp. 157–214). Cheltenham: Elgar.

Reinert, E. S. (2005a). German economics as development economics. From the Thirty Years' War to World War II. In K. S. Jomo, & E. S. Reinert (Eds.), *The origins of development economics* (pp. 48–68). New Delhi: Tulika.

Reinert, E. S. (2005b). Austrian economics and The Other Canon. In J. Backhaus (Ed.), *Modern applications of Austrian thought* (pp. 253–298). Milton Park: Routledge.

Reinert, E. S. (2006). *Institutionalism ancient, old and new: a historical perspective on institutions and uneven development.* Research paper no. 2006/77, United Nations University, WIDER, Helsinki. In H.-J. Chang (Ed.), Institutional change and economic development. Tokyo: United Nations University Press.

Reinert, E. S., & Daastøl, A. (1997). Exploring the genesis of economic innovations: The religious Gestalt-Switch and the duty to invent as preconditions for economic growth. *European Journal of Law and Economics*, 4(2/3), 233–283.

Reinert, E. S., & Reinert, S. (2003). An early national innovation system: the case of Antonio Serra's 1613 'Breve Trattato'. *Institutions and Economic Development/Istituzioni e Sviluppo Economico*, 1(3), 87–129.

Reinert, E. S., & Reinert, S. (2005). Mercantilism and economic development: Schumpeterian dynamics, institution building and international benchmarking. In: K. S. Jomo, & E. S. Reinert (Eds.), *The origins of development economics* (pp. 1–23). New Delhi: Tulika.

Reinert, E. S., & Reinert, H. (2006). Creative destruction in economics: Nietzsche, Sombart, Schumpeter. In J. Backhaus, & W. Drechsler (Eds.), *Friedrich Nietzsche 1844–2000: Economy and society* (pp. 55–85). New York: Springer.

Reinert, S. (2005). The Italian tradition of political economy. Theories and policies of development in the semi-periphery of the enlightenment. In K. S. Jomo, & E. S. Reinert (Eds.), *The origins of development economics* (pp. 24–47). New Delhi: Tulika.

Ricardo, D. (1974[1817]). *The principles of political economy and taxation.* London: Dent, Dutton.

Schumpeter, J. A. (1908). *Wesen und Hauptinhalt der theoretischen Nationalökonomie.* Leipzig: Duncker & Humblot.

Schumpeter, J. A. (1912). *Theorie der wirtschaftlichen Entwicklung.* Leipzig: Duncker & Humblot.

Schumpeter, J. A. (1996). *History of economics analysis*. New York: Oxford University Press.

Serra, A. (1613). *Breve trattato delle cause che possono far abbondare l'oro e l'argento dove non sono miniere*. Naples: Lazzaro Scorriggio.

Singer, H. W. (1950). The distribution of gains between investing and borrowing countries. *American Economic Review*, 40, 473–485.

Smith, A. (1976). *The wealth of nations*. Chicago: University of Chicago Press.

Sombart, W. (1928). *Der moderne Kapitalismus*. Munich: Duncker & Humblot.

Steuart, J. (1767). *An inquiry into the principles of political economy: being an essay on the science of domestic policy in free nations. In which are particularly considered population, agriculture, trade, industry, money, coin, interest, circulation, banks, exchange, public credit, and taxes. 2 volumes*. London: A. Millar & T. Cadell.

Taylor, M. (2004). *What Derrida really meant*. New York Times, October 14, 2004.

Tubaro, P. (2000). Un'esperienza peculiare del Settecento italiano: la 'scuola milanese' di economia matematica. *Studi Settecenteschi*, 20, 193–223.

Vivarelli, M., & Pianta, M. (Eds.) (2000). *The employment impact of innovations*. London: Routledge.

Zeuthen, F (1930). *Problems of monopoly and economic welfare*. London: Routledge.

Chapter Sixteen

THE QUALITATIVE SHIFT IN EUROPEAN INTEGRATION: TOWARDS PERMANENT WAGE PRESSURES AND A 'LATIN-AMERICANIZATION' OF EUROPE?

Erik S. Reinert & Rainer Kattel

Introduction: Types of Economic Integration and Definitions of Capitalism

US economist Hyman Minsky jokingly used to claim that there are as many varieties of capitalism as Heinz has pickles, that is 57 varieties (Minsky 1991). In this paper we argue that economic integration provides a similar analytical problem: economic integration can take many forms, and some are more conducive to wealth and freedom than others. Colonialism was probably the first form of international economic integration, and a very close form of integration at that. Intuitively we understand that what the European Union has attempted to achieve – ever since Winston Churchill called for 'a kind of United States of Europe' in a 1946 Zurich University speech – is something qualitatively very different from colonialism.

In this paper we argue that European economic integration has made a qualitative shift from one type of economic integration to another, from a ***Listian symmetrical economic integration*** to an ***integrative and asymmetrical integration.*** We argue that this change – originating in a new definition of the nature of capitalism – is measurably threatening European welfare, first in the economic periphery and secondly potentially also in the core countries. We argue that the new and enlarged Europe is undergoing structural change towards a *Latin-Americanization*, including a larger spread in wages (more inequality), wages falling as a percentage of GDP (in favour of the FIRE sector: Finance, Insurance & Real Estate), and the formation of pockets of urban wealth and an impoverishment of the countryside. These phenomena, which are clearer in the EU periphery than in the core, will increase the cost of economic cohesion and increase social tension. This development is aggravated by the timing of the enlargement in the

---

The authors would like to express their thanks to Margit Suurna (Tallinn) and Jan Suchacek (Ostrava) for their help with the data. Part of the research has been funded by the Estonian Information Technology Foundation

present phase of the techno-economic paradigm, a period that already under normal circumstances is characterized by deflationary and downward pressures on wages, like in the 1930s.[1]

We argue that this analysis of qualitatively different types of economic integration escapes traditional economic analysis for three basic reasons: a) because of different definitions of capitalism, b) because of what Nobel Laureate James Buchanan refers to as the 'equality assumption' of standard economics (Buchanan 1979: 231ff): that economic activities are qualitatively alike as carriers of economic growth, c) because we assume that a nation or group of nations can be producing far from its production possibility curve; in other words we do not assume full employment.

Today capitalism tends to be defined by the private ownership of assets and market coordination of all activities not organized within firms (Williamson 1985). For Marxists, capitalism tends to be defined as a specific relationship between classes of owners and non-owners of the means of production. Our analysis is a third type, based on understanding of capitalism as ***a system of production***, and follows Werner Sombart's definition in his *opus magnum* on the subject (Sombart 1928). Sombart defines the foundations and preconditions upon which capitalism is built as follows:

1. The business enterpriser (i.e. entrepreneur);
2. The modern state;
3. The machine process (i.e. industrialism), a term defining a dynamic system close to what we today would refer to as the 'national innovation systems'.

With these elements at hand, capitalism – according to Sombart – needs the following factors for full development:

1. Capital;
2. Labour;
3. Markets.

Since the main preconditions for capitalism – the entrepreneur, the modern state, industrial dynamics – did not lend itself particularly well to neo-classical quantitative analysis, this type of economic analysis had to focus on what to Sombart was only *auxiliary elements* in the process; i.e. capital, labour and markets. This removed the causes of capitalist dynamics from economic theory. The real causes of capitalist dynamics, what Nietzsche calls *Geist und Willens-Kapital* (Man's wit and will) – new knowledge, entrepreneurship, innovations and organizational ability – were left out of the analysis. Removing these elements automatically also removed the reasons why dynamic growth is so unevenly distributed between individuals, firms

1 On techno-economic paradigms, see Perez 2002 & 2004.

and nations. Neoclassical economic theory exogenised the dynamic driving forces of capitalism, and came to adopt what Schumpeter calls 'the pedestrian view that it is the accumulation of capital per se that propels the capitalist engine' (Schumpeter 1954: 468). In terms of understanding economic dynamics, neoclassical analysis developed into something akin to playing Hamlet without the participation of the Prince of Denmark.

An important result of this is that late 20th century economic theory came to conceive of economics as a *Harmonielehre* (Robbins 1952). By studying only capital, labour, and markets under 'the equality assumption' the world economy came to be seen as a machine producing automatic harmony. In this way, capitalism as defined by Williamson could not distinguish colonialism from the European Common market as being two qualitatively very different forms of economic integration. The equality assumption – that all economic activities are equally well suited as carriers of innovation and economic growth – leads into economics as a *Harmonielehre*. Not surprisingly, in a theory where all inputs are qualitatively alike – as in Paul Samuelson's trade theory – the outcome is also that all economic factors are alike: the outcome is *factor price equalization* (Samuelson 1948).

It is important to note that capitalism the way Sombart defines it – as a dynamic *industrial system* – never reached the colonies. The essence of colonialism was, from its very inception, precisely to prohibit industrial production there. Neither was agriculture a part of capitalism to Sombart. Successful economic integrations are win-win-situations that extend and develop industrialism and capitalism – as Sombart defines it – to new areas without destroying them in others. Unsuccessful economic integration is, from this point of view, forms of integration where one or both parties are prevented from, or lose, the dynamic economic structures that used to go under the name of *industrialism* (Sombart's definition of capitalism), but today may contain just as much advanced services as physical production.

1. Causes of Uneven Growth as the Basis for a Theory of Types of Economic Integration

A key part of the 18th century scientific revolutions was the development of taxonomies or classification systems as carriers of new and more detailed knowledge of the world that surrounds us. The archetypical case is that of Linnaeus (1707–1778) and his classification systems for living organisms. Distinguishing a good and useful plant from one deadly poisonous and useless was made into a science. As already alluded to when addressing the 'equality assumption', a remarkable feature of modern economics is the complete absence of any taxonomy: the 'equality assumption' is in a sense the mother of all assumptions of the economics profession.

We argue that a key feature of pre-Smithian economics was a taxonomic understanding of the economic world of production. This taxonomy of economic activities led, in turn, to a taxonomy of types of international trade that could, respectively, benefit only one of the trading partners or both. The seeds of this taxonomy can be found already in the 1550s (Ortiz 1558, quoted in Reinert 2003), it solidifies towards the end of the 1600s and is accepted across Europe as common sense in the early 1700s. This theory develops from a pre-scientific common sense to economic science. As English economist Edward Misselden describes this type of development: 'Before we knew it by sense; now we know it by science' (Misselden 1622)

The pre-Smithian taxonomy of 'good' and 'bad' trade was based on the observation of the obvious urban bias of economic development that was found everywhere in Europe. Some, but not all, cities were wealthy, particularly those of Italy and those of the Dutch Republic. It was also a very common observation that the presence of manufacturing spilled over and increased the efficiency of agriculture. 'Promoting husbandry … is never more effectually encouraged than by the increase of manufactures' wrote David Hume, Adam Smith's close friend, in his *History of England* (Hume 1768, vol. 3: 65).

The experience-based economics of the early 1700-century had crystallized the following explanations for why some areas were much wealthier than others (Reinert 2004c):

- Economic development is *activity-specific*, available in some economic activities rather than in others. Development was seen as created by increasing returns and innovations in manufacturing (Botero 1590, Serra 1613, see Reinert and Reinert 2003) and not in agriculture, due to stagnant productivity, diminishing returns and monoculture, and absence of synergies.
- Economic development is a *synergic process*: the greater the division of labour and the number of professions, the greater the wealth (already very clear in Serra 1613, see Reinert & Reinert 2003).
- The targeting, support, and protection of *manufacturing* were argued in terms of
  a) its ability to create wealth
  b) its ability to create employment
  c) its ability to solve balance of payment problems
  d) its ability to increase the velocity of circulation of money
- Starting in the 1700s, great emphasis was put on the beneficial synergies between manufacturing and agriculture: only where there was manufacturing, was there successful agriculture. This crucial understanding – which today is lost – is found not only in Hume in England (see above), but also in the writings of the most influential economists on the continent at the time: Justi in Germany, Montesquieu in France, Galiani in Italy, Uztáriz in Spain and Berch in Sweden.[2] This understanding of synergies also calls for a great variety of manufactures in each country (as in Serra 1613)

[2] Modern economic historians agree with the mercantilist explanation of causality here: 'The bulk of the evidence points to urbanization being the cause of agricultural productivity gain, not a result'. Philip Hoffman quoted in Prak (2001).

This accumulated wisdom was taken over in the economics of Friedrich List (1841), who was the theoretical economist behind the industrialization of continental Europe. List is normally seen as a protectionist, but he was the first visionary of European economic integration once all nations had achieved a comparative advantage in manufacturing (increasing returns industries) (see Reinert 1998). List quotes Serra (1613), and sees manufacturing synergies as being the very basis for civilization, rather than trade:

> Let us compare Poland with England: both nations at one time were in the same stage of culture; and now what a difference. Manufactories and manufactures are the mothers and children of municipal liberty, of intelligence, of the arts and sciences, of internal and external commerce, of navigation and improvements in transport, of civilization and of political power. They are the chief way of liberating agriculture from its chains.... The popular school (i.e. Adam Smith and J. B. Say, authors' note) has attributed this civilizing effect to foreign trade, but in that it has confounded the mere exchanger with the originator. (List 1841: 142)

We shall argue that – regardless of what economic *theory* might have said – the *practice* and history of European economic integration has, until very recently, been based on the understanding expressed here by List: economic integration has essentially taken place between nations that already have achieved a comparative advantage in increasing returns activities (manufacturing) or, alternatively, as colonialism. In fact, economic development and integration of Central European states after the Westphalian Peace of 1648 followed precisely this path laying foundation for the economic success of Europe (see Backhaus 2001). We shall see below that the famous Harvard Commencement Speech by US Secretary of State George Marshall in 1947 – announcing the Marshall Plan – essentially restates the Listian view about the importance of the synergies between city and countryside being the basis of Western civilization.

2. From an Understanding of Uneven Development to a Taxonomy of Economic Integration

Out of this understanding of economic development developed a theory of economic integration that, we claim, was in practice followed in Europe for centuries, including during the gradual buildup of what came to be the European Union over the decades following World War II. An essential feature of this type of economic theory is the understanding of the synergies between increasing return activities (urban/manufacturing activities) and the production of raw materials (rural activities).

The clearest early statement of this theory is found on the first pages of Charles King's three volume work (King 1721, vol. 1: 1–5), a compilation of works published in the previous decade, which was to enjoy unique authority for decades. It is important to note that this scheme is based on a possible discrepancy between the interest of the merchant and the interest of the nation itself: 'There are general Maxims in Trade which are assented to by every body. That a Trade may be of Benefit to the Merchant and Injurious to the Body of the Nation, is one of these Maxims' (King 1721: 1). This is, of course, very different from the later teachings of Adam Smith, who assumes an automatic harmony of interest between merchant and nation. In King's scheme, the normal pre-Smithian scheme, the vested interests of some economic actors will coincide with those of the nation-state – mainly those of the manufacturers – while the vested interests of other economic actors will be at odds with the interests of the nation-state. Yet, it is precisely this crucial link between the interest of the state (higher wealth) and that of industry is essential to the success of modern nation-states in Europe and North-America (a point made already in Schmoller 1884).

In its simple form, the argument presented by King runs like this:

> Good trade is importing raw materials and exporting finished goods. Exporting finished goods produced from native raw materials is the best kind of trade for a nation, but importing raw materials and exporting the finished goods is also good trade.
>
> Importing manufactured goods in exchange for raw materials is bad trade.
>
> But interestingly, exchanging manufactured goods for other manufactured goods is beneficial to both sides, i.e. mutually good trade.

If increasing returns are attributed to manufacturing industries and diminishing returns are attributed to the production of raw materials, King's taxonomy is perfectly compatible with more recent trade theories (Graham 1923) and Krugman 'new trade theory' (Krugman 1980).

We argue that there is a remarkable continuity in the practice – rather than in the theory – of King's principle of economic integration from the early observations in the 1500s (Ortiz 1558 in Reinert 2003, Botero 1590) through the policies of the 1600s and 1700s, to the policies advocated by Friedrich List, and to the European integration as it slowly took form after World War II, assuring the strength and survival of the manufacturing sector in each member country. There is indeed a remarkable similarity between the quote from Friedrich List above and US Secretary of State George Marshall's Harvard Commencement Speech on June 5, 1947, when Marshall says:

> There is a phase of this matter which is both interesting and serious. The farmer has always produced the foodstuffs to exchange with the city dweller for the other necessities of life. ***This division of labour is the basis of modern civilization***. At the present time it is threatened with breakdown. The town and city industries are not producing adequate goods to exchange with the food-producing farmer. Raw materials and fuel are in short supply. Machinery is lacking or worn out. The farmer or the peasant cannot find the goods for sale which he desires to purchase. So the sale of his farm produce for money which he cannot use seems to him an unprofitable transaction. He, therefore, has withdrawn many fields from crop cultivation and is using them for grazing. He feeds more grain to stock and finds for himself and his family an ample supply of food, however short he may be on clothing and the other ordinary gadgets of civilization. Meanwhile, people in the cities are short of food and fuel, and in some places approaching the starvation levels. So the governments are forced to use their foreign money and credits to procure these necessities abroad. This process exhausts funds which are urgently needed for reconstruction. Thus a very serious situation is rapidly developing which bodes no good for the world. The modern system of the division of labour upon which the exchange of products is based is in danger of breaking down. (Emphasis added).

Marshall's remarks were essentially comments on the result of the Morgenthau Plan in Germany (Morgenthau 1943, Reinert 2003). The purpose of this plan, named after Henry Morgenthau, the US Secretary of the Treasury from 1934–1945, was to prevent Germany from ever starting a war again. This was to be achieved by de-industrializing Germany and make it into a pastoral state; closing factories, taking the industrial machinery out of the country and filling the mines with water. The plan was approved in an Allied meeting in 1943 and carried out after the German capitulation in May 1945.

The Morgenthau Plan was abruptly stopped in 1947 when ex-President Herbert Hoover of the United States, on a fact-finding mission, reported back from Germany: 'There is the illusion that the New Germany left after the annexations can be reduced to a 'pastoral state'. It cannot be done unless we exterminate or move 25.000.000 out of it'. Hoover had rediscovered the wisdom of the cameralist and mercantilist population theorists: an industrialized nation has a much larger carrying capacity in terms of population than an agricultural state. The de-industrialization process had led to a sharp fall also in agricultural yields and partly to an institutional collapse, giving evidence to the importance of the linkages between the industrial and agricultural sector that were also a hallmark of cameralist economics. Less than four months after Hoover's alarming reports from Germany, the US government announced the Marshall Plan which aimed to achieve exactly the opposite of the Morgenthau Plan: Germany's industrial capacity was at all cost to be brought back to its 1938 level. It cannot be emphasized enough that the Marshall Plan was not a financial plan, it was a *reindustrialization plan*. It can be argued that early development economics started with very similar ideas. (See, e.g., Rosenstein-Rodan 1943; Singer 1950; Nurkse 1953.)

One of the authors has argued that the type of economic integration that resulted from 'structural adjustment' starting in the 1980s has been of the Morgenthau Plan type (Reinert 2003 & 2004a): a rapid de-industrialization that has threatened what both Friedrich List and US Secretary of State George Marshall saw as the basis of modern civilization. We maintain that a shock-wave of free trade between a relatively advanced nation and a relatively less advanced nation, or group of nations, will tend to kill the most advanced industries in the least advanced countries. We refer to this effect as the Vanek-Reinert Effect (Reinert 1980 & 2004a). This effect can be observed from the 19th century unification of Italy, when Southern Italian industry suffered, to the Czech computer industry as perhaps the earliest casualty of the fall of the COMECON block. As in Mongolia, the last economic activity to survive is subsistence agriculture – in Mongolia in the form of animal herding.

As a continuation of King's principles, and with the experience of 300 more years of economic history, we can establish the taxonomy – based on 'ideal types' – of economic integrations below. There are two main types, ***symmetrical free trade areas,*** i.e. integration among nations at a similar level of economic development and economic sophistication, and ***asymmetrical free trade areas,*** i.e. integration of nations with widely different economic structure, at different levels of development.

I. SYMMETRICAL FREE TRADE AREAS

A. Listian Integration (From Friedrich List)

Examples of Listian economic integration is 19th century Germany and the 'old' European Union. Listian economic integration is between nations on roughly similar levels of GDP/capita, that *all have a comparative advantage in increasing return activities*. This insures that economic integration will not de-industrialize, de-skill or create large-scale unemployment in any of the partner countries. Large Listian areas can, however, absorb small units of relatively more backward countries to the benefit of all parties. An example of this is the integration of Portugal in the old EU, where mature and labour intensive industries could be farmed out to Portugal increasing real wages both in Portugal and in the rest of the EU. In this case integration can be seen as a variant of the flying geese type (see below).

Two main variables determine the ability of a Listian integration to absorb poorer partner countries to mutual benefit. Firstly: The Schumpeterian dynamism of the core (wealthy) countries; i.e. the more dynamic the core countries, the more mature industries they can farm out to the poorer partners without hurting their own employment and wage level. The second variable is the size of the poorer country/countries to be integrated; i.e. the smaller the pool of people to be integrated, the easier the integration becomes.

A symmetrical Listian free trade area can be converted to an integrated welfare state at a relatively low cost. **Listian integration is a typical *win-win* strategy if it does not deteriorate into a Type IIC strategy.**

B. Peripheral Symmetrical Integration

Examples of this type are Pacto Andino and Mercosur. These are cases of economic integration of peripheral nations whose international comparative advantage does not lie in increasing return industries, but that wish to grow such activities and need a bigger market. Included in successful schemes of this types are preferences for relative laggard countries, as for Ecuador and Bolivia *the in Pacto Andino*. The Latin American Free Trade Association (LAFTA/ALALC) is an example of such an integration that failed. A problem with this type of integration is often that such nations have similar economic structures and relatively little to sell to each other.

This type of regional integration is probably a necessary stepping stone before reaching global free trade.

COMECON seems to fall in this symmetrical category because of the emphasis on distribution of increasing return activities, but because of the starting asymmetry it is not clear if this is a third type under category 1.

Peripheral symmetrical integration is also a *win-win* strategy if the right dynamics are achieved.

II. ASYMMETRICAL FREE TRADE AREAS

A. *'Colonial' and Non-Integrative*

In the classical colonial relationship a dynamic industrial nation integrates with a periphery that, whether explicitly stated or not, is not to specialize in innovation and increasing returns activities.

Traditionally 'colonies' specialized in supplying raw materials. Now a more sophisticated neo-colonial division of labour appears as both manufacturing and agriculture sectors split up in a high-tech/capital intensive/innovative/high wage segment on the one hand and a low-tech/low capital intensity/non-innovative/low wage segment on the other hand. Mexico is the country where this development is most visible. The old manufacturing sector, containing 'complete' industries is shrinking and being replaced by the *maquila* sector consisting of unmechanizable fragments of a global value chain seeking low wage and low skilled labour. This development finds its parallel in the Mexican agricultural sector, where highly subsidized US imports of mechanizable grain production is replacing Mexican agriculture even in a traditional product like corn – produced with exceptionally advanced technology including unmanned tractors using global positioning equipment – while Mexico specializes in exporting the unmechanizable agricultural production, some of the fruits and vegetables (e.g. strawberries, cucumbers). The Mexican national innovation system is deteriorating accordingly, and returning to a centre-periphery relationship with the United States (Cimoli 2000).

In asymmetrical trading areas the Vanek-Reinert Effect starts operating, and the least advanced nation concentrates in the low-skilled areas both in manufacturing and also in agriculture. In the worst case this can lead to rampant de-industrialization (Reinert 2003 & 2004b). In Mexico a deteriorating sequence can be observed; first *de-industrialization*, subsequently *de-agriculturalisation* (even of the country's most traditional crop, maize) and finally *de-population*. In many areas of Southern Mexico only the population above 60 years old and below 12 years old is left. The others are working in the United States or further north in Mexico.

The success of this strategy from the colonizing nation's point of view depends on the same variables as mentioned above. If the Schumpeterian dynamics in the rich country is high enough, and the supply of labour to be absorbed is not too big, or protection can be kept at a point securing employment, the rich country may have all the advantages of producing technologically mature and labour-intensive crops with cheap labour, but not the disadvantages.

Classically colonialism is a *win-lose* strategy, the colonial power wins while the colony loses. However, this is potentially a *lose-lose* strategy if the colonial power loses control or loses dynamism. Potentially Mexican real wages may fall while, at the same time, wages fall in the US, when the 'giant sucking sound' Ross Perot used to talk about hits US employment and real wages. If the world moves towards *factor-prize equalization*, this may very well be downwards.

B. Flying Geese, or Sequential Technological Upgrading

The *flying geese* metaphor for economic integrations first appears in a 1935 article by Kaname Akamatsu published in Japanese. His views became known to the West in his 1961 article in *Weltwirtschaftliches Archiv*, and during the 1980s Japanese economist and foreign minister Saburo Okita propagated the concept. As he readily admits, Akamatsu's theory rests on a Germanic conception of society and economy, references to Kant, List, Sombart and Schumpeter – as well as to Russian economist Nikolai Kondratieff – abound. The essence of the flying geese pattern of economic integration is that nations upgrade and catch up technologically by sequentially riding the same technological wave. It essentially describes the way East Asian nations grew. The model builds on Friedrich List's stages of integration. Its dynamics are similar to Michael Porter's stages of national development (Porter 1990) and to Ray Vernon's life-cycle theory of international trade (Vernon 1966), but is both more full-fledged and better integrated into the dynamics of Kondratieff and Schumpeter. Appendix 1 gives graphical representations of this strategy.

To illustrate the process, follow a product: a hairdryer is produced in Japan and exported to the rest of the world. When Japan upgrades her technology and wage level, the production of hairdryers passes on to Korea and is exported from that country. As Korean production after a while also gets more sophisticated, the production of simple hairdryers passes on to Taiwan, where the phenomenon is again repeated. Hairdryer production moves on to Malaysia and Thailand, and finally to Vietnam. On the way all nations have increased their wealth and upgraded technologically, based on the same product.

There are several interesting aspects to this strategy:

1. An intra-industry aspect: product development within a particular developing country, within a single industry, from import to production and then to export (very much List 1841 & Vernon 1966).
2. An inter-industry aspect: sequential appearance and development of industries in a particular developing country, with industries being diversified and upgraded from consumer goods to capital goods and/or from simple to more sophisticated products.
3. An international aspect: subsequent relocation process of industries from advanced to developing countries during the latter's catching-up process. (GRIPS Development Forum, see bibliography)

The flying geese strategy has proved spectacularly successful in East Asia – ***a true win-win form of economic integration*** – where Korea moved up from being poorer than Tanzania in 1950 (see also below). However, the strategy was only possible because it was in the interest of the United States to build a *cordon sanitaire* around the communist world, i.e. an interest in giving the world Marshall Plans rather than Morgenthau Plans. This strategy requires heavy-handed government intervention and is impossible to initiate today under the rule of the Washington Institutions.

Latin American import-substitution initially contained strong elements of *flying geese*, creating a win-win situation where US companies prolonged the life cycle of their products by producing in Latin America. However, Latin America failed to move to the next Listian stage – into regional integration – through the failure of LAFTA/ALALC, and lost its dynamics. It should be noted however, that even the inefficient manufacturing sectors built up in countries like Peru and Mongolia provided much higher real wages than does global capitalism today.

C. Welfare Colonialism

The term welfare colonialism was coined by anthropologist Robert Paine (Paine 1977:1–52) to describe the economic integration of the Arctic population into Canada, and may equally well be applied to the integration of the Saami people in Norway. The essential features of welfare colonialism are: 1) The classical colonial drain is reversed, the net flow of funds is to the colony rather than to the mother country, and 2) the native population is integrated in a way that destroys their previous livelihood, and they are put on the dole. Welfare colonialism identifies welfare as the potential vehicle for a stable internal 'governing at a distance' through the exercise of a particularly subtle, 'non-demonstrative' (Paine 1977:3) and dependency-generating form of neo-colonial social control that pre-empts local autonomy through 'well-intentioned' and 'generous' – but ultimately 'morally wrong' – policies. Welfare colonialism creates paralyzing dependencies on the 'centre' in a peripheral population, a centre exerting control through incentives that create total economic dependency thus preventing political mobilization and autonomy.

Clearly welfare colonialism is a very expensive form of economic integration, essentially paying people not to work. Not unlike the religious missionary element in traditional colonialism, welfare colonialism is in a sense well-intended, but ends up being culturally destructive. Welfare colonialism is a ***lose-lose form of economic integration***: the periphery loses its traditional livelihood and culture and is an economic burden to the colonial power.

D. Integrative and Asymmetrical Integration

This type of economic integration differs from the classical colonial version above in that it attempts to integrate the asymmetrical partners – countries at different levels of economic development – into a welfare state. We see the present European Union enlargement as largely falling under this heading in terms of economic integration. However, the future quality of integration in the new Europe is by no means clear, it may well turn out be a win-win integration or exactly the opposite, a lose-lose one. Europe does not start as *tabula rasa*. In particular, the new member states have, in recent years, experienced unprecedented changes in economic and social terms. The decade of deindustrialisation that preceded the last EU enlargement, in all new member states except Hungary, is an important factor that needs to be taken into account. In what follows, we try to measure the development potential of the new Europe and sketch out the dynamics determining this development.

3. The New Europe: Cost and Nature of the Integration

3.1 Characteristics of Transition

The economic integration of Central and Eastern European (CEE) and newly independent countries from the former Soviet Union (NIS) into world markets after the fall of Berlin Wall in 1989 was based on three basic assumptions shared by most of these countries:

1) economic liberalization through the abolition of controls over prices and production;
2) macro-economic stabilization through control of the money supply and balancing of the government budget;
3) the sale of state property to private individuals. (Kregel et al. 1992:14; also King 2002)

The goal of this architecture of transition was rapid transition to free market economy and, obviously, higher standard of living.

However, the integration of the CEE countries into the EU took place during a particular and peculiar *Zeitgeist*, during the triumphalist euphoria following the fall of the Berlin Wall. With hindsight, this was a period when the West in a sense had come to believe in the propaganda version of their own economic theory, that markets were creators of automatic economic harmony, that immediate opening to international trade would create factor-price equalization (Samuelson 1948). However, in reality this fast integration led to what we have labelled a Vanek-Reinert Effect, a situation where the most advanced economic sectors in the least advanced countries are killed off. In the extreme periphery, Mongolia, most industrial sectors were virtually exterminated, and the only two growing industrial sectors are the collection of bird feathers to produce combed down and the production of alcohol (Reinert 2004b). We have argued that assymetrical shock integration has the same effects as the Morgenthau Plan that was forced on Germany between 1945 and 1947 (see above).

As indicated in Figure 16.1, the integration of the CEE countries into the world economy had – in varying degrees – all the characteristics of a Morgenthau Plan. In all countries except Hungary, industrial employment fell – in several cases dramatically – between 1990 and 2001. Both in post-World War II Germany and in Mongolia during the 1990s this pattern of deindustrialization was accompanied by a rapid growth in agricultural employment and a precipitous fall in agricultural productivity (Reinert 2004b). Figure 16.1 shows two strikingly different patterns. In the least developed countries (Armenia, Azerbaijan, Bulgaria, Kyrgyzstan, and Romania) the surplus labour from deindustrialisation moves back to agriculture – following the Mongolian pattern – lowering labour productivity there. In the slightly less underdeveloped periphery this surplus labour moves into the service sector, including underemployment and informality.

It is important to note that this type of deindustrialization of *low-income countries* is qualitatively very different from the slow 'de-industrialization' of *high-income countries* as they upgrade into a knowledge-intensive service sector (UNCTAD Report reference to follow).

	1990			2001		
Country	Agriculture	Industry	Services	Agriculture	Industry	Services
Armenia[1]	17.7	30.4	38.3	44.4	14.1	37.2
Azerbajan	30.9	22.9	31.1	40.0	10.8	49.3
Bulgaria	18.5	44.2	37.3	26.3	27.6	46.0
Czech Republic	12.3	45.5	42.2	4.8	40.4	54.8
Estonia	21.0	36.8	41.8	6.9	33.0	60.1
Hungary[2]	8.7	33.0	58.1	6.2	34.7	58.9
Kazakhstan[3]	22.3	31.5	40.7	22.0	18.3	59.8
Krygzystan[3]	32.7	27.9	39.4	52.4	11.6	36.1
Lativa	17.4	37.4	45.2	15.0	25.6	59.4
Poland	25.2	37.0	35.8	19.1	30.5	50.4
Romania	29.1	43.5	27.4	42.3	26.2	31.5
Russian Federation[3]	13.9	40.2	45.6	11.8	29.4	58.8
Slovakia[2]	10.1	39.6	50.0	6.1	37.6	56.2
Slovenia[4]	10.7	44.1	45.1	9.8	38.1	50.8

Figure 16.1 Integration and Deindustrialization 1990–2001: Employment Structure by Sector, Selected Transition Economies, 1990 and 2001 (per cent).[3]
Source: International Labour Office 2004.

These problems in the sphere of production rapidly translate into balance of payment problems, and just as there was no Marshall Plan to restore the productive sector of Eastern Europe as there had been in the West after 1947, there were no counterparts in the monetary sphere, nothing similar to the European Payments Union for settling trade balances as in 1950–1958. The emerging divergent developments in CEE and NIS countries were inevitable given the policy framework: increased social stress and constraints in form of a negative current account balance. Indeed, the former was the case in all countries and as Figure 16.2 illustrates, in some CEE countries the current account balance deteriorates starting in 1993. The CEE countries were on their way to what Celso Furtado has called 'the break-down of the capacity to import'.

In 2001, all CEE countries had a negative balance in trade of goods (Sneijers 2004:2). Yet, inflow of foreign direct investments (FDI), gradually picking up after the mid 1990s enabled rapid change and covered some of the negative trade balance consequences (see Figure 16.3). FDI also fuelled rapid privatization of industries: there was a strong correlation between FDI inflow and privatization revenues in CEE and NIS in the 1990s. (EBRD 2000:84). These cannot, of course, be permanent flows.

The financial architecture created for the transition turned both FDI and privatization, especially in the beginning, into means of 'destructive destruction' and Myrdalian vicious circles. The most recent financial transfers by the state to industrial companies of the Soviet period were transferred into loans of newly founded banks to the same companies. Most of the latter were to be privatized. This automatically created liabilities on the balance sheets of companies, in turn making the industrial restructuring of

3 [1] 2000; [2] 1994; [3] 1999; [4] 1994. Numbers do not add up to 100% because some industries are 'not adequately defined'.

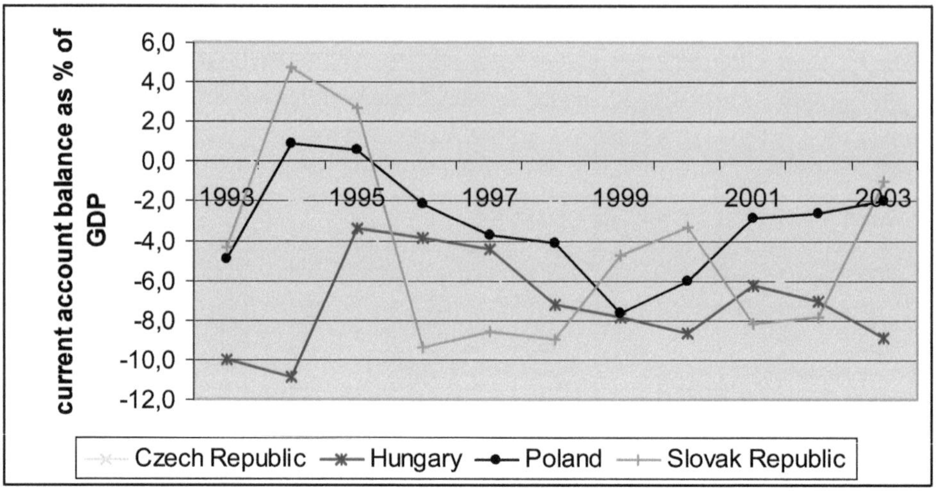

Figure 16.2 Current Account Balance as a Percentage of GPD, Selected CEE Countries, 1993–2003.
Source: OECD 2004.

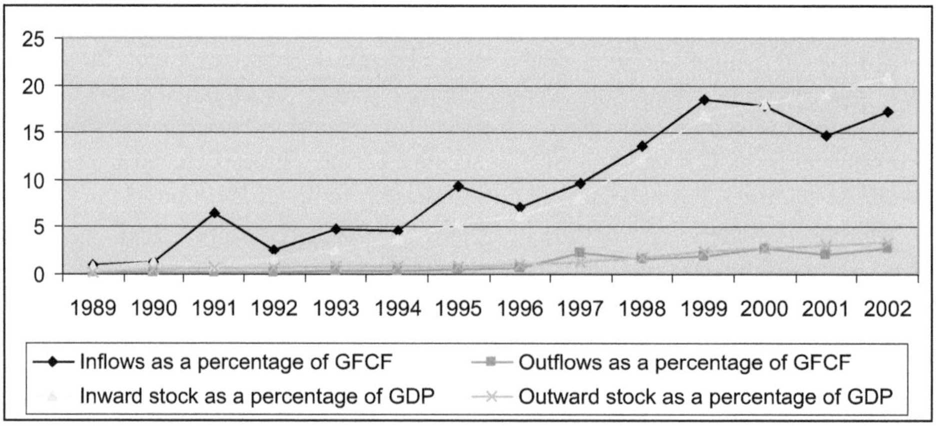

Figure 16.3 Foreign Direct Investments in CEE, 1989–2002.
Source: UNCTAD FDI database.

companies very difficult and creating high risks in the banking sector. The system set up was weak and prone to crisis from the very beginning.

Thus, there was strong 'liability destruction' but hardly any 'asset creation'. (See further Kregel et al. 1992:44–54; King 2002.) This prepared the ground for the Vanek-Reinert Effect, as described above, to rapidly take root in CEE and NIS industries. This, in turn, translated into a sudden and unprecedented onset of social problems: between 1989 and 1996 "the number of poor and unemployed in the region [CEE and NIS] rose respectively by 100 and 10 million while the crime rate tripled' (Cornia 2004). Almost all CEE countries have experienced severe deterioration in life expectancy up to mid 1990s, and the non-EU member countries in CEE and NIS are still seeing lowering life expectancy (Cornia 2004). In addition, all CEE countries experienced growth in regional and income inequality during the 1990s. (See below.)

The positive effects of FDI and privatization were offset by the dramatic rise in social problems as so-called transition costs. Arguably there had to be some rather painful costs as well as uneven development (Hirschmann 1958). Yet, by any standard or understanding of capitalism, the rapid liberalization and onslaught of social problems should have been counterbalanced by creation of new value by upgrading – rather than permanently destroying – large parts of the previous industrial structure. Too little was done to create value by developing the industrial structure of the respective economies towards higher skill and technology intensity. Only if this had been done –as an assisted Listian form of economic integration – the high human costs of transition would have been justified. This would have produced a Schumpeterian creative destruction rather than varying degrees of destructive destruction (Reinert 2004a). The change towards higher skill and technology would have enabled competitive production for export as well as for local markets, thus raising wages, in turn raising government revenues which would, in principle and practice, have allowed for higher investments in education, health and other social services in a virtuous circle of development.

3.2 Quality of Industrial Change

If we look at the development of share of medium and high technology in manufactured exports (international competitiveness) and in manufactured value added (quality of the industrial structure), the new EU member states from CEE were more competitive in 1980 than in 2000.[4] (Figure 16.4) In 1990 CEE countries had qualitatively better industrial structures and were more similar to the East Asian economies than they are today. However, by 2001 the difference between these two groups of countries is truly astonishing. Latin America, by comparison, has fared even worse: if CEE countries have managed to raise the manufactured value added per capita from 1980 to 2000, then Latin America, though more competitive internationally in 2000 than in 1980, has clearly not been able to break out of the vicious circle of uneven development.[5] (See also Cimoli and Correa 2002).

---

4 For specific case studies, see Tiits et al. 2002; King 2002.

5 The development of NIS will not be followed below. It can be argued that most countries in the region are experiencing a rather severe but also novel form of vicious circle of development. The main characteristics of this development, emerging at first almost overnight and then reenforcing itself through 1990s, are: high inflation; strong fall in real wages and productivity; collapse of the productive sector, particularly industry and its capability to export, resulting in severe external constraints in the form of current account deficits and large illegal economic activity; overregulation of the private sector and largely over-bureaucratised state structures disabling cooperative policy actions rendering in turn governance structures disabled to deal

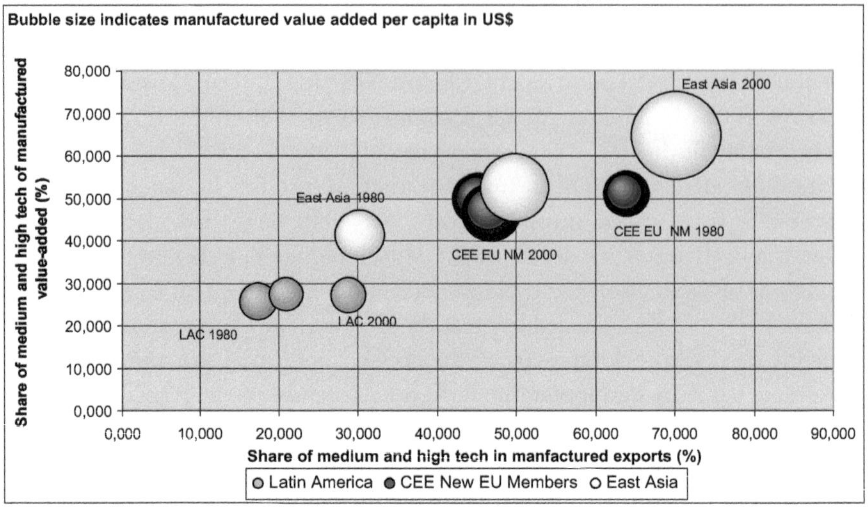

Figure 16.4 Quality of Industrial Change in Selected World Regions, 1980–2000.[6]
Source: UNIDO 2004; calculations by the authors.

In comparison to the EU15, however, the CEE new member states still score lower in terms of the quality of the industrial structure in 2000 than EU15 did in 1980 (Figure 16.5). CEE new member states are slightly more competitive in 2000 than EU15 was in 1980, yet the per capita value added is significantly lower, indicating huge wealth and productivity gaps. Adding up the EU15 with the new member states, the quality of the industrial structure of this new EU23 is catapulted back to a level below the one in 1990. In terms of manufactured value added per capita, the EU23 is catapulted back to the 1980 level. The wealth produced in industry in EU23 in 2000 per capita is similar to that of EU15 in 1980. The fact that the 1990s brought rapid de-industrialisation to the CEE instead of industrial upgrading – the lack of a Listian strategy as in Europe in the 1950s and 1960s – is the explanation for this development

Comparing the integration of the CEE countries with the earlier enlargement of EU – Portugal, Spain and Greece – countries with significantly lower income, skill, and

with existing and emerging problems. These mechanisms are described in detail in Reinert (2004b).

6 Data from the following countries were used in the figures. **Latin America**: Argentina, Bolivia, Brazil, Chile, Colombia, Costa Rica, Ecuador, El Salvador, Haiti, Honduras, Mexico, Paraguay, Peru, Uruguay, Venezuela. **EU15**: Austria, Belgium, Denmark, Finland, France, Germany, Greece, Ireland, Italy, Luxembourg, Netherlands, Portugal, Spain, Sweden, United Kingdom. **CEE New Members EU**: Czech Republic, Estonia, Hungary, Latvia, Lithuania, Poland, Slovakia, Slovenia. **Earlier EU enlargement**: Portugal, Spain, Greece. **Other/ Rest CEE**: Belarus, Bulgaria, Moldova, Romania, Ukraine. **Central Asia**: Armenia, Azerbaijan, Georgia, Kazakhstan, Kyrgyzstan, Mongolia, Tajikistan, Turkmenistan. **East Asia**: Korea, Malaysia, Singapore, Thailand. In all cases averages are calculated.

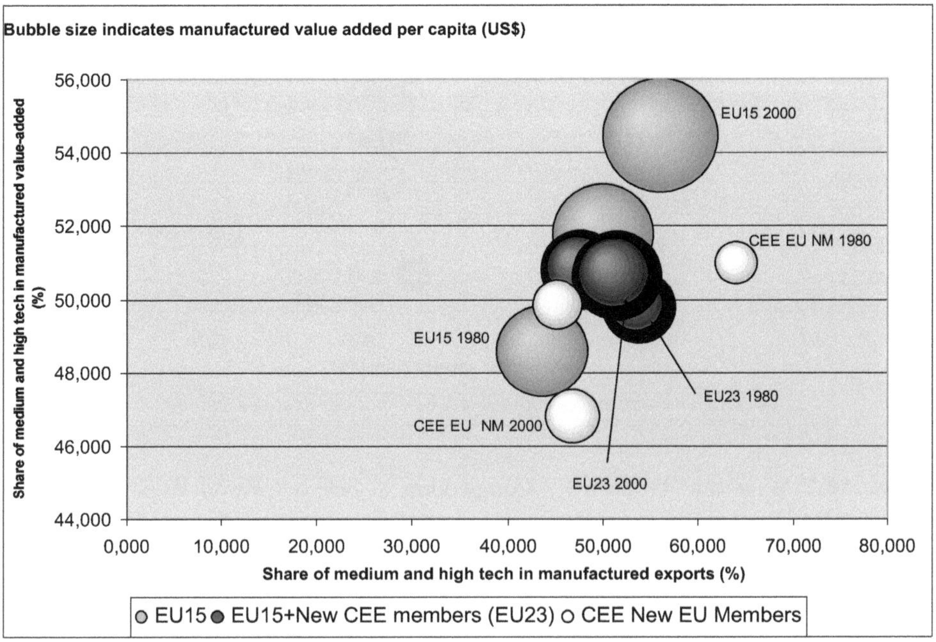

Figure 16.5 The EU Enlargement and Quality of Industrial Change, 1980–2000.
Source: UNIDO 2004; calculations by the authors.

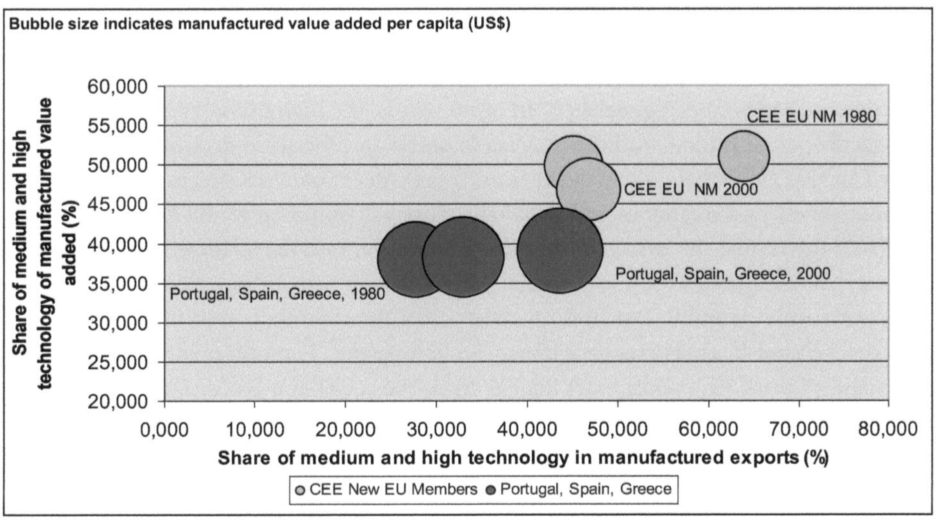

Figure 16.6 Earlier EU Enlargement and Quality of Industrial Change, 1980–2000.
Source: UNIDO 2004; calculations by the authors.

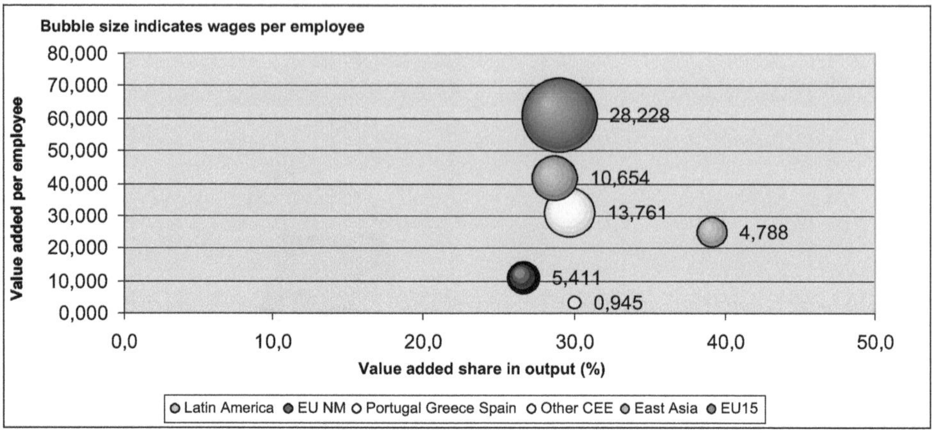

Figure 16.7 Wage and Productivity Competition in Selected World Regions, 2001 (or latest), in US$.[7]

Source: UNIDO Country Statistics database; Götzfried 2001; Eurostat 2004; Mittag 2001; calculations by the authors.

technology levels than the rest, interesting patterns emerge. By 2001 all of these countries are closing in on each other in terms of competitiveness and quality of industrial structure, but significantly differing in wealth and productivity (Figure 16.6). In terms of industrial development the new member states are competing with older enlargement countries.

The quality of industrial change in the CEE countries indicates that the incentives created by the transition architecture for the private sector have not changed significantly over time, nor have these incentives increased productivity of labour and consequently more income has not been generated. In other words, the high human costs of transition have hardly been justified, and the policies initiated and the socio-economic frameworks created in the 1990s have failed to deliver. These developments deteriorate the EU23 competitiveness and quality of industrial structure as compared to the East Asian economies and the rest of the world. Portuguese integration into the CEE served as a pool of relatively cheap labour creating a flying geese win-win integration. Spain's integration was qualitatively different, but in both these cases the slow reduction of tariffs made it possible for Spanish and Portuguese industries to upgrade. This potential has been wasted in the case of the CEE countries. A logical consequence of this is a growing competition of wages and productivity between the EU and other world regions. (Figure 16.7).

In terms of value added share in output most world regions depicted in Figure 16.8 are relatively close. It does not make a huge difference where a company is set up. However, in terms of labour productivity and wages this choice makes a huge difference. As in terms of quality of industrial change, we can also observe here that East Asian economies

[7] In Figures 16.7, 16.8 and 16.10 data is calculated from the same countries as in Figures 16.4–16.6. In all cases averages are calculated.

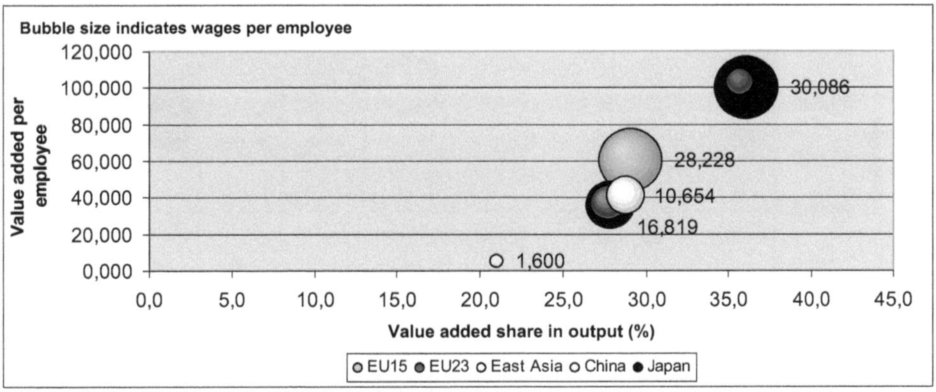

Figure 16.8 Wage and Productivity Competition Between the EU and Asia, 2001 (or latest), in US$.

Source: UNIDO Country Statistics database; Götzfried 2001; Eurostat 2004; Mittag 2001; *China Statistical Yearbook 1999*; calculations by the authors.

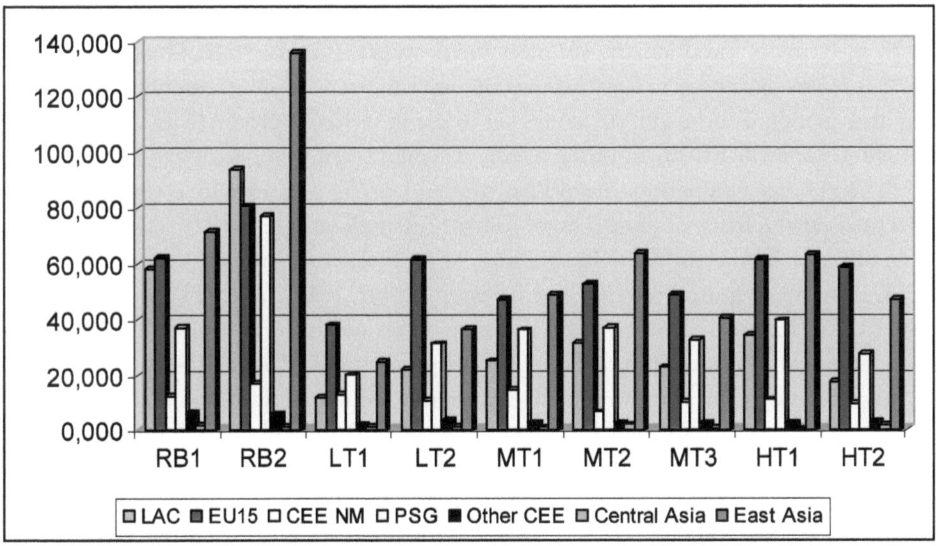

Figure 16.9 Average Value Added per Employee 1997–2001, in US$.[8]

Source: UNIDO Country Statistics Databases, Lall (2000).

[8] The taxonomy follows Lall 2000. RB1 means agro based production, RB2 other resource based production; LT1 (low-tech 1) indicates textile, garment and footwear production, LT2 is other low-tech; MT1 is automotive production, MT2 process technology and MT3 engineering; HT1 means electrical and electronics production and HT2 other technology. LAC signifies Latin America; CEE NM new members of the EU from CEE.

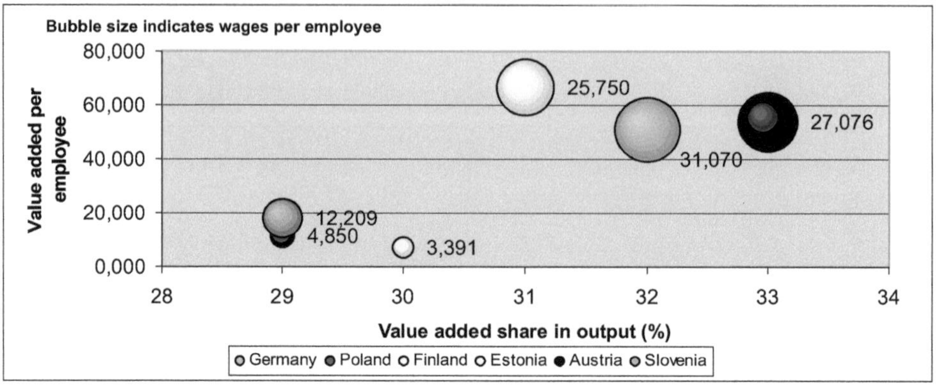

Figure 16.10 Wage and Productivity Competition in Europe, 2001 (or latest), in US$.
Source: UNIDO Country Statistics database; Götzfried 2001; Eurostat 2004; Mittag 2001, calculations by the authors.

outperform Portugal, Spain and Greece. Latin America is in turn outperforming CEE new member states.

If we calculate again the figures for EU23, the East Asian economies outperform EU23 in terms of productivity, yet offer lower wages. (Figure 16.8) Thus, as a region EU23 is relatively similar to East Asian economies in terms of international competitiveness and quality of industrial structure, yet worse in terms of productivity, accompanied by higher wages in EU23. In other words, it would seem that, as an economic region, EU23 faces fierce competition from East Asia and strong pressures to lower salaries and or to raise productivity, or alternatively to raise unemployment.

In terms of labour productivity, the East Asian economies are performing at the level of EU15 in all industrial sectors, and in cases of RB2, MT2 and HT1 actually better than EU15. (Figure 16.9) New CEE member states are in most cases competing with Latin American economies in terms of labour productivity. Portugal, Spain and Greece are outperfoming CEE countries in all sectors, and Latin America in most sectors. Other CEE and NIS countries have extremely low productivity in all sectors. Portugal, Spain and Greece show strong performance in resource-based production as well as in LT1 and MT1. These countries show significant differences to EU15 and East Asia only in high technology sectors. Yet, the fact that Portugal, Spain and Greece show relatively strong productivity in lower technology sectors shows that their integration into EU has been rather successful and that without current enlargement the convergence between older EU and Portugal, Spain and Greece in terms of productivity and living standards would have certainly been rather swift and successful.

The quest for higher productivity is, however, complicated by inner EU wage and productivity competition. (Figure 16.10) If output in most European countries is similar in terms of proportion of value added, then the differences in terms of wages and productivity appear huge. With the common market, an entrepreneur or a company in the old EU member states seems to face two choices in the face of Asian competition: to

Table 16.1 Adjusted Wage Shares of GDP in the European Union, 1961–2000[9]

	1960	1961–70	1971–80	1981–90	1991–2000
Austria	76.4	76.7	78.8	80.0	76.4
Belgium	69.9	70.4	75.8	74.3	72.2
Denmark	71.3	75.2	77.7	70.3	68.3
Finland	73.7	73.1	72.5	71.9	66.5
France	75.2	75.3	76.6	75.4	69.3
Germany*	70.6	71.6	73.7	70.9	67.9
Greece	-	86.1	70.7	74.0	67.2
Ireland	79.4	79.3	77.3	72.5	63.7
Italy	77.2	75.5	76.7	74.3	70.5
Luxembourg	56.3	57.7	65.5	66.5	64.5
Netherlands	63.4	69.4	74.8	68.1	65.9
Portugal	68.5	67.8	81.2	74.0	73.1
Spain	74.4	77.3	79.1	73.0	68.8
Sweden	69.4	72.3	74.1	70.5	68.9
UK	71.3	72.6	73.2	72.7	73.6
European Union	72.7	73.6	75.3	73.0	69.7

Source: European Industrial Relations Observatory On-line, http://www.eiro.eurofound.eu.int/2000/07/study/tn0007402s.html, based on European Commission 1999.

lower wages in the home country or move production into CEE or other parts of the world. (See further UNCTAD 2003). The third possibility, radical product or process innovations, is in many cases just not there. From the CEE perspective, however, this needs to be supplemented by development in the quality and competitiveness of the industrial structure if the newly 'imported' industries are here to stay. Yet, as we have seen above, the lack of industrial upgrading under the transition did not create conditions favourable to this development.

The size of this problem becomes apparent when we look at the share of CEE countries in world manufacturing: This share plummeted from19,3% in 1980 to 2,7% in 2001 (including the non-EU members from CEE and NIS (UNCTAD 2004:89)) Thus, in the CEE we can see a rapid increase in foreign direct investments in the automotive industry (UNCTAD 2003: 60–61) and simultaneously a *relocation in electronics* out of the CEE (particularly from Hungary, UNCTAD 2003: 62; on China in this context, see Boston Consulting Group 2003). Both IBM and Philips decided to move their production from Hungary to China in 2002. (Horvath 2002 and Horvath 2003). This indicates a loss of high-tech industry (electronics) and a specialization in a mature industry (automotive).

Thus, there are hardly any pressures in CEE countries that would significantly push the wages higher, but there also appear to be hardly any pressures for EU15 wages to stay high in the new EU.

9 Adjusted wage share = percentage of GDP at factor costs; * 1961–91 West Germany.

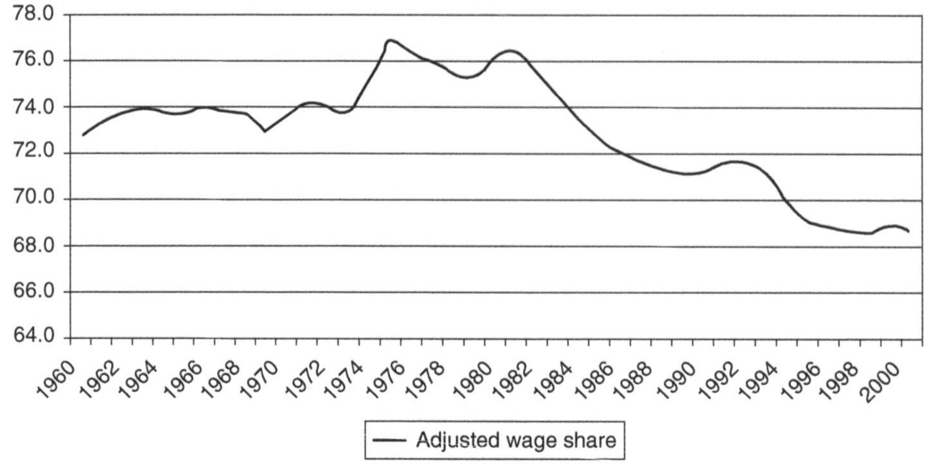

Figure 16.11 Adjusted Wage Share in the European Union 1960–2000.

Source: European Industrial Relations Observatory On-line, http://www.eiro.eurofound.eu.int/2000/07/study/tn0007402s.html, based on European Commission 1999.

3.3 International Trends and Regional Diversity add to the Problems.

The present globalization is taking place against a fairly dramatic backdrop that is rarely discussed. Wages as a percentage of Gross National Product have been falling in the Western World (see Figure 16.11 below). This is all the more surprising because the share of wages in GDP – roughly the division of the fruits of productivity increases between capital and labour – had so far been surprisingly stable through the turbulent 20th century (Krelle 1962). During the 1930s in the United States, the percentage of GDP going to labour even increased, meaning that capital income decreased more than labour income during the crisis. The dramatic losers in the 1930s, however, were the farmers who had no market power or union to protect them.

Table 16.1 and Figure 16.11 show how wages as a percentage of GDP have been declining in Europe since the very early 1980s. The trend is the same in the United States, but starting from a lower level. This is another aspect of *latinamericanization*. In 1990, the year the Peruvian Statistics office stopped collecting this data, the share of wages + income of independent workers reached 23 % of Peruvian GDP.

Clearly globalization as a form of asymmetrical economic integration is playing a crucial role here, and not only for the developing countries. On November 15, 2003, *New York Times*' editorial warned of the Wall-Martization of the US, a continuing drop in real wages that has already been going on for a long time.[10] Two weeks later, *Business Week* followed with the article "Waking up from the American Dream".[11] The essential

[10] http://www.labourrights.org/press/walmart_editorial_112503.htm.

[11] http://www.businessweek.com/@@A50u5oUQ9Q4xyREA/magazine/content/03_48/b3860067_mz021.htm

message of these high profile warning signals is that the challenge of mobility of industries and services posed by economic globalization is threatening to create low-wage peripheries in the US. It took a few months for Europe to follow: on March 25, 2004, Germany's most influential weekly *Der Spiegel* ran a story predicting the loss of 250,000 jobs in German electronics industry in the near future.[12] This was the first public expression of what is still an ongoing debate in Germany about the lowering of wages.

Simultaneously with globalization we observe the decomposition of what used to be nation-based 'industrial sectors' into globally dispersed value-chains in a manner where geographic location and proximity are loosing their importance. (See also Boston Consulting Group 2004; Ernst 1997). This means that high technology sectors of developing countries might become part of larger international value-chains, leaving little reasons for increasing division of labour or clustering in the home (developing) country (Castaldi et al. 2004. For an Estonian case study, see Kalvet 2004). It also means that economic sectors are becoming increasingly different in nature, which makes the traditional liberal policy of treating all sectors the same way impossible. This development opens up for some nations specializing in unskilled and routine (maquila) activities, while others specialize in the innovation-intensive and high-wage areas (the main theme in Reinert 2004a). Such a development will inevitably continue to increase international wage gaps, as some nations specialize in uneducated low-skill labour performing routine operations, while other nations continuously innovate and enjoy innovation rents. This represents a huge challenge for public sector policies: 'the performing state must serve the people, even if doing so requires that it serve them differently' (Schick 2003:72).

The problem of extending the European welfare state to new member states in this situation is best shown by the East German developments. In an ideal world, East Germany could very well serve as the best of all possible forms of globalizations: trade liberalization with social welfare programs at the Western-European level. However, German reunification is turning into an economic nightmare creating such claims as 'economically West Germany has become a colony of the East' (Steingart 2004: 8) because the net flow of funds is going that way. Real wages in Germany peaked as a percentage of GDP already in the 1980s and in real terms in 1990 (Steingart 2004: 48). Also here, the integration did not follow the path of gradual upgrading of East German industry but rather that of swift exchange of production facilities by West German companies in order to capture the market as well as relatively cheaper yet skilled labour.

It is calculated that the costs of the reunification add up to 1, 25 trillion Euro. One should have thought that the high cost of the German unification, with minimal industrial upgrading of the East, would have prevented copying this experiment on an even larger scale with the EU23. If the EU enlargement were to follow the pattern of integration set by German reunification, the costs would be prohibitive. Like most CEE countries, East Germany has experienced highly uneven development with large cities, particularly capitals, growing rapidly, with rural areas constantly falling further behind (See Table 16.2 below). The risk Europe faces is that the there will not be enough new

[12] http://www.spiegel.de/wirtschaft/0,1518,292371,00.html.

Table 16.2. Regional Development in Selected CEE Countries, 2001[13]

	GDP pc 2001, EU 25 = 100	Youth unemploy. 2001	Long-term unemploy., 2001
Czech R.	66,5	16,3	51,5
Prag	148,6	9,2	34,6
Hungary	56,4	10,5	44,8
Budapest	89,2	8,6	50,3
Poland	45,3	41,5	50,1
Warsaw	70,6	32,4	53,1
Slovak R.	49	38,9	58,3
Bratislava	111,7	19,9	39,9

Source: Eurostat 2003; Krueger 2004.

activities to absorb the huge level of rural unemployment in the CEE countries. The modernization of the agricultural sector makes it unlikely that this sector will be able to produce more employment.

The direction of FDI between urban and rural areas shows a very similar pattern. (European Commission 2004). Regional differences in economic performance in the EU are not present only in the new member states (European Commission 2004). This is a historical pattern everywhere, and recent research in the United States shows the income gaps between urban and rural areas increasing also there (Porter 2004). Successful studies of the moving forces behind the urban/rural income gap go all the way back to Serra (1613), and is the main reason behind agriculture support and protection as practiced in all wealthy nations. Yet, in the new member states these developments have surfaced only recently, as opposed to the older member states where these problems last time were acute in the 1930s.

One of the outstanding characteristics of Soviet-style industrialization was the creation of so-called monostructural cities or entire regions that depended on one industry or sometimes even on one single factory. What in the West would be an industrial cluster was in the East often one single firm in one single location. As there was no market for suppliers, these monostructural regions did not develop any high degrees of specialization. The organization of supplies was left to the planning agencies. With the opening of markets most of these companies faced fierce competition, and at the same time they lacked the means and experience to launch efficient restructuring. Most of them probably went bankrupt before they even had a chance to put a costing system into place. In a matter of few years many of these monostructural regions or cities saw massive unemployment and migration, with whole cities developing into ghost towns with depopulated buildings and blocks. Similar developments took place in almost all agricultural centers that used multi-storey buildings to house many people in a relatively

[13] Data for Budapest is for the region of Közep-Magyarorsza; Warsaw for the region of Mazowieckie. Youth unemployment is unemployment in age group 15–24; Long term unemployment is defined as lasting more than one year.

small area. These used to have a living standard comparable to that in the cities. With the collapse of large-scale agriculture, these centres have been depopulated, and the rural standard of living has deteriorated dramatically.

A brief picture of regional disparities: Today, in Siimusti in central Estonia one can buy a fully functional 60 m^2 apartment, for ca 250 US dollars. For the same sum one can *rent* a similar apartment for a month in a modest district of Tallinn, the capital of Estonia. In the same modest district of Tallinn, this apartment would cost about 50 000 US dollars. In the downtown area the price would be doubled. The average wage in Estonia was around 600 US dollars per month in the second quarter of 2004. However, in Chisinau, the capital of Moldova, 250 US dollar would pay the rent of a very nice apartment for an entire year. In 1989, Moldova and Estonia had relatively similar standards of living. The periphery of the periphery is the economically hardest hit.

Also European R&D efforts are highly concentrated. Of the top 15 R&D intensity regions, nine are in Germany, two each in Sweden and Finland (Frank 2004a; on patenting, see Frank 2004b). The EU enlargement compounds the already existing inequality in knowledge production. The difference between old and new member states is almost absolute. For example: per million inhabitants the Czech Republic and Estonia claimed only one patent application for high technology at the European Patent Office in the period 1996–2001; Poland none. On the other hand, Germany has 49 such patent applications per million inhabitants, UK 36 and Sweden 101 (Götzfried 2004:6).

In addition, the change of techno-economic paradigms in the 1980s and 1990s – from Fordist mass-production into one based on ICT – has certainly played a crucial role in the development dynamics of CEE as well as in European integration. The Soviet style economy could cope relatively well with the mass-production paradigm, yet almost by definition networking via backward and forward feedbacks could not develop. This was done centrally. However, networks are perhaps one of the key characteristics of the ICT-led paradigm (Perez 2002 & 2004). Thus, the entire economic culture and structure of the CEE countries was alien to the new paradigm.[14] (Freeman 1998; on European welfare state in this context, see Esping-Andersen 2002).

In addition, the EU enlargement falls into the middle period of the techno-economic paradigm, typically characterized by financial crisis and socio-economic and institutional adaptation to the new paradigm (Perez 2002, 2004). We are at a stage of the techno-economic paradigm where the harvest of the new technologies 'is gathered under recessive symptoms and with more anxiety than rejoicing' (Schumpeter 1939, Vol. 1: 139). Similar wage pressures could be observed in the 1930s where only strong unions kept the industrial sector from the total collapse in real income which happened in the agricultural sector (US rural wages fell 70 per cent in purchasing power during the early 1930s). Such processes feed back into the economy as falling demand, and possibly into a new depression, which – just as the Asian Crisis – cannot happen in neo-classical theory, but may well happen in practice. Thus the EU needs to go through a double institutional

[14] Also, it could be argued that military industry played a crucial part in CEE industrial development prior to 1989.

change: adapting to an enlarged Europe as well as to a new techno-economic paradigm, both under increased wage-pressure from other continents.

Capitalism's most tumultuous periods are characterised by widening gaps between rich and poor. Historically any improvement of this trend – a change in the Kuznets Curve towards a better income distribution – is invariably a result of political decisions, not of market forces (Freeman 2004, Perez 2004). The long way towards the European welfare state started with a description of a situation similar to that of Europe today, by Gustav Schmoller during the very first meeting of the *Verein für Sozialpolitik*, an organisation that during next sixty years was to build the institutional design of generalised European welfare:

> We believe the healthiest and most normal society can be expressed by a ladder containing rungs between different existences, depicting easy access from one step to another. Today's society threatens more and more to look like a ladder which grows fast at the top and at the bottom, but where the middle steps increasingly fall out, and where there is solid hold only at the very top and at the very bottom (Verein für Socialpolitik 1873:5).

4. Conclusion

It can be argued that the European Union enlargement project is laudably idealistic. Whereas the US does not absorb any of the social costs in the Mexican deindustrialization of traditional industry and allows little (legal) immigration, the European integrative model has the disadvantage of possibly accruing very high costs on several counts. The large internal wage differentials are likely to create strong downward pressures on the wage level in the core countries, where the conflicts during the summer of 2004 may have been just preliminary skirmishes for a much larger battle to follow. Just as the free float of alcohol from new member countries has caused a collapse of alcohol prices in a country like Sweden, a large scale free float of labour may very well have a similar effect on labour prices (but some measures have been taken). At the same time the rapid integration into the world economy during the 1990s had already devastated the industrial structures in the new member states, so there is little to build on except moving already existing jobs and purchasing power eastwards in a lose-win, rather than a win-win flying geese type of integration.

An example of the slow advancement of free trade in the post World War II is that for a very long time outright import prohibitions existed. All import of garments into Norway was totally prohibited until 1956, and a shortage of foreign exchange made import licenses for cars last until 1960. Safeguards for the balance of payment also included frequent use of clearing arrangements: i.e. barter agreements that secured a balance on the external account.

The EU enlargement has brought the new EU into a situation where it is difficult to see reasons that would stop pressures towards lower wages, cuts in social benefits etc. An idealistic integration – which at a lower pace of integration could have had more flying geese qualities – **may end up as a lose-lose strategy**. The present European strategy does not capture the benefits from really cheap imports in labour intensive products and crops as the US does from Mexico, but on the cost side it may accrue heavy social expenses associated with integrating with the poor periphery. As with the integration of DDR, a first beneficial 'pipe line effect' will boost sales from the 'old' core, but this benefit is truly transitory.

Turning to the earlier theoretical discussion of types of economic integration, Europe is weak in the win-win categories. The present integration of the European Union is clearly a departure from the slow and careful **Listian form of symmetrical integration** that characterized the growth of the European Common Market, starting in the immediate post-war period. In the old mercantilist tradition, in the first decades of European integration it was made sure that the important paradigm carrier industries – at that time above all the automotive industry – were present in all large countries. When Spain later accessed, this country already had a basic industrial structure which – through gradual rather than abrupt tariff reductions – was able to upgrade and successfully integrate symmetrically with the rest of Europe. The automotive industry with its layers of suppliers is one example of this successful transition. An artificially high exchange rate of the peseta prevented social dumping and wage pressures on the rest of Europe, at the cost of relatively high unemployment in Spain. However, with the former DDR, the exchange rate was so high and the economic structures so rigid that the new *Länder* lost all competitiveness and were largely deindustrialised. All in all, the integration of the large Spanish economy carries all the elements of a carefully planned Listian integration. There is, we argue, **a qualitative quantum leap towards the worse** in the philosophy behind European integration between the careful economic integration of Spain, Portugal and Greece on the one hand, and the May 1, 2004 integration on the other. The first was Listian, the second was much more ideological, a product of economists and politicians who had come to believe in the crude propaganda version of economics, and therefore now threaten European wealth and welfare.

The destructive destruction of the East European industrial structure that took place during the ten years leading up to May 1, 2004, now prevents the very important **flying geese** and technology upgrading aspects of integration to take place as they did on the Iberian Peninsula and even in Greece. In most CEE countries there is too little industry left to upgrade. There are even clear elements of **welfare colonialism** in today's European integration, particularly in the former DDR. The classical colonial drain has been reversed, and now flows from the core country to the colony, while the productive structure of the colony has been greatly reduced and replaced by welfare payments. This is essentially the argument made by Gabor Steingart in his recent book: 'economically West Germany has become a colony of the East' (Steingart 2004: 8). This form of integration carries costs that in the long run are prohibitive.

We would argue that the present problem is that the ruling economic ideology has unlearned the logic and wisdom of Listian integration. Economic activities moving because wages are too high is a completely normal, and even necessary, process in the history of capitalism, and is an integral part of capitalist dynamics. Too high wages in London was the reason why English textile industry moved out of that city many centuries ago. The variables that cause these moves to be problematic and damaging or not to the creation and even maintenance of real wealth are the following:

1. **The degree of dynamics** in the wealthy core, relative to the other world players (US, China, East Asia). Here Europe scores relatively low, in spite of considerable efforts.
2. **The timing of this event in the techno-economic paradigm**. With the Fordist mass production wave near its crest during the 1950s and 1960s, a radical integration would have been easier almost anywhere than now, in the post-financial crisis, deflationary period of the paradigm, resembling in so many ways the 1930s, including politically (Perez 2002, 2004). That financial capitalism, rather than production capitalism, is in charge during such periods further aggravates the problem (Veblen 1899, Hilferding 1912) carrying the focus of the economics profession away from studying production to studying finance.
3. **The size of the poor/unemployed/underemployed population** to be integrated compared to the population of the core countries. Here integrating Portugal and Spain was relatively easy, but again Europe now faces a problem (see Table 16.2).
4. **The ability of the industrial structure in the poor countries to upgrade**. Compared both to the post-WW II situation and to the integration of Spain, Portugal and Greece, the situation in the CEE is very problematic. Instead of the slow reduction of tariffs that made the upgrading of Spanish, Portuguese and even Greek industries survive and upgrade, the CEE countries – with the exception of Hungary – had to varying degrees been subject to de-industrializing Morgenthau Plans that had also created havoc in the agricultural sector.
5. **The wage dynamics of the rest of the world**. Here the dynamics are generally strongly in disfavour of European wages. The Unites States is an innovation powerhouse with creeping Wall-Martization of the labour market, increasing illegal immigration, and falling real wages for last two decades. China is rapidly catching up technologically with minimal increases in real wages, and a virtually unlimited supply of labour from the interior at very low prices. The weakness of labour unions in both these countries will – combined with the other factors on this list – automatically lead to wage pressures in Europe. The efforts needed, and the bottlenecks that will appear, in order to upgrade the Chinese workforce fast enough will be a factor working in the other direction, in favour of a better European wage level.

As Paul Krugman says, there are periods when old economic wisdom is unlearned and has to be rediscovered (Krugman 1996). Or as John Stuart Mill says it, much stronger, 'It often happens that the universal beliefs of one age of mankind – **a belief from which no one *was*, nor without an extraordinary effort of genius and courage *could* at the time be free** – becomes to a subsequent age so palpable an absurdity, that the only difficulty then is to imagine how such a thing can ever have appeared credible…It looks like one of the crude fancies of childhood, instantly corrected by a word from any grown person.' (Mill 1848/1929: 3, emphasis added).

Going back to Hyman Minsky, with whom we started the paper, we just **may** be in a similar situation as regards European wages as Minsky argued regarding financial crises: things happen that theoretically cannot happen, just like a financial crisis. If the world should move towards factor prize equalization under global free trade and relative upskilling of huge numbers of poor (China, India), the huge majority of unemployed, underemployed and poor in the world make it much more likely that equalization will be downwards rather than upwards. For slightly different reasons there was a tremendous pressure in this direction during the 1930s, and the industrial sector wages were only saved by having very strong labour unions as a defense line. If this argument has just a slight validity, we had better turn to a better understanding of Friedrich List.

Now this labour union defence line is seriously weakened, and Europe may be closer than is comfortable to where the agricultural sector was in the 1930s, when the US agricultural sector experienced a 70 per cent fall in income compared to the industrial sector. This catastrophe led to the agricultural policy we still have remnants of today: monopolies to the farmers (US almonds and raisins are still today legal monopolies) and price controls. Farm subsidies have now turned agriculture into an increasing returns activity both in Europe and the US[15], but we otherwise seem, to a large extent, to have forgotten why we have the agricultural policy we have. The Common Agricultural Policy seems to hang in there by inertia and lobby pressures rather than based on any theoretical or historical understanding.

Friedrich List had a very good reason for arguing for economic integration only when an industrial and increasing return sector had been established in each country. The alternatives are either extremely expensive or cause poverty, or both. Industrialization, particularly after the 1848 revolutions, combined enormous productivity increases combined with extremely strong political pressure for increasing wages. This led to what French Regulation School economists refer to as a Fordist wage regime: industrial workers increased their wages roughly at the pace of the productivity improvements in all industrialized countries. For this reason, the huge productivity improvements after World War II did not lead to deflation, and for this same reason the industrialized countries' Terms of Trade with the non-industrialized world did not move in the favour of those nations with fewer productivity improvements. The wealthy nations took their productivity improvements out in the forms of higher wages, not lower prices (Singer 1950). The countervailing forces of capital and labour were in balance, resulting in a situation where their respective shares in GDP were surprisingly stable through business cycles and the depression (Krelle 1962).

Figure 16.11 and Table 16.1 show how the economic power game gradually was lost by the unions. First this only meant that labour was losing its share in GDP without a loss in real income. The further effect is a fall in real wages. This process, which was slow and not clearly noticeable, now is potentially accelerating. Through feed-back through diminishing demand (and a lower and qualitatively different consumption pattern of the rich, whose incomes increase), the falling real wages are likely to start a downward spiral in spending/demand, which again – given Europe's external challenges which we have described – may be difficult to stop even by cutting wages. As England did after the first wave of globalization, the former world leader Europe may have to resort to protectionism again in order to save its welfare. *The Rise and Decline of the Free Trade*

15 We are indebted to Jan Kregel for this point.

Movement was the title of a 1905 book by famous Cambridge economist, William Cunningham. We may get back to a similar situation.

Competition between nations is at times similar to competition between airlines, it becomes a winner-takes it all market (Frank & Cook 1996), but with a difference. Instead of airlines going bankrupt we may have wages falling rapidly. European nations have spent a lot of money propping up their own 'inefficient' national airlines. They may face a similar choice as regards the wage level of their 'inefficient' European workers, compared to extremely efficient and very poor Chinese. The retreat from the first round of globalization, as described in Cunningham's 1905 book was a decision of this type. However, if our possible scenario as described here comes true, it will be a very hard fight, both due to an entrenched ideology and to a relatively recent power imbalance between capital and labour.

Economists have not properly understood that, due to the Fordist wage regime, what we used to call 'Economic Development' was, in effect, a high-tech and dynamic Schumpeterian oligopoly where the fruits of industrialism were shared by capital and labour. The developing countries, lacking this industrialist engine, were not able to catch up. As long as new nations were added to this oligopoly slowly, in a Listian fashion, and with controlled tariff reductions, this shared oligopoly worked very well. This system was not the result of market forces, but of wise political control, and the system functioned well until and including the enlargement of the EU with Spain and Portugal. If the shocks are too big, and the balance of power becomes imbalanced, it is our conviction that the system potentially may deteriorate into a 'race to the bottom' in terms of wages.

Krugman (1996) and Mill (1848), quoted above, argued that economics goes through periods of relative ignorance when previously accumulated knowledge is lost. In our opinion, following the market euphoria and triumphalism of the early 1990s, the West started believing in its own propaganda version of economics, that markets by themselves were creators of automatic harmony. This has previously proved extremely damaging in the periphery, where countries like Peru and Mongolia have experienced a 50 per cent fall in real wages (Reinert 2004a). Now this development is approaching Europe, strongly reinforced by some very unfortunate political decisions in the past. First de-industrializing a group of nations, later to fully integrate them economically, may with hindsight prove to be one of the situations of collective blindness that John Stuart Mill refers to. Such a strategy puts extremely high pressure both on the social fabric and on the resources of the system. Historically this is probably a unique event in this magnitude.

As already mentioned, the free flow of alcohol forces the wealthy European countries to cut their alcohol prices, and in terms of price pressure there is no difference between the effects on a free flow of alcohol and a free flow of labour. Unless something unlikely happens to improve the labour situation in many CEE countries, the West will have to limit labour migration and thus cause political turmoil in CEE countries. Given the international setting, it is simply very difficult to see Europe creating enough industrial dynamics to solve all these challenges without falling wages, spreading from one sector to the other, or without protection of some kind, as happened in the wake of the first wave of globalization. There may be reasons why one need not be alarmist, but the arguments heard in favour of this tend, on both sides of the Atlantic, to be purely ideological, not to discuss the facts, and therefore not to be convincing on a logical level.

In our opinion these issues and mechanisms ought to be put higher up on the agenda. Are the huge pressures for lowering the real wages in Europe this summer a first skirmish in a long and inevitable battle or are they not? The timing in the technology cycles points to a 1930-scenario, where protection is not a beggar-thy-neighbour policy but simply a way to prevent a winner-takes-it all situation. To pick up the airlines industry metaphor again, this means making more than one airline survive, i.e. leaving more than the winner country or area with a decent wage level.

Cambridge economist H. S. Foxwell argued: 'Just as we may avoid widespread physical desolation by rightly turning a stream near its source, so a timely dialectic in the fundamental ideas of social philosophy may spare us untold social wreckage and suffering' (Foxwell 1899: xxi). Clearly the transition and later integration of the CEE countries were not done with these words in mind. We can still limit the damage in Europe by admitting that something went wrong. Hyman Minsky suggests that if something goes wrong and we have not sufficiently understood what is happening, we are just likely to find a scapegoat. Perhaps we can call it 'the Bin Laden Depression' in Europe. Says Minsky: 'A theory that denies that what is happening can happen, that sees unfavourable events as the work of outside forces (such as the oil crisis) rather than as the result of characteristics of the economic mechanism, may satisfy the politicians' need for a villain or scapegoat, but such a theory offers no useful guide to a solution of a problem.' (Minsky 1986).

Appendix 1: The Flying Geese Pattern of Sequential Economic Development.

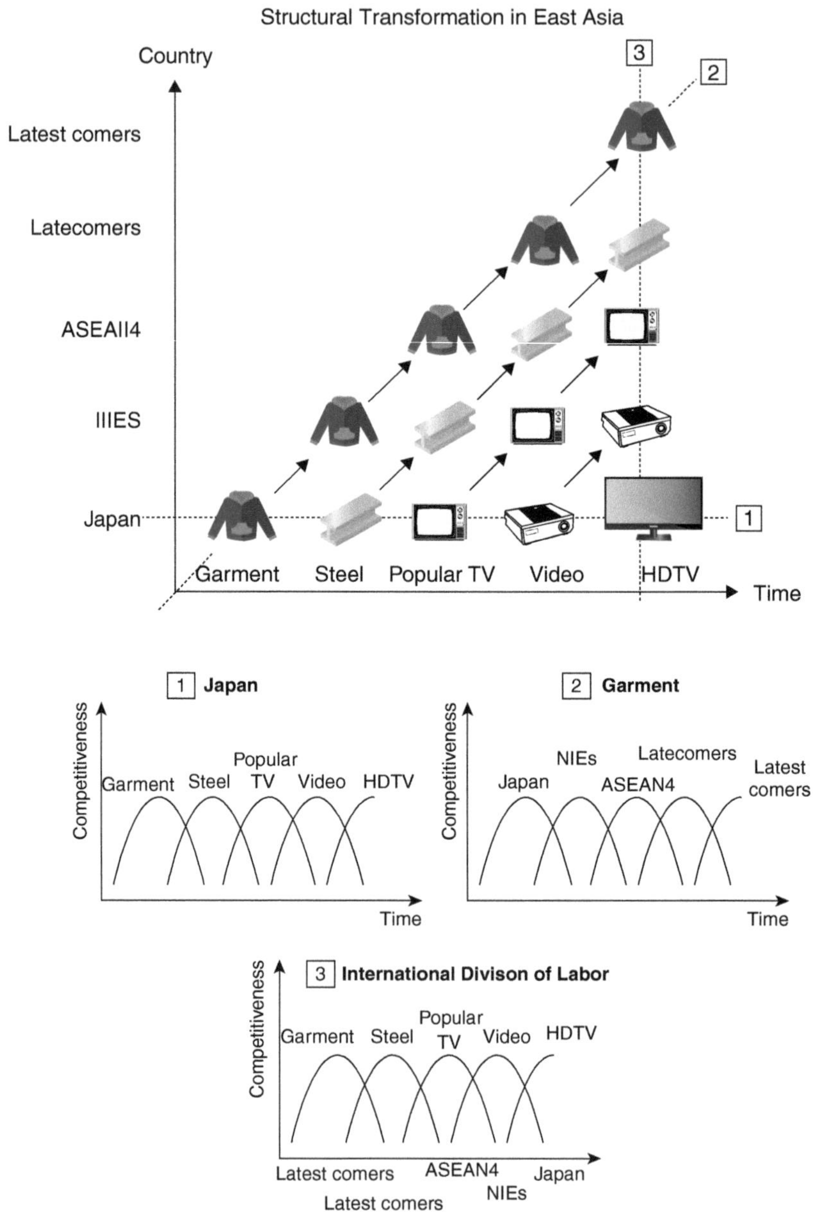

Source: GRIPS Development Forum, http://www.grips.ac.jp/module/prsp/FGeese.htm

Bibliography

Akamatsu, Kaname (1961). 'A Theory of Unbalanced Growth in the World Economy'. *Weltwirtschaftliches Archiv*, 86, 196–217.

Audretsch, David B. (2004). 'Diversity: Implications for Income Distribution'. In Reinert (2004a), *Globalization, Economic Development and Inequality: An Alternative Perspective*, Cheltenham, Elgar.

Backhaus, Jürgen G. (2001) 'Constitutional Causes for Technological Leadership: Why Europe?'. *Independent Institute, Working Paper*, 39.

Boston Consulting Group (2003). 'Made in China: Why Industrial Goods Are Going Next'. Available at http://www.bcg.com/publications/files/Made_%20in%20China_Why%20Industrial_%20Goods_Are%20Going_Next_IG_OfA_%20Nov%2003.pdf.

Boston Consulting Group (2004). 'Riding the Next Wave of Outsourcing'. Available at http://www.bcg.com/publications/files/Riding_the_Next_Wave_of_Outsourcing_Jul04_CP_OfA.pdf.

Botero, Giovanni (1590), *Delle cause della grandezza delle città. Libri tre*, Rome: Presso Vincenzio Pellagallo.

Buchanan, James (1979). *What Should Economists Do?*. Indianapolis: Liberty Fund.

Castaldi, Carolina, Mario Cimoli, Nelson Correa, Giovanni Dosi (2004). 'Technological Learning, Policy Regimes and Growth in a 'Globalized' Economy: General Patterns and the Latin American Experience'. Laboratory of Economics and Management, *Sant'Anna School of Advanced Studies, Working Paper Series*, 01/2004.

Chang, Ha-Joon (ed.) (2003). *Rethinking Economic Development*. London: Anthem.

China Statistical Yearbook (1999). Available at http://www.stats.gov.cn/yearbook/ml/1999_e.htm.

Cimoli, Mario (ed.) (2000). *Developing Innovation Systems: Mexico in a Global Context*. New York, Continuum International Publishing Group.

Cimoli, Mario and Nelson Correa (2002). 'Trade Openness and Technological Gaps in Latin America: A 'Low Growth Gap''. Laboratory of Economics and Management, *Sant'Anna School of Advanced Studies, Working Paper Series*, 14/2002.

Cornia, Giovanni Andrea (2004). ''Rapid Change and Mortality Crises'. Available at www.networkideas.org.

Cunningham, W. (1905), *The Rise and Decline of the Free Trade Movement*, Cambridge: Cambridge University Press.

EBRD (2000). *Transition Report 2000*. London: Hyway Printing Group.

Ernst, Dieter (1997). 'From Partial to Systemic Globalization: International Production Networks in the Electronics Industry'. *The Berkeley Roundtable on the International Economy, Working Paper* 98.

Esping-Andersen, Gösta (2002). 'Towards the Good Society, Once Again?'. In Gösta Esping-Andersen et al. (eds.), *Why We Need a New Welfare State*. Oxford: Oxford University Press, 1–25.

European Commission (1999). *European Economy No. 68. Statistical Annex*. Brussels: European Commission.

European Commission (2004). *Third Report on Economic and Social Cohesion*. Available at http://europa.eu.int/comm/regional_policy/sources/docoffic/official/reports/pdf/cohesion3/cohesion3_part1_ecosoc_en.pdf.

Eurostat (2003). *Employment and Labour Market in Central European Countries*. Detailed Tables, Theme 3, Population and Social Conditions. Eurostat.

Eurostat (2004). *Employment in the Market Economy in the European Union. An Analysis Based on the Structural Business Statistics*. Detailed Tables, Theme 4, Industry, trade and services. Eurostat.

Foxwell, H.S., Introduction to Anton Menger's *The Right to the Whole Produce of Labour*, London, Macmillan, 1899.

Frank, Robert and Philip Cook (1996). *The Winner-Take-All Society*. New York, Penguin.

Frank, Simona (2004a). 'R&D Expenditure in the European Regions'. Statistics in Focus, *Science and Technology*, 3, Eurostat.

Frank, Simona (2004b). 'Patent Applications to the EPO from the EU Regions 1997 to 2002'. Statistics in Focus, *Science and Technology*, 7, Eurostat.

Freeman, Chris (1998). 'Innovation Systems: City-state, National, Continental and Subnational'. Available at http://www.ie.ufrj.br/redesist/P1/texto/NT02.PDF.

Freeman, Chris (2004). 'Income Inequality in Changing Techno-Economic Paradigms'. In Reinert (2004a), *Globalization, Economic Development and Inequality: An Alternative Perspective*, Cheltenham, Elgar.

Graham, Frank (1923), 'Some Aspects of Protection Further Considered', in *Quarterly Journal of Economics*, February, pp. 199–227.

GRIPS Development Forum, http://www.grips.ac.jp/module/prsp/FGeese.htm

Götzfried, August (2004). 'High-Technology and Knowledge-Intensity Leading to More Value Added', Innovation and Patents, Statistics in Focus, *Science and Technology*, 8, Eurostat.

Hilferding, Rudolf (1910), *Das Finanzkapital. Eine Studie über die jüngste Entwicklung des Kapitalismus*, Vienna: Verlag der Wiener Volksbuchhandlung Ignaz Brand & Co.

Hirschmann, Albert O. (1958). *The Strategy of Economic Development*. New Haven: Yale University Press.

Horvath, John (2002). 'Globalisation and the Nature of Networks'. Available at http://www.heise.de/tp/deutsch/html/result.xhtml?url=/tp/english/inhalt/co/13587/1.html&words=Globalisation%20nature%20networks.

Horvath, John (2003). 'Hungary's New Economy'. Available at http://www.heise.de/tp/deutsch/html/result.xhtml?url=/tp/english/inhalt/co/14027/1.html&words=Globalisation%20nature%20networks.

Hume, David (1768). *The History of England*. 6 vols. London: Cadell.

International Labour Office (2004). *Global Employment Trends*. ILO: Geneva.

Kalvet, Tarmo (2004). *The Estonian ICT Manufacturing and Software Industry: Current State and Future Outlook*. Institute for Prospective Technological Studies - Directorate General Joint Research Centre. European Commission: Sevilla.

King, Charles (1721). *The British Merchant or Commerce Preserv'd*. 3 vols. London: John Darby.

King, Lawrence P. (2002) 'Emperor Exposed: Neoliberal Theory and De-modernization in Postcommunist Society'. Available at http://sociology.berkeley.edu/faculty/evans/king_the_emperor_exposed.pdf.

Kregel, Jan, Egon Matzner, Gernot Grabber (eds.) (1992). *The Market Shock. An AGENDA for the Economic and Social Reconstruction of Central and Eastern Europe*. Austrian Academy of Sciences / International Institute for Peace. Ann Arbor: University of Michigan Press.

Krelle, Wilhelm (1962), *Verteilungstheorie*. Tübingen:Mohr.

Krueger, Andreas (2004). 'Regional Gross Domestic Product in the Candidate Countries 2001'. Statistics in Focus, General Statistics, Theme 1, 2, Eurostat

Krugman, Paul (1980), *Rethinking International Trade*, Cambridge, Mass.: MIT Press.

Krugman, Paul (1996), *Development, Geography and Economic Theory*, Cambridge, Mass.: MIT Press

Lall, Sanjaya (2000). 'The Technological Structure and Performance of Developing Country Manufactured Exports, 1985–98'. *Oxford Development Studies*, 28, 3, 337–369.

List, Friedrich (1841), *Das Nationale System der Politischen Ökonomie*, Stuttgart & Tübingen: Cotta.

Mill, John Stuart (148/1929), *Principles of Political Economy*, London: Longmans, Green..

Minsky, Hyman (1991). 'The Transition to a Market Economy'. Working Paper no. 66, Annandale-on-Hudson, N.Y.: The Jerome Levy Economics Institute, November.

Misselden, Edward (1622). *Free Trade or, The Meanes to make Trade florish, wherein the Causes of the Decay of Trade in this Kingdom are discovered*. London: Simon Waterson.[16]

Mittag, Hans-Joachim (2004). 'Labour Costs in Europe 1996–2002'. *Statistics in Focus, Population and Social Conditions*, 9, Eurostat.

[16] Free trade at the time signified the absence of monopolies, not the absence off tariffs.

Morgenthau, Henry, Jr. (1943) *Germany is Our Problem. A Plan for Germany*. New York: Harper.

Nurkse, Ragnar (1953). *Problems of Capital Formation in Underdeveloped Countries*. New York: Oxford University Press.

OECD (2004). *Economic Outlook No. 75*, June 2004. Annex tables available at http://www.oecd.org/dataoecd/5/46/2483884.xls.

Paine, Robert (ed.) (1977). *The White Arctic. Anthropological Essays on Tutelage and Ethnicity*. St John's Memorial University of Newfoundland.

Perez, Carlota (2002). *Technological Revolutions and Financial Capital: The Dynamics of Bubbles and Golden Ages*. Edward Elgar Publications.

Perez, Carlota (2004). 'Technological Revolutions, Paradigm Shifts and Socio-institutional Change'. In Reinert (2004a), *Globalization, Economic Development and Inequality: An Alternative Perspective*. Cheltenham, Elgar.

Porter, Michael (1990), *The Competitive Advantage of Nations*, London: Macmillan.

Porter, Michael (2004), *Competitiveness in Rural U.S. Regions: Learning and Research Agenda*, Boston: Institute for Strategy and Competitiveness, Harvard Business School.

Prak, Maarten (2001). 'Early Modern Capitalism: an Introduction'. In Maarten Prak (ed.) *Early Modern Capitalism: Economic and Social Change in Europe 1400–1800*. London, Routledge, 1–21.

Reinert, Erik (1980). *International Trade and the Economic Mechanisms of Underdevelopment*. Ph D. thesis, Cornell University. Ann Arbor, Michigan, University Microfilms.

Reinert, Erik (1998). 'Raw Materials in the History of Economic Policy; or, Why List (the Protectionist) and Cobden (the Free Trader) both Agreed on Free Trade in Corn.'. In G. Parry (ed.) *Freedom and Trade. 1846–1996*. London: Routledge.

Reinert, Erik (2003). 'Increasing Poverty in a Globalised World: Marshall Plans and Morgenthau Plans as Mechanisms of Polarization of World Incomes'. In Chang (2003) *Rethinking Economic Development*. London: Anthem.

Reinert Erik (ed.) (2004a). *Globalization, Economic Development and Inequality: An Alternative Perspective*. Cheltenham, Elgar.

Reinert, Erik (2004b). 'Globalisation in the Periphery as a Morgenthau Plan: The Underdevelopment of Mongolia in the 1990s'. In Reinert (2004a) *Globalization, Economic Development and Inequality: An Alternative Perspective*. Cheltenham, Elgar.

Reinert, Erik (2004c). *How Rich Nations got Rich. Essays in the History of Economic Policy*. Working paper Nr. 1, 2004, SUM - Centre for Development and the Environment, University of Oslo, Norway. Available on http://www.sum.uio.no/publications

Reinert, Erik S. and Sophus A. Reinert (2003). 'An Early National Innovation System: the Case of Antonio Serra's 1613 *Breve Trattato*'. *Institutions and Economic Development/Istituzioni e Sviluppo Economico*, 1, 3. Available on www.othercanon.org

Robbins, Lionel (1952). *The Theory of Economic Policy in English Classical Political Economy*. London: Macmillan.

Rosenstein-Rodan, P. N. (1943). 'The problems of Industrialization of Eastern and South-Eastern Europe'. *Economic Journal*, 53, 202–211.

Samuelson, Paul (1948). 'International Trade and the Equalization of Factor Prices'. *Economic Journal*, 58, June.

Schick, Allen (2003). 'The Performing State: Reflection on an Idea Whose Time Has Come but Whose Implementation Has Not'. *OECD Journal on Budgeting*, 3, 71–103.

Schmoller, Gustav von ([1884] 1944). *Das Merkantilsystem in seiner Historischen Bedeutung. Städtische, Territoriale und Staatliche Wirtschaftspolitik*. Frankfurt a. M.:Klostermann.

Schumpeter, Joseph (1939). *Business Cycles, a Theoretical, Historical, and Statistical Analysis of the Capitalist Process*. New York: McGraw-Hill.

Schumpeter, Joseph A. (1954). *History of Economic Analysis*. New York: Oxford University Press.

Serra, Antonio (1613). *Breve trattato delle cause che possono far abbondare li regni d'oro & argento dove non sono miniere*. Naples: Lazzaro Scorriggio.

Singer, Hans (1950) 'The Distribution of Gains between Investing and Borrowing Countries', *i American Economic Review*, Papers and Proceedings, vol. II, nr. 2, Mai 1950. reprinted in Singer, Hans W. (1964), *International Development, Growth and Change.* New York: McGraw-Hill.

Sneijers, Petra (2004). 'Industry and construction in the New Member States and Candidate countries'. Statistics in focus, *Industry, Trade and Services*, 23, Eurostat

Sombart, Werner (1928). *Der Moderne Kapitalismus.* 6 Vols. Munich and Leipzig: Duncker & Humblot. The key volumes have been translated into French, Spanish, and Italian. French: *L'Apogée du Capitalisme*, Paris, Pauot, 1932 (2 Vols.). Spanish: *El Apogeo del Capitalismo*, México DF, Fondo de Cultura Económica, 1946 (2 Vols.), Italian: *Il Capitalismo Moderno*, Turin, Unione Tipografico-Editrice Torinese, 1967.

Steingart, Gabor (2004). *Deutschland. Der Abstieg eines Superstars.* Munich: Piper.

Tiits, Marek, Rainer Kattel, Tarmo Kalvet and Rein Kaarli (2002). *The Estonian Economy. Competitiveness & Future Outlooks. R&D and Innovation Policy Review.* Tallinn: R&D Council of the Republic of Estonia.

UNCTAD (2004). *Development and Globalization: Facts and Figures.* New York and Geneva: United Nations.

UNCTAD (2003). *World Investment Report. FDI Policies for Development: National and International Perspectives.* New York and Geneva: United Nations.

UNIDO (2004). *Industrial Development Report 2004. Industrialization, Environment and the Millennium Development Goals in Sub-Saharan Africa.* UNIDO: Vienna.

Veblen, Thorstein (1899). *The Theory of the Leisure Class - An economic Study of Institutions*, New York: Macmillan.

Verein für Sozialpolitik (1873). *Verhandlungen der Eisenacher Versammlung zur Besprechung der Sozialen Frage am 6. und 7. October 1872.* Leipzig, Ducker & Humblot.

Vernon, Raymond (1966), 'International Investment and International Trade in the Product Cycle', *Quarterly Journal of Economics*, May 1966. Vol. 80, pp.190–207.

Williamson, Oliver E. (1985). *The Economic Institutions of Capitalism.* The Free Press: New York.

Chapter Seventeen

PRIMITIVIZATION OF THE EU PERIPHERY: THE LOSS OF RELEVANT KNOWLEDGE

Erik S. Reinert

1 Introduction

The European periphery – from Greece to Spain and the Baltic States – is hard hit by economic crises in the form of unemployment and falling real wages. The immediate reasons for these crises, 'the straw that broke the nations' back' so to say, are not the same. The countries in crisis may have had irresponsible budget deficits or irresponsible housing and property booms, but– as this article argues – the present underlying problems in the European Union can partly be attributed to ignoring previously well-understood economic insights and wisdom based on the interplay between geography, technology, and economic structure. This ignored knowledge abounds in the German-speaking literature, in this chapter represented by three economists: Heinrich von Thünen, Friedrich List, and Joseph Schumpeter, whose collective lives span from 1783 to 1950. Although all three worked in the periphery of what is normally referred to as *The German Historical School of Economics*, they all centered their analysis on a qualitative understanding of economic phenomena which disappeared from ruling economic theory, and consequently also from the understanding of politicians.

It is argued that the European Union was initially built on principles emanating from a type of geography-based economic understanding with old roots, but that the formalization of economics has led to the fact that this previous knowledge has been lost both to economists and policy-makers. This loss occurred in two overlapping stages: after World War II when German economic theory spanning from The Thirty Years' War to World War II[1] was thrown out with the proverbial bathing water of the Hitler regime, and it reached its final blow with the neoliberal 'triumphalism' starting with the Fall of the Berlin Wall.

The type of economic understanding represented by this qualitative economic tradition, as opposed to the incoming neoclassical tradition, continued to be applied in actual

1 See also Reinert 2005.

economic policy until and including the slow integration of Spain into the European Union in the 1980s, thus saving and strengthening Spain's industrial sector. Neoclassical principles only entered policy-making after the Fall of the Berlin Wall in 1989, and – we shall argue – with very negative outcomes: a shock therapy resulting in deindustrialization and ultimately depopulation.

Knowledge Lost: A Brief Aside on the Financial Crisis

Although this article concerns the geography of production, it is relevant to look at a similar case of the loss of relevant knowledge which occurred in the financial sector leading to the financial crisis. Until after World War II financial crises – and the consequent need to control the financial sector – were well understood over the whole political spectrum from left to right: Marx– in Volume 3 of *Das Kapital* – clearly understands financial crises, Lenin sees the end of capitalism when finance capital becomes dominant over industrial capital. Politically conservative writers like Schumpeter and Keynes also had a good understanding of crises, although they differed in their policy recommendations. Schumpeter's differentiation between *Güterwelt* (the world of goods and services) and *Rechenpfennige* (the accounting units or tokens that inhabit the world of the financial sector) shaped Hyman Minsky's understanding of financial crises. He considered them as results of mismatches in the innovation capacity of the two spheres of economy, i.e. the innovative capacity of the financial sector far outstrips the ability of the real economy to use these funds in a profitable way.

Norwegian-American economist Thorstein Veblen (1857–1929) differentiated between wealth created through what Veblen himself called *idle curiosity* and *the instinct of workmanship* (newly created wealth), and wealth created from a *predatory instinct* (appropriating wealth that had already been created by harvesting where others had sown). Veblen's heroes were the innovative entrepreneurs, like Henry Ford, and he disapproved of businessmen making money by 'withdrawing efficiency' – i.e. by creating obstacles to economic innovations and change – and of the vested interest of the financial sector.

In the United States evolutionary and institutional economics, both improbably founded by Thorstein Veblen, played the same role as the historical schools played in Europe. The financial crisis of the 1970s (commonly called the *Oil Crisis*) was solved when Veblen's student's student Arthur F. Burns (1904–1987) was at the helm of the Federal Reserve until 1979. Burns solved the crisis by keeping wages and demand up and creating an inflation which made it very unprofitable to hold idle cash balances, thus forcing speculative capital back into the real economy. In other words: Burns carried out the opposite of the austerity policy being carried out today. So, also in terms of understanding financial crises, there was a lag between the teaching on neoclassical principles and their application in real policy.

2 The Ignored Knowledge of von Thünen, List and Schumpeter

This chapter looks at the insights provided by three German speaking economists from the same historical period who explicitly and implicitly worked with economics in

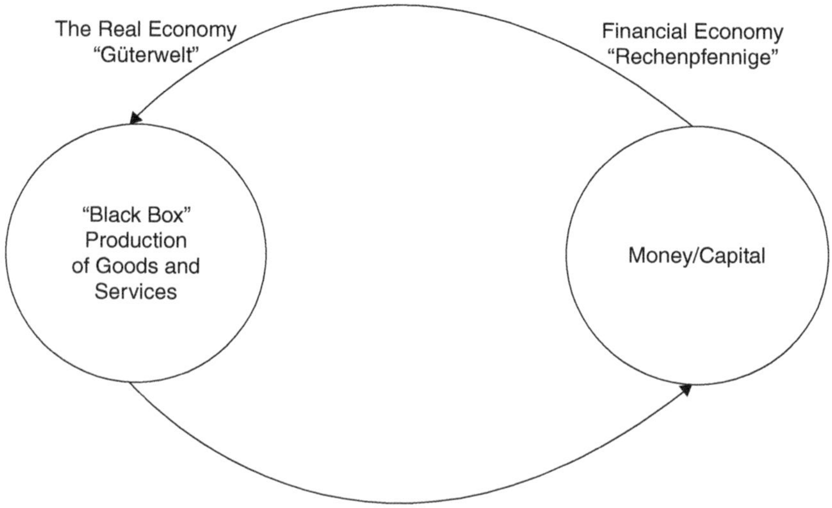

Figure 17.1 Distinguishing the Real Economy from the Accounting Units.
Source: own illustration.

geographical space: Heinrich von Thünen (1783–1850), Friedrich List (1789–1846), and Joseph Schumpeter (1883–1950). It is argued that a main cause of the problems of the European periphery is that these nations have been voided of the core economic area of von Thünen's *Isolirte [sic!] Staat*, that the three core theses of Friedrich List's model for the diffusion of free trade have been violated, and that the qualitative distinction between what we call Schumpeterian and Malthusian activities has been abandoned. Taken together, Thünen, List and Schumpeter provide a qualitative understanding of economic development in space and time, a type of understanding which reigned in Europe until the end of the 1980s, including the policy which integrated Spain into the European Union. The economic ideas which subsequently integrated the former Eastern Block countries had completely lost the insights from von Thünen, List, and Schumpeter. Yet, the utmost importance of including the insights of these three economists shall be discussed in the following.

2.1 Von Thünen's Model of Concentric Circles

While economists have recently attempted to reintroduce geography – a process which has seen Paul Krugman as a major contributor – Heinrich von Thünen (1783–1850) is considered an early protagonist in the field of economic geography. Thünen drew a map of civilized society with four concentric circles around a core of increasing returns activities – the city. Moving outwards from the city core, the use of capital and advanced skills gradually decreases and the use of nature gradually increases. Near the city the most perishable products are produced, such as dairy products, vegetables, and fruit; grain for bread is produced further out, and in the periphery there is hunting in the wilderness. Economists today have rediscovered Thünen's approach to economic

Figure 17.2 Johann Heinrich von Thünen.
Source: Warren J. Samuels Portrait Collection, Rubenstein Rare Book & Manuscript Library, Duke University.

geography, but many miss the crucial point he stresses, namely what stands on the lines on the first page of the *Isolirte Staat*: 'Man denke sich eine sehr große Stadt in der Mitte einer fruchtbaren Ebene gelegen.' The need for the city activities, for example industry, may not be ignored.

Since von Thünen was a farmer and mainly interested in the improvement of agriculture, he does not pay too much attention to the factories in the city, even though they are also mentioned in his book. It was the common sense of the day that the increasing returns of city activities needed tariff protection in order to get the entire system to function; there was no need for von Thünen to argue for or against that established practice. Thünen did not argue against the accepted knowledge of the time that a state needed manufacturing industry. Underlying what happened in Thünen's outer circles was a development machine at the core of the concentric circles – the urban increasing returns industries (manufacturing) – which, at least for a time, needed targeting, nurturing, and protection. In other words, the presence and state of development of the core city would also determine the standard of living in the rest of the country, in these outer circles.

Thünen drew a version of the traditional stage theories (*Stufentheorien*) in economics – what in later German literature came to be called *Wirtschaftsstile* – onto a map where the most 'modern' sector, manufacturing, formed the city core, and the most 'backward' sector, hunting and gathering, formed the periphery furthest from the city. Moving outward away from the city, the use of nature as a factor of production increases and the use of capital decreases. Only the city will have authentic increasing returns, free from nature's flimsy cyclicality and supply of resources (land, minerals) of different qualities.

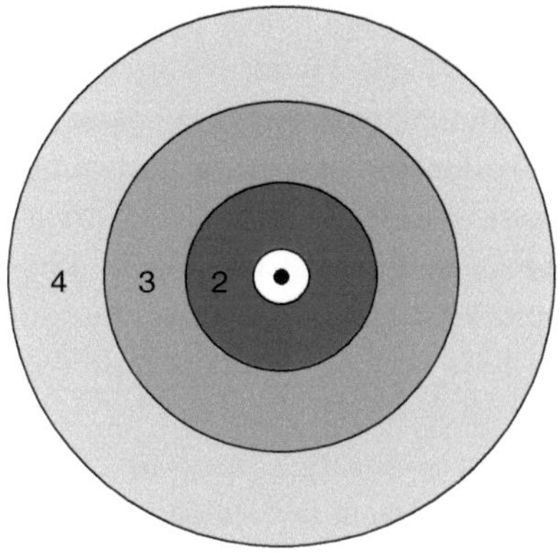

Figure 17.3 Von Thünen's Concentric Circles.
Source: Wikimedia Commons.

As one moves from the city towards the periphery, man-made comparative advantage (subject to increasing returns) gradually diminishes and nature-made comparative advantage (subject to diminishing returns) increases. As we move outwards in the circles, the carrying capacity of the land in terms of population also diminishes.

The importance of the linkages and synergies for agricultural development, seeing the benefits accruing to agriculture from the proximity of manufacturing, was perhaps the most important new insight in economics during the early 1700s. This was also reflected in English literature at that time: 'Husbandry … is never more effectually encouraged than by the increase of manufactures,' says David Hume in his *History of England* (1767: 65, Vol. III).

Thünen's model pictures all the stages of development inside one nation-state, one labour market, one school and university system, and one social security system. The synergies that David Hume points to are partly the result of an equal access to basic institutions and government services accruing to the 'hunters' in the outermost circle as well as to the city dwellers. The local city market does to national agriculture what an international market can never do. Proximity to a city in the same labour market, rather than abroad, assures employment for the second and third son on the farm. The wage pressure from the city activities makes labour more expensive in the countryside, allowing for technological change that would never be profitable with low wage rates. The proximity to the city gives access to advanced technology and expertise that a rural-only nation would never achieve. All in all von Thünen's model provides a useful picture for development as a synergy between town and countryside.

The free trade shock to which the former Soviet Block countries were subject following 1989 thoroughly upset von Thünen's model, killing off a manufacturing sector which had been created in all countries. The most advanced sectors in the least advanced countries died out, not only the European part, but the whole former Soviet Block and its division of labour based on the COMECON trade area was severely deindustrialized. More skill- and capital-intensive activities at the core of the once *Isolirte Staat* died out, and were replaced by activities which take place in the outermost circle, offering much nature and little capital and skills. Handpeeling of shrimps in Holland was moved to locations with cheaper labour like Poland. The Baltic countries closed down their heavy industry and got a formidable comparative advantage in activities like picking wild mushrooms. Today, even outside the EU – in Norway and Switzerland – there are hardly any *Eierschwämme*[2] picked locally any longer. These products, typically from the most nature-intensive and least capital-intensive outermost circle in von Thünen's system, now all come from Eastern Europe. This represents a primitivization of the economies of those countries.

The European periphery has been subject to what I have called the *Vanek-Reinert Effect*: When two nations at widely different technological levels integrate, the first casualty is the most advanced economic activity in the least advanced nation. I argue that this effect represents one of the mechanisms of primitivization that accompany free trade shocks and premature globalization. This effect in turn contributes to falling employment for skilled people, to falling wages and factor price polarization, and consequently to migration of skilled labour. For example, Southern Italy was subject to this effect with the unification of Italy during the late nineteenth century: industry died out and migration resulted. A more current example can be observed in Latvia: more than 20 % of the population has left Latvia since the country joined the EU in 2004.[3]

While neoclassical economics have no tools to comprehend and describe this phenomenon, it can easily be explained in von Thünen's framework where economic activities are qualitatively different, subject to more capital and less nature (*economic progress*), or, conversely, with less capital and more nature (*economic retrogression*). Von Thünen established a framework that enables the study of economic primitivization which occurs when his concentric circles are being hollowed out with the loss of the core city activities.

2.2 Friedrich List's Economic Principles

Even though Friedrich List (1789–1846) is largely ignored in today's economics textbooks, his economic principles not only industrialized Continental Europe in the 19th century, but he was also a very early visionary of a united Europe, and inspired European integration from the early 1950s until and including the successful integration of Spain and Portugal into the EU in 1986. The European Union followed the Listian policy of opening up for free trade between *symmetrical partners* all with a *healthy industri-al fabric*. A slow pace of integration, slowly building down tariff barriers, was done with the preservation and strengthening of the industrial symmetry in mind. So, for a certain period of time, the academic division of labour in Europe was clear: Friedrich List ruled the field of practical policy, while neoclassical economics ruled in the economics textbooks. Slowly, starting with the free trade shock after the Fall of the Berlin Wall, and

2 Chantarelles, a type of mushroom.

3 This was the provisional result of the last Latvian population census.

Figure 17.4 Friedrich List.
Source: Wikimedia Commons.

continuing with the integration of ten new EU countries in 2004, List's principles were abandoned in favour of the same textbook economics that dominate the Washington Consensus.

A worrying aspect of this is that even the countries that are hailed as success stories of the recent European integration have serious problems of social cohesion: apparently successful urban administrative centres contrast starkly with rural poverty. With my Estonian colleague Prof. Rainer Kattel, I attempted to create a rough index for regional inequality. Based on the monthly rent of a city apartment of $100m^2$ in the national capital, we measured the distance to the area where, with the same amount of money, you can purchase a whole house. In Norway this *monthly rental to full ownership index* lies at around 2.000 kilometers, from Oslo to Vardø at the Arctic Sea in the extreme North. In Estonia, this distance is down to less than 100 kilometres from Tallinn. In spite of its success in high-tech innovations Estonia is one of the nations in Europe with the worst income distribution and where the demographic development suggests that the population will be halved by 2050. Unfortunately, instead of facing up to these problems, Europe's present mood is to gloss over reality and present Estonia as an unmitigated European success story.

Table 17.1 shows the contrasting juxtaposition of three of List's key principles with standard textbook economics. The present neoclassical economic principles must be abandoned in favour of the old Listian principles. Just as with von Thünen's insights described above, these Listian principles cannot be captured by the tools of the ruling economic paradigm. Understanding List requires understanding qualitative differences between economic activities, diversity, innovations, synergies and historical sequencing of processes. These are all blind spots in standard economics, especially in their interacting and cumulative totality. The failure to understand the wisdom of the Listian principles

Table 17.1 Contrast of Listian and Neoclassical Principles

Listian Principle	Opposing Neoclassical Principle
The preconditions for wealth, democracy and political freedom are all the same: a diversified manufacturing sector subject to increasing returns (which would historically mean manufacturing, but also includes a knowledge-intensive service sector).	All economic activities are qualitatively alike, so it does not matter what you produce. Ideology based on 'comparative advantage' allowing nations to specialize in economic activities that require little knowledge, operate under perfect competition and diminishing returns, and/or lack any scale economies and technological change. In other words: making it possible for a nation to specialize in being poor.
A nation first industrializes and is then gradually integrated economically into nations at the same level of development.	Free trade is a goal per se, even before the required stage of industrialization is achieved.
Economic welfare is a result of synergy. Investments in infrastructure, education and science are an integral part of this type of policy.	'There is no such thing as society', Margaret Thatcher (1987).

Source: own comparison

which previously upgraded the common interests of Europe has produced an economic and social race to the bottom.

The vision of WTO's first director Renato Ruggiero on the operation of the world market may stand as a prototype for the new view that also penetrated European Union thinking. This global vision was centered around 'the borderless economy's potential to equalize relations between countries and regions'. 'At the global level', Ruggiero says, 'old divisions between North and South are being superseded by new distinctions – between those countries embracing technology and globalization, and those that remain behind' (1998: 130f.). As I see it, the European Union strategy is too simplistically based on this view: an abstract and empirically ungrounded view that technology and innovation are enough to solve most problems, regardless of context.

At the global level, the most populated nations on the planet – China and India – had followed for more than 50 years a Listian economic policy protecting industry. They benefited from globalization, while many small nations in Latin America, in Africa, and in Asia were deindustrialized. Yet, Ruggiero further talks about 'the potential for eradicating global poverty in the early part of the next century – a utopian notion even a few decades ago, but a real possibility today' (ibid.).

2.3 Schumpeter's Concept of Innovation and Creative Destruction

Joseph Schumpeter (1883–1950) was born one hundred years after von Thünen (1783) and also passed away one hundred years after von Thünen did (1850). Adding Schumpeter to our discussion creates a 200 year lasting sequence of visions that are internally

Figure 17.5 Joseph Schumpeter.

Source: Warren J. Samuels Portrait Collection, Rubenstein Rare Book & Manuscript Library, Duke University.

consistent and complementary visions to the problems of Europe today. They stand in sharp contrast to neoclassical economics – individually and as a group of theories.

Schumpeter is increasingly known today for his perspective of *creative destruction*, the idea that economic progress is achieved through incessant innovations which make older technologies obsolete and unprofitable. However, the perspective in Europe today has shifted to a neoclassical view where all economic activities are assumed to be qualitatively alike. If we instead superimpose Schumpeter's world view on a theory based on Heinrich von Thünen and Friedrich List, we get an entirely different picture and entirely different policy recommendations.

Economic activities are not alike; however, neoclassical economic theory implicitly claims exactly the opposite. Table 17.2 explains by which mechanisms some economic activities create more wealth (the Schumpeterian activities listed on the left side), while others make nations stay in poverty (the Malthusian-type economic activities listed to the right). Schumpeterian activities are those which produce the dynamic imperfect competition of creative destruction; innovations which create higher profits, higher wages, higher tax incomes, and higher living standards. Malthusian activities are those which are void of these characteristics, therefore not providing increased welfare but poverty and population pressure.

The present European understanding of innovation tends to apply the term inside a neoclassical framework with an underlying assumption that all economic activities are qualitatively alike. An example shall explain why this approach is wrong: assume the employees of a Berlin hospital are placed in two different countries; the surgeons and other highly qualified personnel are put in one country and the people washing the

Table 17.2 Contrast of Schumpeterian and Malthusian Economic Activities

Characteristics of Schumpeterian activities (= 'good' export activities)	Characteristics of Malthusian activities (= 'bad' export activities if no Schumpeterian sector present)
Increasing returns	Diminishing returns
Dynamic imperfect competition ('rent-seeking')	'Perfect competition' (commodity competition)
Stable prices	Extreme price fluctuations
Generally skilled labour	Generally unskilled labour
Creates a middle class	Creates a 'feudalist' class structure
Irreversible wages ('stickiness' of wages)	Reversible wages
Technical change leads to higher wages for the producer ('Fordist wage regime')	Technical change tends to lower price for the consumer
Creates large synergies (linkages, clusters)	Creates few synergies

Source: Reinert 2007

hospital floors are put in another. If we open up for free trade we will find that the country where the surgeons live will have much higher wages and a much higher standard of living than the country where the people who wash the floors live. The experiment would result in factor-price polarization rather than factor-price equalization.

Modern European Union policy would prescribe innovation as the solution to the nation of floor washing. Apply more capital per employee and employ only people who have Ph.Ds in washing floors could be a start. The problem is that people who wash floors are poorer precisely because there is no way one can profitably add much more capital to that activity, and that for the exact same reason there are just no Ph.Ds in washing floors. The same applies to cleaning shrimps or picking *Eierschwämme*. These are – at the moment – technological dead-ends, corresponding to the outermost circle of von Thünen's concentric circles, corresponding to the kind of economic activities which Friedrich List understood must be complemented with high-tech industrial activities in order to make a country rich, and void of the criteria that inhabit Schumpeterian economic activities as outlined above. The factor-price dilemma created cannot be understood in the present mental framework of the European Union, but may be understood in the frameworks of von Thünen, List, and Schumpeter.

3 Europe's Failed Response: The Lisbon Strategy as a List of Good Intentions

What brought Europe into the present confusion and disorder is a mainstream economic theory that abdicated from studying key aspects of capitalist dynamics, including the dynamics of technology and financial crises. The failure to understand dynamics led to a 'tyranny of good intentions' that frequently produced disasters. Instead of developing Africa through industrialization – as had been the Post World War II project – well-intentioned aid brought the continent from traditional colonialism into an equally humiliating 'welfare colonialism'. The good intention of including Greece in the Euro project ended in an unmitigated disaster produced by the parallel forces of deindustrialization and a financial setup that prevented much-needed exchange-rate flexibility.

The failure to understand what once were basic economic principles of accepted common sense made it possible for European politicians to create a 'united Europe' on a foundation that could not withstand normal economic gravity. The intentions, although noble, produced the opposite result of what was intended: economic and social disharmony rather than harmony. The good intention of including the peripheral EU countries – like Greece – into the common currency, has turned out to be an economic nightmare to the Greeks. In both situations noble intentions in a simplistic neoclassical economic framework created disasters. Europe is now stuck with a dysfunctional economic theory that fails to provide the tools that used to make change happen, presently tearing its economic and social fabric apart. Whereas crises previously could be solved through devaluations in the affected nations, this solution is now blocked. Europe has unknowingly accepted the US model which solves problems by moving people rather than by adjusting currencies.

The same unfortunate combination of noble intentions and lack of understanding of real-world economic dynamics also haunts European technology policy. Having been engaged in a project for the EU Institute for Prospective Technological Studies (IPTS), my conclusion in the IPTS report was that the technology policy of the EU essentially was a laundry list of good intentions, which – because the analysis was framed in a neoclassical framework – failed to cope with the real dynamics of world capitalism:

> 'The Lisbon Strategy appears to have been superimposed on the neoclassical economic framework dominating in the 1990s, where the market is a great equalizer and creator of economic order and harmony. In many parts of the global periphery it is increasingly clear that globalization creates more poverty, not less. It is reasonably clear that such trends – exemplified by East Germany – may be found within the EU. As I see it, the further debate ought to be based on an analysis of what went wrong in the past, and it should move away from the neoclassical tradition of discussing policy void of its context. A policy may be excellent in one set of circumstances, but counterproductive in another. I argue for bringing back the Continental European economic tradition that created Rhine Capitalism: a society where the market is a tool rather than a goal in itself, and where economics is defined as the study of the economy as a real object in a specific context, not defined in terms of the adoption of core assumptions and techniques.' (Reinert 2006)

Both in terms of financial and of technological dynamics the European Union has lived in a fairytale world of simplistic neoclassical economics. Many problems have been evident for a long time, and the specific European Union issues have been covered in detail in two joint papers by an Estonian colleague and myself (Kattel/Reinert 2004, 2007). There are strong parallels between these failures in the policies of finance and of technology. Quoting from my chapter, written for the European Union's own research unit, both discussions appear as 'a long list of good intentions which – it seems implicitly to be assumed – necessarily will lead to success'. In both aspects – in the financial crisis and in terms of its deteriorating ability to employ its population in well-paid jobs (also referred to as *competitiveness*) – Europe has hit a wall. In parallel, the decades of focus on 'limits to growth' have for many Europeans mutated into a belief in 'limits to innovation', at times almost evoking a yearning for some kind of technological retrogression. However, what we measure as GDP and growth is relatively arbitrary. If the clean energy that in the future will substitute oil initially is more expensive than its dirty predecessor, cleaning up the planet will necessarily appear as economic growth.

As Lionel Robbins wrote more than 50 years ago, the basic features of the neoclassical paradigm produce a *Harmonielehre*, a theory where economic harmony is already built into the assumptions on which the theory rests. Today, this paradigm hinders rather than helps our understanding of the reasons behind poverty. As Thomas Kuhn says:

> 'A paradigm can, for that matter, even insulate the community from those socially important problems that are not reducible to the puzzle form, because they cannot be stated in terms of the conceptual and instrumental tools the paradigm supplies.' (1962: 37)

Any long-term solution both for Europe and for the poor nations of the world will have to rest on a *theory of uneven development* – a theory which addresses these blind spots of economics which obfuscate our collective view. Such a theory once existed at a level complete enough to create successful economic policy for 500 years – from Henry VII's policy in England in 1485 to the integration of Spain and Portugal into the European Union in 1986 – but is now virtually extinct in any faculty of economics.

Tensions within the European Community are results of the same economic forces that create poverty in the world periphery. People in the old member states in the European Union feel betrayed because their welfare is being eroded, while people in the new member states feel betrayed because welfare is not arriving as fast as expected. This completely new and unanticipated situation causes people to ask the same way they ask about globalization: what went wrong? The answer lies in the loss of the insights from von Thünen, List and Schumpeter.

4 Conclusion

In the European periphery the advancing financial crisis superimposed austerity and frozen exchange rates on an already advanced process of deindustrialization. In these regions – from Greece to the Baltic States – real wages are falling, both in real terms and as a percentage of GDP. Seen from Heinrich von Thünen's theoretical scheme we can describe what is happening in terms of hollowing out his scheme of concentric circles, killing off the industrial activities of the city which is the nucleus of his system. In terms of Friedrich List's insights, we have neglected the preconditions for successful sequencing of economic integration. As to Schumpeter, we have removed Schumpeterian activities from the peripheral countries. The Listian and Schumpeterian processes of increasing wealth have been put in reverse, now increasing poverty instead of increasing wealth. The sequencing in Greece and Latvia is the same one we recognize from the globalized periphery: first deindustrialization, then deagriculturization (e.g. death of agriculture), and finally depopulation.

What to do? The first age of globalization ended with a return to tariff protection. *The Rise and Fall of the Free Trade Movement* was the appropriate book title published by Cambridge economist William Cunningham in 1905. Today it is clear that while the world took for granted that the factor price equalization produced by free trade would mean an upward adjustment of real wages for all, there are in reality strong pressures towards a downward factor-price equalization combined with increased unemployment. This produces a wake-up call both for the global economy and for the European economy.

'Because the private interest of each individual, when it coincides with the public interests, is always the safest guarantor of public happiness', says Pietro Verri (1771: 42). Adam Smith's (1723–1790) followers – in fact more than Smith himself – changed this into a system where private interests, by definition and in any context, not only coincided with the public interest, but alone were sufficient to create public happiness. In the triumphalism following the Fall of the Berlin Wall it looked as if Smith had been right, now it is increasingly clear that we have to modify this view.

The conclusions of a 2005 meeting of the European Council correctly and importantly stated: 'Europe needs a solid industrial fabric throughout its territory'. This insight was recently 'rediscovered' and restated by the EU in the fall of 2012. To this industrial vision must also be added the importance of the knowledge-intensive service sector which exhibits the same Schumpeterian qualities traditionally associated with industry. However, solely applying a Schumpeterian 'icing on a solid cake of mainstream theory' is an example for the insufficient use of the combined theories of von Thünen, List, and Schumpeter. In the meantime Asia, particularly China, has incorporated the old European type of industrial policy.

In 1841 Friedrich List gave Continental Europe a theory on how to achieve a balanced growth and how to industrialize against the fierce competitiveness of England. List stated that symmetrical integration of industrialized nations where each industrial structure survives is beneficial to all parties, a typical win-win situation. Today, Europe has created a situation which rather appears as a lose-lose situation to many of its inhabitants, both in the old and new member states. As I see it, these are problems that will require the resurrection of some of the recently abolished tools from the policy toolbox, together with the factually based continental economic theories that created them.

Joseph Schumpeter's contrast of the work of Adam Smith and German economist Johann Heinrich Gottlob von Justi (1717–1771) provides a description of economics which can be suggested for the European Union:

> 'He (Justi) saw the practical argument for laissez-faire not less clearly than did A. Smith. (…) Only he saw much more clearly than did the latter all the obstacles that stood in the way of its working according to design. Also, he was much more concerned than A. Smith with the practical problems of government action in the shortrun vicissitudes of his time and country, and with particular difficulties in which private initiative fails or would have failed under the conditions of German industry of his time. His laissez-faire was a laissez-faire plus watchfulness, his private-enterprise economy a machine that was logically automated but exposed to breakdowns and hitches which his government was ready to mend. For instance,

> he accepted as a matter of course that the introduction of labour-saving machinery would cause unemployment: but this was no argument against the mechanization of production because, also as a matter of course, his government would find equally good employment for the unemployed. This, however, is not inconsistency, but sense. And to us who are apt to agree with him much more than we do with A. Smith, his (Justi's) vision of economic policy might look like laissez-faire with the nonsense left out.' (1954: 172)

There is a cyclical element in economics: in the 1840s the economic wisdom of Verri, Justi and their contemporaries had been replaced by Ricardian economics where the market was seen as producing harmony. Contrary to the predictions of Ricardian economics, what was then called 'the social question' shattered Europe and led to revolutions in all large European countries with the exception of England and Russia. However, Marx' spectre of communism sparked economic reform, where the *Verein für Sozialpolitik*, literally the *Association for Social Policy*, produced economic and social institutions that created the European welfare state. Gustav Schmoller took the leadership of the Verein from the start in 1872. Chancellor Bismarck's support of this line of economic research was key to its success.

Following the 1848 upheavals, timely fact-based, context-specific and problem-oriented economics – rather than Ricardo's assumption-based, context-free and highly abstract theories – chased away the 'specter of communism' and laid the foundations for democratic social market economies. As Keynes wisely said, the real issue was 'not one between collectivism and laissez-faire, but between targeted state action and a socialism which was out of date and contrary to human nature'.

In this long term perspective today's political situation in Europe carries with it a strong sense of déjà vu. Again Europe has fallen victim to the simplicities of Ricardian economics, a theory that – as English economic historians readily used to admit – was created in order to let England keep its world industrial monopoly and convince the rest of the world to accept their roles of suppliers of raw materials. Europe has started to believe in what once was the propaganda version of its own economic theory, while China has understood the games of von Thünen, List, and Schumpeter.

It appears we may be doomed to repeat conflicts that we had previously managed to solve. One important reason for this retrogression is that the triumphalism following the Fall of the Berlin Wall made us collectively forget the wise targeted state actions that modified the pure market economy. If communism failed, so Europe seems to have reasoned in the 1990s, the market had to be perfect. Based on this the 2004 enlargement was agreed.

Compared to the rest of the world, many things are not really that bad. If we com-pare European productivity data to those of the United States and correct for the hours worked, we find that European productivity is in fact doing well. The biggest – and rapidly growing – problem is self-inflicted, namely the downward pressure on real wages and the welfare system in 'old Europe' coupled with extremely low real wages and huge un- and underemployment in the new member states. These problems are two sides of the same coin. A widely proclaimed success story of the new member states, Estonia's electronic industry, produces hourly wages of about one Euro, which equates to approximately 10 % of the earnings of someone sweeping the streets of Paris or Frankfurt. Tensions are too big and the number of people and vested interests involved is too high for the market alone to create a happy end. In fact what is missing is old-fashioned *Staatsklugheit*, or experience-based wisdom among the political elites.

The present situation of Europe requires more than the Lisbon Strategy's list of good intentions focusing around innovations, it needs to bring back economic thinking and economic tools that had been abandoned in the 1990s. This includes bringing back the earlier focus on employment that dominated the period after World War II. It also means a qualitatively much more profound and differentiated analysis of technology and innovations and their economic consequences on both wages and employment, at company, community, and national level. A framework of equilibrium theory is neither adequate nor effective to study the phenomena that create the economic differences which now haunt Europe. We are instead in a situation dominated by processes of cumulative causation. The now practically defunct continental European tradition of economics is much better suited to tackle such a task. Above all, the discussion of the Lisbon Strategy must be lifted out of the generic and context-free into a context where present problems – caused both by the shock therapies of the 1990s and the challenges from Asia – are recognized as being the real challenges to European Union policy.

References

Hume, David, 1767: *The History of England from the Invasion of Julius Caesar to the Revolution in 1688.* 6 volumes, London: A. Millar.

Kuhn, Thomas, 1962: *The Structure of Scientific Revolutions.* Chicago: University of Chicago Press.

List, Friedrich (1841), 1959: *Das nationale System der Politischen Ökonomie.* Basel: Kyklos Verlag.

Reinert, Erik S.; Kattel, Rainer, 2004: The Qualitative Shift in European Integration: Towards Permanent Wage Pressures and a 'Latin-Americanization' of Europe? *Praxis Working Paper* no. 17, Praxis Foundation, Estonia. Access: http://pdc.ceu.hu/archive/00002068/01/WP_17_20043.pdf.

Reinert, Erik S., 2005: German Economics as Development Economics: From the Thirty Years War to World War II. In: Jomo, K. S.; Erik S. Reinert (eds.): *Origins of Development Economics.* London: Zed Publications/New Delhi: Tulika, pp. 48–68.

Reinert, Erik S., 2006: European Integration, Innovations and Uneven Economic Growth: Challenges and Problems of EU 2005. Paper prepared for FISTERA (Foresight on Information Society Technologies in the European Research Area). In: Compañó, R, C. Pascu; A. Bianchi; J-C. Burgelman; S. Barrios; M. Ulbrich; I. Maghiros (eds.): *The Future of the Information Society in Europe: Contributions to the Debate.* Seville, Spain: European Commission, Directorate General Joint Research Centre. Institute for Prospective Technological Studies (IPTS), p. 129. Working paper version downloadable on http://hum.ttu.ee/tg/.

Reinert, Erik S.; Kattel, Rainer, 2007: European Eastern Enlargement as Europe's Attempted Economic Suicide? Working Paper No. 14, The Other Canon Foundation – Tallinn University of Technology Working Paper Series. Downloadable on http://hum.ttu.ee/tg/.

Ricardo, David (1817), 1974: *The Principles of Political Economy and Taxation.* London: Dent, Dutton.

Ruggiero, Renato, 1998: Wither the Trade System Next. In: Bhagwati, Jagdish; M. Hirsch (eds.): *The Uruguay Round and Beyond– Essays in Honour of Arthur Dunkel*. Ann Arbor: The University of Michigan Press, pp. 123–141.

Schumpeter, Joseph Alois, 1954: *History of Economic Analysis*. New York: Oxford University Press.

von Thünen, Johann Heinrich, 1826: *Der isolirte Staat mit Beziehung auf Landwirtschaft und Nationalökonomie*. Hamburg: Perthes.

Verri, Pietro, 1771: *Meditazioni sulla economia politica*. Genova: Ivone Gravier.

Chapter Eighteen

MECHANISMS OF FINANCIAL CRISES IN GROWTH AND COLLAPSE: HAMMURABI, SCHUMPETER, PEREZ, AND MINSKY

Erik S. Reinert[1]

Abstract. This paper provides a historical and theoretical overview of the mechanisms leading up to financial crises and financial bubbles. It suggests that the potentially explosive growth of the financial sector at the expense of the real economy fed by compound interest has – since before ancient Mesopotamia under the rule of Hammurabi – represented a real threat for such crises. A more modern and additional factor that builds up crises is Joseph Schumpeter's observation of the clustering of innovations. Carlota Perez has more recently developed Schumpeter's vision into a theory of techno-economic paradigms which – about midway in their trajectory – produce the build-up to financial crises. The theories of Schumpeterian economist Hyman Minsky, describing the mechanisms producing the collapse of financial bubbles complete the overview. The paper ends with recommendations to bring the West out of the present crisis by – once again – putting the real economy rather than the financial economy in the driver's seat of capitalism.

Keywords: Financial crises, innovations, Hammurabi, Joseph Schumpeter, John Maynard Keynes, Hyman Minsky, Carlota Perez.

Introduction

Financial crises occur when the relationship between the *real economy* (the total production of goods and services) and the *financial economy* (money in the widest sense) comes out of balance in such a way that the financial economy no longer primarily supports the

[1] Professor Erik S. Reinert is the holder of the Distinguished Chair of Tun Ismail Ali, Permodalan nasional Berhad (PnB) at the Faculty of Economics and Management, Universiti Kebangsaan Malaysia (2012).

real economy, but takes on an independent life of its own in such a way as to damage the real economy. Today's economics (*neoclassical economics, standard textbook economics, mainstream economics*) accepts such an imbalance between the real economy and the monetary sphere when it comes to inflation (rising price levels) and deflation (decreasing price levels), but not when it comes to financial crises. This is in sharp contrast to other kinds of economics – the experienced-base type of economics I refer to as the other Canon – which traditionally have understood and still understand crises, but which have been marginalized.

Financial crises represent imbalances which – in contrast to inflation and deflation – are not immediately visible in the consumer price index as rising or falling prices, but rather in the form of *asset inflation* and *debt deflation*, which in sum have very important impacts on income distribution. The assets in which massive incomes from the financial sector are invested, will experience an *asset inflation*. On the other hand, the falling levels of prices and wages that result from the crises, will result in *debt deflation*, a continually rising real quantity of outstanding debt.

The transfer of income and assets from the real economy to the financial economy is the most important long-run effect of a financial crisis. If these imbalances are not addressed by making big investments in the real economy, any recovery – in that case by definition weak – will be driven by demand from the financial sector, and the losses in the real economy may be permanent. This is now what is happening in the US and in Europe, where the EU's 'internal devaluations' in the Baltic in some places have reduced real wages by up to 50 per cent, while at the same time unemployment is alarmingly high.

If the financial imbalances in the EU periphery had been addressed by a traditional formula of debt cancellation and devaluation – which was successfully done in Argentina about ten years ago – this would have penalized the financial economy, but in the long run supported the wage level. In the case of the Baltic countries this would have meant letting the (mostly foreign) banks and the financial (real estate) side of the economy take the losses, while saving the production economy. Instead Europe made the decision to 'save' the financial economy in the short run, which is likely to permanently destroy the wage level. This is why Martin Wolf of the *Financial Times* is of the opinion that a possible recovery will be a 'yacht and mansion' recovery. This paper argues that the way the problems of the financial crisis is being solved – under the general heading of austerity – will lead to a permanent domination over the economy by the financial sector at the expense of the real economy, citing examples of this development in Latin America in the 1970s and in the former Soviet sphere in the 1990s.

Financial Crises were understood from left to right – but unlearned all along the political axis

The interesting thing is that once upon a time financial crises were a well known and well understood phenomenon along the whole political axis.[2] Karl Marx wrote about

---

[2] An extensive bibliography and brief overview of previous theories of financial crises is found in Reinert, Erik S. & Arno Daastøl, 'Production Capitalism vs. Financial Capitalism – Symbiosis

them (volume 3 of *Das Kapital*), and Lenin said that control of the financial economy represented the last stage of capitalism. In the theories of the Austrian social democrat Rudolf Hilferding[3], financial crises were once a social democratic strongpoint. Joseph Alois Schumpeter and John Maynard Keynes – possibly the most important theoreticians on financial crises – were politically conservative, and the most important Norwegian representative, Torkel Aschehoug, was head of the conservative party. Even though the present loss in the real economy in favor of the financial sector ought to be extremely important for any government, it is still barely visible on the political agenda. Today's economics – compared to in earlier times – has important blind spots as regards the role of the financial sector, and these blind spots also transfer to the perspective of politicians.

Earlier terminologies, which understood and described the mechanisms of crises, are now largely lacking. Lately some economists, particularly Americans, have 'rediscovered' some of the old theories, Irving Fisher's 'debt deflation' being one of them. However, as this paper argues, many more basic mechanisms and insights are up for rediscovery.

To understand financial crises a terminology distinguishing between the financial economy (what Schumpeter called 'die Rechenpfennige', the 'accounting units') and the real economy (the production of goods and services, Schumpeter's *Güterwelt*) is necessary (See Figure 18.1). The family tree of today's mainstream economics, originating in the late 1700s with Quesnay and the Physiocrats, and continuing with the English economics of David Ricardo (1817), does not have a monetary or financial sector and is therefore generally blind to financial crises, abstaining from studying the relationship between the financial sector and the real economy. In the alternative tradition, The Other Canon in my terminology, this difference has always been important. Starting with the Anti-Physiocrats, who tried to stop the free trade and resulting speculation leading up to the French Revolution, The Other Canon type of economics – where distinguishing between the financial economy and the real economy is a key feature – dominated after the 1848 revolutions. However, as this historical and fact-based economic theory virtually died out after World War II, with it the crisis theories also disappeared along the whole political axis. Under the assumption of perfect competition and in the absence of any conflicts between the financial sector and the real economy, neoclassical economics models the market economy as machinery where friction is absent: a machinery creating automatic harmony. The theories handed down from Ricardo do not contain the categories to make possible the understanding of crises.

---

and Parasitism. An Evolutionary Perspective and Bibliography', *The Other Canon Foundation and Tallinn University of Technology Working Papers in Technology Governance and Economic Dynamics*, no. 36, 2011 (original 1998). This paper is an edited version of the author's report to the Norwegian Parliamentary Commission on the Financial Crisis. The origins of this paper go back to the 1990s and it is influenced by the scholarship and friendship of Jan Kregel and Carlot Perez.

3 On Hilferding, see Smaldone, William, *Rudolf Hilferding. The Tragedy of a German Social Democrat*, DeKalb, Ill, Northern Illinois University Press, 1998.

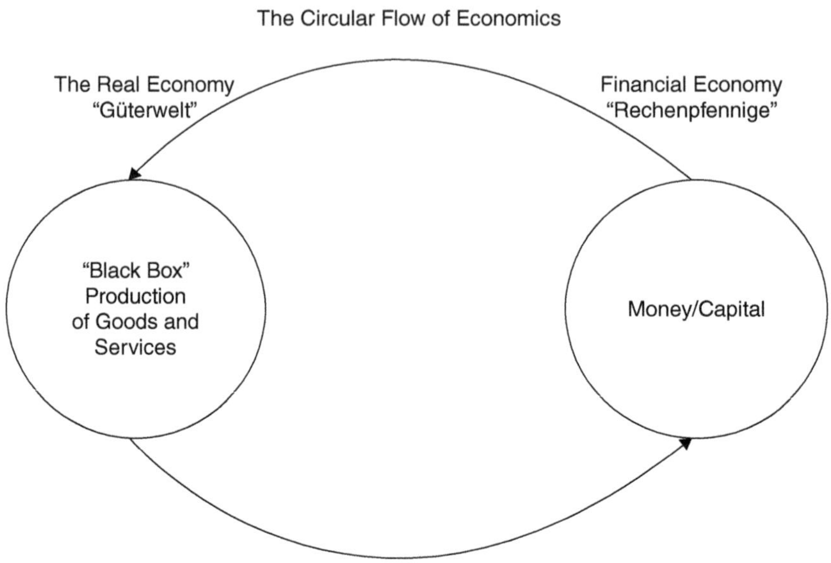

Figure 18.1 The Real Economy and the Financial Economy as Different Spheres.

The Hammurabi Effect and 'Debt Deflation'

The simplest model for understanding the disproportion between the real economy and the financial economy originated in Mesopotamia[4] under Hammurabi (2030–1995 BC). Claiming that the roots of civilization were found here is indeed more than an empty phrase.

Hammurabi's economists calculated that due to compound interest the financial economy would increase far more than the real economy would be able to absorb. After normal bookkeeping principles the assets of the financial economy would have their counterparts as debt in the real economy. Thus did English economist Richard Price (1769) express the force of compound interest:

> 'A shilling invested at 6% interest at the birth of Christ would …have increased to an amount (gold) larger than could be contained in the whole solar system, if this is constructed as a sphere with the diameter of Saturn's bane around the sun'.

As someone must obviously have invested 1 shilling at the time of the birth of Christ, this means that any system permitting compound interest necessarily must break down at intervals. Hammurabi and his descendants took the consequences of this, and irregularly cancelled all debt (except short run commercial debt) to avoid the death of the real

---

[4] For an account of debt dating back to the Sumerian Kingdoms, see Graeber, David, *Debt. The First 5,000 Years*, New York, Melville House, 2011. I am grateful to Michael Hudson for having introduced me to the Hammurabi mechanisms in the eraly 1990s.

economy due to ever increasing debt. In the Old Testament we still find references to this system. The years when debts were cancelled were called *Jubilee Years*.

Money and gold are then conceptually different from the goods and services that can be acquired with their help. History is filled with warnings against what has been called *chrysohedonism*, confusing money with what money can buy. The legend of King Midas, who was granted his wish that whatever he touched should be turned into gold – and then later discovered this to be a curse – is a brilliant example of the danger of confusing riches of money and gold with riches of 'goods and services'. Without *Jubilee Years* the financial sector would end up as a King Midas, with loads of money and gold, but with a real economy extremely weakened – or dead – because of the debt burden. This is the track we are on now.

The Bible (Matthew 25, 14–30) tells us that the coins – the 'talents' – should not be buried, but invested. In the mid 1300s the early money theorist Nicolas Oresme complained about too much money ending in treasure chests instead of being productively invested. This is not why we created money, he writes. Around 1600 Francis Bacon writes that money is like manure, only useful when spread. Through the whole history of Civilization we find as a red thread that the 'financial sector' is only useful when invested in the real economy.

The Muslim prohibition against interest – *riba* – and the Christian prohibition against charging interest up until the 1600s must be seen in this perspective. Amassing fortunes without lifting a finger was seen as qualitatively very different from earning money by 'honest work', commerce and production. That Judaism – as opposed to Christianity and Islam – accepted lending against interest is a historically important point. At the same time Jews were not permitted to own land.

When Western Christianity in the early 1600s started collecting interest, this was with a view – as Francis Bacon's – of the importance of innovation. Innovations required risk capital, and the acceptance of lending out capital against interest seems to have coincided with the discovery of the role of innovations.[5] Capital became, in the words of Keynes, 'a bridge in time', something financed today may last for a very long time.

Here it is important to understand Schumpeter's theory of capital: if nothing new happens in the world (innovations) capital is theoretically without value. If we again look to the bookkeeping perspective – which is absolutely necessary to understand financial crises – all investments in a world without innovations could be covered by depreciation. The innovations give value to capital. Capital in itself is sterile (cf. King Midas/the buried talents).

Financial crises occur when the financial sector stops functioning as a bridge in time for the real economy, and starts earning money on itself in pyramid-scheme

---

5 For a discussion on the changing view on innovations and the growth of Europe, see Reinert, Erik S. & Arno Daastøl, 'Exploring the Genesis of Economic Innovations: The religious gestalt-switch and the **duty to invent** as preconditions for economic growth', in *European Journal of Law and Economics*, Vol 4, No. 2/3, 1997, pp. 233–283, and in *Christian Wolff. Gesammelte Werke*, IIIrd series, Vol. 45, Hildesheim, Georg Olms Verlag, 1998.

type constructions. We shall discuss this in the section on Hyman Minsky. In the inter-war period German discourse sharply distinguished between *schaffendes Kapital* (capital employed in the creation of goods and services) and *raffendes Kapital* (capital that only accumulates more capital without creating anything). Today American economist Bill Lazonick differentiates between wealth creation and wealth extraction. In his *Treatise on Money* (1931) Keynes sees depression approaching when money goes from being in industrial circulation to being in financial circulation. Some years later, in 1936, another conservative Englishman, later prime minister, Harold Macmillan, complained that his own party was dominated by casino capitalism.

Even if Lenin, as above mentioned, concluded that financial capital taking command over the system would mark the final stage of capitalism (it would presumable collapse for lack of demand, as we presently witness in Greece), skepticism towards the financial sector – the whole banking system – has been great also among conservatives. Thomas Jefferson, the most conservative of the US founding fathers, was also the one most critical towards banking and finance. To be conservative (rightist) for Torkel Aschehoug meant that he wanted to protect the real economy from devastating speculations; to be a neo-liberalist (rightist) now means to believe that the market cannot be wrong. For conservative think-tanks to act as claques for the financial sector is a completely new phenomenon. Neoclassical economics and neo-liberalism have replaced the conservative voices that traditionally have acted as a bulwark against the excesses of the financial and speculation economies. This will most likely make the present crisis both deeper and longer lasting.

Conclusion: History has shown that to have a system permitting compound interest makes financial crises a certainty. Historian Reinholdt Mueller at the University of Venice describes how the Venetian State in the 1200s had to step in and save the whole financial system only few years after the first financial center had been established. Capitalism had to be saved by the state right at the start! Since then financial crises have been frequent in capitalism, and – as illustrated in Fig. 2 – are easy to find by checking the quantity of books published about economics and when. The first international financial crisis in 1720 – which simultaneously hit the large financial centers Paris, London, and Amsterdam – shows the same pattern as today's crisis.

The book *This time is different. Eight Centuries of Financial Folly* by Carmen Reinhart and Kenneth Rogoff[6] gives us an historical perspective on financial crises. However, the book contains more data than it contains theory and analysis.

A symbol-filled illustration from one of the many books published in 1720 – Fig. 3 – shows a typical trait of a financial crisis: a stock exchange project artificially kept up by speculators. These are named 'wind merchants' because they buy and sell merchandise which can only be bought and sold in a fantasy world, not in the real economy.

---

6 Princeton, Princeton University Press, 2009. The fact that neither Schumpeter, Keynes, Minsky or Veblen figure in the name index of this 463 page book is remarkable, and certifies to the tendency of present economics to 'reinvent wheels' and not learn from the theories (as opposed to the facts) that grew out of similar experiences in the past.

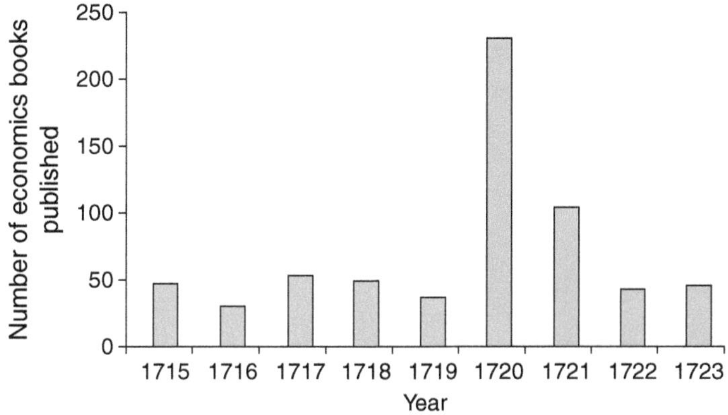

Figure 18.2 Number of Economics Books Published (1715–1723).
Source: Own calculations from the holdings of Kress Library, Harvard University.

Hyman Minsky

In contrast to Hammurabi's model with two sectors, the real economy and the financial sector, the American Schumpeterian economist Hyman Minsky (1919–1996) had other sectors: households and non-financial activities + financial intermediaries and government. Recently US economists have contributed a more precise definition of what we can call the enlarged financial sector: Finance, Insurance, and Real Estate: the FIRE sector.

Hyman Minsky built his theories on earlier insights from Thorstein Veblen, John Maynard Keynes and Joseph Schumpeter. A *leitmotif* in his carrier was that 'it' (i.e. another financial crisis like the one in the 1930s) 'can happen again'. Minsky's two important books were *John Maynard Keynes* (1975) and *Stabilizing an Unstable Economy* (1986). Both were, because of the financial crisis, republished in 2008.[7]

Like Schumpeter, Minsky says that innovations in the financial sector differ from innovations in the rest of the economy, and that economies that have financial innovations (which are both useful and necessary) will necessarily have crises because, a) financial innovations make debts grow faster than the ability to repay these debts (cf. Hammurabi). In other words the capacity of the financial sector to generate funds through new innovations exceeds the ability of the real economy to absorb these funds in a profitable way, and b) such crises move income and wealth to a class of *rentiers* whose tendency to spend is lower than in the real economy (cf. Martin Wolf's yacht and mansion recovery). This way the demand that is needed to help the countries out of the crisis is not created. A typical example is the US today. Real wages are roughly at the level they were in the mid 1970s, which means that most fruits of economic growth since then has gone to the

[7] For an overview of Minsky, see Papadimitriou, Dimitri & L. Randall Wray, *The Elgar Companion to Hyman Minsky*, Cheltenham, Elgar, 2010.

Figure 18.3 Speculative Stock Exchange Projects that Cannot Keep in the air Without artificial Help.

Source: *Het groote tafereel der dwaasheid* ('the Great Mirror of Folly'), Amsterdam 1720.

FIRE sector. Any stimulation packages will not work well unless the balance between the FIRE sector and the real economy is adjusted.

One of Minsky's important contributions was the understanding of the 'destabilizing stability', a point we see clearly already in Torkel Aschehoug's writings: as the good times seem to go on, the banks will take increasingly greater risks. Finally they will finance projects so speculative that they will not even be able to serve the interest on the debt.

Minsky called such loans Ponzi schemes, and the subprime crisis matched this description perfectly. Loans were granted to home owners who could not even pay the interest on the loans. This creates a bubble in the economy – an imbalance between the financial economy and the real economy – which is bound to burst. Understanding Minsky's model it was fairly clear that the Terra scandal – a scandal virtually bankrupting several norwe-gian municipalities – might be the start of a serious financial crisis (e.g. my article in newspaper *Dagbladet*, November 26, 2007).

As Minsky wrote in 1964: 'At present real estate assets seem to be a more important source of financial distress than stock exchange assets... real estate assets are collateral for an extensive amount of debt, both of households and of business firms, owned by financial institutions... If the price of real estate should fall very sharply, not only will the net worth of households and business firms be affected, but also defaults, repossessions, and losses by financial intermediaries would occur.'

This 1964 paragraph is still an adequate description of what happened during the last financial crisis. It is important to note that in this perspective financial crises are no 'black swan' – something happening surprisingly and very seldom. Such crises are endogenous to the technological selection mechanisms of the capitalist system, forming an integral part of the relationship between the innovation cycles in the real economy and the innovations in the financial sector.

Minsky's idea was that anyone can create money, the only problem is to get that money accepted. Minsky imagined a hierarchy – a pyramid – of different kinds of money, organized by solidity and confidence. Before the last financial crisis there were financial innovations that – probably literally – no one understood, like mortgage-based securities (MBS), collateralized debt obligations (CDO), and credit default swaps (CDS). These financial innovations, securitization, created a systemic risk, they created a debt that was larger than the system's capacity for paying back the debt. When the confidence in the less secure financial instruments collapses during crises, people tend to seek the more secure ones, cash, and finally gold (which Keynes called 'a barbaric relic').

My Chilean colleague Gabriel Palma (University of Cambridge) has quantified the increasing imbalance between the real economy and the financial economy in a paper.[8] Figure 18.2 of this paper shows the increase in the balance between financial assets and GDP in the period 2002 to 2007, before the financial crisis. Here Schumpeter's and Minsky's point is clearly illustrated: financial assets increased heavily compared to the size of GDP. In a country like Spain financial assets as a percentage of GDP increased from a little over 300% to more than 550% from 2002 to 2007.

Palma's Figure 18.3 shows growth in GDP and growth in the debts of house-holds and non-financial business firms in the US from 1950 to 2007. He shows that debt growth and economic growth more or less kept pace until 1982, debt grew with 3.8% annually while GDP grew with 3.4%. In the period 1982 to 1987 debt grew with 4.7% annually, while GDP still had a growth of 3.4%. In the period 1988 to 2007 debt grew

---

8 'The Revenge of the Market on the Rentiers. Why neo-liberal reports of the end of history turned out to be premature', *Cambridge Journal of Economics* 33(4), July 2009, pp. 829–869.

with 0.5% annually, while GDP only had a growth of 2.8%. This could not possibly go on for long.

The moment when the market realizes that the financial economy is a non-sustainable pyramid game is now often called 'The Minsky Moment'. Another name is 'The Wile E. Coyote Moment' after the cartoon figure who has rushed over the edge of an American canyon and – in the moment he starts falling – realizes what has happened.

Carlota Perez: Financial Crises and Technological Change

In his three-volume *Social-Oeconomik* (1905–1908) Norwegian economist Torkel Aschehoug points out that financial crises have their origins in technological changes. Venezuelan scholar Carlota Perez has developed this reasoning in a way which in my view is convincing, in her 2003 book *Technological Revolutions and Financial Capital: The Dynamics of Bubbles and Golden Ages.*[9] As Perez herself points out in the introduction, The Other Canon conference in Oslo in 1998, referred to in footnote 2, was important for the development of the theory. Her theories build on the works of Russian economist Nicolay Kontratief (1892–1938) and Joseph Schumpeter (1883–1950).[10]

A main point in her theory is that technological revolutions create new firms with high stock exchange value. Through several hundred years such technological revolutions have created financial bubbles, the canal bubble, the railroad bubble etc. Lastly the IT bubble which burst in 2000. Such bubbles that are a result of a new and revolutionary technology are useful, they seem to be a necessary part of the dynamics of capitalism, and serve to upgrade the whole production system of the real economy. But what we saw after the burst of the IT bubble was bubbles that did nothing for the real economy, on the contrary they weakened it. Figure 18.4 shows that before the IT bubble burst 60% of new companies on the US stock exchanges were (IPO = Initial Public Offering) technological companies (ICT = Information and Communication Technology), while only 10% were companies from the financial sector. In 2003 the roles were changed: 60% of all new companies on the stock exchange were financial ones, while only 10% were from the IT field.

To Perez the rational increase in stock prices of companies with new and revolutionary technologies will spread irrationally also to hopeless projects and to pyramid schemes in the financial sector (see Figures 18.3 and 18.5). In times when capitalism functions well the financial sector and the real economy live in a kind of symbiosis – they support each other – while in times of crisis the financial sector becomes a parasite weakening the real economy. What was rational (investing in new technology) gradually becomes irrational (investing in pyramid games).

An early contribution to this literature was the book 'Extraordinary Popular Delusions and the Madness of Crowds' by Charles Mackay, published in 1841. The former head of the Federal Reserve, Alan Greenspan, described this phenomenon as 'irrational

---

9 Cheltenham, Elgar, 2003.

10 In particular his *Business Cycles*, 2 volumes, New York, Mc-Graw Hill, 1939.

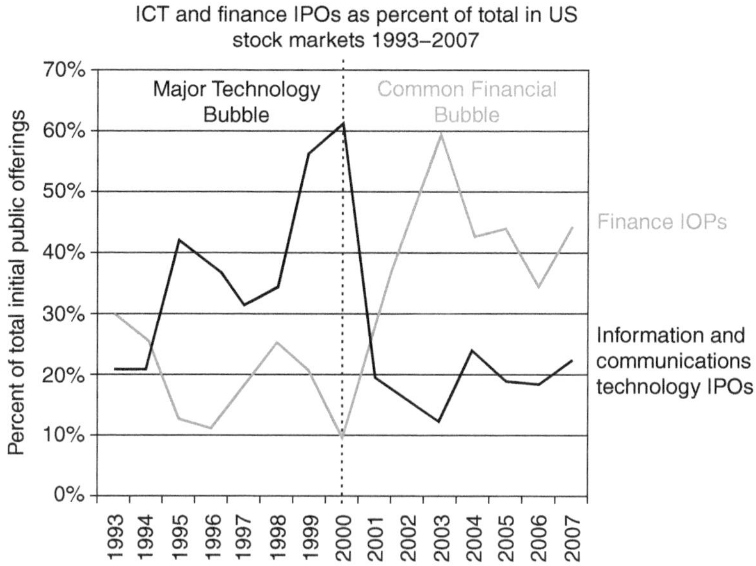

Figure 18.4 Technology Bubble ('Useful Bubble') vs. Finance Bubble ('Useless Bubble').
Source: Carlota Perez.

exuberance'. Figure 18.5 shows how a cartoon author (Dilbert 1999) understood the irrationality of the stock exchange bubble a year before the burst of the bubble. Note the similarity of this to the idea behind the drawing in Figure 18.3.

Defending capitalism as by definition being 'rational' has been a serious hindrance for the economics profession's understanding of financial crises. The present Chairman of the Federal Reserve, Ben Bernanke, wrote a book about the 1929 crisis and the Great Depression. There he mentions Hyman Minsky once, but just in order to dismiss him because Minsky 'had to depart from the theory of rational economic behavior'.[11] To be a 'mainstream' economist the last 30–40 years has meant not to accept mechanisms that doubtlessly are very important in a financial crisis because they were in conflict with the fundamental assumptions of standard economic theory. In this way even the people with the main responsibility for handling the crisis have been isolated from the most relevant theory of crisis.

It is quite clear that for a single individual earning money in the financial sector without at the same time creating real economy values, the speculative build-up towards a financial crisis is rational. The important thing is to be close enough to the door to get out before the rest when 'the Minsky Moment' strikes. That this should be rational from the viewpoint of society is something completely different. Here the markets fail, and regulations are needed. During Clinton's presidency, and with Ayn Rand pupil Alan

[11] Bernanke, Ben S. (editor), *Essays on the The Great Depression.* Princeton, Princeton University Press, 2000, page 43.

Figure 18.5 Finance Capital Goes Berserk During a Techno-Economic Paradigm Shift.
Source: Dilbert cartoons, 1999 (the year before the stock market collapse).

Greenspan at the Head of the Federal Reserve, the very wise and well-built institutional defenses against financial crises that had been erected after the crisis of 1929 (Glass-Steagall act) were removed. A main argument for dismantling the defenses was that there were no crises, so the defenses were not needed. The obvious fact is that the regulations that were removed were indeed the very reasons that there had been no crises!

The tulip bubble in Holland in 1636–37 was also such a bubble, where the tulip bulbs from far countries – this was indeed an innovation – played the role of 'new technology' (see Figure 18.6).

Save the Financial Economy or Save the Real Economy?

Joseph Schumpeter was of the opinion that governments should not intervene in a financial crisis, as such a salvage operation would strengthen the very forces which had created the crisis in the first place. The crisis should burn out by itself. Today we see the wisdom

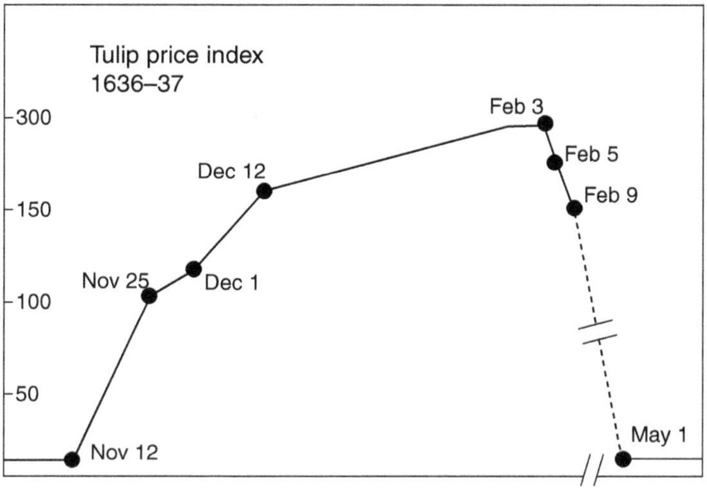

Figure 18.6 The Anatomy of a Bubble. The Tulip Bubble in 1636–37.

of that. But the crisis became so serious that governments had to do something, as Keynes suggested. But we see that Schumpeter's intuition on one level was correct: it is hard to do this without encouraging new speculative bubbles. The huge financial packages that were made to save the real economy by saving the banks, in effect in many countries fail to reach the real economy. at the moment (2012) both banks and large corporations are left with huge cash balances, while lacking demand and consequently lagging investments are preventing a healthy recovery.

Financial crises both create and are results of imbalances. During the Bretton Woods-discussions Keynes suggested a 'tax on imbalances'. As the world's imports must equal its exports, Keynes suggested an international tax on export surpluses over a certain amount. This would avoid international imbalances and prevent some nations from savings glut while others built up enormous debts. It would also serve as an incentive for nations not to keep their exchange rates artificially low, as China has been doing. The suggestion was blocked, mainly by the US, but if Keynes had had his will, the United States would today have been saved from their own irresponsibility, saved from building up such enormous debts to the rest of the world as they have done.

Classical crisis theories operate with the terms 'overproduction' and 'underconsumption'. An important part of today's financial crisis is the Global Savings Glut (GSG). 'Real' saving may be said to occur when it is matched by a dis-saving in form of investment or consumption as a book-keeping counterpart in. In the absence of investment or consumption, without a dis-saving, saving becomes unproductive hoarding. The Quantitative Easing – the creation of huge amounts of money – on both sides of the Atlantic, matched with austerity policies simultaneously reducing demand, are creating the conditions that the Bible (idle 'Talents'), the Midas legend, Oresme, and Lenin all warned against. These all represent a wisdom which cannot seemingly be captured by today's mainstream economics, unable as it apparently is to conceive of the financial economy being something other than the mirror image of the real economy.

The lack of balance between the financial economy and the real economy can only be solved by one part – or both – being adjusted. One can choose to protect the inflated financial sector, or protect the real economy. Often, as during the Asia crisis, production units are left to go broke to save the banks. The Argentine crisis at the end of the 1990s ended up reducing real wages by more than 40%.

EU's handling of the crisis shows us the choices. The deficits in the PIIG countries (Portugal, Italia, Ireland, and Greece) would traditionally have been solved by the countries devaluating, so the local production systems would restore their competitiveness. At the same time the debt, traditionally often in local currency, would be reduced, leading to a loss for foreign creditors.

The alternative to this is what is called internal devaluation. This means that wages are pressed downwards, without touching the exchange rate, while at the same time even larger loans are taken up, to service the debt. This will let the real economy take the whole loss, while downward spirals of lessened buying power and lessened national production start.

The Estonian example shows that these are mechanisms that can be started also without the country in question being in debt. The country has had an internal devaluation reducing wages with more than 20%. Wages have fallen for 9 quarters in a row, and unemployment is high. What gives food for thought is that such internal devaluations now seem to be the model also for the larger countries in the EC periphery. It seems likely that the downward adjustment of people's buying power – the buying power of whole nations – may be permanent.

Traditionally it has been possible to differentiate between two models for economic adjustments, the European model and the American one. The European model had adjusted exchange rates. In the US the whole country of course has the same currency. When one of the states has an economic crisis, like Michigan with its car industry, the adjustment mechanism is that people move to other states. By not giving up the Euro to let countries in crisis devaluate, Europe has in effect chosen the American model. Greeks will have to move to Germany, even though neither Greeks nor Germans see this as an optimal solution. Europe is probably not prepared for the demographic movements which will be the result of the ongoing crisis.

The Growth of the FIRE Sector Displaces the Real Economy

We have earlier referred to Gabriel Palma's article, which shows the disproportionate growth in the financial economy over the real economy. This is a phenomenon that started already in the 1970s in the economic periphery of the world. The period from 1950 to 1973 registered the highest economic growth ever in the world, but after 1973 there was a change in political economic ideology that (consciously) led to a market and free trade shock which again led to the FIRE sector taking over a larger part of the total value of GDP at the expense of wages and the income of the self-employed. Figure 18.7 shows the changes in GDP growth rates in certain countries in the Second (ex communist) World and the Third World.

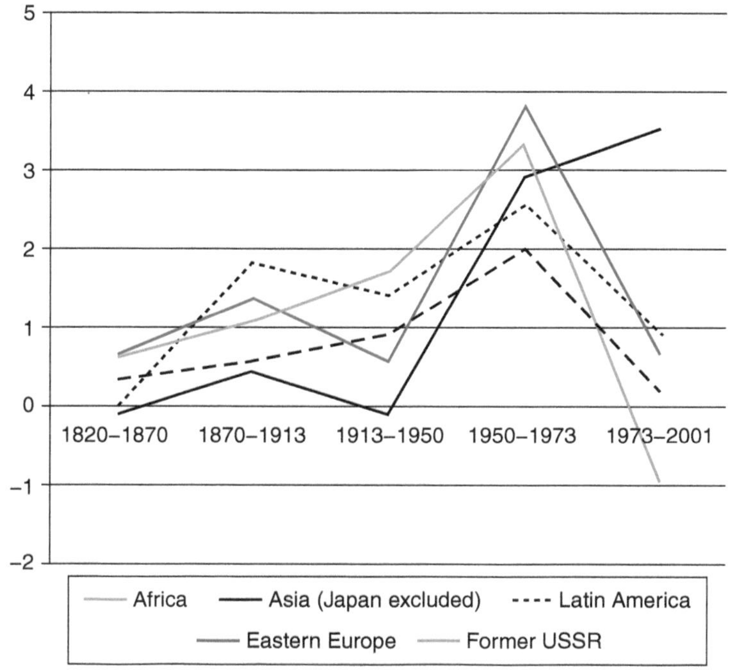

Figure 18.7 Economic Growth Falls Drastically, Except in Asia.
Source: Rainer Kattel, Tallinn University of Technology.

Asia in general, but particularly China and India, avoided this development because of what can be called ideological inertia. While shock therapy and free market logic became the fashion in the rest of the world, China and India stuck to the same conscious industrial strategy they had had since the end of the 1940s. The markets opened, but slowly.

The FIRE Sector Takes Over: The Third World

From the mid 1970s Latin America and Africa were the victims of a so called structural adjustment policy. In several of these countries real wages were more than halved in a very short time. We shall take Peru as an example. The structural changes led to a rapid fall in wages, as a very quick opening up for free trade killed the industry and weakened the unions.

Real wages were more than halved, but on the other hand exports increased rapidly (see Figure 18.8).

The interesting thing here is that just looking at GDP, things do not seem too bad in Peru. But looking at the composition of this GDP, it has changed very much: the FIRE sector has taken over an ever larger percentage of GDP.

The data from Peru's central bank show that in 1972 wages represented 51.2% of GDP, and the income of self-employed 26.5%, total 77.7%. Figure 18.9 shows how

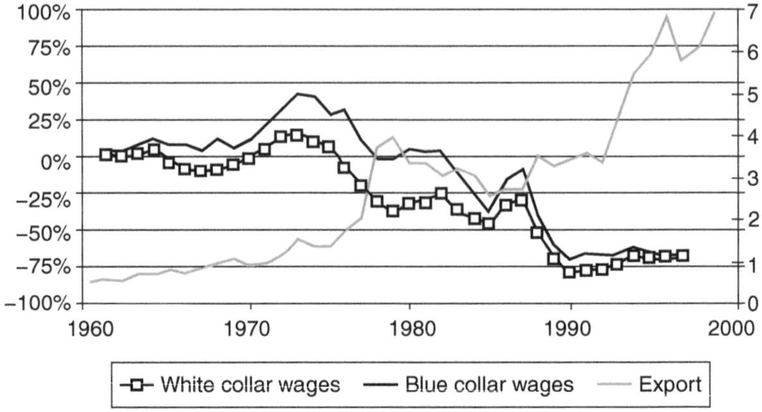

Figure 18.8 Peru: Deindustrialization, Falling Wages and Increasing Raw Materials Exports.
Source: Reinert 2007, p. 162.[12]

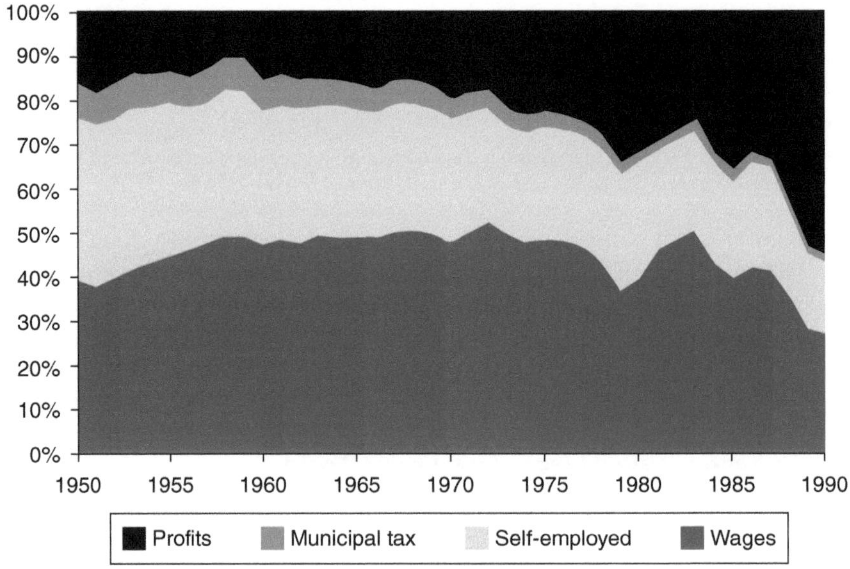

Figure 18.9 Composition of GDP in Peru: The FIRE Sector Takes Over.
Source: Banco Central de Reserva del Perú. These data have not been published after 1990.

this percentage fell with deindustrialization. In 1990, the last year Peru's central bank produced these statistics, the wage part of GDP was almost halved, while the part of the

[12] Reinert, Erik S., *How Rich Countries got Rich…and why Poor Countries stay Poor*, London, Constable, 2007.

self-employed had fallen to 15.9%. In total wages and income of the self-employed had fallen by 45% from 77.7% of GDP to 42.4%.

I spent much time in Peru in those years when wages were halved, and saw poverty increase dramatically. My wife commented that the same children outside the Lima supermarket, who had usually begged for sweets, now begged for canned milk and other food. To me it has always remained a mystery that this development was not regarded as interesting, and why such a dramatic theme has not shown up on an academic or a political agenda.

With Europe's internal devaluations these same dramatic mechanisms have started in Europe. We get a permanent fall in wages and self-employed income as part of GDP and in absolute numbers. In the short run this can look good for industry, as wage costs fall. But still industry as a whole will suffer, as demand contracts dramatically. In Peru the halving of wages led to a brutal closing down of newspapers (before the age of internet). High wages are in many ways very important for development, not only do markets grow through higher demand, high wages are also driving technological development. With the wage reductions Europe now experiences, we risk Hyman Minsky's 'financial fragility' creating a 'technological fragility': Cheap labor makes for less investment in new technology.

The FIRE Sector Takes Over: The Second World

In 2000 I was invited to a conference in Parliament in Mongolia's capital Ulaanbaatar, and was asked to prepare a report on the economic development of the country. Again I found the same pattern as in Latin America: real wages were more than halved. The real interest level was 35%, which made it virtually impossible to start any production, while there was much gain in moving money into the country. This money was not invested in the real economy. I was told that the high real interest was necessary to avoid a financial crisis.

Figure 18.10 shows the fall in production in a typical ex-Soviet republic, Latvia. Production was more than halved, but when this graph was made, in 1994, everybody believed growth would return rapidly. Time has shown, though, that most of the growth in the Baltic really has been housing bubbles. Growth after 1994 has had the same pattern as in Latin America: the wage part has fallen.

Also Russia shows the same kind of development (Figure 18.11). Real wages were halved, but as Russian GDP now gets closer to the 1989 level, income distribution is totally different. Particularly interesting is the observation that a strong overvaluation of the Ruble in the mid 1990s is closely connected to the fall in production and in real wages.

It is worth noting that democracy arrived in Russia at the same time as real wages were halved. The 'oligarchs' who had the economic power earned their money in the financial sector, while the real economy plummeted. A revaluation of the Ruble made it easy to transfer the oligarch's booty from financial speculations abroad at a very high value in dollars or pounds. But this reevaluation at the same time weakened the production economy even more, as Russian produced goods became very expensive and

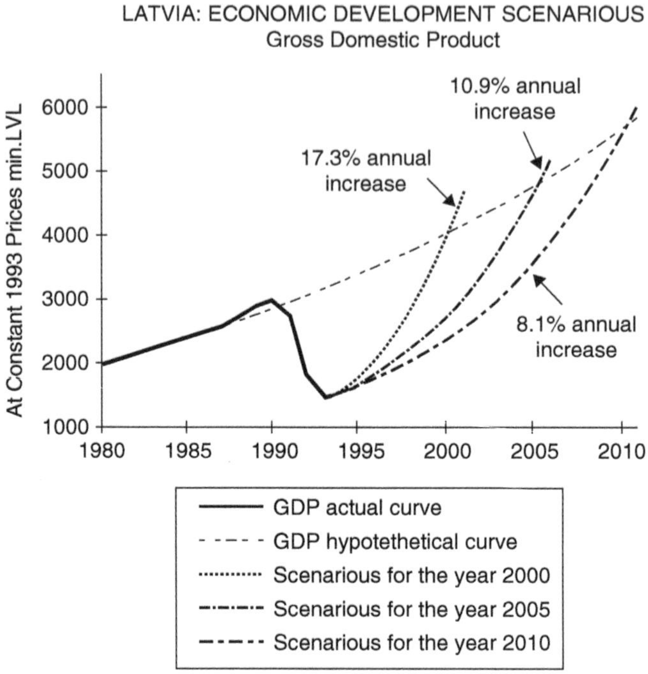

Figure 18.10 The Latvian Economic Collapse after the Fall of the Iron Curtain.
Source: Latvian Ministry of the Economy, 1994.

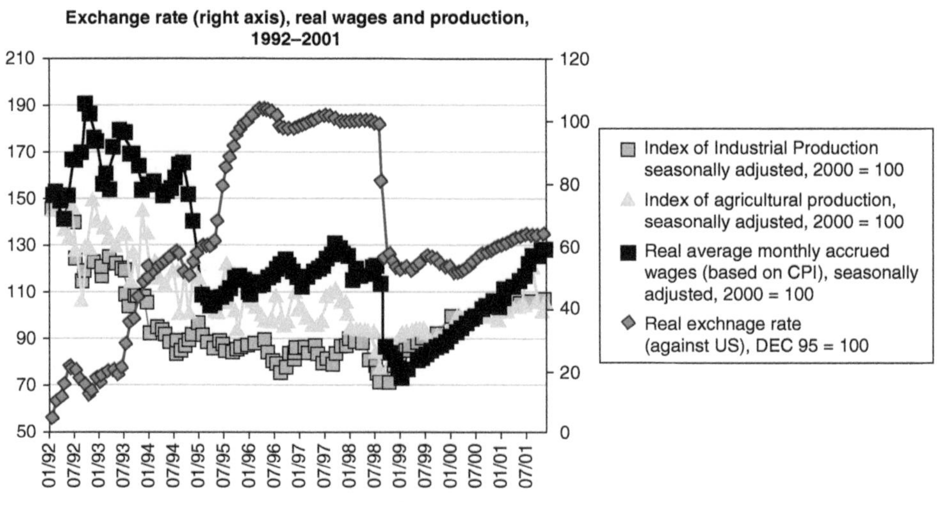

Figure 18.11 Russia: Halving of Production and Wages.
Source: Reinert & Kattel 2010.[13]

[13] Reinert, Erik S. & Rainer Kattel, 'Modernizing Russia: Round III. Russia and the other BRIC countries: forging ahead, catching up or falling behind?', *The Other Canon Foundation and Tallinn*

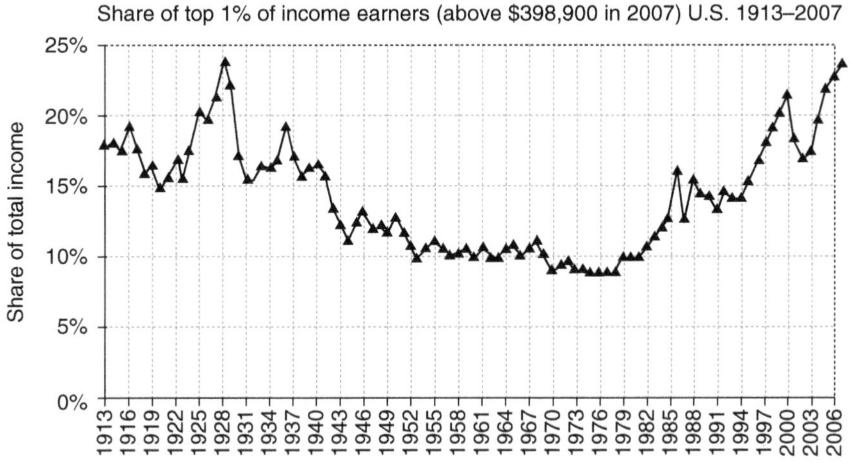

Figure 18.12 Part of Total Income in USA Earned by the Top 1% of the Tax Payers.

imports cheap. As in many other instances, the financial sector and the real economy have opposite interests.

The FIRE Sector Takes Over: The First World

The finance sector's taking over an ever larger part of GDP started in Latin America in the 1970s, hit the earlier Soviet sphere in the 1990s, and is now badly hitting USA and Europe. The destroying effect of overrated currencies is a common element for them all. The Euro as a straightjacket sets off the same mechanisms in Greece and Spain now as they did in Russia in the 1990s (see Figure 18.11), but now through internal devaluations.

Carlota Perez sees this as cyclical movements: during financial crises income is badly distributed, while in times when technological development hits the real economy income distribution improves (see Figure 18.12). Before the financial crises (1928 and 2006) the wealthiest 1% of the tax payers had about 25% of USA's total personal income. In times when technology and the real economy are seen as important, this number falls to about 10%. This will not happen without strong political pressure, as with Roosevelt and his economists' New Deal in the 1930s. It is hard to find anything like that economic and political strength today.

Figure 18.13 shows that the financial sector's part of GDP in USA is under 10%, while Figure 18.14 shows that measured by total income in USA the financial sector's part has at times reached 45%.

University of Technology Working Papers in Technology Governance and Economic Dynamics, no 32, 2010. http://tg.deca.ee/files/main/2010090707562222.pdf

Figure 18.13 The Financial Sector as Part of US GDP.
Source: Philippon, 2008.

Conclusion: The Mentality that Created the Crisis, its Consequences and Possible Remedies

The crisis was made possible by an economics profession that no longer differentiated between financial economy and real economy. Influential economists even came to think that financial economy was the real essence of the economy. One of Obama's main advisor Larry Summers's favorite expressions is 'Financial markets do not just oil the wheels of economic growth. They are the wheels.' Summers is then getting close to what we have called *chrysohedonism*, to confuse money itself with what money can buy. the financial economy became more real than the real economy. Important economists' close connection and common vested interests with the financial sector have become a theme in the discussions about the financial crisis, e.g. in the documentary film *Inside Job*. Another documentary movie on the crisis, *When Bubbles Burst* (2012), bases its understanding on the tradition emphasized in this paper: Schumpeter, Keynes, Veblen, Minsky and Perez.

The counterweight to this understanding is found in a German and American tradition from before World War II. This tradition was cross-disciplinary and covered economic theory and money theory, finance, law, philosophy, and political science, all within the same volumes. Examples are Georg Friedrich Knapp's *The State Theory of Money*

Figure 18.14 The Financial Sector's Part of Total Income in USA.

(1905)[14], Georg Simmel's *Philosophy of Money* (*Philosophie des Geldes*)[15], and Karl Elster's *The Soul of Money* (*Die Seele des Geldes*)[16]. Schumpeter contributed to this debate with an article from 1917 ('Das Sozialprodukt und die Rechenpfennige', roughly 'GDP and the Accounting Units')[17] and his book *Das Wesen des Geldes* (The Nature of Money) written in the late 1920s, but not published until 1970[18]. Schumpeter draws the line between financial economy (the *Rechenpfennige*, accounting units) and the real economy (The *Güterwelt*, 'the world of goods and services'), concepts that are required in order to understand financial crises (Figure 18.1).

The old American institutional school of economics, founded by Norwegian-American Thorstein Veblen, also made important contributions to the study of business

[14] Knapp, Georg Friedrich, *The State Theory of Money*, San Diego, Simon Publications, 2003 (reprint of 1924 English translation).

[15] Simmel, Georg, *Philosophie des Geldes*, Munich & Leipzig, Dunker & Humblot, 1920.

[16] Elster, Karl, *Die Seele des Geldes*, Jena, Fischer, 1923.

[17] Schumpeter, Joseph Alois,' Das Sozialprodukt und die Rechenpfennige: Glossen und Beiträge zur Geldtheorie von heute', *in Archiv für Sozialwissenschaft und Sozialpolitik*, no. 44, 1917–1918, p. 627–715.

[18] Schumpeter, Joseph Alois, *Das Wesen des Geldes*, Göttingen, Vandenhoeck und Ruprecht, 1970.

cycles and crises. Veblen – who predicted the crisis of 1929, but died a couple of months before it started – sharply differentiated between people in 'industrial activities' ('engineers') and speculators who quite peripherally contributed to production. He saw these speculators as the last remnants of the pirates and robber barons of earlier times. In his classic bestseller The Theory of the Leisure Class (1899) Veblen ridicules what he sees as a completely unproductive class, and its rituals, which he compares to the rituals of primitive races.

The US institutional school literally produced massive volumes on financial crises. Veblen's student Wesley Clair Mitchell work *Business Cycles* weighs in at 4 kilos of solid scholarship. Joseph Schumpeter had moved to the US and Harvard in the early 1930s, and his *Business Cycles* fills two heavy volumes. Mitchell's student Arthur F. Burns was the last representative of the old US institutional school to head the Federal Reserve, from 1970 to 1978. His presidency was dominated by a financial crisis – the so-called oil crisis – and under Burns' chairmanship this crises was typically solved by saving the real economy, production and real wages, at the expense of the financial sector (through inflation and negative real interest rates). The negative real interest rate forced money out of banks and into productive investments.

In his 1949 book *The Veil of Money*, Cambridge professor Cecil Pigou described the seesaw of sequential domination of the financial economy, with corresponding crises, and the real and productive economy: 'During the 1920s and 1930s … money, the passive veil, took on the appearance of an evil genius; the garment became a Nessus shirt[19]; the wrapper a thing liable to explode. Money, in short, after being little or nothing, was now everything… then with the Second World War, the tune changed again. Manpower, equipment and organization once more came into their own. The role of money dwindled to insignificance.'[20] This tradition of qualitative understanding in economics disappeared with the mathematization of economics after World War II. The fact that it had disappeared made the coming crisis so much harder to see, and the consequences so much harder to understand and to remedy.

In this old tradition money was seen as created and regulated by society's law and order (German: *Das Geld ist ein Geschöpf der Rechtsordnung*). The business cycles of capitalism were seen as needing continuous adjustments, not only of the interest, but also of the reserves of the banking sector in relation to its loans. My 1970s textbook from the University of St. Gallen in Switzerland[21] teaches the students how the economy must be fine-tuned through the business cycles i.e. by increasing or decreasing the reserve requirements regulating the banking sector. Under the ideological influence of neoliberalism, these adjustments were stopped. The reserve requirements were set very low, and the leveraging and the risks of the global financial system became correspondingly higher. The Basle process is now readjusting this somewhat. But the reserve requirements

[19] The poisoned shirt that killed Hercules.

[20] A. C. Pigou, *The Veil of Money*, London, Macmillan, 1949, pp.18–19.

[21] Schneider, Erik, *Einführung in die Wirtschaftstheorie. Vol. III. Geld, Kredit, Volkseinkommen und Beschäftigung*, Tübingen, Mohr (Siebeck), 1969.

are still low, and do not have to be fully adhered to until 2019, so 'we'll manage to have a couple of financial crises before that time', as Martin Wolf says.[22] Even if regulations tighten a bit, it is very clear that the financial sector is still directing capitalism. As long as this situation remains, it is hard not to expect the crisis to go on, and deepen.

If we take a look at how the crisis which started in 1929 was solved, it is clear that several theoretically radical – though often politically conservative – economists, not only Keynes and Schumpeter, played an important part. It could be said that Schumpeter delivered the theory explaining the crisis, while Keynes delivered the cure. American economist Rexford Tugwell (1891–1979) was an important adviser to Roosevelt and his New Deal. No economists of that kind have any power today. There is no conspiracy, but it seems clear that there exists a powerful political group in the US with the goal to reverse the New Deal reforms. The vested interests of this group overlap with the interests of financial capital. If this group/fraction is successful – as it seems to be – financial capital will take over for a long time, and the fall in real wages will be permanent, also in the developed world.

The process of falling wages and an increasing FIRE sector as a percentage of GDP described in this paper, which started in the economic periphery in the 1970s now has world coverage. The processes in the periphery have been totally neglected and now, as the Americans say, *the chickens are coming home to roost*. The West is itself being overtaken by mistakes made long ago and far away. The crisis theories presented in this paper based on observations of historical facts – what I refer to as The Other Canon of Economics – have now been marginalized by theories which tend to treat the financial sector as a mere mirror image of the real economy. Instead, in the Other Canon tradition, the financial sector may abruptly change from being a faithful servant to the real economy – living in symbiosis – to a parasitic monster feeding on possibly permanent cuts in wages, production, and human welfare such as Greece is experiencing at the moment. Capitalism needs purchasing power, and to remove so much purchasing power from the majority of the population as is now done – with Greece leading the pack – will sooner or later destroy capitalism as we have known it since World War II. What we may be creating in its place is a kind of post-industrial feudalism.

This paper is written from the point of view of oil-rich Norway. The financial crisis will probably force Norway to reconsider the strategy behind the oil fund. Already when visiting Oslo in 2008 Martin Wolf was of the opinion that the Norwegian oil fund was part of GSG, *The Global Savings Glut*. Our first Nobel Prize winner in economics, Ragnar Frisch, once wisely wrote something which is not obviously understandable except in the setting of a financial crisis, as experienced in the 1930s: 'Savings from the point of view of an individual and from the point of view of society as a whole are two entirely different concepts. They ought to be distinguished by using two different labels, not the same as now. This just causes confusion. Society as a whole can only save through productive investments'.[23]

---

22 Martin Wolf, 'The Mouse that did not Roar', *Financial Times*, September 14, 2010.

23 Ragnar Frisch, *Noen Trekk av Konjunkturlæren*, Oslo, Aschehoug, 1947, pages 41 and 42.

This is because financial savings in times of financial crisis will easily lose much of their value. Norway's first reserve fund for a rainy day was established in 1904 and invested in government bonds – which everybody thought was the safest investment. Most of the investments were lost during the crises following World War I. Particularly during times of financial crisis, Ragnar Frisch's advice should be followed: More should be invested in productive investments and less in financial markets. When, sooner or later, the financial sector will receive 'a haircut' through nations defaulting on their debts, while at the same time share prices fall because of diminishing purchasing power (a result of falling wages), part of the Norwegian oil fund will be lost. If the mechanisms of financial crises are properly understood, it is also easy to see that in the long run the oil fund has an aspect of 'Monopoly' money. There are times when savings are counterproductive in all their aspects, and the wisest thing to do is to spend money fast before they lose too much of their value.

The crisis in Europe will probably pass through the same stages as the one in Argentina in the 1990s. Right now we are at the stage of rigidly holding on to the currency exchange rates, while wages are falling (in Argentina this was an exchange rate at 1:1 with the dollar.) Sooner or later the nations of the European periphery will have to do as the Argentinians did, default and at the same time devalue. When the crisis in Argentina was over, real wages had fallen by 40%. The longer one waits, the worse it gets, because with time the productive sectors of the crisis economies are gradually destroyed. Markets dwindle and machines physically rust while the best brains leave the crisis countries.

During the crisis of the 1930 selective protectionism – so called Trade Wars – prevented a very uneven outcome of the crisis among the developed countries. this policy measure prevented a winner-takes-it-all outcome: that the developed world avoided being split into one camp of winners and one camp of losing nations. The Marshall Plan after World War II completed this work, before Europe again could start growing under a symmetrical free trade regime (among industrialized countries at similar levels of development). today the mistaken idea that protectionism caused the crisis is widespread, and instead of Trade Wars the world is embarking on Currency Wars. An important difference between Trade Wars and Currency Wars is that while the former primarily creates jobs, wages, and income in the real economy, the latter primarily creates rents to the financial sectors from bids and speculations. "Trade Wars" aiming at symmetrical industrial development are infinitely superior to Currency Wars. This financial crisis may represent a permanent blow to Western economies, with Asia being the winner that takes it all.

The last period of big shifts in the economic ranking between European states was the 1700s, when small city states were forced to yield economic power to strong nation-states. Venice and Amsterdam declined, while England and France rose. Faced with a growing real economy in Asia and, at home, a vicious circle of financial-sector growth and productive-sector decline, the West now basically has to choose between declining like Amsterdam – relatively, but keeping a healthy productive sector – or declining like Venice – declining absolutely, first losing the productive sector and then the financial sector – in order to become a museum. The former will requires the resurrection of policy instruments which went out of fashion in the 1970s, and started the trend of falling real wages, first in the Third World, then in the Second World, and now in the First World: the West.

Capital in itself – without possibility for investments – is sterile. If the possibilities for investment are lacking, amassing of capital will be counterproductive and prolong the crisis. The world economy is – as it was in 1929 – a pyramid game or Ponzi scheme, which collapses under increasing debt deflation if we do not maintain and increase the speed of innovation in the real economy. In the US the GDP level from 1929 was not reached again until mid World War II. The US stock market did not regain its 1929 level until the early 1950s. War is the ultimate Keynesian machinery for investment and consumption because it creates a situation where political and economic worries about inflation disappear, and enormous amounts of money are invested and spent in the real economy. The world does the opposite of oversaving, it dis-saves. War is also an important driver for technological change, because the state wants and demands products at the limit of what is technologically possible, thus advancing the frontier of knowledge.[24] If these mechanisms are properly understood, it is possible to invest more in the real economy by declaring war against environment pollution and old fashioned energy forms, and obtain the same economic boom that has always been the result of conventional wars. Such massive investments in renewable energy and green technology in my view represent the only way out of the present crisis.

[24] Werner Sombart's 1913 book on War and Kapitalism explains this and other mechanisms (*Krieg und Kapitalismus*, Munich & Leipzig, Duncker & Humblot 1913).

Chapter Nineteen

FULL CIRCLE: ECONOMICS FROM SCHOLASTICISM THROUGH INNOVATION AND BACK INTO MATHEMATICAL SCHOLASTICISM: REFLECTIONS ON A 1769 PRICE ESSAY: "WHY IS IT THAT ECONOMICS SO FAR HAS GAINED SO FEW ADVANTAGES FROM PHYSICS AND MATHEMATICS?"

Erik S. Reinert

Abstract

Through the sixteenth and seventeenth centuries, European science slowly lifted itself out of the fog of Mediaeval scholasticism. A rational, quantified and mechanised world picture emerged. In 1769 an essay questioned why economics benefited so little from the use of mathematics and quantification. Today the opposite may be argued – the increasing loss of relevance of economics is associated with the use of mathematics. Based on Francis Bacon's criticism of scholasticism, it is argued here that strong parallels exist between the decay of scholasticism and the decay of modern economics. From being a science of practice, late neoclassical economics has degenerated into "working upon itself", as Bacon says about late scholasticism. Since the 1769 essay, economics has come "full circle". The problem for economics is not then mathematics per se – mathematics is just one language in which science may decay.

Keywords Economics, History, Mathematics

"Never will man penetrate deeper into error than when he is continuing on a road which has led him to great success", says Hayek (1952) in his book, *The Counter-revolution of Science. Studies in the Abuse of Reason.* In the context of Kuhnian paradigm shifts, Hayek pictures a process of scientific decay that grows out of the excesses that follow from the very success of a particular set of ideas.

Scientific paradigms may, in this way, be seen as moving in trajectories similar to the trajectories of technologies. Mature technologies and mature scientific paradigms unleash search processes for fundamentally new ideas. Confronted with mature technologies, the markets for new ideas often provide a large diversity of solutions – the steam-powered car, the electrical car and the petrol-driven car were all competing at the turn of the last century. The market for ideas in economics, however, seems to become oligopolistic and less diverse, particularly after a great success as described by Hayek.

An increasing number of observers, both inside and outside of the economics profession, argue that the use of mathematics in economics in some areas has reached a point of diminishing or even negative returns. In Hayek's terms, reason is in a sense being "abused". Nowhere is the effect of this abuse more obvious than in the reality of economic development, where the increasingly globalised economy seems to produce opposite effects of what standard economic theory predicts. Instead of a convergence of world income (towards factor-price equalisation), we find that while the rich nations enjoy sustained growth, 90 of the world's nations were poorer in 1997 than in 1990.

In some fields of economics we seem to be at the end of a successful trajectory using quantification and mathematics in economics, a trajectory that had its humble beginnings around 1750. An unknown book that seemingly marks the start of this scientific trajectory or paradigm came up for sale in the fall of 1998. The book with the surprising title, *Why is it that Economics so Far has Gained so Few Advantages from Physics and Mathematics* was written by Johann Jacob Meyen and published in Berlin in 1770. The Royal Academy of Sciences in Berlin gave the title of the book as a price essay, which was won by Meyen.

Meyen's book brings us to the mid-1750s, a period when the "old" science has decayed and the scientific development of the Enlightenment is being diffused to new areas, in this case to economics. A new attitude is about to be formed towards social affairs, due to what Hayek (1952) calls "the new mental habits acquired in the intellectual and material conquest of nature". The price essay offered by the Prussian Academy of Science reflects a conscious concern that this process of learning from the exact sciences to economics was not taking place fast enough. The price essay helps introduce a great innovation, bringing mathematics – which in Meyen's use of the word also means "quantification" – into economics. This was the beginning of the scientific trajectory that many today would claim continued too long on the road to success, and decayed into what Philip Mirowski (1994) calls "physics envy".

The focus of this paper is on the transition period, where the old science has entered into decay, pedantry and irrelevance. We shall argue that there are striking similarities in the process of decay and abuse of science as they gradually lose relevance and "decay" scientifically. The "decay" of the science of the scholastics thus presents surprisingly many similarities to the increasing loss of relevance which many observers and participants perceive in economics today. Based on this, we would argue that mathematics *per se* cannot be blamed for the loss of relevance. The parallel with the decay of the science of scholastics seems to indicate that mathematics is but one language in which a science may lose its relevance to the problems of the real world.

We are thus discussing the birth of quantification and the use of mathematics in economics, a science competing with the decaying and increasingly irrelevant science produced by the schoolmen. Originally the term "scholastic" signified things relating to schools and universities. With the decay of scholasticism, the term also took on a new derogatory sense of a pedantic and formal science dealing in logical subtleties far removed from the problems of real life. Based on Francis Bacon's analysis of the decay of scholasticism, we compare the similarities of late scholasticism and today's mathematical economics, and suggest that the Bacon's formula for the way out is still the valid one.

The schoolmen as a prototype of success and decay of science

Dissatisfaction with the state of economics is growing. The following analysis by a well-known historian of the profession, Mark Blaug, is becoming almost mainstream:

> Modern economics is "sick". Economics has increasingly become an intellectual game played for its own sake and not for its practical consequences. Economists have gradually converted the subject into a sort of social mathematics in which analytical rigor as understood in math departments is everything and empirical relevance (as understood in physics departments) is nothing. If a topic cannot be tackled by formal modelling, it is simply consigned to the intellectual underworld. To pick up a copy of *American Economic Review* or *Economic Journal*, not to mention *Econometrica* or *Review of Economic Studies*, these days is to wonder whether one has landed on a strange planet in which tedium is the deliberate objective of professional publication. Economics was condemned a century ago as "the dismal science", but the dismal science of yesterday was a lot less dismal than the soporific scholasticism of today (Blaug, 1998).

Comparing sterile economics to scholasticism is not new, and the parallel is a good one. Already in 1926 Danish economist L.V. Birck wrote an article in *Weltwirtschaftliches Archiv*, called "Moderne scholastik"[1] ("Modern scholasticism") in which he discusses the theories of Böhm-Bawerk (Birck, 1926). The scholastics – or schoolmen – were the carriers of science in the Middle Ages. Schumpeter ascribes to this early school of economics most of the important principles found in Adam Smith's *Wealth of Nations* (see de Roover, 1957). However, their science decayed and the scientists of the day were increasingly accused of pedantry and irrelevance.

Like neo-classical economics, in its extreme form scholasticism also "proves" things that contradict common sense and intuition. Samuelson's factor-price equalisation, which will happen under free trade, is an example of counterintuitive scholasticism in economics. McCloskey (1985) makes the point about neo-classical economics proving counter-intuitive propositions very clearly. The example he uses is Fogel's (1964) "proof" that the railroad was not important in the development of the USA, because railroads, compared to canals, only improved GDP by 2.5 per cent. This is like proving that the heart is an unimportant organ because it only represents 2.5 per cent of the weight of the human body. Robert Heilbroner (1971) asked the question "Is economics relevant?" The answer to that question has been increasingly "no".

Clearly, the lack of historical knowledge and corresponding *Fingerspitzengefühl* is almost a prerequisite for economic scholasticism. Jacob Viner (1991) makes the point

---

[1] Birck (1926) heads the article with Carlyle's motto as already quoted in this article: "That dismal science!".

that "economists have succeeded in being as ahistorical as an educated man can perhaps possibly be". This lack of historical knowledge contributes to what Veblen calls the contamination of instincts: an irrelevant education blocks what to practical people is "common sense". In a similar vein, a distinguished committee of the American Economic Association pointed in 1991 to the danger that "graduate programs (in economics) may be turning out a generation of too many idiots savants, skilled in technique but innocent in real economic issues" (American Economic Association, 1991).

In the literature of the early eighteenth century, two authors stand out in their criticism of this same kind of pedantry, removed from real life, in contemporary science: Jonathan Swift (1684–1754) in Ireland and Ludvig Holberg (1667–1745) in Denmark-Norway. Swift's *Travels into Several Remote Nations of the World*, published under the pseudonym Lemuel Gulliver, mocks the scientific establishment in England. This is particularly evident in Gulliver's visit to the land of the giants. In his *Erasmus Montanus*, Ludvig Holberg gives us a parody of the decayed logic of the scholastics, when a learned man makes the following proof to a poor woman: "A stone cannot fly. Mother Nille cannot fly. Therefore Mother Nille is a stone".

These authors were both very influential. In the mid-eighteenth century, a list of the ten most sold books in Denmark-Norway would have consisted of the Bible and nine works by Holberg. This mockery of contemporary science was no doubt an important part of the *Zeitgeist*: Swift's Gulliver appeared in 1726 and Holberg's Erasmus *Montanus* was written no later than 1727.

While Swift and Holberg popularised the mockery of scholastic science, the criticism of the schoolmen had started with Francis Bacon more than 100 years earlier. Bacon recognised the enormous potential for development of human knowledge. He consciously tried to infuse the spirit of exploration into his time by writing what he called "feigned history" – fiction written in order to influence the future path of the history of mankind. Bacon's utopia, New Atlantis, presents the world with its first research council, and with a whole range of future inventions. Bacon perceived "the never ending frontier of knowledge" and urged his time to march towards it (see Reinert and Daastøl, 1997).

However, the old scientific order stood in the way of such a task, and Bacon had to fight this state of scientific affairs in order to make way for the new world view. In our view, Bacon's description from 1605 in *An Essay on Human Learning* fits the problems of economics today in a number of ways. We have marked these points in italics:

> Surely, like as many substances in nature which are solid, do putrefy and corrupt into worms; so it is the propriety of good and solid knowledge to putrefy and dissolve into a number of subtle, idle, unwholesome and, as I may term them, vermiculite questions, which have indeed a kind of quickness, and life of spirit, but no soundness of matter, or goodness of quality. This kind of degenerate learning did chiefly reign amongst the schoolmen, who, *having sharp and strong wits, and abundance of leisure, and small variety of reading, but their wits being shut up in the cells of a few authors* (chiefly Aristotle their dictator), *as their persons were shut up in the cells of monasteries and colleges, and knowing little history, either of nature or time, did, out of no great quantity of matter, and infinite agitation of wit, spin out unto us those laborious webs of learning which are extant in their books.* For the wit and mind of man, if it work upon matter, which is the contemplation of the creatures of God,

> worketh according to the stuff, and is limited thereby: but if it work upon itself, as the spider worketh his web, then it is endless, and brings forth indeed cobwebs of learning, admirable for the fineness of thread and work, *but of no substance or profit* (Bacon, 1605).

As in Bacon's analysis, very capable and intelligent individuals produce today's economic scholasticism. However, their limited reading and very limited knowledge of history cause them to produce "webs of learning" which are irrelevant, and even counterproductive.

The advances of the natural sciences slowly increased their influence on economic theory. "Never can pride in the achievements of the natural sciences and confidence in the omnipotence of their methods have been more justified than at the turn of the eighteenth and nineteenth centuries", says Hayek (1952). It is therefore natural that this period represents the start of "physics envy" in economics and, from the point of view of economic policy, David Ricardo was the starting point in this "decay".

Cambridge professor H.R. Foxwell, who was born in 1849, knew the history of economic thought better than most. Foxwell put together the two largest collections of historical economics books and pamphlets that exist to this day; the Goldsmiths' Collection at the University of London and the Kress Collection at Harvard Business School. To Foxwell, the problems in economics started with David Ricardo. In his biographical article on Foxwell, Keynes (1972) informs us that such was Foxwell's dislike of Ricardian economics that he refused to deliver the presidential address on Ricardo to the Royal Economic Society.

Foxwell wrote in 1899:

> Ricardo, and still more those who popularised him, may stand as an example for all time of the extreme danger which may arise from the unscientific use of hypothesis in social speculations, from the failure to appreciate the limited applications to actual affairs of a highly artificial and arbitrary analysis. His ingenious, though perhaps over-elaborated, reasonings became positively mischievous and misleading when they were unhesitatingly applied to determine grave practical issues without the smallest sense of the thoroughly abstract and unreal character of the assumptions on which they were founded (Foxwell, 1899).

This criticism could indeed have been tailor-made today to criticise the devastating affects on welfare in the Second and Third World produced by neoclassical economics. This kind of theoretical "mischief" among other things caused a fairly conscious de-industrialisation of the Second and Third World which has been an important factor in causing the rapid decrease in real wages in these nations.

The start of a new scientific trajectory: Meyen's 1769 price essay, "Why is it that economics so far has gained so few advantages from physics and mathematics?

In the fall of 1998 a book with a surprising title appeared for sale at a Hamburg auction house – *Why Is It that Economics so Far Has Gained so Few Advantages from Physics and Mathematics*, with the subtitle, *And How Could These Sciences be Introduced in Order to be*

Generally Useful in Economics, and How Could One, by Connecting these Sciences, Arrive at Principles which Are of Practical Use? The author of the book was Johann Jacob Meyen, and the date of publication 1770. The original German title is: *Wie kommt es, dass die Oekonomie bisher so wenig Vortheile von der Physik und Mathematik gewonnen hat; und wie kann man diese Wissenschaften zum gemeinen Nutzen in die Oekonomie einführen, und von dieser Verbindung auf Grundsätze kommen, die in die Ausübung brauchbar sind?*

This author acquired the book, which had been published in Berlin by Haude & Spener in 1770. The book is seemingly rare; it does not appear in any of the standard bibliographies and collections of economics books of the period, i.e. Kress, Goldsmith, Einaudi, Humpert or Higgs. A search in the catalogues of German university libraries located four other copies of the book. In the German libraries the book is catalogued under its first title page, in French. The rest of the book is written in German, and there is also a second title page in that language.

The title of Meyen's book is even more interesting when it becomes clear that the title of the book is a question put forward as a price essay by the Royal Academy of Sciences of Prussia for 1769. The subject of the use of mathematics in economics was not the idea of a single outsider, it was a subject important enough to be put forward as a price essay by one of the most prestigious scientific academies of the period. The use of quantitative measures was apparently seen as a way of improving man's lot.

This book won the Academy's prize. The author, Johann Jacob Meyen, is not well known. He was born on November 26, 1731 in Colberg in Hinterpommern (Lower Pomerania) and died on March 8, 1797 in Stettin[2]. Meyen studied in Königsberg, later in Halle, where the first chair in economics had been established in 1728. He studied theology, and at the time he wrote the prize essay, he worked as a priest in Koblenz (not the Koblenz of the confluence of the Moselle and the Rhine, but Koblenz in Upper Pomerania, Vorpommern). He was also a Magister of Philosophy, and from 1774 employed as a professor of physics and mathematics at the academic Gymnasium in Stettin. The biographical dictionary also lists him as a poet in Latin (*lateinischer Dichter*). The French title page confirms that Meyen uses the term "economics" as it was normally still used at the time, as "agricultural economics". But it is clear that the treatise goes beyond that, covering both manufacturing and what the German economist Justi earlier in the 1750s had termed Polizei-Wissenschaft, or "the science of economic policy".

The practical use of the sciences – the subject of the 1769 essay – clearly was close to Meyen's heart. This urge for usefulness and praxisnahe – for closeness to the practice of real life – is typical both of the German philosophers of this period, Leibniz and Christian Wolff, and also of the later reaction of German economics to the more abstract English school of economics. Almost ten years after publishing the book – from November 1787 to March 1788 – Meyen issued a mathematical monthly under the title, *Unknown and Too Little Known Truths of Mathematics, Physics and Philosophy and Their Use for the Common Good, Particularly for the Economy of Pomerania and Neighbouring Provinces.*

2 Bibliographical information from *Allgemeine Deutsche Biographie*, Vol. 21, p. 553.

Meyen's book is significant because it so consciously – and early in the process – discusses the epochal shift from a purely qualitative perception of economic reality to one also including quantification. At the time of Meyen's writing, very few uses of mathematics had been made in economics, perhaps only three[3]. Francois Forbonnais (1722–1800) uses mathematical reasons and symbols in his *Elémens du Commerce* from 1754. Cesare Beccaria (1735–1793), a Milanese economist, used mathematics in the early and mid-1760s. Proposing a metric system for measurements, based on astronomical magnitudes and physical properties, Beccaria clearly qualifies in the category of scientists that Meyen describes as *Messkünstler* ("artists of measuring"). A third mathematical contribution in economics before Meyen was by Giammaria Ortes (1713–1790) – a Venetian monk – in his *Calcolo Sopra il Valore delle Opinione Umane* (1757).

It is worth noticing that two of these early "artists of measuring" in economics – Beccaria and Ortes – were the first harbingers of Malthus' theory of population. The qualitative and knowledge-focused economics of the Renaissance had produced optimistic theories like those of Bacon. In this setting, economic development was dependent on scale and a big market, and consequently a large population was seen as a blessing for a nation. Later quantification and abstract economic reasoning tended to hold the level of human knowledge constant, while disregarding the relationship between scale and technical change. This combination of mechanics and statics came to produce what Carlyle dubbed "the dismal science". Meyen, however, is optimistic. He typically stresses the importance of a large population in order for a nation to achieve wealth.

Meyen (1770) intensely discusses the relationship between theory and practice, and clearly pronounces himself in favour of the *combination* of both theory and practice: "The theoretical truths are reached on a long and barren road, the practical ones on a lighter and fertile one. But the fact that one reaches further on the first road comes from the use that the human spirit makes of both". Meyen clearly admires the rise of the theoretical sciences: "The theoretical sciences rise faster and to higher levels of perfection than the practical ones", commenting on "The propensity of mankind towards 'synthetic' knowledge or 'way of learning' ('*synthetischer Lehrart*')".

The Bible tells us that God "hast ordered all things by measure and number and weight" (*Wisdom of Solomon* 11:20). Not until the thirteenth century, however, did Western civilisation pay much attention to the concept of reality as quantifiable (see Crosby, 1997). Meyen refers to scientists as "measuring artists and persons who understand nature" (*Messkünstler und Naturkundige*), and he clearly uses the term mathematics also to cover measuring and quantification. We are here touching on two phenomena – quantification and the use of mathematics – which occur parallel in history, but which are in fact separate phenomena. From the late Middle Ages onwards one could witness a growing interest in measurement of the surrounding reality (Crosby, 1997). Maps and clocks are two main symbols of this quest for measurement. The Enlightenment saw a related development into a more mechanised world picture, where the emergence of astronomy as a science and of clocks, cogs and wheels, slowly led to a "mechanisation"

3 These early contributions are discussed in Theocharis (1983).

of the world picture (Dijksterhuis, 1986). It was the mindset from these sciences that later came to influence economics. Adam Smith's metaphor of "the invisible hand" appears several times in his early publication on astronomy, but only once in the *Wealth of Nations*.

Meyen's book was published at a time when Justi dominated the *Policey-Wissenschaft*, or science of economic policy, in Germany. Leibniz and Wolff – both referred to by Meyen – were the two prominent philosophers of the time. Meyen also refers to the great agricultural economist of the eighteenth century, Arthur Young. This in spite of the fact that Young was only 27 years old when Meyen's book appeared. Young's *The Farmer's Letters to the People of England* had been published in 1767. All in all we find Meyen representing the *zeitgeist* of his time, a *zeitgeist* that later found its best expression in James Steuart's *Inquiry into the Principles of Political Economy* (Steuart, 1767). Steuart had spent many years in Germany, and his work was much inspired by German economics, and almost immediately there were two different German translations of his voluminous tomes. At this time quantification was still coupled with the dynamic and knowledge-focused view of Francis Bacon.

Meyen on the relationship between agriculture and manufacturing

Meyen, Young, Hume and Steuart had one very important conviction in common, a conviction which in English political economy was to disappear with Adam Smith. This regards the relationship between agriculture and industry. These authors believed, as David Hume put it in his six-volume *History of England*, that the best way to promote agriculture is to promote industry. Also Meyen insists that manufacturing is the key to national improvement, and he puts it very clearly: "it is known that a primitive people (*ein rohes Volk*) does not improve their customs and habits (*Sitten*) later to find useful industries (*Gewerbe*), but the other way around …" (Meyen, 1770, p. 11, emphasis added).

This is the same argument that Mathew Carey highly successfully uses in 1821 in his influential *Address to the Farmers of the United States*, and which Friedrich List uses against English political economy 20 years later. These publications were both important foundations for nineteenth century economic policy. The theoretical argument, however, is seemingly one by the other side, when, in 1846, England convinces the world to stop protecting manufacturing industry because she herself stopped protecting agriculture. However, both Germany and the United States were to follow the advice of Friedrich List, not opening up for world free trade until they had acquired a sufficiently strong industrial base.

It is all too well known that early economists were aware of the importance of money and species. This also led to an awareness of the importance of velocity of circulation. Meyen recognises the connection between the existence of manufacturing industry and a high velocity of circulation ("*Der Flor des Fabrikenwesens giebt nun dem Gelde den vortrefflichsten Umlauf*" (p. 143)).

The pre-Smithian argument against opening a nation to free trade too early was that economic progress was activity-specific, it was tied to certain economic activities which were the carriers of technology to other economic activities. Here Meyen's statement is very clear (see also Meyen, 1770, p. 150). This argument was lost in the mechanised world view of neo-classical economics. In this context the great novelty of Adam Smith was that he – for the first time – made all economic activities qualitatively alike as carriers of economic progress. The importance of this historical controversy for today's economic policy in the Second and Third Worlds cannot be overemphasised (see Reinert, 1999).

Meyen on technology, science and innovations

The general opinion among economic historians is that the first industrial revolution did not have close ties to science. One could, however, argue that this may have been less true in Germany than in England. Meyen was clearly aware of the important role of science in promoting the wealth of nations. A few years after Meyen published his price essay, Johann Beckmann, who was a professor of economics in Göttingen, wrote a book about the role of technology in economics (Beckman, 1780). Also in the 1770s, Goethe's friend Johann Gottfried Herder discusses science policy in a book entitled *On the Influence of Government on the Sciences, and that of the Sciences on Government* (Herder, 1781). In England Charles Babbage raises this same argument in the 1820s (Babbage, 1830).

Innovation is an important subject in English political economy from Francis Bacon's *An Essay on Innovations* (around 1605) to James Steuart's 1767 book. The term innovation is repeatedly used by Steuart, but disappears in the trade-and-barter focused theory of Adam Smith. Meyen belongs to the old school, and stresses the practical goals of the great German philosophers of the day. Their science is not empty like scholasticism, their goals are practical: "Leibniz took great care to improve the machinery used in mining, and the archives of Hanover still contains piles of documents regarding these matters. Wolff introduced suggestions to the propagation of corn, and informed the world thereof – but these improvements are not appreciated" (Meyen, 1770, p. 20).

Meyen on resistance to change

The common people's lack of appreciation of improvements is a recurrent theme in Meyen's book. He often complains of a "hatred against reason" – *Hass gegen den Verstand* – which prevents new discoveries from being put into practical use. Here is one example: "Many nobles of Pomerania and Rügen have properties in Schonen (Skåne, Sweden), where 7 or 8 horses are used to plough, and with a horseman on every horse". Clearly this was a very inefficient and labour intensive way of ploughing. Better harnesses were sent from Pomerania, but alas, the "improvers" were driven away with showers of stones.

Meyen then lists the reasons why practical people do not learn from theoretical knowledge: they are pride (*Hochmut/Stolz*), meanness (*Geiz*), and also because people are simple-minded (*einfältig*), lazy (*faul*), and envious (*neidisch*). We find the same issue addressed by Christian Wolff when he suggests that "It ought to be prohibited to make mockery with inventors" (see Reinert and Daastøl, 1997).

Meyen complains that the normal excuse used to block innovations is the phrase "That may be true in theory, but not in practice". Obviously having heard this excuse over and over, Meyen also repeats it over and over in his book. He also observes that innovators and improvers (*Verbesserer*) fall victim to ostracism ("*Ostracismus*"). Socrates is Meyen's prime example of the "improver" (*Verbesserer*) who is driven away. Meyen describes a world of ignorance in which a sort of "Gresham's Law" drives out good practice and protects old bad practices. Meyen is here very much in line with his ruler, Frederick the Great of Prussia, who describes the "liberation from above", the kind of governmental stimuli which were typical of the premodern age: "The plebs" – his term for the rising bourgeoisie – "will never give up the humdrum tune, unless you drag them by their noses and ears to their profits" (quoted in Cowe, 1988).

In Meyen's opinion revolutions are required in order to improve things: "The discoveries were a fruit of genius, and were normally already around for a long time, but the introduction and feasibility of the improvement came out of the revolutions" (p. 19). In Keynes' world, practical men are all slaves of defunct economists. In Meyen's world practical men were slaves of old habits.

Meyen on "synergies"

Early economists were aware of what we would call synergies between economic activities. In 1613 Antonio Serra says that the wealth of a city can be roughly judged by counting the number of different professions: the larger the number of professions, the wealthier the city. In other words, the greater the division of labour, the greater the wealth (Serra, 1613).

Meyen describes the usefulness of what we would call networks: "A nation is happy when the theoreticians and the economists are in constant activity and in connection, and are aware of the advantages that these sciences may bring to every economic activity (*Gewerbe*) in the nation" (Meyen, 1770, p. 14).

Meyen stresses that "lines of communication" from one science to another bring advantages. Here he uses as one example that artillery and fortifications have achieved several advantages from higher geometry. Meyen also has a clear description of a type of accidental discovery that we would call serendipity (Meyen, 1770, p. 15).

Meyen on types of nations

Meyen produces a typology of nations (1770, pp. 48–9), and argues that national characteristics are important in order to explain to what extent sciences will be put to practical use: "In this way (i.e. through the typology) one can investigate to what extent a nation will tend to connect the theoretical sciences with economics, or what kind of hindrances are in the way of such connections".

Meyen distinguishes between three types of nations:

(1) *When a nation has the character of a soldier* ... sciences will not be held in high esteem. In such a nation the scientists will also try to tyrannise his profession (*Dort wird auch fast ein jeder schlechter Mensch monosyllabisch genug sein, und in seinem Fache tyrannisiren suchen*). Here mathematics will also be little used in the art of war, because empiricism

is used "they will use the contributions from the sable rather than those from mathematics".

(2) *When a nation has the character of a trader* (Kaufmann), everything that regards trade will have good conditions. But as soon as the scientist raises above what causes domestic advantages, like the reduction of imports, he will face the usual problems. The (agricultural) economist will be hated in the nations where the traders are at the steering wheel, and the farmer gets very little respect beyond what respect he gets from producing staples, "Though, the *Teoreticus* has an advantage in this type of nation: the measuring artist (*Messkünstler*) can help shipbuilding and the improvement of machinery (*Maschinen-Wesen*)".

(3) *When a nation is similar to a woman* … the *belle arti*, the poet, the writer of novels, the actor, and the producer of jewellery will find applause. But the agricultural economist will have to be a simple farmer. Mathematics and physics have the worst conditions is such states. The producer finds his inventions from the neighbour, and these are brought to him by the merchant of fashion accessories. Art itself, and even more theoretical sciences, are muted. This is because this kind of nation only considers the beauty of an article.

To Meyen the prospects for science are rather bleak in most, if not all, countries. However, during the next century Germany was to produce a new type of nation, where science was held in higher esteem than probably in any nation, before or after. Germany became a type of nation described by an English foreign minister as "A nation of bloody university professors".

Conclusion: history as the way out of scholasticism

Meyen's economics, while arguing for quantification and mathematisation, still stresses the importance of the non-quantifiable issues like knowledge, science, networks and "national character". In the 1750s a scientific trajectory of "theory with measurement" begins, which now slowly has degenerated to "theory without measurement".

As already mentioned, the affiliation of neo-classical economics with the pedantic and circuitous reasonings of scholasticism is not new. It is in this spirit that the Danish economist L.V. Birck already in 1926 named an article discussing the theories of Böhm-Bawerk "Moderne Scholastik" (Birck, 1926). Like neo-classical economics, in its extreme form scholasticism also "proves" things that contradict common sense and intuition. McCloskey (1985) makes this point very well.

Francis Bacon gave us the formula for escaping scholasticism, a formula that in our opinion is the solution also for today's problems in economics:

> Martin Luther, conducted no doubt by an higher providence, but in discourse of reason, finding what a province he had undertaken against the bishop of Rome, and the degenerate traditions of the church, and finding his own solitude being no ways aided by the opinion of his own time, was enforced to awake all antiquity, and to call former times into his succour, to make a party against the present time. So that the ancient authors, both in divinity and

> in humanity, which had long slept in their libraries, began generally to be read and revolved (Bacon, 1605).

In 1886 Columbia economist Edwin Seligman described how economics in the 1850s freed itself from the claws of Ricardian irrelevance. Seligman's prescription was the same as that of Bacon 300 years earlier: go back to history as the only laboratory we have. He explains the re-development of the alternative economic canon, a reply to the *reductio ad absurdum* of orthodox Ricardian economics:

> The socialists, such as Weitling, Marlo and Proudhon, uttered energetic and effective protests against the prevailing systems; and in England able men like Thompson and Jones wrote large works to countervail the exaggerations of the orthodox school. But the new ideas first obtained a truly scientific basis about the middle of the century, when three young German economists – Roscher, Knies and Hildebrand – proclaimed the necessity of treating economics from the historical standpoint. They initiated a new movement whose leading principles may be thus formulated:
>
> 1. It discards the exclusive use of the deductive method, and stresses the necessity of historical and statistical treatment.
> 2. It denies the existence of immutable natural laws in economics, calling attention to the interdependence of theories and institutions, and showing that different epochs or countries require different systems.
> 3. It disclaims belief in the beneficence of the absolute laissez-faire system; it maintains the close interrelation of law, ethics, and economics; and it refuses to acknowledge the adequacy of a scientific explanation, based the assumption of self-interest as the sole regulator of economic action (Seligman, 1925).

In our opinion this is the path which again has to be followed in order to lead economics out of the barren wastelands of scholasticism. Hopefully this note has illustrated that today's economic scholasticism has not been caused by mathematics *per se*. As Meyen's book shows, the introduction of science, quantification and mathematics in economics was indeed a most useful innovation. The analogy with Bacon's criticism of the schoolmen shows us that mathematics is but one language in which a science may decay to sterility and irrelevance.

References

American Economic Association (1991), "Report of the Commission on Graduate Education in Economics", *Journal of Economic Literature*, September, pp. 1044–5.

Allgemeine Deutsche Biographie, Bibliographical information on Johann Jacob Meyen, Vol. 21, p. 553.

Babbage, C. (1830), *Reflections on the Decline of Science in England and on Some of Its Causes*, B. Fellowes, London.

Bacon, F. (1605), *On the Advancement of Learning.*

Beckmann, J. (1780), *Anleitung zur Technologie, oder zur Kenntniss der Handwerke, Fabriken und Manufacturen, vornehmlich derer, die mit der Landwirthschaft, Polizey und Cameralwissenschaft in nächster Verbindung stehen*, 2nd ed., Wittwe Vandenhoeck, Göttingen.

Birck, L.V. (1926), "Moderne Scholastik. Eine kritische Darstellung der Böhm-Bawerkschen Theorie", *Weltwirtschaftliches Archiv*, Vol. 24 No. 2, pp. 198–227.

Blaug, M. (1998), "Disturbing currents in modern economics", *Challenge*, May/June.

Crosby, A.W. (1997), *The Measure of Reality. Quantification and Western Society 1250–1600*, Cambridge University Press, Cambridge.

de Roover, R. (1957), "Joseph Schumpeter and scholastic economics", *Kyklos*, Vol. 10 No. 2, pp. 115–43.

Dijksterhuis, E.J. (1986), *The Mechanization of the World Picture*, Princeton University Press, Princeton, NJ.

Fogel, R.W. (1964), *Railroads and the American Economic Growth: Essays in Economic History*, John Hopkins, Baltimore, MD.

Foxwell, H.S. (1899), "Foreword", in Menger, A., *The Right of the Whole Produce of Labour*, Macmillan, London, p. xli.

Hayek, F. (1952), *The Counter-Revolution of Science. Studies in the Abuse of Reason*, The Free Press, Glencoe, IL, p. 105.

Heilbroner, R. (1971), *Is Economics Relevant? A Reader in Political Economics,* Goodyear Publishing Company, Pacific Palisades, CA.

Herder, J.G. (1781), *Vom Einfluss der Regierung auf die Wissenschaften, und der Wissenschaften auf die Regiergung*, 2nd ed., Georg Jakob Decker, Berlin.

Keynes, J.M. (1972), "Herbert Somerton Foxwell", *The Collected Writings of John Maynard Keynes*, Vol. 20, Macmillan, London, p. 270.

Lowe, A. (1988), *Has Freedom a Future?*, Praeger, New York, NY.

McCloskey, D. (1985), *The Rhetoric of Economics*, University of Wisconsin Press, Madison, WI, pp. 113–37.

Meyen, J.J. (1770, *Wie kommt es, dass die Oekonomie bisher so wenig Vortheile von der Physik und Mathematik gewonnen hat; und wie kann man diese Wissenschaften zum gemeinen Nutzen in die Oekonomie einführen, und von dieser Verbindung auf Grundsätze kommen, die in die Ausübung brauchbar sind?*, Haude & Spener, Berlin.

Mirowski, P. (1994), *More Heat than Light. Economics as Social Physics, Physics as Nature's Economics*, Cambridge University Press, Cambridge.

Reinert, E.S. (1999), "The role of the state in economic growth", *Journal of Economic Studies*, Vol. 4.

Reinert, E.S. and Daastøl, A. (1997), "Exploring the genesis of economic innovations: the religious *gestalt*-switch and the duty to invent as preconditions for economic growth", *European Journal of Law and Economics*, Vol. 4 No. 2/3.

Seligman, E. (1925), "Continuity in economics" (1886), published in his *Essays in Economics*, Macmillan, New York, NY, pp. 15–16.

Serra, A. (1613), *Breve Trattato delle Cause che Possono far Abbondare li Regni d'Oro e Argento dove non sono Miniere*, Lazzaro Scoriggio, Naples.

Steuart, J. (1767), *An Inquiry into the Principles of Political Economy: Being an Essay on the Science of Domestic Policy in Free Nations*, 2 vols, Millar and Cadell, London.

Theocharis, R. (1983), *Early Developments in Mathematical Economics*, 2nd ed., Macmillan, London.

Viner, J. (1991), *Essays in the Intellectual History of Economics*, Princeton University Press, Princeton, NJ.

Chapter Twenty

WERNER SOMBART (1863–1941) AND THE SWAN SONG OF GERMAN ECONOMICS

Erik S. Reinert

It is probably fair to say that the last German economist in the old tradition was Werner Sombart. What is most noteworthy about Sombart is probably his going from being Germany's best known economist – one of his books was translated into 25 languages – and being acclaimed as 'brilliant', and at his death being honoured with both an obituary and an editorial in New York Times, to being virtually unknown today. In this sense Sombart epitomizes German economic theory itself: its swan song from world centre stage to oblivion. One historian has pertinently characterized Sombart as a seismograph for what happened in Germany: a country diagnosed in 1915 by Thorstein Veblen as having moved too fast from feudalism to machine-age capitalism.[1] Sombart's career is a part explanation why German influence was lost: thrown out as the proverbial baby with the bathing water after World War II. Sombart's life and writings[2] open up for an insight into a process that went very wrong in 20th century Germany.

Three months before Werner Sombart was born, his father had participated in the establishment of *Verein für Sozialpolitik,* a group of economists, under the leadership of Gustav Schmoller (1838–1917), who wanted to 'civilize' capitalism. The members disliked communism just as strongly as they disliked the Manchester liberalism, the neoliberalism of the day: the two ahistorical twins as Gustav Schmoller later referred to them. There is a clear concordance between the members of *Verein für Sozialpolitik* – who by their opponents were called *Kathedersozialisten* ("socialists of the professorial chair") – and the German historical school of economics. One common element was that ethics had to be an integral part of economics.[3] This influential association, which lasted from 1872 to 1936, gradually built up what came to be the social institutions of the welfare state. In most parts of Europe the construction of the welfare state was heavily based on the German experience.

---

1 Veblen, Thorstein, *Imperial Germany and the Industrial Revolution,* introduction by Joseph Dorfman, New York: Macmillan, 1915.

2 The main source of information on Sombart in English remains the three volumes edited by Jürgen Backhaus, *Werner Sombart. Social Scientist,* Marburg: Metropolis. 1996.

3 See e.g. Schmoller, Gustav, *Historisch-ethische Nationalökonomie als Kulturwissenschaft: ausgewählte methodologische Schriften,* (Nau, Heinrich, editor), Marburg: Metropolis, 1998.

Because of bad health, young Sombart did his studies partly in Pisa and Rome, where he also found the theme for his doctoral thesis written under Schmoller in Berlin: 'The economic situation in Campagna', i.e. the rural area around Rome. Here Sombart found a feudal society exploiting the dependent farmers. This probably contributed to the radicalization of his views, and soon he turned to the writings of Marx. Later this made it problematic for him to find a professorship. Friedrich Engels was of the opinion that Sombart was the only German professor who had understood Marx. But even at this early stage Sombart pointed out that socialism had to have a national dimension.

Werner Sombart and the one year younger Max Weber had much in common, they were close friends for a long time and were both among the 1909 founders of the German Sociological Association. Their fathers – Anton Sombart and Max Weber Sr. – were both members of the Prussian House of Representatives and the German Empire Reichstag. Werner Sombart had published his main work, *Der moderne Kapitalismus* (Modern Capitalism), in 1902, and pointed out how the system had originated in the Italian city states of the Renaissance. Max Weber wrote, in 1904 and 1905, articles claiming a near connection between capitalism and 'the spirit of Protestantism'. In 1911 Sombart answered with a book praising the importance of the Jews in the development of capitalism. The discussion on the importance of religion for capitalism was also a debate between two friends and colleagues. The mature Sombart, who lived two decades longer than Weber, was of the meaning that Catholicism, Protestantism, and Judaism all had a part in the creation of capitalism. Today just one half of the debate on religion and capitalism between Sombart and Weber is remembered: Weber and his emphasis on Protestantism.

Modern Capitalism [4] was published in two volumes in the first edition in 1902. Then it was rewritten, a new edition in four volumes was published in 1916, and the final edition, in six volumes, in 1927. This enormous work describes capitalism in a qualitatively understanding – *verstehende* – way. The closest English translation is possibly what Richard Nelson and Sidney Winter call *appreciative theory*.[5] Sombart's massive volumes on capitalism and its history have no parallel in economic literature. A key descriptive term of capitalism – *creative destruction* – was first formulated by Sombart.[6]

Sombart creates a typology of different kinds of capitalism, and points to important elements in the development of the capitalist system, like the introduction of double book-keeping in the 1400s, which made it possible to measure the concept of capital. Sombart, probably better than anyone, understood the 'spirit' of capitalism. Like Thorstein Veblen

---

4 The first English translation of this work, of the four volumes that were first published in 1916, will be published in 2019. Werner Sombart, *Modern Capitalism,* Reinert, Erik S. (ed.), Berlin & Heidelberg: Springer, forthcoming 2019.

5 Nelson, Richard and Sidney Winter, *An Evolutionary Theory of Economic Change,* Cambridge MA: Harvard University Press, 1982. See page 46 for a discussion of *formal* vs. *appreciative* theories.

6 Reinert, Hugo and Erik S. Reinert, 'Creative Destruction in Economics: Nietzsche, Sombart, Schumpeter', in Backhaus, Jürgen and Wolfgang Drechsler (eds.), *Friedrich Nietzsche 1844–2000: Economy and Society*, New York, NY: Springer, 2006,

he thought the basis for understanding capitalism lay in understanding 'the motivation of living people'. Sombart possessed the important insight that capitalism starts when production is no longer only for covering personal and family needs, but going beyond that, including the need to create great things (*magna facere*), something that started in the Italian Renaissance. When trying to understand the difference between today's capitalism in rural Africa and Silicon Valley, this is still an important insight.

Fernand Braudel's three volume work on capitalism from the 1970s[7] is the modern work coming closest to Sombart. Braudel refers approvingly to Sombart, and also describes – as Sombart does – how capitalism came 'out of Italy', as the English title of one of Braudel's books indicates.[8]

One problem with Sombart is that he – as he himself admitted at least once – was making certain historical speculations. Schumpeter comments quite rightly that while Marx was interested in the answers, Sombart was interested in the questions, and he describes Sombart's books as very stimulating, even when the author is wrong. That can hardly be said about any modern economist.

In Sombart's book *Händler und Helden* (*Hucksters and Heroes*) from 1915, where the English are the hucksters and the Germans the heroes, his speculations turn into a not very pleasing piece of warmongering propaganda. In the same year, 1915, Veblen published the book already mentioned, *Imperial Germany and the Industrial Revolution*, where he claimed that industrial technological knowledge combined with feudal traditions and war-related concepts of honor were very dangerous to world peace. Veblen was right. As was Keynes, when he in 1918 warned that the excessive war compensations Germany had to pay after World War I would lead to a new war within a generation.

The usual explanation for Sombart's fall from the peaks of fame is his sympathy for fascism. But here the philosopher Martin Heidegger and the composer Richard Wagner sinned far more than Sombart, and their life works are not forgotten because of it. Sombart's relations with Judaism are complex. Some years ago I talked about Sombart with a Peruvian colleague, a Harvard economist, whose Jewish parents had barely escaped the Holocaust. My friend enthusiastically told me that his father had studied economics under Sombart in Berlin, and had told his son a lot about Sombart. Great was my surprise when I realized that my friend had no idea that Sombart was now viewed as a fascist. Before they had had to flee from Berlin, Sombart had had many Jewish students, several of them Zionists. One of them, David Ben-Gurion, later became Israel's first prime minister, and translated Sombart's 1892 book *Sozialismus und soziale Bewegung*[9] into Hebrew.[10]

Between the first two-volume edition of *Modern Capitalism* (1902) and the second edition, in four volumes (1916)[11], Sombart wrote a series of books describing decisive factors

---

7 In English: *Civilization and Capitalism, 15th–18th Centuries,* 3 vols. New York, NY: HarperCollins, 1985

8 Braudel, Fernand, *Out of Italy: 1450–1650,* Paris: Flammarion, 1991.

9 English translation; *Socialism and the Social Movement in the 19th Century*, New York. NY: Putnam, 1898.

10 The Hebrew translation was published in Jerusalem in 1911 by Achdut.

11 As already mentioned the last edition, in six volumes, would be published in 1927.

shaping capitalism. His 1906 book *Warum gibt es in den Vereinigten Staaten keinen Sozialismus?*[12] is still a very interesting volume. Then followed *Die Juden und das Wirtschaftsleben* (1911)[13], *Der Bourgeois* (1913)[14], *Luxus und Kapitalismus* (1913)[15] und *Krieg und Kapitalismus* (1913).[16] Recently some of Sombart's other writings have been made available in English.[17]

Even if he later flirted with them, the national-socialists were unable to forgive Sombart for his laudatory comments on Jewish culture and its rationality as the origins of capitalism. In reality Sombart's antisemitism consisted in an overestimate of the historical importance of the Jews. In his book *Die Juden und das Wirtschaftsleben* he gives them the credit – or the responsibility – for having financed everything from the discovery of America to colonialism. The book got a mixed reception, but in certain Jewish circles the reaction was positive. Sombart sometimes exaggerated tremendously whatever he at any time focused on, whether it was the importance of love[18] or Judaism for capitalism. A 1909 article in The New York Times[19], a "special cable to the New York Times" reports from a lecture by Sombart in Berlin under a sequence of headlines: 'Jews the Pioneers in the New World. Prof. Sombart says they financed Columbus' Voyages and Formed Part of Crew. Were early Colonizers'. That this and other examples of sometimes overrating the importance of the Jews in capitalism would later be used against the Jews was not to be guessed at when the book appeared in 1911. But that Sombart later should support fascism is rightly a matter for criticism. As he had supported Marxism he now supported Fascism and the '*Führer*' principle. Again we see the exaggeration, the going to extremes. As previously said, Sombart functioned as a seismograph that incarnated the shocks to the intellectual life of Germany. As his friend Max Weber wrote to his wife: 'Sombart always wants to be the last cry (*dernier cri*).'

Schmoller and the generation of the fathers of Sombart and Weber had staked out what was to be the third, and let us call it the 'sufficiently nationalistic' way between the great cosmopolitan ideologies: Communism and Manchester liberalism. Instead Sombart moved first towards a partly cosmopolitan Marxism, before he – when Germany's economy had been destroyed – ended up in a nationalistic extreme. This happened

---

12 *Why is there no socialism in the United States*, White Plains, NY: Sharpe, 1976. The English translation contains a very perceptive introduction by Michael Harrington.

13 English translation, *The Jews and Modern Capitalism,* London: Unwin, 1913.

14 Translated as *The Quintessence of Capitalism,* New York, NY: Howard Fertig, 1967.

15 English translation *Luxury and Capitalism,* Ann Arbor, MI: University of Michigan Press, 1967.

16 Munich and Leipzig: Duncker und Humblot, 1913. The title means 'War and Capitalism'. Unfortunately there is no English translation of this book. It is on the last page of this book Sombart evokes 'the creative spirit of destruction'.

17 Stehr, Nico and Reiner Grundmann (eds.), *Werner Sombart: Economic Life in the Modern Age,* New Brunswick, NJ: Transaction.

18 The latest German edition of *Luxury and Capitalism* carries the title Sombart originally wanted, but it was too daring: *Luxury, Love, and Capitalism: Liebe, Luxus und Kapitalismus. Über die Entstehung der modernen Welt aus dem Geist der Verschwendung,* Berlin: Wagenbach, 1983. Clearly this way of thinking is related to Thorstein Veblen's 'conspicuous consumption' in his 1899 *Theory of the Leisure Class,* New York, NY: Macmillan, 1899.

19 November 20. 1909

while the first wave of globalization collapsed, and it is interesting to note that the two European nations last to be united – Italy and Germany – was where an apparent overdose of nationalism carried the day. When now the globalization wave of neoliberalism is creating poverty also in the centre of capitalism, both in the United States and in the European Union, when the economy of the middle classes – which Sombart tried to defend – again is threatened, we may see similar phenomena. Sombart and Germany may be a guide to future developments as well.

Why the interest in such a controversial and probably rather unpleasant person as Sombart? One reason is that he, in my view, in addition to purely historical work has given us theoretical works[20] that contain some useful taxonomies. Sombart has probably delivered the best definition of capitalism, as needing to comprise 1) the entrepreneur with initiative, 2) the modern state, and 3) the technology, or *innovation system* as we might call it today. When all these three factors have virtually disappeared from economic theory – they are difficult to model – economists, and those who attempt to understand economic development, all have a problem.

Sombart also defines two ideal types of economic theory that appear to have coexisted parallel over an extended period of time. These ideal types can be seen as constituting two separate *filiations*[21] – to use Schumpeter's term – and they come into occasional methodological clashes. Werner Sombart fittingly calls the first tradition *activistic-idealistic*, a tradition born with the Renaissance, what I call The Other Canon of economics. The second type of economic theory he calls *passivistic-materialistic*,[22] a tradition having its origins with Mandeville and Adam Smith and solidifying as the 'a-priori method' with David Ricardo and today's mainstream economics. German economics clearly falls into the *activistic-idealistic* tradition.

In a third set of taxonomies[23] Werner Sombart establishes three categories: *Ordnende Nationalökonomie,* which is concerned with mechanically *organizing* the economic sphere. This tradition represents what today is referred to as *physics envy*.[24] The second tradition is what Sombart calls *verstehende Nationalökonomie*, Nelson and Winter's *appreciative economics.* A third category of economics, *richtende Nationalökonomie* – a tradition that aimed at the 'right' kind of economy, *how things ought to be* – is rejected by Sombart as metaphysics. The first tradition (*ordnende*) typically explains Man's economic activities in terms of physics, of dead matter, the second (*verstehende*) in terms of biology, of living matter *and* of Man's wit and will, the third (*richtende*) in terms of 'metaphysical speculations'.

Sombart's two books from 1913, *War and Capitalism* and *Luxury and Capitalism*, give us unique insights into two main factors responsible for technological change in the West.

---

20 Especially *Die Drei Nationalökonomien,* Munich and Leipzig: Duncker und Humblot, 1930.

21 'The relation of one thing to another from which it may say to be descended or derived; position in a genealogical classification', *The Oxford English Dictionary*, Oxford 1933, Vol. 4, p.212.

22 Sombart, Werner, *Der Moderne Kapitalismus,* Vol. 2, *Das Europäische Wirtschaftsleben im Zeitalter des Frühkapitalismus,* Munich and Leipzig: Duncker & Humblot, 1928, p. 919.

23 Sombart, Werner, *Die Drei Nationalökonomien,* Munich and Leipzig: Duncker und Humblot, 1930.

24 See Mirowski, Philip, *More Heat than Light: Economics as Social Physics, Physics as Nature's Economics,* Cambridge: Cambridge University Press, 1989.

War, conspicuous consumption and prestige among the very different states of Europe created an abundance of ideas, technologies and products that could be tried out against each other. The fact that a similar competition in an enormous and united China was non-existent gives us one of the explanations why Europe, economically, overtook China around 1700. As already mentioned the concept *creative destruction* – later made famous by Schumpeter – turns up in the last sentence of Sombart's *War and Capitalism.*

Joseph Alois Schumpeter (1883–1950) is perceived as extremely original in the Anglo-Saxon environment. As I see it, this is to a large extent a product of the present ignorance of the traditions on which he built and the intellectual context in which he wrote. Part of what Schumpeter did was to filter Sombart's work and the economic debate in Germany between the world wars to the Anglo-Saxon world. Most Schumpeterians, especially non-Germans, would probably be surprised by a German book that describes Schumpeter's 1942 book *Capitalism, Socialism and Democracy* – the work that made him accessible to the layman – as essentially a reworking of a German debate which had taken place decades earlier, where, as this author carefully points out, Schumpeter neither refers to the debate itself, nor to its protagonist Werner Sombart.[25]

Aspects of Sombart's work are occasionally being rediscovered. When *Luxury and Capitalism* was republished in German in 1967, the title was changed to the one Sombart originally had wanted, which was too risqué in 1913: *Love, Luxury, and Capitalism* (*Liebe, Luxus und Capitalismus*). The first English translation was reviewed in *The Economist* under the heading *Sexual Economics* in 1968. Sombart's book *Why is there no Socialism in the United States* (German 1906) resurfaced, and was quoted several times during the last American election campaign. As China now seems to have understood what made the West rich, while the West itself is drowning in the havoc of financial capital, and what German economists called *Mammonismus* – that is: chasing money for money itself, not for production – it may be useful to dig out Sombart's understanding of what for so long made the West so unique, what for so long enabled capitalism to produce such wealth.

A number of issues discussed by Werner Sombart recently reappear in economics and economic history: time and work, bourgeois virtue, the fiscal-military state, the enlightened economy, useful knowledge, and many others. What these approaches have in common is that they resurrect questions that were already handled very well – often better – by Sombart, but mostly without referring to him and his work. Until after World War II, knowledge of German was mandatory for students of economics in the United States. This partly explains why Sombart's monumental *Modern Capitalism* was not published in English until the forthcoming 2019 edition already mentioned.[26]

---

25 'Without referring to Sombart or to the general literature of the twenties and thirties, (in *Capitalism, Socialism and Democracy*) Schumpeter in essence presented only what had already been written and said decades earlier in the German discussion about 'the future of capitalism', in Appel, Michel, *Werner Sombart. Theoretiker und Historiker des modernen Kapitalismus*, Marburg: Metropolis, 1992. p. 260 (my translation).

26 There were translations into French, Italian, Spanish and Russian. Not all of them complete, but voluminous.

Two aspects of Werner Sombart make him a somewhat tragic historical figure. On the one hand on the personal level: during the last years of his life he understood that his great reputation had faded. His flirts with the latest intellectual fashions – first socialism, then fascism – had discredited him. But he is also a tragic figure because Germany – fully understandably – after World War II attempted to distance itself from everything smacking of fascism.[27] Werner Sombart therefore also, for all practical purposes, represents the swan song of a long independent German-language economics tradition. A tradition of qualitative understanding of the economic sphere that had lasted for three centuries – since the end of the Thirty Years' War – was, with Werner Sombart, poured out with the proverbial bathing water after World War II.

Meantime, in the United States, what has been described as a "struggle over the soul of economics" took place.[28] The failure of American institutional economics to reproduce, as one author put it, coincided with death of the German Historical School of economics on the other side of the Atlantic. These developments took place as the Cold War atmosphere increased the latent demand for theories proving that markets were always right, a demand which frictionless neo-classical economics effortlessly provided. When communism promised "from each according to ability, to each according to need", neo-classical economics – during the Berlin Blockade – came up with something even better: under their usual assumptions it could be mathematically "proven" that free trade would produce *factor-price equalization*, everyone would be equally wealthy.[29] The absurdity that free trade, at the time, between Detroit and an Amazon tribe, would make people in the two places equally wealthy faded from the discussion. Given the new rules of the economics game, such discussions came to be considered "unscientific": a type of discussion from which prestigious economists collectively abdicated. As Thorstein Veblen would have put it: useful and comprehensible *exoteric* knowledge was crowded out by irrelevant, but prestigeous, *esoteric* knowledge.

This development, the loss of *appreciative economics*, on both sides of the Atlantic left us with neo-classical economics dominated by *qualitätslose Größen* – by quantities void of any qualities[30] – which severely limits present economic understanding. Parallel to this – as part of the same limited understanding – the economy becomes what Lionel Robbins

---

[27] One great irony here is that the most fascist of the leading German economists was also the most neoclassical of them all: Heinrich von Stackelberg (1905–1946).

[28] Yonay, Yuval P., *The Struggle over the Soul of Economics, Institutional and Neoclassical Economists in America between the Wars,* Princeton, NJ: Princeton University Press, 1998. See also Morgan, Mary S. and Malcolm Rutherford (editors), *From Interwar Pluralism to Postwar Neoclassicism,* Durham, NC: Duke University Press, 1998.

[29] Samuelson, Paul A. 'International Trade and the Equalisation of Factor Prices', *Economic Journal,* June, 1948, pp. 163–184 and his 'International Factor-Price Equalisation Once Again', *The Economic Journal,* June 1949, pp. 181–197.

[30] In the Ricardian tradition, to Samuelson a labour hour in the car industry in Detroit became, in terms of ability to create wealth, qualitatively identical to a labour hour in a Stone Age Amazon tribe. Specializing in a comparative advantage in "Stone Age activities" – activities void of skills and increasing returns – in international trade gradually came not to be seen as a disadvantage.

(1898–1984) called a *Harmonielehre*[31], a system where free trade and free capital creation and transfer are supposed to produce automatic harmony and equilibrium.

In German language theory national wealth is *activity specific,* it needs certain kinds of economic activities. German theory – from Marx to the left to Schumpeter to the right – insisted on a clear separation between the financial capital and the real economy. Now the theories prescribed by Adam Smith and, in particular, David Ricardo hit the West like a boomerang in the form of de-industrialization and financial crises. Asia, particularly China, has learned what used to be our strengths, while we ourselves have unlearned them.[32] Feudalism was a system where 1 per cent owned the land and 99 per cent worked it. Now large parts of the West risk facing a post-industrial neo-feudalism, where 1 per cent own most of the capital and a large part of the 99 per cent increasingly work informally and under falling real wages. It is time we resurrect more realistic economic theories – the historical and institutional schools – on both sides of the Atlantic.

---

31 For a discussion on Robbins' protest against economics as a *Harmonielehre*, see Samuels, Warren, *Erasing the Invisible Hand: Essays on an Elusive and Misused Concept,* Cambridge: Cambridge University Press, 2014, p. 209.

32 This point is made by Mahbubani, Kishore, *The New Asian Hemisphere: The Irresistible Shift of Global Power to the East,* New York, NY, Publicaffairs, 2008.

INDEX

www.ingramcontent.com/pod-product-compliance
Ingram Content Group UK Ltd.
Pitfield, Milton Keynes, MK11 3LW, UK
UKHW041830100926
8556IPUK00002B/98

9 781783 089031